Reading the Gospel of St. Matthew *in Greek*

Reading the Gospel of St. Matthew *in Greek*

A Beginning

WITH INTRODUCTION, NOTES, VOCABULARY, AND GRAMMATICAL APPENDIX

by

NORBERT H. O. DUCKWITZ
Brigham Young University

Bolchazy-Carducci Publishers, Inc.
Mundelein, Illinois USA

Editor: Laurel Draper

Design and Layout: Adam Phillip Velez

Cover Illustration: James C. Christensen *We Three Kings*

Greek Text: Barbara Aland, Kurt Aland, Johannes Karavidopoulos, Carlo M. Martini, and Bruce M. Metzger, eds. *The Greek New Testament*, Fourth Revised Edition Deutsche Bibelgesellschaft 1993 Reprinted with kindly permission.

Reading the Gospel of St. Matthew in Greek
A Beginning

Norbert H. O. Duckwitz

Bolchazy-Carducci Publishers, Inc.
1570 Baskin Road
Mundelein, Illinois 60060
www.bolchazy.com

Printed in the United States of America
2017
by United Graphics

ISBN 978-0-86516-817-6

Library of Congress Cataloging-in-Publication Data

Duckwitz, Norbert H. O., author.
Reading the Gospel of St. Matthew in Greek : a beginning / with introduction, notes, vocabulary, and grammatical appendix by Norbert H. O. Duckwitz.
pages cm
Includes bibliographical references and index.
ISBN 978-0-86516-817-6 (pbk. : alk. paper) 1. Bible. Matthew--Language, style. 2. Greek language, Biblical--Grammar. I. Bible. Matthew. 2013. II. Title.
PA817.D834 2013
487'.4--dc23

2013039877

τοῖς παισί μου,
David, Tamara, Jonathan,
Gregory, Daniel, Justin, and Christel

CONTENTS

PREFACE

It is the purpose of this book to empower students of the New Testament at all levels to learn to read and appreciate the Gospel of Matthew in Greek. For several years now the original book in this series, *Reading the Gospel of St. John in Greek: A Beginning,* and the subsequent *Reading the Gospel of St. Mark in Greek: A Beginning* have been successfully used by students of the New Testament with no prior knowledge of Greek as well as by middle and advanced level Greek students. With perhaps an idealistic goal in mind I proposed an honors course at the university that invited Greekless readers to read the Gospel of John with me in the original language. Because of the scarcity of beginning Greek readers that cover the entire Gospel text and because of student discouragement with the originally assigned text, students proposed that I provide them with running vocabulary to help speed up their reading by not having to thumb through lexica. They then suggested adding notes about grammar, syntax, literary figures of speech, history, contextual questions, and discussions of cruces. Their suggestions and recommendations helped to inform this text along with the most proven methodology of intermediate readers I have used successfully for forty-three years. The new approach and adaptation to a beginning text have turned into a useful reader for any person who desires a self-tutorial, a beginning Greek text, or an aid in a more advanced graduate course at the university level. Its use at the advanced level will allow a teacher more free time to add insights based on the teacher's training and area of specialty or expertise. In beginning classes it may also be useful to supplement the text with an introductory New Testament grammar.

Learning Greek by way of *Reading the Gospel of St. Matthew in Greek: A Beginning* produces distinct advantages for students. Traditionally those interested in reading the GNT (*The Greek New*

Testament, United Bible Societies, 4th Ed. 1993) take two years of classical Greek at the university before moving on to the Greek text. Moreover, many undergraduates never take Greek at all during their college years due to the pressures of completing the coursework for their declared major in time for graduation and yet they find a latent desire to read the New Testament in Greek at a later point of time in their lives. This text obviates the necessity of that sort of time constraint: it allows a person to work in the GNT text immediately. What facilitates the learning process is that a reader is all the while in the familiar context of the New Testament language and does not have to translate ponderous and unfamiliar original Greek sentiments on the one hand or simplistic and fabricated English sentences that have been turned into Greek on the other. Also the reader saves much time because the original text, the vocabulary for translating the Greek text, and the notes for understanding the Greek text all appear on the same page. Thus a student may read more quickly without having to break concentration by going to additional lexica and commentaries. By using this method, beginning students have surpassed expectations and have been able to read, with comprehension and critically, much of the gospel in one semester. The success has been repeated in other honors classes as well. Also, by using this text in the junior and senior level courses, students regularly and easily complete the entire gospel texts of John and Mark, although Matthew presents a good challenge in that regard. The text is primarily designed as a reader, not a grammar.

The introduction presents a summary description of the alphabet, pronunciation, accent, and grammar, making simple and brief comparisons between English and Greek. For a fuller perspective and for purposes of memorization of grammatical forms and concepts, a student is encouraged to turn to the appendix. After memorizing the alphabet, reciting it effortlessly, learning how to pronounce the letters, and becoming acquainted with the rudimentary concepts of grammar, the student is at once introduced to the Greek text of the gospel. For easy reference a running vocabulary list appears beneath the text in the order of the verses. Due to limitation of space, the vocabulary cited does not show an exhaustive list of meanings but does provide a sufficiently comprehensive citing for translation purposes. Except for simple transliterations, vocabulary is repeated approximately ten times for memorization purposes, although a vocabulary item is not repeated in the same passage or even consecutive verses. When it no longer appears in the running vocabulary list, the vocabulary item may be looked up in the dictionary at the end of the book. The cited vocabulary will show basic lexical meanings in addition to specialized meanings (see especially Introduction paragraphs 23, 24, 30, and 52). Notes may occasionally refer to the appendix. It will facilitate and enhance the reading experience to memorize the paradigms and vocabulary either before or after a reading session. Doing so during the reading session may prove disruptive for the reading flow. A reference to the appendix always indicates a paragraph number, not pagination.

A special debt of gratitude is owed to my colleague Steven C. Walker for reading the English text and to James C. Christensen for providing the frontispiece. All suggestions, recommendations, and talents have made a valuable contribution to this text. I wish to thank my students whose enthusiasm for reading the New Testament in Greek have increased my sensitivities to the text and my awareness of their needs. For their assistance in reading the text and for their computer skills and help I am deeply grateful, especially to my son, Daniel. Finally, I express my devotion to my wife, Susan, and my children without whose love, abiding interest, and continuous support this project would not have been possible.

Norbert H. O. Duckwitz
September 2013

INTRODUCTION

1. The Greek alphabet, with pronunciation, is presented here:

LETTER		NAME	PRONUNCIATION
Α	α	alpha	f**a**ther (long); dram**a** (short)
Β	β	beta	**b**ook
Γ	γ	gamma	**g**ardner
Δ	δ	delta	**D**avid
Ε	ε	epsilon	**e**pistle (always short)
Ζ	ζ	zeta	gir**ds** (= dz)
Η	η	eta	b**e**ten (German, always long, never a diphthong)
Θ	θ	theta	bro**th**er
Ι	ι	iota	pol**i**ce (long); s**i**ster (short)
Κ	κ	kappa	**k**insman, **c**risis
Λ	λ	lambda	**l**amp
Μ	μ	mu	**m**urmur
Ν	ν	nu	**n**ight
Ξ	ξ	xi	e**x**istence
Ο	ο	omicron	p**o**sterity (always short)
Π	π	pi	**p**itcher
Ρ	ρ	rho	**r**osa (Spanish)
Σ	σ, ς	sigma	**s**ignal
Τ	τ	tau	**t**emple
Υ	υ	upsilon	s**u**r (French, long); t**u** (French, short)
Φ	φ	phi	**Ph**ilip
Χ	χ	chi	ma**ch**en (German)
Ψ	ψ	psi	perha**ps**
Ω	ω	omega	Br**o**t (German, always long, never a diphthong)

2. The quality of long vowels is maintained by not moving the lower jaw once the proper vowel sound has been produced. The dropping of the jaw will engender an undesired glide or drawl.

3. The sound of the upsilon is produced by first making a long *e* sound and then rounding one's lips: *bee* becomes βυ. Once the sound has been produced, it may be shortened or lengthened as indicated by the vowel.

4. The rho is a tongue trilled rather than a uvular or American *r*.

5. The final sigma (ς) is found only at the end of a word, **σ** everywhere else: κρίσις.

6. The chi is produced by slightly constricting the throat.

7. Theta, phi, and chi were originally voiceless stops with strong aspiration (**Th**omas, u**ph**ill, and bac**kh**and).

8. Greek capital letters occur much less frequently than in English. They are used at the beginning of names, paragraphs, and quotations.

9. The gamma takes on the nasal quality of *ng* (say**ing**) when it precedes **κ**, **γ**, **χ**, or **ξ**: ἄγγελος.

10. **ζ** (pronounced *dz*, derived from **σδ** or *dy*), **ξ**, (a combination of **κσ**, **γσ**, or **χσ**) and **ψ** (a result of **πσ**, **βσ**, or **φσ**) are double consonants.

11. The letter *h* is indicated as a rough breathing (ʽ) over the initial vowel and always pronounced before the vowel sound(s): ὑπέρ; over the second vowel of a diphthong: αἷμα; or before the initial vowel of a capital letter: Ἑβραϊστί. All words beginning with an upsilon and rho take a rough breathing: ὕπνος, ῥαββί. The rho is the only consonant to do so.

12. Every initial vowel or diphthong either shows a rough breathing or indicates the absence thereof by a smooth breathing (ʼ): Ἀβραάμ.

13. Diphthongs combine two vowels that glide into each other and form one syllable. Although the second vowel of the diphthong receives the breathing and/or accent, the stress or breathing applies to both as a single syllable.

DIPHTHONG	PRONUNCIATION	EXAMPLE
αι	C**ai**ro	δαιμόνιον
αυ	h**ou**se	αὐλή
ει	d**eig**n	εἰρήνη
ευ	m**e**t + s**oo**n	πλευρά
ηυ	**eh** + s**oo**n	ηὕρηκα
οι	**oi**l	οἶκος
ου	s**oo**n	οὐρανός
υι	L**ouie**	υἱός

14. When an iota is placed beneath a long vowel (ᾳ, ῃ, ῳ), it is called an *iota subscript* and is not pronounced. A double dot over an iota or upsilon indicates *diaeresis,* a separation from the previous vowel as a separate syllable: Καϊάφας, Μωϋσῆς.

15. A Greek word has as many syllables as it has separate vowels or diphthongs. A consonant between two vowels generally marks the beginning of a new syllable: πυ-ρε-τός. A consonant combination or cluster, as it can be pronounced together at the beginning of a word, initiates syllabification: ἀν-θρω-πο-κτό-νος. However, double consonants are usually divided: ἀν-αγ-γέλ-λω. Lambda and rho stay attached to the preceding consonant: ὑ-δρί-α, τυ-φλός. Compound words constructed with prepositions keep the preposition intact and are divided at the point of juncture: συν-εισ-έρ-χο-μαι.

16. The accent of a Greek word usually falls on one of the last three syllables of a word: the final syllable is called *ultima,* the second from the end *penult,* and the third from the end *antepenult.* There are three accents: *acute* (´), *grave* (`), and *circumflex* (῀). The acute may appear on any one of the three last syllables. An acute accent on the ultima (e.g., θεός) is known as an *oxytone,* on the penult (e.g., λόγος) as a *paroxytone,* and on the antepenult (e.g., ἄνθρωπος) as a *proparoxytone.* The grave is found only on the ultima, in the place of an oxytone, to indicate that another word is following without a mark of punctuation (e.g., πρὸς τὸν θεόν). The circumflex, a combination of the acute and grave accent, stands only on one of the last two syllables and only on long vowels or diphthongs. A circumflex over the ultima

(e.g., Κηφᾶς) is called *perispomenon*, over the penult (e.g., Πιλᾶτος) a *properispomenon*. While these terms may be challenging to learn initially, they prevent cumbersome circumlocution in the end. In modern times the accented syllable is simply given extra stress, but originally it was raised or lowered as a musical pitch. A few words called *proclitics* and *enclitics* receive no accent.

17. Greek has four punctuation marks: the period and comma corresponding to those in English; the high dot (·) indicating a colon or semicolon; the semicolon (;) being a question mark. There are no quotation or exclamation marks.

18. The following words are provided for pronunciation practice:

λόγος	θεός	ζωή
φῶς	ἄνθρωπος	μαρτυρία
ἄγγελος	ἀλόη	βιβλίον
Γαλιλαία	ἔθνος	εἰρήνη
ἑκατόν	Ἕλλην	ἔργον
Ἐφραίμ	Ζεβεδαῖος	Ἠσαΐας
θάλασσα	θεραπεύω	Ἰησοῦς
Ἰόρδανος	Καϊάφας	Καῖσαρ
κεφαλή	κόσμος	κρίσις
λίθος	μαθητής	μέτρον
νεκρός	ὁδός	ὀρφανός
ὀφθαλμός	πατήρ	ποταμός
προφήτης	ῥαββί	σπόγγος
σχίσμα	τόπος	ὕδωρ
φόβος	φωνή	Χριστός
χρόνος	ψεῦδος	ψυχή
ὥρα	φίλος	σῶμα

19. Greek includes the following eight parts of speech: nouns, adjectives, pronouns, verbs, adverbs, conjunctions, prepositions, and particles.

20. Greek has three grammatical genders: *masculine, feminine,* and *neuter.* Nouns of the first declension ending in -α or -η are feminine. Most nouns of the second declension ending in -ος are masculine. Nouns of the second declension ending in -ον are neuter. Nouns of the third and final declension include all genders. The article given in the vocabulary with a noun indicates the gender: ἡ is feminine, ὁ masculine, and τό neuter.

21. The language shows three numbers: *singular, dual,* and *plural.* The dual, refering to two people or things, is used prominently in the epic diction of Homer, declines in classical Greek, and falls out of use in the language of the New Testament. It is replaced by the plural.

22. There are five cases: *nominative, genitive, dative, accusative,* and *vocative.* The case of a noun shows its relationship to another noun or to a verb as a subject or object. In English this is accomplished by word placement: *Peter finds Philip.* Here the subject precedes the verb and the object follows it. A change of word order either changes the meaning or makes it ambiguous. In Greek, the endings of these nouns are inflected to distinguish the subject from the object: Πέτρ**ος** εὑρίσκει Φίλιππ**ον**. No matter what the word order, the context remains clear. Nouns that change their endings according to cases are said to be *declined* and in a *declension.* A discussion of basic meanings of these cases follows, but other uses will be explained in the notes of the text as they appear and further examples will be cited in the appendix.

23. The nominative case (from the Latin *nomino name*) *names* a subject of the verb (e.g., ἠγάπησεν ὁ θεὸς τὸν κόσμον *God loved the world,* τὸ φῶς φαίνει *the light shines*). It also names predicate nouns. A predicate is connected to the subject by a linking verb and so is equated with it (e.g., ἡ ζωὴ ἦν τὸ φῶς *the light was the life,* ὁ λόγος σὰρξ ἐγένετο *the Word was made flesh*). A Greek dictionary listing of a noun indicates the nominative case first: ἀρχή, ῆς, ἡ *beginning.*

24. The genitive case frequently indicates possession or source. It limits another noun and is expressed in English by the preposition *of* (e.g., ὁ υἱὸς τοῦ θεοῦ *the son of God,* ἡ μαρτυρία τοῦ Ἰωάννου *the witness of John,* ὁ ἀμνὸς τοῦ θεοῦ *the lamb of God*). A Greek dictionary listing

cites only the ending of the genitive case after the nominative: ἀρχή, ῆς, ἡ *beginning*. Hence the full genitive form is created by adding the ending to the stem: ἀρχῆς. The dropping of the genitive ending helps to identify the stem of a noun and to distinguish one noun declension from another.

25. The dative case (from the Latin *do give*) often expresses the person *to whom* the action of a verb pertains other than the subject or direct object. It is rendered in English by the prepositions *to* or *for*. One of its main uses includes the indirect object (e.g., ἔδωκεν ἐξουσίαν τοῖς μαθηταῖς *He gave power to the disciples*, πάντα ἔδωκεν τῷ υἱῷ ὁ πατὴρ *the Father gave all things to the son*, ἐφανέρωσεν ἑαυτὸν πάλιν ὁ Ἰησοῦς τοῖς μαθηταῖς *Jesus showed himself again to the disciples*).

26. The accusative case (from the Latin *ad* + *cuso strike against*) designates the direct object of a transitive verb (e.g., ἐθεασάμεθα τὴν δόξαν αὐτοῦ *we saw His glory*, φώνησον τὸν ἄνδρα σου *call your husband*, τὰς ἐντολὰς τὰς ἐμὰς τηρήσετε *keep my commmandments*, καὶ ἐπάρας τοὺς ὀφθαλμοὺς αὐτοῦ *and lifting His eyes*).

27. The vocative case (from the Latin *voco call*) is the case of direct address (e.g., λέγουσιν αὐτῷ, Διδάσκαλε, αὕτη ἡ γυνὴ κατείληπται *they say to Him, Master, this woman has been caught*, Μὴ φοβοῦ, θυγάτηρ Σιών *do not fear, daughter of Sion*, Κύριε, τίς ἐπίστευσεν τῇ ἀκοῇ ἡμῶν; *Lord, who believed our report?*).

28. The genitive, dative, and accusative cases are also frequently used as objects of a preposition: χωρὶς τοῦ λόγου *apart from the Word*, ἐν τῷ λόγῳ *in the Word*, πρὸς τὸν θεόν *with God*.

29. The article ἡ, ὁ, τό *the* is a definite article. It agrees in gender, number, and case with the noun it modifies (e.g., ἐν τῷ κόσμῳ *in the world*, ἐν τῇ σκοτίᾳ *in the darkness*, περὶ τοῦ φωτός *about the light*). For the most part, the use of the Greek article is similar to English. Greek does not have an indefinite article. The notion is expressed in Greek simply by the noun: Ἐγένετο ἄνθρωπος *a man was born*. A Greek dictionary listing cites the article directly after the noun forms: ἀρχή, ῆς, ἡ *beginning*.

30. An adjective agrees in gender, number, and case with the noun it modifies: ὁ καλὸς οἶνος *the good wine*. In this example the adjective is masculine, singular, and nominative and matches its subject. It is here placed between the article and the noun, but other arrangements of word order also occur with the same meaning: ὁ οἶνος ὁ καλός or οἶνος ὁ καλός *the good wine*. As long as the adjective follows the article, it stands in *attributive* position. If an adjective stands outside of this article noun group, it is said to be in *predicate* position and forms a sentence with the verb *to be* understood: ὁ οἶνος καλός or καλὸς ὁ οἶνος means *the wine is good*. A Greek dictionary listing cites only the nominative forms of the adjective: ἀγαθός, ή, όν *good, profitable, upright*.

31. While nouns and adjectives are declined, verbs are conjugated and in a conjugation. These verbs denote person, number, tense, voice, and mood.

32. There are three persons: a first person (*I, we*), a second person (*you*, singular and plural), and a third person (*he, she, it, they*). Since the person is indicated by the ending of the verb, a pronoun subject is usually omitted.

33. There are three numbers: singular, dual, and plural. The dual, rare even in classical Greek, is replaced by the plural.

34. Tense refers to present, past, or future time. The Greek verb has seven tenses in the indicative mood: present, imperfect, future, aorist, perfect, pluperfect, and future perfect. A Greek verb also has three aspects to distinguish the type of action: simple/single, progressive/repeated, and completed.

35. The present tense indicates an action taking place in present time. It can have either simple or progressive/repeated aspect. λύω τὸν ἱμάντα may be translated *I loose the strap* (once and for all) or *I am loosing the strap* or *I am continually loosing the strap*.

36. The imperfect tense describes an action in past time that by definition carries with it progressive/repeated aspect: ἔλυον τὸν ἱμάντα *I was loosing the strap; I used to loose the strap; I continually loosed the strap*.

37. The future tense signals a future action and can have either simple or progressive/repeated aspect: λύσω τὸν ἱμάντα *I shall loose the strap* (once and for all); *I shall be loosing the strap; I shall continually loose the strap.*

38. The aorist tense denotes a single action in past time and always indicates simple aspect: ἔλυσα τὸν ἱμάντα *I loosed the strap* (once and for all).

39. The perfect tense (from the Latin *perfectum completed*) shows present time and completed aspect. It denotes action that is completed near present time and continues with present result: λέλυκα τὸν ἱμάντα *I have loosed the strap.*

40. The pluperfect tense (from the Latin *plus quam perfectum more than perfect*) expresses an action that precedes another past action and by definition denotes a completed aspect: ἐλελύκειν τὸν ἱμάντα *I had loosed the strap.*

41. The future perfect tense marks a future action and completed aspect. The form is rare in classical Greek and does not appear in this text.

42. The tenses of the indicative mood denoting actions in present and future time are called *primary* (or principal) tenses: present, future, perfect, and future perfect. The tenses of the indicative mood expressing actions in the past tense are called *secondary* (or historical) tenses: imperfect, aorist, pluperfect.

43. Secondary tenses receive an *augment*. The augment **ε** preceding the stem signals that this is one of the past tenses in the indicative mood. It is called *syllabic augment* when **ε** is prefixed to a verb beginning with a consonant: ἔλυον, ἔλυσα, ἐλελύκειν. It is a temporal augment when the initial vowel of a verb is lengthened: The initial **ἐ** of the present tense stem of ἐρωτάω *ask* becomes **ἠ** in the aorist: ἠρώτησα.

44. A Greek verb has three voices: *active, passive,* and *middle.*

45. The active voice shows that the subject performs an action: τὸ φῶς φαίνει *the light shines.* The verb in this case is active and *intransitive.* When a verb in the active voice takes an object, it is a *transitive* verb: λύω τὸν ἱμάντα *I loose the strap.*

46. The passive voice indicates that the subject is acted upon by an agent that may or may not be expressed: ὁ ἱμάς λύεται *the strap is loosed* (by John). Only transitive verbs are able to become passive.

47. The middle voice denotes that the subject performs an action for itself or its own interest or its own benefit: λύομαι τὸν ἱμάντα *I loose the strap for myself* or *I have the strap loosed*. Verbs with an active meaning but a middle or passive form are called *deponent* verbs. They are so called (from the Latin *de + pono*) because they *lay aside* their passive meaning.

48. A Greek verb has four moods: *indicative, imperative, subjunctive,* and *optative*. The classical uses of the optative mood have mostly disappeared in the New Testament language. The few forms that occur will be identified and explained in the notes of the text.

49. The indicative mood of a verb *indicates* a statement of fact: how things are, how they will be, and how they were: αὕτη ἐστὶν ἡ μαρτυρία τοῦ Ἰωάννου *this is the witness of John*, ἀναγγελεῖ ἡμῖν ἅπαντα *He will announce all things to us*, ἠρώτησαν αὐτὸν καὶ εἶπαν αὐτῷ *they asked him and said to him*.

50. The imperative mood is used to express commands: Ἔρχου καὶ ἴδε *come and see*. The tenses of the imperative mood are only three: present, aorist, and perfect. They refer to aspect only, not time: the present tense indicates progressive or repeated action; the aorist, simple or single action; the perfect, completed action. The person and number may only be in the second or third person singular or plural. A third person command form is translated by *let:* ἐρχέσθω πρός με καὶ πινέτω *let him come to me and drink*.

51. The subjunctive mood has a great variety of uses. One of the most prominent in the New Testament is the purpose or final clause introduced by the conjunction ἵνα *to, in order to, in order that, that*: οὗτος ἦλθεν, ἵνα μαρτυρήσῃ περὶ τοῦ φωτός, ἵνα πάντες πιστεύσωσιν *this one came to witness about the light, that all might believe*. As with the imperative, the tenses of the subjunctive mood are only three: present, aorist, and perfect. They refer to aspect only, not time: the present tense indicates progressive or repeated action; the aorist, simple or

single action; the perfect, completed action. Other uses of this mood will be explained as they occur in the text.

52. A dictionary generally lists six principal parts of a verb by the first person singular indicative: λύω (present active), λύσω (future active), ἔλυσα (first aorist active), λέλυκα (first perfect active), λέλυμαι (perfect middle), ἐλύθην (first aorist passive). Some verbs take a second form in the aorist active, perfect active, and aorist passive. Few verbs show both the first and second form of the same tense. Many verbs do not have all six principal parts.

ΚΑΤΑ ΜΑΘΘΑΙΟΝ

1 Βίβλος γενέσεως Ἰησοῦ Χριστοῦ υἱοῦ Δαυὶδ υἱοῦ Ἀβραάμ.
1:2 Ἀβραὰμ ἐγέννησεν τὸν Ἰσαάκ, Ἰσαὰκ δὲ ἐγέννησεν τὸν Ἰακώβ,

---

1:1
βίβλος, ου, ἡ scroll, roll, book
γένεσις, εως, ἡ birth; generation, descent, lineage; story; life
Ἰησοῦς, οῦ, ὁ Jesus
Χριστός, οῦ, ὁ Christ
υἱός, οῦ, ὁ son
Δαυίδ, ὁ David (indeclinable)
Ἀβραάμ, ὁ Abraham (indeclinable)

1:2
γεννάω, γεννήσω, ἐγέννησα, γεγέννηκα, γεγέννημαι, ἐγεννήθην beget, father, be father of, have a child, daughter, son; give birth to, bear, bring forth, conceive; be born, be conceived (in passive)
ὁ, ἡ, τό the (definite article)
Ἰσαάκ, ὁ Isaac (indeclinable)
δέ and, but, now (conjunction, postpositive)
Ἰακώβ, ὁ Jacob (indeclinable)

1:1 **βίβλος γενέσεως**: *The book of the life*; verbal echoes invite comparison with the Book of Genesis, where reference is made to the creation of heaven and earth (Gen 2:4) and the posterity of Adam (Gen 5:1–32). Matthew similarly introduces an ancestral catalogue, but his prologue invites us to contemplate an even larger vision of the new birth and life of Christ. The titular nature of this phrase, succinctly annnouncing the theme of the entire gospel, accounts for the lack of articles and verb. **βίβλος**: the noun is in the nominative case. It belongs to the class of second declension masculine nouns ending in **ος** (cf. App. 4). However, this declension includes a few feminines ending in **ος** (App. 5); any modifiers will be feminine. **γενέσεως**: the noun belongs to the class of third declension nouns (App. 6) and stands in the possessive or genitive case. **Ἰησοῦ Χριστοῦ** also stands in the genitive case. The citing of the full name and the repetition of the successive genitive cases suggest an appropriately formal tone in the introductory phrase. The title **Χριστοῦ**, *The Anointed One,* derives from the verb χρίω. **υἱοῦ Δαυὶδ** and **υἱοῦ Ἀβραάμ** stand in apposition, more fully identifying Ἰησοῦ Χριστοῦ: the son of David because He comes from a royal line and is the ultimate king; the son of Abraham because He is the fulfillment of the promise made to Abraham that he and all the families of the earth will be blessed through Him (Gen 12:2–3).

1:2 **Ἀβραὰμ ἐγέννησεν τὸν Ἰσαάκ**: *Abraham had a son Isaac*; the catalogue of ancestry commences with the patriarch Abraham at the head of the list with whom the last verse ends and who thus stands prominently in close proximity to **Ἰησοῦ Χριστοῦ**.

Ἰακὼβ δὲ ἐγέννησεν τὸν Ἰούδαν καὶ τοὺς ἀδελφοὺς αὐτοῦ,
1:3 Ἰούδας δὲ ἐγέννησεν τὸν Φάρες καὶ τὸν Ζάρα ἐκ τῆς Θαμάρ,

1:2
Ἰούδας, α, ὁ Judas (Greek), Judah (Hebrew)
καί and (conjunction)
ἀδελφός, οῦ, ὁ brother
αὐτός, αὐτή, αὐτό self; same; he, she, it, they
1:3
δέ and, but, now (conjunction, postpositive)
γεννάω, γεννήσω, ἐγέννησα, γεγέννηκα, γεγέννημαι, ἐγεννήθην beget, father, be father of, have a child, daughter, son; give birth to, bear, bring forth, conceive; be born, be conceived (in passive)
ὁ, ἡ, τό the (definite article)
Φάρες, ὁ Phares, Perez (indeclinable)
καί and (conjunction)
Ζάρα, ὁ Zara, Zerah (indeclinable)
ἐκ (ἐξ before a vowel) from, out of, of, by (preposition + genitive)
Θαμάρ, ἡ Thamar, Tamar (indeclinable)

1:2 The predominant pattern in this genealogy lists the father begetting the son. The verb **ἐγέννησεν** is a first aorist contracted verb with stem in **α** (cf. App. 55). The tense sign of the first aorist **σ** is added to the stem with the personal active endings: -σα, -σας, -σε(ν), -σαμεν, -σατε, -σαν. A movable **ν** may be added to the third person singular ending in -ε. For personal endings see App. 53, D, 1. The verb is neatly juxtaposed to the noun and main theme of γενέσεως. The augment **ε** preceding the stem signals that this is one of the past tenses in the indicative mood. It is called *syllabic augment* when **ε** is prefixed to a verb beginning with a consonant. Since most of the proper names are indeclinable, the accusative article τὸν (App. 1) helps to clarify the relationship between the nouns. Proper names usually take an article in Greek. **Ἰσαὰκ δὲ**: *but Isaac*; the conjunction **δὲ** does not appear as the first word in its clause and so is called *postpositive*. It signals a slight contrast from a previously made statement. **τὸν Ἰούδαν**: Judah is singled out among his brothers because of Christ's descent through his royal house.

1:3 The verb **ἐγέννησεν** is the third person singular first aorist active indicative of γεννάω. It is formed with an augment and a sigma before its personal endings: -σα, σας, σε(ν), -σαμεν, -σατε, σαν (cf. App. 53, D, 1). **ἐκ τῆς Θαμάρ**: along with Tamar mention is made of four other women in this patriarchal genealogy: Rahab, Ruth, Bathsheba, and Mary. The inclusion of these women thematically brings to light marital relationships that are complex and otherwise difficult to understand. By calling attention to them, Matthew may wish to affirm that although the marriages involve unusual circumstances, they nevertheless produce noble offspring and a legitimate heir. In this case, Tamar, a foreigner and the daughter-in-law of Judah, seduced Judah and gave birth to twins but was accounted by Judah as being more righteous than he himself (Gen 38). ἐκ: a few words called *proclitics* and *enclitics* have no accent and are closely connected with the word they modify.

Φάρες δὲ ἐγέννησεν τὸν Ἑσρώμ, Ἑσρὼμ δὲ ἐγέννησεν τὸν Ἀράμ,
1:4 Ἀρὰμ δὲ ἐγέννησεν τὸν Ἀμιναδάβ, Ἀμιναδὰβ δὲ ἐγέννησεν τὸν
Ναασσών, Ναασσὼν δὲ ἐγέννησεν τὸν Σαλμών, 1:5 Σαλμὼν δὲ
ἐγέννησεν τὸν Βόες ἐκ τῆς Ῥαχάβ, Βόες δὲ ἐγέννησεν τὸν Ἰωβὴδ ἐκ
τῆς Ῥούθ, Ἰωβὴδ δὲ ἐγέννησεν τὸν Ἰεσσαί, 1:6 Ἰεσσαὶ δὲ ἐγέννησεν
τὸν Δαυὶδ τὸν βασιλέα.

1:3

Ἑσρώμ, ὁ Esrom, Hezron (indeclinable)

Ἀράμ, ὁ Aram (indeclinable)

1:4

δέ and, but, now (conjunction, postpositive)

γεννάω, γεννήσω, ἐγέννησα, γεγέννηκα, γεγέννημαι, ἐγεννήθην beget, father, be father of, have a child, daughter, son; give birth to, bear, bring forth, conceive; be born, be conceived (in passive)

ὁ, ἡ, τό the (definite article)

Ἀμιναδάβ, ὁ Aminadab, Amminadab (indeclinable)

Ναασσών, ὁ Naasson, Nahshon (indeclinable)

Σαλμών, ὁ Salmon (indeclinable)

1:5

Βόες, ὁ Booz, Boaz

δέ and, but, now (conjunction, postpositive)

γεννάω, γεννήσω, ἐγέννησα, γεγέννηκα, γεγέννημαι, ἐγεννήθην beget, father, be father of, have a child, daughter, son; give birth to, bear, bring forth, conceive; be born, be conceived (in passive)

ἐκ (ἐξ before a vowel) from, out of, of, by (preposition + genitive)

Ῥαχάβ, ἡ Rachab, Rahab (indeclinable)

Ἰωβήδ, ὁ Obed (indeclinable)

Ῥούθ, ἡ Ruth (indeclinable)

Ἰεσσαί, ὁ Jesse (indeclinable)

1:6

δέ and, but, now (conjunction, postpositive)

βασιλεύς, έως, ὁ king

1:4 The verb **ἐγέννησεν** is the third person singular first aorist active indicative of γεννάω (cf. App. 53, D, 1). The augment **ε** preceding the stem signals that this is one of the past tenses in the indicative mood. It is called *syllabic augment* when **ε** is prefixed to a verb beginning with a consonant.

1:5 **ἐκ τῆς Ῥαχάβ**: both a Canaanite and a harlot, Rahab protected the two spies sent to Jericho by Joshua and was protected in turn by Joshua during and after the war (Josh 2–6). ἐκ: a few words called *proclitics* and *enclitics* have no accent and are closely connected with the word they modify. **ἐκ τῆς Ῥούθ**: Ruth, a Moabite and daughter-in-law of Naomi, was a paradigm of kindness and loyalty. She selflessly desired to follow her mother-in-law and her mother-in-law's traditions and God (Ru).

1:6 **τὸν Δαυὶδ τὸν βασιλέα**: David represents a pivotal point in the triad of the genealogical paragraphs. He comes at the end of the first period and is the fourteenth king.

Δαυὶδ δὲ ἐγέννησεν τὸν Σολομῶνα ἐκ τῆς τοῦ Οὐρίου, 1:7 Σολομὼν δὲ ἐγέννησεν τὸν Ῥοβοάμ, Ῥοβοὰμ δὲ ἐγέννησεν τὸν Ἀβιά, Ἀβιὰ δὲ ἐγέννησεν τὸν Ἀσάφ,1:8 Ἀσὰφ δὲ ἐγέννησεν τὸν Ἰωσαφάτ, Ἰωσαφὰτ δὲ ἐγέννησεν τὸν Ἰωράμ, Ἰωρὰμ δὲ ἐγέννησεν τὸν Ὀζίαν, 1:9 Ὀζίας δὲ ἐγέννησεν τὸν Ἰωαθάμ, Ἰωαθὰμ δὲ ἐγέννησεν τὸν Ἀχάζ, Ἀχὰζ δὲ ἐγέννησεν τὸν Ἑζεκίαν, 1:10 Ἑζεκίας δὲ ἐγέννησεν τὸν Μανασσῆ, Μανασσῆς δὲ ἐγέννησεν τὸν Ἀμώς, Ἀμὼς δὲ ἐγέννησεν τὸν Ἰωσίαν, 1:11 Ἰωσίας δὲ ἐγέννησεν τὸν Ἰεχονίαν καὶ τοὺς ἀδελφοὺς αὐτοῦ

1:6
Σολομών, ῶνος, ὁ Solomon
ἐκ (ἐξ before a vowel) from, out of, of, by (preposition + genitive)
ὁ, ἡ, τό the (definite article)
Οὐρίας, ου, ὁ Urias (Greek), Uriah (Hebrew)
1:7
δέ and, but, now (conjunction, postpositive)
ὁ, ἡ, τό the (definite article)
Ῥοβοάμ, ὁ Roboam, Rehoboam (indeclinable)
Ἀβιά, ὁ Abia, Abijah (indeclinable)
Ἀσάφ, ὁ Asa(ph) (indeclinable)
1:8
δέ and, but, now (conjunction, postpositive)
ὁ, ἡ, τό the (definite article)
Ἰωσαφάτ, ὁ Josaphat, Jehoshaphat (indeclinable)
Ἰωράμ, ὁ Joram (indeclinable)
Ὀζίας, ου, ὁ Ozias, Uzziah
1:9
δέ and, but, now (conjunction, postpositive)
ὁ, ἡ, τό the (definite article)
Ἰωαθάμ, ὁ Joatham, Jotham (indeclinable)
Ἀχάζ, ὁ Achaz, Ahaz (indeclinable)
Ἑζεκίας, ου, ὁ Ezekias, Hezekiah
1:10
δέ and, but, now (conjunction, postpositive)
ὁ, ἡ, τό the (definite article)
Μανασσῆς, ῆ, ὁ Manasses, Manasseh
Ἀμώς, ὁ Amos, Amon (indeclinable)
Ἰωσίας, ου, ὁ Josias, Josiah
1:11
δέ and, but, now (conjunction, postpositive)
ὁ, ἡ, τό the (definite article)
Ἰεχονίας, ου, ὁ Jechonias, Jechoniah
καί and (conjunction)
ἀδελφός, οῦ, ὁ brother
αὐτός, αὐτή, αὐτό self; same; he, she, it, they

1:6 **ἐκ τῆς τοῦ Οὐρίου**: *by the wife of Uriah*; supply γυναικός after the feminine article. The omission of the noun is commonplace in Greek. The circumlocution avoids having to name Bathsheba with whom David committed adultery but calls attention to her husband whom he had killed.

ἐπὶ τῆς μετοικεσίας Βαβυλῶνος.
1:12 Μετὰ δὲ τὴν μετοικεσίαν Βαβυλῶνος Ἰεχονίας ἐγέννησεν
τὸν Σαλαθιήλ, Σαλαθιὴλ δὲ ἐγέννησεν τὸν Ζοροβαβέλ, 1:13
Ζοροβαβὲλ δὲ ἐγέννησεν τὸν Ἀβιούδ, Ἀβιοὺδ δὲ ἐγέννησεν τὸν
Ἐλιακίμ, Ἐλιακὶμ δὲ ἐγέννησεν τὸν Ἀζώρ, 1:14 Ἀζὼρ δὲ ἐγέννησεν
τὸν Σαδώκ, Σαδὼκ δὲ ἐγέννησεν τὸν Ἀχίμ, Ἀχὶμ δὲ ἐγέννησεν
τὸν Ἐλιούδ, 1:15 Ἐλιοὺδ δὲ ἐγέννησεν τὸν Ἐλεάζαρ, Ἐλεάζαρ δὲ
ἐγέννησεν τὸν Ματθάν, Ματθὰν δὲ ἐγέννησεν τὸν Ἰακώβ, 1:16
Ἰακὼβ δὲ ἐγέννησεν τὸν Ἰωσὴφ τὸν ἄνδρα Μαρίας,

1:11
ἐπί in, at; in the time of, at the time of, during (preposition + genitive)
μετοικεσία, ας, ἡ deportation, captivity
Βαβυλών, ῶνος, ἡ Babylon
1:12
μετά after (preposition + accusative)
μετοικεσία, ας, ἡ migration, removal, deportation, captivity
Σαλαθιήλ, ὁ Salathiel, Shealtiel (indeclinable)
Ζοροβαβέλ, ὁ Zorobabel, Zerubbabel
1:13
Ἀβιούδ, ὁ Abiud (indeclinable)
Ἐλιακίμ, ὁ Eliakim (indeclinable)
Ἀζώρ, ὁ Azor (indeclinable)
1:14
Σαδώκ, ὁ Sadoc, Zadok (indeclinable)
Ἀχίμ, ὁ Achim (indeclinable)
Ἐλιούδ, ὁ Eliud (indeclinable)
1:15
Ἐλεάζαρ, ὁ Eleazar (indeclinable)
Ματθάν, ὁ Matthan (indeclinable)
1:16
γεννάω, γεννήσω, ἐγέννησα, γεγέννηκα, γεγέννημαι, ἐγεννήθην beget, father, be father of, have a child, daughter, son; give birth to, bear, bring forth, conceive
Ἰωσήφ, ὁ Joseph (indeclinable)
ἀνήρ, ἀνδρός, ὁ man, male, husband
Μαρία, ας, ἡ Mary

1:11 **ἐπὶ τῆς μετοικεσίας Βαβυλῶνος**: *at the time of the Babylonian captivity*; this event marks the end of the second paragraph and closes out the second period of fourteen patriarchs.

1:16 **τὸν ἄνδρα Μαρίας**: the appositional ἄνδρα could easily have been omitted similarly to γυναικός in 1:6 above, but it is emphatically included to show that Joseph's nobility derives not only through his patriarchal line but also because of his marriage to his wife Mary. The familiar verb pattern of patriarch begetting patriarch changes from the active ἐγέννησεν to the passive **ἐγεννήθη** (cf. App. 53, G, 1). The sign of the first aorist passive is θ. The endings are -θην, -θης, -θη, -θημεν, -θητε, -θησαν. The consistently employed ἐκ still indicates the mother by whom the child is born, but Joseph is not given as the literal father. When Joseph is told by an angel of the unusual circumstance surrounding the birth of Jesus (1:20–21), he accepts not only Mary as his wife but also her son as his legal heir. Thus the birth of Jesus concludes the third paragraph of the genealogical list and stands as the climax of the triadic structure of ancestral fathers.

ἐξ ἧς ἐγεννήθη Ἰησοῦς ὁ λεγόμενος Χριστός.

1:17 Πᾶσαι οὖν αἱ γενεαὶ ἀπὸ Ἀβραὰμ ἕως Δαυὶδ γενεαὶ δεκατέσσαρες,καὶ ἀπὸ Δαυὶδ ἕως τῆς μετοικεσίας Βαβυλῶνος γενεαὶ δεκατέσσαρες, καὶ ἀπὸ τῆς μετοικεσίας Βαβυλῶνος ἕως τοῦ Χριστοῦ γενεαὶ δεκατέσσαρες.

1:18 Τοῦ δὲ Ἰησοῦ Χριστοῦ ἡ γένεσις οὕτως ἦν.

1:16
ἐκ (ἐξ before a vowel) from, out of, of, by (preposition + genitive)
ὅς, ἥ, ὅ who, which, what; he who, that (relative pronoun)
λέγω, ἐρῶ, εἶπον, εἴρηκα, εἴρημαι, ἐρρέθην/ἐρρήθην say, assert, proclaim, tell, declare, call, name
1:17
πᾶς, πᾶσα, πᾶν every, all
οὖν therefore, then, so (conjunction, postpositive)
γενεά, ᾶς, ἡ progeny, generation
ἀπό from, because of, out of, by (preposition + genitive)
ἕως while, as long as, until
δεκατέσσαρες, ων, οἱ, αἱ fourteen
μετοικεσία, ας, ἡ migration, removal, deportation, captivity
Βαβυλών, ῶνος, ἡ Babylon
1:18
γένεσις, εως, ἡ birth; generation, descent, lineage
οὕτως so, thus, in this manner (adverb)
εἰμί, ἔσομαι be

1:16 **ἐξ ἧς**: *by whom*; ἧς is a relative pronoun (App. 49). It agrees in gender and number with its antecedent, Μαρίας. The case of the relative, determined by its use in its own clause, is in the genitive case as the object of the preposition ἐξ. **ὁ λεγόμενος Χριστός**: *who is called Christ*; the present passive participle λεγόμενος is masculine, singular, nominative (cf. App. 30), and, as an adjective, agrees in gender, number, and case with the article ὁ (App. 1). The article with a participle is best translated as a relative clause. Χριστός is predicate nominative.

1:17 **Πᾶσαι** is a feminine plural nominative adjective (App. 27) modifying γενεαὶ. **γενεαὶ δεκατέσσερες**: *are fourteen generations*; supply the appropriate form of the verb εἰμί *to be* (App. 63). It is often omitted in simple sentences with predicate adjectives or nouns as seen here and in the next two clauses.

1:18 **τοῦ δὲ Ἰησοῦ Χριστοῦ ἡ γένεσις**: after a historical review of the genealogy of Christ, Matthew returns to his central theme, His life, echoing the language of the proem in inverted order: βίβλος γενέσεως Ἰησοῦ Χριστοῦ. The conjunction **δὲ** does not appear as the first word in its clause and so is called *postpositive*. It signals a slight contrast from a previously made statement. **οὕτως** anticipates a more detailed narration of the birth of Christ. **ἦν**: *was*; the verb is the third person singular imperfect active indicative of the verb εἰμί (App. 63). The imperfect tense denotes progressive, continued, and repeated action (aspect) in past time.

μνηστευθείσης τῆς μητρὸς αὐτοῦ Μαρίας τῷ Ἰωσήφ, πρὶν ἢ συνελθεῖν αὐτοὺς εὑρέθη

1:18

μνηστεύω, μνηστεύσω, ἐμνηστεύθην to betroth (active), be betrothed (passive)

μήτηρ, τρός, ἡ mother

πρίν ἤ sooner than, before (adverb)

συνέρχομαι, συνελεύσομαι, συνῆλθον (2 aorist), συνελήλυθα come together, go or come with (anyone), accompany

αὐτός, αὐτή, αὐτό self; same; he, she, it, they

εὑρίσκω, εὑρήσω, εὗρον (2 aorist), ηὕρηκα/εὕρηκα, εὑρέθην find, meet, discover, recognize

---

1:18 **μνηστευθείσης . . . μητρὸς αὐτοῦ**: *when His mother had been betrothed*; the construction is a *genitive absolute*. The noun μητρὸς and the circumstantial participle μνηστευθείσης in the genitive case are syntactically independent of the main verb and clause, i.e., the subject of the genitive absolute may not be used as the subject or the object of the main verb. However, New Testament language does not always strictly adhere to classical usage: in this sentence the noun is used both as the subject of the genitive absolute and as the subject of the main verb. A circumstantial participle may express time, cause, concession, condition, and other circumstances. It needs to be sensitively interpreted according to context and translated into English as a clause (App. 65). μητρὸς is a third declension noun (App. 12). μνηστευθείσης is a feminine singular first aorist passive participle in agreement with μητρὸς. The aorist participle usually expresses a single act (aspect) in past time and frequently translates as a pluperfect when a main verb stands in the past tense. The genitive personal pronoun αὐτοῦ (App. 40) is translated as a possessive adjective in English. The article is omitted in translation. **Μαρίας** stands in apposition to μητρὸς. **τῷ Ἰωσήφ**: the participle μνηστευθείσης takes an object in the dative case. **πρὶν ἢ συνελθεῖν αὐτοὺς**: *before they came together*; after an affirmative clause the conjunction πρὶν ἢ means *before* and is followed by an infinitive with a subject accusative. αὐτοὺς: the personal pronoun (App. 40) becomes masculine when both male and female genders combine. συνελθεῖν is a second aorist infinitive of συνέρχομαι (cf. App. 54). The verb is an expression for having marital relations or for taking up common residence. **εὑρέθη**: *she was found*; the main verb is third person singular first aorist passive indicative. The sign of this passive is **θ** and the endings are -θην, -θης, -θη, -θημεν, -θητε, -θησαν (cf. App. 53, G, 1). It is a temporal augment when the initial vowel of a verb is lengthened, but some initial diphthongs may not be augmented.

ἐν γαστρὶ ἔχουσα ἐκ πνεύματος ἁγίου. 1:19 Ἰωσὴφ δὲ ὁ ἀνὴρ αὐτῆς,
δίκαιος ὢν καὶ μὴ θέλων αὐτὴν δειγματίσαι,

1:18
ἐν in, on, among (proclitic; preposition + dative)
γαστήρ, τρός, ἡ belly, womb; ἐν γαστρὶ ἔχειν be with child, be pregnant
ἔχω, ἕξω, ἔσχον (2 aorist), ἔσχηκα have, keep, cause, consider; be (with adverbs and indications of time and age); be able (with infinitive)
ἐκ (ἐξ before a vowel) from, out of, of, by (preposition + genitive)
πνεῦμα, ατος, τό wind, spirit, mind, Spirit
ἅγιος, ια, ιον hallowed, pure, holy
1:19
ἀνήρ, ἀνδρός, ὁ man, male, husband
αὐτός, αὐτή, αὐτό self; same; he, she, it, they
δίκαιος, αία, αιον right, just, honest, good
εἰμί, ἔσομαι be
μή not (particle of negation)
θέλω, θελήσω, ἠθέλησα wish, desire, purpose, want
δειγματίζω, δειγματίσω, ἐδειγμάτισα disgrace, make a public spectacle of, disgrace

---

1:18 **ἐν γαστρὶ ἔχουσα**: γαστρὶ is a third declension noun that declines like μήτηρ (App. 12). ἔχουσα: the feminine singular nominative present active participle (cf. App. 29) agrees with the subject of the main verb *she*. The idiom is easily understood if παιδίον *child* is supplied as the accusative object of the participle. **ἐκ πνεύματος ἁγίου**: the child is begotten in a divine way. ἐκ: a few words called *proclitics* and *enclitics* have no accent and are closely connected with the word they modify. πνεύματος is a third declension neuter noun with stem in **τ** (cf. App. 10). ἁγίου is a first and second declension adjective (cf. App. 17).

1:19 **ὁ ἀνὴρ αὐτῆς**: *her husband*; the third declension noun (App. 12), in the nominative case, stands in apposition to Ἰωσὴφ. The genitive personal pronoun αὐτῆς (App. 40) is translated as a possessive adjective in English. The article is omitted in translation. **δίκαιος ὢν**: *since he was a just man*; ὢν is a masculine singular nominative present active participle of εἰμί (App. 28). As an adjective it agrees in gender, number, and case with its subject Ἰωσὴφ. A present participle indicates continuous and repeated action and is contemporary with the tense of the main verb. A circumstantial participle may express time, cause, concession, condition, and other circumstances. It needs to be sensitively interpreted according to context and translated into English as a clause. δίκαιος is a predicate adjective. **καὶ μὴ θέλων**: *and did not wish*; θέλων is also a present participle. **μὴ** is regularly used as a negation of a participle. **αὐτὴν δειγματίσαι**: the verb is a first aorist active infinitive (cf. App. 53, D, 4); by definition it has no ending as to person or number. It is the complementary infinitive of the participle θέλων. αὐτὴν, the personal pronoun (App. 40), is the direct object of the infinitive.

ἐβουλήθη λάθρᾳ ἀπολῦσαι αὐτήν. 1:20 ταῦτα δὲ αὐτοῦ ἐνθυμηθέντος ἰδοὺ ἄγγελος κυρίου

1:19

βούλομαι, βουλήσομαι, βεβούλημαι, ἐβουλήθην wish, be willing, desire, want

λάθρᾳ in secret, secretly (adverb)

ἀπολύω, ἀπολύσω, ἀπέλυσα, ἀπολέλυκα, ἀπολέλυμαι, ἀπελύθην release, set free, allow to depart; divorce; pardon

αὐτός, αὐτή, αὐτό self; same; he, she, it, they

1:20

οὗτος, αὕτη, τοῦτο this, this one (demonstrative pronoun)

ἐνθυμέομαι, ἐνθυμήσομαι, ἐνεθυμήθην reflect on, ponder, consider, think

ἰδού see, look, behold (demonstrative particle)

ἄγγελος, ου, ὁ messenger, angel

κύριος, ου, ὁ lord, master; Lord

1:19 **ἐβουλήθη**: *desired*; the main verb is the third person singular first aorist passive indicative of the deponent verb βούλομαι. Deponents have middle or passive voice forms but active meanings: ἕπομαι *follow,* γίνομαι *become,* ἔρχομαι *come* or *go,* πορεύομαι *journey* or *travel* are common examples (cf. App. 53, F). It is called *syllabic augment* when **ε** is prefixed to a verb beginning with a consonant. **ἀπολῦσαι**: the first aorist infinitive (App. 53, D, 4) complements the main verb. The aorist tense usually expresses a single act (aspect) in past time.

1:20 **ταῦτα δὲ αὐτοῦ ἐνθυμηθέντος**: *but while he pondered these thoughts*; the conjunction **δὲ** does not appear as the first word in its clause and so is called *postpositive.* It signals a slight contrast from a previously made statement. The verbal construction is a *genitive absolute.* The personal pronoun αὐτοῦ and the circumstantial participle ἐνθυμηθέντος in the genitive case are syntactically independent of the main clause, i.e., the subject of the genitive absolute may not be used as the subject or the object of the main verb. However, New Testament language does not always strictly adhere to classical usage: in this sentence the pronoun is used both as the subject of the genitive absolute and as the dative object of the main verb. A circumstantial participle may express time, cause, concession, condition, and other circumstances. It should be sensitively interpreted and translated into English as a clause (App. 65). ἐνθυμηθέντος, the aorist participle of a deponent verb (cf. App. 34), has active meaning and takes ταῦτα as its direct object. The demonstrative pronoun is a neuter plural substantive and a *cognate accusative.* Obvious examples of such an accusative are *to run a race, to dream a dream, to live a life, to die a death,* where the verb shows linguistic kinship to its noun. Occasionally the cognate accusative construction omits the noun and admits only a demonstrative pronoun or adjective as an object. In translating this construction more idiomatically an accusative noun can be constructed from the verbal form and added to the demonstrative pronoun. **ἰδοὺ** anticipates the divine visitation. **ἄγγελος κυρίου**: Both are second declension nouns (cf. App. 4). The divine event of her pregnancy will now be revealed by a divine messenger.

κατ' ὄναρ ἐφάνη αὐτῷ λέγων, Ἰωσὴφ υἱὸς Δαυίδ, μὴ φοβηθῇς παραλαβεῖν Μαρίαν τὴν γυναῖκά σου·

1:20
κατά in, during, by, in accordance with, after the manner of (preposition + accusative)
ὄναρ, τό dream (indeclinable)
φαίνω, φανῶ, ἔφηνα, πέφαγκα, πέφηνα, πέφασμαι, ἐφάνθην, ἐφάνην shine, give light, be bright; be seen, appear, be visible (middle and passive)
αὐτός, αὐτή, αὐτό self; same; he, she, it, they
λέγω, ἐρῶ, εἶπον, εἴρηκα, εἴρημαι, ἐρρέθην/ἐρρήθην say, assert, proclaim, tell, declare
υἱός, οῦ, ὁ son
μή not (particle of negation)
φοβέομαι, φοβηθήσομαι, ἐφοβήθην be afraid, become frightened
παραλαμβάνω, παραλήμψομαι, παρέλαβον (2 aorist), παρείληφα, παρείλημμαι, παρελήφθην take, receive, accept
γυνή, γυναικός, ἡ woman, wife
σύ, σοῦ (σου) you (personal pronoun)

1:20 **κατ' ὄναρ**: κατ' = κατὰ; the final vowel of a preposition is frequently elided before the initial vowel of the following word; elision is indicated by an apostrophe. **ὄναρ** is a third declension noun used only in the nominative and accusative. **ἐφάνη**: *appeared*; some verbs show a second aorist passive in addition to the first with a distinctive change in meaning. This passive omits θ, and the endings -ην, -ης, -η, -ημεν, -ητε, -ησαν (cf. App. 53, G, 1) are added directly to the stem. It is called *syllabic augment* when **ε** is prefixed to a verb beginning with a consonant. **αὐτῷ λέγων**: the present active participle (cf. App. 29) agrees in gender, number, and case with its subject ἄγγελος and takes a dative object in αὐτῷ. The participle introduces direct speech, which is editorially indicated by the capitalization of the following word. **υἱὸς Δαυίδ**: *son of David*; the nominative is not uncommonly used as a vocative in N.T. Greek (App. 4). **μὴ φοβηθῇς**: *do not be afraid*; the negative particle μὴ and the subjunctive are equivalent to a negative imperative. The first aorist passive (cf. App. 53, G, 2) of a deponent verb is active in meaning. **παραλαβεῖν Μαρίαν τὴν γυναῖκά σου**: *to take Mary as your wife*; the second aorist complementary infinitive (cf. App. 54) takes Μαρίαν as an accusative and γυναῖκά as a predicate accusative. σου is the enclitic second person pronoun. By definition an enclitic *leans on* the previous word so that the two words are counted as one in terms of accent. To compensate for the additional syllable γυναῖκά receives an additional acute accent on the ultima.

τὸ γὰρ ἐν αὐτῇ γεννηθὲν ἐκ πνεύματός ἐστιν ἁγίου. 1:21 τέξεται δὲ υἱόν, καὶ καλέσεις τὸ ὄνομα αὐτοῦ Ἰησοῦν·

1:20
γάρ for, indeed, but (conjunction)
ἐν in, on, among (proclitic; preposition + dative)
αὐτός, αὐτή, αὐτό self; same; he, she, it, they
γεννάω, γεννήσω, ἐγέννησα, γεγέννηκα, γεγέννημαι, ἐγεννήθην beget, father, be father of, have a child, daughter, son; give birth to, bear, bring forth, conceive; be born, be conceived (in passive)
ἐκ (ἐξ before a vowel) from, out of, of, by (preposition + genitive)
πνεῦμα, ατος, τό wind, spirit, mind, Spirit
εἰμί, ἔσομαι be
ἅγιος, ια, ιον hallowed, pure, holy
1:21
τίκτω, τέξομαι, ἔτεκον (2 aorist), τέτοκα, ἐτέχθην give birth, bear, bring forth
υἱός, οῦ, ὁ son
καλέω, καλέσω, ἐκάλεσα, κέκληκα, κέκλημαι, ἐκλήθην call, summon, invite
ὄνομα, ατος, τό name
αὐτός, αὐτή, αὐτό self; same; he, she, it, they

1:20 **τὸ γὰρ ἐν αὐτῇ γεννηθὲν**: *for that which was conceived in her*; the literary figure hyperbaton or separation of two words may introduce a poetic image or paint a picture. The article τὸ and its participle γεννηθὲν are separated by the prepositional phrase ἐν αὐτῇ. Contrary to expectation, the child surrounds the mother. Perhaps the word order suggests that she is being protected by the child or being reborn in a spiritual way by her experience. The aorist tense of the participle focuses on a single act (aspect) in past time. **ἐκ πνεύματός . . . ἁγίου**: the divine voice reveals to Joseph what Matthew has already declared to the reader (1:18).

1:21 **τέξεται**: *she will bear*; the verb form is a third person singular future deponent indicative. Only the future tense of this verb is deponent. The future is formed with a sigma plus the middle endings: -σομαι, -σῃ/-σει, -σεται, -σομεθα, -σεσθε, -σονται (cf. 53, B, Middle). The future sign, sigma, is here included in the letter **ξ** (= **κ** + **σ**). Deponents have middle or passive voice forms but active meanings. **υἱόν** is the direct object of the deponent verb. **καλέσεις**: by naming Him, Joseph will adopt Him and make Him heir to his Davidic line (cf. Isa 43:1). The second person singular future active indicative verb takes a double accusative: in addition to the direct object ὄνομα, it takes a predicate accusative Ἰησοῦν. The sign of the future is a sigma followed by the active endings: -σω, -σεις, -σει, -σομεν, -σετε, -σουσι(ν) (cf. 53, B, 1).

αὐτὸς γὰρ σώσει τὸν λαὸν αὐτοῦ ἀπὸ τῶν ἁμαρτιῶν αὐτῶν. 1:22 Τοῦτο δὲ ὅλον γέγονεν ἵνα πληρωθῇ

1:21
γάρ for, indeed, but (conjunction)
σῴζω, σώσω, ἔσωσα, σέσωκα, σέσωσμαι, ἐσώθην save, rescue
λαός, οῦ, ὁ people
ἀπό from, because of, out of, by (preposition + genitive)
ἁμαρτία, ας, ἡ error, sin
1:22
οὗτος, αὕτη, τοῦτο this, this one (demonstrative pronoun, adjective)
ὅλος, η, ον all, whole, entire, complete
γίνομαι, γενήσομαι, ἐγενόμην, γέγονα/γεγένημαι, ἐγενήθην become, be made, be created; arise, occur, come to pass, happen; be born, come, arrive, be present, be
ἵνα to, in order to, in order that, that (conjunction)
πληρόω, πληρώσω, ἐπλήρωσα, πεπλήρωκα, πεπλήρωμαι, ἐπληρώθην fill, complete, fulfill

1:21 The placement of **αὐτὸς** at the beginning of the sentence makes the pronoun emphatic. When it stands in the nominative case it is called *intensive* (App. 40, note 2). **σώσει**: the verb is a third person singular future active indicative of the **ω** verb (cf. App. 53, B, 1). The verb placement is here at the beginning but may also occur in the middle or at the end of a sentence. Words placed at the beginning and end tend to be emphatic. The three future verbs τέξεται, καλέσεις, and σώσει, all collocated at the beginning of their clauses, constitute a classical tricolon, in which the third element is more fully developed. The repetition creates a poetic crescendo. **τὸν λαὸν αὐτοῦ**: *his people*; the genitive personal pronoun αὐτοῦ (App. 40) is translated as a possessive adjective in English. The article is omitted in translation. **ἁμαρτιῶν** is a first declension noun (cf. App. 2). From the time of Adam and Eve's ejection from the garden, ἁμαρτία has been associated with death, and salvation has always been a hope. The tricolon concludes the angel's remarks.

1:22 **Τοῦτο δὲ ὅλον γέγονεν**: *but all this occurred*; both the demonstrative pronoun (App. 41) and the adjective are neuter and may be changed into a substantive (cf. App. 16). The conjunction **δὲ** does not appear as the first word in its clause and so is called *postpositive*. It signals a slight contrast from a previously made statement. **γέγονεν**: the verbal form is a third person singular perfect active indicative (cf. App. 53, E, 1). The perfect tense denotes action (aspect) that is completed near present time and continues with present result: *All this has occurred* (recently and is happening now). The reduplication or doubling of the stem at the beginning of a word occurs especially in the perfect, pluperfect, and future perfect tenses to indicate completed action. **ἵνα πληρωθῇ τὸ ῥηθὲν**: *in order that what was spoken might be fulfilled*; ἵνα is the usual conjunction to introduce purpose clauses. The first aorist passive verb stands in the subjunctive mood (cf. App. 53, G, 2). The subjunctive mood is regularly formed by the lengthening of the personal endings of the present indicative. The third person singular ending **-ει** becomes **-ῃ**: the **ε** changes to **η**, and the **ι** becomes a subscript.

τὸ ῥηθὲν ὑπὸ κυρίου διὰ τοῦ προφήτου λέγοντος,
1:23 Ἰδοὺ ἡ παρθένος ἐν γαστρὶ ἕξει καὶ τέξεται υἱόν,
καὶ καλέσουσιν τὸ ὄνομα αὐτοῦ Ἐμμανουήλ,

1:22
λέγω, ἐρῶ, εἶπον, εἴρηκα, εἴρημαι, ἐρρέθην/ἐρρήθην say, assert, proclaim, tell, declare
ὑπό by (preposition + genitive of personal agent)
κύριος, ου, ὁ lord, Lord, master
διά through, by (preposition + genitive)
προφήτης, ου, ὁ prophet, seer, revelator
1:23
ἰδού see, look, behold (demonstrative particle)
παρθένος, ου, ἡ virgin
ἐν in, on, among (proclitic; preposition + dative)
γαστήρ, τρός, ἡ belly, womb; ἐν γαστρὶ ἔχειν be with child, be pregnant
ἔχω, ἕξω, ἔσχον (2 aorist), ἔσχηκα have, keep, cause, consider
τίκτω, τέξομαι, ἔτεκον (2 aorist), τέτοκα, ἐτέχθην give birth, bear, bring forth
υἱός, οῦ, ὁ son
καλέω, καλέσω, ἐκάλεσα, κέκληκα, κέκλημαι, ἐκλήθην call, summon
ὄνομα, ατος, τό name
αὐτός, αὐτή, αὐτό self; same; he, she, it, they
Ἐμμανουήλ, ὁ Emmanuel (indeclinable)

1:22 τὸ ῥηθὲν: *that which was spoken* (literally); the verbal form is a neuter singular nominative first aorist passive participle (cf. App. 53, G, 5; 34) of the verb λέγω that translates as a relative clause in conjunction with an article. **ὑπὸ κυρίου διὰ τοῦ προφήτου λέγοντος**: the preposition takes the genitive case expressing agency. διὰ denotes intermediate agency. **τοῦ προφήτου** is a first declension noun ending in **ης** (App. 3). The Lord speaks; the prophet is his mouthpiece. λέγοντος: the masculine singular genitive present active participle (cf. App. 29) may modify either κυρίου or προφήτου or both. The rhetorical figure where one element or word governs a double syntactic function is called *apo koinou* (ἀπὸ κοινοῦ).

1:23 **Ἰδοὺ** again anticipates the divine visitation. **ἡ παρθένος**: the noun is in the nominative case. It belongs to the class of second declension masculine nouns ending in **ος** (cf. App. 4). However, this declension includes a few feminines ending in **ος** (App. 5); any modifiers will be feminine. **γαστρὶ** is a third declension noun that declines like μήτηρ (App. 12). **ἕξει** is a third person singular future active indicative of ἔχω (cf. App. 53, B, 1). The idiom is easily understood if παιδίον *child* is supplied as the accusative object of the finite verb. **τέξεται**: the verb form is a third person singular future deponent indicative. Only the future tense of this verb is deponent (cf. 53, B, Middle). Deponents have middle or passive voice forms but active meanings. **υἱόν** is the direct object of the deponent verb. **καλέσουσιν τὸ ὄνομα αὐτοῦ Ἐμμανουήλ**: the main or finite verb, a third person plural future active indicative, takes a double accusative; in addition to the direct object ὄνομα, it takes a predicate accusative Ἐμμανουήλ. The third person plural may be an impersonal construction or refer to those who believe on His name.

ὅ ἐστιν μεθερμηνευόμενον Μεθ' ἡμῶν ὁ θεός. 1:24 ἐγερθεὶς δὲ ὁ Ἰωσὴφ ἀπὸ τοῦ ὕπνου ἐποίησεν

1:23
ὅς, ἥ, ὅ who, which, what; he who, that (relative pronoun)
εἰμί, ἔσομαι be
μεθερμηνεύω translate, interpret
μετά (μεθ' before a rough breathing) with (preposition + genitive)
ἐγώ, ἐμοῦ (μου) I (personal pronoun)
θεός, οῦ, ὁ God, god
1:24
ἐγείρω, ἐγερῶ, ἤγειρα, ἠγήγερμαι, ἠγέρθην awaken, raise up from the dead, restore, rebuild; arise! get up! come! (intransitive, only in imperative)
ἀπό from, because of, out of, by (preposition + genitive)
ὕπνος, ου, ὁ sleep
ποιέω, ποιήσω, ἐποίησα, πεποίηκα, πεποίημαι, ἐποιήθην make, do, keep, obey

---

1:23 **ὅ ἐστιν μεθερμηνευόμενον**: *which interpreted means*; the phrase is frequently used to explain foreign terms and names. The verb ἐστιν is the third person singular present active indicative of the verb εἰμί, but may be translated more idiomatically. It is conjugated εἰμί, εἶ, ἐστί, ἐσμέν, ἐστέ, εἰσί(ν) (App. 63). All but the second person singular are enclitics and by definition *lean on* the previous word so that the two words are counted as one in terms of accent. The enclitic usually loses its accent. The accent on the relative pronoun stays acute. μεθερμηνευόμενον is a neuter present passive participle (cf. App. 53, A, 5; 30) in agreement with the relative pronoun ὅ (App. 49). **ἡμῶν**, the object of the preposition, is a first person plural personal pronoun (App. 39). The verb placements of the last three verbs in the future tense **ἕξει, τέξεται,** and **καλέσουσιν,** either at the beginning or at the end of a sentence, stand in emphatic position and constitute a classical tricolon. In the arrangement of these clauses, the third element is more fully developed. The repetition creates a poetic crescendo. **ὁ θεός**: supply the appropriate form of the verb εἰμί *to be* (App. 63). It is often omitted in simple sentences. Ellipsis of the copula εἰμί occurs more frequently with some forms of this verb than others. The article is omitted in translation.

1:24 **ἐγερθεὶς** is a first aorist passive participle (cf. App. 34) modifying ὁ Ἰωσήφ. **ὁ Ἰωσὴφ**: proper names usually take an article in Greek. **ἀπὸ τοῦ ὕπνου**: *from his sleep*; the article is used as an unemphatic possessive adjective where ownership or relationship is logically implied. **ἐποίησεν**: this and the following main verbs in the narrative summarize and briskly move the action along. The syllabic augment is prefixed to a verb beginning with a consonant.

ὡς προσέταξεν αὐτῷ ὁ ἄγγελος κυρίου καὶ παρέλαβεν τὴν γυναῖκα αὐτοῦ, 1:25 καὶ οὐκ ἐγίνωσκεν αὐτὴν ἕως οὗ ἔτεκεν υἱόν· καὶ ἐκάλεσεν τὸ ὄνομα αὐτοῦ Ἰησοῦν.

1:24
ὡς as, like, just as
προστάσσω, προστάξω, προσέταξα, προστέταγμαι, προσετάχθην command, order
ἄγγελος, ου, ὁ messenger, angel
κύριος, ου, ὁ lord, Lord, master
καί and (conjunction); even, also, likewise, and yet (adverb)
παραλαμβάνω, παραλήμψομαι, παρέλαβον (2 aorist), παρείληφα, παρείλημμαι, παρελήφθην take, receive, accept
γυνή, γυναικός, ἡ woman, wife
1:25
καί and (conjunction); even, also, likewise, and yet (adverb)
οὐ not (οὐκ before vowels with a smooth breathing, οὐχ before a rough breathing, adverb)
γινώσκω, γνώσομαι, ἔγνων, ἔγνωκα, ἔγνωσμαι, ἐγνώσθην know, learn, understand, know carnally
ἕως while, as long as, until; ἕως οὗ until
τίκτω, τέξομαι, ἔτεκον (2 aorist), τέτοκα, ἐτέχθην give birth, bear, bring forth
υἱός, οῦ, ὁ son
καλέω, καλέσω, ἐκάλεσα, κέκληκα, κέκλημαι, ἐκλήθην call, summon, invite
ὄνομα, ατος, τό name

1:24 **προσέταξεν αὐτῷ**: the verb takes the dative of the person. The syllabic augment is prefixed to a verb beginning with a consonant and follows the preposition.

1:25 **οὐκ ἐγίνωσκεν αὐτὴν**: the verb is the third person singular imperfect of the verb γινώσκω. The imperfect tense denotes progressive, continued, and repeated action (aspect) in past time. It adds its endings to the present stem (cf. App. 53, C). The verb is a common euphemism for sexual intercourse. The tense suggests continued abstinence in the past. The child has not been conceived by human but by divine agency. **ἔτεκεν** is a second aorist tense. Personal endings are -ον, -ες, -ε(ν), -ομεν, -ετε, -ον (cf. App. 54). As an aorist, it expresses a single act (aspect) in past time. A change in stem from the present tense to the aorist distinguishes the second aorist from the first, as with the stem changes observed thus far: γιν-> γεν- (γίνομαι), λαμβ-> λαβ- (λαμβάνω), ερχ-> ελθ- (ἔρχομαι). A movable **ν** may be added to the third person singular ending in -**ε** (cf. App. 54). **ἐκάλεσεν** takes a double accusative; in addition to the direct object ὄνομα, it takes a predicate accusative Ἰησοῦν. Thus Joseph fulfills the prophecy and the command of the angel of the Lord.

2 Τοῦ δὲ Ἰησοῦ γεννηθέντος ἐν Βηθλέεμ τῆς Ἰουδαίας ἐν ἡμέραις Ἡρῴδου τοῦ βασιλέως, ἰδοὺ μάγοι ἀπὸ ἀνατολῶν παρεγένοντο

2:1

γεννάω, γεννήσω, ἐγέννησα, γεγέννηκα, γεγέννημαι, ἐγεννήθην beget, father; give birth to, bear, bring forth, conceive; be born, be conceived (in passive)

ἐν in, on, among (proclitic; preposition + dative)

Βηθλέεμ, ἡ Bethlehem (indeclinable)

Ἰουδαία, ας, ἡ Judaea

ἡμέρα, ας, ἡ day

Ἡρῴδης, ου, ὁ Herod

βασιλεύς, έως, ὁ king

ἰδού see, look, behold (demonstrative particle)

μάγος, ου, ὁ magus, wise man, magian

ἀπό from, because of, out of, by (preposition + genitive)

ἀνατολή, ῆς, ἡ rising, east, orient

παραγίνομαι, παραγενήσομαι, παρεγενόμην come, arrive, be present

---

2:1 **Τοῦ δὲ Ἰησοῦ γεννηθέντος**: *Now when Jesus was born*; the construction is a *genitive absolute*. The conjunction **δὲ** does not appear as the first word in its clause and so is called *postpositive*. It signals a slight contrast from a previously made statement. The noun Ἰησοῦ and the circumstantial participle γεννηθέντος in the genitive case are syntactically independent of the main clause, i.e., the subject of the genitive absolute may not be used as the subject or the object of the main verb. Although New Testament language does not always strictly adhere to classical usage, in this sentence it does. A circumstantial participle may express time, cause, concession, condition, and other circumstances. It should be sensitively interpreted and translated into English as a clause (App. 65). γεννηθέντος is a first aorist passive participle (cf. App. 34). The name, conspicuous at the beginning and end of chapters and paragraphs, dominates the beginning of the Gospel of Matthew. **ἐν Βηθλέεμ τῆς Ἰουδαίας**: Jesus came not only through the royal house of David but also from his city (Jn 7:42) as prophesied (Mic 5:2). The text specifies which Bethlehem is meant. **ἐν ἡμέραις Ἡρῴδου τοῦ βασιλέως**: the article is often omitted in expressions of time. **Ἡρῴδου** is a first declension noun ending in **ης** (App. 3). The meaning of the idiomatic expression is clear enough. The genitive may be construed as a simple possessive: the days are Herod's to rule. τοῦ βασιλέως: the third declension noun (App. 14) stands in apposition to Ἡρῴδου. **ἰδοὺ**: the demonstrative particle introduces an extraordinary mortal visitation. **μάγοι**: the text does not further identify who they are, but it makes clear that they are well disposed, have a deep sense of recognition as to who they are, who the newborn child is, and what their relationship is to the child. **ἀπὸ ἀνατολῶν παρεγένοντο εἰς Ἱεροσόλυμα**: collocation of words suggests having to travel a long journey between east and west. The theme is that of home and distance. Again, the text does not specify from where they are coming, but perhaps by not doing so generalizes and hints at a more universal journey of spiritual and cosmic significance. **ἀπὸ ἀνατολῶν**: the noun often occurs in the plural.

εἰς Ἱεροσόλυμα 2:2 λέγοντες, Ποῦ ἐστιν ὁ τεχθεὶς βασιλεὺς τῶν Ἰουδαίων; εἴδομεν γὰρ αὐτοῦ τὸν ἀστέρα ἐν τῇ ἀνατολῇ

2:1
εἰς to, into, on, in; for, as; with respect to (preposition + accusative)
Ἱεροσόλυμα, τά and ἡ Jerusalem (indeclinable)
2:2
λέγω, ἐρῶ, εἶπον, εἴρηκα, εἴρημαι, ἐρρέθην/ἐρρήθην say, assert, proclaim, tell, declare
ποῦ where? in what place? (interrogative adverb)
εἰμί, ἔσομαι be
τίκτω, τέξομαι, ἔτεκον (2 aorist), τέτοκα, ἐτέχθην give birth, bear, bring forth
βασιλεύς, έως, ὁ king
Ιουδαῖος, αία, αῖον Jewish, Jew
ὁράω, ὄψομαι, εἶδον (2 aorist), ἑώρακα/ἑόρακα, φθην see, catch sight of, notice, look, observe, perceive, experience, witness
γάρ for, indeed, but (conjunction)
ἀστήρ, ἀστέρος, ὁ star
ἐν in, on, among (proclitic; preposition + dative)
ἀνατολή, ῆς, ἡ rising, rising of the sun, east, orient

2:2 **λέγοντες**: the masculine plural nominative present active participle (cf. App. 29) at the end modifies the subject μάγοι at the beginning of the sentence. The hyperbaton or lengthy separation of the two words may be a poetic expression to underscore the length of the journey. The two hyperbatons are part of a more intricate pattern. The symmetrical structure of the word order A, B, C, B, A with the verb in the center produces a golden chiasm: μάγοι . . . ἀπὸ ἀνατολῶν . . . παρεγένοντο . . . εἰς Ἱεροσόλυμα . . . λέγοντες. This is no simple journey. **ἐστιν**: the verb is the third person singular present active indicative of the verb εἰμί. It is conjugated εἰμί, εἶ, ἐστί, ἐσμέν, ἐστέ, εἰσί(ν) (App. 63). All but the second person singular are enclitics and by definition *lean on* the previous word so that the two words are counted as one in terms of accent. The enclitic usually loses its accent. **ὁ τεχθεὶς**: *he who was born*; the verbal form is a first aorist passive participle (cf. App. 53, G, 5; 34), that translates as a relative clause in conjunction with an article. **βασιλεὺς**: the third declension noun (App. 14) stands in apposition to the nominative article ὁ. **εἴδομεν γὰρ αὐτοῦ τὸν ἀστέρα**: the astrological phenomenon of the star attests to the cosmic significance of the birth. Recognition of the sign speaks to the wisdom and spirituality of the magi. εἴδομεν is a first person plural second aorist active indicative of the verb ὁράω. Personal endings are -ον, -ες, -ε(ν), -ομεν, -ετε, -ον (cf. App. 54). As an aorist, it expresses a single act (aspect) in past time. A change in stem from the present tense to the aorist distinguishes the second aorist from the first, as with the stem changes observed thus far: γιν-> γεν- (γίνομαι), λαμβ-> λαβ- (λαμβάνω), ερχ-> ελθ- (ἔρχομαι). Personal endings are added to the second aorist stem. τὸν ἀστέρα: the third declension noun is in the accusative case (cf. App. 12). The genitive personal pronoun αὐτοῦ (App. 40) is translated as a possessive adjective in English. The article is omitted in translation.

καὶ ἤλθομεν προσκυνῆσαι αὐτῷ. 2:3 ἀκούσας δὲ ὁ βασιλεὺς Ἡρῴδης ἐταράχθη

2:2

καί and (conjunction); even, also, likewise, and yet (adverb)

ἔρχομαι, ἐλεύσομαι, ἦλθον (2 aorist), ἐλήλυθα come, go

προσκυνέω, προσκυνήσω, προσεκύνησα worship, prostrate oneself before, reverence before, reverence

2:3

ἀκούω, ἀκούσω, ἤκουσα, ἀκήκοα, ἤκουσμαι, ἠκούσθην hear, obey, understand (+ genitive or accusative)

βασιλεύς, έως, ὁ king

Ἡρῴδης, ου, ὁ Herod

ταράσσω, ταράξω, ἐτάραξα, τετάραγμαι, ἐταράχθην stir up, disturb, trouble

---

2:2 **ἤλθομεν προσκυνῆσαι**: their observation leads the magi to great effort of making the journey to adore the child. The main or finite verb is a first person plural second aorist active indicative. For personal endings see App. 54. προσκυνῆσαι is an aorist active infinitive (cf. App. 53, D, 4) of a contracted verb with stem in **ε** (cf. App. 56). By definition an infinitive has no ending as to person or number. It functions here as an infinitive of purpose and is equivalent to the more commonly used ἵνα clause. This purpose construction is particularly prevalent after main verbs of motion like ἔρχομαι. **αὐτῷ**: the compound verb (προς + κυνεω) governs the dative case (App. 40).

2:3 **ἀκούσας δὲ ὁ βασιλεὺς Ἡρῴδης**: *but when Herod the king had heard this*; supply ταῦτα, a neuter plural accusative of οὗτος (App. 41), as the object of the participle. Translate as *these things* or simply *this*. ἀκούσας is a masculine singular nominative first aorist active participle (cf. App. 31) in agreement with its subject Ἡρῴδης, a first declension noun ending in **ης** (App. 3). Since the action of the aorist participle precedes that of the main verb and represents a single action in the past, it has the force of an English pluperfect. The conjunction **δὲ** does not appear as the first word in its clause and so is called *postpositive*. It signals a slight contrast from a previously made statement. The juxtaposition of βασιλεὺς τῶν Ἰουδαίων in the previous verse with ὁ βασιλεὺς Ἡρῴδης points out an obvious conflict of kingship. Although Herod will soon die, he has been ruthless in guarding his dynasty and will continue to do so. **ἐταράχθη**: *was troubled*; the form is a third person singular first aorist passive indicative. The sign of this passive is **θ** and the endings are -θην, -θης, -θη, -θημεν, -θητε, -θησαν (App. 53, G, 1).

καὶ πᾶσα Ἱεροσόλυμα μετ᾽ αὐτοῦ, 2:4 καὶ συναγαγὼν πάντας τοὺς ἀρχιερεῖς καὶ γραμματεῖς τοῦ λαοῦ ἐπυνθάνετο παρ᾽ αὐτῶν

2:3
καί and (conjunction); even, also, likewise, and yet (adverb)
πᾶς, πᾶσα, πᾶν every, all
Ἱεροσόλυμα, τά and ἡ Jerusalem
μετ᾽ = μετά with (preposition + genitive)
2:4
καί and (conjunction); even, also, likewise, and yet (adverb)
συνάγω, συνάξω, συνήγαγον (2 aorist), συνῆγμαι, συνήχθην gather, gather in, gather up, bring together; convene, come together, meet (passive)
πᾶς, πᾶσα, πᾶν every, all
ἀρχιερεύς, έως, ὁ high priest
γραμματεύς, έως, ὁ secretary, clerk, scholar versed in law, scribe
λαός, οῦ, ὁ people
πυνθάνομαι, πεύσομαι, ἐπυθόμην (2 aorist) inquire, ask
παρ᾽ = παρά from (the side of), from, issuing from, by (preposition + genitive)
αὐτός, αὐτή, αὐτό self; same; he, she, it, they

2:3 **καὶ πᾶσα Ἱεροσόλυμα μετ᾽ αὐτοῦ**: the statement is a hyperbole, a rhetorical exaggeration. Matthew makes reference to the corrupt political and religious leadership of the city, not to the Jewish people as a whole. **πᾶσα** is a feminine singular nominative adjective (App. 27) modifying Ἱεροσόλυμα.

2:4 **συναγαγὼν**: *when he had gathered*; is a masculine singular nominative second aorist active participle (cf. App. 54; 29 note) modifying the pronoun of the verb as its subject. Since the action of the aorist participle precedes that of the main verb and represents a single action in the past, it has the force of an English pluperfect. **τοὺς ἀρχιερεῖς καὶ γραμματεῖς**: both third declension nouns are masculine plural accusative (cf. App. 14). The declensional pattern is that of βασιλεύς except the accusative plural looks like the nominative plural. **ἐπυνθάνετο**: *he began to inquire*; the verb is third person singular imperfect middle indicative of a deponent verb. The imperfect tense denotes progressive, continued, repeated, and beginning action (aspect) in past time. Deponents have middle or passive voice forms but active meanings. The imperfect deponent, formed by adding an augment to the present stem, takes the same personal endings as that of the second aorist: -μην, -ου, -το, -μεθα, -σθε, -ντο (App. 54). However, in contrast to the aorist, its aspect shows action in the past that is continuing (*was inquiring*), customary (*used to inquire*), conative (*attempted to inquire*), inchoative (*began to inquire*), etc. The verb frequently takes the preposition παρά.

ποῦ ὁ Χριστὸς γεννᾶται.
2:5 οἱ δὲ εἶπαν αὐτῷ, Ἐν Βηθλέεμ τῆς Ἰουδαίας· οὕτως γὰρ
γέγραπται διὰ τοῦ προφήτου·
2:6 Καὶ σὺ Βηθλέεμ, γῆ Ἰούδα,
οὐδαμῶς ἐλαχίστη εἶ ἐν τοῖς ἡγεμόσιν Ἰούδα·

2:4
ποῦ where? in what place? (interrogative adverb)
γεννάω, γεννήσω, ἐγέννησα, γεγέννηκα, γεγέννημαι, ἐγεννήθην beget, father, be father of, have a child, daughter, son; give birth to, bear, bring forth, conceive; be born, be conceived (in passive)
2:5
λέγω, ἐρῶ, εἶπον, εἴρηκα, εἴρημαι, ἐρρέθην/ἐρρήθην say, assert, proclaim, tell, declare
ἐν in, on, among (proclitic; preposition + dative)
Βηθλέεμ, ἡ Bethlehem (indeclinable)
Ἰουδαία, ας, ἡ Judaea
οὕτως so, thus, in this manner (adverb)
γράφω, γράψω, ἔγραψα, γέγραφα, γέγραμμαι, ἐγράφθην engrave, write
διά through, by (preposition + genitive)
προφήτης, ου, ὁ prophet, seer, revelator
2:6
σύ, σοῦ (σου) you (personal pronoun)
γῆ, γῆς, ἡ soil, land, region, country
Ἰούδας, α, ὁ Judas (Greek), Judah (Hebrew)

2:4 **ποῦ ὁ Χριστὸς γεννᾶται**: *where Christ was being born*; ποῦ introduces an indirect question. In indirect questions Greek retains the original mood and tense. In Herod's original question, *Where is Christ being born?*, the mood is indicative and the tense present (cf. App. 55). In English the verb of the indirect question matches the tense of the verb introducing the indirect question. Since ἐπυνθάνετο is a past, γεννᾶται is translated as a past.

2:5 **εἶπαν**: occasionally this second aorist stem takes first aorist endings without the **σ**. The present tense of this second aorist form (cf. App. 54) has gone out of use and is supplied by λέγω, φημί, or ἀγορεύω. The verb takes the dative of the person. After a verb of speaking follows a direct statement. **Ἐν Βηθλέεμ**: a quote usually begins with capitalization. **γέγραπται** is the impersonal use of the third person singular perfect passive indicative of γράφω (cf. App. 53, E, 1). The perfect tense denotes action (aspect) that is completed near present time and continues with present result: *it has been written* (and is so now). **διὰ τοῦ προφήτου**: the preposition takes the genitive case expressing agency. διὰ denotes intermediate agency. **τοῦ προφήτου** is a first declension noun ending in **ης** (App. 3).

2:6 **σὺ Βηθλέεμ, γῆ Ἰούδα**: Βηθλέεμ is in the vocative, the case of direct address. γῆ stands in apposition to Βηθλέεμ, and Ἰούδα is an appositional genitive (cf. App. 65): *the land of Judah*, naming the land more specifically. The change from normal discourse to the direct address in the second person (App. 39), called *apostrophe*, is a poetic figure that enhances interest. The quotation from Mic 5:2 is not a verbatim citation.

ἐκ σοῦ γὰρ ἐξελεύσεται ἡγούμενος,
ὅστις ποιμανεῖ τὸν λαόν μου τὸν Ἰσραήλ.
2:7 Τότε Ἡρῴδης λάθρᾳ καλέσας τοὺς μάγους

2:6
οὐδαμῶς by no means, not at all (adverb)
ἐλάχιστος, η, ον smallest, least
εἰμί, ἔσομαι be
ἐν in, on, among (proclitic; preposition + dative)
ἡγεμών, όνος, ὁ guide, leader, prince
ἐκ (ἐξ before a vowel) from, out of, of, by (preposition + genitive)
σύ, σοῦ (σου) you (personal pronoun)
γάρ for, indeed, but (conjunction)
ἐξέρχομαι, ἐξελεύσομαι, ἐξῆλθον (2 aorist), ἐξελήλυθα go or come out of, go out
ἡγέομαι, ἡγήσομαι lead, preside, govern, rule
ὅστις, ἥτις, ὅ τι whoever, whatever (indefinite relative pronoun)
ποιμαίνω, ποιμανῶ, ἐποίμανα feed, herd, tend
λαός, οῦ, ὁ people
ἐγώ, ἐμοῦ (μου) I (personal pronoun)
Ἰσραήλ, ὁ Israel (indeclinable)
2:7
τότε then, at that time, thereupon, thereafter (adverb)
Ἡρῴδης, ου, ὁ Herod
λάθρᾳ in secret, secretly (adverb)
καλέω, καλέσω, ἐκάλεσα, κέκληκα, κέκλημαι, ἐκλήθην call, summon, invite
μάγος, ου, ὁ magus, wise man, magian

2:6 **ἐλαχίστη**, a superlative adjective of μικρός: *small*, stands in predicate position to the subject pronoun in the verb εἶ. It is a first and second declension adjective (cf. App. 16). **ἡγεμόσιν** is a third declension dative plural noun (cf. App. 11). **ἐκ σοῦ**: the threefold repetition of the second person pronoun constitutes a tricolon, emphasizing the importance of the town of Bethlehem. The third element, frequently more fully developed, creates a poetic crescendo. **ὅστις**: *who*; the indefinite relative pronoun is occasionally used instead of the simple relative. The use will generally be made clear by the context. **ποιμανεῖ**: *will shepherd*; the verb changes its stem and accent in the future. It may be well to maintain the metaphor in translation since He is ὁ ποιμὴν ὁ καλός. **τὸν Ἰσραήλ** stands in apposition to λαόν, naming the people more specifically.

2:7 **καλέσας**: *after he had summoned*; the first aorist active participle is masculine, singular, nominative, and, as an adjective, agrees in gender, number, and case with its subject Ἡρῴδης, a first declension noun ending in **ης** (App. 3). As a participle it also has the capacity to take an object: τοὺς μάγους. The aorist participle usually expresses a single act (aspect) in past time and frequently translates as a pluperfect when a main verb stands in the past tense.

ἠκρίβωσεν παρ' αὐτῶν τὸν χρόνον τοῦ φαινομένου ἀστέρος,
2:8 καὶ πέμψας αὐτοὺς εἰς Βηθλέεμ εἶπεν, Πορευθέντες ἐξετάσατε
ἀκριβῶς περὶ τοῦ παιδίου·

2:7
ἀκριβόω, ἀκριβώσω, ἠκρίβωσα, ἠκρίβωκα ascertain exactly
παρ' = παρά from (the side of), from, issuing from, by (preposition + genitive)
χρόνος, ου, ὁ time
φαίνω, φανῶ, ἔφηνα, πέφαγκα, πέφηνα, πέφασμαι, ἐφάνθην, ἐφάνην shine, give light, be bright; be seen, appear, be visible (middle and passive)
ἀστήρ, ἀστέρος, ὁ star
2:8
πέμπω, πέμψω, ἔπεμψα, πέπομφα, ἐπέμφθην send
εἰς to, into, on, in; for, as; with respect to (preposition + accusative)
λέγω, ἐρῶ, εἶπον, εἴρηκα, εἴρημαι, ἐρρέθην/ἐρρήθην say, assert, proclaim, tell, declare
πορεύομαι, πορεύσομαι, πεπόρευμαι, ἐπορεύθην go, proceed, travel
ἐξετάζω, ἐξετάσω, ἐξήτασα inquire, interrogate
ἀκριβῶς diligently, accurately (adverb)
περί about, concerning (preposition + genitive); about, around (+ accusative)
παιδίον, ου, τό infant, young child, little boy, little girl

2:7 **ἠκρίβωσεν** takes the preposition παρά with the genitive of the person interrogated and an accusative of the thing asked τὸν χρόνον. **τοῦ φαινομένου ἀστέρος**: *of the appearing star* or *of the star that appeared*; the participle placed in attributive position, i.e., between the article and its noun, is called an *attributive* participle. The time of its appearance proved critical for Herod's plot in determining the span of time designated for the murder of children.

2:8 **πέμψας αὐτοὺς . . . εἶπεν**: *as he sent them, he said*; the first aorist here has no temporal value but indicates a single act (aspect) only. Context will help to determine whether the time of the participle precedes the action of the main verb or is simultaneous. **Πορευθέντες ἐξετάσατε ἀκριβῶς**: *go and inquire diligently*; when a participle modifies an imperative, it is commonly changed into an imperative and the two verbs are coordinated in translation. Πορευθέντες is the first aorist passive participle of a deponent verb (cf. App. 34). Deponents have middle or passive voice forms but active meanings. **ἐξετάσατε** is a second person plural first aorist active imperative; imperatives drop the augment (cf. App. 53, D, 3). **παιδίου**, the diminutive of παῖς, is a neuter second declension noun (cf. App. 5).

ἐπὰν δὲ εὕρητε, ἀπαγγείλατέ μοι, ὅπως κἀγὼἐλθὼν προσκυνήσω αὐτῷ.

2:8

ἐπάν whenever, as soon as (conjunction)

εὑρίσκω, εὑρήσω, εὗρον (2 aorist), ηὕρηκα/εὕρηκα, εὑρέθην find, meet, discover, recognize

ἀπαγγέλλω, ἀπαγγελῶ, ἀπήγγειλα (1 aorist), ἀπηγγέλην (2 aorist passive) bring back word, report, declare, announce, tell

ἐγώ, ἐμοῦ (μου) I (personal pronoun)

ὅπως how, in what way (adverb); that, in order that (conjunction)

κἀγώ = καὶ ἐγώ I also, even I

ἔρχομαι, ἐλεύσομαι, ἦλθον (2 aorist), ἐλήλυθα come, go

προσκυνέω, προσκυνήσω, προσεκύνησα worship, prostrate oneself before, reverence before, reverence

---

2:8 **ἐπὰν δὲ εὕρητε, ἀπαγγείλατέ μοι**: *but when you find him, tell me*; ἐπὰν, the temporal conjunction followed by a subjunctive, introduces a future more vivid condition (App. 70). The conjunction **δὲ** does not appear as the first word in its clause and so is called *postpositive*. It signals a slight contrast from a previously made statement. The verb of the protasis or the condition is a second aorist subjunctive (cf. App. 54). ἀπαγγείλατε is a first or liquid aorist imperative; some verbs ending in a liquid or nasal (**λ, μ, ν,** or **ρ**) add the first aorist endings -σα, -σας, -σε, -σαμεν, -σατε, -σαν to the stem but omit the **-σ-**. To compensate for the loss of the **-σ-**, the vowel stem is usually lengthened (compensatory lengthening): **ε** becomes **ει**. The imperative in the apodosis or conclusion serves as an equivalent form for the commonly used future indicative. Since both the subjunctive and the imperative commonly connote a future, the tenses refer to aspect rather than time: the present indicates progressive/repeated action; the aorist expresses a single act. **ὅπως**: the conjunction with the subjunctive is used to indicate purpose. **κἀγὼ**: *I also*; the combining of two words καὶ ἐγὼ to avoid vowel succession in adjoining words is called *crasis*. The breathing mark is retained over the contraction. To assure their good will, Herod identifies himself with the magi. **ἐλθὼν προσκυνήσω αὐτῷ**: *may come and worship Him*; he echoes and feigns their words: ἤλθομεν προσκυνῆσαι αὐτῷ (2:2). ἐλθὼν: the second aorist participle stands in predicate position, i.e., it is not modified by an article, and is called a *circumstantial* participle. A circumstantial participle may express time, cause, concession, condition, manner, means, and other circumstances. It needs to be interpreted sensitively according to context and translated into English as a clause. In this case it may be better to coordinate the participle and the finite verb. προσκυνήσω: the future active indicative (cf. 53, B, 1) and the first aorist active subjunctive (cf. 53, D, 2) look alike in the first person. The use will be made clear by the context: the conjunction ὅπως requires the subjunctive. The compound verb (προς + κυνεω) governs the dative case.

2:9 οἱ δὲ ἀκούσαντες τοῦ βασιλέως ἐπορεύθησαν καὶ ἰδοὺ ὁ ἀστήρ, ὃν εἶδον ἐν τῇ ἀνατολῇ,προῆγεν αὐτούς,

---

2:9
ἀκούω, ἀκούσω, ἤκουσα, ἀκήκοα, ἤκουσμαι, ἠκούσθην hear, obey, understand (+ genitive or accusative)
βασιλεύς, έως, ὁ king
πορεύομαι, πορεύσομαι, πεπόρευμαι, ἐπορεύθην go, proceed, travel
ἰδού see, look, behold (demonstrative particle)
ἀστήρ, ἀστέρος, ὁ star
ὅς, ἥ, ὅ who, which, what; he who, that (relative pronoun)
ὁράω, ὄψομαι, εἶδον (2 aorist), ἑώρακα/ἑόρακα, ὤφθην see, catch sight of, notice, look, observe, perceive, experience, witness
ἀνατολή, ῆς, ἡ rising, rising of the sun, east, orient
προάγω, προάξω, προήγαγον (2 aorist) lead forward, bring out (transitive); go before, precede (intransitive)

2:9 **οἱ δὲ**: *but they*; the article is used as a pronoun here for the finite verb. The conjunction **δὲ** does not appear as the first word in its clause and so is called *postpositive*. It signals a slight contrast from a previously made statement. **ἀκουσάντες**: *after they had heard*; the circumstantial participle refers to the simple act of listening. Context suggests that the magi journey on their own volition and not out of obedience to Herod (2:12). The verb ἀκούω is construed with the genitive of person. This is one of six participles that describes the activities of the magi at the beginning of their sentences or clauses in the next three verses: ἀκουσάντες, ἰδόντες (2:10), ἐλθόντες (2:11), πεσόντες (2:11), ἀνοίξαντες (2:11), and χρηματισθέντες (2:12). The first and the last describe their relationship with Herod: they hear and are warned not to return. The next four tell of their journey and visit with the young child: they see, they come, and they worship. **ἐπορεύθησαν** is third person plural first aorist passive indicative of a deponent verb (cf. App. 53, G, 1). Deponents have middle or passive voice forms but active meanings. **ἰδοὺ** anticipates the divine astrological phenomenon. **ὁ ἀστήρ**: the third declension noun is masculine singular nominative. **ὃν εἶδον**: *which they saw*; ὃν is a relative pronoun (App. 49). It agrees in gender and number with its antecedent ὁ ἀστήρ. The relative, whose case is determined by its use in its own clause, is in the accusative case. **προῆγεν αὐτούς**: *continually went before them*; the intransitive verb, construed with the accusative of the person, is a third person singular imperfect active indicative. It is formed by adding an augment to the present stem and takes the personal endings: -ον, -ες, -ε(ν), -ομεν, -ετε, -ον (cf. App. 53, C). The imperfect tense denotes progressive, continued, and repeated action (aspect) in past time and should not be slighted in translation. It adds its endings to the present stem.

ἕως ἐλθὼν ἐστάθη ἐπάνω οὗ ἦν τὸ παιδίον. 2:10 ἰδόντες δὲ τὸν ἀστέρα ἐχάρησαν χαρὰν μεγάλην σφόδρα.

2:9

ἕως while, as long as, until

ἔρχομαι, ἐλεύσομαι, ἦλθον (2 aorist), ἐλήλυθα come, go

ἵστημι, στήσω, ἔστησα, ἔστην (2 aorist), ἕστηκα, ἐστάθην put, place, set, cause to stand (transitive); stand, be (intransitive)

ἐπάνω above, over, upon (adverb)

οὗ where, in what place (adverb)

εἰμί, ἔσομαι be

παιδίον, ου, τό infant, young child, little boy, little girl

2:10

ὁράω, ὄψομαι, εἶδον (2 aorist), ἑώρακα/ἑόρακα, ὤφθην see, catch sight of, notice, look, observe, perceive, experience, witness

ἀστήρ, ἀστέρος, ὁ star

χαίρω, χαρήσομαι, ἐχάρην (2 aorist passive) rejoice, be glad; χαῖρε, χαίρετε hail, greetings, welcome (as a form of greeting)

χαρά, ᾶς, ἡ joy

μέγας, μεγάλη, μέγα large, great

σφόδρα greatly, exceedingly (adverb)

2:9 **ἕως ἐλθὼν ἐστάθη ἐπάνω**: *until it came and stood above*; the aorist participle, in agreement with ὁ ἀστήρ, may be changed into a finite verb and coordinated with the main verb in translation. ἐστάθη is a third person singular first aorist passive indicative of ἵστημι used intransitively (cf. App. 53, G, 1). The star, by its threefold repetition as subject, object, and subject again, is the focus not only of the sentence but also of the magi. **ἦν**: *was*; the verb is the third person singular imperfect of the verb εἰμί (App. 63). The imperfect tense denotes progressive, continued, and repeated action (aspect) in past time. **παιδίον** is a neuter noun of the second declension (cf. App. 5) and the subject of the sentence. Since the nominative and accusative neuters look alike, context will determine proper usage.

2:10 **ἐχάρησαν χαρὰν μεγάλην σφόδρα**: *they rejoiced with exceedingly great joy*; when the noun in the accusative derives from the same root as the verb, the direct object is a cognate accusative. The alliterative sounds of the cognate words express intense joy of the occasion. The adverb modifies the adjective.

2:11 καὶ ἐλθόντες εἰς τὴν οἰκίαν εἶδον τὸ παιδίον μετὰ Μαρίας τῆς μητρὸς αὐτοῦ, καὶ πεσόντες προσεκύνησαν αὐτῷ καὶ ἀνοίξαντες τοὺς θησαυροὺς αὐτῶν προσήνεγκαν αὐτῷ δῶρα, χρυσὸν καὶ λίβανον καὶ σμύρναν.

2:11
ἔρχομαι, ἐλεύσομαι, ἦλθον (2 aorist), ἐλήλυθα come, go
εἰς to, into, on, in; for, as; with respect to (preposition + accusative)
οἰκία, ας, ἡ building; house, household, family
ὁράω, ὄψομαι, εἶδον (2 aorist), ἑώρακα/ἑόρακα, ὤφθην see, catch sight of, notice, look, observe, perceive, experience, witness
παιδίον, ου, τό infant, young child, little boy, little girl
μετά with (preposition + genitive)
μήτηρ, τρός, ἡ mother
πίπτω, πεσοῦμαι, ἔπεσα, ἔπεσον (2 aorist), πέπτωκα fall, fall prostrate, fall down
προσκυνέω, προσκυνήσω, προσεκύνησα worship, prostrate oneself before, reverence before, reverence
ἀνοίγω, ἀνοίξω, ἀνέῳξα/ἤνοιξα, ἀνέῳγα, ἀνέῳγμαι, ἠνεῴχθην open
θησαυρός, οῦ, ὁ treasure box, treasury, treasure
προσφέρω, προσοίσω, προσήνεγκα, προσήνεγκον (2 aorist), προσηνέχθην bring, offer, present
δῶρον, ου, τό gift, present
χρυσός, οῦ, ὁ gold
λίβανος, ου, ὁ frankincense
σμύρνα, ης, ἡ myrrh

2:11 **καὶ ἐλθόντες . . . εἶδον τὸ παιδίον . . . καὶ πεσόντες προσεκύνησαν αὐτῷ καὶ ἀνοίξαντες . . . προσήνεγκαν αὐτῷ δῶρα**: a fullness of joy is realized by the actual visit, which is described by an extraordinary tricolon of participles, verbs, and references to the child that ends with a threefold number gifts: **χρυσὸν καὶ λίβανον καὶ σμύρναν. τὸ παιδίον . . . αὐτῷ . . . αὐτῷ:** the child, as the object of their adoration, is the object of each action in all three verbs, creating a poetic climax. The thrice repeated use of the conjunction καὶ (polysyndeton) before each participle slows the narrative and savors the action. The single aspect of successive aorist participles and finite verbs speeds up the narrative and maintains interest. προσήνεγκαν, the first aorist of προσφέρω, also shows a second aorist in προσήνεγκον. The distinction between the first and second aorist is only one of form, not tense or meaning.

2:12 καὶ χρηματισθέντες κατ' ὄναρ μὴ ἀνακάμψαι πρὸς Ἡρῴδην, δι' ἄλλης ὁδοῦ ἀνεχώρησαν εἰς τὴν χώραν αὐτῶν.

2:13 Ἀναχωρησάντων δὲ αὐτῶν

2:12

χρηματίζω, χρηματίσω, ἐχρημάτισα, κεχρημάτισμαι, ἐχρημάτισθην have dealings, negotiate; be divinely instructed, receive a revelation or warning from God

κατά in, during, by, in accordance with, after the manner of (preposition + accusative)

ὄναρ, τό dream (indeclinable)

μή not (particle of negation)

ἀνακάμπτω, ἀνακάμψω, ἀνέκαμψα return

πρός to, towards, unto (+ accusative)

δι' = διά through, by (preposition + genitive)

ἄλλος, η, ο other, another

ὁδός, οῦ, ἡ road, way, journey

ἀναχωρέω, ἀναχωρήσω, ἀνεχώρησα go away, depart, withdraw, retire

εἰς to, into, on, in; for, as; with respect to (preposition + accusative)

χώρα, ας, ἡ country, land, field

2:13

ἀναχωρέω, ἀναχωρήσω, ἀνεχώρησα go away, depart, withdraw, retire

---

2:12 **καὶ χρηματισθέντες**: *and since they had been warned of God*; the participle connotes divine warning or instruction. The aorist participle usually expresses a single act (aspect) in past time and frequently translates as a pluperfect when a main verb stands in the past tense. A circumstantial participle may express time, cause, concession, condition, and other circumstances. It needs to be sensitively interpreted according to context and translated into English as a clause. **κατ' ὄναρ**: κατ' = κατὰ; the final vowel of a preposition is frequently elided before the initial vowel of the following word; elision is indicated by an apostrophe. **ὄναρ** is a third declension noun used only in the nominative and accusative. **μὴ ἀνακάμψαι**: *not to return*; the infinitive depends on the participle χρηματισθέντες for its construction. The negative of an infinitive is usually μή. **δι' ἄλλης ὁδοῦ**: *by another way*; the second declension includes a few feminine nouns ending in ος (App. 5); any modifiers will be feminine.

2:12–13 **ἀνεχώρησαν . . . χώραν . . . Ἀναχωρησάντων**: the repetition of the same sound of words in close proximity to each other emphatically announces the departure of the magi and serves as an appropriate transition to the imminent flight by Joseph to Egypt. **Ἀναχωρησάντων δὲ αὐτῶν**: *now when they had departed*; the conjunction **δὲ** does not appear as the first word in its clause and so is called *postpositive*. It signals a slight contrast from a previously made statement. The verbal construction is a *genitive absolute*. The circumstantial participle **Ἀναχωρησάντων** and the pronoun **αὐτῶν** in the genitive case are syntactically independent of the main clause, i.e., the subject of the genitive absolute may not be used as the subject or the object of the main verb.

ἰδοὺ ἄγγελος κυρίου φαίνεται κατ' ὄναρ τῷ Ἰωσὴφ λέγων, Ἐγερθεὶς παράλαβε

2:13
ἰδού see, look, behold (demonstrative particle)
ἄγγελος, ου, ὁ messenger, angel
κύριος, ου, ὁ lord, Lord, master
φαίνω, φανῶ, ἔφηνα, πέφαγκα, πέφηνα, πέφασμαι, ἐφάνθην, ἐφάνην shine, give light, be bright; be seen, appear, be visible (middle and passive)
κατά in, during, by, in accordance with, after the manner of (preposition + accusative)
ὄναρ, τό dream (indeclinable)
λέγω, ἐρῶ, εἶπον, εἴρηκα, εἴρημαι, ἐρρέθην/ἐρρήθην say, assert, proclaim, tell, declare
ἐγείρω, ἐγερῶ, ἤγειρα, ἠγήγερμαι, ἠγέρθην awaken, raise up from the dead, restore, rebuild; arise! get up! come! (intransitive, only in imperative)
παραλαμβάνω, παραλήμψομαι, παρέλαβον (2 aorist), παρείληφα, παρείλημμαι, παρελήφθην take, receive, accept

2:13 (continued from p. 27) Although New Testament language does not always strictly adhere to classical usage, in this sentence it does. A circumstantial participle may express time, cause, concession, condition, and other circumstances. It should be sensitively interpreted and translated into English as a clause (App. 65). **ἰδοὺ** again anticipates the divine visitation. Both language and structure resemble that of the first visit by the angel (1:20–23). **ἄγγελος κυρίου**: both are second declension nouns (cf. App. 4). The divine messenger discloses the need for flight. **φαίνεται**: *appeared*; the verb is a third person singular present middle indicative (cf. App. 53, A, 1). The personal endings are best seen in the middle or passive endings of the perfect tense (cf. App. 53, E, 1): -μαι, -σαι, -ται, -μεθα, -σθε, -νται. The **ε** preceding the personal ending is called a thematic vowel. The present used for a past tense is called *historical present* and is frequently seen in vivid narrative accounts. **κατ' ὄναρ**: κατ' = κατὰ; the final vowel of a preposition is frequently elided before the initial vowel of the following word; elision is indicated by an apostrophe. **ὄναρ** is a third declension noun used only in the nominative and accusative. **τῷ Ἰωσὴφ λέγων**: the present active participle (cf. App. 29) agrees in gender, number, and case with its subject ἄγγελος and takes a dative object in τῷ Ἰωσὴφ. The participle introduces direct speech, which is editorially indicated by the capitalization of the following word. **Ἐγερθεὶς παράλαβε**: *arise and take*; when a participle modifies an imperative, it is commonly changed into an imperative and the two verbs are coordinated in translation. Ἐγερθεὶς, the first aorist passive participle of ἐγείρω (cf. App. 34), shows intransitive meaning. παράλαβε is a second person singular second aorist active imperative (cf. App. 54). A change in stem from the present tense to the aorist distinguishes the second aorist from the first.

τὸ παιδίον καὶ τὴν μητέρα αὐτοῦ καὶ φεῦγε εἰς Αἴγυπτον καὶ ἴσθι ἐκεῖ ἕως ἂν εἴπω σοι· μέλλει γὰρ Ἡρῴδης ζητεῖν τὸ παιδίον τοῦ ἀπολέσαι αὐτό.

2:13
παιδίον, ου, τό infant, young child, little boy, little girl
μήτηρ, τρός, ἡ mother
φεύγω, φεύξομαι, ἔφυγον (2 aorist) flee, flee from, avoid, shun
εἰς to, into, on, in; for, as; with respect to (preposition + accusative)
Αἴγυπτος, ου, ἡ Egypt
εἰμί, ἔσομαι be
ἕως while, as long as, until
ἄν (a conditional particle indicating contingency in certain constructions)
λέγω, ἐρῶ, εἶπον, εἴρηκα, εἴρημαι, ἐρρέθην/ἐρρήθην say, assert, proclaim, tell, declare
σύ, σοῦ (σου) you (personal pronoun)
μέλλω, μελλήσω be about to, be on the point of
γάρ for, indeed, but (conjunction)
ζητέω, ζητήσω, ἐζήτησα, ἐζητήθην seek, desire, ask for
παιδίον, ου, τό infant, young child, little boy, little girl
ἀπόλλυμι/ἀπολλύω, ἀπολέσω/ἀπολῶ, ἀπώλεσα, ἀπολώλεκα, ἀπόλωλα (2 perfect) lose, destroy, ruin, kill; perish (middle)

2:13 **τὸ παιδίον καὶ τὴν μητέρα αὐτοῦ**: the nouns are in reverse order of customary usage. Attention is focused particularly on τὸ παιδίον (cf. 2:11). μητέρα is a feminine singular accusative third declension noun (App. 12). **φεύγε** is a second person singular present active imperative (cf. App. 53, A, 3). **ἴσθι ἐκεῖ**: *stay there*; the form is the second person singular present active imperative of the irregular verb εἰμί (App. 63). The arrangement of the three imperatives παράλαβε, φεύγε, and ἴσθι is structurally similar to the three future verbs τέξεται, καλέσεις, and σώσει in the first visit by the angel (1:20–23). All collocated at the beginning of their clauses, they constitute a classical tricolon. In the arrangement of these clauses, the third element is more fully developed. **ἕως ἂν εἴπω σοι**: *until I tell you*; the temporal conjunction with the aorist subjunctive and the particle ἄν refers indefinitely to the future and denotes that the commencement of one event is dependent on another. σοι is the enclitic second person pronoun (App. 39). By definition an enclitic *leans on* the previous word so that the two words are counted as one in terms of accent. **μέλλει . . . ζητεῖν**: the finite verb takes a complementary infinitive. The complementary infinitive is a present active infinitive of a contracted verb with stem in **ε** (App. 56). It takes a circumflex over the contraction. **τοῦ ἀπολέσαι αὐτό**: *in order to kill it*; the construction is called an *articular infinitive*. A purpose clause may be expressed by the neuter article in the genitive case, followed by an infinitive. It is an alternate construction where ἕνεκα *for the sake of* is usually employed with the genitive article. In this construction the article has the power to turn the infinitive into a substantive. As a verbal noun or gerund it continues to show verbal force and takes an object in αὐτό.

2:14 ὁ δὲ ἐγερθεὶς παρέλαβεν τὸ παιδίον καὶ τὴν μητέρα αὐτοῦ νυκτὸς καὶ ἀνεχώρησεν εἰς Αἴγυπτον, 2:15 καὶ ἦν ἐκεῖ ἕως τῆς τελευτῆς Ἡρῴδου· ἵνα πληρωθῇ τὸ ῥηθὲν

2:14
ἐγείρω, ἐγερῶ, ἤγειρα, ἠγήγερμαι, ἠγέρθην awaken, lift, raise up from the dead, restore, rebuild; arise! get up! come! (intransitive, only in imperative)
παραλαμβάνω, παραλήμψομαι, παρέλαβον (2 aorist), παρείληφα, παρείλημμαι, παρελήφθην take, receive, accept
παιδίον, ου, τό infant, young child, little boy, little girl
μήτηρ, τρός, ἡ mother
νύξ, νυκτός, ἡ night
ἀναχωρέω, ἀναχωρήσω, ἀνεχώρησα go away, depart, withdraw, retire
εἰς to, into, on, in; for, as; with respect to (preposition + accusative)
Αἴγυπτος, ου, ἡ Egypt
2:15
εἰμί, ἔσομαι be
ἐκεῖ there, in that place (adverb)
ἕως while, as long as, until
τελευτή, ῆς, ἡ end; end of life, death
ἵνα to, in order to, in order that, that (conjunction)
πληρόω, πληρώσω, ἐπλήρωσα, πεπλήρωκα, πεπλήρωμαι, ἐπληρώθην fill, complete, fulfill
λέγω, ἐρῶ, εἶπον, εἴρηκα, εἴρημαι, ἐρρέθην/ἐρρήθην say, assert, proclaim, tell, declare

2:14 **Ἐγερθεὶς**: this and the following main verbs show Joseph's obedience, summarize the previous events, and quickly move the narrative along as in 1:24. **νυκτὸς**: *at night*; the genitive of time expresses time at which an action takes place.

2:15 **ἦν**: *was*; the verb is the third person singular imperfect active indicative of the verb εἰμί (App. 63). The imperfect tense denotes progressive, continued, and repeated action (aspect) in past time. The subject of the verb is still Joseph. **ἕως τῆς τελευτῆς Ἡρῴδου**: *until the death of Herod* (literally: *until the end of Herod*); as a preposition of time ἕως is construed with the genitive of the noun. τελευτῆς is a euphemism for death. Ἡρῴδου, a first declension noun ending in **ης** (App. 3), is a subjective genitive, i.e., Herod died. Supply **τοῦτο δὲ ὅλον γέγονεν** (cf. 1:22): *but all this occurred* before the ἵνα clause. ἵνα is the usual conjunction to introduce purpose clauses. **ἵνα πληρωθῇ τὸ ῥηθὲν**: *in order that what was spoken might be fulfilled*; fulfillment of prophecy dominates as a salient feature of Matthew's literary programme. ἵνα is the usual conjunction to introduce purpose clauses. The first aorist passive verb stands in the subjunctive mood (cf. App. 53, G, 2). The subjunctive mood is regularly formed by the lengthening of the personal endings of the present indicative. The third person singular ending **-ει** becomes **-ῃ**: the **ε** changes to **η**, and the **ι** becomes a subscript. τὸ ῥηθὲν: *that which was spoken* (literally); the verbal form is a neuter singular nominative first aorist passive participle (cf. App. 53, G, 5; 34) of the verb λέγω that translates as a relative clause in conjunction with an article.

ὑπὸ κυρίου διὰ τοῦ προφήτου λέγοντος, Ἐξ Αἰγύπτου ἐκάλεσα τὸν υἱόν μου.

2:16 Τότε Ἡρῴδης ἰδὼν ὅτι ἐνεπαίχθη ὑπὸ τῶν μάγων ἐθυμώθη λίαν,

---

2:15

ὑπό by (preposition + genitive of personal agent)
κύριος, ου, ὁ lord, Lord, master
διά through, by (preposition + genitive)
προφήτης, ου, ὁ prophet, seer, revelator
λέγω, ἐρῶ, εἶπον, εἴρηκα, εἴρημαι, ἐρρέθην/ἐρρήθην say, assert, proclaim, tell, declare
ἐκ (ἐξ before a vowel) from, out of, of, by (preposition + genitive)
καλέω, καλέσω, ἐκάλεσα, κέκληκα, κέκλημαι, ἐκλήθην call, summon
υἱός, οῦ, ὁ son
ἐγώ, ἐμοῦ (μου) I (personal pronoun)

2:16

τότε then, at that time, thereupon, thereafter (adverb)
ὁράω, ὄψομαι, εἶδον (2 aorist), ἑώρακα/ἑόρακα, φθην see, notice, look, observe, perceive
ὅτι that, because, since (conjunction)
ἐμπαίζω, ἐμπαίξω, ἐνέπαιξα, ἐνεπαίχθην ridicule, make fun of, mock; deceive, trick
ὑπό by (preposition + genitive of personal agent)
θυμόω, θυμώσω, ἐθυμώθην provoke to anger, make angry; become angry, enraged (passive)
λίαν greatly, exceedingly (adverb)

2:15 **ὑπὸ κυρίου διὰ τοῦ προφήτου λέγοντος**: the preposition ὑπὸ takes the genitive case expressing agency. διὰ denotes intermediate agency. The Lord speaks; the prophet is his mouthpiece. **τοῦ προφήτου** is a first declension noun ending in ης (App. 3). The masculine singular genitive present active participle (cf. App. 29) may modify either κυρίου or προφήτου or both. The rhetorical figure where one element or word governs a double syntactic function is called *apo koinou* (ἀπὸ κοινοῦ). **τὸν υἱόν μου**: thus far the divine nature of Jesus has been declared: He is born ἐκ πνεύματος ἁγίου (1:18, 20), He is the one to save His people from their sins (1:22), and He is the one whom the people will call Emmanuel meaning *God is with us* (1:23). Now Matthew sees in Him the fulfillment of prophecy in Hos 11:1 and identifies Him by *the Son of God*.

2:16 **ἰδὼν**: *when he saw*; the form is a second aorist circumstantial participle (cf. App. 54; 29 note). **ὅτι ἐνεπαίχθη**: *that he had been mocked*; the finite verb is third person singular first aorist passive indicative. The sign of this passive is **θ** and the endings are -θην, -θης, -θη, -θημεν, -θητε, -θησαν (App. 53, G, 1). Since the action of the clause precedes that of the main verb, the verb of the clause is translated as a pluperfect. The verb characterizes the perspective of Herod.

καὶ ἀποστείλας ἀνεῖλεν πάντας τοὺς παῖδας τοὺς ἐν Βηθλέεμ καὶ ἐν πᾶσι τοῖς ὁρίοις αὐτῆς ἀπὸ διετοῦς καὶ κατωτέρω, κατὰ τὸν χρόνον ὃν ἠκρίβωσεν παρὰ τῶν μάγων.

2:16
ἀποστέλλω, ἀποστελῶ, ἀπέστειλα, ἀπέσταλκα, ἀπέσταλμαι, ἀπεστάλην send, send away, send out
ἀναιρέω, ἀναιρήσω, ἀνεῖλον (2 aorist), ἀνηρέθην take away, destroy, kill, put to death, murder
πᾶς, πᾶσα, πᾶν every, all
παῖς, παιδός, ὁ child, boy, youth
ὅριον, ου, τό boundary; region, territory, district (plural)
διετής, ές two years old
κατωτέρω under; lower, further down (adverb)
κατά near, towards, by, in accordance with, after the manner of (preposition + accusative)
χρόνος, ου, ὁ time
ὅς, ἥ, ὅ who, which, what; he who, that (relative pronoun)
ἀκριβόω, ἀκριβώσω, ἠκρίβωσα, ἠκρίβωκα ascertain exactly
παρά from (the side of), from, issuing from, by (preposition + genitive)

2:16 **ἀποστείλας**: supply τοὺς ὑπηρέτας: *his servants, assistants,* or *officers.* The circumstantial participle is a liquid aorist (cf. App. 31); some verbs ending in a liquid or nasal (**λ**, **μ**, **ν**, or **ρ**) add the first aorist endings -σα, -σας, -σε, -σαμεν, -σατε, -σαν to the stem but omit the -**σ**-. To compensate for the loss of the -**σ**-, the vowel stem is usually lengthened (compensatory lengthening): **ε** becomes **ει**. **ἀνεῖλεν**: this liquid verb shows a second aorist but appears also in the form ἀνεῖλα. **πάντας τοὺς παῖδας τοὺς ἐν Βηθλέεμ**: *all the children in Bethlehem*; πάντας is a masculine plural accusative adjective (App. 27) modifying παῖδας and standing in predicate position (i.e., not immediately preceded by a definite article). παῖδας is a third declension noun (cf. App. 6). The repetition of the article with the prepositional phrase is an alternate construction for τοὺς ἐν Βηθλέεμ παῖδας. In both cases the prepositional phrase is in attributive position (i.e., immediately preceded by a definite article) and forms a substantive with the article. **ἀπὸ διετοῦς καὶ κατωτέρω** *and from the age of two and under*; διετοῦς is a third declension adjective turned substantive (cf. App. 21). **ὃν** is a relative pronoun (App. 49). It agrees in gender and number with its antecedent τὸν χρόνον. The case of the relative, determined by its use in its own clause, is in the accusative case.

2:17 τότε ἐπληρώθη τὸ ῥηθὲν διὰ Ἰερεμίου τοῦ προφήτου λέγοντος,
2:18 Φωνὴ ἐν Ῥαμὰ ἠκούσθη,
κλαυθμὸς καὶ ὀδυρμὸς πολύς·
Ῥαχὴλ κλαίουσα τὰ τέκνα αὐτῆς,

2:17
τότε then, at that time, thereupon, thereafter (adverb)
πληρόω, πληρώσω, ἐπλήρωσα, πεπλήρωκα, πεπλήρωμαι, ἐπληρώθην fill, complete, fulfill
διά through, by (preposition + genitive)
Ἰερεμίας, ου, ὁ Jeremiah
προφήτης, ου, ὁ prophet, seer, revelator
2:18
φωνή, ῆς, ἡ voice, sound
Ῥαμά, ἡ Rama (indeclinable)
ἀκούω, ἀκούσω, ἤκουσα, ἀκήκοα, ἤκουσμαι, ἠκούσθην hear, obey, understand (+ genitive or accusative)
κλαυθμός, ου, ὁ weeping
ὀδυρμός, ου, ὁ lamentation, mourning
πολύς, πολλή, πολύ much, large, many (in plural)
Ῥαχήλ, ἡ Rachel (indeclinable)
κλαίω, κλαύσω/κλαύσομαι, ἔκλαυσα weep, shed tears
τέκνον, ου, τό child, descendant, posterity

2:17 **τότε ἐπληρώθη**: *then was fulfilled*; the adverb is frequently used by Matthew to introduce a sentence. The finite verb is third person singular first aorist passive indicative. The sign of this passive is **θ** and the endings are -θην, -θης, -θη, -θημεν, -θητε, -θησαν (App. 53, G, 1). **τὸ ῥηθὲν**: *that which was spoken* (literally); the verbal form is a neuter singular nominative first aorist passive participle (cf. App. 53, G, 5; 34) that translates as a relative clause in conjunction with an article. **διὰ Ἰερεμίου τοῦ προφήτου λέγοντος**: the preposition takes the genitive case expressing agency. διὰ denotes intermediate agency. The Lord speaks; the prophet is his mouthpiece. Ἰερεμίου is a first declension noun ending in ας (App. 3). τοῦ προφήτου, a first declension noun ending in **ης** (App. 3), stands in apposition to Ἰερεμίου. λέγοντος: the masculine singular genitive present active participle (cf. App. 29) modifies Ἰερεμίου as its subject.

2:18 **Φωνὴ . . . κλαυθμὸς και ὀδυρμὸς πολύς**: while the tricolon of nouns includes the prepositional phrase, the adjective, and the finite verb, the meaning of Φωνὴ is more specifically identified by its two appositional nouns. **ἠκούσθη**: the finite verb is third person singular aorist passive indicative. The sign of this passive is **θ** and the endings are -θην, -θης, -θη, -θημεν, -θητε, -θησαν (App. 53, G, 1). **κλαίουσα** is a feminine present active participle (cf. App. 29) that agrees with its subject Ῥαχὴλ in gender, number, and case and shows transitive meaning, taking τὰ τέκνα as its object: *weeping for*. **τὰ τέκνα** belongs to the class of second declension neuter nouns ending in -ον (App. 5).

καὶ οὐκ ἤθελεν παρακληθῆναι, ὅτι οὐκ εἰσίν.
2:19 Τελευτήσαντος δὲ τοῦ Ἡρῴδου ἰδοὺ ἄγγελος κυρίου φαίνεται

2:18
οὐ not (οὐκ before vowels with a smooth breathing, οὐχ before a rough breathing, adverb)
θέλω, θελήσω, ἠθέλησα wish to have, desire, purpose, want
παρακαλέω, παρακαλέσω, παρεκάλεσα, παρακέκληκα, παρακέκλημαι, παρεκλήθην call upon, exhort, persuade; beg, entreat; comfort, encourage, cheer up
ὅτι that, because, since (conjunction)
εἰμί, ἔσομαι be

2:19
τελευτάω, τελευτήσω, ἐτελεύτησα, τετελεύτηκα end, finish, die
ἰδού see, look, behold (demonstrative particle)
ἄγγελος, ου, ὁ messenger, angel
κύριος, ου, ὁ lord, Lord, master
φαίνω, φανῶ, ἔφηνα, πέφαγκα, πέφηνα, πέφασμαι, ἐφάνθην, ἐφάνην shine, give light, be bright; be seen, appear, be visible (middle and passive)

2:18 **ἤθελεν**: the finite verb is third person imperfect active indicative. The imperfect tense denotes progressive, continued, and repeated action (aspect) in past time. It is formed by adding an augment to the present stem and takes the personal endings -ον, -ες, -ε(ν), -ομεν, -ετε, -ον (cf. App. 53, C). However, in contrast to the single action or aspect of the aorist, its aspect shows action in the past that is continuing. In the context of a negative statement, the imperfect frequently indicates resistance or refusal (*would not* or *could not*). The finite verb takes a complementary infinitive in παρακληθῆναι (cf. App. 56). **ὅτι οὐκ εἰσίν** is a euphemistic way of saying that the children have been brutally murdered.

2:19 **Τελευτήσαντος δὲ τοῦ Ἡρῴδου**: *Now when Herod had died:* the construction is a *genitive absolute*. The noun Ἡρῴδου and the circumstantial participle Τελευτήσαντος in the genitive case are syntactically independent of the main clause, i.e., the subject of the genitive absolute may not be used as the subject or the object of the main verb. Although New Testament language does not always strictly adhere to classical usage, in this sentence it does. A circumstantial participle may express time, cause, concession, condition, and other circumstances. It should be sensitively interpreted and translated into English as a clause (App. 65). Τελευτήσαντος is an aorist active participle (cf. App. 34). The verb means *to end, finish, complete,* but in an absolute sense it means *to finish or end one's life, to die.* The aorist participle shows aspect of a single act and often precedes that of the main verb. Since the main verb φαίνεται is a historical present and therefore translated as a past tense, the aorist participle may be construed as a pluperfect. **φαίνεται**: *appeared*; the verb is a third person singular present middle indicative (cf. App. 53, A, 1). The personal endings are best seen in the middle or passive endings of the perfect tense (cf. App. 53, E, 1): -μαι, -σαι, -ται, -μεθα, -σθε, -νται. The **ε** preceding the personal ending is called a thematic vowel. The present used for a past tense is frequently seen in vivid narrative accounts.

κατ' ὄναρ τῷ Ἰωσὴφ ἐν Αἰγύπτῳ 2:20 λέγων, Ἐγερθεὶς παράλαβε τὸ παιδίον καὶ τὴν μητέρα αὐτοῦ καὶ πορεύου εἰς γῆν Ἰσραήλ·

2:19
κατά in, during, by, in accordance with, after the manner of (preposition + accusative)
ὄναρ, τό dream (indeclinable)
2:20
ἐγείρω, ἐγερῶ, ἤγειρα, ἠγήγερμαι, ἠγέρθην awaken, lift, raise up from the dead, restore, rebuild; arise! get up! come! (intransitive, only in imperative)
παραλαμβάνω, παραλήμψομαι, παρέλαβον (2 aorist), παρείληφα, παρείλημμαι, παρελήφθην take, receive, accept
παιδίον, ου, τό infant, young child, little boy, little girl
μήτηρ, τρός, ἡ mother
πορεύομαι, πορεύσομαι, πεπόρευμαι, ἐπορεύθην go, proceed, travel
εἰς to, into, on, in; for, as; with respect to (preposition + accusative)
γῆ, γῆς, ἡ soil, land, region, country

2:19 **κατ' ὄναρ**: κατ' = κατὰ; the final vowel of a preposition is frequently elided before the initial vowel of the following word; elision is indicated by an apostrophe. **ὄναρ** is a third declension noun used only in the nominative and accusative.

2:20 **λέγων**: the present active participle (cf. App. 29) agrees in gender, number, and case with its subject ἄγγελος in the previous verse and takes a dative object in τῷ Ἰωσὴφ above. The participle introduces direct speech, which is editorially indicated by the capitalization of the following word. **Ἐγερθεὶς παράλαβε**: *arise and take*; when a participle modifies an imperative, it is commonly changed into an imperative and the two verbs are coordinated in translation. Ἐγερθεὶς, the first aorist passive participle of ἐγείρω (cf. App. 34), shows intransitive meaning. παράλαβε is a second person singular second aorist active imperative (cf. App. 54). A change in stem from the present tense to the aorist distinguishes the second aorist from the first. **πορεύου** is second person singular present middle imperative (cf. App. 53, A, 3). **Ἰσραήλ** stands in apposition to γῆν and more specifically identifies it. **τεθνήκασιν** is third person plural perfect active indicative (cf. App. 53, E, 1).

τεθνήκασιν γὰρ οἱ ζητοῦντες τὴν ψυχὴν τοῦ παιδίου. 2:21 ὁ δὲ ἐγερθεὶς παρέλαβεν τὸ παιδίον καὶ τὴν μητέρα αὐτοῦ καὶ εἰσῆλθεν εἰς γῆν Ἰσραήλ. 2:22 ἀκούσας δὲ ὅτι Ἀρχέλαος βασιλεύει τῆς Ἰουδαίας

2:20
θνήσκω, θανοῦμαι, ἔθανον (2 aorist), τέθνηκα die, face death
ζητέω, ζητήσω, ἐζήτησα, ἐζητήθην seek, desire, ask for
ψυχή, ῆς, ἡ breath, life, soul, heart
παιδίον, ου, τό infant, young child, little boy, little girl
2:21
ἐγείρω, ἐγερῶ, ἤγειρα, ἠγήγερμαι, ἠγέρθην awaken, lift, raise up from the dead, restore, rebuild
παραλαμβάνω, παραλήμψομαι, παρέλαβον (2 aorist), παρείληφα, παρείλημμαι, παρελήφθην take, receive, accept
παιδίον, ου, τό infant, young child
μήτηρ, τρός, ἡ mother
εἰσέρχομαι, εἰσελεύσομαι, εἰσῆλθον (2 aorist), εἰσελήλυθα come (in, into), go (in, into), enter into, share in
2:22
ἀκούω, ἀκούσω, ἤκουσα, ἀκήκοα, ἤκουσμαι, ἠκούσθην hear, obey, understand (+ genitive or accusative)
ὅτι that, because, since (conjunction)
Ἀρχέλαος, ου, ὁ Archelaus
βασιλεύω, βασιλεύσω, ἐβασίλευσα be king, rule

2:20 The context (2:19) indicates that only one person has died, Herod. A single person may be referred to in the plural when the person is a royal. Although he had many of his leaders killed at the time of his death to evoke greater mourning, it is a hyperbole to say that πᾶσα Ἱεροσόλυμα (2:3) has died μετ᾽ αὐτοῦ. The perfect tense denotes action (aspect) that is completed near present time and continues with present result: *He has died* (recently and is dead now; cf. App. 53, E).

2:21 **ὁ δὲ ἐγερθεὶς**: *but he, after he had arisen*; a circumstantial participle may express time, cause, concession, condition, and other circumstances. It needs to be interpreted according to context and translated as a clause (App. 65).

2:22 **ἀκούσας δὲ ὅτι Ἀρχέλαος βασιλεύει**: *But when he had heard that Archelaus was ruling*; the participle introduces an indirect statement with ὅτι, followed by a nominative subject and a finite verb in the indicative mood. In this construction Greek retains the tense and the mood of the direct speech, i.e., the present tense, but in translation the verb is changed to the past tense. After Herod died, the kingdom was divided among his sons, Philip, Antipas, and Archelaus. Tetrarch Archelaus, who showed a cruel and tyrannical disposition similar to that of his father, ruled over Judea, Samaria, and Idumea. Antipas was originally designated as heir to the kingdom but was ultimately appointed by his father's will as tetrarch over Galilee and Perea. He ruled until 39 AD. Tetrarch Philip received Trachonitis and Iturea. **τῆς Ἰουδαίας**: verbs of ruling generally govern the genitive case.

ἀντὶ τοῦ πατρὸς αὐτοῦ Ἡρῴδου ἐφοβήθη ἐκεῖ ἀπελθεῖν·
χρηματισθεὶς δὲ κατ' ὄναρ ἀνεχώρησεν εἰς τὰ μέρη τῆς Γαλιλαίας,
2:23 καὶ ἐλθὼν κατῴκησεν εἰς πόλιν λεγομένην Ναζαρέτ·

2:22
ἀντί in place of, for, upon (preposition + genitive)
πατήρ, πατρός, ὁ father, parent, ancestor
φοβέομαι, φοβηθήσομαι, ἐφοβήθην be afraid, become frightened
ἐκεῖ there, in that place; thither, to that place (adverb)
ἀπέρχομαι, ἀπελεύσομαι, ἀπῆλθον, ἀπελήλυθα go, go away, depart
χρηματίζω, χρηματίσω, ἐχρημάτισα, κεχρημάτισμαι, ἐχρημάτισθην have dealings, negotiate; be divinely instructed, receive a revelation or warning from God
κατά in, during, by, in accordance with, after the manner of (preposition + accusative)
ὄναρ, τό dream (indeclinable)
ἀναχωρέω, ἀναχωρήσω, ἀνεχώρησα go away, depart, withdraw, retire
εἰς to, into, on, in; for, as; with respect to (preposition + accusative)
μέρος, ους, τό part, portion, share
Γαλιλαία, ας, ἡ Galilee
2:23
ἔρχομαι, ἐλεύσομαι, ἦλθον (2 aorist), ἐλήλυθα come, go
κατοικέω, κατοικήσω, κατῴκησα live, dwell, reside, settle; inhabit (transitive)
εἰς to, into, on, in; for, as; with respect to (preposition + accusative)
πόλις, εως, ἡ city
Ναζαρέτ, ἡ (indeclinable) Nazareth

2:22 **Ἡρῴδου**, a first declension noun ending in ης, stands in apposition to τοῦ πατρὸς αὐτοῦ. **ἐφοβήθη** is a first aorist passive deponent. The personal endings are -θην, -θης, -θη, -θημεν, -θητε, -θησαν (App. 53, G, 1). Deponents have middle or passive voice forms but active meanings. **ἀπελθεῖν** is a second aorist infinitive; it takes the ending of the present infinitive (App. 53, A, 4) with an accent change (cf. App. 54). **χρηματισθεὶς**: *since he had been divinely instructed*; the participle is masculine singular first aorist passive (cf. App. 53, G, 5; 34). Although he is instructed by an angel of the Lord to return to the land of Israel in general, his prudence leads him to seek the safety of Galilee specifically. **τὰ μέρη** is a third declension noun (cf. App. 15).

2:23 **κατῴκησεν**: in the aorist tense the verb takes a temporal augment: the initial vowel of the verb is lengthened: **ο** becomes **ω**. The **ι** is added to the vowel as a subscript. **εἰς** (+ accusative) is frequently equivalent to ἐν (+ dative). **πόλιν** is a third declension noun with stem in **ι** (App. 13). **λεγομένην**: *called*; the form is a feminine singular accusative present passive participle (cf. App. 53, A, 4) standing in agreement with its subject πόλιν. **Ναζαρέτ** is a predicate accusative noun.

ὅπως πληρωθῇ τὸ ῥηθὲν διὰ τῶν προφητῶν ὅτι Ναζωραῖος κληθήσεται.

2:23
ὅπως that, in order that (conjunction)
πληρόω, πληρώσω, ἐπλήρωσα, πεπλήρωκα, πεπλήρωμαι, ἐπληρώθην fill, complete, fulfill
διά through, by (preposition + genitive)
προφήτης, ου, ὁ prophet, seer, revelator
διά through, by (preposition + genitive)
προφήτης, ου, ὁ prophet, seer, revelator
ὅτι that, because, since (conjunction)
Ναζωραῖος, ου, ὁ Nazorean, Nazarene, inhabitant of Nazareth
καλέω, καλέσω, ἐκάλεσα, κέκληκα, κέκλημαι, ἐκλήθην call, summon, invite

---

2:23 **ὅπως πληρωθῇ**: supply ταῦτα ἐγένετο before the purpose clause. The conjunction with the subjunctive is used to indicate purpose. The first aorist passive verb stands in the subjunctive mood (cf. App. 53, G, 2). The subjunctive mood is regularly formed by the lengthening of the personal endings of the present indicative. The third person singular ending -**ει** becomes -**ῃ**: the **ε** changes to **η**, and the **ι** becomes a subscript. **τὸ ῥηθὲν**: *that which was spoken* (literally); the verbal form is a neuter singular nominative first aorist passive participle (cf. App. 53, G, 5; 34) that translates as a relative clause in conjunction with an article. **διὰ τῶν προφητῶν**: usually the evangelist cites a singular rather than a more generalized plural. **ὅτι** introduces a direct statement and is equivalent to our quotation marks. **Ναζωραῖος κληθήσεται**: *He will be called a Nazorean*; the verb is a third person singular first future passive indicative. It is conjugated κληθήσομαι, κληθήσῃ/κληθήσει, κληθήσεται, κληθησόμεθα, κληθήσεσθε, κληθήσονται (cf. App. 53, G, 1). The subject of the verb is Jesus. The change of subject from Joseph to Jesus is readily anticipated, since fulfillment of prophecies frequently involves Jesus. The precise wording of the prophecy is not found in the Old Testament.

3 Ἐν δὲ ταῖς ἡμέραις ἐκείναις παραγίνεται Ἰωάννης ὁ βαπτιστὴς κηρύσσων ἐν τῇ ἐρήμῳ τῆς Ἰουδαίας 3:2 [καὶ] λέγων, Μετανοεῖτε· ἤγγικεν γὰρ

3:1
ἡμέρα, ας, ἡ day
ἐκεῖνος, η, ον that, that one, the former
παραγίνομαι, παραγενήσομαι, παρεγενόμην come, arrive, be present
Ἰωάννης, ου, ὁ John
βαπτιστής, οῦ, ὁ one who baptises, Baptist, Baptizer
κηρύσσω, κηρύξω, ἐκήρυξα, ἐκηρύχθην announce openly, proclaim aloud
ἔρημος, ου, ἡ wilderness, desert, grassland
3:2
μετανοέω, μετανοήσω, μετανόησα change one's mind, repent
ἐγγίζω, ἐγγίσω, ἤγγισα, ἤγγικα approach, draw near
γάρ for, indeed, but (conjunction)

3:1 **ἐκείναις** is a demonstrative pronoun. When demonstrative pronouns are used as adjectives they must stand in predicate position, i.e., either in front of or after the article and noun group which they modify. A large space of time has elapsed between the time Joseph returned from Egypt and the preaching of John the Baptist. **παραγίνεται** is a third person present deponent indicative verb. The present used for a past tense is called *historical present* and is frequently seen in vivid narrative accounts and translated as a past tense. **Ἰωάννης ὁ βαπτιστὴς**: the title more specifically identifies John and stands in apposition to the name. **κηρύσσων** is a masculine singular nominative present active participle (cf. App. 29) in agreement with its subject Ἰωάννης. While the same participle is used in the other Synoptic Gospels, in the Gospel of John he came ἵνα μαρτυρήσῃ περὶ τοῦ φωτός. **ἐν τῇ ἐρήμῳ**: the location runs from Jerusalem and Bethlehem east to the lower Jordan and south to the Dead Sea, a place to which John had accustomed himself and where he found solitude in preparation of his work to preach and baptize.

3:2 **Μετανοεῖτε** is, according to Matthew, a key message of his ministry. The verb is a second person plural present active imperative of a contracted verb in **ε** (cf. App. 56). The forms of the second person plural present active indicative and this imperative look alike and must be distinguished by context. **ἤγγικεν** is third person singular perfect active indicative. The perfect tense denotes action (aspect) that is completed near present time and continues with present result: *The kingdom of heaven has approached* (recently and is now here). The verb expresses great urgency. Verbs beginning with a short vowel lengthen the vowel to show reduplication. The reduplication or doubling of the sound at the beginning of a word occurs especially in the perfect, pluperfect, and future perfect tenses to indicate completed action.

ἡ βασιλεία τῶν οὐρανῶν. 3:3 οὗτος γάρ ἐστιν ὁ ῥηθεὶς διὰ Ἠσαΐου
τοῦ προφήτου λέγοντος,

Φωνὴ βοῶντος ἐν τῇ ἐρήμῳ·
Ἑτοιμάσατε τὴν ὁδὸν κυρίου,
εὐθείας ποιεῖτε τὰς τρίβους αὐτοῦ.

3:2
βασιλεία, ας, ἡ kingship, royal power, kingdom
οὐρανός, οῦ, ὁ heaven
3:3
οὗτος, αὕτη, τοῦτο this, this one (demonstrative pronoun)
εἰμί, ἔσομαι be
διά through, by (preposition + genitive)
Ἠσαΐας, ου, ὁ Isaiah
φωνή, ῆς, ἡ voice, sound
βοάω, βοήσω, ἐβόησα shout, cry out
ἔρημος, ου, ἡ wilderness, desert, grassland
ἑτοιμάζω, ἑτοιμάσω, ἡτοίμασα, ἡτοίμακα, ἡτοίμασμαι, ἡτοιμάσθην make ready, prepare
ὁδός, οῦ, ἡ road, way, journey
κύριος, ου, ὁ lord, Lord, master
εὐθύς, εῖα, ύ straight; right, upright, true
ποιέω, ποιήσω, ἐποίησα, πεποίηκα, πεποίημαι, ἐποιήθην make, do, keep, obey
τρίβος, ου, ἡ a beaten track; path, road, highway

3:2 **ἡ βασιλεία τῶν οὐρανῶν**: a phrase particularly identified with Matthew: the other Synoptic Gospels use *the kingdom of God*. The kingdom of heaven is heralded as beginning with the advent of Jesus and its identification becomes a recurring theme in the first Gospel. It is the same message that Jesus teaches (4:17).

3:3 **οὗτος** is a demonstrative pronoun (App. 41) and the subject of the verb. It refers to John the Baptist. **ὁ ῥηθεὶς**: *he who was spoken of*; the verbal form is a masculine singular nominative first aorist passive participle (cf. App. 53, G, 5; 34) that translates as a relative clause in conjunction with an article. The introductory formula changes from the neuter τὸ ῥηθὲν to the masculine form, making the reference to John the Baptist a more personal one. **Ἠσαΐου**: the two dots over the **ι** indicate diaeresis: the vowel is treated as a separate syllable. **Φωνὴ βοῶντος**: *the voice of one crying*; βοῶντος is the masculine singular present active participle of a contracted verb in αω (cf. App. 35). All four evangelists cite this passage in reference to John the Baptist. **Ἑτοιμάσατε** is a second person plural aorist active imperative; imperatives drop the augment (cf. App. 53, D, 3). **εὐθείας ποιεῖτε τὰς τρίβους**: the adjective εὐθείας is feminine plural accusative in agreement with its subject τρίβους. Since it stands outside of the article and noun group τὰς τρίβους, it is a predicate adjective. Both verbs Ἑτοιμάσατε and εὐθείας ποιεῖτε along with their parallel constructions are doublets and have similar meaning. Such preparation involves a change of heart as required by John the Baptist's Μετανοεῖτε (3:2).

3:4 Αὐτὸς δὲ ὁ Ἰωάννης εἶχεν τὸ ἔνδυμα αὐτοῦ ἀπὸ τριχῶν καμήλου καὶ ζώνην δερματίνην περὶ τὴν ὀσφὺν αὐτοῦ, ἡ δὲ τροφὴ ἦν αὐτοῦἀκρίδες καὶ μέλι ἄγριον.

3:4

ἔχω, ἕξω, ἔσχον (2 aorist), ἔσχηκα have, keep, cause, consider; be (with adverbs and indications of time and age); be able (with infinitive)

ἔνδυμα, ατος, τό garment, clothing; cloak, mantle

ἀπό from, because of, out of, by (preposition + genitive)

θρίξ, τριχός, ἡ hair

κάμηλος, ου, ὁ and ἡ camel

ζώνη, ης, ἡ belt, girdle

δερμάτινος, η, ον made of skin, leather

περί about, concerning (preposition + genitive); about, around (+ accusative)

ὀσφύς, ύος, ἡ waist

τροφή, ῆς, ἡ nourishment, food

ἀκρίς, ίδος, ἡ grasshopper, locust

μέλι, ιτος, τό honey

ἄγριος, ία, ιον wild

3:4 **Αὐτὸς δὲ ὁ Ἰωάννης**: *Now John himself*; the intensive pronoun stands in predicate position with the subject ὁ Ἰωάννης (App. 40). **εἶχεν**: *used to wear*; the verb is the third person singular imperfect active indicative of the verb ἔχω. It is formed by adding an augment to the present stem and takes the endings -ον, -ες, -ε(ν), -ομεν, -ετε, -ον (cf. App. 53, C). In contrast to the aorist, its aspect shows action in the past that is continuing (*was wearing*), customary (*used to wear*), conative (*attempted to wear*), inchoative (*began to wear*), etc., and should not be slighted in translation. **ἀπὸ τριχῶν καμήλου**: *of camel's hair*; the preposition ἀπὸ with the genitive τριχῶν expresses the material *out of* or *from which* something is made. The plural of τριχῶν, a third declension noun with stem in guttural **χ** (App. 7), is translated into the singular as a collective noun. **ζώνην δερματίνην**: prophets regularly distinguished themselves by wearing rough clothing of sheepskins or goatskins (Zech 13:4, Heb 11:37) and a leather belt (1 Kgs 18:46). He may be compared particularly to Elijah in regard to his clothing. **ὀσφὺν** is a feminine singular accusative third declension noun with stem in **υ** (cf. App. 13). **ἦν**: *was*; the verb is the third person singular imperfect active indicative of the verb εἰμί (App. 63). The imperfect tense denotes progressive, continued, and repeated action (aspect) in past time. **ἀκρίδες** are considered clean and represent a simple and not uncommon food in desert lands (Lev 11:21–22). The form is a feminine plural nominative third declension noun with stem in dental (cf. App. 8). **μέλι** is considered one *of the best products of the land* (Gen 43:11). The form is a neuter singular accusative third declension noun with stem **τ** (cf. App. 10).

3:5 τότε ἐξεπορεύετο πρὸς αὐτὸν Ἱεροσόλυμα καὶ πᾶσα ἡ Ἰουδαία καὶ πᾶσα ἡ περίχωρος τοῦ Ἰορδάνου, 3:6 καὶ ἐβαπτίζοντο ἐν τῷ Ἰορδάνῃ ποταμῷ ὑπ' αὐτοῦ ἐξομολογούμενοι τὰς ἁμαρτίας αὐτῶν.
3:7 Ἰδὼν δὲ πολλοὺς τῶν Φαρισαίων καὶ Σαδδουκαίων

3:5
τότε then, at that time, thereupon, thereafter (adverb)
ἐκπορεύομαι, ἐκπορεύσομαι, ἐκπεπόρευμαι, ἐξεπορεύθην come out, go out, proceed
πρός to, towards, for, for the purpose of (+ accusative)
πᾶς, πᾶσα, πᾶν every, all
περίχωρος, ὁ, ἡ adjacent region; inhabitants of the region around
Ἰόρδανος, ου, ὁ Jordan
3:6
βαπτίζω, βαπτίσω, ἐβάπτισα, βεβάπτισμαι, ἐβαπτίσθην dip, immerse, baptize
ἐν in, on, among (proclitic; preposition + dative)
Ἰορδάνης, ου, ὁ Jordan
ποταμός, οῦ, ὁ river, stream, torrent
ὑπό by (preposition + genitive of personal agent)
ἐξομολογέω, ἐξομολογήσω, ἐξωμολόγησα consent, agree; confess, admit, acknowledge; praise, give praise (middle)
ἁμαρτία, ας, ἡ error, sin
3:7
ὁράω, ὄψομαι, εἶδον (2 aorist), ἑώρακα/ἑόρακα, φθην see, notice, look, perceive, experience, witness
πολύς, πολλή, πολύ much, large, many (in plural)
Φαρισαῖος, ου, ὁ a Pharisee
Σαδδουκαῖος, ου, ὁ Sadducee

3:5 **ἐξεπορεύετο** is a third person singular imperfect deponent indicative (App. 53, C). The singular verb agrees in number with its nearest subject Ἱεροσόλυμα only. **πᾶσα** modifies Ἰουδαία. This and the subsequent adjective speak to the great popularity of John the Baptist.

3:6 **ἐβαπτίζοντο**: *they were baptized*; the form is third person plural imperfect passive indicative. It is formed by adding an augment to the present stem and adding to the stem the endings -ομην, -ου, -ετο, -ομεθα, -εσθε, -οντο (App. 53, C). The **ε/ο** preceding the personal ending is called a *thematic vowel*. The imperfect tense denotes progressive, continued, and repeated action (aspect) in past time. Agency is usually expressed, as here, by the preposition **ὑπό** and a noun or pronoun in the genitive case. **ἐξομολογούμενοι**: *as they confessed*; the form is a present middle participle of a contracted verb with stem in **ε** (cf. App. 56). The endings of a contracted participle are those of a regular **ω** verb (App. 30). The middle voice denotes that the subject performs an action for itself or its own interest or benefit. The present tense of the participle generally agrees in time with that of the main verb.

3:7 **Ἰδὼν**: *when he saw*; the verbal form is a second aorist active participle (App. 29, note). The aorist tense expresses a single act (aspect) in past time. **πολλοὺς τῶν Φαρισαίων**: the irregular adjective, used as a substantive, is declined with stems in πολυ- and πολλο- (App. 38). Φαρισαίων and Σαδδυκαίων are partitive genitives since they follow a word denoting part of a whole (App. 65).

ἐρχομένους ἐπὶ τὸ βάπτισμα αὐτοῦ εἶπεν αὐτοῖς, Γεννήματα ἐχιδνῶν, τίς ὑπέδειξεν ὑμῖν φυγεῖν ἀπὸ τῆς μελλούσης ὀργῆς;

3:7
ἔρχομαι, ἐλεύσομαι, ἦλθον (2 aorist), ἐλήλυθα come, go
ἐπί upon, on (preposition + genitive); on, in, above, at, by, near, at the time of, during (+ dative); on, to, near, by, against (+ accusative)
βαπτίσμα, ατος, τό immersion, baptism
γέννημα, ατος, τό offspring, progeny, brood
ἔχιδνα, ης, ἡ viper, poisonous serpent
τίς, τί, (τίνος) who? what? why? (interrogative pronoun)
ὑποδείκνυμι/ὑποδεικνύω, ὑποδείξω, ὑπέδειξα, ὑποδέδειχα, ὑπεδείχθην show, point out, make known, demonstrate, announce
σύ, σοῦ (σου) you (personal pronoun)
φεύγω, φεύξομαι, ἔφυγον (2 aorist) flee, flee from, avoid, shun
ἀπό from, because of, out of, by (preposition + genitive)
μέλλω, μελλήσω be about to, be on the point of
ὀργή, ῆς, ἡ anger, wrath, indignation

3:7 **ἐρχομένους**: the present deponent participle agrees in gender, number, and case with its subject πολλοὺς. **βάπτισμα** is a neuter singular accusative third declension noun with stem in **τ**. Both the nominative and the accusative forms look alike in the neuter (cf. App. 10). **Γεννήματα ἐχιδνῶν** is a neuter plural vocative third declension noun with stem in τ. Both the nominative and the vocative forms look alike (cf. App. 10). ἐχιδνῶν is an appositional genitive (cf. App. 65) more specifically identifying Γεννήματα. John at once recognizes their malicious intent and verbally confronts them. Their relationship with John the Baptist foreshadows their antagonism toward Jesus, who frequently addresses them as ὑποκριταί. **τίς ὑπέδειξεν ὑμῖν φυγεῖν ἀπὸ τῆς μελλούσης ὀργῆς;** *Who warned you to flee from the coming wrath?* Who, indeed? The rhetorical question is filled with irony. John has been teaching repentence and either they have heard him but not heeded his exhortation or they have not been willing to hear him at all. In neither case will they avoid eschatological judgment. The interrogative pronoun is τίς (App. 47). The interrogative pronoun distinguishes itself from the indefinite pronoun by the accent (cf. App. 48). The semicolon also indicates a direct question. ὑπέδειξεν ὑμιν φυγεῖν: the verb takes a dative personal pronoun (App. 39) and an infinitive construction. φυγεῖν is a second aorist infinitive; it takes the ending of the present infinitive with an accent change and loses its augment (cf. App. 54). μελλούσης is a present active participle that agrees in gender, number, and case with its subject ὀργῆς. The endings are those of the present active participle added to the stem (cf. App. 53, A, 5; 29).

3:8 ποιήσατε οὖν καρπὸν ἄξιον τῆς μετανοίας 3:9 καὶ μὴ δόξητε λέγειν ἐν ἑαυτοῖς, Πατέρα ἔχομεν τὸν Ἀβραάμ. λέγω γὰρ ὑμῖν

3:8
ποιέω, ποιήσω, ἐποίησα, πεποίηκα, πεποίημαι, ἐποιήθην make, do, keep, obey
οὖν therefore, then, so (conjunction, postpositive)
καρπός, οῦ, ὁ fruit, crop; result, gain
ἄξιος, ία, ιον worthy
μετάνοια, ας, ἡ change of mind, remorse, repentance
3:9
μή not (particle of negation)
δοκέω, δόξω, ἔδοξα think (mistakenly), believe, suppose, consider
ἐν in, on, among (proclitic; preposition + dative)
ἑαυτοῦ, ῆς, οῦ himself, herself, itself; themselves, ourselves, yourselves (reflexive pronoun)
πατήρ, πατρός, ὁ father, parent, ancestor
ἔχω, ἕξω, ἔσχον (2 aorist), ἔσχηκα have, keep, cause, consider; be (with adverbs and indications of time and age); be able (with infinitive)
Ἀβραάμ, ὁ Abraham (indeclinable)
σύ, σοῦ (σου) you (personal pronoun)

3:8 **ποιήσατε** is second person plural first aorist active imperative (cf. App. 53, D, 3). **καρπὸν ἄξιον τῆς μετανοίας**: *fruit worthy of repentence*; in this context, his challenge to produce good works includes especially ἐξομολογούμενοι τὰς ἁμαρτίας αὐτῶν (3:6) and τὸ βάπτισμα (3:11). ἄξιον takes a genitive when followed by a noun.

3:9 **μὴ δόξητε λέγειν ἐν ἑαυτοῖς**: *do not mistakenly think to say among yourselves*; the negative particle in μὴ and the subjunctive combine to produce a prohibitive subjunctive. The aorist indicates the aspect of a single act. The subjunctive mood is regularly formed by lengthening the thematic vowel of the present indicative: **ε/ο** become **η/ω** (cf. App. 53, D, 2). λέγειν is a present active infinitive (cf. 53, A, 4). ἑαυτοῖς is a third person plural reflexive pronoun (App. 46). **Πατέρα ἔχομεν τὸν Ἀβραάμ**: *We have Abraham as our father*; Πατέρα is a predicate accusative which does not usually have an article. It is a third declension noun with stems in **ερ** alternating with **ρ** (App. 12). John anticipates their argument and at once gives a specific example of what they should repent of: excessive pride in Abrahamic descent and supposing that their lineage was a sufficient condition for salvation and that they had no need of repentence and baptism. The same argument is made before Jesus (Jn 8:39). **λέγω . . . ὑμῖν**: λέγω is a present active indicative form of the regular **ω** verb with endings in -ω, -εις, -ει, -ομεν, -ετε, -ουσι(ν) (App. 53, A, 1). The movable **ν** appears when the following word begins with a vowel or when it occurs at the end of a sentence. The verb takes a dative object. ὑμῖν is a second person plural personal pronoun in the dative case (App. 39).

ὅτι δύναται ὁ θεὸς ἐκ τῶν λίθων τούτων ἐγεῖραι τέκνα τῷ Ἀβραάμ.
3:10 ἤδη δὲ ἡ ἀξίνη πρὸς τὴν ῥίζαν τῶν δένδρων κεῖται· πᾶν οὖν
δένδρον μὴ

3:9
ὅτι that, because, since (conjunction)
δύναμαι, δυνήσομαι, ἠδυνήθην be able
θεός, οῦ, ὁ God, god
ἐκ (ἐξ before a vowel) from, out of, of, by (preposition + genitive)
λίθος, ου, ὁ stone
οὗτος, αὕτη, τοῦτο this, this one (demonstrative pronoun)
ἐγείρω, ἐγερῶ, ἤγειρα, ἠγήγερμαι, ἠγέρθην awaken, lift raise up from the dead, restore, rebuild; get up!, come! (intransitive, only in imperative)
τέκνον, ου, τό child, descendant, posterity
Ἀβραάμ, ὁ Abraham (indeclinable)
3:10
ἤδη now, already (adverb)
ἀξίνη, ης, ἡ ax
πρός for, for the purpose of (preposition + genitive); to, towards, unto, for, for the purpose of (+ accusative)
ῥίζα, ης, ἡ root
δένδρον, ου, τό tree
κεῖμαι, κείσομαι, lie, be laid, be placed, be set
πᾶς, πᾶσα, πᾶν every, all
οὖν therefore, then, so (conjunction, postpositive)
μή not (particle of negation)

3:9 **ὅτι** introduces an indirect statement. **δύναται**, a deponent verb, takes a complementary infinitive in ἐγεῖραι. **ἐκ τῶν λίθων τούτων**: demonstrative pronouns, used as adjectives, must agree in gender, number, and case with their noun and stand in predicate position, i.e., either in front of or after the article and noun group which they modify. Since the article and demonstrative may be construed as deictic, John may indeed be pointing to the stones along the Jordan. **ἐγεῖραι** is a liquid aorist infinitive: a verb stem ending in a liquid or nasal (**λ**, **μ**, **ν**, or **ρ**) adds the first aorist ending -σαι to the stem but omits the -**σ**- (cf. App. 53, D, 4). **τέκνα τῷ Ἀβραάμ**: by his seemingly hyperbolic imagery John asserts that children of the covenant community of Abraham can be born outside of the covenant community of a traditional Jewish family. To suggest that paronomasia or a word play is at work because of the close linguistic relationship between the Hebrew words for children and stones tends to obfuscate the meaning somewhat. John primarily discusses the stones as the source (ἐκ τῶν λίθων τούτων), not as the offspring. Nonetheless, John's imagery of stones may not be that far afield given how God formed man: χοῦν ἀπὸ τῆς γῆς: *dust from the earth* (Gen 2:7).

3:10 **ἤδη δὲ ἡ ἀξίνη . . . τὴν ῥίζαν**: the collocation of the adverb in emphatic position at the beginning of the sentence and the metaphorical language vividly indicate the impendence of the final judgment. **πᾶν . . . δένδρον μὴ ποιοῦν**: *every tree that does not produce* (literally: *every tree, if it [whichever] does not produce*); the use of μὴ as negation of a participle that has an indefinite antecedent indicates conditional force and the participial construction is equivalent to a conditional relative clause.

ποιοῦν καρπὸν καλὸν ἐκκόπτεται καὶ εἰς πῦρ βάλλεται. 3:11 ἐγὼ μὲν ὑμᾶς βαπτίζω ἐν ὕδατι εἰς μετάνοιαν, ὁ δὲ ὀπίσω μου ἐρχόμενος

3:10

ποιέω, ποιήσω, ἐποίησα, πεποίηκα, πεποίημαι, ἐποιήθην make, produce, do, keep, obey

καρπός, οῦ, ὁ fruit, crop; result, gain

καλός, ή, όν good, useful, choice

ἐκκόπτω, ἐκκόψω, ἐξέκοψα, ἐξεκόπην cut out, cut off

εἰς to, into, on, in; for, as; with respect to (preposition + accusative)

πῦρ, πυρός, τό fire

βάλλω, βαλῶ, ἔβαλον, βέβληκα, βέβλημαι, ἐβλήθην throw, sow, cast, place, put, bring

3:11

ἐγώ, ἐμοῦ (μου) I (personal pronoun)

μέν on the one hand; ὁ μέν . . . ὁ δέ the one . . . the other; οἱ μέν . . . ἄλλοι δέ some . . . others

σύ, σοῦ (σου) you (personal pronoun)

βαπτίζω, βαπτίσω, ἐβάπτισα, βεβάπτισμαι, ἐβαπτίσθην dip, immerse, baptize

ἐν in, on, among (proclitic; preposition + dative)

ὕδωρ, ὕδατος, τό water

μετάνοια, ας, ἡ change of mind, remorse, repentance

ὀπίσω behind, after (adverb; preposition + genitive); εἰς τὰ ὀπίσω back, backward

ἔρχομαι, ἐλεύσομαι, ἦλθον (2 aorist), ἐλήλυθα come, go

3:10 ποιοῦν is a present active participle of a contracted verb with stem in **ε** (cf. App. 56; 36). It agrees with its subject δένδρον in gender, number, and case and takes καρπὸν as its object. **ἐκκόπτεται . . . βάλλεται**: both verbs are third person singular present passive indicative (cf. App. 53, A, 1). The personal endings are best seen in the middle or passive endings of the perfect tense (cf. App. 53, E, 1): -μαι, -σαι, -ται, -μεθα, -σθε, -νται. The vowel **ε/ο** preceding the personal ending is called a *thematic* vowel. The second person singular has a change of form due to consonant omission and vowel contraction.

3:11 **μὲν . . . δὲ**: the postpositive particles indicate contrast and may be rendered *on the one hand . . . on the other hand, indeed . . . but*; but they are often left untranslated. They closely follow the words they modify: ἐγὼ μὲν . . . ὁ δὲ, and frequently occur at the beginning of their clause, in an emphatic position. Here the contrast is between the baptism of John and that of Jesus. **ὑμᾶς βαπτίζω**: the verb is a present active indicative form of the regular **ω** verb with endings in -ω, -εις, -ει, -ομεν, -ετε, -ουσι(ν) (App. 53, A, 1). The movable nu appears when the following word begins with a vowel or when it occurs at the end of a sentence. The verb takes an accusative object. ὑμᾶς is a second person plural personal pronoun (App. 39). **ἐν ὕδατι**: *with water*; while the preposition indicates instrument or means, it also carries the primary meaning of baptizing or immersing *in* water. **ὁ δὲ ὀπίσω μου ἐρχόμενος**: *He who comes after me*; the attributive participle, which regularly stands right after the noun or pronoun, is here immediately preceded by its own modifiers, the prepositional phrase. The pronoun μου has optional enclitic forms in the genitive, dative, and accusative singular forms (App. 39).

ἰσχυρότερός μού ἐστιν, οὗ οὐκ εἰμὶ ἱκανὸς τὰ ὑποδήματα βαστάσαι· αὐτὸς ὑμᾶς βαπτίσει ἐν πνεύματι ἁγίῳ καὶ πυρί· 3:12 οὗ τὸ πτύον ἐν τῇ χειρὶ αὐτοῦ καὶ διακαθαριεῖ τὴν ἅλωνα αὐτοῦ

3:11

ἰσχυρός, ά, όν strong, mighty, powerful

ὅς, ἥ, ὅ who, which, what; he who, that (relative pronoun)

οὐκ not (a form of οὐ used before vowels with a smooth breathing, adverb)

ἱκανός, ή, όν sufficient, enough; adequate, competent, qualified; fit, worthy

ὑπόδημα, ατος, τό sandal

βαστάζω, βαστάσω, ἐβάστασα lift, bear, take up; carry away, remove, steal

σύ, σοῦ (σου) you (personal pronoun)

βαπτίζω, βαπτίσω, ἐβάπτισα, βεβάπτισμαι, ἐβαπτίσθην dip, immerse, baptize

πνεῦμα, ατος, τό wind, spirit, mind, Holy Spirit

ἅγιος, ια, ιον hallowed, pure, holy

πῦρ, πυρός, τό fire

3:12

ὅς, ἥ, ὅ who, which, what; he who, that (relative pronoun)

πτύον, ου, τό winnowing shovel

χείρ, χειρός, ἡ hand

διακαθαρίζω, διακαθαριῶ clean out

ἅλων, ωνος, ἡ threshing floor

3:11 **ἰσχυρότερός μού**: *more powerful than I*; John has a true sense of recognition of who he is, who Jesus is, and what their relationship is. ἰσχυρότερός is a comparative adjective in predicate position. The first/second declension adjective is formed by adding a vowel between the stem ἰσχυρ- and the comparative ending -τερός. The vowel is an omicron if the final vowel of the stem contains a diphthong, a long vowel, or a vowel long by position, i.e., a short vowel followed by two consonants. A word with an acute accent on the antepenult (third syllable from the end) takes an additional accent on the ultima when followed by an enclitic. The enclitic takes no accent. The case use of μού is a genitive of comparison. It requires a comparative adjective. According to rules of accent, a proclitic or enclitic takes an accent when followed by a consecutive enclitic. **οὗ . . . ὑποδήματα**: *whose sandals*; the lengthy separation of the two words that are usually closely connected is called *hyperbaton*. **ἱκανὸς** requires an infinitive βαστάσαι for completion. **ἐν πνεύματι ἁγίῳ καὶ πυρί**: *with the fire of the Holy Spirit*; this figure of speech, hendiadys, expands a single idea into a compound one for purposes of emphasis. John metaphorically likens the Holy Spirit to fire, a traditional image used to describe divinity. The similarity of the language with βαπτίζω ἐν ὕδατι suggests envelopment of the Holy Spirit. Both water and fire are cleansing agents.

3:12 **οὗ τὸ πτύον**: *His winnowing shovel*; the relative pronoun (App. 49) carries demonstrative force. Supply ἐστιν as the finite verb of the sentence. John associates the first coming of Jesus with both His second coming and the final judgment.

καὶ συνάξει τὸν σῖτον αὐτοῦ εἰς τὴν ἀποθήκην, τὸ δὲ ἄχυρον κατακαύσει πυρὶ ἀσβέστῳ.

3:13 Τότε παραγίνεται ὁ Ἰησοῦς ἀπὸ τῆς Γαλιλαίας ἐπὶ τὸν Ἰορδάνην πρὸς τὸν Ἰωάννην τοῦ βαπτισθῆναι ὑπ' αὐτοῦ. 3:14 ὁ δὲ Ἰωάννης διεκώλυεν αὐτὸν λέγων,

---

3:12
συνάγω, συνάξω, συνήγαγον (2 aorist), συνῆγμαι, συνήχθην gather in, gather up, bring together; convene, come together, meet (passive)
σῖτος, ου, ὁ wheat, grain
ἀποθήκη, ης, ἡ granary, storehouse, barn
ἄχυρον, ου, τό chaff, straw
κατακαίω, κατακαύσω, κατέκαυσα, κατεκαύθην light, cause to burn, kindle, burn up, burn down, consume by fire (active); burn, be burned, be consumed with fire (passive)
πῦρ, πυρός, τό fire
ἄσβεστος, ον inextinguishable, unquenchable
3:13
τότε then, at that time, thereupon, thereafter (adverb)
παραγίνομαι, παραγενήσομαι, παρεγενόμην come, arrive, be present
ἀπό from, because of, out of, by (preposition + genitive)
ἐπί upon, on (preposition + genitive); on, in, above, at, by, near, at the time of, during (+ dative); on, to, near, by, against (+ accusative)
Ἰορδάνης, ου, ὁ Jordan
πρός for, for the purpose of (preposition + genitive); with, to, towards, unto, for, for the purpose of, with reference to, in relation to, of, concerning (+ accusative); near, at, by (preposition + dative)
βαπτίζω, βαπτίσω, ἐβάπτισα, βεβάπτισμαι, ἐβαπτίσθην dip, immerse, baptize
ὑπό by (preposition + genitive of personal agent)
3:14
διακωλύω, διακωλύσω hinder, restrain, prevent, prohibit

3:13 **τοῦ βαπτισθῆναι**: *to be baptized*; the construction is an articular infinitive. A purpose clause may be expressed by the neuter article in the genitive case followed by an infinitive. It is an alternate construction where ἕνεκα *for the sake of* is usually employed with the genitive article. In this construction the article has the power to turn the infinitive into a substantive. As a verbal noun or gerund it continues to show verbal force. The passive infinitive (cf. App. 53, G, 4) takes a preposition ὑπ' with a genitive pronoun to show agency. The final vowel of a preposition is frequently elided before the initial vowel of the following word; elision is indicated by an apostrophe.

3:14 **διεκώλυεν**: *tried to deter*; the aspect of the imperfect tense shows action in the past that is continuing (*was deterring*), customary (*used to deter*), conative (*tried to deter*), inchoative (*began to deter*), etc.

Ἐγὼ χρείαν ἔχω ὑπὸ σοῦ βαπτισθῆναι, καὶ σὺ ἔρχῃ πρός με; 3:15
ἀποκριθεὶς δὲ ὁ Ἰησοῦς εἶπεν πρὸς αὐτόν, Ἄφες ἄρτι, οὕτως γὰρ
πρέπον ἐστὶν ἡμῖν πληρῶσαι πᾶσαν δικαιοσύνην.

3:14

χρεία, ας, ἡ need, necessity

ἔχω, ἕξω, ἔσχον (2 aorist), ἔσχηκα have, keep, cause, consider; be (with adverbs and indications of time and age); be able (with infinitive)

ὑπό by (preposition + genitive of personal agent)

σύ, σοῦ (σου) you (personal pronoun)

βαπτίζω, βαπτίσω, ἐβάπτισα, βεβάπτισμαι, ἐβαπτίσθην dip, immerse, baptize

ἔρχομαι, ἐλεύσομαι, ἦλθον (2 aorist), ἐλήλυθα come, go

πρός to, towards, unto, for, for the purpose of, with reference to, in relation to, of, concerning (+ accusative)

3:15

ἀποκρίνομαι, ἀπεκρινάμην, ἀπεκρίθην answer, reply

ἀφίημι, ἀφήσω, ἀφῆκα, ἀφῆν (2 aorist), ἀφεῖκα, ἀφεῖμαι, ἀφέθην let go, permit, suffer, leave, forgive

ἄρτι now (adverb)

οὕτως so, thus, in this manner (adverb)

γάρ for, indeed, but (conjunction)

πρέπον fitting, proper, right (+ dative and infinitive)

πληρόω, πληρώσω, ἐπλήρωσα, πεπλήρωκα, πεπλήρωμαι, ἐπληρώθην fill, complete, fulfill

πᾶς, πᾶσα, πᾶν every, all

δικαιοσύνη, ης, ἡ justice, righteousness, godliness

3:14 **χρείαν . . . βαπτισθῆναι**: the infinitive serves to define or explain the meaning of the noun. It follows especially nouns that denote ability, fitness, and necessity. **σὺ ἔρχῃ**: since it is not strictly necessary, the pronoun takes on emphasis by its mere use and prominent placement at the beginning of the sentence. The verbal form is a second person singular present deponent indicative of ἔρχομαι. The second person singular has optional endings in **η/ει**.

3:15 **ἀποκριθεὶς**: *in reply*; the verbal form is a first aorist passive participle (cf. App. 34) modifying ὁ Ἰησοῦς. The participle loses its verbal force in this formulaic phrase. **Ἄφες ἄρτι**: *let it be so now*; that is the meaning of the verb in an absolute sense. The verbal form is a second person singular second aorist imperative (cf. App. 59). **πρέπον ἐστὶν ἡμῖν . . . πληρῶσαι πᾶσαν δικαιοσύνην**: the infinitive is the subject of the quasi-impersonal verb. It follows especially verbs that denote ability, fitness, and necessity. The subject of the infinitive is in the dative plural. While a person speaking of himself may use the first person plural as a modest form of statement, the speaker may also suggest a shift from a particular to a general statement. In this He not only does what is right but serves as an example.

τότε ἀφίησιν αὐτόν. 3:16 βαπτισθεὶς δὲ ὁ Ἰησοῦς εὐθὺς ἀνέβη ἀπὸ τοῦ ὕδατος· καὶ ἰδοὺ ἠνεῴχθησαν [αὐτῷ] οἱ οὐρανοί, καὶ εἶδεν [τὸ] πνεῦμα [τοῦ] θεοῦ καταβαῖνον ὡσεὶ περιστερὰν [καὶ] ἐρχόμενον ἐπ' αὐτόν·

3:16
βαπτίζω, βαπτίσω, ἐβάπτισα, βεβάπτισμαι, ἐβαπτίσθην dip, immerse, baptize
εὐθύς immediately, at once (adverb)
ἀναβαίνω, ἀναβήσομαι, ἀνέβην, ἀναβέβηκα go up, ascend, rise
ἀπό from, because of, out of, by (preposition + genitive)
ὕδωρ, ὕδατος, τό water
ἰδού see, look, behold (demonstrative particle)
ἀνοίγω, ἀνοίξω, ἀνέῳξα/ἤνοιξα, ἀνέῳγα, ἀνέῳγμαι, ἠνεῴχθην open
οὐρανός, οῦ, ὁ heaven
ὁράω, ὄψομαι, εἶδον (2 aorist), ἑώρακα/ἑόρακα, ὤφθην see, catch sight of, notice, look
πνεῦμα, ατος, τό wind, spirit, mind, Holy Spirit
θεός, οῦ, ὁ God, god
καταβαίνω, καταβήσομαι, κατέβην, καταβέβηκα come down, go down, descend, fall
ὡσεί as if, as, like (adverb)
περιστερά, ᾶς, ἡ dove, pigeon
ἔρχομαι, ἐλεύσομαι, ἦλθον (2 aorist), ἐλήλυθα come, go
ἐπί on, to, upon, towards, against (+ accusative)
ἀφίημι, ἀφήσω, ἀφῆκα, ἀφῆν (2 aorist), ἀφεῖκα, ἀφεῖμαι, ἀφέθην let go, permit, suffer, leave, forgive

---

3:15 **ἀφίησιν αὐτόν**: *he allowed Him* (supply βαπτισθῆναι): the verbal form is a third person singular present active indicative of a μι verb (cf. App. 59).

3:16 **βαπτισθεὶς**: *as soon as He had been baptized*; the participle is masculine singular first aorist passive (cf. App. 53, G, 5; 34). The aorist participle usually expresses a single act (aspect) in past time and frequently translates as a pluperfect when a main verb stands in the past tense. **ἠνεῴχθησαν** takes not only a double augment of the stem but also an augmented prefix. **καταβαῖνον ὡσεὶ περιστερὰν**: *descending like a dove*; the neuter singular accusative present active participle (cf. App. 29) modifies its subject πνεῦμα. ὡσεὶ introduces a simile, not an allegory. It makes only a single comparison between τὸ πεῦμα and περιστερὰν: the manner of the descent.

3:17 καὶ ἰδοὺ φωνὴ ἐκ τῶν οὐρανῶν λέγουσα, Οὗτός ἐστιν ὁ υἱός μου ὁ ἀγαπητός, ἐν ᾧ εὐδόκησα.

3:17
ἰδού see, look, behold (demonstrative particle)
φωνή, ῆς, ἡ voice, sound
ἐκ (ἐξ before a vowel) from, out of, of, by (preposition + genitive)
οὐρανός, οῦ, ὁ heaven
οὗτος, αὕτη, τοῦτο this, this one (demonstrative pronoun)
ἐγώ, ἐμοῦ (μου) I (personal pronoun)
ἀγαπητός, ή, όν beloved, dear
ἐν in, on, among (proclitic; preposition + dative)
ὅς, ἥ, ὅ who, which, what; he who, that (relative pronoun)
εὐδοκέω, εὐδοκήσω, εὐδόκησα/ηὐδόκησα be well pleased, take delight

3:17 **φωνὴ . . . λέγουσα**: supply a finite verb like ἐγένετο or ἦλθε. **ὁ υἱός μου ὁ ἀγαπητός**: *my Beloved Son*; The repetition of the article with the adjective is an alternate construction for ὁ ἀγαπητὸς υἱός. In both cases the adjective is in attributive position, i.e., it follows the article. However, in the alternate construction greater emphasis falls on the noun: *my Son who is Beloved*. **εὐδόκησα**: *I am well pleased*; the verbal form is a gnomic aorist. The aorist may be used to express a general truth where the experience of an action in the past suggests an action that is likely to be repeated.

4 Τότε ὁ Ἰησοῦς ἀνήχθη εἰς τὴν ἔρημον ὑπὸ τοῦ πνεύματος
πειρασθῆναι ὑπὸ τοῦ διαβόλου. 4:2 καὶ νηστεύσας ἡμέρας
τεσσεράκοντα καὶ νύκτας τεσσεράκοντα, ὕστερον ἐπείνασεν. 4:3
Καὶ προσελθὼν ὁ πειράζων εἶπεν αὐτῷ, Εἰ υἱὸς εἶ τοῦ θεοῦ, εἰπὲ ἵνα

4:1
τότε then, at that time, thereupon, thereafter (adverb)
ἀνάγω, ἀνάξω, ἀνήγαγον (2 aorist), ἀνήχθην lead up, bring up
ἔρημος, ου, ἡ wilderness, desert, grassland
ὑπό by (preposition + genitive of personal agent)
πνεῦμα, ατος, τό wind, spirit, mind, Holy Spirit
πειράζω, πειράσω, ἐπείρασα, πεπείρασμαι, ἐπειράσθην try, test, tempt, prove
διάβολος, ου, ὁ slanderer, devil
4:2
νηστεύω, νηστεύσω, ἐνήστευσα fast
ἡμέρα, ας, ἡ day
τεσσεράκοντα forty (indeclinable)
νύξ, νυκτὸς, ἡ night
ὕστερος, α, ον later; ὕστερον later, afterwards (adverb)
πεινάω, πεινάσω/πεινήσω, ἐπείνασα hunger, be hungry
4:3
προσέρχομαι, προσελεύσομαι, προσῆλθον, προσελήλυθα come to, go to, approach
πειράζω, πειράσω, ἐπείρασα, πεπείρασμαι, ἐπειράσθην try, test, tempt, prove
εἰ if, whether
υἱός, οῦ, ὁ son
θεός, οῦ, ὁ God, god
ἵνα to, in order to, in order that, that (conjunction)

4:1 **πειρασθῆναι**: *to be tempted;* the verbal form is a first aorist passive infinitive (cf. App. 53, G, 4); by definition it has no ending as to person or number. It functions here as an infinitive of purpose and is equivalent to the more commonly used ἵνα clause.

4:2 **νηστεύσας**: *when he had fasted;* is a masculine singular nominative first aorist active participle (cf. App. 31). **ἡμέρας . . . νύκτας**: the accusative case expresses duration of time.

4:3 **Εἰ . . . εἶ . . . εἰπὲ**: *if you are . . . command;* εἰ with the indicative in both clauses introduces a simple or particular condition (App. 70). Conditions consist of a protasis, i.e., that which is put forth or proposed, and an apodosis, the conclusion. Note the difference in accent between εἰ and εἶ. In this simple condition the imperative is substituted for the indicative. **ἵνα . . . γένωνται**: ἵνα is the usual conjunction to introduce purpose clauses. The second aorist deponent verb stands in the subjunctive mood (cf. App. 54). The subjunctive mood is regularly formed by lengthening the thematic vowel of the personal endings of the present indicative. The third person plural ending -ονται becomes -ωνται.

οἱ λίθοι οὗτοι ἄρτοι γένωνται. 4:4 ὁ δὲ ἀποκριθεὶς εἶπεν, Γέγραπται,
Οὐκ ἐπ' ἄρτῳ μόνῳ ζήσεται ὁ ἄνθρωπος,
ἀλλ' ἐπὶ παντὶ ῥήματι ἐκπορευομένῳ
διὰ στόματος θεοῦ.

4:3

λίθος, ου, ὁ stone

οὗτος, αὕτη, τοῦτο this, this one (demonstrative pronoun)

ἄρτος, ου, ὁ bread, loaf of bread

γίνομαι, γενήσομαι, ἐγενόμην, γέγονα/γεγένημαι, ἐγενήθην become, be made, be created, be born, come, arrive, be present

4:4

ἀποκρίνομαι, ἀπεκρινάμην, ἀπεκρίθην answer, reply

γράφω, γράψω, ἔγραψα, γέγραφα, γέγραμμαι, ἐγράφθην engrave, write

οὐκ not (a form of οὐ used before vowels with a smooth breathing, adverb)

ἐπί upon, on (preposition + genitive); on, in, in dependence upon, above, at, by, near, at the time of, during (+ dative); on, to, near, by, against (+ accusative)

ἄρτος, ου, ὁ bread, loaf of bread

μόνος, η, ον only, alone

ζάω, ζήσω/ζήσομαι, ἔζησα, ἔζηκα live

ἄνθρωπος, ου, ὁ human being, person, man

ἀλλ' = ἀλλά but, yet (conjunction)

πᾶς, πᾶσα, πᾶν every, all

ῥῆμα, ατος, τό word, saying, speech, declaration

ἐκπορεύομαι, ἐκπορεύσομαι, ἐκπεπόρευμαι, ἐξεπορεύθην come out, go out, proceed

διά through, by (preposition + genitive); because of, for the sake of (+ accusative)

στόμα, ατος, τό mouth

θεός, οῦ, ὁ God, god

4:4 **ἀποκριθεὶς**: *in reply*; the verbal form is a first aorist passive participle (cf. App. 34) modifying ὁ Ἰησοῦς. The participle virtually loses its verbal force in this formulaic phrase. **Γέγραπται**: *it is written*; the formulaic verb used to introduce scripture is third person singular perfect passive indicative. The stem ending in the consonant **φ** changes to **π** before **τ**. The perfect tense denotes action (aspect) that is completed and continues with present result. The reduplication or doubling of the stem at the beginning of a word occurs especially in the perfect, pluperfect, and future perfect tenses to indicate completed action. **ἐπ'**: *by*; more specifically, the preposition denotes that the action of living is *based on* bread. **ὁ ἄνθρωπος**: the generic article in the singular is included in Greek to denote a whole class and so to distinguish humans from other beings. **ζήσεται**: the optional future deponent is a later but more commonly used form of the verb. **ἐκπορευομένῳ**: *that proceeds*; the present deponent participle agrees in gender, number, and case with its subject ῥήματι. **διὰ στόματος θεοῦ** simply means *out of the mouth of God*. Jesus cites Deut 8:3.

4:5 Τότε παραλαμβάνει αὐτὸν ὁ διάβολος εἰς τὴν ἁγίαν πόλιν καὶ
ἔστησεν αὐτὸν ἐπὶ τὸ πτερύγιον τοῦ ἱεροῦ 4:6 καὶ λέγει αὐτῷ, Εἰ
υἱὸς εἶ τοῦ θεοῦ, βάλε σεαυτὸν κάτω· γέγραπται γὰρ ὅτι
Τοῖς ἀγγέλοις αὐτοῦ ἐντελεῖται περὶ σοῦ

4:5

τότε then, at that time, thereupon, thereafter (adverb)

παραλαμβάνω, παραλήμψομαι, παρέλαβον (2 aorist), παρείληφα, παρείλημμαι, παρελήφθην take, receive, accept

διάβολος, ου, ὁ slanderer, devil

ἅγιος, ια, ιον hallowed, pure, holy

πόλις, εως, ἡ city

ἵστημι, στήσω, ἔστησα, ἔστην (2 aorist), ἕστηκα, ἐστάθην put, place, set, cause to stand (transitive); stand, be (intransitive)

ἐπί upon, on, at the time of, during (preposition + genitive); on, in, above, at, by, near, during, at the time of (+ dative); on, to, near, by, against (+ accusative)

πτερύγιον, ου, τό little wing; pinnacle, summit

ἱερόν, οῦ, τό temple

4:6

εἰ if, whether

υἱός, οῦ, ὁ son

βάλλω, βαλῶ, ἔβαλον (2 aorist), βέβληκα, βέβλημαι, ἐβλήθην throw, sow, cast, place, put, bring

σεαυτοῦ, ῆς, οῦ yourself (reflexive pronoun)

κάτω downward, down, below

γράφω, γράψω, ἔγραψα, γέγραφα, γέγραμμαι, ἐγράφθην engrave, write

γάρ for, indeed, but (conjunction)

ὅτι that, because, since (conjunction); (used as our quotation marks to introduce direct discourse)

ἄγγελος, ου, ὁ messenger, angel

ἐντέλλομαι, ἐντελοῦμαι, ἐνετειλάμην, ἐντέταλμαι command, order, enjoin

περί about, concerning (preposition + genitive); about, around (+ accusative)

4:5 **παραλαμβάνει**: the present used for a past tense is called *historical present* and is frequently seen in vivid narrative accounts. **τὴν ἁγίαν πόλιν**: the attributive adjective traditionally describes Jerusalem for its association with the temple or holy *house*. πόλιν is a third declension noun (App. 13). **ἔστησεν**: the second aorist tense of this verb regularly shows transitive meaning.

4:6 **Εἰ . . . εἶ . . . βάλε**: *if you are . . . cast*; εἰ with the indicative in both clauses introduces a simple or particular condition. In this simple condition the imperative is substituted for the indicative. **γέγραπται**: *it is written*; the formulaic verb used to introduce scripture mocks the verb above and ignites a scriptural challenge. **Τοῖς ἀγγέλοις . . . ἐντελεῖται**: this third person singular future deponent indicative verb takes a dative case of persons commanded. The subject, not named by Satan, is God. ἐντελεῖται is a third person singular future liquid verb. Its basic stem ends in a liquid (**λ**, **μ**, **ν**, or **ρ**). The future stem –**εσ** + personal endings passes through two changes: the intervocalic **σ** drops out and the **ε** contracts with the following vowel. It is thus formed like verbs contracted with stem in **ε** (App. 56), and takes a circumflex over the contraction.

καὶ ἐπὶ χειρῶν ἀροῦσίν σε,
μήποτε προσκόψῃς πρὸς λίθον τὸν πόδα σου.
4:7 ἔφη αὐτῷ ὁ Ἰησοῦς, Πάλιν γέγραπται, Οὐκ ἐκπειράσεις κύριον τὸν θεόν σου.

4:6

ἐπί upon, on, at the time of, during (preposition + genitive); on, in, above, at, by, near, during, at the time of (+ dative); on, to, near, by, against (+ accusative)

χείρ, χειρός, ἡ hand

αἴρω, ἀρῶ, ἦρα, ἦρκα, ἦρμαι, ἤρθην take up, bear, take away, lift, carry, remove; keep in suspense; destroy, kill

μήποτε not; that . . . not, lest, (in order) that . . . not

προσκόπτω, προσκόψω, προσέκοψα dash against, beat upon, strike (the foot) against; stumble

πρός for, for the purpose of (preposition + genitive); with, to, towards, unto, for, for the purpose of, with reference to, in relation to, of, concerning, against (+ accusative); near, at, by (preposition + dative)

λίθος, ου, ὁ stone

πούς, ποδός, ὁ foot

4:7

φημί, φήσω, ἔφησα say

πάλιν again (adverb)

γράφω, γράψω, ἔγραψα, γέγραφα, γέγραμμαι, ἐγράφθην engrave, write

οὐκ not (a form of οὐ used before vowels with a smooth breathing, adverb)

ἐκπειράζω, ἐκπειράσω, ἐκεπείρασα, ἐκπεπείρασμαι, ἐκεπειράσθην try, put to the test, tempt

κύριος, ου, ὁ lord, Lord, master

θεός, οῦ, ὁ God, god

4:6 **ἐπὶ χειρῶν**: *with their hands* (literally: *on their hands*). χειρῶν is a third declension noun (cf. App. 11). **ἀροῦσίν** is a third person plural future liquid verb. The enclitic pronoun **σε** adds an additional accent over the ultima of a previous word with a properispomenon accent (= a circumflex [˜] over the second syllable from the end). **μήποτε προσκόψῃς**; the conjunction introduces a negative clause of pupose. The verb is a second person singular aorist active subjunctive (cf. App. 53, D, 2).

4:7 **ἔφη** is third person singular imperfect active indicative. **Πάλιν γέγραπται**: the second temptation is again met by a scriptural passage: ὁ πειράζων may tempt the Son of God, but Jesus does not need to put God to the test and make trial of God's faithfulness.

4:8 Πάλιν παραλαμβάνει αὐτὸν ὁ διάβολος εἰς ὄρος ὑψηλὸν λίαν καὶ δείκνυσιν αὐτῷ πάσας τὰς βασιλείας τοῦ κόσμου καὶ τὴν δόξαν αὐτῶν 4:9 καὶ εἶπεν αὐτῷ, Ταῦτά σοι πάντα δώσω, ἐὰν πεσὼν προσκυνήσῃς μοι.

4:8
πάλιν again (adverb)
παραλαμβάνω, παραλήμψομαι, παρέλαβον, παρείληφα, παρείλημμαι, παρελήφθην take, receive, accept
διάβολος, ου, ὁ slanderer, devil
ὄρος, ους, τό mountain, hill
ὑψηλός, ή, όν high; exalted, proud, haughty
λίαν greatly, exceedingly (adverb)
δείκνυμι/δεικνύω, δείξω, ἔδειξα, δέδειχα, ἐδείχθην show, point out, make known, demonstrate, announce
πᾶς, πᾶσα, πᾶν every, all
βασιλεία, ας, ἡ kingship, royal power, kingdom
κόσμος, ου, ὁ order, world, universe
δόξα, ης, ἡ glory, honor, majesty
4:9
οὗτος, αὕτη, τοῦτο this, this one (demonstrative pronoun)
πᾶς, πᾶσα, πᾶν every, all
δίδωμι, δώσω, ἔδωκα, δέδωκα, δέδομαι, ἐδόθην give
ἐάν if (conditional particle)
πίπτω, πεσοῦμαι, ἔπεσα, ἔπεσον (2 aorist), πέπτωκα fall, fall prostrate, fall down
προσκυνέω, προσκυνήσω, προσεκύνησα worship, prostrate oneself before, reverence before, reverence
ἐγώ, ἐμοῦ (μου) I (personal pronoun)

4:8 **εἰς ὄρος**: the noun is a neuter singular accusative third declension with stem in **σ** (cf. App. 15, and note). **τὴν δόξαν αὐτῶν**: *their glory*; the genitive personal pronoun αὐτῶν (App. 40) is translated as a possessive adjective in English.

4:9 **Ταῦτά . . . δώσω, ἐὰν . . . προσκυνήσῃς** is a future more vivid condition (cf. App. 70), which makes a positive statement that the action is likely to take place in the future. The apodosis or conclusion precedes the protasis here and thus emphasises the more positive side of the condition. The condition is formed by ἐὰν with a subjunctive προσκυνήσῃς in the protasis and a future indicative δώσω in the apodosis. The condition conspicuously lacks a parallel scriptural passage but speaks most directly to the true intent of Satan's temptations.

4:10 τότε λέγει αὐτῷ ὁ Ἰησοῦς, Ὕπαγε, Σατανᾶ· γέγραπται γάρ,
Κύριον τὸν θεόν σου προσκυνήσεις
καὶ αὐτῷ μόνῳ λατρεύσεις.
4:11 Τότε ἀφίησιν αὐτὸν ὁ διάβολος, καὶ ἰδοὺ ἄγγελοι προσῆλθον καὶ διηκόνουν αὐτῷ.

4:10
τότε then, at that time, thereupon, thereafter (adverb)
ὑπάγω, ὑπάξω, ὑπήγαγον, ὑπήχθην go, go away, go home
Σατανᾶς, ᾶ, ὁ Satan
γράφω, γράψω, ἔγραψα, γέγραφα, γέγραμμαι, ἐγράφθην engrave, write
γάρ for, indeed, but (conjunction)
θεός, οῦ, ὁ God, god
προσκυνέω, προσκυνήσω, προσεκύνησα worship, prostrate oneself before, reverence before, reverence
μόνος, η, ον only, alone
λατρεύω, λατρεύσω, ἐλάτρευσα serve
4:11
τότε then, at that time, thereupon, thereafter (adverb)
ἀφίημι, ἀφήσω, ἀφῆκα, ἀφῆν (2 aorist), ἀφεῖκα, ἀφεῖμαι, ἀφέθην let go, forgive, leave
ἰδού see, look, behold (demonstrative particle)
ἄγγελος, ου, ὁ messenger, angel
προσέρχομαι, προσελεύσομαι, προσῆλθον, προσελήλυθα come to, go to, approach
διακονέω, διακονήσω, διηκόνησα, δεδιηκόνηκα, διηκονήθην wait on, attend upon, serve

---

4:10 **Ὕπαγε**: this is the only time Jesus uses the imperative mood in His encounter with Satan. Satan had used the imperatives εἰπὲ (4:3) and βάλε (4:6) only to be rebuffed. Changing his tactics and employing a more positive condition also proves to no avail. He is rebuked by the imperative mood and a scriptural passage (Deut 6:13).

4:11 **ἀφίησιν αὐτὸν ὁ διάβολος**: Jesus commands, Satan obeys. **ἄγγελοι . . . διηκόνουν αὐτῷ**: *angels continually attended him*. The **α** in the verb is lengthened to **η** to form the temporal augment. The imperfect tense denotes progressive, continued, and repeated action (aspect) in past time and should not be slighted in translation. At the end of the temptations angels visit Him and attend Him not because He has jumped off the pinnacle of the temple but because of his devotion to the Lord. The three temptations with their scriptural responses form a tricolon, which emphasises one and the same point: constancy of devotion to God. Instead of yielding to display of power, to self-aggrandizement, and ultimately to Satan, Jesus relies ἐπὶ παντὶ ῥήματι ἐκπορευμένῳ διὰ στόματος θεοῦ, trusts and does not question τὸν θεόν, and worships τὸν θεόν and serves αὐτῷ. In the scriptures cited by Jesus, the noun God is also emphatically collocated both at the end of the sentence in the first two passages and at the beginning of the sentence in the third.

4:12 Ἀκούσας δὲ ὅτι Ἰωάννης παρεδόθη ἀνεχώρησεν εἰς τὴν Γαλιλαίαν. 4:13 καὶ καταλιπὼν τὴν Ναζαρὰ ἐλθὼν κατῴκησεν εἰς Καφαρναοὺμ τὴν παραθαλασσίαν ἐν ὁρίοις Ζαβουλὼν καὶ Νεφθαλίμ·

4:12

ἀκούω, ἀκούσω, ἤκουσα, ἀκήκοα, ἤκουσμαι, ἠκούσθην hear, obey, understand

ὅτι that, because, since (conjunction); (used as our quotation marks to introduce direct discourse)

παραδίδωμι, παραδώσω, παρέδωκα, παρέδων (2 aorist), παραδέδωκα, παραδέδομαι, παρεδόθην give, hand over, give over, deliver up, give up, arrest, betray

ἀναχωρέω, ἀναχωρήσω, ἀνεχώρησα go away, depart, withdraw, retire

4:13

καταλείπω, καταλείψω, κατέλειψα, κατέλιπον (2 aorist), κατελείφθην leave behind (active); remain behind (passive)

ἔρχομαι, ἐλεύσομαι, ἦλθον (2 aorist), ἐλήλυθα come, go

κατοικέω, κατοικήσω, κατῴκησα inhabit (transitive); live, dwell, reside, settle down (intransitive)

Καφαρναούμ, ἡ Capernaum

παραθαλάσσιος, ία, ιον by the sea, maritime, by the lake

ὅριον, ου, τό boundary; region, territory, district (plural)

Ζαβουλών, ὁ Zebulun

Νεφθαλίμ, ὁ Nephthali

4:12 **Ἀκούσας** is a masculine singular nominative first aorist active participle (cf. App. 31) in agreement with the subject of the main verb ἀνεχώρησεν, who is Jesus. Since the action of the aorist participle precedes that of the main verb and represents a single action in the past, it has the force of an English pluperfect.

4:13 **καταλιπὼν** is a second aorist participle. A change in stem from the present to the aorist distinguishes the second aorist from the first: λειπ- becomes λιπ-. **κατῴκησεν εἰς**: *lived in*; the verb may take the prepositions ἐν, εἰς, or the accusative case to indicate place where.

4:14 ἵνα πληρωθῇ τὸ ῥηθὲν διὰ Ἠσαΐου τοῦ προφήτου λέγοντος,
4:15 Γῆ Ζαβουλὼν καὶ γῆ Νεφθαλίμ,
ὁδὸν θαλάσσης, πέραν τοῦ Ἰορδάνου,
Γαλιλαία τῶν ἐθνῶν,
4:16 ὁ λαὸς ὁ καθήμενος ἐν σκότει

4:14
ἵνα to, in order to, in order that, that (conjunction)
πληρόω, πληρώσω, ἐπλήρωσα, πεπλήρωκα, πεπλήρωμαι, ἐπληρώθην fill, complete, fulfill
διά through, by (preposition + genitive)
προφήτης, ου, ὁ prophet, seer, revelator
4:15
γῆ, γῆς, ἡ soil, land, region, country
ὁδός, οῦ, ἡ road, way, journey
θάλασσα, ης, ἡ sea, inland sea, lake
πέραν across, beyond, on the other side of (preposition + genitive)
ἔθνος, ους, τό nation, people
4:16
λαός, οῦ, ὁ people
κάθημαι, καθήσομαι sit, stay, reside
σκότος, ους, τό darkness, gloom

4:14 Supply **τοῦτο δὲ ὅλον γέγονεν** (cf. 1:22): *but all this occurred* before the ἵνα clause. **ἵνα πληρωθῇ τὸ ῥηθὲν**: *in order that what was spoken might be fulfilled*; fulfillment of prophecy dominates as a salient feature of Matthew's literary programme. ἵνα is the usual conjunction to introduce purpose clauses. The first aorist passive verb stands in the subjunctive mood (cf. App. 53, G, 2). τὸ ῥηθὲν: *that which was spoken* (literally); the verbal form is a neuter singular nominative first aorist passive participle (cf. App. 53, G, 5; 34) of the verb λέγω that translates as a relative clause in conjunction with an article. **διὰ Ἠσαΐου τοῦ προφήτου λέγοντος**: the preposition διὰ denotes intermediate agency. The Lord speaks; the prophet is his mouthpiece. **τοῦ προφήτου** stands in apposition and is a first declension noun ending in **ης** (App. 3).

4:15 **Γῆ Ζαβουλὼν καὶ γῆ Νεφθαλίμ**: *O land of Zebulun and land of Naphtali*; Γῆ is in the vocative or case of direct address. Both Zebulun and Naphtali are appositional genitives and serve to identify the land more specifically (cf. App. 65). **ὁδὸν θαλάσσης**: *by way of the sea*; ὁδὸν is an adverbial accusative of manner. **Γαλιλαία τῶν ἐθνῶν**: *Galilee of the Gentiles*. Γαλιλαία is in the vocative case.

4:16 **ὁ λαὸς ὁ καθήμενος**: *the people who are sitting*; the repetition of the article with the adjective is an alternate construction for **ὁ καθήμενος λαὸς**. In both cases the adjective is in attributive position, i.e., it follows the article. The article and the present participle are best translated as a relative clause.

φῶς εἶδεν μέγα,
καὶ τοῖς καθημένοις ἐν χώρᾳ καὶ σκιᾷ θανάτου
φῶς ἀνέτειλεν αὐτοῖς.

4:17 Ἀπὸ τότε ἤρξατο ὁ Ἰησοῦς κηρύσσειν καὶ λέγειν, Μετανοεῖτε· ἤγγικεν γὰρ ἡ βασιλεία τῶν οὐρανῶν.

4:16
φῶς, φωτός, τό light
ὁράω, ὄψομαι, εἶδον (2 aorist), ἑώρακα/ἑόρακα, ὤφθην see, catch sight of, notice, look, observe, perceive, experience, witness
μέγας, μεγάλη, μέγα large, great
χώρα, ας, ἡ country, land, field
σκιά, ᾶς, ἡ shade, shadow; gloom; darkness
θάνατος, ου, ὁ death
ἀνατέλλω, ἀνατελῶ, ἀνέτειλα (1 aorist) cause to rise; rise, spring up (intransitive)
4:17
ἀπὸ τότε from then on
ἄρχω, ἄρξω, ἦρξα, ἦρχα, ἦργμαι, ἤρχθην rule (active); begin (middle)
κηρύσσω, κηρύξω, ἐκήρυξα, ἐκηρύχθην announce openly, proclaim aloud
μετανοέω, μετανοήσω, μετανόησα change one's mind, repent
ἐγγίζω, ἐγγίσω, ἤγγισα, ἤγγικα approach, draw near
γάρ for, indeed, but (conjunction)
βασιλεία, ας, ἡ kingship, royal power, kingdom
οὐρανός, οῦ, ὁ heaven

4:16 **φῶς εἶδεν μέγα**: the hyperbaton or separation of the two words usually connected may be a poetic expression to paint a picture of people looking on as they are surrounded by light. The LXX shows the more usual prose word order: ἴδετε φῶς μέγα. **τοῖς καθημένοις . . . αὐτοῖς**: *for those who are sitting*; the personal pronoun may be translated as a demonstrative. **ἐν χώρᾳ καὶ σκιᾷ θανάτου**: *in the land of death's shadow*; the καὶ explains and more specifically identifies the land. The figure of speech, hendiadys, expands a single idea into a compound one for purposes of emphasis. The juxtaposition of light and darkness in the center and the people τοῖς καθημένοις . . . αὐτοῖς at the beginning and end of the phrase develops more fully the chiastic construction begun in the previous half of the verse.

4:17 **Ἀπὸ τότε**: from the time of John's arrest He began to preach John's message of repentance and the imminence of the kingdom.

4:18 Περιπατῶν δὲ παρὰ τὴν θάλασσαν τῆς Γαλιλαίας εἶδεν δύο ἀδελφούς, Σίμωνα τὸν λεγόμενον Πέτρον καὶ Ἀνδρέαν τὸν ἀδελφὸν αὐτοῦ, βάλλοντας ἀμφίβληστρον εἰς τὴν θάλασσαν· ἦσαν γὰρ ἁλιεῖς.

4:18

περιπατέω, περιπατήσω, περιεπάτησα walk, walk about

παρά from (the side of), from, issuing from, by (preposition + genitive); with, by (+ dative); by, near to, along; to, at; by, near, at the side of (+ accusative)

θάλασσα, ης, ἡ sea, inland sea, lake

ὁράω, ὄψομαι, εἶδον (2 aorist), ἑώρακα/ἑόρακα, ὤφθην see, catch sight of, notice, look, observe, perceive, experience, witness

δύο two

ἀδελφός, οῦ, ὁ brother

Σίμων, Σίμωνος, ὁ Simon

Πέτρος, ου, ὁ Peter

Ἀνδρέας, ου, ὁ Andrew

ἀδελφός, οῦ, ὁ brother

βάλλω, βαλῶ, ἔβαλον, βέβληκα, βέβλημαι, ἐβλήθην throw, sow, cast, place, put, bring

ἀμφίβληστρον, ου, τό casting-net

εἰμί, ἔσομαι be

ἁλιεύς, έως, ὁ fisherman

4:18 **Περιπατῶν**: the form is a present active participle of a contracted verb with stem in **ε** (cf. App. 56). The endings of a contracted participle are those of a regular **ω** verb (App. 30). The present tense of the participle generally agrees in time with that of the main verb, whose subject is ὁ Ἰησοῦς from the verse above. **τὸν λεγόμενον Πέτρον**: *who is called Peter*; the article and the present participle are best translated as a relative clause. **βάλλοντας ἀμφίβληστρον**: *as they were casting their net*; the present active participle agrees with its subject ἀδελφούς in gender, number, and case and takes ἀμφίβληστρον as its direct object. A circumstantial participle may express time, cause, concession, condition, and other circumstances. It needs to be sensitively interpreted according to context and translated into English as a clause. **ἁλιεῖς** is predicate nominative.

4:19 καὶ λέγει αὐτοῖς, Δεῦτε ὀπίσω μου, καὶ ποιήσω ὑμᾶς ἁλιεῖς ἀνθρώπων. 4:20 οἱ δὲ εὐθέως ἀφέντες τὰ δίκτυα ἠκολούθησαν αὐτῷ. 4:21 Καὶ προβὰς ἐκεῖθεν εἶδεν ἄλλους δύο ἀδελφούς,

---

4:19
δεῦτε come! come here! (adverb)
ὀπίσω behind, after (adverb; preposition + genitive)
ποιέω, ποιήσω, ἐποίησα, πεποίηκα, πεποίημαι, ἐποιήθην make, do, keep, obey
ἄνθρωπος, ου, ὁ human being, person, man
4:20
εὐθέως at once, immediately (adverb)
ἀφίημι, ἀφήσω, ἀφῆκα, ἀφῆν (2 aorist), ἀφεῖκα, ἀφεῖμαι, ἀφέθην let go, forgive, leave
δίκτυον, ου, τό net
ἀκολουθέω, ἀκολουθήσω, ἠκολούθησα, ἠκολούθηκα follow (+ dative)
4:21
προβαίνω, προβήσομαι, προέβην (2 aorist) go forward, go ahead, advance
ἐκεῖθεν from there, from that place (adverb)
ὁράω, ὄψομαι, εἶδον (2 aorist), ἑώρακα/ἑόρακα, φθην see, catch sight of, notice, look, observe, perceive, experience, witness
ἄλλος, η, ο other, another
δύο two
ἀδελφός, οῦ, ὁ brother
Ἰάκωβος, ου, ὁ Jacob = James (Greek form of Ἰακώβ)
Ζεβεδαῖος, ου, ὁ Zebedee
πλοῖον, ου, τό ship, boat
μετά with (preposition + genitive); after (+ accusative)
πατήρ, πατρός, ὁ father, parent, ancestor
καταρτίζω, καταρτίσω, κατήρτισα, κατήρτισμαι put in order, restore to its former condition; prepare, make, create; prepare for oneself (middle)
δίκτυον, ου, τό net
καλέω, καλέσω, ἐκάλεσα, κέκληκα, κέκλημαι, ἐκλήθην call, summon, invite

---

4:19 **Δεῦτε ὀπίσω μου**: *Come, follow me.* **ἁλιεῖς ἀνθρώπων**: ἁλιεῖς is predicate accusative. ἀνθρώπων is an objective genitive (cf. App. 65). The metaphor must not be pressed too far: the disciples will share in missionary activity and Jesus's unique work of salvation.

4:20 **οἱ δὲ**: *but they*; the article is used as a pronoun here. **ἀφέντες**: the second aorist participle is declined like the aorist passive participle of the **ω** verb (cf. App. 34).

4:21 **προβὰς**: the second aorist participle is declined like the first aorist participle (cf. App. 31). **τὸν τοῦ**: *the son of.* **καταρτίζοντας**: the present participle agrees in gender, number, and case with its subject ἀδελφούς.

Ἰάκωβον τὸν τοῦ Ζεβεδαίου καὶ Ἰωάννην τὸν ἀδελφὸν αὐτοῦ, ἐν τῷ πλοίῳ μετὰ Ζεβεδαίου τοῦ πατρὸς αὐτῶν καταρτίζοντας τὰ δίκτυα αὐτῶν, καὶ ἐκάλεσεν αὐτούς. 4:22 οἱ δὲ εὐθέως ἀφέντες τὸ πλοῖον καὶ τὸν πατέρα αὐτῶν ἠκολούθησαν αὐτῷ.

4:23 Καὶ περιῆγεν ἐν ὅλῃ τῇ Γαλιλαίᾳ διδάσκων ἐν ταῖς συναγωγαῖς αὐτῶν καὶ κηρύσσων τὸ εὐαγγέλιον τῆς βασιλείας καὶ θεραπεύων πᾶσαν νόσον καὶ πᾶσαν μαλακίαν ἐν τῷ λαῷ. 4:24 καὶ ἀπῆλθεν ἡ ἀκοὴ αὐτοῦ εἰς ὅλην τὴν Συρίαν·

4:22
εὐθέως at once, immediately (adverb)
ἀφίημι, ἀφήσω, ἀφῆκα, ἀφῆν (2 aorist), ἀφεῖκα, ἀφεῖμαι, ἀφέθην let go, forgive, leave
πλοῖον, ου, τό ship, boat
πατήρ, πατρός, ὁ father, parent, ancestor
ἀκολουθέω, ἀκολουθήσω, ἠκολούθησα, ἠκολούθηκα follow (+ dative)
4:23
περιάγω, περιάξω lead around; traverse
ὅλος, η, ον all, whole, entire, complete
διδάσκω, διδάξω, ἐδίδαξα, ἐδιδάχθην teach, instruct
συναγωγή, ῆς, ἡ synagogue
κηρύσσω, κηρύξω, ἐκήρυξα, ἐκηρύχθην announce openly, proclaim aloud
εὐαγγέλιον, ου, τό good news, gospel, glad tidings
βασιλεία, ας, ἡ kingship, royal power, kingdom
θεραπεύω, θεραπεύσω, ἐθεράπευσα, ἐθεραπεύθην care for, heal, restore
νόσος, ου, ἡ disease, sickness, illness
μαλακία, ας, ἡ softness, weakness, infirmity
λαός, οῦ, ὁ people
4:24
ἀπέρχομαι, ἀπελεύσομαι, ἀπῆλθον, ἀπελήλυθα go, go away, depart; go forth, pervade
ἀκοή, ῆς, ἡ hearing, fame, report, account
ὅλος, η, ον all, whole, entire, complete
Συρία, ας, ἡ Syria

4:22 **εὐθέως**: both here and in the previous calling (4:20) there is no hesitation in following Jesus.

4:23 **περιῆγεν**: the imperfect tense denotes progressive, continued, and repeated action (aspect) in past time. **ἐν ὅλῃ τῇ Γαλιλαίᾳ**: *in all Galilee*; the adjective never stands in attributive position. **διδάσκων . . . κηρύσσων . . . θεραπεύων**: after having called His disciples, Jesus shows them by example what it means to be fishers of men in this tricolon of participles.

4:24 **εἰς ὅλην τὴν Συρίαν**: as He was ministering ἐν ὅλῃ τῇ Γαλιλαίᾳ, His report spread far and wide to Jews and Gentiles alike.

καὶ προσήνεγκαν αὐτῷ πάντας τοὺς κακῶς ἔχοντας ποικίλαις νόσοις καὶ βασάνοις συνεχομένους [καὶ] δαιμονιζομένους καὶ σεληνιαζομένους καὶ παραλυτικούς, καὶ ἐθεράπευσεν αὐτούς.
4:25 καὶ ἠκολούθησαν αὐτῷ ὄχλοι πολλοὶ ἀπὸ τῆς Γαλιλαίας καὶ Δεκαπόλεως καὶ Ἱεροσολύμων καὶ Ἰουδαίας καὶ πέραν τοῦ Ἰορδάνου.

4:24
προσφέρω, προσοίσω, προσήνεγκα, προσήνεγκον (2 aorist), προσηνέχθην bring, offer, present
κακῶς ill, badly, wickedly, wrongly (adverb)
ἔχω, ἕξω, ἔσχον (2 aorist), ἔσχηκα have, keep, cause, consider; be (with adverbs and indications of time and age); be able (with infinitive)
ποικίλος, η, ον various, diverse
νόσος, ου, ἡ disease, sickness, illness
βάσανος, ου, ἡ torture, torment
συνέχω, συνέξω hold together; be seized with, be affected with (passive)
δαιμονίζομαι, δαιμονίσομαι, ἐδαιμονίσθην be possessed, tormented, afflicted, by a demon
σεληνιάζομαι, σεληνιάσομαι be lunatic, be moon-struck
παραλυτικός, ή, όν lame person, paralytic, palsied
θεραπεύω, θεραπεύσω, ἐθεράπευσα, ἐθεραπεύθην care for, heal, restore

4:25
ἀκολουθέω, ἀκολουθήσω, ἠκολούθησα, ἠκολούθηκα follow (+ dative)
ὄχλος, ου, ὁ crowd, throng, multitude
πολύς, πολλή, πολύ much, large, many (in plural)
ἀπό from, because of, out of, by (preposition + genitive)
Δεκάπολις, εως, ἡ Decapolis
πέραν across, beyond, on the other side of (preposition + genitive)

4:24 **τοὺς κακῶς ἔχοντας**: *those who were ill.* **νόσοις** is a dative of means or cause. **σεληνιαζομένους**: the ancients probably associated epileptical seizures with the moon σελήνη, the Latin *luna*.

4:25 **ὄχλοι πολλοὶ**: both the catalogue of the sick and that of the cities serve to emphasize the immense numbers surrounding Jesus.

5 Ἰδὼν δὲ τοὺς ὄχλους ἀνέβη εἰς τὸ ὄρος, καὶ καθίσαντος αὐτοῦ
προσῆλθαν αὐτῷ οἱ μαθηταὶ αὐτοῦ· 5:2 καὶ ἀνοίξας τὸ στόμα αὐτοῦ
ἐδίδασκεν αὐτοὺς λέγων,
5:3 Μακάριοι οἱ πτωχοὶ τῷ πνεύματι,

5:1
ὁράω, ὄψομαι, εἶδον (2 aorist), ἑώρακα/ἑόρακα, ὤφθην see, catch sight of, notice, look, observe, perceive, experience, witness
ὄχλος, ου, ὁ crowd, throng, multitude
ἀναβαίνω, ἀναβήσομαι, ἀνέβην, ἀναβέβηκα go up, ascend, rise
ὄρος, ους, τό mountain, hill
καθίζω, καθίσω, ἐκάθισα, κεκάθικα cause to sit down, seat, set (transitive); sit, sit down; remain, stay, continue, rest (intransitive)
προσέρχομαι, προσελεύσομαι, προσῆλθον, προσελήλυθα come to, go to, approach
μαθητής, οῦ, ὁ disciple
5:2
ἀνοίγω, ἀνοίξω, ἀνέῳξα/ἤνοιξα, ἀνέῳγα, ἀνέῳγμαι, ἠνεῴχθην open
στόμα, ατος, τό mouth
διδάσκω, διδάξω, ἐδίδαξα, ἐδιδάχθην teach, instruct
5:3
μακάριος, ία, ιον blessed, happy, fortunate
πτωχός, ή, όν poor, indigent, needy, lowly, contrite
πνεῦμα, ατος, τό wind, spirit, mind, Holy Spirit

5:1 **καθίσαντος αὐτοῦ**: *as He sat down*; the construction is a *genitive absolute*. The pronoun αὐτοῦ and the circumstantial participle καθίσαντος in the genitive case are syntactically independent of the main verb and clause, i.e., the subject of the genitive absolute may not be used as the subject or the object of the main verb. However, New Testament language does not always strictly adhere to classical usage: in this sentence the noun is used both as the subject of the genitive absolute and as the object of the main verb. A circumstantial participle may express time, cause, concession, condition, and other circumstances. It needs to be sensitively interpreted according to context and translated into English as a clause (App. 65). The mountainside provides an appropriate setting to teach these large crowds (7:28).

5:2 **ἀνοίξας τὸ στόμα** introduces a more lengthy and formal discourse intended not only for an audience of his disciples but also for the large crowds of sick he had healed and townspeople who had followed (4:24, 25).

5:3 **Μακάριοι**: supply εἰσίν. The adjective initiates a commonplace formula in Greek, Latin, and Hebrew literature. **οἱ πτωχοὶ τῷ πνεύματι**: *the contrite in spirit*; the dative article is omitted in translation. πνεύματι is a dative of respect. The attitude suggests a reverence toward God and man and a recognition of his relationship to both. The beatitude properly takes its position at the head of the catalogue.

ὅτι αὐτῶν ἐστιν ἡ βασιλεία τῶν οὐρανῶν.
5:4 μακάριοι οἱ πενθοῦντες,
ὅτι αὐτοὶ παρακληθήσονται.
5:5 μακάριοι οἱ πραεῖς,
ὅτι αὐτοὶ κληρονομήσουσιν τὴν γῆν.
5:6 μακάριοι οἱ πεινῶντες καὶ διψῶντες τὴν δικαιοσύνην,
ὅτι αὐτοὶ χορτασθήσονται.

5:3
ὅτι that, because, since (conjunction)
βασιλεία, ας, ἡ kingship, royal power, kingdom
οὐρανός, οῦ, ὁ heaven
5:4
πενθέω, πενθήσω, ἐπένθησα be sad, grieve, mourn
παρακαλέω, παρακαλέσω, παρεκάλεσα, παρακέκληκα, παρακέκλημαι, παρεκλήθην call upon, exhort, persuade; beg, entreat; comfort, encourage, cheer up
5:5
πραΰς, πραεῖα, πραΰ meek, gentle, humble, considerate, kind, forgiving; mild, benevolent, humane
κληρονομέω, κληρονομήσω, ἐκληρονόμησα, κεκληρονόμηκα inherit; obtain, acquire, receive
γῆ, γῆς, ἡ earth, soil, land, region, country
5:6
πεινάω, πεινάσω/πεινήσω, ἐπείνασα hunger, be hungry; hunger after, long for
διψάω, διψήσω, ἐδίψησα thirst, be thirsty
δικαιοσύνη, ης, ἡ justice, righteousness, godliness
ὅτι that, because, since (conjunction)
χορτάζω, χορτάω, εχόρτασα, ἐχορτάσθην feed, fill, satisfy

5:4 **οἱ πενθοῦντες**: perhaps an intense emotion that draws them closer to God. We vainly look for one exclusive universal reason for godly sorrow. The experience of such sorrow may vary with each individual, but the blessing is the same.

5:5 **οἱ πραεῖς**: the attribute involves gentleness, kindliness, and consideration for others. **τὴν γῆν**: they may be trampled upon by the world but *inherit the earth*. The idiom suggests that they will be heirs in the kingdom of heaven.

5:6 **πεινῶντες καὶ διψῶντες τὴν δικαιοσύνην**: the metaphor suggests that seeking righteousness requires a desire that is as essential for the growth of the spirit as food and drink are for the development of the body. τὴν δικαιοσύνην may be defined as living a life that is justified by God and leads to the kingdom of heaven. Abstract nouns are generally modified by an article, which is omitted in translation.

5:7 μακάριοι οἱ ἐλεήμονες,
ὅτι αὐτοὶ ἐλεηθήσονται.
5:8 μακάριοι οἱ καθαροὶ τῇ καρδίᾳ,
ὅτι αὐτοὶ τὸν θεὸν ὄψονται.
5:9 μακάριοι οἱ εἰρηνοποιοί,
ὅτι αὐτοὶ υἱοὶ θεοῦ κληθήσονται.
5:10 μακάριοι οἱ δεδιωγμένοι ἕνεκεν δικαιοσύνης,
ὅτι αὐτῶν ἐστιν ἡ βασιλεία τῶν οὐρανῶν.

5:7
ἐλεήμων, ον merciful, compassionate
ἐλεέω, ἐλεήσω, ἠλέησα, ἠλέημαι, ἠλεήθην pity, show mercy
5:8
καθαρός, ά, όν clean, pure
καρδία, ας, ἡ heart
θεός, οῦ, ὁ God, god
ὁράω, ὄψομαι, εἶδον (2 aorist), ἑώρακα/ἑόρακα, ὤφθην see, catch sight of, notice, look, observe, perceive, experience, witness
5:9
εἰρηνοποιός, οῦ, ὁ/ἡ peace-maker
καλέω, καλέσω, ἐκάλεσα, κέκληκα, κέκλημαι, ἐκλήθην call, summon, invite
5:10
διώκω, διώξω, ἐδίωξα, δεδίωγμαι, ἐδιώχθην persecute, pursue, seek after
ἕνεκεν/ἕνεκα because of, on account of, for the sake of (preposition + genitive)
δικαιοσύνη, ης, ἡ justice, righteousness, godliness
βασιλεία, ας, ἡ kingship, royal power, kingdom
οὐρανός, οῦ, ὁ heaven

5:7 **ἐλεήμονες . . . ἐλεηθήσονται**: in accordance with the law of the harvest, they will reap what they sow.

5:8 **οἱ καθαροὶ τῇ καρδίᾳ . . . τὸν θεὸν ὄψονται**: those who are both physically and spiritually washed and cleansed from the sins of the world and who have no desire to do evil will enter into the presence of God.

5:9 **οἱ εἰρηνοποιοί** will proclaim the message of peace and salvation, strive to be at peace with everyone, and promote peace as an essential part of the kingdom of heaven. **υἱοὶ θεοῦ**: in the kingdom of heaven they will enjoy a special relationship with God as His sons and daughters.

5:10 **δικαιοσύνης**: here the abstract noun is not modified by the article. **ὅτι αὐτῶν ἐστιν ἡ βασιλεία τῶν οὐρανῶν**: the line repeats the second half of the first beatitude and marks the end of the poetry by formally bracketing it.

5:11 μακάριοί ἐστε ὅταν ὀνειδίσωσιν ὑμᾶς καὶ διώξωσιν καὶ εἴπωσιν πᾶν πονηρὸν καθ' ὑμῶν [ψευδόμενοι] ἕνεκεν ἐμοῦ. 5:12 χαίρετε καὶ ἀγαλλιᾶσθε, ὅτι ὁ μισθὸς ὑμῶν πολὺς ἐν τοῖς οὐρανοῖς· οὕτως γὰρ ἐδίωξαν τοὺς προφήτας τοὺς πρὸ ὑμῶν.

5:11

ὅταν when, whenever (conjunction)

ὀνειδίζω, ὀνειδίσω, ὠνείδισα reproach, revile, heap insults upon

διώκω, διώξω, ἐδίωξα, δεδίωγμαι, ἐδιώχθην persecute, pursue, seek after

πονηρός, ά, όν bad, evil, wicked

κατά near, towards, by, in accordance with, after the manner of (preposition + accusative); against (+ genitive)

ψεύδομαι, ψεύσομαι, ἐψευσάμην lie, tell a falsehood

ἕνεκεν/ἕνεκα because of, on account of, for the sake of (preposition + genitive)

5:12

χαίρω, χαρήσομαι, ἐχάρην (2 aorist passive) rejoice, be glad; χαῖρε, χαίρετε hail, greetings, welcome (as a form of greeting)

ἀγαλλιάω, ἀγαλλιάσω, ἠγαλλίασα celebrate, praise, rejoice (usually deponent)

μισθός, οῦ, ὁ pay, wages, reward

πολύς, πολλή, πολύ much, large, great, many (in plural)

οὐρανός, οῦ, ὁ heaven

οὕτως so, thus, in this manner (adverb)

διώκω, διώξω, ἐδίωξα, δεδίωγμαι, ἐδιώχθην persecute, pursue, seek after

προφήτης, ου, ὁ prophet, seer, revelator

πρό before (preposition + genitive)

5:11 **μακάριοί ἐστε**: the person changes from a third person plural to a second person plural and the verse from a couplet to a tricolon construction: **ὀνειδίσωσιν . . . διώξωσιν . . . εἴπωσιν**. The indefinite relative adverb **ὅταν** replaces ἐάν or ἄν in this present general condition (App. 70). It takes a subjunctive in the protasis and a present indicative in the apodosis. The tense of the first two subjunctives is first aorist (cf. App. 53, D, 2); that of the third is second aorist (cf. App. 54). The poetical structure of the tricolon and the similarity of themes of blessedness and persecution produce a smooth transition from the previous verse, but the admonition now becomes more personalized.

5:12 The doublet of imperatives **χαίρετε καὶ ἀγαλλιᾶσθε** poetically encourages the disciples to rejoice, continues to be personalized, and summarizes the theme of μακάριοι in the first line of the formal couplet of the beatitudes. **ὅτι ὁ μισθὸς . . . τοῖς οὐρανοῖς** echoes the reward of the second line of the couplet of the beatitudes. **τοὺς προφήτας** serve as past examples of future persecutions.

5:13 Ὑμεῖς ἐστε τὸ ἅλας τῆς γῆς· ἐὰν δὲ τὸ ἅλας μωρανθῇ, ἐν τίνι ἁλισθήσεται; εἰς οὐδὲν ἰσχύει ἔτι εἰ μὴ βληθὲν ἔξω

5:13
σύ, σοῦ (σου) you (personal pronoun)
ἅλας, ατος, τό salt
γῆ, γῆς, ἡ earth, soil, land, region, country
ἐάν if (conditional particle)
μωραίνω, μωρανῶ, ἐμώρανα, ἐμωράνθην make foolish, make tasteless; become foolish, become tasteless, insipid (passive)
τίς, τί, (τίνος) who? what? why? (interrogative pronoun)
ἁλίζω, ἁλίσω, ἡλίσθην salt
οὐδείς, οὐδεμία, οὐδέν no (adjective); no one, nobody, nothing (substantive)
ἰσχύω, ἰσχύσω, ἴσχυσα be good, be strong, be powerful, be well
ἔτι yet, still (adverb)
εἰ if, whether; εἰ μή unless, except
βάλλω, βαλῶ, ἔβαλον, βέβληκα, βέβλημαι, ἐβλήθην throw, sow, cast, place, put, bring
ἔξω outside, out (adverb)

5:13 **Ὑμεῖς ἐστε**: the combination of the second person plural pronoun and the second person plural verb occurring at the beginning of the sentence makes an emphatic statement and a smooth transition from the previous two verses to the parables. **τὸ ἅλας**: the metaphor may refer to purification, sacrificing, preservation, friendship, and wisdom. In this context it is particularly suited to 5:8 but may refer more broadly to all qualities of the beatitudes. **ἐὰν . . . μωρανθῇ, ἐν τίνι ἁλισθήσεται** is a future more vivid condition introduced by ἐὰν with a subjunctive μωρανθῇ in the protasis and a future indicative ἁλισθήσεται in the apodosis. Since the subjunctive commonly connotes a future, the aorist tense here has no temporal value but indicates aspect only. The comparison implies that just as salt loses its potency by being mixed with impurities of the earth, so the disciples lose their power by embracing impure activities of the world. ἐν τίνι: the form of the pronoun is the neuter interrogative of τίς (App. 47). The interrogative pronoun distinguishes itself from the indefinite pronoun by the accent (cf. App. 48). The semicolon also indicates a direct question. The verb ἁλισθήσεται is third person singular first future passive indicative (cf. App. 53, G, 1). **εἰς οὐδὲν ἰσχύει ἔτι**: *is good for nothing hereafter*; οὐδὲν is used as a substantive. The adverb may be translated in this sense after a future: the present tense ἰσχύει connotes a future. **εἰ μὴ**: *but*; the two particles are equivalent to ἀλλά when preceded by οὐδὲν. **βληθὲν ἔξω**: *after it has been cast out*; the verbal form is a first aorist passive participle (cf. App. 34) modifying τὸ ἅλας, the subject of the finite verb. A circumstantial participle may express time, cause, concession, condition, and other circumstances. It needs to be sensitively interpreted according to context and translated into English as a clause.

καταπατεῖσθαι ὑπὸ τῶν ἀνθρώπων. 5:14 Ὑμεῖς ἐστε τὸ φῶς τοῦ κόσμου. οὐ δύναται πόλις κρυβῆναι ἐπάνω ὄρους κειμένη· 5:15 οὐδὲ καίουσιν λύχνον καὶ τιθέασιν αὐτὸν ὑπὸ τὸν μόδιον ἀλλ' ἐπὶ τὴν λυχνίαν, καὶ λάμπει πᾶσιν τοῖς ἐν τῇ οἰκίᾳ.

5:13

καταπατέω, καταπατήσω, κατεπάτησα, κατεπατήθην trample under foot; treat with disdain

ὑπό by (preposition + genitive of personal agent)

ἄνθρωπος, ου, ὁ human being, person, man

5:14

φῶς, φωτός, τό light

κόσμος, ου, ὁ order, world, universe

οὐκ not (a form of οὐ used before vowels with a smooth breathing, adverb)

δύναμαι, δυνήσομαι, ἠδυνήθην be able

πόλις, εως, ἡ city

κρύπτω, κρύψω, ἔκρυψα, κέκρυμμαι, ἐκρύβην hide, conceal, cover

ἐπάνω above, over, upon (adverb; preposition + genitive)

ὄρος, ους, τό mountain, hill

κεῖμαι, κείσομαι lie, be laid, be placed, be set

5:15

οὐδέ and not, nor (conjunction and adverb)

καίω, καύσω, ἔκαυσα, ἐκαύθην light, cause to burn, kindle (active); burn, be burned, be consumed with fire (passive)

λύχνος, ου, ὁ lamp

τίθημι, θήσω, ἔθηκα, τέθεικα, τέθειμαι, ἐτέθην place, set, lay, serve, give

ὑπό by (preposition + genitive of personal agent); under (+ accusative)

μόδιος, ου, ὁ corn measure, vessel, bushel

ἐπί upon, on, at the time of, during (preposition + genitive); on, in, above, at, by, near, during, at the time of (+ dative); on, to, near, by, against (+ accusative)

λυχνία, ας, ἡ lampstand, stand

λάμπω, λάμψω, ἔλαμψα shine, shine forth, give light

οἰκία, ας, ἡ house, household, family

5:13 **καταπατεῖσθαι**: the passive infinitive (cf. App. 53, G, 4) serves as a complementary infinitive to the main verb ἰσχύει.

5:14 **Ὑμεῖς ἐστε**: the combination of the second person plural pronoun and the second person plural verb occurring at the beginning of the sentence makes an emphatic statement and connects the two parables. **κρυβῆναι**: the second aorist passive infinitive serves as a complementary infinitive to the main verb δύναται. In the second aorist passive, the infinitive ending is directly added to the passive stem of the verb (cf. App. 53, G, 4). **κειμένη**: *when it is situated*; the present participle agrees in gender, number, and case with its subject πόλις. The metaphor suggests that the disciples bring the light of the gospel as a beacon to the world abroad.

5:15 **λύχνον**: in contrast to the first, the second metaphor with its domestic images confines their activity locally to their home.

5:16 οὕτως λαμψάτω τὸ φῶς ὑμῶν ἔμπροσθεν τῶν ἀνθρώπων, ὅπως
ἴδωσιν ὑμῶν τὰ καλὰ ἔργα καὶ δοξάσωσιν τὸν πατέρα ὑμῶν τὸν ἐν
τοῖς οὐρανοῖς.
5:17 Μὴ νομίσητε ὅτι ἦλθον καταλῦσαι τὸν νόμον ἢ τοὺς
προφήτας· οὐκ ἦλθον καταλῦσαι ἀλλὰ πληρῶσαι. 5:18 ἀμὴν γὰρ
λέγω ὑμῖν·

5:16
οὕτως so, thus, in this manner (adverb)
λάμπω, λάμψω, ἔλαμψα shine, shine forth, give light
φῶς, φωτός, τό light
ἔμπροσθεν in front of, before, in the presence of (adverb; preposition + genitive)
ἄνθρωπος, ου, ὁ human being, person, man
ὅπως that, in order that (conjunction)
καλός, ή, όν good, useful, choice
ἔργον, ου, τό work, deed, action
δοξάζω, δοξάσω, ἐδόξασα, δεδόξασμαι, ἐδοξάσθην praise, honor, magnify, glorify
πατήρ, πατρός, ὁ father, parent, ancestor
οὐρανός, οῦ, ὁ heaven
5:17
μή not (particle of negation)
νομίζω, νομίσω, ἐνόμισα, νενόμικα think, believe, consider
ὅτι that, because, since (conjunction)
καταλύω, καταλύσω, κατέλυσα, κατελύθην throw down, destroy, abolish
νόμος, ου, ὁ law, custom, ordinance
ἤ either, or, than (conjunction)
ἀλλά but, yet (conjunction)
πληρόω, πληρώσω, ἐπλήρωσα, πεπλήρωκα, πεπλήρωμαι, ἐπληρώθην fill, complete, fulfill
5:18
ἀμήν in truth, verily (Hebrew)

5:16 **λαμψάτω τὸ φῶς ὑμῶν**: *let your light shine*; the verbal form is a third person singular aorist active imperative (cf. App. 53, D, 3). **τῶν ἀνθρώπων** refers to Jews and Gentiles alike. The generic article is included in Greek to denote a whole class and so to distinguish humans from other beings. **ὅπως ἴδωσιν . . . καὶ δοξάσωσιν**: *that they may see . . . and glorify*; the conjunction with the subjunctive is used to indicate purpose. **τὸν πατέρα ὑμῶν τὸν ἐν τοῖς οὐρανοῖς**: *your Father in heaven*; the repetition of the article with the prepositional phrase is an alternate construction for τὸν ἐν τοῖς οὐρανοῖς πατέρα. In both cases the prepositional phrase is in attributive position (i.e., immediately preceded by a definite article) and forms a substantive with the article.

5:17 **Μὴ νομίσητε**: the negative imperative (cf. App. 53, D, 2) makes an asseveration against a prevalent misconception. **καταλῦσαι . . . πληρῶσαι** are infinitives of purpose: *to abolish . . . to fulfill*.

5:18 **ἀμὴν γὰρ λέγω ὑμῖν**: the formulaic language occurs frequently and with slight variations in these teachings. Jesus begins with a solemn declaration.

ἕως ἂν παρέλθῃ ὁ οὐρανὸς καὶ ἡ γῆ, ἰῶτα ἓν ἢ μία κεραία οὐ μὴ παρέλθῃ ἀπὸ τοῦ νόμου, ἕως ἂν πάντα γένηται. 5:19 ὃς ἐὰν οὖν λύσῃ μίαν τῶν ἐντολῶν τούτων τῶν ἐλαχίστων καὶ διδάξῃ οὕτως τοὺς ἀνθρώπους,

---

5:18
ἕως while, as long as, until
ἄν (a conditional particle indicating contingency)
παρέρχομαι, παρελεύσομαι, παρῆλθον (2 aorist), παρελήλυθα pass, pass by; pass away
οὐρανός, οῦ, ὁ heaven
γῆ, γῆς, ἡ earth, soil, land, region
ἰῶτα, τό iota, yod, jot, the least bit (indeclinable)
εἷς, μία, ἕν one, single (numeral)
ἤ either, or, than (conjunction)
κεραία, ας, ἡ point, minutest part
οὐ μή never, certainly not
ἀπό from, because of, out of, by (preposition + genitive)
νόμος, ου, ὁ law, custom, ordinance
γίνομαι, γενήσομαι, ἐγενόμην, γέγονα/γεγένημαι, ἐγενήθην become, be made, be fulfilled, come, arrive, be present
5:19
ὅς, ἥ, ὅ who, which, what; he who, that (relative pronoun)
ἐάν if (conditional particle)
οὖν therefore, then, so (conjunction, postpositive)
λύω, λύσω, ἔλυσα, λέλυκα, λέλυμαι, ἐλύθην loose, break, destroy
εἷς, μία, ἕν one, single (numeral)
ἐντολή, ῆς, ἡ command, commandment
οὗτος, αὕτη, τοῦτο this, this one (demonstrative pronoun)
ἐλάχιστος, η, ον smallest, least
διδάσκω, διδάξω, ἐδίδαξα, ἐδιδάχθην teach, instruct
οὕτως so, thus, in this manner (adverb)
ἄνθρωπος, ου, ὁ human, person, man

5:18 **ἕως ἂν παρέλθῃ**: *until . . . pass away*; the temporal conjunction, the aorist subjunctive, and the particle ἂν refer indefinitely to the future and denote that the commencement of one event is dependent on another. **ὁ οὐρανὸς καὶ ἡ γῆ . . . ἰῶτα ἓν ἢ μία κεραία . . . ἀπὸ τοῦ νόμου**: the chiastic structure suggests an inner order between the cosmos and the law. **οὐ μὴ παρέλθῃ**: *will never pass away*; the double negative indicates a strong negation and usually takes an aorist subjunctive that is translated as a future. The hyperbole stresses the validity of the law in every detail and its perpetuity until it has been completely fulfilled. **πάντα** refers to the law and the prophets in the previous verse.

5:19 **ὃς ἐὰν . . . λύσῃ . . . καὶ διδάξῃ . . . κληθήσεται**: *whoever breaks . . . and teaches . . . will be called*; the condition is future more vivid (App. 70), introduced by a relative pronoun and a particle with a verb in the subjunctive of a double protasis and a future indicative in the apodosis. **μίαν τῶν ἐντολῶν τούτων τῶν ἐλαχίστων**: *one of the least of these commandments*; the adjective with the article is a substantive. They are partitive genitives since they follow a word denoting part of a whole μίαν (App. 65). τῶν ἐντολῶν τούτων is in turn a partitive genitive because it depends on the superlative τῶν ἐλαχίστων, part of a whole. The bracketing may suggest that the least of the commandments are on the fringes.

ἐλάχιστος κληθήσεται ἐν τῇ βασιλείᾳ τῶν οὐρανῶν· ὃς δ' ἂν ποιήσῃ καὶ διδάξῃ, οὗτος μέγας κληθήσεται ἐν τῇ βασιλείᾳ τῶν οὐρανῶν.
5:20 λέγω γὰρ ὑμῖν ὅτι ἐὰν μὴ περισσεύσῃ ὑμῶν ἡ δικαιοσύνη πλεῖον τῶν γραμματέων καὶ Φαρισαίων, οὐ μὴ εἰσέλθητε εἰς τὴν βασιλείαν τῶν οὐρανῶν.

5:19

καλέω, καλέσω, ἐκάλεσα, κέκληκα, κέκλημαι, ἐκλήθην call, summon, invite

βασιλεία, ας, ἡ kingship, royal power, kingdom

οὐρανός, οῦ, ὁ heaven

ὅς, ἥ, ὅ who, which, what; he who, that (relative pronoun)

ἄν (a conditional particle indicating contingency in certain constructions)

ποιέω, ποιήσω, ἐποίησα, πεποίηκα, πεποίημαι, ἐποιήθην make, do, keep, obey

διδάσκω, διδάξω, ἐδίδαξα, ἐδιδάχθην teach, instruct

οὗτος, αὕτη, τοῦτο this, this one (demonstrative pronoun)

μέγας, μεγάλη, μέγα large, great

καλέω, καλέσω, ἐκάλεσα, κέκληκα, κέκλημαι, ἐκλήθην call, summon, invite

5:20

ἐάν if (conditional particle); ἐὰν μή if not, unless, except

περισσεύω, περισσεύσω, ἐπερίσσευσα be left over, abound

δικαιοσύνη, ης, ἡ justice, righteousness, godliness

πλείων, πλεῖον or πλέον more, greater, larger; πλέον more (comparative adverb)

γραμματεύς, έως, ὁ secretary, clerk, scholar versed in law

Φαρισαῖος, ου, ὁ a Pharisee

οὐ μή never, certainly not

εἰσέρχομαι, εἰσελεύσομαι, εἰσῆλθον (2 aorist), εἰσελήλυθα come (in, into), go (in, into), enter into, share in, come to enjoy

βασιλεία, ας, ἡ kingship, royal power, kingdom

5:19 **ἐλάχιστος κληθήσεται**: the superlative adjective stands in predicate position. The verb is third person singular first future passive indicative (cf. App. 53, G, 1). The word play or paronomasia argues: the commandment thought to be the least of the commandments turns out not to be so, but the person who breaks it is the least in the kingdom of heaven. **ὃς δ' ἂν ποιήσῃ . . . ἐν τῇ βασιλείᾳ τῶν οὐρανῶν**: the parallel construction is given in the positive for purposes of emphasis.

5:20 **περισσεύῃ . . . πλεῖον τῶν γραμματέων**: *is more abundant than that of the scribes;* the comparative adverb takes a genitive of comparison (App. 65). In an abbreviated construction (brachylogy or ellipsis) the Greek frequently omits the second element of the comparison when it is the same as the first. It is supplied in English by the demonstrative pronoun *that.* **οὐ μὴ εἰσέλθητε**: *you will never enter;* the double negative indicates a strong negation and usually takes an aorist subjunctive that is translated as a future.

5:21 Ἠκούσατε ὅτι ἐρρέθη τοῖς ἀρχαίοις,Οὐ φονεύσεις· ὃς δ' ἂν φονεύσῃ, ἔνοχος ἔσται τῇ κρίσει. 5:22 ἐγὼ δὲ λέγω ὑμῖν ὅτι πᾶς ὁ ὀργιζόμενος τῷ ἀδελφῷ αὐτοῦ ἔνοχος ἔσται τῇ κρίσει· ὃς δ' ἂν εἴπῃ τῷ ἀδελφῷ αὐτοῦ,

---

5:21

ἀκούω, ἀκούσω, ἤκουσα, ἀκήκοα, ἤκουσμαι, ἠκούσθην hear, obey, understand

ἀρχαῖος, αία, αῖον old, ancient

οὐ not (οὐκ before vowels with a smooth breathing, οὐχ before a rough breathing, adverb)

φονεύω, φονεύσω, ἐφόνευσα murder, kill, commit murder

ὅς, ἥ, ὅ who, which, what; he who, that (relative pronoun)

ἄν (a conditional particle indicating contingency in certain constructions)

ἔνοχος, ον subjected to, liable to

κρίσις, εως, ἡ judgment, justice, righteousness, condemnation

5:22

ὀργίζω, ὀργίσω, ὠργίσθην provoke to anger; be angry at, be enraged at (passive + dative)

ἀδελφός, οῦ, ὁ brother

ἔνοχος, ον subjected to, liable to

κρίσις, εως, ἡ judgment, justice, righteousness, condemnation

---

5:21 **ἐρρέθη τοῖς ἀρχαίοις**: *it was said to the people of old*; the word is spoken by the Lord, the Lawgiver, and passed on through his mouthpiece, the prophets, to the people of old. Although it is grammatically possible for the dative with the passive to replace ὑπό with the genitive, a formulaic pattern has been established in regard to speaker and audience (1:22, 2:5, 2:15, 2:17, 3:3). **Οὐ φονεύσεις**: *You shall not commit murder*; the future indicative verb has an absolute sense. The future may be used to express a command, like the imperative: *Do not commit murder*; the negative is οὐ. **ὃς δ' ἂν φονεύσῃ . . . ἔσται**: *whoever commits murder will be*; the condition is future more vivid (App. 70), introduced by a relative pronoun and a particle with a verb in the subjunctive and a future indicative in the apodosis.

5:22 **ἐγὼ δὲ λέγω ὑμῖν**: the combination of the first person singular pronoun and the first person singular verb occurring at the beginning of the sentence makes an emphatic statement. ὑμῖν stands parallel to τοῖς ἀρχαίοις in the previous verse. The conjunction δὲ, unlike ἀλλά, signals a slight contrast from a previously made statement. Jesus does not contradict the law but adds a fuller, more spiritual dimension to the letter of the law. **τῷ ἀδελφῷ** may mean a close relative, disciple, neighbor, fellow countryman, or foreigner.

Ῥακά, ἔνοχος ἔσται τῷ συνεδρίῳ· ὃς δ' ἂν εἴπῃ, Μωρέ, ἔνοχος ἔσται εἰς τὴν γέενναν τοῦ πυρός. 5:23 ἐὰν οὖν προσφέρῃς τὸ δῶρόν σου ἐπὶ τὸ θυσιαστήριον κἀκεῖ μνησθῇς ὅτι ὁ ἀδελφός σου ἔχει τι κατὰ σοῦ,

---

5:22

ῥακά empty one, empty-head, numbskull, fool (Aramaic term of abuse and derision)

συνέδριον, ίου, τό assembly, high council, Sanhedrin

μωρός, ά, όν foolish, wicked, impious

γέεννα, ης, ἡ Gehenna, Valley of Hinnom, hell, the fires of Tartarus (a place known for sacrifices to Moloch, pollution, pestilence, punishment of malefactors, and continually burning fires)

πῦρ, πυρός, τό fire

5:23

ἐάν if (conditional particle); ἐὰν μή if not, unless, except

οὖν therefore, then, so (conjunction, postpositive)

προσφέρω, προσοίσω, προσήνεγκα (1 aorist), προσήνεγκον (2 aorist), προσηνέχθην bear to, carry to, bring to or before; offer, present

δῶρον, ου, τό gift, present

ἐπί upon, on, at the time of, during (preposition + genitive); on, in, above, at, by, near, during, at the time of (+ dative); on, to, near, by, against (+ accusative)

θυσιαστήριον, ίου, τό altar

κἀκεῖ = καί ἐκεῖ and there, and in that place (adverb)

μιμνήσκομαι, μνησθήσομαι, μέμνημαι, ἐμνήσθην remember, recollect, call to mind

ἀδελφός, οῦ, ὁ brother

ἔχω, ἕξω, ἔσχον (2 aorist), ἔσχηκα have, keep, cause, consider; be (with adverbs and indications of time and age); be able (with infinitive)

τις, τι anyone, anything, someone, something, a certain one, a certain thing (indefinite pronoun)

κατά near, towards, by, in accordance with, after the manner of (preposition + accusative); against (+ genitive)

5:22 **ἔνοχος ἔσται τῇ κρίσει**: although the language echoes that of the verse above, the punishment of murder and of growing angry are not the same. Nonetheless anger and the following two vices may lead to murder and are therefore condemned. **Ῥακά . . . Μωρέ** are both abusive terms that probably carry similar meaning. Such offenses will exact both mortal and divine punishment.

5:23 **ἐὰν . . . προσφέρῃς . . . κἀκεῖ μνησθῇς**: the conjunction with verbs in the subjunctive introduces a double protasis of a future more vivid condition. The combining of two words καί ἐκεῖ to avoid vowel succession in adjoining words is called *crasis*. The breathing mark is retained over the contraction. μνησθῇς is a first aorist subjunctive (cf. App. 53, G, 2) of a deponent verb. The tense has no temporal value here but indicates single aspect only. **ἔχει τι**: *holds some grudge* or *has some complaint* (literally: *has anything*).

5:24 ἄφες ἐκεῖ τὸ δῶρόν σου ἔμπροσθεν τοῦ θυσιαστηρίου καὶ ὕπαγε πρῶτον διαλλάγηθι τῷ ἀδελφῷ σου, καὶ τότε ἐλθὼν πρόσφερε τὸ δῶρόν σου. 5:25 ἴσθι εὐνοῶν τῷ ἀντιδίκῳ σου ταχύ, ἕως ὅτου εἶ μετ' αὐτοῦ ἐν τῇ ὁδῷ, μήποτέ σε παραδῷ

5:24
ἀφίημι, ἀφήσω, ἀφῆκα, ἀφῆν (2 aorist), ἀφεῖκα, ἀφεῖμαι, ἀφέθην let go, forgive, leave
ἐκεῖ there, in that place (adverb)
δῶρον, ου, τό gift, present
ἔμπροσθεν in front of, before, in the presence of (adverb; preposition + genitive)
θυσιαστήριον, ίου, τό altar
ὑπάγω, ὑπάξω, ὑπήγαγον, ὑπήχθην go, go away, go home
διαλλάσσομαι, διηλλάγην (2 aorist passive) become reconciled to (+ dative)
ἀδελφός, οῦ, ὁ brother
τότε then, at that time, thereupon, thereafter (adverb)
προσφέρω, προσοίσω, προσήνεγκα (1 aorist), προσήνεγκον (2 aorist), προσηνέχθην bear to, carry to, bring to or before; offer, present
δῶρον, ου, τό gift, present
5:25
εὐνοέω be well disposed to, make friends with (+ dative)
ἀντίδικος, ου, ὁ opponent, adversary, enemy
ταχύς, εῖα, ύ quick, swift, fleet; ταχύ quickly, speedily, hastily (adverb)
ἕως ὅτου while, as long as, until
μετ' = μετά with (preposition + genitive); after (+ accusative)
ὁδός, οῦ, ἡ road, way, journey
μήποτε not; that . . . not, lest, (in order) that . . . not
παραδίδωμι, παραδώσω, παρέδωκα, παρέδων (2 aorist), παραδέδωκα, παραδέδομαι, παρεδόθην give, hand over, give over, deliver, give up, betray

---

5:24 **ἄφες** is a second person singular second aorist imperative (cf. App. 59). This and the next four imperatives serve as an equivalent form of the future indicative in the apodosis of a future more vivid condition. **ὕπαγε . . . διαλλάγηθι**: *go and be reconciled*; ὕπαγε is a second person singular present active imperative (cf. App. 53, A, 3). Supply καὶ: the imperative is usually found without a conjunction when followed by another imperative. The ending of the second person singular aorist passive imperative is regularly -θι, but when the stem ends in an aspirated consonant it beomes -τι to avoid two consecutive aspirations (cf. App. 53, G, 3). **ἐλθὼν πρόσφερε**: *go and bring*; a participle is coordinated when combined with an imperative.

5:25 **ἴσθι**: the form is the second person singular present active imperative of the irregular verb εἰμί (App. 63). **εἶ**: the verb is the second person singular present active indicative of the verb εἰμί. It is conjugated εἰμί, εἶ, ἐστί, ἐσμέν, ἐστέ, εἰσί(ν), (App. 63). All but the second person singular are enclitics and by definition *lean on* the previous word so that the two words are counted as one in terms of accent. The enclitic usually loses its accent. **μήποτέ . . . παραδῷ**: the conjunction introduces a negative clause of pupose. The verb is a third person singular aorist active subjunctive (cf. App. 58).

ὁ ἀντίδικος τῷ κριτῇ καὶ ὁ κριτὴς τῷ ὑπηρέτῃ καὶ εἰς φυλακὴν
βληθήσῃ· 5:26 ἀμὴν λέγω σοι, οὐ μὴ ἐξέλθῃς ἐκεῖθεν, ἕως ἂν ἀποδῷς
τὸν ἔσχατον κοδράντην.
5:27 Ἠκούσατε ὅτι ἐρρέθη, Οὐ μοιχεύσεις. 5:28 ἐγὼ δὲ λέγω ὑμῖν

5:25
ἀντίδικος, ου, ὁ opponent, adversary, enemy
κριτής, ου, ὁ judge
ὑπηρέτης, ου, ὁ servant, helper, assistant, attendant, officer
φυλακή, ῆς, ἡ watch, guard, prison
βάλλω, βαλῶ, ἔβαλον, βέβληκα, βέβλημαι, ἐβλήθην throw, sow, cast, place, put, bring
5:26
ἀμήν in truth, verily (Hebrew)
οὐ μή never, certainly not
ἐξέρχομαι, ἐξελεύσομαι, ἐξῆλθον (2 aorist), ἐξελήλυθα go or come out of, go out
ἐκεῖθεν from there, from that place (adverb)
ἕως while, as long as, until
ἄν (a conditional particle indicating contingency in certain constructions)
ἀποδίδωμι, ἀποδώσω, ἀπέδωκα, ἀποδέδωκα, ἀποδέδομαι, ἀπεδόθην give away, pay
ἔσχατος, η, ον last
κοδράντης, ου, ὁ Roman brass coin, penny, cent (the actual value is approximately one quarter of an as)
5:27
ἀκούω, ἀκούσω, ἤκουσα, ἀκήκοα, ἤκουσμαι, ἠκούσθην hear, obey, understand
οὐκ not (a form of οὐ used before vowels with a smooth breathing, adverb)
μοιχεύω, μοιχεύσω, ἐμοίχευσα commit adultery
5:28
ἐγώ, ἐμοῦ (μου) I (personal pronoun)

5:25 **καὶ εἰς φυλακὴν βληθήσῃ**: *and you will be cast into prison*; the verbal form is a second person singular first future passive indicative (cf. App. 53, G, 1). The future indicative, connected by καὶ to a negative clause of purpose, indicates more vividly the reality of some further consequence.

5:26 **οὐ μὴ ἐξέλθῃς**: *you will never get out*; the double negative indicates a strong negation and usually takes an aorist subjunctive that is translated as a future. The hyperbole stresses the seriousness of obedience to the law and its consequences of losing time and money. **ἕως ἂν ἀποδῷς**: the temporal conjunction with the aorist subjunctive and the particle ἂν refers indefinitely to the future and denotes that the commencement of one event is dependent on another.

5:27 **Οὐ μοιχεύσεις**: *you shall not commit adultery*; the future may be used to express a command, like the imperative. The negative is οὐ.

5:28 **ἐγὼ δὲ λέγω ὑμῖν**: the conjunction δὲ, unlike ἀλλά, signals a slight contrast from a previously made statement. Jesus does not contradict the law but adds a fuller, more spiritual dimension to the letter of the law.

ὅτι πᾶς ὁ βλέπων γυναῖκα πρὸς τὸ ἐπιθυμῆσαι αὐτὴν ἤδη ἐμοίχευσεν αὐτὴν ἐν τῇ καρδίᾳ αὐτοῦ. 5:29 εἰ δὲ ὁ ὀφθαλμός σου ὁ δεξιὸς σκανδαλίζει σε, ἔξελε αὐτὸν καὶ βάλε ἀπὸ σοῦ· συμφέρει γάρ σοι ἵνα ἀπόληται ἓν τῶν μελῶν σου

5:28
βλέπω, βλέψω, ἔβλεψα see, behold, perceive
γυνή, γυναικός, ἡ woman, wife
πρός for, for the purpose of (preposition + genitive); with, to, towards, unto, for, for the purpose of, with reference to, in relation to, of, concerning (+ accusative); near, at, by (preposition + dative)
ἐπιθυμέω, ἐπιθυμήσω, ἐπεθύμησα desire, long for
ἤδη now, already (adverb)
μοιχεύω, μοιχεύσω, ἐμοίχευσα commit adultery with, debauch (+ accusative)
καρδία, ας, ἡ heart
5:29
εἰ if, whether
ὀφθαλμός, οῦ, ὁ eye
δεξιός, ά, όν right (as opposed to left)
σκανδαλίζω, σκανδαλίσω, ἐσκανδάλισα, ἐσκανδαλίσθην offend, anger, shock
ἐξαιρέω, ἐξελῶ, ἐξεῖλον take out, tear out
βάλλω, βαλῶ, ἔβαλον, βέβληκα, βέβλημαι, ἐβλήθην throw, sow, cast, place, put, bring
συμφέρει it is profitable, expedient, advantageous, good or better (impersonal verb)
ἀπόλλυμι/ἀπολλύω, ἀπολέσω/ἀπολῶ, ἀπώλεσα, ἀπολώλεκα, ἀπόλωλα (2 perfect) lose, destroy, ruin, kill; perish (middle)
εἷς, μία, ἕν one, single (numeral)
μέλος, ους, τό member, limb, part

5:28 **πρὸς τὸ ἐπιθυμῆσαι αὐτὴν**: *for the purpose of arousing his desires for her*; the verbal construction is an articular infinitive. As a noun the infinitive takes an article which is the object of the preposition πρὸς: *for the purpose of.* As a verbal form the Greek infinitive may additionally take an accusative subject and govern an object. If αὐτὴν is taken as the subject of the infinitive, the phrase reads: *for the purpose of arousing her desires.* In that case the pronoun αὐτόν: *for him* would be understood as the object. Both readings are grammatically possible. The same verb is also used in the decalogue.

5:29 **εἰ δὲ ὁ ὀφθαλμός . . . σκανδαλίζει σε, ἔξελε . . . καὶ βάλε**: εἰ with the indicative in both clauses introduces a simple or particular condition (App. 70). In this condition the imperative is substituted for the indicative in both clauses of the apodosis. The hyperbole stresses the seriousness of obedience to the law and the importance of rooting out and casting away, like a cancerous growth, the desire to lust or covet. **συμφέρει** may be followed by a ἵνα clause, i.e., one that explains the impersonal verb συμφέρει, or by an accusative and an infinitive. **ἀπόληται** is a second aorist middle subjunctive (cf. App. 54). The three indications are the stem change, the lengthened thematic vowel, and the ending.

καὶ μὴ ὅλον τὸ σῶμά σου βληθῇ εἰς γέενναν. 5:30 καὶ εἰ ἡ δεξιά σου
χεὶρ σκανδαλίζει σε, ἔκκοψον αὐτὴν καὶ βάλε ἀπὸ σοῦ· συμφέρει
γάρ σοι ἵνα ἀπόληται ἓν τῶν μελῶν σου καὶ μὴ ὅλον τὸ σῶμά σου εἰς
γέενναν ἀπέλθῃ.

5:31 Ἐρρέθη δέ,

5:29

μή not (particle of negation); that not, lest (conjunction)

ὅλος, η, ον all, whole, entire, complete

σῶμα, ατος, τό body

βάλλω, βαλῶ, ἔβαλον, βέβληκα, βέβλημαι, ἐβλήθην throw, sow, cast, place, put, bring

γέεννα, ης, ἡ Gehenna, Valley of Hinnom, hell, the fires of Tartarus (a place known for sacrifices to Moloch, pollution, pestilence, punishment of malefactors, and continually burning fires)

5:30

εἰ if, whether

δεξιός, ά, όν right (as opposed to left)

χείρ, χειρός, ἡ hand

σκανδαλίζω, σκανδαλίσω, ἐσκανδάλισα, ἐσκανδαλίσθην offend, anger, shock

ἐκκόπτω, ἐκκόψω, ἐξέκοψα, ἐξεκόπην cut out, cut off

βάλλω, βαλῶ, ἔβαλον, βέβληκα, βέβλημαι, ἐβλήθην throw, sow, cast, place, put, bring

συμφέρει it is profitable, expedient, advantageous, good or better (impersonal verb)

ἀπόλλυμι/ἀπολλύω, ἀπολέσω/ἀπολῶ, ἀπώλεσα, ἀπολώλεκα, ἀπόλωλα (2 perfect) lose, destroy, ruin, kill; perish (middle)

εἷς, μία, ἕν one, single (numeral)

μέλος, ους, τό member, limb, part

μή not (particle of negation); that not, lest (conjunction)

ὅλος, η, ον all, whole, entire, complete

σῶμα, ατος, τό body

γέεννα, ης, ἡ Gehenna, Valley of Hinnom, hell, the fires of Tartarus (a place known for sacrifices to Moloch, pollution, pestilence, punishment of malefactors, and continually burning fires)

ἀπέρχομαι, ἀπελεύσομαι, ἀπῆλθον, ἀπελήλυθα go, go away, depart

---

5:29 **βληθῇ** is a first aorist passive subjunctive (cf. App. 53, G, 2).

5:30 **καὶ εἰ ἡ δεξιά σου χεὶρ . . . εἰς γέενναν ἀπέλθῃ**: the verse runs parallel in structure and sentiment to the verse above and thus emphasizes the need to eradicate lusts and passions that lead to adultery.

5:31 **Ἐρρέθη** is an abbreviation of 5:21: *it was said to the people of old*; the word is spoken by the Lord, the Lawgiver, and passed on through his mouthpiece, the prophets, to the people of old. Although it is grammatically possible for the dative with the passive to replace ὑπό with the genitive, a formulaic pattern has been established in regard to speaker and audience (1:22, 2:5, 2:15, 2:17, 3:3).

Ὃς ἂν ἀπολύσῃ τὴν γυναῖκα αὐτοῦ, δότω αὐτῇ ἀποστάσιον.
5:32 ἐγὼ δὲ λέγω ὑμῖν ὅτι πᾶς ὁ ἀπολύων τὴν γυναῖκα αὐτοῦ
παρεκτὸς λόγου πορνείας ποιεῖ αὐτὴν μοιχευθῆναι, καὶ ὃς ἐὰν
ἀπολελυμένην γαμήσῃ, μοιχᾶται.

5:31
ἄν (a conditional particle indicating contingency in certain constructions)
ἀπολύω, ἀπολύσω, ἀπέλυσα, ἀπολέλυκα, ἀπολέλυμαι, ἀπελύθην release, set free, allow to depart; pardon
γυνή, γυναικός, ἡ woman, wife
δίδωμι, δώσω, ἔδωκα, ἔδων (2 aorist), δέδωκα, δέδομαι, ἐδόθην give
ἀποστάσιον, ου, τό certificate of divorce
5:32
ἐγώ, ἐμοῦ (μου) I (personal pronoun)
ἀπολύω, ἀπολύσω, ἀπέλυσα, ἀπολέλυκα, ἀπολέλυμαι, ἀπελύθην release, set free, allow to depart; pardon
γυνή, γυναικός, ἡ woman, wife
παρεκτός except for, apart from (preposition + genitive)
λόγος, ου, ὁ word, doctrine, account, reason, statement, saying
πορνεία, ας, ἡ immorality, prostitution, fornication, adultery
ποιέω, ποιήσω, ἐποίησα, πεποίηκα, πεποίημαι, ἐποιήθην make, do, cause, keep, obey
μοιχεύω, μοιχεύσω, ἐμοίχευσα commit adultery
ἐάν if (conditional particle)
ἀπολύω, ἀπολύσω, ἀπέλυσα, ἀπολέλυκα, ἀπολέλυμαι, ἀπελύθην release, set free, allow to depart; pardon
γαμέω, γαμήσω, ἔγημα/ἐγάμησα, γεγάμηκα, ἐγαμήθην marry, take a wife
μοιχάομαι, μοιχήσομαι defile a married woman, commit adultery, be guilty of adultery

---

5:31 **Ὃς ἂν ἀπολύσῃ . . . δότω**: *whoever divorces . . . let him give*; the future more vivid condition (App. 70) is introduced by a relative pronoun and a particle with a verb in the first aorist subjunctive (cf. App. 53, D, 2) in the protasis and a third person singular second aorist imperative (cf. App. 58) instead of a future indicative in the apodosis. The teaching about divorce follows hard on the heels on that of adultery because the action of divorce and remarriage constitutes adultery.

5:32 **παρεκτὸς λόγου πορνείας**: *except for reason of marital infidelity*; scarcely to be differentiated from μοιχεία, πορνεία is the sexual unfaithfulness of a married woman. **ποιεῖ αὐτὴν μοιχευθῆναι**: *causes her to commit adultery.* In this teaching about divorce, the man who divorces his wife is responsible of a heinous deed when he divorces his wife for any reason other than adultery. He forces his wife, not legally, but morally, to commit adultery as soon as she marries another man. **ὃς ἐὰν . . . γαμήσῃ, μοιχᾶται**: the man who marries her commits adultery because morally, not legally, she is still married to her first husband. At a time when divorce grew rampant and was easily granted for trivial reasons, Jesus asserts the sanctity of the divine law of marriage.

5:33 Πάλιν ἠκούσατε ὅτι ἐρρέθη τοῖς ἀρχαίοις, Οὐκ ἐπιορκήσεις,
ἀποδώσεις δὲ τῷ κυρίῳ τοὺς ὅρκους σου. 5:34 ἐγὼ δὲ λέγω ὑμῖν μὴ
ὀμόσαι ὅλως· μήτε ἐν τῷ οὐρανῷ, ὅτι θρόνος ἐστὶν τοῦ θεοῦ,
5:35 μήτε ἐν τῇ γῇ, ὅτι ὑποπόδιόν ἐστιν τῶν ποδῶν αὐτοῦ,

5:33
πάλιν again (adverb)
ἀκούω, ἀκούσω, ἤκουσα, ἀκήκοα, ἤκουσμαι, ἠκούσθην hear, obey, understand
ἀρχαῖος, αία, αῖον old, ancient
οὐκ not (a form of οὐ used before vowels with a smooth breathing, adverb)
ἐπιορκέω, ἐπιορκήσω swear falsely, perjure oneself; break one's oath
ἀποδίδωμι, ἀποδώσω, ἀπέδωκα, ἀποδέδωκα, ἀποδέδομαι, ἀπεδόθην give away, pay, keep, perform
ὅρκος, ου, ὁ oath
5:34
ἐγώ, ἐμοῦ (μου) I (personal pronoun)
μή not (particle of negation)
ὀμνύω/ὄμνυμι, ὀμοῦμαι, ὤμοσα, ὀμώμοκα swear, promise with an oath
ὅλως wholly, altogether; at all (adverb; with a negative)
μήτε . . . μήτε neither . . . nor
ἐν in, on, among; by (in oaths)
θρόνος, ου, ὁ seat, throne; power, dominion
θεός, οῦ, ὁ God, god
5:35
μήτε . . . μήτε neither . . . nor
γῆ, γῆς, ἡ earth, soil, land, region, country
ὑποπόδιον, ιου, τό footstool
πούς, ποδός, ὁ foot

5:33 **Οὐκ ἐπιορκήσεις**: *you shall not break your oath*; although the oath may be between people, it must nevertheless not be taken lightly. **ἀποδώσεις . . . τοὺς ὅρκους**: the positive command makes explicit that the swearing of an oath inherently involves invocation of deity and that therefore all oaths must be faithfully kept.

5:34 **λέγω ὑμῖν μὴ ὀμόσαι ὅλως**: *I command you not to swear at all*; the active forms of λέγω with the infinitive mean *command*. The person commanded usually stands in the accusative but may also occur in the dative as the subject of the infinitive. μὴ is the usual particle used with an infinitive in a negation. The infinitive is used as the object of the verb of saying in indirect discourse. The aorist is the usual tense after verbs of *will* or *desire*. ὑμῖν stands parallel to τοῖς ἀρχαίοις in the previous verse. The statement again expresses a hyperbole to stress the offensiveness of oaths that profane God and the need for honesty and integrity in daily speech and communications. Jesus does not categorically reject all oaths and covenants. Those made by Abraham, Isaac, and Jacob will always be in effect. The people of Israel were a nation of covenant and promise: solemn oaths on sacred occasions were a requirement by the Lord. **μήτε ἐν τῷ οὐρανῷ**: in mundane daily circumstances it is inappropriate to swear either by God, the Creator, or by His creations.

5:35 **ὑποπόδιόν ἐστιν**: a proparoxytone, i.e., an acute accent on the third syllable from the end, receives an additional accent on the ultima when followed by a disyllabic enclitic. The noun receives no article because it is in predicate position.

μήτε εἰς Ἱεροσόλυμα, ὅτι πόλις ἐστὶν τοῦ μεγάλου βασιλέως, 5:36 μήτε ἐν τῇ κεφαλῇ σου ὀμόσῃς, ὅτι οὐ δύνασαι μίαν τρίχα λευκὴν ποιῆσαι ἢ μέλαιναν. 5:37 ἔστω δὲ ὁ λόγος ὑμῶν ναὶ ναί, οὒ οὔ·

5:35
εἰς to, into, on, in; for, as; by (in oaths)
πόλις, εως, ἡ city
μέγας, μεγάλη, μέγα large, great
βασιλεύς, έως, ὁ king
5:36
κεφαλή, ῆς, ἡ head
ὀμνύω/ὄμνυμι, ὀμοῦμαι, ὤμοσα, ὀμώμοκα swear, promise with an oath
οὐ not (οὐκ before vowels with a smooth breathing, οὐχ before a rough breathing, adverb)
δύναμαι, δυνήσομαι, ἠδυνήθην be able
εἷς, μία, ἕν one, single (numeral)
θρίξ, τριχός, ἡ hair
λευκός, ή, όν bright, shining, gleaming, white
ποιέω, ποιήσω, ἐποίησα, πεποίηκα, πεποίημαι, ἐποιήθην make, do, keep, obey
ἤ either, or, than (conjunction)
μέλας, αινα, αν black
5:37
λόγος, ου, ὁ word, speech, saying, doctrine, account, reason, statement
ναί yes, indeed, certainly (particle of affirmation)
οὐ not (οὐκ before vowels with a smooth breathing, οὐχ before a rough breathing, adverb)

5:35 **εἰς** stands for the more commonly used ἐν in the oath formula. **τοῦ μεγάλου βασιλέως**: Jerusalem is the city of the Lord (Ps. 48:2).

5:36 **μήτε . . . ὀμόσῃς**: *and you shall not swear*; the negative particle introduces a second person aorist subjunctive which often expresses prohibitions and is called *prohibitive subjunctive*. It has the force of (take care that you) *do not swear*. **ἐν τῇ κεφαλῇ**: the formula of swearing by the head may have been a common practice since shaving the head or wearing long hair was a sign of a vow or religious observance. However, as a part of the whole, the head governs the σῶμα and may metaphorically mean *life*. **ὅτι οὐ δύνασαι**: God is the creator who formed man in His image. **μίαν τρίχα λευκὴν ποιῆσαι ἢ μέλαιναν**: a sprinkling of white hair indicates advancing age. God provides for a person in old age as well as in youth. The arrangement of reversing the natural order of time, hysteron proteron, and placing old age before youth gives emphasis to the aged. A person, therefore, indebted to God for creating life and sustaining it from birth to old age, offends God by profaning the sanctity of life when he swears by his head.

5:37 **ἔστω δὲ ὁ λόγος ὑμῶν**: *but let your speech be*; the verbal form is third person singular present active imperative of the verb εἰμί (App. 63) and stands in agreement with its subject ὁ λόγος. **ναὶ ναί, οὒ οὔ**: *a clear 'yes', a clear 'no'*; the doublets in each case express a solemn assurance, and the dependability of the statement is such so as to obviate the need for an oath. The lack of conjunction or asyndeton intensifies the antithesis between the positive and negative particles.

τὸ δὲ περισσὸν τούτων ἐκ τοῦ πονηροῦ ἐστιν.
5:38 Ἠκούσατε ὅτι ἐρρέθη, Ὀφθαλμὸν ἀντὶ ὀφθαλμοῦ καὶ
ὀδόντα ἀντὶ ὀδόντος. 5:39 ἐγὼ δὲ λέγω ὑμῖν μὴ ἀντιστῆναι τῷ
πονηρῷ·

5:37

περισσός, ή, όν over and above, extraordinary, excessive; more, greater

πονηρός, ά, όν bad, evil, wicked

5:38

ἀκούω, ἀκούσω, ἤκουσα, ἀκήκοα, ἤκουσμαι, ἠκούσθην hear, obey, understand

ὀφθαλμός, οῦ, ὁ eye

ἀντί in place of, for, upon (preposition + genitive)

ὀδούς, ὀδόντος, ὁ tooth

5:39

ἀνθίστημι, ἀντέστην (2 aorist), ἀνθέστηκα, ἀντεστάθην oppose, resist, withstand (+ dative)

πονηρός, ά, όν bad, evil, wicked

5:37 **τὸ δὲ περισσὸν τούτων**: *but whatever goes beyond this*; any expression that misses the mark is a lie. **ἐκ τοῦ πονηροῦ ἐστιν**: the substantive may either be neuter or masculine: *is from that which is evil* or *is from the Evil One*. The latter seems preferable: the devil is the source of evil and the father of lies. Inherent in his name διάβολος, commonly translated as *slanderer*, is also the notion of *one who misses the mark*, a primary meaning of the verb διαβάλλω and a metaphor from the field of archery. As one who profoundly missed the mark in choosing to oppose the will of God, he causes others to do the same—to miss the mark.

5:38 **ἐρρέθη** is an abbreviation of 5:21: *it was said to the people of old*; the word is spoken by the Lord, the Lawgiver, and passed on through his mouthpiece, the prophets, to the people of old. Although it is grammatically possible for the dative with the passive to replace ὑπό with the genitive, a formulaic pattern has been established in regard to speaker and audience (1:22, 2:5, 2:15, 2:17, 3:3). **Ὀφθαλμὸν . . . ὀδόντα**: the nouns in the accusative case require a subject and a transitive verb. Supply something like ὁ ὀφειλέτης ἀποδώσει *the guilty will repay*. The *lex talionis* or punishment in kind provided a measure of legal recourse and justice in the law courts of a society that would otherwise have been at the mercy of a continuous cycle of extreme personal retaliations and blood feuds.

5:39 **λέγω ὑμῖν μὴ ἀντιστῆναι τῷ πονηρῷ**: *I command you not to resist the evildoer*; the active forms of λέγω with the infinitive mean *command*. The person commanded usually stands in the accusative but may also occur in the dative as the subject of the infinitive. μή is the usual particle used with an infinitive in a negation. The infinitive is used as the object of the verb of saying in indirect discourse. The aorist is the usual tense after verbs of *will* or *desire*. The command does not supplant the *lex talionis* but additionally requires of the disciples long-suffering in the face of persecution for His sake and the sake of righteousness (5:10–11) with an eschatological promise (5:12) for the persecuted and punishment (Rom 12:19) for the evildoer.

ἀλλ' ὅστις σε ῥαπίζει εἰς τὴν δεξιὰν σιαγόνα [σου], στρέψον αὐτῷ καὶ τὴν ἄλλην· 5:40 καὶ τῷ θέλοντί σοι κριθῆναι καὶ τὸν χιτῶνά σου λαβεῖν, ἄφες αὐτῷ

5:39

ἀλλ' = ἀλλά but, yet (conjunction)

ὅστις, ἥτις, ὅ τι whoever, whatever (indefinite relative pronoun)

ῥαπίζω, ῥαπίσω, ἐρράπισα beat with rods; strike with the palm of the hands; strike, slap

δεξιός, ά, όν right (as opposed to left)

σιαγών, όνος, ἡ cheek

στρέφω, στρέψω, ἔστρεψα, ἔστραμμαι, ἐστρέφθην, ἐστράφην (2 aorist passive) turn, make a change, change

καί and (conjunction); even, also, likewise, and yet (adverb)

ἄλλος, η, ο other, another

5:40

θέλω, θελήσω, ἠθέλησα wish to have, desire, purpose, want

κρίνω, κρινῶ, ἔκρινα, κέκρικα, κέκριμαι, ἐκρίθην separate, select, judge, condemn; dispute, quarrel, debate, sue (middle and passive)

χιτών, ῶνος, ὁ tunic, inner garment, shirt

λαμβάνω, λήμψομαι, ἔλαβον, εἴληφα, εἴλημμαι, ἐλήφθην take, receive, accept

ἀφίημι, ἀφήσω, ἀφῆκα, ἀφῆν (2 aorist), ἀφεῖκα, ἀφεῖμαι, ἀφέθην let go, forgive, leave, let (someone) have (something), give up

---

5:39 **ὅστις σε ῥαπίζει . . . στρέψον**: in this simple or particular condition (App. 70) the indefinite relative pronoun introduces the protasis instead of εἰ, and the imperative is substituted for the indicative in the apodosis. To smite someone's right cheek backhandedly is a most humiliating and insulting blow. **καὶ** functions as an adverb here.

5:40 **τῷ θέλοντί σοι κριθῆναι**: *that person who* (i.e., *if anyone*) *wishes to go to court with you*; an attributive participle may be circumstantial. A circumstantial participle may be interpreted conditionally and so replace the protasis of any condition. It is used here instead of εἰ and the imperative is substituted for the indicative in the apodosis to create a simple or particular condition (App. 70). τῷ θέλοντί is the object of the main verb **ἄφες** and takes two complementary infinitives κριθῆναι καὶ . . . λαβεῖν. It also receives an additional accent because it is a proparoxytone, i.e., an acute accent on the third syllable from the end, followed by a disyllabic enclitic. The hyperbaton between the subject and the object of the verb poetically suggests that the principals are at odds with each other: the court and the shirt stand between them. σοι: the dative pronoun linked to the verb κριθῆναι may be an ethical dative, dative of disadvantage, or dative of accompaniment. **χιτῶνά σου**: The linen garment was worn under the ἱμάτιον next to the skin. The properispomenon, i.e., a circumflex accent on the penult, receives an additional accent on the ultima because it is followed by a disyllabic enclitic. **αὐτῷ** emphatically resumes the object τῷ θέλοντί at the beginning of the sentence.

καὶ τὸ ἱμάτιον· 5:41 καὶ ὅστις σε ἀγγαρεύσει μίλιον ἕν, ὕπαγε
μετ᾽ αὐτοῦ δύο. 5:42 τῷ αἰτοῦντί σε δός, καὶ τὸν θέλοντα ἀπὸ σοῦ
δανίσασθαι μὴ ἀποστραφῇς.

5:40
καί and (conjunction); even, also, likewise, and yet (adverb)
ἱμάτιον, ου, τό garment, clothing; cloak, robe
5:41
ὅστις, ἥτις, ὅ τι whoever, whatever (indefinite relative pronoun)
ἀγγαρεύω, ἀγγαρεύσω, ἠγγάρευσα force, press, compel (someone) to go
μίλιον, ίου, τό (Roman) mile = 1000 paces
εἷς, μία, ἕν one, single (numeral)
ὑπάγω, ὑπάξω, ὑπήγαγον, ὑπήχθην go, go away, go home
μετ᾽ = μετά with (preposition + genitive); after (+ accusative)
δύο two
5:42
αἰτέω, αἰτήσω, ᾔτησα, ᾔτηκα ask, ask for, make a request
δίδωμι, δώσω, ἔδωκα, ἔδων (2 aorist), δέδωκα, δέδομαι, ἐδόθην give
θέλω, θελήσω, ἠθέλησα wish to have, desire, purpose, want
δαν(ε)ίζω, δανίσω, ἐδάνισα lend money (active); borrow money (middle)
μή not (particle of negation)
ἀποστρέφω, ἀποστρέψω, ἀπέστρεψα, ἀπέστραμμαι, ἀπεστράφην (2 aorist passive) turn away, remove; turn away (intransitive in middle and 2 aorist passive)

5:40 **καὶ** functions as an adverb here.

5:41 **ὅστις . . . ἀγγαρεύσει . . . ὕπαγε**: in this simple or particular condition (App. 70) the indefinite relative pronoun introduces the protasis instead of εἰ, and the imperative is substituted for the indicative in the apodosis. The main verb of the protasis, a future active indicative, is a Persian loanword that refers to an ἄγγαρος: *a mounted courier* carrying royal dispatches at regular stages throughout Persia.

5:42 **τῷ αἰτοῦντί σε δός**: *that person who* (i.e., *if anyone*) *asks you*; an attributive participle may be circumstantial. A circumstantial participle may be interpreted conditionally and so replace the protasis of any condition. It is the indirect object of the imperative and used here instead of εἰ. σε is the direct object of the participle. The imperative is substituted for the indicative in the apodosis to create a simple or particular condition (App. 70). **τὸν θέλοντα . . . μὴ ἀποστραφῇς**: the use of the participle is the same as that above in a parallel construction with slight variations. It is the direct object of the main verb. The negative particle introduces a second person aorist subjunctive which often expresses prohibitions and is called *prohibitive subjunctive*. It has the force of (take care that you) *do not turn away*. Like the imperative, it is substituted for the indicative in the apodosis to create a simple or particular condition (App. 70). **δανίσασθαι** is a complementary infinitive of θέλοντα.

5:43 Ἠκούσατε ὅτι ἐρρέθη, Ἀγαπήσεις τὸν πλησίον σου καὶ μισήσεις τὸν ἐχθρόν σου. 5:44 ἐγὼ δὲ λέγω ὑμῖν, ἀγαπᾶτε τοὺς ἐχθροὺς ὑμῶν καὶ προσεύχεσθε ὑπὲρ τῶν διωκόντων ὑμᾶς, 5:45 ὅπως γένησθε υἱοὶ τοῦ πατρὸς ὑμῶν τοῦ ἐν οὐρανοῖς,

---

5:43

ἀκούω, ἀκούσω, ἤκουσα, ἀκήκοα, ἤκουσμαι, ἠκούσθην hear, obey, understand

ἀγαπάω, ἀγαπήσω, ἠγάπησα, ἠγάπηκα, ἠγάπημαι, ἠγαπήθην love, cherish, value

πλησίον near, close to (adverb, preposition + genitive); ὁ πλησίον neighbor; a friendly neighbor

μισέω, μισήσω, ἐμίσησα, μεμίσηκα hate, detest, abhor

ἐχθρός, ά, όν hostile, inimical; enemy, adversary (substantive)

5:44

ἀγαπάω, ἀγαπήσω, ἠγάπησα, ἠγάπηκα, ἠγάπημαι, ἠγαπήθην love, cherish, value

ἐχθρός, ά, όν hostile, inimical; enemy, adversary (substantive)

προσεύχομαι, προσεύξομαι, προσηυξάμην pray

ὑπέρ above, in behalf of, about, for (preposition + genitive)

διώκω, διώξω, ἐδίωξα, δεδίωγμαι, ἐδιώχθην persecute, pursue, seek after

5:45

ὅπως that, in order that (conjunction)

υἱός, οῦ, ὁ son

πατήρ, πατρός, ὁ father, parent, ancestor

5:43 **ἐρρέθη** is an abbreviation of 5:21: *it was said to the people of old*; the word is spoken by the Lord, the Lawgiver, and passed on through his mouthpiece, the prophets, to the people of old. Although it is grammatically possible for the dative with the passive to replace ὑπό with the genitive, a formulaic pattern has been established in regard to speaker and audience (1:22, 2:5, 2:15, 2:17, 3:3). **Ἀγαπήσεις τὸν πλησίον σου**: the sentiment is expressed in Lev 19:18. **μισήσεις τὸν ἐχθρόν σου**: while the expression is not found in the O.T., the sentiment is commonplace in the ancient world. τὸν ἐχθρόν: the word usually refers to one's personal enemy but in the O.T. it includes also the enemy of the State.

5:44 **ἀγαπᾶτε** is a second person plural present active imperative of a contracted verb with stem in **α** (cf. App. 55). The verb looks similar to the second person plural present active indicative. Context helps to determine appropriate usage. For the disciples, love may not be restricted: everyone is a neighbor, including the enemy. The enemies are probably more specifically identified by those for whom they are commanded to pray: **ὑπὲρ τῶν διωκόντων ὑμᾶς**.

5:45 **ὅπως γένησθε υἱοὶ τοῦ πατρὸς**: the reward will be eschatological. The conjunction with the subjunctive is used to indicate purpose. υἱοὶ stands in predicate position.

ὅτι τὸν ἥλιον αὐτοῦ ἀνατέλλει ἐπὶ πονηροὺς καὶ ἀγαθοὺς καὶ βρέχει ἐπὶ δικαίους καὶ ἀδίκους. 5:46 ἐὰν γὰρ ἀγαπήσητε τοὺς ἀγαπῶντας ὑμᾶς, τίνα μισθὸν ἔχετε; οὐχὶ καὶ οἱ τελῶναι τὸ αὐτὸ ποιοῦσιν;

5:45
ἥλιος, ου, ὁ sun
ἀνατέλλω, ἀνατελῶ, ἀνέτειλα (1 aorist) cause to rise; rise, spring up (intransitive)
ἐπί upon, on, at the time of, during (preposition + genitive); on, in, above, at, by, near, during, at the time of (+ dative); on, to, near, by, against (+ accusative)
πονηρός, ά, όν bad, evil, wicked
ἀγαθός, ή, όν good, profitable, upright
βρέχω, βρέξω, ἔβρεξα wet, moisten; rain, cause to rain, send rain
δίκαιος, αία, αιον right, just, honest, good
ἄδικος, ον unjust, unrighteous, dishonest, untrustworthy
5:46
ἐάν if (conditional particle)
ἀγαπάω, ἀγαπήσω, ἠγάπησα, ἠγάπηκα, ἠγάπημαι, ἠγαπήθην love, cherish, value
τίς, τί, (τίνος) who? what? why? (interrogative pronoun and adjective)
μισθός, οῦ, ὁ pay, wages, reward
ἔχω, ἕξω, ἔσχον (2 aorist), ἔσχηκα have, keep, cause, consider; be (with adverbs and indications of time and age); be able (with infinitive)
οὐχί not; no, by no means (adverb; more intensive form of οὐ)
καί and (conjunction); even, also, likewise, and yet (adverb)
τελώνης, ου, ὁ tax-collector, publican
ποιέω, ποιήσω, ἐποίησα, πεποίηκα, πεποίημαι, ἐποιήθην make, do, keep, obey

---

5:45 **ἀνατέλλει . . . βρέχει**: both verbs are causative, denoting *to cause* or *to make,* and indicate an action performed at the bidding of the subject. Their subject is God. **ἐπὶ πονηροὺς καί ἀγαθοὺς . . . ἐπὶ δικαίους καὶ ἀδίκους**: the chiastic order suggests that evil and unjust people surround the good and the just, at least until the eschatological judgment.

5:46 **ἐὰν γὰρ ἀγαπήσητε . . . ἔχετε**: a present general condition (App. 70) is introduced by ἐάν or ἄν with a subjunctive in the protasis and a present indicative in the apodosis. **ἀγαπήσητε τοὺς ἀγαπῶντας**: the repetition of the same verb as the subject and object may convey a simplicity of the action involved. **οὐχὶ καὶ**: *not also*; the negative is a strengthened form of οὐ; as an interrogative word in a question, it expects an affirmative answer. **τὸ αὐτὸ**: *the same*; when αὐτός (App. 40) stands in attributive position it is an adjective meaning *same.*

5:47 καὶ ἐὰν ἀσπάσησθε τοὺς ἀδελφοὺς ὑμῶν μόνον, τί περισσὸν ποιεῖτε; οὐχὶ καὶ οἱ ἐθνικοὶ τὸ αὐτὸ ποιοῦσιν; 5:48 Ἔσεσθε οὖν ὑμεῖς τέλειοι ὡς ὁ πατὴρ ὑμῶν ὁ οὐράνιος τέλειός ἐστιν.

5:47
ἐάν if (conditional particle)
ἀσπάζομαι, ἀσπάσομαι, ἠσπασάμην, ἤσπασμαι welcome; treat with affection, be fond of, cherish
ἀδελφός, οῦ, ὁ brother
μόνον only (adverb)
τίς, τί, (τίνος) who? what? why? (interrogative pronoun and adjective)
περισσός, ή, όν extraordinary, excessive; more, greater
ποιέω, ποιήσω, ἐποίησα, πεποίηκα, πεποίημαι, ἐποιήθην make, do, keep, obey
οὐχί not; no, by no means (adverb; more intensive form of οὐ)
ἐθνικός, ή, όν gentile, heathen
5:48
οὖν therefore, then, so (conjunction, postpositive)
τέλειος, εία, ειον complete, perfect, fully developed, consecrated
ὡς as, like, when, after, about (with numerals), how, provided that (adverb, conjunction)
πατήρ, πατρός, ὁ father, parent, ancestor
οὐράνιος, ία, ιον heavenly, celestial

5:47 **καὶ ἐὰν ἀσπάσησθε . . . ποιεῖτε**: the construction and sentiment run parallel to the verse above. ἀσπάσησθε is a second person plural first aorist middle subjunctive (cf. App. 53, D, 2). ποιεῖτε is a second person plural present active indicative of a verb contracted with stem in **ε** (cf. App. 56). It takes a circumflex over the contraction.

5:48 **Ἔσεσθε οὖν ὑμεῖς τέλειοι**: *you will then be perfect*; the combination of the pronoun and the verb occurring at the beginning of the sentence makes an emphatic statement to His listeners. The verb is second person plural future active indicative of the verb εἰμί (App. 63). The future may be construed in two ways: it may express a command or indicate a future event. Commands have been prominently used in verses 21, 27, 33, and 43 of this chapter in quotes from the O.T. However, they are notably not accompanied by the emphatic pronoun. Also, the imperatival future suggests that a command can potentially be carried out. While mortals may attain the end or purpose of their lives in keeping the aforementioned commandments and may even be perfect in their generation by comparison with mortals (Gen 6:9), it is impossible to match the perfection of God here on earth, no matter how we interpret the meaning of that perfection. A simple future indicative, more commonly accompanied by the emphatic pronoun, may prove the better alternative. It refers to eschatological time, when the Father will be surrounded by perfection, his own and that of others: **τέλειοι ὡς ὁ πατὴρ . . . ὁ οὐράνιος τέλειός**, as the collocation of the text suggests, and when οἱ μακάριοι τὸν θεὸν ὄψονται, αὐτοὶ υἱοὶ θεοῦ κληθήσονται and αὐτῶν ἐστιν ἡ βασιλεία τῶν οὐρανῶν. The text thus represents the apodosis of a future more vivid condition (App. 70): (If you keep these commandments,) *you will then be perfect.*

6 Προσέχετε [δὲ] τὴν δικαιοσύνην ὑμῶν μὴ ποιεῖν ἔμπροσθεν τῶν
ἀνθρώπων πρὸς τὸ θεαθῆναι αὐτοῖς· εἰ δὲ μή γε, μισθὸν οὐκ ἔχετε
παρὰ τῷ πατρὶ ὑμῶν τῷ ἐν τοῖς οὐρανοῖς.
6:2 Ὅταν οὖν ποιῇς ἐλεημοσύνην,

6:1

προσέχω, προσέξω, προσέσχον (2 aorist) pay attention to, give heed to, consider; beware of, take heed of, guard against (followed by ἀπό, μή)

δικαιοσύνη, ης, ἡ justice, righteousness, godliness, generosity, alms

ποιέω, ποιήσω, ἐποίησα, πεποίηκα, πεποίημαι, ἐποιήθην make, do, keep, obey

ἔμπροσθεν in front of, before, in the presence of (adverb; preposition + genitive)

ἄνθρωπος, ου, ὁ human, person, man

πρός for, for the purpose of (preposition + genitive); with, to, towards, unto, for, for the purpose of, with reference to, in relation to, of, concerning (+ accusative); near, at, by (preposition + dative)

θεάομαι, θεάσομαι, ἐθεασάμην, τεθέαμαι, ἐθεάθην see, look at, gaze upon, discern with the eyes

εἰ δὲ μή if not, otherwise

γε at least, indeed (an enclitic particle emphasizing the preceding word; often untranslatable)

μισθός, οῦ, ὁ pay, wages, reward

οὐκ not (a form of οὐ used before vowels with a smooth breathing, adverb)

παρά from (the side of), from, issuing from, by (preposition + genitive); with, by; in the sight of, in the judgment of (+ dative)

πατήρ, πατρός, ὁ father, parent, ancestor

6:2

ὅταν when, whenever (conjunction)

οὖν therefore, then, so (conjunction, postpositive)

ποιέω, ποιήσω, ἐποίησα, πεποίηκα, πεποίημαι, ἐποιήθην make, do, keep, obey

ἐλεημοσύνη, ης, ἡ kind deed, alms, charitable giving

6:1 **τὴν δικοιοσύνην**: *acts of righteousness*; the noun encompasses the activities of righteousness specified below. **πρὸς τὸ θεαθῆναι αὐτοῖς**: *for the purpose of being seen by them*; the construction is an articular infinitive. In this construction the article has the power to turn the infinitive into a substantive which is the object of the preposition πρὸς: *for the purpose of.* Since the verbal noun is passive, agency may be, and is here, expressed by the dative of agency rather than by the more usual preposition ὑπό and the genitive case. **εἰ δὲ μή** introduces a simple or particular condition (App. 70) with ellipsis of the verb in the protasis. **παρὰ τῷ πατρὶ ὑμῶν**: *before your Father*; they have already been seen before men and have their reward.

6:2 **Ὅταν . . . ποιῇς . . . μὴ σαλπίσῃς**: *whenever you offer . . . do not sound a trumpet*; the indefinite relative adverb ὅταν replaces ἐάν or ἄν in this future more vivid condition (App. 70). It takes a subjunctive in the protasis. The apodosis of a negative future more vivid condition frequently takes a subjunctive with μή which is equivalent to a future indicative.

μὴ σαλπίσῃς ἔμπροσθέν σου, ὥσπερ οἱ ὑποκριταὶ ποιοῦσιν ἐν ταῖς συναγωγαῖς καὶ ἐν ταῖς ῥύμαις, ὅπως δοξασθῶσιν ὑπὸ τῶν ἀνθρώπων· ἀμὴν λέγω ὑμῖν, ἀπέχουσιν τὸν μισθὸν αὐτῶν. 6:3 σοῦ δὲ ποιοῦντος ἐλεημοσύνην μὴ γνώτω ἡ ἀριστερά σου τί ποιεῖ ἡ δεξιά σου,

---

6:2
σαλπίζω, σαλπίσω, ἐσάλπισα sound a trumpet, trumpet forth
ἔμπροσθεν in front of, before, in the presence of (adverb; preposition + genitive)
ὥσπερ as, just as (adverb)
ὑποκριτής, οῦ, ὁ hypocrite, pretender, dissembler
συναγωγή, ῆς, ἡ synagogue
ῥύμη, ης, ἡ narrow street, lane, alley
ὅπως that, in order that (conjunction)
δοξάζω, δοξάσω, ἐδόξασα, δεδόξασμαι, ἐδοξάσθην praise, honor, magnify, glorify
ἄνθρωπος, ου, ὁ human being, person, man
ἀμήν in truth, verily (Hebrew)
ἀπέχω, ἀφέξω have in full, receive in full; be distant, be away
μισθός, οῦ, ὁ pay, wages, reward
6:3
ἐλεημοσύνη, ης, ἡ kind deed, alms, charitable giving
γινώσκω, γνώσομαι, ἔγνων, ἔγνωκα, ἔγνωσμαι, ἐγνώσθην know, learn, understand
ἀριστερός, ά, όν left
τίς, τί, (τίνος) who? what? why? (interrogative pronoun)
δεξιός, ά, όν right (as opposed to left)

6:2 **οἱ ὑποκριταὶ** serve as stock characters and foils. The context in the following verses describes sufficiently enough who they are, what they do, and what their purpose is. **ὅπως δοξασθῶσιν**: *that they may be praised*; the conjunction with the subjunctive is used to indicate purpose. The verb is third person plural first aorist passive subjunctive (cf. App. 53, G, 2). Agency is usually expressed by the preposition **ὑπό** and a noun or pronoun in the genitive case. **τῶν ἀνθρώπων**: the generic article is included in Greek to denote a whole class and so to distinguish humans from other beings.

6:3 **σοῦ δὲ ποιοῦντος**: *but whenever you offer*; the construction is a *genitive absolute*. The pronoun σοῦ and the circumstantial participle ποιοῦντος in the genitive case are syntactically independent of the main verb and clause. A circumstantial participle may express time, cause, concession, condition, and other circumstances. It needs to be sensitively interpreted according to context and translated into English as a clause (App. 65). The present participle usually expresses progressive, continued, and repeated action (aspect) in present time. **μὴ γνώτω**: *let not . . . know*; the verb is third person singular second aorist active imperative. Several **ω** verbs form their second aorists without a thematic vowel, being similar to **μι** verbs (App. 61). **τί ποιεῖ**: the interrogative pronoun keeps its acute accent (App. 47). It introduces an indirect question. An indirect question retains both the mood and the tense of the direct question. The verb is third person singular present active indicative of a contracted verb with stem in **ε** (cf. App. 56).

6:4 ὅπως ᾖ σου ἡ ἐλεημοσύνη ἐν τῷ κρυπτῷ· καὶ ὁ πατήρ σου ὁ βλέπων ἐν τῷ κρυπτῷ ἀποδώσει σοι.

6:5 Καὶ ὅταν προσεύχησθε, οὐκ ἔσεσθε ὡς οἱ ὑποκριταί, ὅτι φιλοῦσιν ἐν ταῖς συναγωγαῖς καὶ ἐν ταῖς γωνίαις τῶν πλατειῶν

6:4

ὅπως that, in order that (conjunction)

ἐλεημοσύνη, ης, ἡ kind deed, alms, charitable giving

κρυπτός, ή, όν hidden, secret (adjective); hidden thing, hidden place, secret (noun)

πατήρ, πατρός, ὁ father, parent, ancestor

βλέπω, βλέψω, ἔβλεψα see, behold, perceive

ἀποδίδωμι, ἀποδώσω, ἀπέδωκα, ἀπέδων (2 aorist), ἀποδέδωκα, ἀποδέδομαι, ἀπεδόθην give away, give out; give back, return; render in full, reward, recompense

6:5

ὅταν when, whenever (conjunction)

προσεύχομαι, προσεύξομαι, προσηυξάμην pray, offer prayer

οὐκ not (a form of οὐ used before vowels with a smooth breathing, adverb)

ὡς as, like, when, after, about (with numerals), how, provided that (adverb, conjunction)

ὑποκριτής, οῦ, ὁ hypocrite, pretender, dissembler

φιλέω, φιλήσω, ἐφίλησα, πεφίληκα love; like, be fond of

συναγωγή, ῆς, ἡ synagogue

γωνία, ας, ἡ corner

πλατεῖα, ας, ἡ wide road, street

6:4 **ὅπως ᾖ**: the conjunction with the subjunctive is used to indicate purpose. The verb is third person singular present active subjunctive of the verb εἰμί (App. 63). **ὁ πατήρ σου ὁ βλέπων**: *your Father who sees*; the repetition of the article with the present participle is an alternate construction for **ὁ βλέπων πατήρ**. In both cases the participle stands in attributive position (i.e., immediately preceded by a definite article). The article with a participle is translated as a relative clause. **ἐν τῷ κρυπτῷ**: the article is omitted in translation.

6:5 **ὅταν προσεύχησθε, οὐκ ἔσεσθε**: the indefinite relative adverb ὅταν replaces ἐάν or ἄν in this future more vivid condition (App. 70). It takes a subjunctive in the protasis and a future indicative connoting an imperative in the apodosis. προσεύχησθε is second person plural present middle subjunctive of a deponent verb (cf. App. 53, A, 2). **φιλοῦσιν . . . ἑστῶτες προσεύχεσθαι**: *they love to pray as they stand*; the finite verb is third person plural present active indicative of a contracted verb with stem in **ε** (cf. App. 56). ἑστῶτες is masculine plural nominative perfect active participle (cf. App. 61; 33) modifying the subject of the main verb. A circumstantial participle may express time, cause, concession, condition, and other circumstances. It needs to be sensitively interpreted according to context and translated into English as a clause. προσεύχεσθαι is a complementary infinitive of the deponent verb (cf. App. 53, A, 4).

ἑστῶτες προσεύχεσθαι, ὅπως φανῶσιν τοῖς ἀνθρώποις· ἀμὴν λέγω ὑμῖν, ἀπέχουσιν τὸν μισθὸν αὐτῶν. 6:6 σὺ δὲ ὅταν προσεύχῃ, εἴσελθε εἰς τὸ ταμεῖόν σου καὶ κλείσας τὴν θύραν σου πρόσευξαι τῷ πατρί σου τῷ ἐν τῷ κρυπτῷ·

6:5
ἵστημι, στήσω, ἔστησα, ἔστην (2 aorist), ἕστηκα, ἐστάθην put, place, set, cause to stand (transitive); stand, be (intransitive)
προσεύχομαι, προσεύξομαι, προσηυξάμην pray, offer prayer
ὅπως that, in order that (conjunction)
φαίνω, φανῶ, ἔφηνα, πέφαγκα, πέφηνα, πέφασμαι, ἐφάνθην, ἐφάνην shine, give light, be bright; be seen, appear, be visible (middle and passive)
ἄνθρωπος, ου, ὁ human, person, man
ἀμήν in truth, verily (Hebrew)
ἀπέχω, ἀφέξω have in full, receive in full; be distant, be away
μισθός, οῦ, ὁ pay, wages, reward
6:6
ὅταν when, whenever (conjunction)
προσεύχομαι, προσεύξομαι, προσηυξάμην pray, offer prayer
εἰσέρχομαι, εἰσελεύσομαι, εἰσῆλθον (2 aorist), εἰσελήλυθα come (in, into), go (in, into), enter into, share in, come to enjoy
ταμεῖον, ου, τό storehouse, barn; inner chamber, private room, secret room
κλείω, κλείσω, ἔκλεισα, κέκλεισμαι, ἐκλείσθην close, shut, lock
θύρα, ας, ἡ door, entrance
προσεύχομαι, προσεύξομαι, προσηυξάμην pray, offer prayer
πατήρ, πατρός, ὁ father, parent, ancestor
κρυπτός, ή, όν hidden, secret (adjective); hidden thing, hidden place, secret (noun)

6:5 **ὅπως φανῶσιν τοῖς ἀνθρώποις**: *that they may be seen by men*; ὅπως introduces a purpose clause. φανῶσιν is third person plural second aorist passive subjunctive. τοῖς ἀνθρώποις is a dative of agency. The passive verb may express agency by the dative case.

6:6 **ὅταν προσεύχῃ, εἴσελθε**: the indefinite relative adverb ὅταν replaces ἐάν or ἄν in this future more vivid condition (App. 70). It takes a subjunctive in the protasis and may substitute an imperative for a future indicative in the apodosis. προσεύχῃ is a second person singular present middle subjunctive of a deponent verb (cf. App. 53, A, 2). εἴσελθε is a second person singular second aorist active imperative (cf. App. 54). **κλείσας τὴν θύραν σου πρόσευξαι**: *close your door and pray*; when a participle modifies an imperative, it is commonly changed into an imperative and the two verbs are coordinated in translation. **κλείσας** is the first aorist active participle (cf. App. 53, D, 5; 31). **πρόσευξαι** is the second person singular first aorist imperative of a deponent verb (cf. 53, D, 3). **τῷ πατρί σου τῷ ἐν τῷ κρυπτῷ**: *your Father who is in secret*; the article followed by a prepositional phrase stands in attributive position as part of the substantive. The adjective following an article becomes a substantive. The secret place may well refer to heaven, where He is not seen but where He *sees in secret*. The context suggests because He is in His hiding place, He can see yours.

καὶ ὁ πατήρ σου ὁ βλέπων ἐν τῷ κρυπτῷ ἀποδώσει σοι. 6:7
Προσευχόμενοι δὲ μὴ βατταλογήσητε ὥσπερ οἱ ἐθνικοί, δοκοῦσιν
γὰρ ὅτι ἐν τῇ πολυλογίᾳ αὐτῶν εἰσακουσθήσονται. 6:8 μὴ οὖν
ὁμοιωθῆτε αὐτοῖς· οἶδεν γὰρ ὁ πατὴρ ὑμῶν ὧν χρείαν ἔχετε

6:6

βλέπω, βλέψω, ἔβλεψα see, behold, perceive

ἀποδίδωμι, ἀποδώσω, ἀπέδωκα, ἀπέδων (2 aorist), ἀποδέδωκα, ἀποδέδομαι, ἀπεδόθην give away, give out; give back, return; render in full, reward, recompense

6:7

προσεύχομαι, προσεύξομαι, προσηυξάμην pray, offer prayer

βατταλογέω, βατταλογήσω babble, prate, speak idly, use vain repetitions

ὥσπερ as, just as (adverb)

ἐθνικός, ή, όν gentile, heathen

δοκέω, δόξω, ἔδοξα think (mistakenly), believe, suppose, consider

πολυλογία, ας, ἡ wordiness

εἰσακούω, εἰσακούσομαι, εἰσήκουσα, εἰσηκούσθην listen to, hear, obey

6:8

οὖν therefore, then, so (conjunction, postpositive)

ὁμοιόω, ὁμοιώσω, ὁμοίωσα, ὡμοιώθην make like, liken, compare; be like, be made like, become like, resemble (passive)

οἶδα know

χρεία, ας, ἡ need, necessity

6:7 **Προσευχόμενοι**: *as you pray*; the present middle participle (cf. App. 30) stands in agreement with the subject of the finite verb. A circumstantial participle may express time, cause, concession, condition, and other circumstances. **μὴ βατταλογήσητε**: the negative particle introduces a second person plural aorist active subjunctive which often expresses prohibitions and is called *prohibitive subjunctive*. It has the force of (take care that you) *do not babble*. The Greek, like the English verb, has onomatopoeic qualities. **ἐν τῇ πολυλογίᾳ**: *because of their loquaciousness*; the preposition may indicate cause or reason. **εἰσακουσθήσονται** is third person plural first future passive indicative (cf. App. 53, G, 1).

6:8 **μὴ . . . ὁμοιωθῆτε αὐτοῖς**: *do not be like them*; the negative particle introduces a prohibitive subjunctive (cf. App. 53, G, 2). It is second person plural first aorist passive subjunctive and distinguishes itself from the first aorist passive imperative (cf. App. 53, G, 3) only by its accent. It has the force of (take care that you) *do not be like them*. The verb governs the dative case. **οἶδεν**: *knows*; the perfect οἶδα (App. 62), from the stem ειδ-, is used as a present. **ὧν χρείαν ἔχετε**: *what you need* (literally: *those things of which you have need*); the construction is equivalent to ἐκεῖνα ὧν. In the abbreviated form the antecedent of the relative pronoun is missing. Since the relative pronoun is the object of the noun χρείαν, it is an objective genitive (cf. App. 65).

πρὸ τοῦ ὑμᾶς αἰτῆσαι αὐτόν. 6:9 Οὕτως οὖν προσεύχεσθε ὑμεῖς·
Πάτερ ἡμῶν ὁ ἐν τοῖς οὐρανοῖς·
ἁγιασθήτω τὸ ὄνομά σου·
6:10 ἐλθέτω ἡ βασιλεία σου·
γενηθήτω τὸ θέλημά σου,
ὡς ἐν οὐρανῷ καὶ ἐπὶ γῆς·
6:11 τὸν ἄρτον ἡμῶν τὸν ἐπιούσιον δὸς ἡμῖν σήμερον·

6:8
πρό before (preposition + genitive)
αἰτέω, αἰτήσω, ᾔτησα, ᾔτηκα ask, ask for, make a request
6:9
οὕτως so, thus, in this manner (adverb)
οὖν therefore, then, so (conjunction, postpositive)
προσεύχομαι, προσεύξομαι, προσηυξάμην pray, offer prayer
ἁγιάζω, ἁγιάσω, ἡγίασα, ἡγίακα, ἡγίασμαι, ἡγιάσθην separate, consecrate; cleanse, purify, sanctify; regard as holy, hold in reverence, hallow
ὄνομα, ατος, τό name
6:10
γίνομαι, γενήσομαι, ἐγενόμην, γέγονα/γεγένημαι, ἐγενήθην become, be made, be done, be created, be born, come, arrive, be present
θέλημα, ατος, τὸ will; wish, desire
ὡς as, like, when, after, about (with numerals), how, provided that (adverb, conjunction)
γῆ, γῆς, ἡ earth, soil, land, region, country
6:11
ἄρτος, ου, ὁ bread, loaf of bread
ἐπιούσιος, ιον daily
δίδωμι, δώσω, ἔδωκα, ἔδων (2 aorist), δέδωκα, δέδομαι, ἐδόθην give
σήμερον today, this day (adverb)

6:8 **πρὸ τοῦ ὑμᾶς αἰτῆσαι αὐτόν**: *before you ask Him*; the construction is an articular infinitive. As a noun the infinitive takes an article which is the object of the preposition πρὸ: *before the circumstance* or *time*. As a verbal form the Greek infinitive may additionally have an accusative subject and govern an accusative object: *that you ask him*. In the event of two accusatives the context will be decisive.

6:9 **προσεύχεσθε** is a second person plural present middle imperative of a deponent verb (cf. App. 53, A, 3). **ὁ ἐν τοῖς οὐρανοῖς**: *who is in heaven*; the article may be followed by a prepositional phrase and stand in attributive position. **ἁγιασθήτω** is a third person singular first aorist passive imperative (cf. App. 53, G, 3), as are the two verbs in the following verse.

6:11 **δὸς** is a second person singular second aorist active imperative (App. 58).

6:12 καὶ ἄφες ἡμῖν τὰ ὀφειλήματα ἡμῶν,
ὡς καὶ ἡμεῖς ἀφήκαμεν τοῖς ὀφειλέταις ἡμῶν·
6:13 καὶ μὴ εἰσενέγκῃς ἡμᾶς εἰς πειρασμόν,
ἀλλὰ ῥῦσαι ἡμᾶς ἀπὸ τοῦ πονηροῦ.
6:14 Ἐὰν γὰρ ἀφῆτε τοῖς ἀνθρώποις τὰ παραπτώματα αὐτῶν, ἀφήσει καὶ ὑμῖν ὁ πατὴρ ὑμῶν ὁ οὐράνιος·

6:12
ἀφίημι, ἀφήσω, ἀφῆκα, ἀφῆν (2 aorist), ἀφεῖκα, ἀφεῖμαι, ἀφέθην let go, forgive, leave
ὀφείλημα, ατος, τό debts; offense, fault, sin
ὡς as, like, when, after, about (with numerals), how, provided that (adverb, conjunction)
ὀφειλέτης, ου, ὁ debtor; offender; sinner
6:13
εἰσφέρω, εἰσοίσω, εἰσήνεγκα (1 aorist), εἰσήνεγκον (2 aorist), εἰσηνέχθην bear in, carry to; bring or lead (someone) into
πειρασμός, οῦ, ὁ test, trial; temptation
ῥύομαι, ῥύσομαι, ἐρ(ρ)υσάμην, ἐρ(ρ)ύσθην save, deliver, rescue, preserve
πονηρός, ά, όν bad, evil, wicked
6:14
ἐάν if (conditional particle)
ἀφίημι, ἀφήσω, ἀφῆκα, ἀφῆν (2 aorist), ἀφεῖκα, ἀφεῖμαι, ἀφέθην let go, forgive, leave
ἄνθρωπος, ου, ὁ human being, person, man
παράπτωμα, ατος, τό transgression, sin
οὐράνιος, ία, ιον heavenly, celestial

6:12 **ἄφες,** a second person singular second aorist imperative (cf. App. 59), takes an accusative of the thing and a dative of person. **ἀφήκαμεν**: *we forgive*; the verbal form is a gnomic aorist. The aorist may be used to express a general truth where the experience of an action in the past suggests an action that is likely to be repeated: it is always our part to forgive.

6:13 **μὴ εἰσενέγκῃς ἡμᾶς εἰς πειρασμόν**: *lead us not into sore trials*; the verb is a second person singular either first or second aorist active subjunctive. The two aorist forms look alike in the subjunctive and show no difference in meaning between them. The negative particle introduces a prohibitive subjunctive, regularly formed with the aorist tense (cf. App. 53, D, 2; 54). The *tempter* entices the world to sin and death. God's purposes bring about the immortality and eternal life of men, and He sends them trials to prove themselves true (Jn 6:6). As Jesus, each person is *tested* πεπειραμένος, surely not as intensely as He, but nonetheless tested *in all things* κατὰ πάντα (Hb 4:15). Perhaps the plea here expressed seeks avoidance of persecutions too difficult to bear, or an amelioration of the intensity of afflictions or trials. **ἀλλὰ ῥῦσαι ἡμᾶς ἀπὸ τοῦ πονηροῦ**: *but deliver us from evil*; ῥῦσαι is a first aorist imperative (cf. App. 53, D, 3). The context suggests that τοῦ πονηροῦ is the abstract noun rather than a personification. The evil results from painful trials sent by God may include loss of faith.

6:14 **Ἐὰν γὰρ ἀφῆτε . . . ἀφήσει** is a future more vivid condition (App. 70). The verb takes an accusative of the thing and a dative of person.

6:15 ἐὰν δὲ μὴ ἀφῆτε τοῖς ἀνθρώποις, οὐδὲ ὁ πατὴρ ὑμῶν ἀφήσει τὰ παραπτώματα ὑμῶν.

6:16 Ὅταν δὲ νηστεύητε, μὴ γίνεσθε ὡς οἱ ὑποκριταὶ σκυθρωποί, ἀφανίζουσιν γὰρ τὰ πρόσωπα αὐτῶν ὅπως φανῶσιν τοῖς ἀνθρώποις νηστεύοντες· ἀμὴν λέγω ὑμῖν, ἀπέχουσιν τὸν μισθὸν αὐτῶν.

6:15
ἐάν if (conditional particle)
οὐδέ and not, nor (conjunction and adverb)
παράπτωμα, ατος, τό transgression, sin
6:16
ὅταν when, whenever (conjunction)
νηστεύω, νηστεύσω, ἐνήστευσα fast
γίνομαι, γενήσομαι, ἐγενόμην, γέγονα/γεγένημαι, ἐγενήθην become, be made, be done, be created, be born, come, arrive, be present
ὡς as, like, when, after, about (with numerals), how, provided that (adverb, conjunction)
ὑποκριτής, οῦ, ὁ hypocrite, pretender, dissembler
σκυθροπός, ή, όν with a sad face, of a gloomy countenance, with a sullen look
ἀφανίζω, ἀφανίσω, ἠφανίσθην render unrecognizable; destroy, consume; spoil, deform, disfigure
πρόσωπον, ου, τό face, countenance
ὅπως that, in order that (conjunction)
φαίνω, φανῶ, ἔφηνα, πέφαγκα, πέφηνα, πέφασμαι, ἐφάνθην, ἐφάνην shine, give light, be bright; be seen, appear, be visible (middle and passive)
ἄνθρωπος, ου, ὁ human being, person, man
νηστεύω, νηστεύσω, ἐνήστευσα fast
ἀμήν in truth, verily (Hebrew)
ἀπέχω, ἀφέξω have in full, receive in full; be distant, be away
μισθός, οῦ, ὁ pay, wages, reward

6:15 **ἐὰν δὲ μὴ ἀφῆτε . . . ἀφήσει** is a parallel construction in the negative.

6:16 **Ὅταν δὲ νηστεύητε, μὴ γίνεσθε**: the indefinite relative adverb ὅταν replaces ἐάν or ἄν in this future more vivid condition (App. 70). It takes a subjunctive in the protasis and may substitute an imperative for a future indicative in the apodosis. **ἀφανίζουσιν γὰρ τὰ πρόσωπα . . . ὅπως φανῶσιν τοῖς ἀνθρώποις**: *they disfigure their faces* (literally: *they make their faces unseen*)*that they may be seen by men*; visible signs of fasting include placing sackcloth and ashes on their head and tearing their clothing. ὅπως introduces a purpose clause. φανῶσιν is third person plural second aorist passive subjunctive. τοῖς ἀνθρώποις is a dative of agency. The passive verb may express agency by the dative case. The two antithetical verbs introduce a play on words or paronomasia which exposes the hypocrites as playing a game. **νηστεύοντες**: *as though they are fasting*; the verbal form is a masculine plural nominative present active participle (cf. App. 29) in agreement with the subject of the verb φανῶσιν. A circumstantial participle may express time, cause, concession, condition, and other circumstances. It needs to be sensitively interpreted according to context and translated into English as a clause.

6:17 σὺ δὲ νηστεύων ἄλειψαί σου τὴν κεφαλὴν καὶ τὸ πρόσωπόν σου νίψαι, 6:18 ὅπως μὴ φανῇς τοῖς ἀνθρώποις νηστεύων ἀλλὰ τῷ πατρί σου τῷ ἐν τῷ κρυφαίῳ· καὶ ὁ πατήρ σου ὁ βλέπων ἐν τῷ κρυφαίῳ ἀποδώσει σοι.

6:19 Μὴ θησαυρίζετε ὑμῖν θησαυροὺς ἐπὶ τῆς γῆς,

6:17
νηστεύω, νηστεύσω, ἐνήστευσα fast
ἀλείφω, ἀλείψω, ἤλειψα anoint
κεφαλή, ῆς, ἡ head
πρόσωπον, ου, τό face, countenance
νίπτω, νίψω, ἔνιψα wash (active); wash oneself (middle)
6:18
ὅπως that, in order that (conjunction)
φαίνω, φανῶ, ἔφηνα, πέφαγκα, πέφηνα, πέφασμαι, ἐφάνθην, ἐφάνην shine, give light, be bright; be seen, appear, be visible (middle and passive)
νηστεύω, νηστεύσω, ἐνήστευσα fast
κρυφαῖος, αία, αῖον secret, hidden; ἐν τῷ κρυφαίῳ in secret
βλέπω, βλέψω, ἔβλεψα see, behold, perceive
ἀποδίδωμι, ἀποδώσω, ἀπέδωκα, ἀπέδων (2 aorist), ἀποδέδωκα, ἀποδέδομαι, ἀπεδόθην give away, give out; give back, return; render in full, reward, recompense
6:19
θησαυρίζω, θησαυρίσω, ἐθησαύρισα store up, gather, save
θησαυρός, οῦ, ὁ treasury, store, treasure
γῆ, γῆς, ἡ earth, soil, land, region, country

6:17 **σὺ δὲ**: the disciple, by contrast, internalizes the fast and goes about his daily activities in an ordinary way. **ἄλειψαί . . . νίψαι** are two aorist active imperatives. The aorist aspect may be particularly significant since it expresses a single act (aspect) in time that quickly moves on.

6:18 **τῷ ἐν τῷ κρυφαίῳ**: *who is in secret*; the article may be followed by a prepositional phrase and stand in attributive position as part of the substantive. The adjective following an article is a substantive. The secret place may well refer to heaven, where He is not seen but where He *sees in secret*. The context suggests that because He is in His hiding place, He can see yours.

6:19 **Μὴ θησαυρίζετε ὑμῖν θησαυροὺς**: *do not heap up for yourselves treasures* (literally: *do not treasure up for yourselves treasures*); when the noun in the accusative derives from the same root as the verb, the direct object is a cognate accusative. In translation, the verb may be flattened out appropriately according to context. The collocation of the words paints a picture depicting a person surrounded by treasures.

ὅπου σὴς καὶ βρῶσις ἀφανίζει καὶ ὅπου κλέπται διορύσσουσιν καὶ κλέπτουσιν· 6:20 θησαυρίζετε δὲ ὑμῖν θησαυροὺς ἐν οὐρανῷ, ὅπου οὔτε σὴς οὔτε βρῶσις ἀφανίζει καὶ ὅπου κλέπται οὐ διορύσσουσιν οὐδὲ κλέπτουσιν· 6:21 ὅπου γάρ ἐστιν ὁ θησαυρός σου, ἐκεῖ ἔσται καὶ ἡ καρδία σου.

6:19
ὅπου where (adverb)
σής, σεός/σητός, ὁ moth
βρῶσις, εως, ἡ eating; food, meat; canker, rust, corrosion
ἀφανίζω, ἀφανίσω, ἠφανίσθην render unseen or unrecognizable; destroy, consume; spoil, deform, disfigure
κλέπτης, ου, ὁ thief
διορύσσω, διορύξω break through, break in
κλέπτω, κλέψω, ἔκλεψα, κέκλοφα, ἐκλάπην (2 aorist passive) steal
6:20
θησαυρίζω, θησαυρίσω, ἐθησαύρισα store up, gather, save
θησαυρός, οῦ, ὁ treasury, store, treasure
ὅπου where (adverb)
οὔτε and not, not even (conjunction); οὔτε . . . οὔτε neither . . . nor
σής, σεός/σητός, ὁ moth
βρῶσις, εως, ἡ eating; food, meat; canker, rust, corrosion
ἀφανίζω, ἀφανίσω, ἠφανίσθην render unseen or unrecognizable; destroy, consume; spoil, deform, disfigure
κλέπτης, ου, ὁ thief
διορύσσω, διορύξω break through, break in
οὐδέ and not, nor (conjunction and adverb)
κλέπτω, κλέψω, ἔκλεψα, κέκλοφα, ἐκλάπην (2 aorist passive) steal
6:21
ὅπου where (adverb)
θησαυρός, οῦ, ὁ treasury, store, treasure
ἐκεῖ there, in that place (adverb)
καρδία, ας, ἡ heart

6:19 **σὴς καὶ βρῶσις ἀφανίζει**: *the consuming moth corrupts* (literally: *the moth and eating*); the singular verb requires a singular subject, which is constructed here by way of hendiadys, where, for purposes of rhetorical emphasis, two substantives are combined by a conjunction instead of one substantive and an adjective. Costly apparel appropriately identifies the rich and their plight of temporal wealth because their dress is ostentatious but easily subject to the ravages of the moth. The rich in possession of gold, silver, diamonds, pearls, and other jewelry do not fear rust but thieves. Like the ephemeral garment, all worldly treasures are fleeting.

6:20 **θησαυρίζετε . . . ὑμῖν θησαυροὺς**: the parallel wording introduces an antithetical statement to the one in the previous verse. **οὔτε σὴς οὔτε βρῶσις ἀφανίζει**: *the consuming moth does not corrupt* (literally: *neither the moth nor eating*); the two substantives stay intact in the emphatic negative statement. οὔτε . . . οὔτε correlate single words. Spiritual treasures are an eternal possession.

6:21 **καὶ**: *also*; the word functions as an adverb here.

6:22 Ὁ λύχνος τοῦ σώματός ἐστιν ὁ ὀφθαλμός. ἐὰν οὖν ᾖ ὁ ὀφθαλμός σου ἁπλοῦς, ὅλον τὸ σῶμά σου φωτεινὸν ἔσται· 6:23 ἐὰν δὲ ὁ ὀφθαλμός σου πονηρὸς ᾖ, ὅλον τὸ σῶμά σου σκοτεινὸν ἔσται. εἰ οὖν τὸ φῶς τὸ ἐν σοὶ σκότος ἐστίν, τὸ σκότος πόσον.

6:24 Οὐδεὶς δύναται δυσὶ κυρίοις δουλεύειν·

6:22
λύχνος, ου, ὁ lamp
σῶμα, ατος, τό body
ὀφθαλμός, οῦ, ὁ eye
οὖν therefore, then, so (conjunction, postpositive)
ἁπλοῦς, ῆ, οῦν simple, single, sincere; clear, sound, healthy
ὅλος, η, ον all, whole, entire, complete
φωτεινός, ή, όν radiant, bright, shining; full of light, enlightened, illuminated
6:23
ὀφθαλμός, οῦ, ὁ eye
πονηρός, ά, όν bad, evil, wicked
ὅλος, η, ον all, whole, entire, complete
σῶμα, ατος, τό body
σκοτεινός, ή, όν dark
εἰ if, whether
φῶς, φωτός, τό light
σκότος, ους, τό darkness, gloom
πόσος, η, ον how great? how much?
6:24
οὐδείς, οὐδεμία, οὐδέν no (adjective); no one, nobody, nothing (substantive)
δύναμαι, δυνήσομαι, ἠδυνήθην be able
δύο two
δουλεύω, δουλεύσω, ἐδούλευσα, δεδούλευκα be a slave, be subjected, serve as a slave, serve

---

6:22 **ὁ λύχνος τοῦ σώματός ἐστιν ὁ ὀφθαλμός**: collocation of words shows that light emphatically at the beginning and at the end of the sentence shines around the body and from the body, the center and the source. **ἐὰν οὖν ᾖ . . . ἔσται** is a future more vivid condition (App. 70). The lamp or the eye indicates the quality of the source.

6:23 **ἐὰν δὲ . . . ᾖ . . . ἔσται**: the parallel wording introduces a future more vivid condition (App. 70) antithetical to the one in the previous verse. **εἰ . . . ἐστίν, τὸ σκότος πόσον** is a simple or particular condition (App. 70). Supply ἐστίν for the apodosis from the protasis. The interrogative agrees with its subject τὸ σκότος in gender, number, and case.

6:24 **Οὐδεὶς δύναται** at the beginning of the sentence emphasizes the nature of the difficulty of serving two masters and begins the chiastic verse. **δυσὶ κυρίοις δουλεύειν**: the complementary infinitive governs the dative case. δυσὶ is an additional form probably created by analogy to the declension of the numeral three. The regular declension of the dual form is δυοῖν both in the genitive and in the dative (App. 51). δύο may also appear as indeclinable.

ἢ γὰρ τὸν ἕνα μισήσει καὶ τὸν ἕτερον ἀγαπήσει, ἢ ἑνὸς ἀνθέξεται καὶ τοῦ ἑτέρου καταφρονήσει. οὐ δύνασθε θεῷ δουλεύειν καὶ μαμωνᾷ.
6:25 Διὰ τοῦτο λέγω ὑμῖν, μὴ μεριμνᾶτε τῇ ψυχῇ ὑμῶν τί φάγητε [ἢ τί πίητε],

---

6:24
ἤ either, or, than (conjunction)
εἷς, μία, ἕν one, single (numeral)
μισέω, μισήσω, ἐμίσησα, μεμίσηκα hate, detest, abhor; love less, esteem less
ἕτερος, α, ον other, another
ἀγαπάω, ἀγαπήσω, ἠγάπησα, ἠγάπηκα, ἠγάπημαι, ἠγαπήθην love, cherish, value
ἤ either, or, than (conjunction)
ἀντέχω, ἀνθέξομαι cling to, adhere to, be devoted to
καταφρονέω, καταφρονήσω, κατεφρόνησα look down on, scorn, despise
οὐ not (οὐκ before vowels with a smooth breathing, οὐχ before a rough breathing, adverb)
δύναμαι, δυνήσομαι, ἠδυνήθην be able
θεός, οῦ, ὁ God, god
δουλεύω, δουλεύσω, ἐδούλευσα, δεδούλευκα be a slave, be subjected, serve as a slave, serve
μαμωνᾶς, ᾶ, ὁ wealth, property, Mammon
6:25
διά through, by (preposition + genitive); because of, for the sake of (+ accusative); διὰ τοῦτο therefore, for this reason
μεριμνάω, μεριμνήσω, ἐμερίμνησα have anxiety, be anxious; expend careful thought, concern oneself
ψυχή, ῆς, ἡ breath, life, soul, heart
τίς, τί, (τίνος) who? what? why? (interrogative pronoun)
ἐσθίω, φάγομαι, ἔφαγον (2 aorist) eat
ἤ either, or, than (conjunction)
πίνω, πίομαι, ἔπιον, πέπωκα drink

6:24 **μισήσει . . . ἀγαπήσει . . . ἀνθέξεται . . . καταφρονήσει**: the chiastic order in the middle of the verse makes emphatic the dilemma of serving two masters. **οὐ δύνασθε** at the beginning of the line repeats the negation at the beginning of the verse and ends the chiasmus. However, the last line personalizes the servant by the second person and the masters as **θεῷ . . . καὶ μαμωνᾷ**.

6:25 **Διὰ τοῦτο**: *for this reason*; the prepositional phrase resumes the preceding theme of not being a slave to wealth. **μὴ μερινᾶτε τῇ ψυχῇ ὑμῶν**: *do not be anxious for your life*; the prohibitive subjunctive takes a dative of advantage and introduces indirect questions, before which supply *about.*

μηδὲ τῷ σώματι ὑμῶν τί ἐνδύσησθε. οὐχὶ ἡ ψυχὴ πλεῖόν ἐστιν τῆς τροφῆς καὶ τὸ σῶμα τοῦ ἐνδύματος; 6:26 ἐμβλέψατε εἰς τὰ πετεινὰ τοῦ οὐρανοῦ ὅτι οὐ σπείρουσιν οὐδὲ θερίζουσιν οὐδὲ συνάγουσιν εἰς ἀποθήκας, καὶ ὁ πατὴρ ὑμῶν ὁ οὐράνιος τρέφει αὐτά·

6:25

μηδέ and not, but not, nor (following a negation)

σῶμα, ατος, τό body

τίς, τί, (τίνος) who? what? why? (interrogative pronoun)

ἐνδύω, ἐνδύσω, ἐνέδυσα dress, clothe; clothe oneself in, put on, wear (middle)

οὐχί not; no, by no means (adverb; more intensive form of οὐ)

ψυχή, ῆς, ἡ breath, life, soul, heart

πλείων, πλεῖον or πλέον more, greater, larger; πλεῖον/πλέον more (comparative adverb)

τροφή, ῆς, ἡ nourishment, food

σῶμα, ατος, τό body

ἔνδυμα, ατος, τό garment, clothing; cloak, mantle

6:26

ἐμβλέπω, ἐμβλέψω, ἐνέβλεψα see, behold, perceive, look attentively at

πετεινόν, οῦ, τό bird, fowl

οὐ not (οὐκ before vowels with a smooth breathing, οὐχ before a rough breathing, adverb)

σπείρω, σπερῶ, ἔσπειρα, ἔσπαρμαι, ἐσπάρην sow

οὐδέ and not, nor (conjunction and adverb)

θερίζω, θερίσω, ἐθέρισα reap, harvest

συνάγω, συνάξω, συνήγαγον (2 aorist), συνῆγμαι, συνήχθην gather in, gather up, bring together; convene, come together, meet (passive)

ἀποθήκη, ης, ἡ granary, storehouse, barn

οὐράνιος, ία, ιον heavenly, celestial

τρέφω, θρέψω, ἔθρεψα feed, nourish, support

6:25 **τί φάγητε . . . τί πίητε . . . τί ἐνδύσησθε**: *what you will eat . . . what you will drink . . . what you will wear*; indirect questions retain the mood and the tense of the direct question. Since these are originally deliberative questions, they retain the subjunctive mood. The deliberative subjunctive (present or aorist) is used when the speaker is perplexed about *what he is to do* or *say* or *think*, etc. Since the future is also used in deliberate questions, the subjunctive is appropriately translated by the future. **πλεῖόν . . . τῆς τροφῆς . . . τοῦ ἐνδύματος**: the comparative adverb takes a genitive of comparison (App. 65). Supply πλεῖον in the parallel but slightly elliptical second clause.

6:26 **ἐμβλέψατε**: the prefixed preposition is commonly repeated either by the same or a similar preposition; before a **β** the **ν** becomes **μ**. **ὅτι . . . καὶ**: *because . . . and yet*. **οὐ** begins a tricolon of negatives and finite verbs.

οὐχ ὑμεῖς μᾶλλον διαφέρετε αὐτῶν; 6:27 τίς δὲ ἐξ ὑμῶν μεριμνῶν δύναται προσθεῖναι ἐπὶ τὴν ἡλικίαν αὐτοῦ πῆχυν ἕνα; 6:28 καὶ περὶ ἐνδύματος τί μεριμνᾶτε; καταμάθετε τὰ κρίνα τοῦ ἀγροῦ

6:26

μᾶλλον more, to a greater degree, rather (adverb)

διαφέρω, διοίσω, διήνεγκα carry through; differ, be different; be better, be worth more than, be superior to

6:27

τίς, τί, (τίνος) who? what? why? (interrogative pronoun)

μεριμνάω, μεριμνήσω, ἐμερίμνησα have anxiety, be anxious; expend careful thought, concern oneself

δύναμαι, δυνήσομαι, ἠδυνήθην be able

προστίθημι, προσθήσω, προσέθηκα, προστέθεικα, προστέθειμαι, προσετέθην add; provide, give, grant, do

ἡλικία, ας, ἡ age, time of life; stature

πῆχυς, εως, ὁ cubit (17 to 18 inches)

εἷς, μία, ἕν one, single (numeral)

6:28

περί about, concerning (preposition + genitive); about, around (+ accusative)

ἔνδυμα, ατος, τό garment, clothing; cloak, mantle

τίς, τί, (τίνος) who? what? why? (interrogative pronoun)

μεριμνάω, μεριμνήσω, ἐμερίμνησα have anxiety, be anxious; expend careful thought, concern oneself

καταμανθάνω, καταμαθήσομαι, κατέμαθον (2 aorist), καταμεμάθηκα observe, consider, contemplate

κρίνον, ου, τό lily

ἀγρός, οῦ, ὁ field

6:26 **μᾶλλον διαφέρετε αὐτῶν**: *much more valuable than they*; the comparative adverb modifies the verb. The verb governs a genitive of comparison. The argument *a minori ad maius* runs: if God takes care of the birds, how much more will He take care of you.

6:27 **τίς . . . ἐξ ὑμῶν**: *who of you*; the partitive idea is expressed with ἐξ and the genitive after τίς (App. 47). The accent distinguishes the interrogative pronoun from the indefinite. **μεριμνῶν**: *by constantly worrying*; a circumstantial participle may express time, cause, concession, condition, and other circumstances. It needs to be sensitively interpreted according to context. The present participle here expresses *means,* which regularly does not require an adverbial clause to bring out the idea latent in the participle, but it does indicate progressive, continued, and repeated action (aspect) in present time, which should not be slighted in translation. **προσθεῖναι ἐπὶ τὴν ἡλικίαν αὐτοῦ πῆχυν ἕνα** may be translated in two ways: *to add one measure of time to his age* or *to add one cubit to his stature*; in the first instance, the primary meaning of measurement of space πῆχυν ἕνα is used metaphorically in reference to time. In the second, τὴν ἡλικίαν, whose primary meaning is *age,* refers to physical height. Whatever the difficulty of the text, it is clear that worrying extends neither life nor stature.

6:28 **καταμάθετε**: the structure runs almost parallel to that of verse 26.

πῶς αὐξάνουσιν· οὐ κοπιῶσιν οὐδὲ νήθουσιν· 6:29 λέγω δὲ ὑμῖν ὅτι οὐδὲ Σολομὼν ἐν πάσῃ τῇ δόξῃ αὐτοῦ περιεβάλετο ὡς ἓν τούτων. 6:30 εἰ δὲ τὸν χόρτον τοῦ ἀγροῦ σήμερον ὄντα καὶ αὔριον εἰς κλίβανον βαλλόμενον ὁ θεὸς οὕτως ἀμφιέννυσιν, οὐ πολλῷ μᾶλλον ὑμᾶς, ὀλιγόπιστοι;

6:28
πῶς how? in what way? in what sense? (interrogative adverb)
αὐξάνω/αὔξω, αὐξήσω, ηὔξησα, ηὐξήθην grow, increase
κοπιάω, κοπιάσω, ἐκοπίασα, κεκοπίακα be weary, be tired, work hard, toil
οὐδέ and not, nor (conjunction and adverb)
νήθω, νήσω spin
6:29
οὐδέ not even (when single); and not, neither, nor (conjunction and adverb)
Σολομών, ῶνος, ὁ Solomon
δόξα, ης, ἡ glory, honor, majesty
περιβάλλω, περιβαλῶ, περέβαλον, περιβέβληκα, περεβλήθην cast around, throw around; clothe; clothe oneself, be clothed (middle)
ὡς as, like, when, after, about (with numerals), how, provided that (adverb, conjunction)
εἷς, μία, ἕν one, single (numeral)
6:30
εἰ if, whether
χόρτος, ου, ὁ grass
ἀγρός, οῦ, ὁ field
σήμερον today, this day (adverb)
αὔριον tomorrow (adverb)
κλίβανος, ου, ὁ oven, furnace
βάλλω, βαλῶ, ἔβαλον, βέβληκα, βέβλημαι, ἐβλήθην throw, sow, cast, place, put, bring
οὕτως so, thus, in this manner (adverb)
ἀμφιέννυμι, ἀμφιέσω, ἠμφίεσμαι clothe, dress
πολύς, πολλή, πολύ much, large, many (in plural); πολλῷ by far (adverb)
μᾶλλον more, to a greater degree, rather (adverb)
ὀλιγόπιστος, ον of little faith

6:29 **ἐν πάσῃ τῇ δόξῃ αὐτοῦ**: *in all his splendor*; the adjective stands in predicate position (App. 27).

6:30 **εἰ . . . αμφιέννυσιν**: the verb of the protasis is third person singular present active indicative of a **μι** verb (cf. App. 58). In this simple condition supply the future of the verb from the protasis ἀμφιέσει in this slightly elliptical apodosis. **σήμερον ὄντα καὶ αὔριον εἰς κλίβανον βαλλόμενον**: *although it exists today and tomorrow is cast into the furnace*; ὄντα and βαλλόμενον are circumstantial participles that express concession: the brevity of a season of grass contrasts to the length of life of a person. **πολλῷ μᾶλλον**: *much more* (literally: *more by much*); πολλῷ is a dative of degree of difference (App. 66). The argument *a minori ad maius* runs: if God takes care of the grass, how much more will He take care of you. **ὀλιγόπιστοι**: *o you of little faith*; the adjective turned substantive is in the vocative or case of address.

6:31 μὴ οὖν μεριμνήσητε λέγοντες, Τί φάγωμεν; ἤ, Τί πίωμεν; ἤ, Τί περιβαλώμεθα; 6:32 πάντα γὰρ ταῦτα τὰ ἔθνη ἐπιζητοῦσιν· οἶδεν γὰρ ὁ πατὴρ ὑμῶν ὁ οὐράνιος ὅτι χρῄζετε τούτων ἁπάντων. 6:33 ζητεῖτε δὲ πρῶτον τὴν βασιλείαν [τοῦ θεοῦ] καὶ τὴν δικαιοσύνην αὐτοῦ,

---

6:31
μεριμνάω, μεριμνήσω, ἐμερίμνησα have anxiety, be anxious; expend careful thought, concern oneself
τίς, τί, (τίνος) who? what? why? (interrogative pronoun)
ἐσθίω, φάγομαι, ἔφαγον (2 aorist) eat
ἤ either, or, than (conjunction)
περιβάλλω, περιβαλῶ, περέβαλον, περιβέβληκα, περεβλήθην cast around, throw around; clothe; put (something) on oneself, clothe oneself, be clothed (middle)
6:32
ἔθνος, ους, τό nation, people
ἐπιζητέω, ἐπιζητήσω, ἐπεζήτησα, ἐπεζητήθην search for, seek after; strive for, wish for; demand, desire
οἶδα know
οὐράνιος, ία, ιον heavenly, celestial
χρῄζω need, have need of, want, desire
ἅπας, ἅπασα, ἅπασαν all, whole, every
6:33
ζητέω, ζητήσω, ἐζήτησα, ἐζητήθην seek, desire, ask for
πρῶτον first (in time; adverb)
βασιλεία, ας, ἡ kingship, royal power, kingdom
δικαιοσύνη, ης, ἡ justice, righteousness, godliness

6:31 **μὴ ... μεριμνήσητε**: the negative particle introduces a second person aorist subjunctive which often expresses prohibitions and is called *prohibitive subjunctive*. It has the force of (take care that you) *do not worry.* **Τί φάγωμεν ... Τί πίωμεν ... Τί περιβαλώμεθα**: *what are we to eat ... what are we to drink ... what are we to wear*; this tricolon of direct questions in the subjunctive mood poses deliberative questions. The deliberative subjunctive (present or aorist) is used when the speaker is perplexed about *what he is to do* or *say* or *think*, etc. It is usually in the first person. Since the future is also used in deliberate questions, the subjunctive may also be translated by the future.

6:32 **πάντα ... ταῦτα** are a sytactical unit. **τὰ ἔθνη ἐπιζητοῦσιν**: neuter plural subjects are considered as collective nouns and regularly take a singular verb. However, a plural verb may be used when stress is laid on the plurality of persons or parts. **χρῄζετε τούτων ἁπάντων**: the verb takes an objective genitive (cf. App. 65). ἅπας is a strengthened form of πᾶς (App. 27). The prefix ἀ- or ἁ- (alpha copulative) may indicate union, likeness, and intensity and is derived from ἅμα *together.*

6:33 **ζητεῖτε δὲ πρῶτον τὴν βασιλείαν**: in contrast to what the Gentiles do (32). πρῶτον is an adverb of degree: *above all.*

καὶ ταῦτα πάντα προστεθήσεται ὑμῖν. 6:34 μὴ οὖν μεριμνήσητε εἰς τὴν αὔριον, ἡ γὰρ αὔριον μεριμνήσει ἑαυτῆς· ἀρκετὸν τῇ ἡμέρᾳ ἡ κακία αὐτῆς.

6:33

προστίθημι, προσθήσω, προσέθηκα, προστέθεικα, προστέθειμαι, προσετέθην add, add to; provide, give, grant, do

6:34

μεριμνάω, μεριμνήσω, ἐμερίμνησα have anxiety, be anxious; expend careful thought, concern oneself

αὔριον tomorrow (adverb)

ἑαυτοῦ, ῆς, οῦ himself, herself, itself; themselves, ourselves, yourselves (in plural)

ἀρκετός, ή, όν sufficient, enough, adequate

ἡμέρα, ας, ἡ day

κακία, ας, ἡ depravity, wickedness, vice; evil, trouble, misfortune

---

6:33 **ταῦτα πάντα προστεθήσεται ὑμῖν**: neuter plural subjects are considered as collective nouns and regularly take a singular verb. The verb is third person singular first future passive indicative (cf. App. 53, G, 1) and takes a dative object.

6:34 **μὴ μεριμνήσητε**: the negative particle introduces a prohibitive subjunctive. **εἰς τὴν ἄυριον**: *about the next day*; the article combines with the adverb to form a substantive. **μεριμνήσει ἑαυτῆς**: *will worry about itself*; the verb takes an objective genitive reflexive pronoun (App. 46). **ἀρκετὸν τῇ ἡμέρᾳ ἡ κακία αὐτῆς**: *a sufficient task for the day is its trouble*; ἀρκετὸν is used as a substantive (literally: *a sufficient thing*), which may be interpreted according to context; it is not a predicate adjective in agreement with ἡ κακία. It takes the dative case. Supply the verb ἐστί in this sentential statement.

7 Μὴ κρίνετε, ἵνα μὴ κριθῆτε· 7:2 ἐν ᾧ γὰρ κρίματι κρίνετε
κριθήσεσθε, καὶ ἐν ᾧ μέτρῳ μετρεῖτε μετρηθήσεται ὑμῖν. 7:3 τί δὲ
βλέπεις τὸ κάρφος τὸ ἐν τῷ ὀφθαλμῷ τοῦ ἀδελφοῦ σου, τὴν δὲ ἐν τῷ
σῷ ὀφθαλμῷ δοκὸν οὐ κατανοεῖς; 7:4 ἢ πῶς ἐρεῖς τῷ ἀδελφῷ σου,

---

7:1
κρίνω, κρινῶ, ἔκρινα, κέκρικα, κέκριμαι, ἐκρίθην separate, select, judge, condemn
ἵνα to, in order to, in order that, that (conjunction)
7:2
κρίμα, ατος, τό judging, judgment, condemnation
κρίνω, κρινῶ, ἔκρινα, κέκρικα, κέκριμαι, ἐκρίθην separate, select, judge, condemn
μέτρον, ου, τό measure
μετρέω, μετρήσω, ἐμέτρησα measure; give out, apportion
7:3
βλέπω, βλέψω, ἔβλεψα see, behold, perceive
κάρφος, ους, τό speck, bit, small particle (of straw, chaff, wood)
ὀφθαλμός, οῦ, ὁ eye
ἀδελφός, οῦ, ὁ brother
σός, σή, σόν your, yours
δοκός, οῦ, ἡ beam of wood
κατανοέω, κατανοήσω notice, observe; look at, mark, discern; consider
7:4
ἤ either, or, than (conjunction)
πῶς how? in what way? in what sense? (interrogative adverb)

7:1 **Μὴ κρίνετε**: the command is qualified by the following verses and John adds: κατ' ὄψιν, ἀλλὰ τὴν δικαίαν κρίσιν κρίνετε (7:24).

7:2 **ἐν ᾧ γὰρ κρίματι**: *for with what judgment* (literally: *for by the judgment with which*); κρίματι is a dative of means and serves as the antecedent to the relative pronoun. **ἐν ᾧ μέτρῳ** parallels the construction above. **μετρηθήσεται**: *it will be measured*; is an impersonal third person singular first future passive indicative. The interchange of the active and passive of the same verbs and the repetition of nouns and relative pronouns stress the standard of fairness of the true judge.

7:3 **τί**: *why*; The interrogative pronoun (App. 47) distinguishes itself from the indefinite pronoun (cf. App. 48) by the accent. **τὸ ἐν τῷ ὀφθαλμῷ**: the article may be followed by a prepositional phrase and stand in attributive position as part of the substantive. **τὴν δὲ ἐν τῷ σῷ ὀφθαλμῷ δοκὸν**: the hyperbaton of the article at the beginning and its noun at the end of the phrase suggests that the wooden beam across the eye completely covers it.

7:4 **ἐρεῖς** is the second person singular future active indicative of the verb λέγω. The future is conjugated like the present active indicative of a contracted verb with stem in **ε** (cf. App. 56).

Ἄφες ἐκβάλω τὸ κάρφος ἐκ τοῦ ὀφθαλμοῦ σου, καὶ ἰδοὺ ἡ δοκὸς ἐν τῷ ὀφθαλμῷ σοῦ; 7:5 ὑποκριτά, ἔκβαλε πρῶτον ἐκ τοῦ ὀφθαλμοῦ σοῦ τὴν δοκόν, καὶ τότε διαβλέψεις ἐκβαλεῖν τὸ κάρφος ἐκ τοῦ ὀφθαλμοῦ τοῦ ἀδελφοῦ σου. 7:6 Μὴ δῶτε τὸ ἅγιον τοῖς κυσὶν μηδὲ βάλητε τοὺς μαργαρίτας ὑμῶν ἔμπροσθεν τῶν χοίρων,

---

7:4
ἀφίημι, ἀφήσω, ἀφῆκα, ἀφῆν (2 aorist), ἀφεῖκα, ἀφεῖμαι, ἀφέθην let go, forgive, leave
ἐκβάλλω, ἐκβαλῶ, ἐξέβαλον, ἐκβέβληκα, ἐξεβλήθην drive out, expel, disdain, spurn, send out, lead out, take out, bring out
κάρφος, ους, τό speck, bit, small particle (of straw, chaff, wood)
ὀφθαλμός, οῦ, ὁ eye
ἰδού see, look, behold (demonstrative particle)
δοκός, οῦ, ἡ beam of wood
7:5
ὑποκριτής, οῦ, ὁ hypocrite, pretender, dissembler
ἐκβάλλω, ἐκβαλῶ, ἐξέβαλον, ἐκβέβληκα, ἐξεβλήθην drive out, expel, disdain, spurn, send out, lead out, take out
πρῶτον first (in time; adverb)
ὀφθαλμός, οῦ, ὁ eye
δοκός, οῦ, ἡ beam of wood
διαβλέπω, διαβλέψω, διέβλεψα look intently; see clearly (+ infinitive)
κάρφος, ους, τό speck, bit, small particle (of straw, chaff, wood)
7:6
δίδωμι, δώσω, ἔδωκα, ἔδων (2 aorist), δέδωκα, δέδομαι, ἐδόθην give
ἅγιος, ια, ιον hallowed, pure, holy, sacred
κύων, κυνός, ὁ dog
βάλλω, βαλῶ, ἔβαλον, βέβληκα, βέβλημαι, ἐβλήθην throw, sow, cast, place, put, bring
μαργαρίτης, ου, ὁ pearl
ἔμπροσθεν in front of, before, in the presence of (adverb; preposition + genitive)
χοῖρος, ου, ὁ young pig, swine
μήποτε not; that . . . not, lest, (in order) that . . . not

7:4 **Ἄφες ἐκβάλω**: *let me take out*; the imperative of this verb is used with the subjunctive especially in the first person to emphasize the idea of *let, allow, permit,* already inherent in the subjunctive. ἐκβάλω is a first person singular second aorist active subjunctive (cf. App. 54), used as a hortatory subjunctive. Like the prohibitive and deliberative, it is an independent subjunctive. It is used to express a request or a proposal in the first person.

7:5 **ὑποκριτά** is in the vocative or case of address (cf. App. 3). **ἐκβαλεῖν** is second aorist infinitive. It functions as an infinitive of purpose and is equivalent to the more commonly used ἵνα clause.

7:6 **Μὴ δῶτε τὸ ἅγιον**: Μὴ introduces a prohibitive subjunctive. The finite form is second person plural second aorist active subjunctive (cf. App. 58). τὸ ἅγιον: *that which is holy*; the article and the adjective combine to form a substantive. **μηδὲ βάλητε**: μὴ introduces a prohibitive subjunctive. The form of the verb is second person plural second aorist active subjunctive (cf. App. 54).

μήποτε καταπατήσουσιν αὐτοὺς ἐν τοῖς ποσὶν αὐτῶν καὶ στραφέντες ῥήξωσιν ὑμᾶς.

7:7 Αἰτεῖτε καὶ δοθήσεται ὑμῖν, ζητεῖτε καὶ εὑρήσετε, κρούετε καὶ
ἀνοιγήσεται ὑμῖν· 7:8 πᾶς γὰρ ὁ αἰτῶν λαμβάνει καὶ ὁ ζητῶν εὑρίσκει
καὶ τῷ κρούοντι ἀνοιγήσεται.

7:6

καταπατέω, καταπατήσω trample upon, tread upon; disdain, treat with disdain

πούς, ποδός, ὁ foot

στρέφω, στρέψω, ἔστρεψα, ἔστραμμαι, ἐστρέφθην, ἐστράφην (2 aorist passive) turn, make a change, change

ῥήγνυμι/ῥήσσω, ῥήξω, ἔρ(ρ)ηξα tear in pieces; break, burst

7:7

αἰτέω, αἰτήσω, ᾔτησα, ᾔτηκα ask, ask for, make a request

δίδωμι, δώσω, ἔδωκα, ἔδων (2 aorist), δέδωκα, δέδομαι, ἐδόθην give

ζητέω, ζητήσω, ἐζήτησα, ἐζητήθην seek, desire, ask for

εὑρίσκω, εὑρήσω, εὗρον (2 aorist), ηὕρηκα/εὕρηκα, εὑρέθην find, meet, discover, recognize

κρούω, κρούσω, ἔκρουσα knock (at a door)

ἀνοίγω, ἀνοίξω, ἀνέῳξα/ἤνοιξα, ἀνέῳγα, ἀνέῳγμαι, ἠνεῴχθην open

7:8

αἰτέω, αἰτήσω, ᾔτησα, ᾔτηκα ask, ask for, make a request

λαμβάνω, λήμψομαι, ἔλαβον, εἴληφα, εἴλημμαι, ἐλήφθην take, receive, accept

ζητέω, ζητήσω, ἐζήτησα, ἐζητήθην seek, desire, ask for

εὑρίσκω, εὑρήσω, εὗρον (2 aorist), ηὕρηκα/εὕρηκα, εὑρέθην find, meet, discover, recognize

κρούω, κρούσω, ἔκρουσα knock (at a door)

ἀνοίγω, ἀνοίξω, ἀνέῳξα/ἤνοιξα, ἀνέῳγα, ἀνέῳγμαι, ἠνεῴχθην open

---

7:6 **μήποτε καταπατήσουσιν**: *lest they trample*; a negative purpose clause may use the future indicative instead of the subjunctive with no difference in sense. **καὶ στραφέντες**: *and after they turn themselves around*; the verbal form is a masculine plural nominative second aorist passive participle (cf. App. 34) with reflexive meaning. The context indicates that their turning signals an attack.

7:7 **Αἰτεῖτε . . . ζητεῖτε** are second person plural present active imperatives of a contracted verb with stem in **ε** (cf. App. 56). **δοθήσεται** is an impersonal third person singular first future passive (cf. App. 53, G, 1), formed from the first aorist passive stem. **ἀνοιγήσεται** is an impersonal third person singular second future passive, formed from the second aorist passive stem (cf. App. 53, G, 1). The tricolon of imperatives and responses emphasizes the importance of human initiative in receiving divine guidance.

7:8 **πᾶς γὰρ ὁ αἰτῶν**: *for everyone who asks*; the article and the participle combine to form a substantive. **λαμβάνει . . . εὑρίσκει . . . ἀνοιγήσεται**: while the present tense of the first two verbs connotes a future, the third is future in both form and meaning.

7:9 ἢ τίς ἐστιν ἐξ ὑμῶν ἄνθρωπος, ὃν αἰτήσει ὁ υἱὸς αὐτοῦ ἄρτον,
μὴ λίθον ἐπιδώσει αὐτῷ; 7:10 ἢ καὶ ἰχθὺν αἰτήσει, μὴ ὄφιν ἐπιδώσει
αὐτῷ; 7:11 εἰ οὖν ὑμεῖς πονηροὶ ὄντες οἴδατε δόματα ἀγαθὰ διδόναι
τοῖς τέκνοις ὑμῶν, πόσῳ μᾶλλον ὁ πατὴρ ὑμῶν ὁ ἐν τοῖς οὐρανοῖς
δώσει ἀγαθὰ

7:9
ἤ either, or, than (conjunction)
αἰτέω, αἰτήσω, ᾔτησα, ᾔτηκα ask, ask for, make a request
υἱός, οῦ, ὁ son
ἄρτος, ου, ὁ bread, loaf of bread
λίθος, ου, ὁ stone
ἐπιδίδωμι, ἐπιδώσω give to

7:10
ἤ either, or, than (conjunction)
ἰχθύς, ύος, ὁ fish
αἰτέω, αἰτήσω, ᾔτησα, ᾔτηκα ask, ask for, make a request
ὄφις, εως, ὁ snake, serpent
ἐπιδίδωμι, ἐπιδώσω give to

7:11
εἰ if, whether
πονηρός, ά, όν bad, evil, wicked
οἶδα know how to (+ infinitive)
δόμα, ατος, τό gift, present
ἀγαθός, ή, όν good, profitable, upright
τέκνον, ου, τό child, descendant, posterity
πόσος, η, ον how great? how much?
μᾶλλον more, to a greater degree, rather (adverb)
δίδωμι, δώσω, ἔδωκα, ἔδων (2 aorist), δέδωκα, δέδομαι, ἐδόθην give

---

7:9 **ἢ τίς ἐστιν ἐξ ὑμῶν ἄνθρωπος**: the first correlative conjunction anticipates the second and may be omitted in translation. τίς functions as an interrogative adjective (App. 47) modifying ἄνθρωπος. ἐστιν: *is there*. The partitive idea is expressed with ἐξ and the genitive after τίς ἄνθρωπος. The slight hyperbaton gives pause in the rhythm of the sentence and invites reflection. **ὃν αἰτήσει ὁ υἱὸς αὐτοῦ ἄρτον, μὴ λίθον ἐπιδώσει αὐτῷ**: *if ever (whomever) his son asks (will ask) for bread, he will not give him a stone, will he*; the construction is a future most vivid conditional relative clause. It is introduced by a relative pronoun instead of εἰ and takes a future in both the protasis and apodosis. αἰτήσει takes a double accusative: one of the thing asked for and one of the person asked. The future may be replaced by the present. μή: the negative interrogative particle is used when a negative answer is expected: *he will not . . . , will he?*

7:10 **ἢ καὶ ἰχθὺν αἰτήσει**: *or likewise if he asks (will ask) for a fish*; the construction is the same as in the verse above.

7:11 **πονηροὶ ὄντες**: *although you are wicked*; the circumstantial participle expresses concession: the contrast is between mortals and God. **οἴδατε . . . διδόναι**: *you know how to give*; with the infinitive the verb means *know* or *understand how*. **πόσῳ μᾶλλον**: *(by) how much more*; πόσῳ is a dative of degree of difference (App. 66).

τοῖς αἰτοῦσιν αὐτόν. 7:12 Πάντα οὖν ὅσα ἐὰν θέλητε ἵνα ποιῶσιν ὑμῖν οἱ ἄνθρωποι, οὕτως καὶ ὑμεῖς ποιεῖτε αὐτοῖς· οὗτος γάρ ἐστιν ὁ νόμος καὶ οἱ προφῆται.

7:13 Εἰσέλθατε διὰ τῆς στενῆς πύλης· ὅτι πλατεῖα ἡ πύλη καὶ εὐρύχωρος ἡ ὁδὸς ἡ ἀπάγουσα εἰς τὴν ἀπώλειαν καὶ πολλοί εἰσιν οἱ εἰσερχόμενοι δι' αὐτῆς·

7:11
αἰτέω, αἰτήσω, ᾔτησα, ᾔτηκα ask, ask for, make a request
7:12
ὅσος, η, ον how large, how great; as many as (plural); whosoever, whatsoever
θέλω, θελήσω, ἠθέλησα wish to have, desire, purpose, want
ἵνα to, in order to, in order that, that (conjunction)
οὕτως so, thus, in this manner (adverb)
νόμος, ου, ὁ law, custom, ordinance
προφήτης, ου, ὁ prophet, seer, revelator
7:13
εἰσέρχομαι, εἰσελεύσομαι, εἰσῆλθον (2 aorist), εἰσελήλυθα come (in, into), go (in, into), enter into, share in, come to enjoy
στενός, ή, όν narrow, straight
πύλη, ης, ἡ gate
πλατύς, εῖα, ύ broad, wide
εὐρύχωρος, ον broad, spacious, wide
ὁδός, οῦ, ἡ road, way, journey
ἀπάγω, ἀπάξω, ἀπήγαγον, ἀπήχθην lead away; lead away (of a road; intransitive)
ἀπώλεια, ας, ἡ destruction; misery, eternal ruin
πολύς, πολλή, πολύ much, large, many (in plural)
εἰσέρχομαι, εἰσελεύσομαι, εἰσῆλθον (2 aorist), εἰσελήλυθα come (in, into), go (in, into), enter into, share in, come to enjoy
δι' = διά through, by (preposition + genitive); because of, for the sake of (+ accusative)

7:11 **τοῖς αἰτοῦσιν αὐτόν**: *to those who ask Him*; the article and present participle combine to form a substantive, but the participle (cf. App. 36) retains its ability to take an object. The form may be easily confused with a finite verb because it looks like a third person plural present active indicative (cf. App. 56).

7:12 **Πάντα οὖν ὅσα ἐὰν θέλητε**: *therefore, all that you desire*; ἐὰν introduces the protasis of a future more vivid condition. **ἵνα ποιῶσιν ὑμῖν οἱ ἄνθρωποι**: *that men do to you*; ἵνα introduces a final clause. **ποιεῖτε**: the construction may substitute an imperative for a future indicative in the apodosis.

7:13 **Εἰσέλθατε**: occasionally this second aorist stem takes first aorist endings without the **σ**. πλατεῖα ἡ πύλη: *wide is the gate*; the adjective outside of the article noun group stands in predicate position. **ἡ ἀπάγουσα**: *which leads away*; the participle stands in attributive position. Supply the verb ἐστίν. **τὴν ἀπώλειαν**: abstract nouns are generally modified by an article.

7:14 τί στενὴ ἡ πύλη καὶ τεθλιμμένη ἡ ὁδὸς ἡ ἀπάγουσα εἰς τὴν ζωὴν
καὶ ὀλίγοι εἰσὶν οἱ εὑρίσκοντες αὐτήν.
7:15 Προσέχετε ἀπὸ τῶν ψευδοπροφητῶν, οἵτινες ἔρχονται πρὸς
ὑμᾶς ἐν ἐνδύμασιν προβάτων, ἔσωθεν δέ εἰσιν λύκοι ἅρπαγες. 7:16
ἀπὸ τῶν καρπῶν αὐτῶν ἐπιγνώσεσθε αὐτούς. μήτι συλλέγουσιν ἀπὸ
ἀκανθῶν σταφυλὰς ἢ ἀπὸ τριβόλων σῦκα;

7:14

τίς, τί, (τίνος) who? what? why? (interrogative pronoun); τί how! (in exclamations)

στενός, ή, όν narrow, straight

πύλη, ης, ἡ gate

θλίβω, θλίψω, τέθλιμμαι press upon, make narrow; be restricted, narrow (passive)

ὁδός, οῦ, ἡ road, way, journey

ἀπάγω, ἀπάξω, ἀπήγαγον, ἀπήχθην lead away; lead away (of a road; intransitive)

ζωή, ῆς, ἡ life, life eternal

ὀλίγος, η, ον little, small; few (plural)

εὑρίσκω, εὑρήσω, εὗρον (2 aorist), ηὕρηκα/εὕρηκα, εὑρέθην find, meet, discover, recognize

7:15

προσέχω, προσέξω, προσέσχον (2 aorist) pay attention to, give heed to, consider; beware of, take heed of, guard against (followed by ἀπό, μή)

ψευδοπροφήτης, ου, ὁ false prophet

ὅστις, ἥτις, ὅ τι whoever, whatever; who, which, what (indefinite relative pronoun)

πρός for, for the purpose of (preposition + genitive); with, to, towards, unto, for, for the purpose of, with reference to, in relation to, of, concerning (+ accusative); near, at, by (preposition + dative)

ἔνδυμα, ατος, τό garment, clothing; cloak, mantle

πρόβατον, ου, τό sheep

ἔσωθεν from inside; inside, within (adverb)

λύκος, ου, ὁ wolf

ἅρπαξ, αγος ravenous; rapacious

7:16

καρπός, οῦ, ὁ fruit, crop; result, gain

ἐπιγινώσκω, ἐπιγνώσομαι, ἐπέγνων (2 aorist), ἐπέγνωκα, ἐπεγνώσθην know, understand, recognize; discern, detect

μήτι (interrogative particle in questions expecting a negative answer)

συλλέγω, συλλέξω, συνέλεξα collect, gather

ἄκανθα, ης, ἡ thorn

σταφυλή, ῆς, ἡ cluster or bunch of grapes, grapes

τρίβολος, ου, ὁ thistle

σῦκον, ου, τό fig

7:14 **τί στενὴ**: *how narrow*; **εἰς τὴν ζωὴν**: as often, life refers to life eternal.

7:15 **τῶν ψευδοπροφητῶν . . . ἐν ἐνδύμασιν προβάτων**: false prophets, similarly to the hypocrites, cover their true purposes by their appearance. The metaphor may refer to their use of flattering and sophistic language.

7:16 **ἐπιγνώσεσθε**: the verb is deponent only in the future tense. **ἀπὸ ἀκανθῶν σταφυλὰς ἢ ἀπὸ τριβόλων σῦκα** are traditional conceits of *adynaton* in themes of golden age literature.

7:17 οὕτως πᾶν δένδρον ἀγαθὸν καρποὺς καλοὺς ποιεῖ, τὸ δὲ σαπρὸν δένδρον καρποὺς πονηροὺς ποιεῖ. 7:18 οὐ δύναται δένδρον ἀγαθὸν καρποὺς πονηροὺς ποιεῖν οὐδὲ δένδρον σαπρὸν καρποὺς καλοὺς ποιεῖν. 7:19 πᾶν δένδρον μὴ ποιοῦν καρπὸν καλὸν ἐκκόπτεται καὶ εἰς πῦρ βάλλεται. 7:20 ἄρα γε ἀπὸ τῶν καρπῶν αὐτῶν ἐπιγνώσεσθε αὐτούς.

7:21 Οὐ πᾶς ὁ λέγων μοι, Κύριε κύριε, εἰσελεύσεται εἰς τὴν βασιλείαν τῶν οὐρανῶν, ἀλλ' ὁ ποιῶν τὸ θέλημα τοῦ πατρός μου τοῦ ἐν τοῖς οὐρανοῖς.

7:17
οὕτως so, thus, in this manner (adverb)
δένδρον, ου, τό tree
ἀγαθός, ή, όν good, profitable, upright
καρπός, οῦ, ὁ fruit, crop; result, gain
καλός, ή, όν good, useful, choice
σαπρός, ά, όν spoiled, rotten; bad, evil
πονηρός, ά, όν bad, evil, wicked
7:18
δύναμαι, δυνήσομαι, ἠδυνήθην be able
δένδρον, ου, τό tree
ἀγαθός, ή, όν good, profitable, upright
καρπός, οῦ, ὁ fruit, crop; result, gain
πονηρός, ά, όν bad, evil, wicked
οὐδέ and not, nor (conjunction and adverb)
σαπρός, ά, όν spoiled, rotten; bad, evil
καλός, ή, όν good, useful, choice
7:19
δένδρον, ου, τό tree
καρπός, οῦ, ὁ fruit, crop; result, gain
καλός, ή, όν good, useful, choice
ἐκκόπτω, ἐκκόψω, ἐξέκοψα, ἐξεκόπην cut out, cut off
πῦρ, πυρός, τό fire
βάλλω, βαλῶ, ἔβαλον, βέβληκα, βέβλημαι, ἐβλήθην throw, sow, cast, place, put, bring
7:20
ἄρα therefore, then, consequently (particle)
γε at least, indeed (an enclitic particle emphasizing the preceding word; often untranslatable)
καρπός, οῦ, ὁ fruit, crop; result, gain
ἐπιγινώσκω, ἐπιγνώσομαι, ἐπέγνων (2 aorist), ἐπέγνωκα, ἐπεγνώσθην know, understand, recognize; discern, detect
7:21
εἰσέρχομαι, εἰσελεύσομαι, εἰσῆλθον (2 aorist), εἰσελήλυθα come (in, into), go (in, into), enter into, share in, come to enjoy
θέλημα, ατος, τό will, desire

7:19 **πᾶν δένδρον μὴ ποιοῦν . . . ἐκκόπτεται**: *every tree, if it does not produce . . . is cut down*; since the circumstantial participle may express a condition, μὴ and the participle constitute the protasis of a simple or particular condition (App. 70) with the verb of the apodosis standing in the indicative.

7:20 **ἐπιγνώσεσθε**: the verb is deponent only in the future tense.

7:21 **Οὐ πᾶς ὁ λέγων μοι, Κύριε**: *not everyone who says to me, Lord*; an outward confession does not prove a true inner conviction.

7:22 πολλοὶ ἐροῦσίν μοι ἐν ἐκείνῃ τῇ ἡμέρᾳ, Κύριε κύριε, οὐ τῷ σῷ ὀνόματι ἐπροφητεύσαμεν, καὶ τῷ σῷ ὀνόματι δαιμόνια ἐξεβάλομεν, καὶ τῷ σῷ ὀνόματι δυνάμεις πολλὰς ἐποιήσαμεν; 7:23 καὶ τότε ὁμολογήσω αὐτοῖς ὅτι Οὐδέποτε ἔγνων ὑμᾶς· ἀποχωρεῖτε ἀπ' ἐμοῦ οἱ ἐργαζόμενοι τὴν ἀνομίαν.

7:22
πολύς, πολλή, πολύ much, large, many (in plural)
ἐκεῖνος, η, ον that, that one, the former
ἡμέρα, ας, ἡ day
σός, σή, σόν your, yours
ὄνομα, ατος, τό name
προφητεύω, προφητεύσω, ἐπροφήτευσα proclaim a divine revelation, prophetically reveal, prophesy
δαιμόνιον, ου, τό deity, divinity; demon, evil spirit
ἐκβάλλω, ἐκβαλῶ, ἐξέβαλον, ἐκβέβληκα, ἐξεβλήθην drive out, expel, disdain, spurn, send out, lead out
δύναμις, εως, ἡ power; ability; deed of power, miracle, wonder
7:23
ὁμολογέω, ὁμολογήσω, ὡμολόγησα assure, admit, confess, declare (publicly)
οὐδέποτε never (adverb)
γινώσκω, γνώσομαι, ἔγνων, ἔγνωκα, ἔγνωσμαι, ἐγνώσθην know, learn, understand
ἀποχωρέω, ἀποχωρήσω go from, go away, depart
ἐργάζομαι, ἐργάσομαι, ἠργασάμην/εἰργασάμην, εἴργασμαι work, do, accomplish, perform
ἀνομία, ας, ἡ lawlessness, iniquity, sin

7:22 **Κύριε . . . ἐπροφεύσαμεν . . . δαιμόνια ἐξεβάλομεν . . . δυνάμεις πολλὰς ἐποιήσαμεν**: the impressive tricolon of verbs does not impress the Lord: even outwardly proper actions do not prove proper motives; only the meek ὁ ποιῶν τὸ θέλημα τοῦ πατρός (21) will be acknowledged.

7:23 **Οὐδέποτε ἔγνων ὑμᾶς**: *I never knew you*; the form of the verb is a third person singular. The personal endings of the second aorist of γινώσκω are inflected: ἔγνων, ἔγνως, ἔγνω, ἔγνωμεν, ἔγνωτε, ἔγνωσαν (App. 61). **ἀποχωρεῖτε . . . οἱ ἐργαζόμενοι τὴν ἀνομίαν**: *depart . . . you who perform iniquity*; the participle agrees in person with the subject of the imperative. Abstract nouns are generally modified by an article.

7:24 Πᾶς οὖν ὅστις ἀκούει μου τοὺς λόγους τούτους καὶ ποιεῖ αὐτούς, ὁμοιωθήσεται ἀνδρὶ φρονίμῳ, ὅστις ᾠκοδόμησεν αὐτοῦ τὴν οἰκίαν ἐπὶ τὴν πέτραν· 7:25 καὶ κατέβη ἡ βροχὴ καὶ ἦλθον οἱ ποταμοὶ καὶ ἔπνευσαν οἱ ἄνεμοι καὶ προσέπεσαν τῇ οἰκίᾳ ἐκείνῃ, καὶ οὐκ ἔπεσεν, τεθεμελίωτο γὰρ ἐπὶ τὴν πέτραν.

7:24

ὅστις, ἥτις, ὅ τι whoever, whatever; who, which, what (indefinite relative pronoun)

λόγος, ου, ὁ word, doctrine, account, reason, statement, saying

ὁμοιόω, ὁμοιώσω, ὁμοίωσα, ὡμοιώθην make like, liken, compare; be like, be made like, become like, resemble (passive)

ἀνήρ, ἀνδρός, ὁ man, male, husband

φρόνιμος, η, ον thoughtful, prudent, wise

ὅστις, ἥτις, ὅ τι whoever, whatever; who, which, what (indefinite relative pronoun)

οἰκοδομέω, οἰκοδομήσω, ᾠκοδόμησα, ᾠκοδομήθην build, construct, establish

οἰκία, ας, ἡ house, household, family

πέτρα, ας, ἡ rock

7:25

καταβαίνω, καταβήσομαι, κατέβην, καταβέβηκα come down, go down, descend, fall

βροχή, ῆς, ἡ rain

ποταμός, οῦ, ὁ river, stream, torrent

πνέω, πνεύσω, ἔπνευσα blow

ἄνεμος, ου, ὁ wind

προσπίπτω, προσπεσοῦμαι, προσέπεσον (2 aorist) fall upon; rush upon, beat against

οἰκία, ας, ἡ house, household, family

ἐκεῖνος, η, ον that, that one, the former

πίπτω, πεσοῦμαι, ἔπεσα, ἔπεσον (2 aorist), πέπτωκα fall, fall prostrate, fall down

θεμελιόω, θεμελιώσω, ἐθεμελίωσα, τεθεμελίωκα, τεθεμελίωμαι found, establish

πέτρα, ας, ἡ rock

7:24 **τοὺς λόγους τούτους**: *these sayings*; demonstrative pronouns (App. 41; 42) stand in predicate position. **ὁμοιωθήσεται ἀνδρὶ φρονίμῳ**: *will be likened to a wise man*; the verb is a third person plural first future passive indicative (cf. App. 53, G, 1) and governs a dative object. **ἐπὶ τὴν πέτραν**: *on rock*; the generic article in the singular is included in Greek to denote a whole class and so to distinguish one type of material from another. Rock, as opposed to sand, is a suitable foundation for the buiding of a house.

7:25 **καὶ . . . καὶ . . . καὶ . . . καὶ . . . καὶ . . .** : the polysyndeton or repetition of conjunctions in the series of coordinate phrases intensifies the overwhelming nature of the disasters and the resolution. **τεθεμελίωτο**: *it had been founded*; the verb is a third person singular pluperfect passive indicative of a contracted verb with stem in **ο** (cf. App. 53, F).

7:26 καὶ πᾶς ὁ ἀκούων μου τοὺς λόγους τούτους καὶ μὴ ποιῶν αὐτοὺς ὁμοιωθήσεται ἀνδρὶ μωρῷ, ὅστις ᾠκοδόμησεν αὐτοῦ τὴν οἰκίαν ἐπὶ τὴν ἄμμον· 7:27 καὶ κατέβη ἡ βροχὴ καὶ ἦλθον οἱ ποταμοὶ καὶ ἔπνευσαν οἱ ἄνεμοι καὶ προσέκοψαν τῇ οἰκίᾳ ἐκείνῃ, καὶ ἔπεσεν καὶ ἦν ἡ πτῶσις αὐτῆς μεγάλη.

7:26

λόγος, ου, ὁ word, doctrine, account, reason, statement, saying

ὁμοιόω, ὁμοιώσω, ὁμοίωσα, ὡμοιώθην make like, liken, compare; be like, be made like, become like, resemble (passive)

ἀνήρ, ἀνδρός, ὁ man, male, husband

μωρός, ά, όν foolish, wicked, impious

ὅστις, ἥτις, ὅ τι whoever, whatever; who, which, what (indefinite relative pronoun)

οἰκοδομέω, οἰκοδομήσω, ᾠκοδόμησα, ᾠκοδομήθην build, construct, establish

οἰκία, ας, ἡ house, household, family

ἄμμος, ου, ἡ sand

7:27

καταβαίνω, καταβήσομαι, κατέβην, καταβέβηκα come down, go down, descend, fall

βροχή, ῆς, ἡ rain

ποταμός, οῦ, ὁ river, stream, torrent

πνέω, πνεύσω, ἔπνευσα blow

ἄνεμος, ου, ὁ wind

προσκόπτω, προσκόψω, προσέκοψα dash against, beat upon, strike (the foot) against; stumble

οἰκία, ας, ἡ house, household, family

ἐκεῖνος, η, ον that, that one, the former

πίπτω, πεσοῦμαι, ἔπεσα, ἔπεσον (2 aorist), πέπτωκα fall, fall prostrate, fall down

πτῶσις, εως, ἡ fall, crash, ruin

μέγας, μεγάλη, μέγα large, great

7:26 **καὶ πᾶς ὁ ἀκούων . . . καὶ μὴ ποιῶν . . . ὁμοιωθήσεται**: *and every one, if he hears . . . and does not carry out . . . will be likened to*; an attributive participle may be circumstantial. A circumstantial participle may be interpreted conditionally and so replace the protasis of any condition. It is used instead of ἐάν with the subjunctive in the protasis. The protasis and the future indicative in the apodosis form a future more vivid condition (App. 70). This and the next verse are antithetical to the previous two.

7:28 Καὶ ἐγένετο ὅτε ἐτέλεσεν ὁ Ἰησοῦς τοὺς λόγους τούτους, ἐξεπλήσσοντο οἱ ὄχλοι ἐπὶ τῇ διδαχῇ αὐτοῦ· 7:29 ἦν γὰρ διδάσκων αὐτοὺς ὡς ἐξουσίαν ἔχων καὶ οὐχ ὡς οἱ γραμματεῖς αὐτῶν.

7:28

γίνομαι, γενήσομαι, ἐγενόμην, γέγονα/γεγένημαι, ἐγενήθην become, be made, be created; arise, occur, come to pass, happen; be born, come, arrive, be present

ὅτε when, whenever (adverb)

τελέω, τελέσω, ἐτέλεσα, τετέλεκα, τετέλεσμαι, ἐτελέσθην finish, end, fulfill, accomplish

λόγος, ου, ὁ word, doctrine, account, reason, statement, saying

ἐκπλήσσω, ἐκπλήξω, ἐξέπληξα, ἐξεπλάγην amaze, astound, overwhelm

ὄχλος, ου, ὁ crowd, throng, multitude

διδαχή, ῆς, ἡ teaching, instruction

7:29

διδάσκω, διδάξω, ἐδίδαξα, ἐδιδάχθην teach, instruct

ὡς as, like, when, after, about (with numerals), how, provided that (adverb, conjunction)

ἐξουσία, ας, ἡ authority, right, ability, might, power

ἔχω, ἕξω, ἔσχον (2 aorist), ἔσχηκα have, keep, cause, consider; be (with adverbs and indications of time and age); be able (with infinitive)

γραμματεύς, έως, ὁ secretary, clerk, scholar versed in law, scribe

---

7:28 **ὅτε ἐτέλεσεν ὁ Ἰησοῦς . . . ἐξεπλήσσοντο οἱ ὄχλοι**: *When Jesus had made an end of . . . the crowds were amazed*; since the action of the aorist precedes that of the imperfect (ἐξεπλήσσοντο), it is translated as a pluperfect. The audience, consisting initially of disciples (5:1), has turned into crowds by the end of His teaching on the mount.

7:29 **ἦν . . . διδάσκων** is a periphrastic construction. The periphrastic construction of the imperfect of εἰμί and a present participle is used to form an imperfect tense instead of the imperfect active indicative. **ὡς ἐξουσίαν ἔχων**: Jesus spoke authoritatively because He had been sent by the Father and had been given authority by Him (11:27). The source and authority of commission is also an important theme in the Gospel of John: the son μονογενής was sent παρὰ πατρός (Jn 1:14), John the Baptist was sent ἀπεσταλμένος παρὰ θεοῦ (Jn 1:6), the priests and Levites (Jn 1:19) were sent ἀπεσταλμένοι ἐκ τῶν Φαρισαίων.

8 Καταβάντος δὲ αὐτοῦ ἀπὸ τοῦ ὄρους ἠκολούθησαν αὐτῷ ὄχλοι πολλοί. 8:2 καὶ ἰδοὺ λεπρὸς προσελθὼν προσεκύνει αὐτῷ λέγων, Κύριε, ἐὰν θέλῃς δύνασαί με καθαρίσαι.

8:1
καταβαίνω, καταβήσομαι, κατέβην, καταβέβηκα come down, go down, descend, fall
ὄρος, ους, τό mountain, hill
ἀκολουθέω, ἀκολουθήσω, ἠκολούθησα, ἠκολούθηκα follow (+ dative)
ὄχλος, ου, ὁ crowd, throng, multitude
πολύς, πολλή, πολύ much, large, many (in plural)
8:2
λεπρός, οῦ, ὁ leper
προσέρχομαι, προσελεύσομαι, προσῆλθον, προσελήλυθα come to, go to, approach
προσκυνέω, προσκυνήσω, προσεκύνησα worship, prostrate oneself before, reverence before, reverence
θέλω, θελήσω, ἠθέλησα wish to have, desire, purpose, want
δύναμαι, δυνήσομαι, ἠδυνήθην be able
καθαρίζω, καθαρίσω, ἐκαθάρισα cleanse, render pure

8:1 **Καταβάντος δὲ αὐτοῦ**: *as He came down*; the construction is a *genitive absolute*. The pronoun αὐτοῦ and the circumstantial participle Καταβάντος in the genitive case are syntactically independent of the main verb and clause, i.e., the subject of the genitive absolute may not be used as the subject or the object of the main verb. However, New Testament language does not commonly adhere to classical usage: in this sentence the pronoun is used both as the subject of the genitive absolute and as the dative object of the main verb. A circumstantial participle may express time, cause, concession, condition, and other circumstances. It needs to be sensitively interpreted according to context and translated into English as a clause (App. 65). The healings in this section frequently follow a formulaic pattern: a participial construction with Jesus as the subject, a prepositional phrase indicating direction where or from where, a person addressing Jesus, an expression of ready willingness, a miracle, and words of instruction.

8:2 **ἐὰν θέλῃς δύνασαί με καθαρίσαι** is a present general condition (App. 70). Since this condition makes a factual statement about something that is always true in present time, the leper exhibits true faith. The complementary infinitive καθαρίσαι modifies both verbs θέλῃς and δύνασαί. The term where one element is shared by two constructions is called *apo koinou* (ἀπὸ κοινοῦ).

8:3 καὶ ἐκτείνας τὴν χεῖρα ἥψατο αὐτοῦ λέγων, Θέλω, καθαρίσθητι· καὶ εὐθέως ἐκαθαρίσθη αὐτοῦ ἡ λέπρα. 8:4 καὶ λέγει αὐτῷ ὁ Ἰησοῦς, Ὅρα μηδενὶ εἴπῃς,

---

8:3
ἐκτείνω, ἐκτενῶ, ἐξέτεινα stretch out, hold out
χείρ, χειρός, ἡ hand
ἅπτω, ἅψω, ἧψα fasten; light, kindle; touch (middle)
θέλω, θελήσω, ἠθέλησα wish to have, desire, purpose, want
καθαρίζω, καθαρίσω, ἐκαθάρισα cleanse, render pure
εὐθέως at once, immediately (adverb)
λέπρα, ας, ἡ leprosy
8:4
ὁράω, ὄψομαι, εἶδον (2 aorist), ἑώρακα/ἑόρακα, ὤφθην see, catch sight of, notice, look, observe, perceive, experience, witness
μηδείς, μηδεμία, μηδέν not one, none, no one, nothing

8:3 **ἐκτείνας . . . ἥψατο αὐτοῦ**: *after He had stretched forth . . . He touched him*; the first verbal form is an aorist active participle of a liquid verb; the endings are those of the aorist active participle, but it omits the **-σ-** (cf. App. 31). Since the action of the aorist participle precedes that of the aorist tense of the main verb, it is translated as a pluperfect. The main verb governs the genitive case. **Θέλω**: supply καθαρίσαι σε. **καθαρίσθητι** is second person singular first aorist passive imperative (cf. App. 53, G, 3).

8:4 **Ὅρα μηδενὶ εἴπῃς**: *take care not to speak to anyone*; Ὅρα is second person singular present active imperative of a contracted verb with stem in **α**. The verb takes a form of μὴ and an aorist subjunctive to indicate prohibition. The injunction to silence prohibits the leper to speak to anyone until he has been pronounced clean by the priest and has made appropriate sacrifices in accordance with the laws, rites, and sacrifices revealed for cleansing lepers (Lev 13, 14).

ἀλλὰ ὕπαγε σεαυτὸν δεῖξον τῷ ἱερεῖ καὶ προσένεγκον τὸ δῶρον ὃ προσέταξεν Μωϋσῆς, εἰς μαρτύριον αὐτοῖς.

8:5 Εἰσελθόντος δὲ αὐτοῦ εἰς Καφαρναοὺμ προσῆλθεν αὐτῷ ἑκατόνταρχος παρακαλῶν αὐτὸν 8:6 καὶ λέγων,

---

8:4

ἀλλά but, yet (conjunction)

ὑπάγω, ὑπάξω, ὑπήγαγον, ὑπήχθην go, go away, go home

σεαυτοῦ, ῆς, οῦ yourself (reflexive pronoun)

δείκνυμι/δεικνύω, δείξω, ἔδειξα, δέδειχα, ἐδείχθην show, point out, make known, demonstrate, announce

ἱερεύς, έως, ὁ priest

προσφέρω, προσοίσω, προσήνεγκα, προσήνεγκον (2 aorist), προσηνέχθην bring, offer, present

δῶρον, ου, τό gift, present

προστάσσω, προστάξω, προσέταξα, προστέταγμαι, προσετάχθην, προσετάγην (2 aorist passive) command, order, prescribe

Μωϋσῆς, έως, ὁ Moses

μαρτύριον, ίου, τό proof, testimony, evidence

8:5

εἰσέρχομαι, εἰσελεύσομαι, εἰσῆλθον (2 aorist), εἰσελήλυθα come (in, into), go (in, into), enter into, share in, come to enjoy

Καφαρναούμ, ἡ Capernaum (indeclinable)

προσέρχομαι, προσελεύσομαι, προσῆλθον, προσελήλυθα come to, go to, approach

ἑκατόνταρχος, ου, ὁ commander of 100 men, centurion

παρακαλέω, παρακαλέσω, παρεκάλεσα, παρακέκληκα, παρακέκλημαι, παρεκλήθην call for, summon, invite; appeal to, urge, encourage; request, implore entreat; comfort, cheer up

---

8:4 **ὕπαγε σεαυτὸν δεῖξον**: ὕπαγε is a second person singular present active imperative (cf. App. 53, A, 3). Supply καὶ: the imperative is usually found without a conjunction when followed by another imperative. **δεῖξον** is a second person singular aorist active imperative (cf. App. 53, D, 3). **προσένεγκον** is second person singular first aorist active imperative (cf. App. 53, D, 3). προσήνεγκα is used as a first aorist and, like liquid verbs, loses the intervocalic **σ**. **τῷ ἱερεῖ . . . αὐτοῖς**: whether because of lending dignity or an *allusive plural*, the figure *enallage* (interchange) allows a substitution of the plural for the singular. At any rate, the priest closely examines the leper, makes a pronouncement of clean or unclean, and presents the clean person at the door of the tabernacle of the congregation to offer sacrifices (Lev 13, 14).

8:5 **ἑκατόνταρχων** or centurion was captain over a hundred footsoldiers in the Roman army and and as a Gentile would have been considered on the fringes of society, like the leper.

Κύριε, ὁ παῖς μου βέβληται ἐν τῇ οἰκίᾳ παραλυτικός, δεινῶς βασανιζόμενος. 8:7 καὶ λέγει αὐτῷ, Ἐγὼ ἐλθὼν θεραπεύσω αὐτόν. 8:8 καὶ ἀποκριθεὶς ὁ ἑκατόνταρχος ἔφη, Κύριε, οὐκ εἰμὶ ἱκανὸς ἵνα μου ὑπὸ τὴν στέγην εἰσέλθῃς, ἀλλὰ μόνον εἰπὲ λόγῳ, καὶ ἰαθήσεται ὁ παῖς μου.

8:6

παῖς, παιδός, ὁ child, boy; servant

βάλλω, βαλῶ, ἔβαλον, βέβληκα, βέβλημαι, ἐβλήθην throw, sow, cast; lay, place, put; bring

οἰκία, ας, ἡ house, household, family

παραλυτικός, ή, όν lame, paralytic

δεινῶς dreadfully, greatly (adverb)

βασανίζω, βασανίσω, ἐβασάνισα, ἐβασανίσθην afflict, torment

8:7

θεραπεύω, θεραπεύσω, ἐθεράπευσα, ἐθεραπεύθην care for, heal, restore

8:8

ἀποκρίνομαι, ἀπεκρινάμην, ἀπεκρίθην answer, reply

ἑκατόνταρχος, ου, ὁ commander of 100 men, centurion

φημί, φήσω, ἔφησα say, speak

ἱκανός, ή, όν sufficient, enough; adequate, competent, qualified; fit, worthy

ἵνα to, in order to, in order that, that (conjunction)

ὑπό by (preposition + genitive of personal agent); under (+ accusative)

στέγη, ης, ἡ roof

εἰσέρχομαι, εἰσελεύσομαι, εἰσῆλθον (2 aorist), εἰσελήλυθα come (in, into), go (in, into), enter into

ἀλλά but, yet (conjunction)

μόνον only (adverb)

λόγος, ου, ὁ word, doctrine, account, reason, statement, saying

ἰάομαι, ἰάσομαι, ἰασάμην, ἴαμαι, ἰάθην heal, cure, restore

παῖς, παιδός, ὁ child, boy, youth; servant

8:6 **ὁ παῖς μου**: while the noun may refer to his servant, the centurion is probably concerned about the welfare of his son. In his account he seems to distinguish between his son, ὁ παῖς μου, and his servant, and τῷ δούλῳ μου (9). In John's account he is referred to as his son, ὁ υἱὸς, τὸ παιδίον, and ὁ παῖς (Jn 4:43–54); however, in Luke's he is called his servant, δοῦλος (Lk 7:1–10). **βέβληται . . . παραλυτικός**: *lies paralyzed*; the verb form is third person singular perfect passive indicative. The perfect tense denotes action (aspect) that is completed near present time and continues with present result: *he has been placed* (recently and *he lies* now). The reduplication or doubling of the stem at the beginning of a word occurs especially in the perfect, pluperfect, and future perfect tenses to indicate completed action. παραλυτικός is a predicate adjective.

8:7 **ἐλθὼν θεραπεύσω**: *I will go and heal*; a participle may receive as much emphasis as the finite verb and be coordinated with it.

8:8 **ἔφη** is third person singular imperfect active indicative. **οὐκ εἰμὶ ἱκανὸς**: the words, used also by John the Baptist, indicate an attitude in harmony with the first beatitude. **ἀλλὰ μόνον εἰπὲ λόγῳ**: *but say the word only* (literally: *but speak by way of command only*); λόγῳ is a dative of means. The statement shows a surprising amount of faith.

8:9 καὶ γὰρ ἐγὼ ἄνθρωπός εἰμι ὑπὸ ἐξουσίαν, ἔχων ὑπ᾽ ἐμαυτὸν
στρατιώτας, καὶ λέγω τούτῳ, Πορεύθητι, καὶ πορεύεται, καὶ ἄλλῳ,
Ἔρχου, καὶ ἔρχεται, καὶ τῷ δούλῳ μου, Ποίησον τοῦτο, καὶ ποιεῖ.
8:10 ἀκούσας δὲ ὁ Ἰησοῦς ἐθαύμασεν καὶ εἶπεν τοῖς ἀκολουθοῦσιν,
Ἀμὴν λέγω ὑμῖν, παρ᾽ οὐδενὶ τοσαύτην πίστιν ἐν τῷ Ἰσραὴλ εὗρον.

8:9

ὑπό by (preposition + genitive of personal agent); under (+ accusative)

ἐξουσία, ας, ἡ authority, command, right, ability, might, power

ἐμαυτοῦ, ῆς myself

στρατιώτης, ου, ὁ soldier

πορεύομαι, πορεύσομαι, πεπόρευμαι, ἐπορεύθην go, proceed, travel

ἄλλος, η, ο other, another

δοῦλος, ου, ὁ slave, servant

8:10

θαυμάζω, θαυμάσομαι, ἐθαύμασα, ἐθαυμάσθην wonder, marvel, be astonished

ἀκολουθέω, ἀκολουθήσω, ἠκολούθησα, ἠκολούθηκα follow (+ dative)

παρά from (the side of), from, issuing from, by (preposition + genitive); with, by (+ dative); by, near to, along; to, at; by, near, at the side of (+ accusative)

οὐδείς, οὐδεμία, οὐδέν no (adjective); no one, nobody, nothing (substantive)

τοσοῦτος, τοσαύτη, τοσοῦτο so great, so much, so large

πίστις, εως, ἡ faith, trust

εὑρίσκω, εὑρήσω, εὗρον (2 aorist), ηὕρηκα/εὕρηκα, εὑρέθην find, meet, discover, recognize

---

8:9 **ὑπὸ ἐξουσίαν . . . ἔχων ὑπ᾽ ἐμαυτὸν στρατιώτας**: he is both a man under authority and a man of authority. ἔχων: *although I have*; the participle may be construed concessively. The argument *a minori ad maius* runs thus: if he, a lowly centurion, obeys the orders of his superior and has his own orders obeyed, Jesus just needs to speak and his son will be healed.

8:10 **ὁ Ἰησοῦς ἐθαύμασεν**: in a reversal, the verb expresses an emotion of Jesus usually reserved for the crowds, disciples, or followers. **τοῖς ἀκολουθοῦσιν**: *to those who followed*; the article and present participle combine to form a substantive. The masculine plural dative present active participial form (cf. App. 36) may easily be confused with a third person plural present active indicative finite verb (cf. App. 56).

8:11 λέγω δὲ ὑμῖν ὅτι πολλοὶ ἀπὸ ἀνατολῶν καὶ δυσμῶν ἥξουσιν καὶ ἀνακλιθήσονται μετὰ Ἀβραὰμ καὶ Ἰσαὰκ καὶ Ἰακὼβ ἐν τῇ βασιλείᾳ τῶν οὐρανῶν, 8:12 οἱ δὲ υἱοὶ τῆς βασιλείας ἐκβληθήσονται εἰς τὸ σκότος τὸ ἐξώτερον· ἐκεῖ ἔσται ὁ κλαυθμὸς καὶ ὁ βρυγμὸς τῶν ὀδόντων. 8:13 καὶ εἶπεν ὁ Ἰησοῦς τῷ ἑκατοντάρχῃ, Ὕπαγε, ὡς ἐπίστευσας γενηθήτω σοι. καὶ ἰάθη ὁ παῖς [αὐτοῦ] ἐν τῇ ὥρᾳ ἐκείνῃ.

8:11

πολύς, πολλή, πολύ much, large, many (in plural)

ἀνατολή, ῆς, ἡ rising, rising of the sun, east, orient

δυσμή, ῆς, ἡ sinking, setting; setting of the sun, west (plural)

ἥκω, ἥξω have come, be present (the present is supplied by ἔρχομαι)

ἀνακλίνω, ἀνακλινῶ, ἀνέκλινα, ἀνεκλίθην cause to lie down; lie down, recline at meal (passive)

μετά with (preposition + genitive); after (+ accusative)

Ἰσαάκ, ὁ Isaac (indeclinable)

8:12

ἐκβάλλω, ἐκβαλῶ, ἐξέβαλον, ἐκβέβληκα, ἐξεβλήθην drive out, expel, disdain, spurn, send out, lead out

σκότος, ους, τό darkness, gloom

ἐξώτερος, α, ον outer, external

ἐκεῖ there, in that place (adverb)

κλαυθμός, ου, ὁ weeping

βρυγμός, οῦ, ὁ chattering (of teeth), gnashing (of teeth)

ὀδούς, ὀδόντος, ὁ tooth

8:13

ἑκατόνταρχος, ου, ὁ commander of 100 men, centurion

ὑπάγω, ὑπάξω, ὑπήγαγον, ὑπήχθην go, go away, go home

ὡς as, like, when, after, about (with numerals), how, provided that (adverb, conjunction)

πιστεύω, πιστεύσω, ἐπίστευσα, πεπίστευκα, πεπίστευμαι, ἐπιστεύθην believe, entrust

γίνομαι, γενήσομαι, ἐγενόμην, γέγονα/γεγένημαι, ἐγενήθην become, be made, be done, be created, be born, come, arrive, be present

ἰάομαι, ἰάσομαι, ἰασάμην, ἴαμαι, ἰάθην heal, cure, restore

παῖς, παιδός, ὁ child, boy, youth; servant

ὥρα, ας, ἡ hour

ἐκεῖνος, η, ον that, that one, the former

8:11 **πολλοὶ . . . ἥξουσιν καὶ ἀνακλιθήσονται**: the humility and faith of the Gentile centurion provides a suitable occasion to proclaim the universality of the messianic feast where the righteous of all nations will join with the patriarchs in the kingdom of heaven. ἀνακλιθήσονται: in Greek fashion, the ancients reclined on couches at banquets.

8:12 **οἱ . . . υἱοὶ τῆς βασιλείας** are those who thought their descent from Abraham as natural and rightful heirs of the kingdom granted them automatic access to the kingdom of heaven (Jn 8:39–59).

8:13 **γενηθήτω σοι**: *let it be done to you*; the verb form is an impersonal third person singular first aorist passive imperative.

8:14 Καὶ ἐλθὼν ὁ Ἰησοῦς εἰς τὴν οἰκίαν Πέτρου εἶδεν τὴν πενθερὰν αὐτοῦ βεβλημένην καὶ πυρέσσουσαν· 8:15 καὶ ἥψατο τῆς χειρὸς αὐτῆς, καὶ ἀφῆκεν αὐτὴν ὁ πυρετός, καὶ ἠγέρθη καὶ διηκόνει αὐτῷ. 8:16 Ὀψίας δὲ γενομένης προσήνεγκαν αὐτῷ δαιμονιζομένους πολλούς· καὶ ἐξέβαλεν τὰ πνεύματα λόγῳ καὶ πάντας τοὺς κακῶς ἔχοντας ἐθεράπευσεν,

---

8:14
οἰκία, ας, ἡ house, household, family
πενθερά, ᾶς, ἡ mother-in-law
πυρέσσω, πυρέξω suffer with a fever
8:15
ἅπτω, ἅψω, ἧψα fasten; light, kindle; touch, take hold of, hold (middle)
χείρ, χειρός, ἡ hand
πυρετός, οῦ, ὁ fever
ἐγείρω, ἐγερῶ, ἤγειρα, ἠγήγερμαι, ἠγέρθην awaken, lift, raise up from the dead, restore, rebuild; get up!, come! (intransitive, only in imperative)
διακονέω, διακονήσω, διηκόνησα, δεδιηκόνηκα, διηκονήθην wait on, attend upon, serve
8:16
ὀψία, ας, ἡ evening
γίνομαι, γενήσομαι, ἐγενόμην, γέγονα/γεγένημαι, ἐγενήθην become, be made, be created, be born, come, arrive, be present
προσφέρω, προσοίσω, προσήνεγκα, προσήνεγκον (2 aorist), προσηνέχθην bring, offer, present
δαιμονίζομαι, δαιμονίσομαι, ἐδαιμονίσθην be possessed by a demon
πολύς, πολλή, πολύ much, large, many (in plural)
ἐκβάλλω, ἐκβαλῶ, ἐξέβαλον, ἐκβέβληκα, ἐξεβλήθην drive out, expel, disdain, spurn, send out, lead out
πνεῦμα, ατος, τό wind, spirit, mind, Holy Spirit
λόγος, ου, ὁ word, doctrine, account, reason, statement, saying
κακῶς ill, badly, wickedly, wrongly (adverb)
ἔχω, ἕξω, ἔσχον (2 aorist), ἔσχηκα have, keep, cause, consider; be (with adverbs and indications of time and age); be able (with infinitive)
θεραπεύω, θεραπεύσω, ἐθεράπευσα, ἐθεραπεύθην care for, heal, restore

---

8:15 **ἥψατο . . . ἀφῆκεν . . . ἠγέρθη . . . διηκόνει**: the rapid succession of verbs suggests quick action on the part of Jesus who, without being asked, relieved her pain, and a speedy resumption of activities on her part.

8:16 **Ὀψίας δὲ γενομένης**: *but when evening came*; the verbal construction is a genitive absolute (cf. App. 65). **προσήνεγκαν** is used as a first aorist (cf. App. 53, D, 1) and, like liquid verbs, it loses the intervocalic **σ**. **λόγῳ** is a dative of means. **τοὺς κακῶς ἔχοντας**: *those who were ill.*

8:17 ὅπως πληρωθῇ τὸ ῥηθὲν διὰ Ἠσαΐου τοῦ προφήτου λέγοντος,
Αὐτὸς τὰς ἀσθενείας ἡμῶν ἔλαβεν
καὶ τὰς νόσους ἐβάστασεν.
8:18 Ἰδὼν δὲ ὁ Ἰησοῦς ὄχλον περὶ αὐτὸν ἐκέλευσεν ἀπελθεῖν εἰς τὸ πέραν. 8:19 καὶ προσελθὼν εἷς γραμματεὺς εἶπεν αὐτῷ,

---

8:17
ὅπως that, in order that (conjunction)
πληρόω, πληρώσω, ἐπλήρωσα, πεπλήρωκα, πεπλήρωμαι, ἐπληρώθην fill, complete, fulfill
προφήτης, ου, ὁ prophet, seer, revelator
ἀσθένεια, ας, ἡ weakness, sickness, disease
λαμβάνω, λήμψομαι, ἔλαβον, εἴληφα, εἴλημμαι, ἐλήφθην take, receive, accept
νόσος, ου, ὁ disease, sickness, illness
βαστάζω, βαστάσω, ἐβάστασα lift, bear, take up; carry away, remove, steal
8:18
ὄχλος, ου, ὁ crowd, throng, multitude
περί about, concerning (preposition + genitive); about, around (+ accusative)
κελεύω, κελεύσω, ἐκέλευσα give order, command, urge, direct, bid
ἀπέρχομαι, ἀπελεύσομαι, ἀπῆλθον, ἀπελήλυθα go, go away, depart
πέραν across, beyond, on the other side of (preposition + genitive); τὸ πέραν farther side, the other side
8:19
προσέρχομαι, προσελεύσομαι, προσῆλθον, προσελήλυθα come to, go to, approach
εἷς, μία, ἕν one, single; a (numeral and indefinite article)
γραμματεύς, έως, ὁ secretary, clerk, scholar versed in law, scribe

---

8:17 **ὅπως πληρωθῇ**: supply ταῦτα ἐγένετο before the purpose clause. **τὸ ῥηθὲν**: *that which was spoken*; the verbal form is a neuter singular nominative first aorist passive participle (cf. App. 53, G, 5; 34). **Αὐτὸς . . . ἔλαβεν**: *He himself took up*; Αὐτὸς is an intensive pronoun standing in predicate position with the finite verb (App. 40 and notes).

8:18 **ἐκέλευσεν ἀπελθεῖν**: *gave orders to go over*; the context requires an absolute sense of the verb. Verbs indicating *will* or *desire* are often followed by an accusative infinitive construction. The accusative subject of the infinitive may not be included. However, in this sentence ὄχλον may, by *apo koinou* (ἀπὸ κοινοῦ), function both as the object of the participle Ἰδὼν and as the object of the main verb ἐκέλευσεν: *he ordered the crowd to go over.* **τὸ πέραν** refers to the lake.

8:19 **προσελθὼν**: *as he approached.* **εἷς γραμματεὺς**: *a scribe*; εἷς is used as an indefinite article.

Διδάσκαλε, ἀκολουθήσω σοι ὅπου ἐὰν ἀπέρχῃ. 8:20 καὶ λέγει αὐτῷ ὁ Ἰησοῦς, Αἱ ἀλώπεκες φωλεοὺς ἔχουσιν καὶ τὰ πετεινὰ τοῦ οὐρανοῦ κατασκηνώσεις, ὁ δὲ υἱὸς τοῦ ἀνθρώπου οὐκ ἔχει ποῦ τὴν κεφαλὴν κλίνῃ. 8:21 ἕτερος δὲ τῶν μαθητῶν [αὐτοῦ] εἶπεν αὐτῷ, Κύριε, ἐπίτρεψόν μοι πρῶτον ἀπελθεῖν καὶ θάψαι τὸν πατέρα μου.

8:19
διδάσκαλος, ου, ὁ master, teacher
ἀκολουθέω, ἀκολουθήσω, ἠκολούθησα, ἠκολούθηκα follow (+ dative)
ὅπου where (adverb); ὅπου ἐάν wherever (with present subjunctive)
ἀπέρχομαι, ἀπελεύσομαι, ἀπῆλθον, ἀπελήλυθα go, go away, depart
8:20
ἀλώπηξ, ἀλώπεκος, ἡ fox; crafty man
φωλεός, οῦ, ὁ den, lair, hole
πετεινόν, οῦ, τό bird, fowl
κατασκήνοσις, εως, ἡ tent; dwelling-place, place to live; nest (of birds)
ποῦ where? in what place? (interrogative adverb)
κεφαλή, ῆς, ἡ head
κλίνω, κλινῶ, ἔκλινα (1 aorist), κέκλικα bend, bow; lay down (to rest)
8:21
ἕτερος, α, ον other, another
μαθητής, οῦ, ὁ disciple
ἐπιτρέπω, ἐπιτρέψω, ἐπέτρεψα, ἐπιτέτραμμαι, ἐπετράπην (2 aorist passive) give over; permit, allow
πρῶτον first (in time; adverb)
ἀπέρχομαι, ἀπελεύσομαι, ἀπῆλθον, ἀπελήλυθα go, go away, depart
θάπτω, θάψω, ἔθαψα, τέταφα, ἐτάφην (2 aorist passive) bury

8:19 **ἀκολουθήσω ... ὅπου ἐὰν ἀπέρχῃ** is a future more vivid condition (App. 70). A conditional relative clause is here introduced by the indefinite relative adverb ὅπου. ἀπέρχῃ is a second person singular present middle subjunctive of a deponent verb (cf. App. 53, A, 2).

8:20 **ἔχουσιν καὶ**: supply the verb in the next sightly elliptical clause. **οὐκ ἔχει ποῦ ... κλίνῃ** is a present general condition (App. 70). A conditional relative clause is here introduced by the direct interrogative adverb ποῦ instead of the usual relative adverb οὗ. The protasis follows the apodosis. ἔχει: supply an object like τόπον: *place* (cf. Lk 2:7) for the verb.

8:21 **ἕτερος δὲ τῶν μαθητῶν**: ἕτερος is used with a partitive genitive (cf. App. 65). **ἐπίτρεψόν**: the verb calls for a dative and infinitive construction.

8:22 ὁ δὲ Ἰησοῦς λέγει αὐτῷ, Ἀκολούθει μοι καὶ ἄφες τοὺς νεκροὺς θάψαι τοὺς ἑαυτῶν νεκρούς.

8:23 Καὶ ἐμβάντι αὐτῷ εἰς τὸ πλοῖον ἠκολούθησαν αὐτῷ οἱ μαθηταὶ αὐτοῦ. 8:24 καὶ ἰδοὺ σεισμὸς μέγας ἐγένετο ἐν τῇ θαλάσσῃ, ὥστε τὸ πλοῖον καλύπτεσθαι ὑπὸ τῶν κυμάτων, αὐτὸς δὲ ἐκάθευδεν.

8:22
ἀκολουθέω, ἀκολουθήσω, ἠκολούθησα, ἠκολούθηκα follow (+ dative)
ἀφίημι, ἀφήσω, ἀφῆκα, ἀφῆν (2 aorist), ἀφεῖκα, ἀφεῖμαι, ἀφέθην let go, send away; forgive, pardon; allow, let, permit, leave
νεκρός, ά, όν dead
θάπτω, θάψω, ἔθαψα, τέταφα, ἐτάφην (2 aorist passive) bury
ἑαυτοῦ, ῆς, οῦ himself, herself, itself; themselves, ourselves, yourselves (in plural)
8:23
ἐμβαίνω, ἐμβήσομαι, ἐνέβην, ἐμβέβηκα step in, embark
πλοῖον, ου, τό ship, boat
ἀκολουθέω, ἀκολουθήσω, ἠκολούθησα, ἠκολούθηκα follow (+ dative)
μαθητής, οῦ, ὁ disciple
8:24
σεισμός, ου, ὁ shaking; earthquake; tempest
μέγας, μεγάλη, μέγα large, great
γίνομαι, γενήσομαι, ἐγενόμην, γέγονα/γεγένημαι, ἐγενήθην become, be made, be created, be born; come, arrive, be present; arise, occur
θάλασσα, ης, ἡ sea, inland sea, lake
ὥστε so that, so as to (conjunction)
πλοῖον, ου, τό ship, boat
καλύπτω, καλύψω, ἐκάλθψα, κεκάλυμμαι cover; hide, conceal
κῦμα, ατος, τό wave, surge, billow
καθεύδω, καθευδήσω sleep, be fast asleep

8:22 **Ἀκολούθει** is a second person singular present active imperative of a contracted verb with stem in **ε** (cf. App. 56). **ἄφες τοὺς νεκροὺς θάψαι τοὺς ἑαυτῶν νεκρούς**: the imperative takes an accusative infinitive construction. The terseness of the word play or paronomasia comes across as harsh but argues: the disciple's mission requires full attention among the living. He can do nothing more for the dead father because eternal life can come about only through the resurrection of Jesus. Therefore, the spiritually dead benefit by taking pause from their worldly pursuits and reflecting on the dead as they bury their dead.

8:23 **ἐμβάντι αὐτῷ . . . ἠκολούθησαν αὐτῷ**: *they followed Him as He embarked;* the second personal pronoun is pleonastic.

8:24 **ὥστε τὸ πλοῖον καλύπτεσθαι**: *so that the boat was covered;* ὥστε, followed by the accusative with infinitive, introduces a result clause. **ἐκάθευδεν**: continued to sleep. The imperfect tense denotes progressive, continued, and repeated action (aspect) in past time.

8:25 καὶ προσελθόντες ἤγειραν αὐτὸν λέγοντες, Κύριε, σῶσον, ἀπολλύμεθα. 8:26 καὶ λέγει αὐτοῖς, Τί δειλοί ἐστε, ὀλιγόπιστοι; τότε ἐγερθεὶς ἐπετίμησεν τοῖς ἀνέμοις καὶ τῇ θαλάσσῃ, καὶ ἐγένετο γαλήνη μεγάλη. 8:27 οἱ δὲ ἄνθρωποι ἐθαύμασαν λέγοντες, Ποταπός ἐστιν οὗτος ὅτι καὶ οἱ ἄνεμοι καὶ ἡ θάλασσα αὐτῷ ὑπακούουσιν;

8:25

προσέρχομαι, προσελεύσομαι, προσῆλθον, προσελήλυθα come to, go to, approach

ἐγείρω, ἐγερῶ, ἤγειρα, ἠγήγερμαι, ἠγέρθην awaken, lift, raise up from the dead, restore, rebuild; get up!, come! (intransitive, only in imperative)

σῴζω, σώσω, ἔσωσα, σέσωκα, σέσωσμαι, ἐσώθην save, rescue, preserve safe and unharmed

ἀπόλλυμι/ἀπολλύω, ἀπολέσω/ἀπολῶ, ἀπώλεσα, ἀπολώλεκα, ἀπόλωλα (2 perfect) lose, destroy, ruin, kill; perish (middle)

8:26

δειλός, ή, όν timid, fearful

ὀλιγόπιστος, ον of little faith

ἐγείρω, ἐγερῶ, ἤγειρα, ἠγήγερμαι, ἠγέρθην awaken, lift, raise up from the dead, restore, rebuild; get up!, come! (intransitive, only in imperative)

ἐπιτιμάω, ἐπιτιμήσω, ἐπετίμησα set a value on; assess a penalty; rebuke, reprove, censure, reprimand; admonish, enjoin

ἄνεμος, ου, ὁ wind

θάλασσα, ης, ἡ sea, inland sea, lake

γίνομαι, γενήσομαι, ἐγενόμην, γέγονα/γεγένημαι, ἐγενήθην become, be made, be created; arise, occur, come to pass, happen; be born, come, arrive, be present

γαλήνη, ης, ἡ calm, tranquility

μέγας, μεγάλη, μέγα large, great

8:27

θαυμάζω, θαυμάσομαι, ἐθαύμασα, ἐθαυμάσθην wonder, marvel, be astonished

ποταπός, ή, όν what? of what manner? of what sort?

ἄνεμος, ου, ὁ wind

θάλασσα, ης, ἡ sea, inland sea, lake

ὑπακούω, ὑπακούσομαι hear, listen, obey

8:25 **ἤγειραν** is a third person plural first aorist active indicative (cf. App. 53, D, 1). The liquid aorist omits the intervocalic **σ** and shows compensatory lengthening in the stem. **σῶσον** is a second person singular first aorist active imperative (cf. App. 53, D, 3).

8:26 **ἐπετίμησεν**: the compound verb governs the dative case.

8:27 **καὶ . . . καὶ**: *both . . . and*. **αὐτῷ ὑπακούουσιν**: the compound verb governs the dative case.

8:28 Καὶ ἐλθόντος αὐτοῦ εἰς τὸ πέραν εἰς τὴν χώραν τῶν Γαδαρηνῶν ὑπήντησαν αὐτῷ δύο δαιμονιζόμενοι ἐκ τῶν μνημείων ἐξερχόμενοι, χαλεποὶ λίαν, ὥστε μὴ ἰσχύειν τινὰ παρελθεῖν διὰ τῆς ὁδοῦ ἐκείνης. 8:29 καὶ ἰδοὺ ἔκραξαν λέγοντες, Τί ἡμῖν καὶ σοί, υἱὲ τοῦ θεοῦ; ἦλθες ὧδε πρὸ καιροῦ βασανίσαι ἡμᾶς; 8:30 ἦν δὲ μακρὰν ἀπ' αὐτῶν ἀγέλη χοίρων πολλῶν βοσκομένη.

8:28

πέραν across, beyond, on the other side of (preposition + genitive); τὸ πέραν farther side, the other side

χώρα, ας, ἡ country, land, field

Γαδαρηνός, ή, όν from Gadara

ὑπαντάω, ὑπαντήσω, ὑπήντησα meet (+ dative)

δύο two

δαιμονίζομαι, δαιμονίσομαι, ἐδαιμονίσθην be possessed by a demon

μνημεῖον, ου, τό monument, grave, tomb

ἐξέρχομαι, ἐξελεύσομαι, ἐξῆλθον (2 aorist), ἐξελήλυθα go or come out of, go out

χαλεπός, ή, όν hard, difficult; hard to deal with, violent, dangerous; bad, evil

λίαν greatly, exceedingly (adverb)

ὥστε so that, so as to (conjunction)

ἰσχύω, ἰσχύσω, ἴσχυσα be strong, be well; have power, be able

τις, τι anyone, anything, someone, something, a certain one, a certain thing (indefinite pronoun)

παρέρχομαι, παρελεύσομαι, παρῆλθον (2 aorist), ἐλήλυθα pass, pass along, pass by; pass away, come to an end

ὁδός, οῦ, ἡ road, way, journey

ἐκεῖνος, η, ον that, that one, the former

8:29

κράζω, κεκράξομαι/κράξω, ἐκέκραξα/ἔκραξα, κέκραγα cry out, scream; call, call out, cry

ὧδε here (adverb)

πρό before (preposition + genitive)

καιρός, οῦ, ὁ time, appointed time; season; time of crisis, end-time

βασανίζω, βασανίσω, ἐβασάνισα, ἐβασανίσθην afflict, torment, torture

8:30

μακράν far, far off, far away (adverb)

ἀγέλη, ής, ἡ herd

χοῖρος, ου, ὁ young pig, swine

βόσκω, βοσκήσω, ἐβόσκησα feed, tend; graze, feed (passive)

8:28 **ὥστε μὴ ἰσχύειν τινὰ παρελθεῖν**: *so that no one was able to pass by*; ὥστε μὴ, followed by the accusative with infinitive, introduces a negative result clause.

8:29 **Τί ἡμῖν καὶ σοί**: the idiom expresses indignation, rejection, and indifference: *What business do we have with you? What do we have in common? What do you want with us?* They know both Jesus and a time of torment.

8:30 **ἦν δὲ . . . ἀγέλη**: *there was a herd*; the third person singular imperfect active indicative is frequently used at the beginning of a sentence to introduce past tense narratives.

8:31 οἱ δὲ δαίμονες παρεκάλουν αὐτὸν λέγοντες, Εἰ ἐκβάλλεις ἡμᾶς, ἀπόστειλον ἡμᾶς εἰς τὴν ἀγέλην τῶν χοίρων. 8:32 καὶ εἶπεν αὐτοῖς, Ὑπάγετε. οἱ δὲ ἐξελθόντες ἀπῆλθον εἰς τοὺς χοίρους· καὶ ἰδοὺ ὥρμησεν πᾶσα ἡ ἀγέλη κατὰ τοῦ κρημνοῦ εἰς τὴν θάλασσαν καὶ ἀπέθανον ἐν τοῖς ὕδασιν. 8:33 οἱ δὲ βόσκοντες ἔφυγον, καὶ ἀπελθόντες εἰς τὴν πόλιν ἀπήγγειλαν πάντα καὶ τὰ τῶν δαιμονιζομένων.

8:31

δαίμων, ονος, ὁ demon, evil spirit

παρακαλέω, παρακαλέσω, παρεκάλεσα, παρακέκληκα, παρακέκλημαι, παρεκλήθην call upon, exhort, persuade; beg, entreat; comfort, encourage, cheer up

εἰ if, whether

ἐκβάλλω, ἐκβαλῶ, ἐξέβαλον, ἐκβέβληκα, ἐξεβλήθην drive out, expel, disdain, spurn, send out, lead out

ἀποστέλλω, ἀποστελῶ, ἀπέστειλα, ἀπέσταλκα, ἀπέσταλμαι, ἀπεστάλην send, send away, send out

ἀγέλη, ής, ἡ herd

χοῖρος, ου, ὁ young pig, swine

8:32

ὑπάγω, ὑπάξω, ὑπήγαγον, ὑπήχθην go, go away, go home

ἐξέρχομαι, ἐξελεύσομαι, ἐξῆλθον (2 aorist), ἐξελήλυθα go or come out of, go out

ἀπέρχομαι, ἀπελεύσομαι, ἀπῆλθον, ἀπελήλυθα go, go away, depart

χοῖρος, ου, ὁ young pig, swine

ὁρμάω, ὁρμήσω, ὥρμησα put in motion, incite; rush (intransitive)

ἀγέλη, ής, ἡ herd

κατά near, towards, by, in accordance with, after the manner of (preposition + accusative); down from, against (+ genitive)

κρημνός, οῦ, ὁ precipice, steep slope or bank, cliff

θάλασσα, ης, ἡ sea, inland sea, lake

ἀποθνήσκω, ἀποθανοῦμαι, ἀπέθανον (2 aorist) die, face death, decay

ὕδωρ, ὕδατος, τό water

8:33

βόσκω, βοσκήσω, ἐβόσκησα feed, tend

φεύγω, φεύξομαι, ἔφυγον (2 aorist) flee, flee from, avoid, shun

ἀπέρχομαι, ἀπελεύσομαι, ἀπῆλθον, ἀπελήλυθα go, go away, depart

πόλις, εως, ἡ city

ἀπαγγέλλω, ἀπαγγελῶ, ἀπήγγειλα (1 aorist), ἀπηγγέλην (2 aorist passive) bring back word, report, declare, announce, tell

δαιμονίζομαι, δαιμονίσομαι, ἐδαιμονίσθην be possessed by a demon

---

8:31 **ἀπόστειλον** is a second person singular first aorist active imperative of a liquid verb (cf. App. 53, D, 3). The liquid aorist omits the intervocalic **σ** and shows compensatory lengthening in the stem. In this simple or particular condition the imperative is substituted for the indicative in the apodosis (App. 70).

8:33 **οἱ δὲ βόσκοντες**: the herdsmen panicked at the sight. **ἀπήγγειλαν πάντα καὶ τὰ τῶν δαιμονιζομένων**: πάντα is a cognate accusative: supply something like τὰ πράγματα *the events* to complete the object of the verb.

8:34 καὶ ἰδοὺ πᾶσα ἡ πόλις ἐξῆλθεν εἰς ὑπάντησιν τῷ Ἰησοῦ καὶ ἰδόντες αὐτὸν παρεκάλεσαν ὅπως μεταβῇ ἀπὸ τῶν ὁρίων αὐτῶν.

8:34

πόλις, εως, ἡ city

ἐξέρχομαι, ἐξελεύσομαι, ἐξῆλθον (2 aorist), ἐξελήλυθα go or come out of, go out

ὑπάντησις, εως, ἡ coming to meet; εἰς ὑπάντησιν to meet (+ dative)

παρακαλέω, παρακαλέσω, παρεκάλεσα, παρακέκληκα, παρακέκλημαι, παρεκλήθην call upon, exhort, persuade; beg, entreat; comfort, encourage, cheer up

μεταβαίνω, μεταβήσομαι, μετέβην, μεταβέβηκα go, pass over, move; go away, depart

ὅριον, ου, τό boundary; region, territory, district (plural)

8:34 **παρεκάλεσαν ὅπως μεταβῇ**: *they entreated him to leave*; they are more concerned about the physical loss of the swine and reject the spiritual work of the miracle that restores the demoniac to health.

9 Καὶ ἐμβὰς εἰς πλοῖον διεπέρασεν καὶ ἦλθεν εἰς τὴν ἰδίαν πόλιν.
9:2 καὶ ἰδοὺ προσέφερον αὐτῷ παραλυτικὸν ἐπὶ κλίνης βεβλημένον.
καὶ ἰδὼν ὁ Ἰησοῦς τὴν πίστιν αὐτῶν εἶπεν τῷ παραλυτικῷ, Θάρσει,
τέκνον, ἀφίενταί σου αἱ ἁμαρτίαι. 9:3 καὶ ἰδού τινες τῶν γραμματέων
εἶπαν ἐν ἑαυτοῖς,

9:1
ἐμβαίνω, ἐμβήσομαι, ἐνέβην, ἐμβέβηκα step in, embark
πλοῖον, ου, τό ship, boat
διαπεράω, διαπεράσω, διεπέρησα cross over
ἴδιος, ία, ιον one's own
πόλις, εως, ἡ city
9:2
προσφέρω, προσοίσω, προσήνεγκα, προσήνεγκον (2 aorist), προσηνέχθην bring, offer, present
παραλυτικός, ή, όν lame person, paralytic, palsied
κλίνη, ης, ἡ bed, couch; pallet, stretcher
πίστις, εως, ἡ faith, trust
θαρσέω, θαρσήσω, ἐθάρσησα be of good courage, be cheerful
τέκνον, ου, τό child, descendant, posterity
ἁμαρτία, ας, ἡ error, sin
9:3
τις, τι anyone, anything, someone, something; a certain one, a certain thing; some, certain, several (plural; indefinite pronoun)
γραμματεύς, έως, ὁ secretary, clerk, scholar versed in law, scribe
ἑαυτοῦ, ῆς, οῦ himself, herself, itself; themselves, ourselves, yourselves (in plural)

9:1 **εἰς τὴν ἰδίαν πόλιν**: *to his own city*; the adjective stands in attributive position. The city is not Nazareth but Capernaum (4:13), where He was staying in Peter's house (8:14).

9:2 **παραλυτικὸν ἐπὶ κλίνης βεβλημένον**: *a paralytic lying on a mat*; the verb form is third person singular perfect passive indicative. The perfect tense of the participle denotes action (aspect) that is completed near present time and continues with present result: *he has been placed* (recently and *he lies* now). The reduplication or doubling of the stem at the beginning of a word occurs especially in the perfect, pluperfect, and future perfect tenses to indicate completed action. **τὴν πίστιν αὐτῶν**: it is expressly the faith of those who bring him that commands attention. **τέκνον**: *my son*; the vocative may be used figuratively to address a fully grown person. **ἀφίενταί σου αἱ ἁμαρτίαι**: the verb is a third person plural present passive indicative (cf. App. 59) with a single act (aspect) in time. The ancients, including his disciples (Jn 9:1–3), commonly believed that illnesses came about as a direct result of sin. Jesus undoubtedly knows the circumstances of this case and responds appropriately.

Οὗτος βλασφημεῖ. 9:4 καὶ ἰδὼν ὁ Ἰησοῦς τὰς ἐνθυμήσεις αὐτῶν εἶπεν, Ἱνατί ἐνθυμεῖσθε πονηρὰ ἐν ταῖς καρδίαις ὑμῶν; 9:5 τί γάρ ἐστιν εὐκοπώτερον, εἰπεῖν, Ἀφίενταί σου αἱ ἁμαρτίαι, ἢ εἰπεῖν, Ἔγειρε καὶ περιπάτει; 9:6 ἵνα δὲ εἰδῆτε ὅτι ἐξουσίαν ἔχει ὁ υἱὸς τοῦ ἀνθρώπου ἐπὶ τῆς γῆς ἀφιέναι ἁμαρτίας - τότε λέγει τῷ παραλυτικῷ, Ἐγερθεὶς ἆρόν

9:3
βλασφημέω, βλασφημήσω, ἐβλασφήμησα, βεβλασφήμηκα, ἐβλασφημήθην blaspheme, speak irreverently of
9:4
ἐνθύμησις, εως, ἡ thought, reflection, idea
ἱνατί why, for what reason (adverb)
ἐνθυμέομαι, ἐνθυμήσομαι, ἐνεθυμήθην reflect on, ponder, consider, think
πονηρός, ά, όν bad, evil, wicked
καρδία, ας, ἡ heart
9:5
εὐκοπώτερος, α, ον easier
ἁμαρτία, ας, ἡ error, sin
ἐγείρω, ἐγερῶ, ἤγειρα, ἐγήγερμαι, ἠγέρθην awaken, lift, raise up from the dead, restore, rebuild; appear (passive); arise! get up! come! (intransitive, only in imperative)
περιπατέω, περιπατήσω, περιεπάτησα walk, walk about
9:6
ἵνα to, in order to, in order that, that (conjunction)
ἐξουσία, ας, ἡ authority, right, ability, might, power
γῆ, γῆς, ἡ earth, soil, land, region, country
ἁμαρτία, ας, ἡ error, sin
παραλυτικός, ή, όν lame person, paralytic, palsied
αἴρω, ἀρῶ, ἦρα, ἦρκα, ἦρμαι, ἤρθην take up, bear, take away, lift, carry, remove; keep in suspense; destroy, kill

---

9:3 **Οὗτος βλασφημεῖ**: the scribes wrongly believe that only God can forgive sins.

9:4 **ἰδὼν ὁ Ἰησοῦς τὰς ἐνθυμήσεις**: *since Jesus knew their thoughts*; the verbal form is a second aorist active participle (App. 29 and note) indicating mental perception. **Ἱνατί ἐνθυμεῖσθε πονηρὰ**: *why do you ponder wicked thoughts*; πονηρὰ is a cognate accusative: supply a noun from the verb to complete its meaning.

9:5 **τί γάρ ἐστιν εὐκοπώτερον, εἰπεῖν**: *which is easier: to say*; εὐκοπώτερον is a comparative degree of the adjective.

9:6 **ἵνα δὲ εἰδῆτε**: *that is, that you may know*; the particle is used here to insert an explanation. The δὲ suggests a phrase like ἐγὼ δὲ λέγω ταῦτα ὑμῖν before the purpose clause. **Ἐγερθεὶς ἆρόν**: *Arise and take*; when a participle modifies an imperative, it is commonly changed into an imperative and the two verbs are coordinated in translation. Ἐγερθεὶς, the first aorist passive participle of ἐγείρω (cf. App. 34), shows intransitive meaning. ἆρόν is a second person singular second aorist active imperative (cf. App. 54). A change in stem from the present tense to the aorist distinguishes the second aorist from the first.

σου τὴν κλίνην καὶ ὕπαγε εἰς τὸν οἶκόν σου. 9:7 καὶ ἐγερθεὶς
ἀπῆλθεν εἰς τὸν οἶκον αὐτοῦ. 9:8 ἰδόντες δὲ οἱ ὄχλοι ἐφοβήθησαν καὶ
ἐδόξασαν τὸν θεὸν τὸν δόντα ἐξουσίαν τοιαύτην τοῖς ἀνθρώποις.
9:9 Καὶ παράγων ὁ Ἰησοῦς ἐκεῖθεν εἶδεν ἄνθρωπον καθήμενον
ἐπὶ τὸ τελώνιον, Μαθθαῖον λεγόμενον, καὶ λέγει αὐτῷ, Ἀκολούθει
μοι. καὶ ἀναστὰς ἠκολούθησεν αὐτῷ.

9:6
κλίνη, ης, ἡ bed, couch; pallet, stretcher
ὑπάγω, ὑπάξω, ὑπήγαγον, ὑπήχθην go, go away, go home
οἶκος, ου, ὁ house, dwelling
9:7
ἀπέρχομαι, ἀπελεύσομαι, ἀπῆλθον, ἀπελήλυθα go, go away, depart
9:8
ὄχλος, ου, ὁ crowd, throng, multitude
φοβέομαι, φοβηθήσομαι, ἐφοβήθην be afraid, become frightened
δοξάζω, δοξάσω, ἐδόξασα, δεδόξασμαι, ἐδοξάσθην praise, honor, magnify, glorify
δίδωμι, δώσω, ἔδωκα, ἔδων (2 aorist), δέδωκα, δέδομαι, ἐδόθην give
ἐξουσία, ας, ἡ authority, right, ability, might, power
τοιοῦτος, τοιαύτη, τοιοῦτο such, of such kind, such as this, so great
9:9
παράγω, παράξω lead beside, bring in (transitive); pass by, depart, go away (intransitive)
ἐκεῖθεν from there, from that place (adverb)
κάθημαι, καθήσομαι sit, stay, reside
τελώνιον, ου, τό tax office, custom house, toll office
Μαθθαῖος/Ματθαῖος, ου, ὁ Matthew
ἀκολουθέω, ἀκολουθήσω, ἠκολούθησα, ἠκολούθηκα follow (+ dative)
ἀνίστημι, ἀναστήσω, ἀνέστησα, ἀνέστην (2 aorist) cause to rise, raise up (transitive); rise, stand up, get up (2 aorist and all middle forms are intransitive)

9:7 **ἐγερθεὶς**: *after he had arisen.*

9:8 **τὸν θεὸν τὸν δόντα ἐξουσίαν τοιαύτην**: *God who gave such authority*; δόντα is a masculine singular accusative second aorist active participle (App. 58; 29 and note).

9:9 **παράγων**: *as . . . passed on*; the verbal form has an intransitive meaning. **ἄνθρωπον . . . Μαθθαῖον λεγόμενον**: *a man, named Matthew*; the participle agrees in gender, number, and case with its subject ἄνθρωπον. Μαθθαῖον is a predicate accusative. In the active the verb λέγω takes a double accusative, e.g., *he named his son Matthew.*

9:10 Καὶ ἐγένετο αὐτοῦ ἀνακειμένου ἐν τῇ οἰκίᾳ, καὶ ἰδοὺ πολλοὶ τελῶναι καὶ ἁμαρτωλοὶ ἐλθόντες συνανέκειντο τῷ Ἰησοῦ καὶ τοῖς μαθηταῖς αὐτοῦ. 9:11 καὶ ἰδόντες οἱ Φαρισαῖοι ἔλεγον τοῖς μαθηταῖς αὐτοῦ, Διὰ τί μετὰ τῶν τελωνῶν καὶ ἁμαρτωλῶν ἐσθίει ὁ διδάσκαλος ὑμῶν; 9:12 ὁ δὲ ἀκούσας εἶπεν, Οὐ χρείαν ἔχουσιν οἱ ἰσχύοντες ἰατροῦ ἀλλ' οἱ κακῶς ἔχοντες.

9:10
ἀνάκειμαι, ἀνακείσομαι lie down, recline at table as a dinner guest
οἰκία, ας, ἡ house, household, family
τελώνης, ου, ὁ tax-collector, publican
ἁμαρτωλός, όν sinful
συνανάκειμαι, συνανακείσομαι recline at table with, eat with
μαθητής, οῦ, ὁ disciple
9:11
Φαρισαῖος, ου, ὁ a Pharisee
διὰ τί why?
μετά with (preposition + genitive); after (+ accusative)
τελώνης, ου, ὁ tax-collector, publican
ἁμαρτωλός, όν sinful
ἐσθίω, φάγομαι, ἔφαγον (2 aorist) eat
διδάσκαλος, ου, ὁ master, teacher
9:12
χρεία, ας, ἡ need, necessity
ἰσχύω, ἰσχύσω, ἴσχυσα be good, be strong, be powerful, be well
ἰατρός, οῦ, ὁ physician
κακῶς ill, badly, wickedly, wrongly (adverb)

9:10 **Καὶ ἐγένετο αὐτοῦ ἀνακειμένου**: the finite verb, usually omitted in translation, is translated in older versions *and it came to pass*. It is followed by a genitive absolute: *as He was reclining at table*. **ἐν τῇ οἰκίᾳ**: Both here and in Mark (2:15), it is not clear in whose house they are dining. Luke (5:29) identifies it as that of Matthew, whom Mark and Luke call Levi in their accounts.

9:11 **ἰδόντες**: *when they saw this*; supply an object pronoun for the participle. **Διὰ τί;** means *why?* in direct questions.

9:12 **Οὐ χρείαν ἔχουσιν . . . ἰατροῦ**: *do not need a doctor* (literally: *have no need of a doctor*); ἰατροῦ is an objective genitive (cf. App. 65). **ἀλλ' οἱ κακῶς ἔχοντες**: *but those who are sick*; ἔχοντες: the participle translates as the verb *to be* with adverbs.

9:13 πορευθέντες δὲ μάθετε τί ἐστιν, Ἔλεος θέλω καὶ οὐ θυσίαν· οὐ γὰρ ἦλθον καλέσαι δικαίους ἀλλὰ ἁμαρτωλούς.
9:14 Τότε προσέρχονται αὐτῷ οἱ μαθηταὶ Ἰωάννου λέγοντες, Διὰ τί ἡμεῖς καὶ οἱ Φαρισαῖοι νηστεύομεν [πολλά], οἱ δὲ μαθηταί σου οὐ νηστεύουσιν;
9:15 καὶ εἶπεν αὐτοῖς ὁ Ἰησοῦς, Μὴ δύνανται οἱ υἱοὶ τοῦ νυμφῶνος πενθεῖν ἐφ' ὅσον μετ' αὐτῶν ἐστιν ὁ νυμφίος;

9:13
πορεύομαι, πορεύσομαι, πεπόρευμαι, ἐπορεύθην go, proceed, travel
μανθάνω, μαθήσομαι, ἔμαθον (2 aorist), μεμάθηκα learn
ἔλεος, εως, τό/ὁ pity, mercy, compassion, clemency
θέλω, θελήσω, ἠθέλησα wish to have, desire, purpose, want
θυσία, ας, ἡ sacrifice, offering; victim
δίκαιος, αία, ον right, just, honest, good
ἁμαρτωλός, όν sinful
9:14
προσέρχομαι, προσελεύσομαι, προσῆλθον, προσελήλυθα come to, go to, approach
μαθητής, οῦ, ὁ disciple
διὰ τί why?
Φαρισαῖος, ου, ὁ a Pharisee
νηστεύω, νηστεύσω, ἐνήστευσα fast
9:15
δύναμαι, δυνήσομαι, ἠδυνήθην be able
νυμφών, ῶνος, ὁ wedding hall, bridal chamber
πενθέω, πενθήσω, ἐπένθησα be sad, grieve, lament, mourn
ὅσος, η, ον how large, how great; as many as (plural); ἐφ' ὅσον while, as long as
μετ' = μετά with (preposition + genitive); after (+ accusative)
νυμφίος, ου, ὁ bridegroom

9:13 **τί ἐστιν**: *what it means.* **Ἔλεος** is a neuter singular accusative third declension noun (cf. App. 15). **καλέσαι** is a first aorist active infinitive (cf. App. 53, D, 4); by definition it has no ending as to person or number. It functions here as an infinitive of purpose and is equivalent to the more commonly used ἵνα clause. In the parallel passage by Luke (5:32), he adds εἰς μετανοίαν: *to repentance.*

9:14 **προσέρχονται αὐτῷ**: the compound verb governs the dative case. **ἡμεῖς καὶ οἱ Φαρισαῖοι νηστεύομεν**: when the subjects refer to different persons, the verb prefers the first over the third person. **νηστεύομεν πολλά**: *we keep many fasts;* although the neuter accusative plural may be used as an adverb, it is a cognate accusative.

9:15 **Μὴ δύνανται**: the negative interrogative particle is used when a negative answer is expected: *they are not able to . . . are they?* **οἱ υἱοὶ τοῦ νυμφῶνος**: *the children of the bridegroom;* οἱ υἱοὶ refers, in a more extended sense, to those who are closely associated with the bridegroom. Jesus compares himself to a groom and His disciples to his family members. A wedding is a time of joy and celebration. How inappropriate to fast and grieve on such an occasion. This and the next two examples are commonplace paradigms of inappropriate actions.

ἐλεύσονται δὲ ἡμέραι ὅταν ἀπαρθῇ ἀπ᾽ αὐτῶν ὁ νυμφίος, καὶ τότε νηστεύσουσιν. 9:16 οὐδεὶς δὲ ἐπιβάλλει ἐπίβλημα ῥάκους ἀγνάφου ἐπὶ ἱματίῳ παλαιῷ· αἴρει γὰρ τὸ πλήρωμα αὐτοῦ ἀπὸ τοῦ ἱματίου καὶ χεῖρον σχίσμα γίνεται. 9:17 οὐδὲ βάλλουσιν οἶνον νέον εἰς ἀσκοὺς παλαιούς·

9:15
ἡμέρα, ας, ἡ day
ὅταν when, whenever (conjunction)
ἀπαίρω, ἀπαρῶ, ἀπήρθην take away; is taken away (passive)
νηστεύω, νηστεύσω, ἐνήστευσα fast
9:16
οὐδείς, οὐδεμία, οὐδέν no (adjective); no one, nobody, nothing (substantive)
ἐπιβάλλω, ἐπιβαλῶ, ἐπέβαλον, ἐπιβέβληκα, ἐπεβλήθην lay, put on
ἐπίβλημα, ατος, τό patch
ῥάκος, ους, τό tattered garment; piece of cloth, patch
ἄγναφος, ον unbleached, unshrunken, unsized, new
ἱμάτιον, ου, τό garment, clothing; cloak, robe
παλαιός, ά, όν old
αἴρω, ἀρῶ, ἦρα, ἦρκα, ἦρμαι, ἤρθην take up, bear, take away, lift, carry, remove; keep in suspense; destroy, kill
πλήρωμα, ατος, τό that which fills, that which replaces, patch
χείρων, ον worse, more severe (comparative of κακός)
σχίσμα, ατος, τό split, tear, division, dissension
9:17
οὐδέ and not, nor (conjunction and adverb)
οἶνος, ου, ὁ wine
νέος, α, ον new, fresh, young
ἀσκός, οῦ, ὁ leather bag, wine-skin
παλαιός, ά, όν old

9:16 **ἐπιβάλλει . . . ἐπὶ**: the prefixed preposition is commonly repeated either by the same or a similar preposition. **ἐπίβλημα ῥάκους ἀγνάφου**: *a patch of new cloth*; the genitive of material expresses what something consists of. **χεῖρον** is a predicate adjective.

9:17 **οὐδὲ βάλλουσιν**: the verb is an impersonal third person plural.

εἰ δὲ μή γε, ῥήγνυνται οἱ ἀσκοὶ καὶ ὁ οἶνος ἐκχεῖται καὶ οἱ ἀσκοὶ ἀπόλλυνται· ἀλλὰ βάλλουσιν οἶνον νέον εἰς ἀσκοὺς καινούς, καὶ ἀμφότεροι συντηροῦνται.

9:18 Ταῦτα αὐτοῦ λαλοῦντος αὐτοῖς ἰδοὺ ἄρχων εἷς ἐλθὼν προσεκύνει αὐτῷ λέγων ὅτι Ἡ θυγάτηρ μου ἄρτι ἐτελεύτησεν· ἀλλὰ ἐλθὼν ἐπίθες τὴν χεῖρά σου ἐπ' αὐτήν, καὶ ζήσεται. 9:19 καὶ ἐγερθεὶς ὁ Ἰησοῦς ἠκολούθησεν αὐτῷ καὶ οἱ μαθηταὶ αὐτοῦ.

9:17

εἰ δὲ μή if not, otherwise

γε at least, indeed (an enclitic particle emphasizing the preceding word; often untranslatable)

ῥήγνυμι/ῥήσσω, ῥήξω, ἔρ(ρ)ηξα tear in pieces; break, burst

ἐκχέω, ἐκχέω/ἐκχεῶ, ἐξέχεα (1 aorist), ἐκκέχυκα, ἐκκέχυμαι, ἐξεχύθην pour out, spill, scatter

ἀπόλλυμι/ἀπολλύω, ἀπολέσω/ἀπολῶ, ἀπώλεσα, ἀπολώλεκα, ἀπόλωλα (2 perfect) lose, destroy, ruin, kill; perish (middle)

ἀλλά but, yet (conjunction)

οἶνος, ου, ὁ wine

νέος, α, ον new, fresh, young

ἀσκός, οῦ, ὁ leather bag, wine-skin

καινός, ή, όν new

ἀμφότεροι, αι, α both

συντηρέω, συντηρήσω protect, defend; be saved, be preserved (passive)

9:18

ἄρχων, οντος, ὁ chief, ruler, magistrate, prince

εἷς, μία, ἕν one, single; a (numeral and indefinite article)

προσκυνέω, προσκυνήσω, προσεκύνησα worship, prostrate oneself before, reverence before, reverence

θυγάτηρ, τρός, ἡ daughter

ἄρτι now, just now (adverb)

τελευτάω, τελευτήσω, ἐτελεύτησα, τετελεύτηκα end, finish, die

ἐπιτίθημι, ἐπιθήσω, ἐπέθηκα, ἐπιτέθεικα, ἐπιτέθειμαι, ἐπετέθην lay upon, put on

χείρ, χειρός, ἡ hand

ζάω, ζήσω/ζήσομαι, ἔζησα, ἔζηκα live

9:19

ἀκολουθέω, ἀκολουθήσω, ἠκολούθησα, ἠκολούθηκα follow (+ dative)

μαθητής, οῦ, ὁ disciple

9:17 **εἰ δὲ μή**: *if not, otherwise.*

9:18 **Ταῦτα αὐτοῦ λαλοῦντος**: *while He was speaking these words*; the participle of the genitive absolute takes a cognate accusative. **ἄρχων εἷς**: εἷς is used as an indefinite article. **ὅτι** is used as our quotation marks to introduce direct discourse. **ἐτελεύτησεν** is euphemistically used and almost always means *to die.* **ἐλθὼν ἐπίθες**: *come and place*; when a participle modifies an imperative, it is commonly changed into an imperative and the two verbs are coordinated.

9:20 Καὶ ἰδοὺ γυνὴ αἱμορροοῦσα δώδεκα ἔτη προσελθοῦσα ὄπισθεν ἥψατο τοῦ κρασπέδου τοῦ ἱματίου αὐτοῦ· 9:21 ἔλεγεν γὰρ ἐν ἑαυτῇ, Ἐὰν μόνον ἅψωμαι τοῦ ἱματίου αὐτοῦ σωθήσομαι. 9:22 ὁ δὲ Ἰησοῦς στραφεὶς καὶ ἰδὼν αὐτὴν εἶπεν, Θάρσει, θύγατερ· ἡ πίστις σου σέσωκέν σε. καὶ ἐσώθη ἡ γυνὴ ἀπὸ τῆς ὥρας ἐκείνης.

9:20
γυνή, γυναικός, ἡ woman, wife
αἱμορροέω, αἱμορροήσω suffer with hemorrhage, have a flux of blood
δώδεκα twelve (indeclinable)
ἔτος, ους, τό year
προσέρχομαι, προσελεύσομαι, προσῆλθον, προσελήλυθα come to, go to, approach
ὄπισθεν from behind
ἅπτω, ἅψω, ἧψα fasten; light, kindle; touch (middle)
κράσπεδον, ου, τό edge, border, hem; tassel
ἱμάτιον, ου, τό garment, clothing; cloak, robe
9:21
ἑαυτοῦ, ῆς, οῦ himself, herself, itself; themselves, ourselves, yourselves (in plural)
μόνον only (adverb)
ἅπτω, ἅψω, ἧψα fasten; light, kindle; touch (middle)
ἱμάτιον, ου, τό garment, clothing; cloak, robe
9:22
στρέφω, στρέψω, ἔστρεψα, ἔστραμμαι, ἐστρέφθην, ἐστράφην (2 aorist passive) turn, make a change, change
θαρσέω, θαρσήσω, ἐθάρσησα be of good courage, be cheerful
θυγάτηρ, τρός, ἡ daughter
πίστις, εως, ἡ faith, trust
σῴζω, σώσω, ἔσωσα, σέσωκα, σέσωσμαι, ἐσώθην save, rescue, preserve safe and unharmed
γυνή, γυναικός, ἡ woman, wife
ὥρα, ας, ἡ hour

9:20 **Καὶ ἰδοὺ**: at this point the narrative is interrupted as is Jesus. **αἱμορροοῦσα** is a feminine singular nominative present active participle of a contracted verb with stem in **ε** (cf. App. 56; 29). **δώδεκα ἔτη**: *for twelve years*; while the numeral is indeclinable, the third declension noun (cf. App. 15), with stem in **σ** elided, is neuter plural accusative. It is an accusative of duration of time. **ἥψατο τοῦ κρασπέδου**: the verb governs the genitive case.

9:21 **Ἐὰν . . . ἅψωμαι . . . σωθήσομαι**: the future more vivid condition expresses a positive statement of faith. ἅψωμαι is a first person singular aorist middle subjunctive (cf. App. 53, D, 2). **σωθήσομαι** is a first future passive indicative (cf. App. 53, G, 1).

9:22 **στραφεὶς καὶ ἰδὼν . . . εἶπεν**: *when He had turned around and seen . . . said*; στραφεὶς is a masculine singular nominative second aorist passive participle (cf. App. 34) with reflexive meaning.

9:23 Καὶ ἐλθὼν ὁ Ἰησοῦς εἰς τὴν οἰκίαν τοῦ ἄρχοντος καὶ ἰδὼν τοὺς αὐλητὰς καὶ τὸν ὄχλον θορυβούμενον 9:24 ἔλεγεν, Ἀναχωρεῖτε, οὐ γὰρ ἀπέθανεν τὸ κοράσιον ἀλλὰ καθεύδει. καὶ κατεγέλων αὐτοῦ. 9:25 ὅτε δὲ ἐξεβλήθη ὁ ὄχλος εἰσελθὼν ἐκράτησεν τῆς χειρὸς αὐτῆς, καὶ ἠγέρθη τὸ κοράσιον. 9:26 καὶ ἐξῆλθεν ἡ φήμη αὕτη εἰς ὅλην τὴν γῆν ἐκείνην.

9:23
οἰκία, ας, ἡ house, household, family
ἄρχων, οντος, ὁ chief, ruler, magistrate, prince
αὐλητής, οῦ, ὁ flute player
ὄχλος, ου, ὁ crowd, throng, multitude
θορυβέω, θορυβήσω disturb, throw into disorder; be troubled, be distressed (passive)
9:24
ἀναχωρέω, ἀναχωρήσω, ἀνεχώρησα go away, depart, withdraw, retire
ἀποθνήσκω, ἀποθανοῦμαι, ἀπέθανον (2 aorist) die, face death, decay
κοράσιον, ου, τό girl
καθεύδω, καθευδήσω sleep, be fast asleep
καταγελάω, καταγελάσω/καταγελάσομαι laugh at, deride, jeer, ridicule
9:25
ὅτε when, whenever (adverb)
ἐκβάλλω, ἐκβαλῶ, ἐξέβαλον, ἐκβέβληκα, ἐξεβλήθην drive out, expel, disdain, spurn, send out, lead out
εἰσέρχομαι, εἰσελεύσομαι, εἰσῆλθον (2 aorist), εἰσελήλυθα come (in, into), go (in, into), enter into, share in, come to enjoy
κρατέω, κρατήσω, ἐκράτησα, κεκράτηκα, κεκράτημαι lay hold of, grasp; retain, not remit
χείρ, χειρός, ἡ hand
κοράσιον, ου, τό girl
9:26
ἐξέρχομαι, ἐξελεύσομαι, ἐξῆλθον (2 aorist), ἐξελήλυθα go or come out of, go out
φήμη, ης, ἡ fame, rumor, report
ὅλος, η, ον all, whole, entire, complete

9:23 **Καὶ ἐλθὼν** resumes again the narrative, in the pattern of ring composition, of Jesus following the ruler (19). **αὐλητὰς**: flute players were brought in at funeral rites to play lyrical compositions expressive of grief or to accompany psalms sung for a departed soul.

9:24 **κατεγέλων αὐτοῦ**: *they continually laughed at him*; the finite verb is third person plural imperfect active indicative of a contracted verb with stem in **α** (cf. App. 55). The imperfect tense denotes progressive, continued, and repeated action (aspect) in past time. The compound verb governs the genitive case.

9:25 **εἰσελθὼν ἐκράτησεν τῆς χειρὸς**: the subject is Jesus. The verb governs the genitive case.

9:26 **εἰς ὅλην τὴν γῆν ἐκείνην**: *in all that land*; εἰς (+ accusative) is frequently equivalent to ἐν (+ dative, 9:31).

9:27 Καὶ παράγοντι ἐκεῖθεν τῷ Ἰησοῦ ἠκολούθησαν [αὐτῷ] δύο τυφλοὶ κράζοντες καὶ λέγοντες, Ἐλέησον ἡμᾶς, υἱὸς Δαυίδ.
9:28 ἐλθόντι δὲ εἰς τὴν οἰκίαν προσῆλθον αὐτῷ οἱ τυφλοί, καὶ λέγει αὐτοῖς ὁ Ἰησοῦς, Πιστεύετε ὅτι δύναμαι τοῦτο ποιῆσαι; λέγουσιν αὐτῷ, Ναὶ κύριε.
9:29 τότε ἥψατο τῶν ὀφθαλμῶν αὐτῶν λέγων, Κατὰ τὴν πίστιν ὑμῶν γενηθήτω ὑμῖν.
9:30 καὶ ἠνεῴχθησαν αὐτῶν οἱ ὀφθαλμοί. καὶ ἐνεβριμήθη αὐτοῖς ὁ Ἰησοῦς λέγων,

---

9:27
παράγω, παράξω lead beside, bring in (transitive); pass by, depart, go away (intransitive)
ἐκεῖθεν from there, from that place (adverb)
δύο two
τυφλός, ή, όν blind
κράζω, κεκράξομαι/κράξω, ἐκέκραξα/ἔκραξα, κέκραγα cry out, scream; call, call out, cry
ἐλεέω, ἐλεήσω, ἠλέησα, ἠλέημαι, ἠλεήθην pity, show mercy
9:28
προσέρχομαι, προσελεύσομαι, προσῆλθον, προσελήλυθα come to, go to, approach
τυφλός, ή, όν blind
πιστεύω, πιστεύσω, ἐπίστευσα, πεπίστευκα, πεπίστευμαι, ἐπιστεύθην believe, entrust
δύναμαι, δυνήσομαι, ἠδυνήθην be able
ναί yes, indeed, certainly (particle of affirmation)
9:29
ἅπτω, ἅψω, ἧψα fasten; light, kindle; touch (middle)
ὀφθαλμός, οῦ, ὁ eye
κατά near, towards, by, in accordance with, after the manner of (preposition + accusative); down from, against (+ genitive)
πίστις, εως, ἡ faith, trust
9:30
ἀνοίγω, ἀνοίξω, ἀνέῳξα/ἤνοιξα, ἀνέῳγα, ἀνέῳγμαι, ἠνεῴχθην open
ὀφθαλμός, οῦ, ὁ eye
ἐμβριμάομαι, ἐμβριμήσομαι, ἐνεβριμησάμην, ἐνεβριμήθην be deeply moved, groan deeply; charge, forbid, warn sternly

---

9:27 **παράγοντι**: *as He passed on*; the verbal form has an intransitive meaning. **αὐτῷ**: the personal pronoun is pleonastic. **Ἐλέησον** is a second person singular aorist active imperative (cf. App. 53, D, 3).

9:28 **εἰς τὴν οἰκίαν**: the reference is probably to Peter's house (8:14), where He was staying. Although the two blind have made their plea for healing a public issue, Jesus prefers to resolve the matter in the privacy of the home.

9:29 **ἥψατο τῶν ὀφθαλμῶν**: the verb governs the genitive case. **γενηθήτω ὑμῖν**: *let it be done to you*; the verb form is an impersonal third person singular first aorist passive imperative (cf. App. 53, G, 3). The pronoun is a dative of advantage.

9:30 **ἠνεῴχθησαν** takes not only a double augment of the stem but also an augmented prefix. **ἐνεβριμήθη αὐτοῖς**: *warned them sternly*; the verb takes a dative of the person scolded.

Ὁρᾶτε μηδεὶς γινωσκέτω. 9:31 οἱ δὲ ἐξελθόντες διεφήμισαν αὐτὸν ἐν
ὅλῃ τῇ γῇ ἐκείνῃ.
9:32 Αὐτῶν δὲ ἐξερχομένων ἰδοὺ προσήνεγκαν αὐτῷ ἄνθρωπον
κωφὸν δαιμονιζόμενον. 9:33 καὶ ἐκβληθέντος τοῦ δαιμονίου
ἐλάλησεν ὁ κωφός.

9:30
μηδείς, μηδεμία, μηδέν not one, none, no one, nothing
γινώσκω, γνώσομαι, ἔγνων, ἔγνωκα, ἔγνωσμαι, ἐγνώσθην know, learn, understand
9:31
ἐξέρχομαι, ἐξελεύσομαι, ἐξῆλθον (2 aorist), ἐξελήλυθα go or come out of, go out
διαφημίζω, διαφημίσω, διεφήμισα report, proclaim, spread news about, spread widely, disseminate
ὅλος, η, ον all, whole, entire, complete
9:32
προσφέρω, προσοίσω, προσήνεγκα, προσήνεγκον (2 aorist), προσηνέχθην bring, offer, present
κωφός, ή, όν blunt, dull; dull of hearing, deprived of hearing; deaf; dumb, mute
δαιμονίζομαι, δαιμονίσομαι, ἐδαιμονίσθην be possessed by a demon
9:33
ἐκβάλλω, ἐκβαλῶ, ἐξέβαλον, ἐκβέβληκα, ἐξεβλήθην drive out, expel, disdain, spurn, send out, lead out
δαιμόνιον, ου, τό deity, divinity; demon, evil spirit
λαλέω, λαλήσω, ἐλάλησα, λελάληκα, λελάλημαι, ἐλαλήθην speak, address, preach
κωφός, ή, όν blunt, dull; dull of hearing, deprived of hearing; deaf; dumb, mute

---

9:30 **Ὁρᾶτε μηδεὶς γινωσκέτω**: *take care and let no one know*; Ὁρᾶτε is a second person plural present active imperative of a contracted verb with stem in **α** (cf. App. 55). Supply καὶ: the imperative is usually found without a conjunction (asyndeton) when followed by another imperative.

9:31 **διεφήμισαν**: through faith they gained physical sight, through disobedience they incurred spiritual blindness.

9:32 **Αὐτῶν δὲ ἐξερχομένων**: the subject of the genitive absolute is the two men formerly blind. **προσήνεγκαν** is used as a first aorist (cf. App. 53, D, 1) and, like liquid verbs, it loses the intervocalic **σ**. **ἄνθρωπον κωφὸν δαιμονιζόμενον**: *a mute man because he was possessed by an evil spirit.*

9:33 **ἐκβληθέντος τοῦ δαιμονίου**: *after the evil spirit had been cast out*; the construction is a genitive absolute. Since the action of the aorist participle precedes that of the aorist verb **ἐλάλησεν**, it has the force of an English pluperfect.

καὶ ἐθαύμασαν οἱ ὄχλοι λέγοντες, Οὐδέποτε ἐφάνη οὕτως ἐν τῷ Ἰσραήλ. 9:34 οἱ δὲ Φαρισαῖοι ἔλεγον, Ἐν τῷ ἄρχοντι τῶν δαιμονίων ἐκβάλλει τὰ δαιμόνια.

9:35 Καὶ περιῆγεν ὁ Ἰησοῦς τὰς πόλεις πάσας καὶ τὰς κώμας διδάσκων ἐν ταῖς συναγωγαῖς αὐτῶν καὶ κηρύσσων τὸ εὐαγγέλιον τῆς βασιλείας καὶ θεραπεύων πᾶσαν νόσον καὶ πᾶσαν μαλακίαν. 9:36 Ἰδὼν δὲ τοὺς ὄχλους ἐσπλαγχνίσθη περὶ αὐτῶν,

---

9:33

θαυμάζω, θαυμάσομαι, ἐθαύμασα, ἐθαυμάσθην wonder, marvel, be astonished

ὄχλος, ου, ὁ crowd, throng, multitude

οὐδέποτε never (adverb)

φαίνω, φανῶ, ἔφηνα, πέφαγκα, πέφηνα, πέφασμαι, ἐφάνθην, ἐφάνην shine, give light, be bright; be seen, appear, be visible (middle and passive)

9:34

ἄρχων, οντος, ὁ chief, ruler, magistrate, prince

δαιμόνιον, ου, τό deity, divinity; demon, evil spirit

ἐκβάλλω, ἐκβαλῶ, ἐξέβαλον, ἐκβέβληκα, ἐξεβλήθην drive out, expel, disdain, spurn, send out, lead out

9:35

περιάγω, περιάξω lead around; traverse

πόλις, εως, ἡ city

κώμη, ης, ἡ village, small town

διδάσκω, διδάξω, ἐδίδαξα, ἐδιδάχθην teach, instruct

κηρύσσω, κηρύξω, ἐκήρυξα, ἐκηρύχθην announce openly, proclaim aloud

εὐαγγέλιον, ου, τό good news, gospel, glad tidings

θεραπεύω, θεραπεύσω, ἐθεράπευσα, ἐθεραπεύθην care for, heal, restore

νόσος, ου, ἡ disease, sickness, illness

μαλακία, ας, ἡ softness, weakness, infirmity

9:36

ὄχλος, ου, ὁ crowd, throng, multitude

σπλαγχνίζομαι, σπλαγχνίσομαι, ἐσπλαγχνίσθην have compassion, feel sympathy, be moved with pity

---

9:33 **Οὐδέποτε ἐφάνη οὕτως**: *nothing like this was ever seen.*

9:34 **Ἐν τῷ ἄρχοντι**: *by the prince;* the preposition with a person expresses agency: *with the help of, through, by.*

9:35 **περιῆγεν . . . τὰς πόλεις . . . καὶ τὰς κώμας**: *went through the towns and villages;* the intransitive verb takes an accusative of places travelled through.

9:36 **ἐσπλαγχνίσθη** is a third person singular first aorist middle indicative of a deponent verb (cf. App. 53, D, 1).

ὅτι ἦσαν ἐσκυλμένοι καὶ ἐρριμμένοι ὡσεὶ πρόβατα μὴ ἔχοντα
ποιμένα. 9:37 τότε λέγει τοῖς μαθηταῖς αὐτοῦ, Ὁ μὲν θερισμὸς
πολύς, οἱ δὲ ἐργάται ὀλίγοι· 9:38 δεήθητε οὖν τοῦ κυρίου τοῦ
θερισμοῦ ὅπως ἐκβάλῃ ἐργάτας εἰς τὸν θερισμὸν αὐτοῦ.

9:36
σκύλλω, σκυλλῶ, ἔσκυλμαι weary, harass; trouble, bother, annoy
ῥίπτω/ῥιπτέω, ῥίψω, ἔρριψα, ἔρριμαι hurl, throw; lay down, set on the ground; be dispersed, be scattered (passive)
ὡσεί as if, as, like (adverb)
πρόβατον, ου, τό sheep
ποιμήν, ένος, ὁ shepherd, herdsman, guardian
9:37
μαθητής, οῦ, ὁ disciple
θερισμός, οῦ, ὁ harvest
πολύς, πολλή, πολύ much, large, many (in plural)
ἐργάτης, ου, ὁ workman, laborer
ὀλίγος, η, ον little, small; few (plural)
9:38
δέομαι, δεήσομαι, ἐδεήθην ask, request; pray, beseech, supplicate
θερισμός, οῦ, ὁ harvest
ἐκβάλλω, ἐκβαλῶ, ἐξέβαλον, ἐκβέβληκα, ἐξεβλήθην drive out, expel, disdain, spurn, send out, lead out
ἐργάτης, ου, ὁ workman, laborer
θερισμός, οῦ, ὁ harvest

9:36 **ὡσεὶ** is a particle, similar to ὡς, introducing a simile: the crowds are compared to sheep without a shepherd. **μὴ ἔχοντα**: the negative μὴ regularly negates participles in Koine.

9:37 **Ὁ μὲν . . . οἱ δὲ:** supply the appropriate forms of εἰμί (App. 63) in these two antithetical clauses.

9:38 **δεήθητε . . . τοῦ κυρίου**: *ask the Lord*; the verb form is a second person plural first aorist middle imperative (cf. App. 53, G, 3) of a deponent verb. The verb governs the genitive case.

10 Καὶ προσκαλεσάμενος τοὺς δώδεκα μαθητὰς αὐτοῦ ἔδωκεν αὐτοῖς ἐξουσίαν πνευμάτων ἀκαθάρτων ὥστε ἐκβάλλειν αὐτὰ καὶ θεραπεύειν πᾶσαν νόσον καὶ πᾶσαν μαλακίαν. 10:2 Τῶν δὲ δώδεκα ἀποστόλων τὰ ὀνόματά ἐστιν ταῦτα· πρῶτος Σίμων ὁ λεγόμενος Πέτρος καὶ Ἀνδρέας ὁ ἀδελφὸς αὐτοῦ, καὶ Ἰάκωβος ὁ τοῦ Ζεβεδαίου καὶ Ἰωάννης ὁ ἀδελφὸς αὐτοῦ,

---

10:1
προσκαλέω, προσκαλέσω, προσεκάλεσα, προσκέκληκα, προσκέκλημαι, προσεκλήθην call on, summon, invite, call to oneself
δώδεκα twelve (indeclinable)
μαθητής, οῦ, ὁ disciple
δίδωμι, δώσω, ἔδωκα, ἔδων (2 aorist), δέδωκα, δέδομαι, ἐδόθην give
ἐξουσία, ας, ἡ authority, right, ability, might, power
πνεῦμα, ατος, τό wind, spirit, mind, Holy Spirit
ἀκάθαρτος, ον unclean, impure; lewd; foul
ὥστε so that, so as to (conjunction)
θεραπεύω, θεραπεύσω, ἐθεράπευσα, ἐθεραπεύθην care for, heal, restore
νόσος, ου, ἡ disease, sickness, illness
μαλακία, ας, ἡ softness, weakness, infirmity
10:2
δώδεκα twelve (indeclinable)
ἀπόστολος, ου, ὁ messenger, agent, delegate, apostle
ὄνομα, ατος, τό name
πρῶτος, η, ον first, before, earlier, foremost
Φίλιππος, ου, ὁ Philip
Βαρθολομαίος, ου, ὁ Bartholomew
Θωμᾶς, ᾶ, ὁ Thomas (Aramaic = "twin")
τελώνης, ου, ὁ tax-collector, publican
Ἀλφαῖος, ου, ὁ Alphaeus
Θαδδαῖος, ου, ὁ Thaddaeus

10:1 **ἐξουσίαν πνευμάτων ἀκαθάρτων**: *authority over unclean spirits*; πνευμάτων is an objective genitive (cf. App. 65): they control and drive the unclean spirits out.

10:2 **τὰ ὀνόματά ἐστιν**: Neuter plural subjects are considered as collective nouns and regularly take a singular verb. **Ἰάκωβος ὁ τοῦ Ζεβεδαίου**: James, the son of Zebedee; ὁ τοῦ Ζεβεδαίου is an abbreviated form for **ὁ υἱὸς τοῦ Ζεβεδαίου**.

10:3 Φίλιππος καὶ Βαρθολομαῖος, Θωμᾶς καὶ Μαθθαῖος ὁ τελώνης,
Ἰάκωβος ὁ τοῦ Ἁλφαίου καὶ Θαδδαῖος, 10:4 Σίμων ὁ Καναναῖος καὶ
Ἰούδας ὁ Ἰσκαριώτης ὁ καὶ παραδοὺς αὐτόν.
10:5 Τούτους τοὺς δώδεκα ἀπέστειλεν ὁ Ἰησοῦς παραγγείλας
αὐτοῖς λέγων, Εἰς ὁδὸν ἐθνῶν μὴ ἀπέλθητε καὶ εἰς πόλιν Σαμαριτῶν
μὴ εἰσέλθητε·

10:4
Καναναῖος, ου, ὁ Cananaean
Ἰούδας, α, ὁ Judas (Greek), Judah (Hebrew)
Ἰσκαριώτης, ου, ὁ Iscariot
παραδίδωμι, παραδώσω, παρέδωκα, παρέδων (2 aorist), παραδέδωκα, παραδέδομαι, παρεδόθην give, hand over, give over, deliver, give up, betray
10:5
δώδεκα twelve (indeclinable)
ἀποστέλλω, ἀποστελῶ, ἀπέστειλα, ἀπέσταλκα, ἀπέσταλμαι, ἀπεστάλην send, send away, send out
παραγγέλλω, παραγγελλῶ announce, notify; command, direct
ὁδός, οῦ, ἡ road, way, journey
ἔθνος, ους, τό nation, people
ἀπέρχομαι, ἀπελεύσομαι, ἀπῆλθον, ἀπελήλυθα go, go away, depart
πόλις, εως, ἡ city
Σαμαρίτης, ου, ὁ Samaritan
εἰσέρχομαι, εἰσελεύσομαι, εἰσῆλθον (2 aorist), εἰσελήλυθα come (in, into), go (in, into), enter into, share in, come to enjoy

---

10:3 **ὁ τελώνης** stands in apposition to Matthew.

10:4 **ὁ Καναναῖος**: the name stands in apposition to Simon to distinguish him from Simon Peter. The cognomen does not refer to an inhabitant of Cana but to a party member of the Zealots. Luke (6:15) calls him τὸν Ζηλωτήν *the Zealot.* **Ἰσκαριώτης** is the surname of both Judas and Simon, his father. **ὁ . . . παραδοὺς**: the verbal form is a masculine singular nominative second aorist active participle of a **μι** verb with stem in **δο** (cf. App. 58).

10:5 **ἀπέστειλεν**: the liquid aorist omits the intervocalic **σ** and shows compensatory lengthening in the stem. **παραγγείλας**: *after He had instructed them*: the verbal form is an aorist active participle of a liquid verb; the endings are those of the aorist active participle, but the liquid omits the -σ- (cf. App. 31). Since the action of the aorist participle precedes that of the aorist tense of the main verb, it is translated as a pluperfect. The participle governs the dative case. **λέγων**: *by saying*; the circumstantial participle expresses means. **Εἰς ὁδὸν ἐθνῶν μὴ ἀπέλθητε**: *do not go on a journey to the Gentiles*; **ἐθνῶν** is an objective genitive (cf. App. 65): do not visit the Gentiles. **μὴ ἀπέλθητε . . . μὴ εἰσέλθητε** are prohibitive subjunctives. After the resurrection, they are commanded to preach the gospel to all the world (Lk 16:15).

10:6 πορεύεσθε δὲ μᾶλλον πρὸς τὰ πρόβατα τὰ ἀπολωλότα οἴκου Ἰσραήλ. 10:7 πορευόμενοι δὲ κηρύσσετε λέγοντες ὅτι Ἤγγικεν ἡ βασιλεία τῶν οὐρανῶν. 10:8 ἀσθενοῦντας θεραπεύετε, νεκροὺς ἐγείρετε, λεπροὺς καθαρίζετε, δαιμόνια ἐκβάλλετε·δωρεὰν ἐλάβετε, δωρεὰν δότε.

10:6

πορεύομαι, πορεύσομαι, πεπόρευμαι, ἐπορεύθην go, proceed, travel

μᾶλλον more, to a greater degree, rather (adverb)

πρός for, for the purpose of (preposition + genitive); with, to, towards, unto, for, for the purpose of, with reference to, in relation to, of, concerning (+ accusative); near, at, by (preposition + dative)

πρόβατον, ου, τό sheep

ἀπόλλυμι/ἀπολλύω, ἀπολέσω/ἀπολῶ, ἀπώλεσα, ἀπολώλεκα, ἀπόλωλα (2 perfect) lose, destroy, ruin, kill; perish, die, be lost (middle)

οἶκος, ου, ὁ house, dwelling

10:7

πορεύομαι, πορεύσομαι, πεπόρευμαι, ἐπορεύθην go, proceed, travel

κηρύσσω, κηρύξω, ἐκήρυξα, ἐκηρύχθην announce openly, proclaim aloud

ἐγγίζω, ἐγγίσω, ἤγγισα, ἤγγικα approach, draw near

10:8

ἀσθενέω, ἀσθενήσω, ἠσθένησα be weak, be sick

θεραπεύω, θεραπεύσω, ἐθεράπευσα, ἐθεραπεύθην care for, heal, restore

νεκρός, ά, όν dead

καθαρίζω, καθαρίσω, ἐκαθάρισα cleanse, render pure

δαιμόνιον, ου, τό deity, divinity; demon, evil spirit

δωρεάν as a gift, without payment, freely (used as an adverb)

λαμβάνω, λήμψομαι, ἔλαβον, εἴληφα, εἴλημμαι, ἐλήφθην take, receive, accept

δίδωμι, δώσω, ἔδωκα, ἔδων (2 aorist), δέδωκα, δέδομαι, ἐδόθην give

---

10:6 **τὰ πρόβατα τὰ ἀπολωλότα οἴκου Ἰσραήλ**: for now they are commanded to teach and preach and minister only to the house of Israel. The people, like sheep, are lost because their shepherds have strayed. Ἰσραήλ is an appositional genitive, identifying οἴκου more specifically (cf. App. 65).

10:7 **πορευόμενοι δὲ κηρύσσετε**: when a participle modifies an imperative, it is commonly changed into an imperative and the two verbs are coordinated in translation. **ὅτι** introduces a direct statement and is equivalent to our quotation marks.

10:8 **ἀσθενοῦντας . . . νεκροὺς . . . λεπροὺς . . . δαιμόνια**: the article, included in translation, may be omitted in Greek if the noun is suficiently definite by itself. **ἐλάβετε** is a second person plural second aorist active indicative (cf. App. 54). **δότε** is a second person plural second aorist active imperative (cf. App. 58).

10:9 Μὴ κτήσησθε χρυσὸν μηδὲ ἄργυρον μηδὲ χαλκὸν εἰς τὰς ζώνας ὑμῶν, 10:10 μὴ πήραν εἰς ὁδὸν μηδὲ δύο χιτῶνας μηδὲ ὑποδήματα μηδὲ ῥάβδον· ἄξιος γὰρ ὁ ἐργάτης τῆς τροφῆς αὐτοῦ. 10:11 εἰς ἣν δ' ἂν πόλιν ἢ κώμην εἰσέλθητε, ἐξετάσατε τίς ἐν αὐτῇ ἄξιός ἐστιν· κἀκεῖ μείνατε ἕως ἂν ἐξέλθητε.

10:9

κτάομαι, κτήσομαι, ἐκτησάμην, κέκτημαι procure, acquire, get; make gain, gain; preserve, save

χρυσός, οῦ, ὁ gold

ἄργυρος, ου, ὁ silver; money

χαλκός, οῦ, ὁ copper, bronze; copper money; money

ζώνη, ης, ἡ belt, girdle

10:10

πήρα, ας, ἡ leather bag, traveler's bag, knapsack

ὁδός, οῦ, ἡ road, way, journey

χιτών, ῶνος, ὁ tunic, inner garment, shirt

ὑπόδημα, ατος, τό sandal

ῥάβδος, ου, ἡ rod, staff, stick

ἄξιος, ία, ιον worthy

ἐργάτης, ου, ὁ workman, laborer

τροφή, ῆς, ἡ nourishment, food

10:11

ὅς, ἥ, ὅ + ἄν (ἐάν) whoever, whatever

πόλις, εως, ἡ city

κώμη, ης, ἡ village, small town

ἐξετάζω, ἐξετάσω, ἐξήτασα search out, inquire, interrogate

ἄξιος, ία, ιον worthy

κἀκεῖ = καί ἐκεῖ and there, and in that place (adverb)

μένω, μενῶ, ἔμεινα, μεμένηκα stay, rest, dwell

ἐξέρχομαι, ἐξελεύσομαι, ἐξῆλθον (2 aorist), ἐξελήλυθα go or come out of, go out

---

10:9 **μὴ κτήσησθε** is a prohibitive subjunctive. **εἰς τὰς ζώνας**: εἰς (+ accusative) is frequently equivalent to ἐν (+ dative). These belts are used to carry money.

10:10 **μὴ πήραν** is a continuation of the catalogue, the object of Μὴ κτήσησθε in the previous verse. **εἰς ὁδὸν**: *for the journey*; here the preposition introduces a notion of purpose. **ἄξιος . . . τῆς τροφῆς**: the adjective, as in English, governs the genitive case. Supply the verb ἐστίν.

10:11 **εἰς ἣν δ' ἂν πόλιν** introduces a future more vivid condition (App. 70). **ἐξετάσατε** introduces an indirect question. **ἕως ἂν ἐξέλθητε**: *until you depart*; ἕως with the aorist subjunctive generally requires ἂν to denote that the commencement of one event depends on another.

10:12 εἰσερχόμενοι δὲ εἰς τὴν οἰκίαν ἀσπάσασθε αὐτήν· 10:13 καὶ ἐὰν μὲν ᾖ ἡ οἰκία ἀξία, ἐλθάτω ἡ εἰρήνη ὑμῶν ἐπ᾽ αὐτήν, ἐὰν δὲ μὴ ᾖ ἀξία, ἡ εἰρήνη ὑμῶν πρὸς ὑμᾶς ἐπιστραφήτω. 10:14 καὶ ὃς ἂν μὴ δέξηται ὑμᾶς μηδὲ ἀκούσῃ τοὺς λόγους ὑμῶν, ἐξερχόμενοι ἔξω τῆς οἰκίας ἢ τῆς πόλεως ἐκείνης ἐκτινάξατε τὸν κονιορτὸν τῶν ποδῶν ὑμῶν. 10:15 ἀμὴν λέγω ὑμῖν, ἀνεκτότερον ἔσται

10:12
ἀσπάζομαι, ἀσπάσομαι, ἠσπασάμην, ἤσπασμαι salute, greet, welcome; treat with affection, be fond of, cherish; embrace
10:13
ἄξιος, ία, ιον worthy
εἰρήνη, ης, ἡ peace
ἐπιστρέφω, ἐπιστρέψω, ἐπέστρεψα, ἐπέστραμμαι, ἐπεστρέφθην, ἐπεστράφην (2 aorist passive) turn, turn around, return
10:14
ὅς, ἥ, ὅ + ἄν (ἐάν) whoever, whatever
δέχομαι, δέξομαι, ἐδεξάμην, δέδεγμαι take, receive, welcome, accept
μηδέ and not, but not, nor (following a negation)
λόγος, ου, ὁ word, doctrine, account, reason, statement, saying
ἐξέρχομαι, ἐξελεύσομαι, ἐξῆλθον (2 aorist), ἐξελήλυθα go or come out of, go out
ἔξω outside, out (adverb); out of (preposition)
ἐκεῖνος, η, ον that, that one, the former
ἐκτινάσσω, ἐκτινάξω, ἐξετίναξα shake off
κονιορτός, οῦ, ὁ dust
πούς, ποδός, ὁ foot
10:15
ἀμήν in truth, verily (Hebrew)
ἀνεκτότερος, α, ον more bearable, endurable, tolerable (comparative of ἀνεκτός, ή, όν)

10:12 **εἰσερχόμενοι δὲ εἰς τὴν οἰκίαν**: *as you enter the home*; the prefixed preposition is commonly repeated by either the same or a similar preposition.

10:13 **καὶ ἐὰν μὲν ᾖ** introduces a future more vivid condition (App. 70). **ἐλθάτω ἡ εἰρήνη ὑμῶν**: *let your peace come*; the verb is a third person singular first aorist imperative. Occasionally the second aorist stem takes first aorist endings without the **σ** (cf. App. 53, D, 3). The form predominates especially in the imperative. The condition may substitute an imperative for a future indicative in the apodosis. **ἡ εἰρήνη ὑμῶν πρὸς ὑμᾶς ἐπιστραφήτω**: in a negative situation, they are not to grow angry.

10:14 **ἐκτινάξατε τὸν κονιορτὸν τῶν ποδῶν ὑμῶν**: the action symbolizes abrogation of responsibility and rejection of those who reject the disciples.

10:15 **ἀνεκτότερον . . . γῇ Σοδόμων . . . ἢ τῇ πόλει**: the comparative adjective governs the dative case and is followed by the conjunction **ἤ**. In this construction, both members being compared must be in the same case. Σοδόμων is an appositional genitive, identifying γῇ more specifically (cf. App. 65).

γῇ Σοδόμων καὶ Γομόρρων ἐν ἡμέρᾳ κρίσεως ἢ τῇ πόλει ἐκείνῃ.
10:16 Ἰδοὺ ἐγὼ ἀποστέλλω ὑμᾶς ὡς πρόβατα ἐν μέσῳ λύκων·
γίνεσθε οὖν φρόνιμοι ὡς οἱ ὄφεις καὶ ἀκέραιοι ὡς αἱ περιστεραί.
10:17 προσέχετε δὲ ἀπὸ τῶν ἀνθρώπων· παραδώσουσιν γὰρ ὑμᾶς
εἰς συνέδρια καὶ ἐν ταῖς συναγωγαῖς αὐτῶν μαστιγώσουσιν ὑμᾶς·
10:18 καὶ ἐπὶ ἡγεμόνας δὲ καὶ βασιλεῖς ἀχθήσεσθε ἕνεκεν ἐμοῦ εἰς
μαρτύριον αὐτοῖς καὶ τοῖς ἔθνεσιν.

10:15
Σόδομα, ων, τά Sodom
Γόμορρα, ων, τά and ας, ἡ Gomorrah
ἡμέρα, ας, ἡ day
κρίσις, εως, ἡ judgment, justice, righteousness, condemnation
ἐκεῖνος, η, ον that, that one, the former
10:16
ἀποστέλλω, ἀποστελῶ, ἀπέστειλα, ἀπέσταλκα, ἀπέσταλμαι, ἀπεστάλην send, send away, send out
ὡς as, like, when, after, about (with numerals), how, provided that (adverb, conjunction)
πρόβατον, ου, τό sheep
μέσος, η, ον middle, in, among (as adjective + genitive); the middle (as noun τὸ μέσον)
λύκος, ου, ὁ wolf
φρόνιμος, η, ον thoughtful, prudent, wise
ὄφις, εως, ὁ snake, serpent
ἀκέραιος, ον unmixed; pure, innocent, sincere, without guile, blameless
περιστερά, ᾶς, ἡ dove, pigeon
10:17
προσέχω, προσέξω, προσέσχον (2 aorist) pay attention to, give heed to, consider; beware of, take heed of, guard against (followed by ἀπό, μή)
παραδίδωμι, παραδώσω, παρέδωκα, παρέδων (2 aorist), παραδέδωκα, παραδέδομαι, παρεδόθην give, hand over, give over, deliver, give up, betray
συνέδριον, ίου, τό assembly, high council, Sanhedrin
μαστιγόω, μαστιγώσω, ἐμαστίγωσα, ἐμαστιγώθην scourge, whip, flog, beat
10:18
ἡγεμών, όνος, ὁ guide, leader, prince
βασιλεύς, έως, ὁ king
ἄγω, ἄξω, ἤγαγον, ἦχα, ἦγμαι, ἤχθην lead, bring, arrest
ἕνεκεν/ἕνεκα because of, on account of, for the sake of (preposition + genitive)
μαρτύριον, ίου, τό proof, testimony, evidence
ἔθνος, ους, τό nation, people

10:16 **ὡς**: the conjunction introduces a comparison. **ἐν μέσῳ λύκων**: the preposition without the article and a genitive noun can carry the meaning of *in the middle of* or *among*. **ὡς . . . ὡς** continues the comparison: the snake is desribed as φρονιμώτατος *the wisest* of animals (Gen 3:2); the dove represents purity and harmlessness.

10:17 **παραδώσουσιν γὰρ ὑμᾶς . . . μαστιγώσουσιν ὑμᾶς**: the chiastic order of the verse emphasizes the systematic hostility of men.

10:18 **εἰς μαρτύριον**: *as proof*; the preposition introduces the notion of purpose. The disciples will become witnesses of the truth.

10:19 ὅταν δὲ παραδῶσιν ὑμᾶς, μὴ μεριμνήσητε πῶς ἢ τί λαλήσητε· δοθήσεται γὰρ ὑμῖν ἐν ἐκείνῃ τῇ ὥρᾳ τί λαλήσητε· 10:20 οὐ γὰρ ὑμεῖς ἐστε οἱ λαλοῦντες ἀλλὰ τὸ πνεῦμα τοῦ πατρὸς ὑμῶν τὸ λαλοῦν ἐν ὑμῖν. 10:21 παραδώσει δὲ ἀδελφὸς ἀδελφὸν εἰς θάνατον καὶ πατὴρ τέκνον, καὶ ἐπαναστήσονται τέκνα ἐπὶ γονεῖς καὶ θανατώσουσιν αὐτούς.

10:19

ὅταν when, whenever (conjunction)

παραδίδωμι, παραδώσω, παρέδωκα, παρέδων (2 aorist), παραδέδωκα, παραδέδομαι, παρεδόθην give, hand over, give over, deliver, give up, betray

μεριμνάω, μεριμνήσω, ἐμερίμνησα have anxiety, be anxious; expend careful thought, concern oneself

πῶς how? in what way? in what sense? (interrogative adverb)

λαλέω, λαλήσω, ἐλάλησα, λελάληκα, λελάλημαι, ἐλαλήθην speak, address, preach

ἐκεῖνος, η, ον that, that one, the former

ὥρα, ας, ἡ hour

10:20

λαλέω, λαλήσω, ἐλάλησα, λελάληκα, λελάλημαι, ἐλαλήθην speak, address, preach

πνεῦμα, ατος, τό wind, spirit, mind, Holy Spirit

10:21

παραδίδωμι, παραδώσω, παρέδωκα, παρέδων (2 aorist), παραδέδωκα, παραδέδομαι, παρεδόθην give, hand over, give over, deliver, give up, betray

θάνατος, ου, ὁ death

τεκνίον, ου, τό little child

ἐπανίστημι raise up against; rise up against (middle)

γονεύς, έως, ὁ father; parents (plural)

θανατόω, θανατώσω, ἐθανάτωσα kill, put to death, deliver to death

---

10:19 **μὴ μεριμνήσητε**: the prohibitive subjunctive introduces indirect questions, before which supply *about*. **πῶς ἢ τί λαλήσητε**: *how or what you shall speak*; indirect questions retain the mood and the tense of the direct question. Since these are originally deliberative questions, they retain the subjunctive mood. The deliberative subjunctive (present or aorist) is used when the speaker is perplexed about *what he is to do* or *say* or *think*, etc. Since the future is also used in deliberative questions, the subjunctive is appropriately translated by the future. **δοθήσεται . . . τί λαλήσητε**: the first future passive introduces an indirect question that was originally a deliberative question.

10:20 **οὐ γὰρ ὑμεῖς ἐστε οἱ λαλοῦντες**: *you are not the ones who are speaking*; the combination of the second person plural pronoun and the second person plural verb occurring at the beginning of the clause contrasts sharply with the subject of the next clause. **ἀλλὰ τὸ πεῦμα . . . τὸ λαλοῦν**: *but it is the Spirit . . . that speaks*; supply the verb ἐστίν in this slightly elliptical construction.

10:21 **ἐπαναστήσονται** is a third person plural future middle indicative (cf. App. 53, B, 1).

10:22 καὶ ἔσεσθε μισούμενοι ὑπὸ πάντων διὰ τὸ ὄνομά μου· ὁ δὲ ὑπομείνας εἰς τέλος οὗτος σωθήσεται. 10:23 ὅταν δὲ διώκωσιν ὑμᾶς ἐν τῇ πόλει ταύτῃ, φεύγετε εἰς τὴν ἑτέραν· ἀμὴν γὰρ λέγω ὑμῖν, οὐ μὴ τελέσητε τὰς πόλεις τοῦ Ἰσραὴλ ἕως ἂν ἔλθῃ ὁ υἱὸς τοῦ ἀνθρώπου.

10:24 Οὐκ ἔστιν μαθητὴς ὑπὲρ τὸν διδάσκαλον οὐδὲ δοῦλος ὑπὲρ τὸν κύριον αὐτοῦ.

10:22
μισέω, μισήσω, ἐμίσησα, μεμίσηκα hate, detest, abhor; love less, esteem less
ὄνομα, ατος, τό name
ὑπομένω, ὑπομενῶ remain; remain constant, persevere
τέλος, ους, τό end
σῴζω, σώσω, ἔσωσα, σέσωκα, σέσωσμαι, ἐσώθην save, rescue, preserve safe and unharmed
10:23
ὅταν when, whenever (conjunction)
διώκω, διώξω, ἐδίωξα, δεδίωγμαι, ἐδιώχθην persecute, pursue, seek after
φεύγω, φεύξομαι, ἔφυγον (2 aorist) flee, flee from, avoid, shun
ἕτερος, α, ον other, another
ἀμήν in truth, verily (Hebrew)
τελέω, τελέσω, ἐτέλεσα, τετέλεκα, τετέλεσμαι, ἐτελέσθην finish, finish (going through), fulfill, accomplish
ἄν (a conditional particle indicating contingency in certain constructions)
10:24
μαθητής, οῦ, ὁ disciple
ὑπέρ above, in behalf of, about, for (preposition + genitive)
διδάσκαλος, ου, ὁ master, teacher
οὐδέ and not, nor (conjunction and adverb)
δοῦλος, ου, ὁ slave, servant

10:22 **ἔσεσθε μισούμενοι** is a periphrastic construction. The periphrase of εἰμί in the future (App. 63) and a present participle (cf. App. 56) to form a future tense is not an unusual construction. **ὑπὸ πάντων**: the preposition takes the genitive case expressing agency. **ὑπομείνας** is the first aorist active participle of the liquid verb ὑπομένω. The basic stem ends in a liquid (**λ, μ, ν,** or **ρ**). The aorist stem passes through two changes: intervocalic **σ** drops out and the **ε** is lengthened in compensation (compensatory lengthening). **οὗτος** resumes the article and participle for emphasis.

10:23 **ὅταν** introduces a future more vivid condition (App. 70). **οὐ μὴ τελέσητε**: *you will never finish going through;* the double negative indicates a strong negation and usually takes an aorist subjunctive that is translated as a future. **ἕως ἂν ἔλθῃ**: the temporal conjunction with the aorist subjunctive and the particle ἄν refers indefinitely to the future and denotes that the commencement of one event is dependent on another.

10:24 **ὑπὲρ**: *above;* i.e., in rank or station.

10:25 ἀρκετὸν τῷ μαθητῇ ἵνα γένηται ὡς ὁ διδάσκαλος αὐτοῦ καὶ ὁ δοῦλος ὡς ὁ κύριος αὐτοῦ. εἰ τὸν οἰκοδεσπότην Βεελζεβοὺλ ἐπεκάλεσαν, πόσῳ μᾶλλον τοὺς οἰκιακοὺς αὐτοῦ.

10:26 Μὴ οὖν φοβηθῆτε αὐτούς· οὐδὲν γάρ ἐστιν κεκαλυμμένον ὃ οὐκ ἀποκαλυφθήσεται καὶ κρυπτὸν ὃ οὐ γνωσθήσεται.

10:25
ἀρκετός, ή, όν sufficient, enough, adequate
μαθητής, οῦ, ὁ disciple
ἵνα to, in order to, in order that, that (conjunction)
διδάσκαλος, ου, ὁ master, teacher
δοῦλος, ου, ὁ slave, servant
εἰ if, whether
οἰκοδεσπότης, ου, ὁ master of the house
βεελζεβούλ/βεελζεβούβ and βεεζεβούλ, ὁ Beelzebub (indeclinable)
ἐπικαλέω, ἐπικαλέσω, ἐπεκάλεσα, ἐπικέκληκα, ἐπικέκλημαι, ἐπεκλήθην call, name
πόσος, η, ον how great? how much?
μᾶλλον more, to a greater degree, rather (adverb)
οἰκιακός, ου, ὁ member of a household

10:26
φοβέομαι, φοβηθήσομαι, ἐφοβήθην fear, dread; be afraid, become frightened
οὐδείς, οὐδεμία, οὐδέν no (adjective); no one, nobody, nothing (substantive)
καλύπτω, καλύψω, ἐκάλυθψα, κεκάλυμμαι cover; hide, conceal
ἀποκαλύπτω, ἀποκαλύψω, ἀπεκάλυψα, ἀπεκαλύφθην uncover, reveal, disclose
κρυπτός, ή, όν hidden, concealed, secret
γινώσκω, γνώσομαι, ἔγνων, ἔγνωκα, ἔγνωσμαι, ἐγνώσθην know, learn, understand

---

10:25 **ἀρκετὸν τῷ μαθητῇ ἵνα γένηται ὡς ὁ διδάσκαλος**: *it is enough for the student to be like his teacher*; ἀρκετὸν: supply the verb ἐστίν for the adjective, which governs the dative case. **ἵνα** with the subjunctive is equivalent to an infinitive construction and the actual subject of the sentence. **εἰ τὸν οἰκοδεσπότην βεελζεβοὺλ ἐπεκάλεσαν**: *if they called the master of the house Beelzebub*; εἰ introduces a simple or particular condition (App. 70). The verb is a first aorist active indicative. The Pharisees, although not mentioned, are the likely subject of the verb. τὸν οἰκοδεσπότην, the direct object, is the the Son of Man (13:27, 37; 24:43). βεελζεβοὺλ stands in predicate position. The Pharisees associate Him with the prince of evil spirits (9:34). **πόσῳ μᾶλλον τοὺς οἰκιακοὺς αὐτοῦ**: *how much more the members of His household*; the argument runs: if they demonize the master, how much more will they demonize his servants. The comparative adverb is accompanied by a dative of degree of difference.

10:26 **ἐστιν κεκαλυμμένον**: the periphrastic construction, a present of εἰμί and a perfect participle, is a substitute construction for the present passive of καλύπτω. The doubled antithesis in this and the next clause emphasizes a reversal of the presently impending misfortune and provides ultimate hope in the end-time.

10:27 ὃ λέγω ὑμῖν ἐν τῇ σκοτίᾳ εἴπατε ἐν τῷ φωτί, καὶ ὃ εἰς τὸ οὖς ἀκούετε κηρύξατε ἐπὶ τῶν δωμάτων. 10:28 καὶ μὴ φοβεῖσθε ἀπὸ τῶν ἀποκτεννόντων τὸ σῶμα, τὴν δὲ ψυχὴν μὴ δυναμένων ἀποκτεῖναι· φοβεῖσθε δὲ μᾶλλον τὸν δυνάμενον καὶ ψυχὴν καὶ σῶμα ἀπολέσαι ἐν γεέννῃ. 10:29 οὐχὶ δύο στρουθία ἀσσαρίου πωλεῖται;

10:27
σκοτία, ας, ἡ darkness, gloom
φῶς, φωτός, τό light
οὖς, ὠτός, τό ear
κηρύσσω, κηρύξω, ἐκήρυξα, ἐκηρύχθην announce openly, proclaim aloud
δῶμα, ατος, τό house; housetop, roof
10:28
φοβέομαι, φοβηθήσομαι, ἐφοβήθην fear, dread; be afraid, become frightened
ἀποκτείνω/ἀποκτέννω, ἀποκτενῶ, ἀπέκτεινα, ἀπεκτάνθην kill, put to death, murder
σῶμα, ατος, τό body
ψυχή, ῆς, ἡ breath, life, soul, heart
ἀποκτείνω, ἀποκτενῶ, ἀπέκτεινα, ἀπεκτάνθην kill
μᾶλλον more, to a greater degree, rather (adverb)
ἀπόλλυμι/ἀπολλύω, ἀπολέσω/ἀπολῶ, ἀπώλεσα, ἀπολώλεκα, ἀπόλωλα (2 perfect) lose, destroy, ruin, kill; perish (middle)
γέεννα, ης, ἡ Gehenna, Valley of Hinnom, hell, the fires of Tartarus (a place known for sacrifices to Moloch, pollution, pestilence, punishment of malefactors, and continually burning fires)
10:29
οὐχί not; no, by no means (adverb; more intensive form of οὐ)
στρουθίον, ίου, τό small bird; sparrow
ἀσσάριον, ου, τό as, assarian, (Roman) copper coin
πωλέω, πωλήσω, ἐπώλησα sell

10:27 **ἐν τῇ σκοτίᾳ . . . ἐν τῷ φωτί . . . εἰς τὸ οὖς . . . ἐπὶ τῶν δωμάτων**: the repeated antithesis with same meaning continues boldly in the same vein as in the previous verse.

10:28 **μὴ φοβεῖσθε ἀπὸ**: *do not be afraid of.* **τὸ σῶμα, τὴν δὲ ψυχὴν**: the word order, collocated as the two nouns are, provides an emphatic juxtaposition. **δὲ . . . μὴ δυναμένων**: *but are not able*; μὴ regularly introduces a participle. The participle depends on its subject τῶν ἀποκτεννόντων and takes a complementary infinitive. The chiastic structure centers on τὸ σῶμα and τὴν δὲ ψυχὴν. **τὸν δυνάμενον**: the periphrasis elegantly avoids giving the name directly but indirectly refers to the prince of evil spirits, διάβολος. **ἀπολέσαι** is an aorist active (cf. App. 53, D, 4) complementary infinitive. **ἐν γεέννῃ**: what ultimately happens in the end-time is what matters.

10:29 **οὐχὶ**: the negative is a strengthened form of οὐ; as an interrogative word in a question, it expects an affirmative answer. **δύο στρουθία . . . πωλεῖται**: neuter plural subjects are considered as collective nouns and regularly take a singular verb. **ἀσσαρίου**: *for a penny*; the case is a genitive of price or value. In the context of buying or selling the genitive is used to indicate what something is worth.

καὶ ἓν ἐξ αὐτῶν οὐ πεσεῖται ἐπὶ τὴν γῆν ἄνευ τοῦ πατρὸς ὑμῶν.
10:30 ὑμῶν δὲ καὶ αἱ τρίχες τῆς κεφαλῆς πᾶσαι ἠριθμημέναι εἰσίν.
10:31 μὴ οὖν φοβεῖσθε· πολλῶν στρουθίων διαφέρετε ὑμεῖς.
10:32 Πᾶς οὖν ὅστις ὁμολογήσει ἐν ἐμοὶ ἔμπροσθεν τῶν
ἀνθρώπων, ὁμολογήσω κἀγὼ ἐν αὐτῷ ἔμπροσθεν τοῦ πατρός μου
τοῦ ἐν [τοῖς] οὐρανοῖς·

10:29
πίπτω, πεσοῦμαι, ἔπεσα, ἔπεσον (2 aorist), πέπτωκα fall, fall prostrate, fall down
ἄνευ without (preposition + genitive)
10:30
θρίξ, τριχός, ἡ hair
κεφαλή, ῆς, ἡ head
ἀριθμέω, ἀριθμήσω, ἠρίθμησα, ἠρίθμημαι count, number
10:31
φοβέομαι, φοβηθήσομαι, ἐφοβήθην fear, dread; be afraid, become frightened
στρουθίον, ίου, τό small bird; sparrow
διαφέρω, διοίσω, διήνεγκα carry through; differ, be different; be better, be worth more than, be superior to
10:32
ὅστις, ἥτις, ὅ τι whoever, whatever (indefinite relative pronoun)
ὁμολογέω, ὁμολογήσω, ὡμολόγησα assure, admit, confess, declare (publicly); confess someone (+ ἐν)
ἔμπροσθεν in front of, before, in the presence of (adverb; preposition + genitive)
κἀγώ = καὶ ἐγώ I also

10:30 **ἠριθμημέναι εἰσίν**: the periphrastic construction, a present of εἰμί and a perfect participle, is a substitute construction for the present passive of ἀριθμέω.

10:31 **πολλῶν στρουθίων διαφέρετε ὑμεῖς**: *you are more valuable than many sparrows*; the verb governs a genitive of comparison. The argument *a minori ad maius* runs: if God takes care of the birds, how much more will He take care of you.

10:32 **Πᾶς** combines with **ὅστις** to express *whoever.* ὅστις: the indefinite relative pronoun introduces a future most vivid condition instead of εἰ and takes a future in both the protasis and apodosis. **ὁμολογήσει ἐν ἐμοὶ**: *acknowledges (will acknowledge) me*; instead of an accusative of the person, the verb takes a preposition with a dative. In translation, the future of the protasis is usually translated as a present both in the future most and the future more vivid conditions. The future most vivid expresses threats and warnings most intently.

10:33 ὅστις δ’ ἂν ἀρνήσηταί με ἔμπροσθεν τῶν ἀνθρώπων,
ἀρνήσομαι κἀγὼ αὐτὸν ἔμπροσθεν τοῦ πατρός μου τοῦ ἐν [τοῖς]
οὐρανοῖς.
10:34 Μὴ νομίσητε ὅτι ἦλθον βαλεῖν εἰρήνην ἐπὶ τὴν γῆν· οὐκ
ἦλθον βαλεῖν εἰρήνην ἀλλὰ μάχαιραν. 10:35 ἦλθον γὰρ διχάσαι
ἄνθρωπον κατὰ τοῦ πατρὸς αὐτοῦ
καὶ θυγατέρα κατὰ τῆς μητρὸς αὐτῆς
καὶ νύμφην κατὰ τῆς πενθερᾶς αὐτῆς,
10:36 καὶ ἐχθροὶ τοῦ ἀνθρώπου οἱ οἰκιακοὶ αὐτοῦ.

10:33
ὅστις, ἥτις, ὅ τι whoever, whatever (indefinite relative pronoun)
ἀρνέομαι, ἀρνήσομαι, ἠρνησάμην, ἤρνημαι deny, disown
ἔμπροσθεν in front of, before, in the presence of (adverb; preposition + genitive)
10:34
νομίζω, νομίσω, ἐνόμισα, νενόμικα think, believe, consider
εἰρήνη, ης, ἡ peace
ἀλλά but, yet (conjunction)
μάχαιρα, ας, ἡ sword
10:35
διχάζω, διχάσω, ἐδίχασα divide, separate; turn someone against someone
θυγάτηρ, τρός, ἡ daughter
μήτηρ, τρός, ἡ mother
νύμφη, ης, ἡ bride; daughter-in-law
πενθερά, ᾶς, ἡ mother-in-law
10:36
ἐχθρός, ά, όν hostile, hated; hating; personal enemy (substantive)
οἰκιακός, ου, ὁ member of a household

10:33 **ὅστις δ’ ἂν ἀρνήσηταί . . . ἀρνήσομαι**: *but whoever denies . . . I will deny*; the indefinite relative pronoun with ἂν and the verb in the subjunctive introduces a future more vivid condition. The future more vivid is less emotional than the future most vivid.

10:34 **Μὴ νομίσητε ὅτι ἦλθον βαλεῖν εἰρήνην**: Jesus has not come to usher in the golden-age peace either of the garden of Eden or of the messianic era (Mic 4:3). βαλεῖν is an infinitive of purpose, particularly prevalent after a verb of motion. **ἀλλὰ μάχαιραν**: before the ultimate era of peace can be established, the sword will be raised for the present time against the powers of evil which may separate from each other family members, citizens, and nations.

10:35 **ἄνθρωπον κατὰ τοῦ πατρὸς**: actions against one’s own family members are emphasized in this catalogue and in the next verse because they are the most tragic of all.

10:36 **ἐχθροὶ τοῦ ἀνθρώπου**: *a man’s enemies*; the generic article in the singular is included in Greek to denote a whole class and so to distinguish humans from other beings. **οἱ οἰκιακοὶ αὐτοῦ**: *his own household members*; supply the verb εἰσίν.

10:37 Ὁ φιλῶν πατέρα ἢ μητέρα ὑπὲρ ἐμὲ οὐκ ἔστιν μου ἄξιος, καὶ
ὁ φιλῶν υἱὸν ἢ θυγατέρα ὑπὲρ ἐμὲ οὐκ ἔστιν μου ἄξιος· 10:38 καὶ ὃς
οὐ λαμβάνει τὸν σταυρὸν αὐτοῦ καὶ ἀκολουθεῖ ὀπίσω μου, οὐκ ἔστιν
μου ἄξιος. 10:39 ὁ εὑρὼν τὴν ψυχὴν αὐτοῦ ἀπολέσει αὐτήν, καὶ ὁ
ἀπολέσας τὴν ψυχὴν αὐτοῦ ἕνεκεν ἐμοῦ εὑρήσει αὐτήν.
10:40 Ὁ δεχόμενος ὑμᾶς ἐμὲ δέχεται, καὶ ὁ ἐμὲ δεχόμενος δέχεται
τὸν ἀποστείλαντά με.

10:37
φιλέω, φιλήσω, ἐφίλησα, πεφίληκα love
μήτηρ, τρός, ἡ mother
ὑπέρ above, in behalf of, about, for (preposition + genitive); over, beyond; more than (+ accusative)
ἄξιος, ία, ιον worthy
10:38
λαμβάνω, λήμψομαι, ἔλαβον, εἴληφα, εἴλημμαι, ἐλήφθην take, receive, accept
σταυρός, οῦ, ὁ cross
ὀπίσω behind, after (adverb; preposition + genitive)
ἄξιος, ία, ιον worthy
10:39
εὑρίσκω, εὑρήσω, εὗρον (2 aorist), ηὕρηκα/εὕρηκα, εὑρέθην find, meet, discover, recognize
ψυχή, ῆς, ἡ breath, life, soul, heart
ἀπόλλυμι/ἀπολλύω, ἀπολέσω/ἀπολῶ, ἀπώλεσα, ἀπολώλεκα, ἀπόλωλα (2 perfect) lose, destroy, ruin, kill; perish (middle)
ἕνεκεν/ἕνεκα because of, on account of, for the sake of (preposition + genitive)
10:40
δέχομαι, δέξομαι, ἐδεξάμην, δέδεγμαι take, receive, welcome, accept
ἀποστέλλω, ἀποστελῶ, ἀπέστειλα, ἀπέσταλκα, ἀπέσταλμαι, ἀπεστάλην send, send away, send out

---

10:37 **Ὁ φιλῶν**: *he who (if he) loves*; an attributive participle may be circumstantial. A circumstantial participle may be interpreted conditionally and so replace the protasis of any condition. It is used here instead of εἰ and the indicative verb in the protasis to create a simple or particular condition (App. 70). **οὐκ ἔστιν μου ἄξιος**: the change of accent from ἐστί takes place when it follows enclitic οὐκ. The verb in the indicative completes the protasis of the condition. ἄξιος governs the genitive case. The simple or present condition will be repeated in this verse and in the following four.

10:38 **ὅς**: the relative pronoun introduces a condition.

10:39 **ὁ εὑρὼν**: *he who finds*; the aorist participle shows aspect of a single act rather than time both here and in the next participle: **ὁ ἀπολέσας**. The chiastic construction emphasizes the reversal of events when they are done for His sake.

10:40 **Ὁ δεχόμενος ὑμᾶς ἐμὲ δέχεται**: the chiasm centers on the closeness of the relationship between Jesus and the disciple. **ὁ ἐμὲ δεχόμενος δέχεται τὸν ἀποστείλαντα με**: the chiastic structure becomes extended: it centers on the disciple and his relationship with both Jesus on one side and the Father on the other.

10:41 ὁ δεχόμενος προφήτην εἰς ὄνομα προφήτου μισθὸν προφήτου λήμψεται, καὶ ὁ δεχόμενος δίκαιον εἰς ὄνομα δικαίου μισθὸν δικαίου λήμψεται. 10:42 καὶ ὃς ἂν ποτίσῃ ἕνα τῶν μικρῶν τούτων ποτήριον ψυχροῦ μόνον εἰς ὄνομα μαθητοῦ, ἀμὴν λέγω ὑμῖν, οὐ μὴ ἀπολέσῃ τὸν μισθὸν αὐτοῦ.

10:41
δέχομαι, δέξομαι, ἐδεξάμην, δέδεγμαι take, receive, welcome, accept
ὄνομα, ατος, τό name
μισθός, οῦ, ὁ pay, wages, reward
λαμβάνω, λήμψομαι, ἔλαβον, εἴληφα, εἴλημμαι, ἐλήφθην take, receive, accept
δίκαιος, αία, αιον right, just, honest, good, righteous
10:42
ὅς, ἥ, ὅ + ἄν (ἐάν) whoever, whatever
ποτίζω, ποτίσω, ἐπότισα, πεπότικα cause someone to drink, give someone something to drink
μικρός, ά, όν small, short, little, humble
ποτήριον, ου, τό cup
ψυχρός, ά, όν cool, cold; cold water (substantive)
μόνον only (adverb)
ὄνομα, ατος, τό name
ἀμήν in truth, verily (Hebrew)
οὐ μή never, certainly not
ἀπόλλυμι/ἀπολλύω, ἀπολέσω/ἀπολῶ, ἀπώλεσα, ἀπολώλεκα, ἀπόλωλα (2 perfect) lose, destroy, ruin, kill; perish (middle)
μισθός, οῦ, ὁ pay, wages, reward

10:41 **εἰς ὄνομα προφήτου**: *because he is a prophet*; the phrase means that the host has a clear sense of recognition of who the prophet is and is willing to give him hospitality as a servant of the Lord. The practice of hospitality or *ξενία* met an important need of an itinerant prophet, teacher, or righteous disciple in antiquity.

10:42 **ποτίσῃ** takes an accusative of the person and of the thing. **ἕνα τῶν μικρῶν τούτων**: *one of these little ones*; the numeral governs a partitive genitive or genitive of the whole (cf. App. 65). The context clarifies that *little ones* refers to the disciples: εἰς ὄνομα μαθητοῦ: *because he is my disciple.* **οὐ μὴ ἀπολέσῃ**: *he will never lose*; the double negative indicates a strong negation and usually takes an aorist subjunctive that is translated as a future.

11 Καὶ ἐγένετο ὅτε ἐτέλεσεν ὁ Ἰησοῦς διατάσσων τοῖς δώδεκα μαθηταῖς αὐτοῦ, μετέβη ἐκεῖθεν τοῦ διδάσκειν καὶ κηρύσσειν ἐν ταῖς πόλεσιν αὐτῶν.

11:2 Ὁ δὲ Ἰωάννης ἀκούσας ἐν τῷ δεσμωτηρίῳ τὰ ἔργα τοῦ Χριστοῦ πέμψας διὰ τῶν μαθητῶν αὐτοῦ 11:3 εἶπεν αὐτῷ, Σὺ εἶ ὁ ἐρχόμενος ἢ ἕτερον προσδοκῶμεν;

11:1
τελέω, τελέσω, ἐτέλεσα, τετέλεκα, τετέλεσμαι, ἐτελέσθην finish, fulfill, accomplish, make an end
διατάσσω, διατάξω, διέταξα, διετάχθην order, direct, charge, command
δώδεκα twelve (indeclinable)
μεταβαίνω, μεταβήσομαι, μετέβην, μεταβέβηκα go, pass over, move
ἐκεῖθεν from there, from that place (adverb)
διδάσκω, διδάξω, ἐδίδαξα, ἐδιδάχθην teach, instruct
κηρύσσω, κηρύξω, ἐκήρυξα, ἐκηρύχθην announce openly, proclaim aloud, preach
11:2
δεσμωτήριον, ίου, τό prison
ἔργον, ου, τό work, deed, action
πέμπω, πέμψω, ἔπεμψα, πέπομφα, ἐπέμφθην send; send word
11:3
ἕτερος, α, ον other, another
προσδοκάω, προσδοκήσω, προσεδόκησα wait for, look for, expect; think, anticipate

---

11:1 **Καὶ ἐγένετο**: the finite verb, usually omitted in translation, is translated in older versions: *and it came to pass.* **ὅτε ἐτέλεσεν ὁ Ἰησοῦς ... μετέβη**: *when Jesus had finished ... He departed*; since the action of ἐτέλεσεν takes place prior to the time of μετέβη, it is translated as a pluperfect. **διατάσσων**: the participle governs the dative case. **τοῦ διδάσκειν καὶ κηρύσσειν**: *to teach and preach*; the construction is an articular infinitive. A purpose clause may be expressed by the neuter article in the genitive case followed by an infinitive.

11:2 **ἀκούσας**: *when he had heard of*; the participle precedes the following participle and verb in time and is translated as a pluperfect. It takes an accusative object. **πέμψας διὰ τῶν μαθητῶν αὐτοῦ**: *He sent word by his disciples and asked*; the cumbersome nature of the sentence may be resolved by coordinating the participle with the main verb εἶπεν in the next verse. Supply *message* or *word* as the object of πέμψας.

11:3 **εἶπεν**: *and asked*; when followed by a direct question the verb has the meaning *ask.* **ὁ ἐρχόμενος**: the appearance of the Messiah is prophesied in the Old Testament by the title ὁ ἐρχόμενος, and He is called by the same appellation in the New Testament. προδοκῶμεν is a first person plural present active indicative of a contracted verb with stem in **α** (cf. App. 55).

11:4 καὶ ἀποκριθεὶς ὁ Ἰησοῦς εἶπεν αὐτοῖς, Πορευθέντες
ἀπαγγείλατε Ἰωάννῃ ἃ ἀκούετε καὶ βλέπετε· 11:5 τυφλοὶ
ἀναβλέπουσιν καὶ χωλοὶ περιπατοῦσιν, λεπροὶ καθαρίζονται καὶ
κωφοὶ ἀκούουσιν, καὶ νεκροὶ ἐγείρονται καὶ πτωχοὶ εὐαγγελίζονται·
11:6 καὶ μακάριός ἐστιν ὃς ἐὰν μὴ σκανδαλισθῇ ἐν ἐμοί.
11:7 Τούτων δὲ πορευομένων ἤρξατο ὁ Ἰησοῦς λέγειν τοῖς ὄχλοις
περὶ Ἰωάννου, Τί ἐξήλθατε εἰς τὴν ἔρημον θεάσασθαι;

11:4
ἀποκρίνομαι, ἀπεκρινάμην, ἀπεκρίθην answer, reply
πορεύομαι, πορεύσομαι, πεπόρευμαι, ἐπορεύθην go, proceed, travel
ἀπαγγέλλω, ἀπαγγελῶ, ἀπήγγειλα (1 aorist), ἀπηγγέλην (2 aorist passive) bring back word, report, declare, announce, tell
βλέπω, βλέψω, ἔβλεψα see, behold, perceive
11:5
τυφλός, ή, όν blind
ἀναβλέπω, ἀναβλέψω, ἀνέβλεψα look up, regain sight, receive sight
χωλός, ή, όν lame, crippled
περιπατέω, περιπατήσω, περιεπάτησα walk, walk about
λεπρός, οῦ, ὁ leper
καθαρίζω, καθαρίσω, ἐκαθάρισα cleanse, render pure
κωφός, ή, όν blunt, dull; dull of hearing, deprived of hearing; deaf; dumb, mute
νεκρός, ά, όν dead
πτωχός, ή, όν poor, indigent, needy
εὐαγγελίζω, εὐαγγελίσω, εὐηγγέλισα, εὐηγγέλισμαι, εὐηγγελίσθην bring or announce good news, address with good tidings, announce good tidings
11:6
μακάριος, ία, ιον blessed, happy, fortunate
σκανδαλίζω, σκανδαλίσω, ἐσκανδάλισα, ἐσκανδαλίσθην offend, anger, shock
11:7
πορεύομαι, πορεύσομαι, πεπόρευμαι, ἐπορεύθην go, proceed, travel; go away, depart
ἄρχω, ἄρξω, ἦρξα, ἦρχα, ἦργμαι, ἤρχθην rule (active); begin (middle)
ὄχλος, ου, ὁ crowd, throng, multitude
ἐξέρχομαι, ἐξελεύσομαι, ἐξῆλθον (2 aorist), ἐξελήλυθα go or come out of, go out
ἔρημος, ου, ἡ wilderness, desert, grassland
θεάομαι, θεάσομαι, ἐθεασάμην, τεθέαμαι see, look at, gaze upon, discern with the eyes

---

11:4 **ἃ**: supply the omitted antecedent ταῦτα.

11:5 **εὐαγγελίζονται**: *have good news (the gospel) preached to them.*

11:6 **ὃς ἐὰν**: *whoever*; the relative pronoun with ἐὰν introduces a present general condition (App. 70).

11:7 **Τούτων δὲ πορευομένων**: *as the messengers departed*; the messengers from John are the subject of the genitive absolute. The present participle agrees in time with the tense of the main verb **ἤρξατο. θεάθασθαι** is an infinitive of purpose.

κάλαμον ὑπὸ ἀνέμου σαλευόμενον; 11:8 ἀλλὰ τί ἐξήλθατε ἰδεῖν; ἄνθρωπον ἐν μαλακοῖς ἠμφιεσμένον; ἰδοὺ οἱ τὰ μαλακὰ φοροῦντες ἐν τοῖς οἴκοις τῶν βασιλέων εἰσίν. 11:9 ἀλλὰ τί ἐξήλθατε ἰδεῖν; προφήτην; ναὶ λέγω ὑμῖν, καὶ περισσότερον προφήτου. 11:10 οὗτός ἐστιν περὶ οὗ γέγραπται,

---

11:7
κάλαμος, ου, ὁ reed, cane; staff
ἄνεμος, ου, ὁ wind
σαλεύω, σαλεύσω, ἐσάλευσα, ἐσαλεύθην shake; shake down or together; agitate, disturb
11:8
ἀλλά but, yet (conjunction)
μαλακός, ή, όν soft, delicate clothes
ἀμφιέννυμι, ἀμφιέσω, ἠμφίεσμαι clothe, dress
φορέω, φορήσω/φορέσω, ἐφόρεσα, πεφόρηκα bear, wear
οἶκος, ου, ὁ house, dwelling
βασιλεύς, έως, ὁ king
11:9
ναί yes, indeed, certainly (particle of affirmation)
περισσός, ή, όν over and above, extraordinary, excessive; περισσῶς in full abundance (adverb); περισσότερος, α, ον more, greater (comparative)
11:10
περί about, concerning (preposition + genitive); about, around (+ accusative)
γράφω, γράψω, ἔγραψα, γέγραφα, γέγραμμαι, ἐγράφθην engrave, write
ἀποστέλλω, ἀποστελῶ, ἀπέστειλα, ἀπέσταλκα, ἀπέσταλμαι, ἀπεστάλην send, send away, send out
ἄγγελος, ου, ὁ messenger, angel
πρόσωπον, ου, τό face, countenance

11:7 **κάλαμον ὑπὸ ἀνέμου σαλευόμενον** may be used literally of an ordinary event or as a metaphor of a person perhaps waivering ἐν πίστει (Js 1:6) or affected by παντὶ ἀνέμῳ τῆς διδασκαλίας (Eph 4:14).

11:8 **ἄνθρωπον** suggests that κάλαμον above is used metaphorically. **ἠμφιεσμένον**: *dressed*; the form is a perfect passive participle. The initial ἠ-, formed like the temporal augment, is a sign of reduplication. Perfect tenses beginning with a vowel show reduplication by a lengthened vowel. **ἐν μαλακοῖς**: the adjective is used as a substantive.

11:9 **προφήτην**: the rhetorical question, now emphatically posed three times, is answered by a question. **ναὶ λέγω ὑμῖν**: the question is at last averred and climactically brought to conclusion. **περισσότερον προφήτου**: the comparative adjective takes a genitive of comparison.

11:10 **οὗτος ἐστιν**: *this is he.* **γέγραπται** is the impersonal third person singular perfect passive indicative of γράφω (cf. App. 53, E, 1). The perfect tense denotes action (aspect) that is completed near present time and continues with present result: *It has been written* (and is so now).

Ἰδοὺ ἐγὼ ἀποστέλλω τὸν ἄγγελόν μου πρὸ προσώπου σου,
ὃς κατασκευάσει τὴν ὁδόν σου ἔμπροσθέν σου.
11:11 ἀμὴν λέγω ὑμῖν· οὐκ ἐγήγερται ἐν γεννητοῖς γυναικῶν
μείζων Ἰωάννου τοῦ βαπτιστοῦ· ὁ δὲ μικρότερος ἐν τῇ βασιλείᾳ τῶν
οὐρανῶν μείζων αὐτοῦ ἐστιν. 11:12 ἀπὸ δὲ τῶν ἡμερῶν Ἰωάννου τοῦ
βαπτιστοῦ ἕως ἄρτι ἡ βασιλεία τῶν οὐρανῶν βιάζεται καὶ βιασταὶ
ἁρπάζουσιν αὐτήν.

11:10
κατασκευάζω, κατασκευάσω, κατεσκεύασα, κατεσκευάσθην prepare, make ready; build, construct
ὁδός, οῦ, ἡ road, way, journey
ἔμπροσθεν in front of, before, in the presence of (adverb; preposition + genitive)
11:11
ἀμήν in truth, verily (Hebrew)
γεννητός, ή, όν born
γυνή, γυναικός, ἡ woman, wife
μείζων, μεῖζον greater, larger (comparative of μέγας)
μικρότερος, έρα, ον smaller, littler; smallest, least (the comparative of μικρός; also used as the superlative)
11:12
ἡμέρα, ας, ἡ day
ἄρτι now (adverb)
βιάζω, βιάσω apply force, urge, overpower; press forward; be oppressed, suffer violence (passive)
βιαστής, ου, ὁ violent man, impetuous man
ἁρπάζω, ἁρπάσω, ἥρπασα, ἡρπάσθην, ἡρπάγην (2 aorist passive) steal, carry off, drag away, take away

---

11:10 **ἀποστέλλω**: the present tense connotes a future.

11:11 **ἐγήγερται** is an impersonal third person singular perfect passive indicative. **ἐν γεννητοῖς γυναικῶν**: *among those born of women*; supply τοῖς or τούτοις with γεννητοῖς. γυναικῶν is a genitive of source. **Ἰωάννου τοῦ βαπτιστοῦ**: *than John the Baptist*; the noun is a genitive of comparison after a comparative degree of the adjective μείζων (App. 22). τοῦ βαπτιστοῦ stands in apposition. **ὁ δὲ μικρότερος**: *but he who is smaller*; the article turns the adjective into a noun. However, the comparative probably stands for a superlative: *but the one of least importance.*

11:12 **ἕως ἄρτι**: *until now.* **ἡ βασιλεία τῶν οὐρανῶν βιάζεται καὶ βιασταὶ ἁρπάζουσιν αὐτήν**: *the kingdom of heaven is suffering violence and violent men take it by force*; while βιάζεται may be construed as middle or passive, the juxtaposition of the common roots of these verbs, the repetition of similarity of meaning in the context, and the chiastic construction centering on violence against the kingdom of heaven suggest that καὶ is coordinating similar clauses, and that the passive voice is preferable.

11:13 πάντες γὰρ οἱ προφῆται καὶ ὁ νόμος ἕως Ἰωάννου ἐπροφήτευσαν· 11:14 καὶ εἰ θέλετε δέξασθαι, αὐτός ἐστιν Ἠλίας ὁ μέλλων ἔρχεσθαι. 11:15 ὁ ἔχων ὦτα ἀκουέτω.

11:16 Τίνι δὲ ὁμοιώσω τὴν γενεὰν ταύτην; ὁμοία ἐστὶν παιδίοις καθημένοις ἐν ταῖς ἀγοραῖς ἃ προσφωνοῦντα τοῖς ἑτέροις 11:17 λέγουσιν,

---

11:13
νόμος, ου, ὁ law, custom, ordinance
ἕως while, as long as, until; ἕως ἄνω to the brim; ἕως οὗ until; ἕως πότε; how long? (conjunction); until (preposition + genitive)
προφητεύω, προφητεύσω, ἐπροφήτευσα proclaim a divine revelation, prophetically reveal, prophesy
11:14
θέλω, θελήσω, ἠθέλησα wish to have, desire, purpose, want
δέχομαι, δέξομαι, ἐδεξάμην, δέδεγμαι take, receive, welcome, accept
Ἠλίας, ου, ὁ Elijah
μέλλω, μελλήσω be about to, be on the point of
11:15
οὖς, ὠτός, τό ear
11:16
ὁμοιόω, ὁμοιώσω, ὁμοίωσα, ὡμοιώθην make like, liken, compare; be like, be made like, become like, resemble (passive)
γενεά, ᾶς, ἡ generation
ὅμοιος, οία, οιον like, similar (+ dative)
παιδίον, ου, τό infant, young child, little boy, little girl
κάθημαι, καθήσομαι sit, stay, reside
ἀγορά, ᾶς, ἡ marketplace
προσφωνέω, προσφωνήσω, προσεφώνησα call out, address
ἕτερος, α, ον other, another

11:13 **ἐπροφήτευσαν**: *proclaimed these prophesies*; supply ταῦτα.

11:14 **εἰ θέλετε δέξασθαι**: εἰ introduces a simple or particular condition. The complementary infinitive requires ταῦτα as an object. **αὐτός ἐστιν**: *he is*; contrary to classical usage, αὐτός stands here by itself in the nominative case as a personal pronoun (cf. App. 40, notes). **ὁ μέλλων ἔρχεσθαι**: *the One About To Come*; the title, used similarly of Jesus as ὁ ἐρχόμενος, applies to John: the one comes in anticipation and preparation of the other.

11:15 **ὦτα** is a monosyllabic third declension neuter noun with stem in **τ** (cf. App. 10, φῶς). **ἀκουέτω** is a third person singular present active imperative (cf. App. 53, A, 3).

11:16 **Τίνι**: *to what*; the form is an interrogative pronoun. **ὁμοιώσω**: the verb governs an accusative and a dative object. **ὁμοία ἐστὶν παιδίοις**: ὁμοία: the adjective takes the dative case and introduces a simile. **ἃ προσφωνοῦντα τοῖς ἑτέροις**: the neuter plural nominative relative pronoun has an antecedent in **παιδίοις**. The participle, in agreement with the relative, governs the dative case. The generation is likened to two groups of children, the one beckoning the other.

Ηὐλήσαμεν ὑμῖν καὶ οὐκ ὠρχήσασθε,
ἐθρηνήσαμεν καὶ οὐκ ἐκόψασθε.
11:18 ἦλθεν γὰρ Ἰωάννης μήτε ἐσθίων μήτε πίνων, καὶ λέγουσιν,
Δαιμόνιον ἔχει. 11:19 ἦλθεν ὁ υἱὸς τοῦ ἀνθρώπου ἐσθίων καὶ πίνων,
καὶ λέγουσιν, Ἰδοὺ ἄνθρωπος φάγος καὶ οἰνοπότης, τελωνῶν φίλος
καὶ ἁμαρτωλῶν. καὶ ἐδικαιώθη ἡ σοφία ἀπὸ τῶν ἔργων αὐτῆς.
11:20 Τότε ἤρξατο ὀνειδίζειν τὰς πόλεις

11:17
αὐλέω, αὐλήσω, ηὔλησα play the flute
ὀρχέομαι, ὀρχήσομαι, ὠρχησάμην dance
θρηνέω, θρηνήσω, ἐθρήνησα lament, mourn
κόπτω, κόψω, ἔκοψα, ἐκόπην (2 aorist passive) smite, cut, cut off; beat one's breast (in mourning), mourn, lament (middle)
11:18
μήτε . . . μήτε neither . . . nor
ἐσθίω, φάγομαι, ἔφαγον (2 aorist) eat
πίνω, πίομαι, ἔπιον, πέπωκα drink
δαιμόνιον, ου, τό deity, divinity; demon, evil spirit
11:19
φάγος, ου, ὁ glutton
οἰνοπότης, ου, ὁ wine-drinker, drunkard
φίλος, ου, ὁ friend
τελώνης, ου, ὁ tax-collector, publican
ἁμαρτωλός, όν sinful; sinner (substantive)
δικαιόω, δικαιώσω, ἐδικαίωσα, ἐδικαιώθην justify, vindicate
σοφία, ας, ἡ wisdom, prudence
ἔργον, ου, τό work, deed, action
11:20
ἄρχω, ἄρξω, ἦρξα, ἦρχα, ἦργμαι, ἤρχθην rule (active); begin (middle)
ὀνειδίζω, ὀνειδίσω, ὠνείδισα reproach, revile, heap insults upon

---

11:17 **Ηὐλήσαμεν . . . οὐκ ὠρχήσασθε**: an invitation to rejoice in celebration is rejected. **ἐθρηνήσαμεν . . . οὐκ ἐκόψασθε**: a somber call to sing laments is not accepted.

11:18 **Ἰωάννης μήτε ἐσθίων μήτε πίνων**: *John, by neither eating nor drinking*; the simile is discussed in chiastic order. John is demonized for his sober ways of calling people to repentance.

11:19 **ὁ υἱὸς τοῦ ἀνθρώπου ἐσθίων καὶ πίνων**: Jesus is rejected for socializing in society and calling sinners to repentance. **καὶ ἐδικαιώθη ἡ σοφία ἀπὸ τῶν ἔργων αὐτῆς**: *but wisdom is proved right by her works*; ἐδικαιώθη is a gnomic aorist in this sententious statement. The aorist may be used to express a general truth where the experience of an action in the past suggests an action that is likely to be repeated. ἡ σοφία may be construed as personification or simply as an abstract noun. Abstract nouns are generally modified by an article, which is omitted in translation.

11:20 **Τότε ἤρξατο ὀνειδίζειν τὰς πόλεις**: this turning aside to address cities, poetically called *apostrophe*, becomes a prominent theme in the next five verses.

ἐν αἷς ἐγένοντο αἱ πλεῖσται δυνάμεις αὐτοῦ, ὅτι οὐ μετενόησαν·
11:21 Οὐαί σοι, Χοραζίν, οὐαί σοι, Βηθσαϊδά· ὅτι εἰ ἐν Τύρῳ καὶ
Σιδῶνι ἐγένοντο αἱ δυνάμεις αἱ γενόμεναι ἐν ὑμῖν, πάλαι ἂν ἐν
σάκκῳ καὶ σποδῷ μετενόησαν. 11:22 πλὴν λέγω ὑμῖν, Τύρῳ καὶ
Σιδῶνι ἀνεκτότερον ἔσται ἐν ἡμέρᾳ κρίσεως ἢ ὑμῖν.

11:20

πλεῖστος, η, ον most, very great (superlative of πολύς)

δύναμις, εως, ἡ power; strength, ability; authority; might, majesty; omnipotence; miraculous power, miracle

μετανοέω, μετανοήσω, μετανόησα change one's mind, repent

11:21

οὐαί woe! alas! (interjection)

Χοραζίν, ἡ Chorazin (indeclinable)

Βηθσαϊδά, ἡ Bethsaida (indeclinable)

εἰ if, whether

Τύρος, ου, ἡ Tyre

Σιδών, ῶνος, ἡ Sidon

δύναμις, εως, ἡ power; strength, ability; authority; might, majesty; omnipotence; miraculous power, miracle

πάλαι long ago, formerly; for a long time; already (adverb)

σάκκος, ου, ὁ sack, sackcloth

σποδός, οῦ, ἡ ashes

μετανοέω, μετανοήσω, μετανόησα change one's mind, repent

11:22

πλήν besides, except (adverb); but, however, nevertheless (conjunction)

ἀνεκτότερος, α, ον more bearable, endurable, tolerable (comparative of ἀνεκτός, ή, όν)

ἡμέρα, ας, ἡ day

κρίσις, εως, ἡ judgment, justice, righteousness, condemnation

---

11:20 **ἐν αἷς ἐγένοντο αἱ πλεῖσται δυνάμεις αὐτοῦ**: *in which most of His miracles had been performed*; the verb is a second aorist third person plural (cf. App. 54). Since the action of the verb of the relative clause precedes that of the main verb in time, it is translated as a pluperfect.

11:21 **Οὐαί σοι**: *woe to you*; the exclamatory interjection governs the dative of person or thing. **εἰ ἐν Τύρῳ . . . ἐγένοντο αἱ δυνάμεις . . . ἂν . . . μετενόησαν**: *if the miracles . . . would have been performed in Tyre, they would have repented*; the past contrary to fact condition indicates that the action is not fulfilled in the past time. It is formed with εἰ plus the aorist indicative in the protasis and the aorist indicative plus ἄν in the apodosis (App. 70).

11:22 **Τύρῳ . . . ἀνεκτότερον ἔσται . . . ἢ ὑμῖν**: ἀνεκτότερον: the neuter singular nominative comparative adjective stands in predicate position to the impersonal verb, governs a dative of advantage, and introduces a comparison. In a comparative statement with ἤ, the second member of the comparison, ὑμῖν, will be in the same case as that of the first, Τύρῳ, but is a dative of disadvantage.

11:23 καὶ σύ, Καφαρναούμ,
μὴ ἕως οὐρανοῦ ὑψωθήσῃ;
ἕως ᾄδου καταβήσῃ·
ὅτι εἰ ἐν Σοδόμοις ἐγενήθησαν αἱ δυνάμεις αἱ γενόμεναι ἐν σοί,
ἔμεινεν ἂν μέχρι τῆς σήμερον. 11:24 πλὴν λέγω ὑμῖν ὅτι γῇ Σοδόμων
ἀνεκτότερον ἔσται ἐν ἡμέρᾳ κρίσεως ἢ σοί.
11:25 Ἐν ἐκείνῳ τῷ καιρῷ ἀποκριθεὶς ὁ Ἰησοῦς εἶπεν,

11:23
Καφαρναούμ, ἡ Capernaum (indeclinable)
ἕως while, as long as, until; ἕως ἄνω to the brim; ἕως οὗ until; ἕως πότε how long? (conjunction); until; to, even to (preposition + genitive)
οὐρανός, οῦ, ὁ heaven
ὑψόω, ὑψώσω, ὕψωσα, ὑψώθην lift up, raise high, exalt
ᾅδης, ου, ὁ Hades, underworld, abode of the dead; place of punishment, hell; the lowest place
καταβαίνω, καταβήσομαι, κατέβην, καταβέβηκα come down, go down, descend, fall
Σόδομα, ων, τά Sodom
δύναμις, εως, ἡ power; strength, ability; authority; might, majesty; omnipotence; miraculous power, miracle
μένω, μενῶ, ἔμεινα, μεμένηκα stay, rest, dwell
μέχρι to, even to; until, till (preposition + genitive)
σήμερον today, this day, now, our time
11:24
πλήν besides, except (adverb); but, however, nevertheless (conjunction)
ἀνεκτότερος, α, ον more bearable, endurable, tolerable (comparative of ἀνεκτός, ή, όν)
ἡμέρα, ας, ἡ day
κρίσις, εως, ἡ judgment, justice, righteousness, condemnation
11:25
ἐκεῖνος, η, ον that, that one, the former
καιρός, οῦ, ὁ time, appointed time; season; time of crisis, end-time
ἀποκρίνομαι, ἀπεκρινάμην, ἀπεκρίθην answer, reply

11:23 **μὴ ἕως οὐρανοῦ ὑψοθήσῃ**: *you will not be lifted up to heaven, will you*; the negative interrogative particle is used when a negative answer is expected. The verb is second person singular first future passive indicative (cf. App. 53, G, 1). **καταβήσῃ**: *you will descend*; the verb is second person singular future middle indicative. The verb is deponent only in the future. **ᾅδου**: the name of the Greek god of the underworld also serves as the name of the underworld itself. **εἰ** introduces a past contrary to fact condition (App. 70). **Σοδόμοις**: the name of the city is in the plural, as is the case for many Greek city names.

11:24 **γῇ Σοδόμων**: *for the land of Sodom*; Σοδόμων is an appositional genitive more specifically identifying the land (cf. App. 65).

11:25 **ἀποκριθεὶς**: *continuing*; the participle with a verb of speaking may be used to indicate the continuation of discourse.

Ἐξομολογοῦμαί σοι, πάτερ, κύριε τοῦ οὐρανοῦ καὶ τῆς γῆς, ὅτι ἔκρυψας ταῦτα ἀπὸ σοφῶν καὶ συνετῶν καὶ ἀπεκάλυψας αὐτὰ νηπίοις· 11:26 ναὶ ὁ πατήρ, ὅτι οὕτως εὐδοκία ἐγένετο ἔμπροσθέν σου. 11:27 Πάντα μοι παρεδόθη ὑπὸ τοῦ πατρός μου, καὶ οὐδεὶς ἐπιγινώσκει τὸν υἱὸν εἰ μὴ ὁ πατήρ,

---

11:25

ἐξομολογέω, ἐξομολογήσω, ἐξωμολόγησα consent, agree; confess, admit, acknowledge; praise, give praise (middle)

κρύπτω, κρύψω, ἔκρυψα, κέκρυμμαι, ἐκρύβην hide, conceal, cover

σοφός, ή, όν wise; clever, skillful; learned, intelligent

συνετός, ή, όν intelligent, wise, prudent

ἀποκαλύπτω, ἀποκαλύψω, ἀπεκάλυψα, ἀπεκαλύφθην uncover, reveal, disclose

νήπιος, ία, ιον unlearned, simple, young; infant, babe, child (substantive)

11:26

ναί yes, indeed, certainly (particle of affirmation)

εὐδοκία, ας, ἡ goodwill; favor, good pleasure, purpose, intention; wish, desire

ἔμπροσθεν in front of, before, in the presence of (adverb; preposition + genitive)

11:27

παραδίδωμι, παραδώσω, παρέδωκα, παρέδων (2 aorist), παραδέδωκα, παραδέδομαι, παρεδόθην give, hand over, give over, deliver, give up, betray

οὐδείς, οὐδεμία, οὐδέν no (adjective); no one, nobody, nothing (substantive)

ἐπιγινώσκω, ἐπιγνώσομαι, ἐπέγνων (2 aorist), ἐπέγνωκα, ἐπεγνώσθην know, understand, recognize; discern, detect

εἰ μή unless, except

11:25 **Ἐξομολογοῦμαί σοι**: the compound verb in the middle governs the dative case. **κύριε τοῦ οὐρανοῦ καὶ τῆς γῆς**: the vocative case (cf. App. 4) takes an objective genitive (cf. App. 65), i.e., *He rules heaven and earth.* **ἀπὸ σοφῶν καὶ συνετῶν** are those who are skillful and clever in the ways of the world and those who rely on their own intellect and good sense. There is probably little distinction between the two. **νηπίοις** are those who, unspoiled by worldly learning, heed the Spirit of God and with whom God is pleased.

11:26 **ναὶ ὁ πατήρ**: *yes, Father*; the article and the noun in the nominative are used as a vocative (cf. App. 12). **οὕτως εὐδοκία ἐγένετο ἔμπροσθέν σου**: *in this way your good will was done* (literally: *in this way good will in your sight was done*).

11:27 **Πάντα μοι παρεδόθη**: neuter plural subjects are considered as collective nouns and regularly take a singular verb. **εἰ μὴ**: *except.*

οὐδὲ τὸν πατέρα τις ἐπιγινώσκει εἰ μὴ ὁ υἱὸς καὶ ᾧ ἐὰν βούληται ὁ υἱὸς ἀποκαλύψαι. 11:28 Δεῦτε πρός με πάντες οἱ κοπιῶντες καὶ πεφορτισμένοι, κἀγὼ ἀναπαύσω ὑμᾶς. 11:29 ἄρατε τὸν ζυγόν μου ἐφ' ὑμᾶς καὶ μάθετε ἀπ' ἐμοῦ, ὅτι πραΰς εἰμι καὶ ταπεινὸς τῇ καρδίᾳ, καὶ εὑρήσετε ἀνάπαυσιν ταῖς ψυχαῖς ὑμῶν· 11:30 ὁ γὰρ ζυγός μου χρηστὸς καὶ τὸ φορτίον μου ἐλαφρόν ἐστιν.

11:27

οὐδέ and not, nor (conjunction and adverb)

τις, τι anyone, anything, someone, something, a certain one, a certain thing (indefinite pronoun)

βούλομαι, βουλήσομαι, βεβούλημαι, ἐβουλήθην wish, be willing, desire, want

ἀποκαλύπτω, ἀποκαλύψω, ἀπεκάλυψα, ἀπεκαλύφθην uncover, reveal, disclose

11:28

δεῦτε come! come here! (adverb)

κοπιάω, κοπιάσω, ἐκοπίασα, κεκοπίακα be weary, be tired, work hard, toil

φορτίζω, φορτίσω, πεφόρτισμαι load, burden

κἀγώ = καὶ ἐγώ

ἀναπαύω, ἀναπαύσω, ἀνέπαυσα, ἀναπέπαυμαι, ἀνεπαύθην give rest, refresh, revive

11:29

αἴρω, ἀρῶ, ἦρα, ἦρκα, ἦρμαι, ἤρθην take up, take, bear, take away, lift, carry, remove; keep in suspense; destroy, kill

ζυγός, οῦ, ὁ yoke

μανθάνω, μαθήσομαι, ἔμαθον (2 aorist), μεμάθηκα learn

πραΰς, πραεῖα, πραΰ meek, gentle, humble, considerate, kind, forgiving; mild, benevolent, humane

ταπεινός, ή, όν humble, poor, lowly

καρδία, ας, ἡ heart

εὑρίσκω, εὑρήσω, εὗρον (2 aorist), ηὕρηκα/εὕρηκα, εὑρέθην find, meet, discover, recognize

ἀνάπαυσις, εως, ἡ ceasing; rest; resting place

ψυχή, ῆς, ἡ breath, life, soul, heart

11:30

ζυγός, οῦ, ὁ yoke

χρηστός, ή, όν useful, suitable, worthy; good, pleasant, agreeable; easy; gentle, kind, gracious

φορτίον, ου, τό load, burden

ἐλαφρός, ά, όν light, easy to bear

11:27 **ᾧ ἐὰν**: the relative pronoun with ἐὰν introduces a present general condition (App. 70).

11:28 **Δεῦτε**: in an absolute sense the adverb functions as an imperative.

11:29 **ταπεινὸς τῇ καρδίᾳ**: *humble in heart*; τῇ καρδίᾳ is a dative of respect.

11:30 **ζυγός μου χρηστὸς καὶ τὸ φορτίον μου ἐλαφρόν ἐστιν**: the paradoxical statement rings true especially when one considers the alternative of μου, which is stressed by repetition. Ultimately the yoke and burden of Christ bring eternal life and freedom from the yoke and burden of eternal bondage of Satan.

12 Ἐν ἐκείνῳ τῷ καιρῷ ἐπορεύθη ὁ Ἰησοῦς τοῖς σάββασιν διὰ
τῶν σπορίμων· οἱ δὲ μαθηταὶ αὐτοῦ ἐπείνασαν καὶ ἤρξαντο τίλλειν
στάχυας καὶ ἐσθίειν. 12:2 οἱ δὲ Φαρισαῖοι ἰδόντες εἶπαν αὐτῷ, Ἰδοὺ
οἱ μαθηταί σου ποιοῦσιν ὃ οὐκ ἔξεστιν ποιεῖν ἐν σαββάτῳ. 12:3 ὁ δὲ
εἶπεν αὐτοῖς, Οὐκ ἀνέγνωτε τί ἐποίησεν Δαυὶδ ὅτε ἐπείνασεν καὶ
οἱ μετ' αὐτοῦ, 12:4 πῶς εἰσῆλθεν εἰς τὸν οἶκον τοῦ θεοῦ καὶ τοὺς
ἄρτους τῆς προθέσεως ἔφαγον, ὃ οὐκ ἐξὸν ἦν αὐτῷ φαγεῖν οὐδὲ τοῖς
μετ' αὐτοῦ εἰ μὴ τοῖς ἱερεῦσιν μόνοις;

12:1
καιρός, οῦ, ὁ time, appointed time; season; time of crisis, end-time
πορεύομαι, πορεύσομαι, πεπόρευμαι, ἐπορεύθην go, proceed, travel
σάββατον, ου, τό Sabbath; week (both in singular and in plural)
σπόριμος, ου, ὁ sown; standing grain, fields of grain, cornfields (plural)
πεινάω, πεινάσω/πεινήσω, ἐπείνασα hunger, be hungry
ἄρχω, ἄρξω, ἦρξα, ἦρχα, ἦργμαι, ἤρχθην rule (active); begin (middle)
τίλλω, τιλῶ pick, pluck
στάχυς, υος, ὁ ear of corn, head of wheat
ἐσθίω, φάγομαι, ἔφαγον (2 aorist) eat
12:3
ἀναγινώσκω, ἀναγνώσομαι, ἀνέγνων (2 aorist), ἀνέγνωκα, ἀνέγνωσμαι, ἀνεγνώσθην read, read aloud, read in public
πεινάω, πεινάσω/πεινήσω, ἐπείνασα hunger, be hungry
12:4
πῶς how? in what way? in what sense? (interrogative adverb)
οἶκος, ου, ὁ house, dwelling
ἄρτος, ου, ὁ bread, loaf of bread
πρόθεσις, εως, ἡ putting out, setting forth, presentation
ἐσθίω, φάγομαι, ἔφαγον (2 aorist) eat
ἐξόν it is possible, it is proper, it is permitted (participle of ἔξεστι(ν), an impersonal verb)
εἰ μή unless, except
ἱερεύς, έως, ὁ priest
μόνος, η, ον only, alone

12:1 **τοῖς σάββασιν**: *on the Sabbath*; the use of the case is a dative of time when. The dative is used without a preposition to indicate a definite time at which an action occurs.

12:2 **ὃ**: *that which*; the antecedent of the relative pronoun is often omitted. Supply the appropriate form of the demonstrative pronoun: ἐκεῖνο (App. 42).

12:3 **Οὐκ ἀνέγνωτε**: *have you not read*; the direct question introduces indirect questions in this and the next verse: **τί . . . πῶς**.

12:4 **ὃ οὐκ ἐξὸν ἦν**: *which was not permitted*; the present participle of ἔξεστι and the imperfect of εἰμί form a periphrastic construction. **τοῖς μετ' αὐτοῦ**: *those with him*; the article is used as a demonstrative.

12:5 ἢ οὐκ ἀνέγνωτε ἐν τῷ νόμῳ ὅτι τοῖς σάββασιν οἱ ἱερεῖς ἐν τῷ ἱερῷ τὸ σάββατον βεβηλοῦσιν καὶ ἀναίτιοί εἰσιν; 12:6 λέγω δὲ ὑμῖν ὅτι τοῦ ἱεροῦ μεῖζόν ἐστιν ὧδε. 12:7 εἰ δὲ ἐγνώκειτε τί ἐστιν, Ἔλεος θέλω καὶ οὐ θυσίαν, οὐκ ἂν κατεδικάσατε τοὺς ἀναιτίους.

12:5
ἀναγινώσκω, ἀναγνώσομαι, ἀνέγνων (2 aorist), ἀνέγνωκα, ἀνέγνωσμαι, ἀνεγνώσθην read, read aloud, read in public
νόμος, ου, ὁ law, custom, ordinance
σάββατον, ου, τό Sabbath; week (both in singular and in plural)
ἱερεύς, έως, ὁ priest
ἱερόν, οῦ, τό temple
βεβηλόω, βεβηλώσω, ἐβεβήλωσα desecrate, profane, pollute, violate
ἀναίτιος, ον blameless, guiltless, innocent
12:6
ἱερόν, οῦ, τό temple
μείζων, μεῖζον greater, larger (comparative of μέγας)
ὧδε here (adverb)
12:7
γινώσκω, γνώσομαι, ἔγνων, ἔγνωκα, ἔγνωσμαι, ἐγνώσθην know, learn, understand
ἔλεος, εως, τό/ὁ pity, mercy, compassion, clemency
θέλω, θελήσω, ἠθέλησα wish to have, desire, purpose, want
θυσία, ας, ἡ sacrifice, offering
καταδικάζω, καταδικάσω, κατεδίσα, κατεδικάσθην condemn, find guilty
ἀναίτιος, ον blameless, guiltless, innocent

12:5 **τὸ σάββατον βεβηλοῦσιν**: they do so by working in the temple on the sabbath. The doublet of οὐκ ἀνέγνωτε and the tricolon of precedence in the last three verses argue incisively.

12:6 **τοῦ ἱεροῦ μεῖζόν ἐστιν ὧδε**: *here is something greater than the temple*; μεῖζόν: the comparative adjective is neuter, not masculine, and takes a genitive of comparison. Jesus claims that His work takes priority over temple work. The argument runs: if temple workers are allowed to labor in the temple on the sabbath, His disciples are allowed to do so the more because of the nature of His work.

12:7 **εἰ δὲ ἐγνώκειτε . . . οὐκ ἂν κατεδικάσατε**: *if you had come to understand (and knew now) . . . you would not have condemned*; on rare occasions the pluperfect indicative is used instead of the aorist in a protasis of a past contrary to fact condition to indicate a completed act in past time and its continuance to the present. **Ἔλεος θέλω καὶ οὐ θυσίαν**: His work of mercy takes precedence over the priests' sacrifice of animals.

12:8 κύριος γάρ ἐστιν τοῦ σαββάτου ὁ υἱὸς τοῦ ἀνθρώπου.
12:9 Καὶ μεταβὰς ἐκεῖθεν ἦλθεν εἰς τὴν συναγωγὴν αὐτῶν·
12:10 καὶ ἰδοὺ ἄνθρωπος χεῖρα ἔχων ξηράν. καὶ ἐπηρώτησαν αὐτὸν
λέγοντες, Εἰ ἔξεστιν τοῖς σάββασιν θεραπεῦσαι; ἵνα κατηγορήσωσιν
αὐτοῦ. 12:11 ὁ δὲ εἶπεν αὐτοῖς, Τίς ἔσται ἐξ ὑμῶν ἄνθρωπος ὃς
ἕξει πρόβατον ἓν καὶ ἐὰν ἐμπέσῃ τοῦτο τοῖς σάββασιν εἰς βόθυνον,
οὐχὶ κρατήσει αὐτὸ καὶ ἐγερεῖ; 12:12 πόσῳ οὖν διαφέρει ἄνθρωπος
προβάτου.

12:8

σάββατον, ου, τό Sabbath; week (both in singular and in plural)

12:9

μεταβαίνω, μεταβήσομαι, μετέβην, μεταβέβηκα go, pass over, move; go away, depart

ἐκεῖθεν from there, from that place (adverb)

12:10

χείρ, χειρός, ἡ hand

ξηρός, ά, όν withered, paralyzed

ἐπερωτάω, ἐπερωτήσω, ἐπηρώτησα ask, ask a question, interrogate, question; inquire after

εἰ if, whether; an interrogatory particle introducing a direct question

ἔξεστι(ν) it is permitted, it is possible (impersonal verb)

θεραπεύω, θεραπεύσω, ἐθεράπευσα, ἐθεραπεύθην care for, heal, restore

ἵνα to, in order to, in order that, that (conjunction)

κατηγορέω, κατηγορήσω, κατηγόρησα accuse, bring charges against, speak against

12:11

πρόβατον, ου, τό sheep

ἐμπίπτω, ἐμπεσοῦμαι, ἐνέπεσον (2 aorist) fall (in, into, among)

βόθυνος, ου, ὁ pit, well, cistern

κρατέω, κρατήσω, ἐκράτησα, κεκράτηκα, κεκράτημαι lay hold of, grasp; retain, not remit

12:12

πόσος, η, ον how great? how much?

διαφέρω, διοίσω, διήνεγκα carry through; differ, be different; be better, be worth more than, be superior to

πρόβατον, ου, τό sheep

12:8 **κύριος . . . τοῦ σαββάτου**: the predicate noun κύριος governs an objective genitive (cf. App. 65), i.e., He rules the Sabbath.

12:10 **κατηγορήσωσιν αὐτοῦ** is an aorist subjunctive (cf. App. 53, D, 2). The compound verb governs the genitive case.

12:11 **ἕξει** is the third person singular future active indicative of ἔχω. **ἐὰν** introduces a future more vivid condition. **τοῖς σάββασιν**: *on the Sabbath*; the use of the case is a dative of time when. The dative is used without a preposition to indicate a definite time at which an action occurs.

12:12 **πόσῳ** is a dative of degree of difference. **προβάτου** is a genitive of comparison. The comparative idea is expressed inherently in the verb **διαφέρει. τῷ ἀνθρώπῳ** resumes again the narrative, interrupted by the questioning of the Pharisees, of Jesus and the man with the withered hand (10).

ὥστε ἔξεστιν τοῖς σάββασιν καλῶς ποιεῖν. 12:13 τότε λέγει τῷ ἀνθρώπῳ, Ἔκτεινόν σου τὴν χεῖρα. καὶ ἐξέτεινεν καὶ ἀπεκατεστάθη ὑγιὴς ὡς ἡ ἄλλη. 12:14 ἐξελθόντες δὲ οἱ Φαρισαῖοι συμβούλιον ἔλαβον κατ᾽ αὐτοῦ ὅπως αὐτὸν ἀπολέσωσιν.

12:15 Ὁ δὲ Ἰησοῦς γνοὺς ἀνεχώρησεν ἐκεῖθεν. καὶ ἠκολούθησαν αὐτῷ [ὄχλοι] πολλοί, καὶ ἐθεράπευσεν αὐτοὺς πάντας 12:16 καὶ ἐπετίμησεν αὐτοῖς ἵνα μὴ φανερὸν αὐτὸν ποιήσωσιν,

---

12:12
ὥστε so that (conjunction)
ἔξεστι(ν) it is permitted, it is possible (impersonal verb)
καλῶς well (adverb)
12:13
ἐκτείνω, ἐκτενῶ, ἐξέτεινα stretch out, hold out
χείρ, χειρός, ἡ hand
ἀποκαθίστημι/ἀποκαθιστάνω, ἀποκαταστήσω, ἀπεκατέστην (2 aorist), ἀπεκατεστάθην restore, bring back, give back
ὑγιής, ές healthy, sound
ὡς as, like, when, after, about (with numerals), how, provided that (adverb, conjunction)
12:14
συμβούλιον, ίου, τό counsel, plan, consultation; συμβούλιον λαμβάνειν form a plan, consult, plot
κατά near, towards, by, in accordance with, after the manner of (preposition + accusative); down from, against (+ genitive)
ἀπόλλυμι/ἀπολλύω, ἀπολέσω/ἀπολῶ, ἀπώλεσα, ἀπολώλεκα, ἀπόλωλα (2 perfect) lose, destroy, ruin, kill; perish (middle)
12:15
γινώσκω, γνώσομαι, ἔγνων, ἔγνωκα, ἔγνωσμαι, ἐγνώσθην know, learn, understand
ἀναχωρέω, ἀναχωρήσω, ἀνεχώρησα go away, depart, withdraw, retire
ἐκεῖθεν from there, from that place (adverb)
ὄχλος, ου, ὁ crowd, throng, multitude
θεραπεύω, θεραπεύσω, ἐθεράπευσα, ἐθεραπεύθην care for, heal, restore
12:16
ἐπιτιμάω, ἐπιτιμήσω, ἐπετίμησα set a value on; assess a penalty; rebuke, reprove, censure, reprimand; admonish, enjoin
φανερός, ά, όν visible, clear, known

12:13 **ἀπεκατεστάθη**: the subject of the verb is *the hand*.

12:14 **ὅπως αὐτὸν ἀπολέσωσιν**: the conjunction with the subjunctive is used to indicate purpose. The verb is an aorist subjunctive (cf. App. 53, D, 2).

12:15 **γνοὺς**: *since He knew*; supply ταῦτα, referring to their plans to kill him (14). The verbal form is a masculine singular nominative second aorist particple (App. 61; 29, note).

12:16 **ἐπετίμησεν αὐτοῖς**: the compound verb governs the dative case. **ἵνα μὴ φανερὸν αὐτὸν ποιήσωσιν**: *not to make Him known*; ἵνα μὴ introduces a negative clause of purpose.

12:17 ἵνα πληρωθῇ τὸ ῥηθὲν διὰ Ἠσαΐου τοῦ προφήτου λέγοντος,
12:18 Ἰδοὺ ὁ παῖς μου ὃν ᾑρέτισα,
ὁ ἀγαπητός μου εἰς ὃν εὐδόκησεν ἡ ψυχή μου·
θήσω τὸ πνεῦμά μου ἐπ' αὐτόν,
καὶ κρίσιν τοῖς ἔθνεσιν ἀπαγγελεῖ.
12:19 οὐκ ἐρίσει οὐδὲ κραυγάσει,
οὐδὲ ἀκούσει τις ἐν ταῖς πλατείαις τὴν φωνὴν αὐτοῦ.
12:20 κάλαμον συντετριμμένον οὐ κατεάξει

12:18
παῖς, παιδός, ὁ child, boy, youth; servant
αἱρετίζω, αἱρετίσω, ᾑρέτισα choose
ἀγαπητός, ή, όν beloved, dear
εὐδοκέω, εὐδοκήσω, εὐδόκησα/ηὐδόκησα be well pleased, take delight
ψυχή, ῆς, ἡ breath, life, soul, heart
τίθημι, θήσω, ἔθηκα, τέθεικα, τέθειμαι, ἐτέθην place, set, put, lay, serve, give
πνεῦμα, ατος, τό wind, spirit, mind, Holy Spirit
κρίσις, εως, ἡ judgment, justice, righteousness, condemnation
ἔθνος, ους, τό nation, people
ἀπαγγέλλω, ἀπαγγελῶ, ἀπήγγειλα (1 aorist), ἀπηγγέλην (2 aorist passive) bring back word, report, declare, announce, tell

12:19
ἐρίζω, ἐρίσω quarrel, wrangle
κραυγάζω, κραυγάσω, ἐκραύγασα cry out, exclaim
οὐδέ and not, nor (conjunction and adverb)
πλατεῖα, ας, ἡ wide road, street
φωνή, ῆς, ἡ voice, sound

12:20
κάλαμος, ου, ὁ reed, cane; staff
συντρίβω, συντρίψω, συνέτριψα, συντέτριμμαι, συνετρίβην rub together; shiver; break, bruise, crush; deprive of strength, debilitate; be broken in heart, be contrite (passive)
κατάγνυμι, κατεάξω, κατέαξα, κατεάγην (2 aorist passive) break, break in pieces, break in two, crush

---

12:17 **ἵνα πληρωθῇ**: supply ταῦτα ἐγένετο before the purpose clause. The conjunction with the subjunctive is used to indicate purpose.

12:18 **Ἰδοὺ ὁ παῖς μου**: *behold, my servant*; the demonstrative particle with a noun without a finite verb means *here is*.

12:19 **οὐκ ἐρίσει οὐδὲ κραυγάσει**: as the humble servant of the Lord, He does not seek quarrels and strife with adversaries but quietly and calmly performs His works. **οὐδὲ ἀκούσει τις ἐν ταῖς πλατείας τὴν φωνὴν αὐτοῦ**: He does not seek public attention or notoriety.

12:20 **κάλαμον συντετριμμένον . . . λίνον τυφόμενον**: the metaphors probably refer to the sick, weary, afflicted, and outcasts of society who come to Him with a broken heart and a contrite spirit.

καὶ λίνον τυφόμενον οὐ σβέσει,
ἕως ἂν ἐκβάλῃ εἰς νῖκος τὴν κρίσιν.
12:21 καὶ τῷ ὀνόματι αὐτοῦ ἔθνη ἐλπιοῦσιν.

12:22 Τότε προσηνέχθη αὐτῷ δαιμονιζόμενος τυφλὸς καὶ κωφός, καὶ ἐθεράπευσεν αὐτόν, ὥστε τὸν κωφὸν λαλεῖν καὶ βλέπειν.

12:20
λίνον, ου, τό flax, linen; flaxen wick, lamp-wick
τύφω, θύψω give off smoke; smoke, smolder (passive)
σβέννυμι, σβέσω, ἔσβεσα extinguish, put out
νῖκος, ους, τό victory
κρίσις, εως, ἡ judgment, justice, righteousness, condemnation
12:21
ὄνομα, ατος, τό name
ἔθνος, ους, τό nation, people
ἐλπίζω, ἐλπίσω/ἐλπιῶ, ἤλπισα, ἤλπικα hope, hope for, expect
12:22
προσφέρω, προσοίσω, προσήνεγκα, προσήνεγκον (2 aorist), προσηνέχθην bring, offer, present
δαιμονίζομαι, δαιμονίσομαι, ἐδαιμονίσθην be possessed by a demon
τυφλός, ή, όν blind
κωφός, ή, όν blunt, dull; dull of hearing, deprived of hearing; deaf; dumb, mute
θεραπεύω, θεραπεύσω, ἐθεράπευσα, ἐθεραπεύθην care for, heal, restore
ὥστε so that (conjunction)
λαλέω, λαλήσω, ἐλάλησα, λελάληκα, λελάλημαι, ἐλαλήθην speak, address, preach
βλέπω, βλέψω, ἔβλεψα see, behold, perceive

12:20 **ἕως ἂν ἐκβάλῃ**: *until He leads*; the temporal conjunction with the aorist subjunctive and the particle ἂν refers indefinitely to the future and denotes that the commencement of one event is dependent on another. **τὴν κρίσιν**: abstract nouns are generally modified by an article, which is omitted in translation.

12:21 **τῷ ὀνόματι αὐτοῦ ἔθνη ἐλπιοῦσιν**: *in His name nations will place their hope*; neuter plural subjects are considered as collective nouns and regularly take a singular verb. However, a plural verb may be used when stress is laid on the plurality of persons or parts. The verb has an absolute sense and takes a dative of person or thing in whom hope is placed.

12:22 **ὥστε τὸν κωφὸν λαλεῖν καὶ βλέπειν**: *so that the (mute) man talked and saw*; ὥστε, followed by the accusative with infinitive, introduces a result clause. Although the man is also blind and possessed by an evil spirit, for sake of brevity (brachylogy), he is only referred to as mute in the result clause.

12:23 καὶ ἐξίσταντο πάντες οἱ ὄχλοι καὶ ἔλεγον, Μήτι οὗτός ἐστιν
ὁ υἱὸς Δαυίδ; 12:24 οἱ δὲ Φαρισαῖοι ἀκούσαντες εἶπον, Οὗτος οὐκ
ἐκβάλλει τὰ δαιμόνια εἰ μὴ ἐν τῷ Βεελζεβοὺλ ἄρχοντι τῶν δαιμονίων.
12:25 εἰδὼς δὲ τὰς ἐνθυμήσεις αὐτῶν εἶπεν αὐτοῖς, Πᾶσα βασιλεία
μερισθεῖσα καθ' ἑαυτῆς ἐρημοῦται καὶ πᾶσα πόλις ἢ οἰκία μερισθεῖσα
καθ' ἑαυτῆς οὐ σταθήσεται.

12:23

ἐξίστημι/ἐξιστάω, ἐκστήσω, ἐξέστησα, ἐξέστην (2 aorist), ἐξέστακα to put out of its place; to astonish, amaze; be astonished (2 aorist and middle)

μήτι (interrogative particle in questions expecting a negative answer)

12:24

δαιμόνιον, ου, τό deity, divinity; demon, evil spirit

εἰ μή unless, except

βεελζεβούλ/βεελζεβούβ and βεεζεβούλ, ὁ Beelzebub (indeclinable)

ἄρχων, οντος, ὁ chief, ruler, magistrate, prince

12:25

ἐνθύμησις, εως, ἡ thought, reflection, idea

μερίζω, μερίσω, ἐμέρισα, μεμέρικα, μεμέρισμαι, ἐμερίσθην divide, separate; be at variance (passive)

κατά near, towards, by, in accordance with, after the manner of (preposition + accusative); down from, against (+ genitive)

ἑαυτοῦ, ῆς, οῦ himself, herself, itself; themselves, ourselves, yourselves (in plural)

ἐρημόω, ἐρημώσω, ἠρήμωμαι, ἠρημώθην lay waste, bring to ruin, depopulate

ἵστημι, στήσω, ἔστησα, ἔστην (2 aorist), ἕστηκα, ἐστάθην put, place, set, cause to stand (transitive); stand, be (intransitive)

12:23 **Μήτι** is an interrogative particle that expects a negative answer.

12:24 **εἰ μὴ**: *except*. **ἐν τῷ Βεελζεβοὺλ ἄρχοντι τῶν δαιμονίων**: *by Beelzebul, prince of the demons*; the preposition with a person expresses agency: *with the help of, through, by*. ἄρχοντι stands in apposition to Βεελζεβοὺλ.

12:25 **εἰδὼς** is the perfect active participle of οἶδα (App. 62; cf. 33). **μερισθεῖσα**, the feminine singular nominative aorist passive participle (cf. App. 34), stands in agreement with its subject βασιλεία. **σταθήσεται**: the first future passive is intransitive.

12:26 καὶ εἰ ὁ Σατανᾶς τὸν Σατανᾶν ἐκβάλλει, ἐφ᾽ ἑαυτὸν ἐμερίσθη· πῶς οὖν σταθήσεται ἡ βασιλεία αὐτοῦ; 12:27 καὶ εἰ ἐγὼ ἐν Βεελζεβοὺλ ἐκβάλλω τὰ δαιμόνια, οἱ υἱοὶ ὑμῶν ἐν τίνι ἐκβάλλουσιν; διὰ τοῦτο αὐτοὶ κριταὶ ἔσονται ὑμῶν. 12:28 εἰ δὲ ἐν πνεύματι θεοῦ ἐγὼ ἐκβάλλω τὰ δαιμόνια, ἄρα ἔφθασεν ἐφ᾽ ὑμᾶς ἡ βασιλεία τοῦ θεοῦ. 12:29 ἢ πῶς δύναταί τις εἰσελθεῖν εἰς τὴν οἰκίαν τοῦ ἰσχυροῦ καὶ τὰ σκεύη αὐτοῦ ἁρπάσαι,

---

12:26

μερίζω, μερίσω, ἐμέρισα, μεμέρικα, μεμέρισμαι, ἐμερίσθην divide, separate; be at variance (passive)

πῶς how? in what way? in what sense? (interrogative adverb)

ἵστημι, στήσω, ἔστησα, ἔστην (2 aorist), ἕστηκα, ἐστάθην put, place, set, cause to stand (transitive); stand, be (intransitive)

12:27

βεελζεβούλ/βεελζεβούβ and βεεζεβούλ, ὁ Beelzebub (indeclinable)

δαιμόνιον, ου, τό deity, divinity; demon, evil spirit

κριτής, ου, ὁ judge

12:28

δαιμόνιον, ου, τό deity, divinity; demon, evil spirit

ἄρα therefore, then, consequently (particle)

φθάνω, φθήσομαι, φθάσω, ἔφθασα, ἔφθην (2 aorist passive) outstrip; advance, come before, precede; come, arrive; come upon, overtake

12:29

πῶς how? in what way? in what sense? (interrogative adverb)

ἰσχυρός, ά, όν strong, mighty, powerful

σκεῦος, ους, τό vessel, jar, container

ἁρπάζω, ἁρπάσω, ἥρπασα, ἡρπάσθην, ἡρπάγην (2 aorist passive) steal, carry off, drag away, take away

---

12:26 **εἰ ὁ Σατανᾶς . . . ἐκβάλλει . . . ἐμερίσθη**: *if Satan casts out . . . he is divided*; the simple or particular condition shows a gnomic aorist in the apodosis. The aorist may be used to express a general truth where the experience of an action in the past suggests an action that is likely to be repeated.

12:27 **οἱ υἱοὶ ὑμῶν**: the noun may be used of members of a large and coherent group, e.g., υἱοὶ Ἀβρααμ, and here refers to the Pharisees (24). Logic makes clear that demons cannot be driven out by both God and Satan. **διὰ τοῦτο**: *for this reason*. **κριταὶ** is a predicate nominative.

12:28 **εἰ** introduces a simple or particular condition.

12:29 **ἢ πῶς δύναταί τις**: Jesus introduces a parable in which He is the principal opponent of Satan in the battle for the souls of mortals and the sacker of his kingdom. **εἰσελθεῖν εἰς τὴν οἰκίαν τοῦ ἰσχυροῦ**: εἰσελθεῖν εἰς, occasionally used of Satan or evil spirits entering into the body of humans and taking possession (Lk 22:3, Mk 9:25), is used here of Jesus entering the kingdom of Satan and sacking it. **τὰ σκεύη αὐτοῦ ἁρπάσαι**: by driving out the demons He plunders Satan of the vessels of human bodies that he thinks belong to him.

ἐὰν μὴ πρῶτον δήσῃ τὸν ἰσχυρόν; καὶ τότε τὴν οἰκίαν αὐτοῦ διαρπάσει. 12:30 ὁ μὴ ὢν μετ' ἐμοῦ κατ' ἐμοῦ ἐστιν, καὶ ὁ μὴ συνάγων μετ' ἐμοῦ σκορπίζει. 12:31 Διὰ τοῦτο λέγω ὑμῖν, πᾶσα ἁμαρτία καὶ βλασφημία ἀφεθήσεται τοῖς ἀνθρώποις, ἡ δὲ τοῦ πνεύματος βλασφημία οὐκ ἀφεθήσεται. 12:32 καὶ ὃς ἐὰν εἴπῃ λόγον κατὰ τοῦ υἱοῦ τοῦ ἀνθρώπου, ἀφεθήσεται αὐτῷ·

12:29

ἐὰν μή if not, unless, except

πρῶτον first (in time; adverb)

δέω, δήσω, ἔδησα, δέδεκα, δέδεμαι, ἐδέθην bind, tie, impede

ἰσχυρός, ά, όν strong, mighty, powerful

διαρπάζω, διαρπάσω plunder, rob, steal; snatch, abduct, take captive

12:30

κατά near, towards, by, in accordance with, after the manner of (preposition + accusative); down from, against (+ genitive)

συνάγω, συνάξω, συνήγαγον (2 aorist), συνῆγμαι, συνήχθην gather in, gather up, bring together; convene, come together, meet (passive)

σκορπίζω, σκορπίσω, ἐσκόρπισα, ἐσκορπίσθην scatter, disperse

12:31

ἁμαρτία, ας, ἡ error, sin

βλασφημία, ίας, ἡ slander, abusive speech, blasphemy

ἀφίημι, ἀφήσω, ἀφῆκα, ἀφῆν (2 aorist), ἀφεῖκα, ἀφεῖμαι, ἀφέθην let go, forgive, leave

12:32

λόγος, ου, ὁ word, doctrine, account, reason, statement, saying

κατά near, towards, by, in accordance with, after the manner of (preposition + accusative); down from, against (+ genitive)

12:29 **ἐὰν μὴ πρῶτον δήσῃ τὸν ἰσχυρόν**: in a reversal of fortunes, the one who binds (Lk 13:16) is bound.

12:30 **ὁ μὴ . . . ὁ μὴ**: the antithetical couplets of parallel construction are simple or particular conditions (App. 70). **πᾶσα ἁμαρτία καὶ βλασφημία ἀφεθήσεται τοῖς ἀνθρώποις**: the verb in the singular agrees with the nearest subject and governs a dative of person in the passive construction.

12:31 **ἡ δὲ τοῦ πνεύματος βλασφημία**: *blasphemy against the Spirit*; abstract nouns are generally modified by an article, which is omitted in translation. τοῦ πνεύματος is an objective genitive (cf. App. 65). It may be one thing to commit offenses against God unwittingly but quite another to do so wittingly, after having been enlightend by the Holy Spirit (Hb 6:4–8, 2 Pt 2:20–22).

12:32 **ὃς ἐὰν**: the relative pronoun and the particle introduce a future more vivid condition. **ἀφεθήσεται αὐτῷ**: *he will be forgiven* (literally: *it will be forgiven him*); the impersonal verb governs the dative of the person. The construction is translated as a personal one.

ὃς δ' ἂν εἴπῃ κατὰ τοῦ πνεύματος τοῦ ἁγίου, οὐκ ἀφεθήσεται αὐτῷ οὔτε ἐν τούτῳ τῷ αἰῶνι οὔτε ἐν τῷ μέλλοντι.

12:33 Ἢ ποιήσατε τὸ δένδρον καλὸν καὶ τὸν καρπὸν αὐτοῦ καλόν, ἢ ποιήσατε τὸ δένδρον σαπρὸν καὶ τὸν καρπὸν αὐτοῦ σαπρόν· ἐκ γὰρ τοῦ καρποῦ τὸ δένδρον γινώσκεται. 12:34 γεννήματα ἐχιδνῶν, πῶς δύνασθε ἀγαθὰ λαλεῖν πονηροὶ ὄντες; ἐκ γὰρ τοῦ περισσεύματος τῆς καρδίας τὸ στόμα λαλεῖ. 12:35 ὁ ἀγαθὸς ἄνθρωπος ἐκ τοῦ ἀγαθοῦ θησαυροῦ ἐκβάλλει ἀγαθά, καὶ ὁ πονηρὸς ἄνθρωπος ἐκ τοῦ πονηροῦ θησαυροῦ ἐκβάλλει πονηρά.

12:32
οὔτε and not, not even (conjunction); οὔτε . . . οὔτε neither . . . nor
αἰών, αἰῶνος, ὁ eternity, perpetuity, life
μέλλω, μελλήσω be about to, be on the point of
12:33
δένδρον, ου, τό tree
καλός, ή, όν good, useful, choice
καρπός, οῦ, ὁ fruit, crop; result, gain
σαπρός, ά, όν spoiled, rotten; bad, evil
γινώσκω, γνώσομαι, ἔγνων, ἔγνωκα, ἔγνωσμαι, ἐγνώσθην know, learn, understand
12:34
γέννημα, ατος, τό offspring, progeny, brood
ἔχιδνα, ης, ἡ viper, poisonous serpent
πῶς how? in what way? in what sense? (interrogative adverb)
ἀγαθός, ή, όν good, profitable, upright
λαλέω, λαλήσω, ἐλάλησα, λελάληκα, λελάλημαι, ἐλαλήθην speak, address, preach
περίσσευμα, ατος, τό abundance, fullness, exuberance
καρδία, ας, ἡ heart
στόμα, ατος, τό mouth
λαλέω, λαλήσω, ἐλάλησα, λελάληκα, λελάλημαι, ἐλαλήθην speak, address, preach
12:35
ἀγαθός, ή, όν good, profitable, upright
θησαυρός, οῦ, ὁ treasure box, treasury, treasure

12:32 **οὔτε ἐν τῷ μέλλοντι**: *nor in that to come.*

12:33 **Ἢ . . . ἢ**: *either . . . or*; the correlative conjunctions introduce an antithetical parallel couplet. **ποιήσατε** is a second person plural first aorist active imperative (cf. App. 53, D, 3). **καλὸν** is a predicate accusative adjective.

12:34 **γεννήματα ἐχιδνῶν**: the vocative (cf. App. 10) governs an appositional genitive identifying it more specifically (cf. App. 65).

12:36 λέγω δὲ ὑμῖν ὅτι πᾶν ῥῆμα ἀργὸν ὃ λαλήσουσιν οἱ ἄνθρωποι ἀποδώσουσιν περὶ αὐτοῦ λόγον ἐν ἡμέρᾳ κρίσεως· 12:37 ἐκ γὰρ τῶν λόγων σου δικαιωθήσῃ, καὶ ἐκ τῶν λόγων σου καταδικασθήσῃ.

12:38 Τότε ἀπεκρίθησαν αὐτῷ τινες τῶν γραμματέων καὶ Φαρισαίων λέγοντες, Διδάσκαλε, θέλομεν ἀπὸ σοῦ σημεῖον ἰδεῖν.

12:36
ῥῆμα, ατος, τό word, saying, expression, speech
ἀργός, ή, όν inactive, unemployed; idle, lazy; useless, unproductive, careless, unprofitable, hollow
λαλέω, λαλήσω, ἐλάλησα, λελάληκα, λελάλημαι, ἐλαλήθην speak, address, preach
ἀποδίδωμι, ἀποδώσω, ἀπέδωκα, ἀποδέδωκα, ἀποδέδομαι, ἀπεδόθην give, give away, pay, keep, perform
λόγος, ου, ὁ word, doctrine, account, reason, statement, saying
κρίσις, εως, ἡ judgment, justice, righteousness, condemnation

12:37
δικαιόω, δικαιώσω, ἐδικαίωσα, ἐδικαιώθην justify, vindicate
καταδικάζω, καταδικάσω, κατεδίσα, κατεδικάσθην condemn, find guilty

12:38
ἀποκρίνομαι, ἀπεκρινάμην, ἀπεκρίθην answer, reply
τις, τι anyone, anything, someone, something, a certain one, a certain thing (indefinite pronoun)
γραμματεύς, έως, ὁ secretary, clerk, scholar versed in law, scribe
διδάσκαλος, ου, ὁ master, teacher
σημεῖον, ου, τό sign, token, miracle

12:36 **πᾶν ῥῆμα . . . περὶ αὐτοῦ** is an anacoluthon or a syntactic non sequitur in which πᾶν ῥῆμα starts as the subject, but ends up as the object of the preposition. The construction (*casus pendens*) imitates the compression of natural speech and is found more commonly in John than in the other Gospels. However, in this case it may be due to the chiastic nature of the construction. οἱ ἄνθρωποι at the center of the chiasm serves as the subject of λαλήσουσιν and ἀποδώσουσιν. The rhetorical figure where one element or word governs a double syntactic function is called *apo koinou* (ἀπὸ κοινοῦ). **λόγον ἐν ἡμέρᾳ κρίσεως**: in a slight twist, the addition of λόγον changes the meaning of the verb from its absolute sense of *making recompense* to *giving an account*. The phrase added at the end, outside of the chiastic structure, stresses the importance of the eschatological event.

12:37 **δικαιωθήσῃ . . . καταδικασθήσῃ**: the antithetical verbs are second person singular first future passive indicative (cf. App. 53, G, 1).

12:38 **τινες τῶν γραμματέων**: *some of the scribes*; the partitive idea is expressed with the genitive after τινες. The lack of accent distinguishes the indefinite from the interrogative pronoun.

12:39 ὁ δὲ ἀποκριθεὶς εἶπεν αὐτοῖς, Γενεὰ πονηρὰ καὶ μοιχαλὶς σημεῖον ἐπιζητεῖ, καὶ σημεῖον οὐ δοθήσεται αὐτῇ εἰ μὴ τὸ σημεῖον Ἰωνᾶ τοῦ προφήτου. 12:40 ὥσπερ γὰρ ἦν Ἰωνᾶς ἐν τῇ κοιλίᾳ τοῦ κήτους τρεῖς ἡμέρας καὶ τρεῖς νύκτας, οὕτως ἔσται ὁ υἱὸς τοῦ ἀνθρώπου ἐν τῇ καρδίᾳ τῆς γῆς τρεῖς ἡμέρας καὶ τρεῖς νύκτας. 12:41 ἄνδρες Νινευῖται ἀναστήσονται ἐν τῇ κρίσει μετὰ τῆς γενεᾶς ταύτης καὶ κατακρινοῦσιν αὐτήν, ὅτι μετενόησαν εἰς τὸ κήρυγμα Ἰωνᾶ,

---

12:39
ἀποκρίνομαι, ἀπεκρινάμην, ἀπεκρίθην answer, reply
γενεά, ᾶς, ἡ progeny, generation, age
μοιχαλίς, ίδος, ἡ adulteress; adulterous, faithless, ungodly (adjective)
σημεῖον, ου, τό sign, token, miracle
ἐπιζητέω, ἐπιζητήσω, ἐπεζήτησα, ἐπεζητήθην search for, seek after; strive for, wish for; demand, desire
εἰ μή unless, except
Ἰωνᾶς, ᾶ, ὁ Jonah
12:40
ὥσπερ as, just as (adverb)
κοιλία, ας, ἡ stomach, belly, womb
κῆτος, ους, τό large fish, sea monster, whale
τρεῖς, τρία three
νύξ, νυκτός, ἡ night
καρδία, ας, ἡ heart
12:41
ἀνήρ, ἀνδρός, ὁ man, male, husband
Νινευίτης, ου, ὁ Ninevite
ἀνίστημι, ἀναστήσω, ἀνέστησα, ἀνέστην (2 aorist) cause to rise, raise up (transitive); rise, stand up, get up (2 aorist and all middle forms are intransitive)
κρίσις, εως, ἡ judgment, justice, righteousness, condemnation
γενεά, ᾶς, ἡ progeny, generation, age
κατακρίνω, κατακρινῶ, κατέκρινα, κατακέκρικα, κατακέκριμαι, κατεκρίθην condemn, pronounce sentence
μετανοέω, μετανοήσω, μετανόησα change one's mind, repent
κήρυγμα, ατος, τό proclaiming, preaching

12:39 **μοιχαλὶς**: a generation becomes adulterous by abandoning its spiritual relationship with God and worshiping idols (Hos 1–3). **τὸ σημεῖον Ἰωνᾶ τοῦ προφητοῦ**: τὸ σημεῖον takes two appositional genitives. Each identifies its previous noun more specifically.

12:40 **ὥσπερ . . . οὕτως**: the two adverbs introduce a protasis and apodosis of a comparison.

12:41 **μετὰ τῆς γενεᾶς ταύτης**: *with this generation.* **εἰς τὸ κήρυγμα**: *at the preaching.*

καὶ ἰδοὺ πλεῖον Ἰωνᾶ ὧδε. 12:42 βασίλισσα νότου ἐγερθήσεται ἐν τῇ κρίσει μετὰ τῆς γενεᾶς ταύτης καὶ κατακρινεῖ αὐτήν, ὅτι ἦλθεν ἐκ τῶν περάτων τῆς γῆς ἀκοῦσαι τὴν σοφίαν Σολομῶνος, καὶ ἰδοὺ πλεῖον Σολομῶνος ὧδε.

12:43 Ὅταν δὲ τὸ ἀκάθαρτον πνεῦμα ἐξέλθῃ ἀπὸ τοῦ ἀνθρώπου, διέρχεται δι' ἀνύδρων τόπων ζητοῦν ἀνάπαυσιν καὶ οὐχ εὑρίσκει.

12:41
πλείων, πλεῖον or πλέον more, greater, larger; πλέον more (comparative adverb)
ὧδε here (adverb)
12:42
βασίλισσα, ης, ἡ queen
νότος, ου, ὁ, south wind; south
κρίσις, εως, ἡ judgment, justice, righteousness, condemnation
γενεά, ᾶς, ἡ progeny, generation, age
κατακρίνω, κατακρινῶ, κατέκρινα, κατακέκρικα, κατακέκριμαι, κατεκρίθην condemn, pronounce sentence
πέρας, ατος, τό end, limit, boundary
σοφία, ας, ἡ wisdom, prudence
πλείων, πλεῖον or πλέον more, greater, larger; πλέον more (comparative adverb)
ὧδε here (adverb)
12:43
ὅταν when, whenever (conjunction)
ἀκάθαρτος, ον unclean, impure; lewd; foul
διέρχομαι, διελεύσομαι, διῆλθον pass through, pass over, cross, pass along; proceed; travel through, wander about; transfix, pierce; spread abroad
ἄνυδρος, ον waterless, dry, barren
τόπος, ου, ὁ place, position, region
ζητέω, ζητήσω, ἐζήτησα, ἐζητήθην seek, desire, ask for
ἀνάπαυσις, εως, ἡ ceasing; rest; resting place, place of rest
εὑρίσκω, εὑρήσω, εὗρον (2 aorist), ηὕρηκα/εὕρηκα, εὑρέθην find, meet, discover, recognize

---

12:41 **πλεῖον Ἰωνᾶ ὧδε**: *something more than Jonah is here*; the comparative adjective is neuter singular nominative. The statement suggests that the actual resurrection transcends the sign of the resurrection. Supply ἐστί.

12:42 **βασίλισσα νότου**: the queen of Sheba (1 Kgs 10:1) will be an additional witness against the generation. **ἀκοῦσαι τὴν σοφίαν Σολομῶνος**: the infinitive introduces a purpose clause. **πλεῖον Σολομῶνος ὧδε**: the statement suggests that the message of Jesus surpasses the wisdom of Solomon.

12:43 **Ὅταν** introduces a present general condition. **ἐξέλθῃ**: the unclean spirit has been driven out. **δι' ἀνύδρων τόπων**: apart from humans, dry places seem to be the *locus amoenus* for demons (cf. Is 13:21, 34:14; Rev 18:2). **ζητοῦν ἀνάπαυσιν**: the verbal form is an infinitive of purpose. Ironically, ἀνάπαυσιν is not *rest* at all: for the unclean spirit finds respite only by doing evil, not by abstaining from it, in the desert.

12:44 τότε λέγει, Εἰς τὸν οἶκόν μου ἐπιστρέψω ὅθεν ἐξῆλθον· καὶ ἐλθὸν εὑρίσκει σχολάζοντα σεσαρωμένον καὶ κεκοσμημένον. 12:45 τότε πορεύεται καὶ παραλαμβάνει μεθ' ἑαυτοῦ ἑπτὰ ἕτερα πνεύματα πονηρότερα ἑαυτοῦ καὶ εἰσελθόντα κατοικεῖ ἐκεῖ· καὶ γίνεται τὰ ἔσχατα τοῦ ἀνθρώπου ἐκείνου χείρονα τῶν πρώτων.

12:44

οἶκος, ου, ὁ house, dwelling
ἐπιστρέφω, ἐπιστρέψω, ἐπέστρεψα, ἐπέστραμμαι, ἐπεστρέφθην, ἐπεστράφην (2 aorist passive) turn, turn around
ὅθεν from where, whence, from which (adverb)
εὑρίσκω, εὑρήσω, εὗρον (2 aorist), ηὕρηκα/εὕρηκα, εὑρέθην find, meet, discover, recognize
σχολάζω, σχολάσω, ἐσχόλασα be at leisure; be unoccupied, be empty
σαρόω, σαρώσω, ἐσάρωσα, σεσάρωμαι, ἐσαρώθην sweep clean, cleanse with a broom, cleanse
κοσμέω, κοσμήσω, ἐκόσμησα, κεκόσμηκα, κεκόσμημαι set in order, arrange; prepare, trim; decorate, adorn

12:45

παραλαμβάνω, παραλήψομαι, παρέλαβον, παρείληφα, παρείλημμαι, παρελήφθην take, receive, accept
ἑαυτοῦ, ῆς, οῦ himself, herself, itself; themselves, ourselves, yourselves (in plural)
ἑπτά seven (indeclinable)
ἕτερος, α, ον other, another
πονηρότερος, α, ον more evil, more wicked (comparative of πονηρός)
κατοικέω, κατοικήσω, κατῴκησα live, dwell, reside (intransitive); inhabit (transitive)
ἔσχατος, η, ον last
χείρων, ον worse, more severe (comparative of κακός)
πρῶτος, η, ον first, before, earlier, foremost

12:44 **Εἰς τὸν οἶκόν μου**: he goes back to the person from whom he had been expelled. **ἐλθὸν** is a neuter singular nominative second aorist active participle that stands in agreement with τὸ ἀκάθαρτον πνεῦμα (43). **σχολάζοντα σεσαρωμένον καὶ κεκοσμημένονον**: the subject of these participles is τὸν οἶκόν. The house, spiritually void, becomes accessible to the same unclean spirit.

12:45 **πονηρότερα ἑαυτοῦ**: *more wicked than himself*; the comparative adjective governs a genitive of comparison. ἑαυτοῦ is a third person reflexive pronoun (App. 46). The man's lack of attention to spiritual matters has compounded his evils. **καὶ εἰσελθόντα κατοικεῖ ἐκεῖ**: *and they entered and lived there*; the cumbersome nature of the sentence may be resolved by dividing it and coordinating the participle with the main verb. **εἰσελθόντα**: the subject of the participle is ἑπτὰ ἕτερα πνεύματα. Neuter plural subjects are considered as collective nouns and regularly take a singular verb. **τὰ ἔσχατα**: *the last evils*; supply κακὰ: *evils, ills, misfortunes*. **χείρονα τῶν πρώτων**: the comparative adjective governs a genitive of comparison.

οὕτως ἔσται καὶ τῇ γενεᾷ ταύτῃ τῇ πονηρᾷ.

12:46 Ἔτι αὐτοῦ λαλοῦντος τοῖς ὄχλοις ἰδοὺ ἡ μήτηρ καὶ οἱ ἀδελφοὶ αὐτοῦ εἱστήκεισαν ἔξω ζητοῦντες αὐτῷ λαλῆσαι. [12:47 εἶπεν δέ τις αὐτῷ, Ἰδοὺ ἡ μήτηρ σου καὶ οἱ ἀδελφοί σου ἔξω ἑστήκασιν ζητοῦντές σοι λαλῆσαι.] 12:48 ὁ δὲ ἀποκριθεὶς εἶπεν τῷ λέγοντι αὐτῷ, Τίς ἐστιν ἡ μήτηρ μου καὶ τίνες εἰσὶν οἱ ἀδελφοί μου; 12:49 καὶ ἐκτείνας τὴν χεῖρα αὐτοῦ ἐπὶ τοὺς μαθητὰς αὐτοῦ εἶπεν, Ἰδοὺ ἡ μήτηρ μου καὶ οἱ ἀδελφοί μου. 12:50 ὅστις γὰρ ἂν ποιήσῃ τὸ θέλημα τοῦ πατρός μου τοῦ ἐν οὐρανοῖς αὐτός μου ἀδελφὸς καὶ ἀδελφὴ καὶ μήτηρ ἐστίν.

12: 45
γενεά, ᾶς, ἡ progeny, generation, age
12:46
ἔτι yet, still (adverb)
λαλέω, λαλήσω, ἐλάλησα, λελάληκα, λελάλημαι, ἐλαλήθην speak, address, preach
μήτηρ, τρός, ἡ mother
ἵστημι, στήσω, ἔστησα, ἔστην (2 aorist), ἕστηκα, ἐστάθην put, place, set, cause to stand (transitive); stand, be (intransitive)
ζητέω, ζητήσω, ἐζήτησα, ἐζητήθην seek, desire, ask for
λαλέω, λαλήσω, ἐλάλησα, λελάληκα, λελάλημαι, ἐλαλήθην speak, address, preach
12:47
τις, τι anyone, anything, someone, something, a certain one, a certain thing (indefinite pronoun)
12:48
ἀποκρίνομαι, ἀπεκρινάμην, ἀπεκρίθην answer, reply
μήτηρ, τρός, ἡ mother
12:49
ἐκτείνω, ἐκτενῶ, ἐξέτεινα stretch out, hold out
χείρ, χειρός, ἡ hand
12:50
ὅστις, ἥτις, ὅ τι whoever, whatever (indefinite relative pronoun)
θέλημα, ατος, τό will, desire
ἀδελφή, ῆς, ἡ sister

12:45 **τῇ γενεᾷ ταύτῃ τῇ πονηρᾷ**: the repetition of the article with the demonstrative pronoun in the center stresses the wickedness of the generation.

12:46 **εἱστήκεισαν**: *stood*; the form is pluperfect and intransitive. The endings are -κειν, -κεις, -κει(ν), -κειμεν, -κειτε, -κεισαν (cf. App. 53, F).

12:48 **Τίς . . . τίνες** are interrogative pronouns (App. 47). The interrogative pronoun distinguishes itself from the indefinite pronoun by the accent (cf. App. 48).

12:50 **ὅστις γὰρ ἂν**: the indefinite relative pronoun with ἂν introduces a present general condition.

13 Ἐν τῇ ἡμέρᾳ ἐκείνῃ ἐξελθὼν ὁ Ἰησοῦς τῆς οἰκίας ἐκάθητο παρὰ τὴν θάλασσαν· 13:2 καὶ συνήχθησαν πρὸς αὐτὸν ὄχλοι πολλοί, ὥστε αὐτὸν εἰς πλοῖον ἐμβάντα καθῆσθαι, καὶ πᾶς ὁ ὄχλος ἐπὶ τὸν αἰγιαλὸν εἱστήκει.

13:1
κάθημαι, καθήσομαι sit, stay, reside
παρά from (the side of), from, issuing from, by (preposition + genitive); with, by (+ dative); by, near to, along; to, at; by, near, at the side of (+ accusative)
θάλασσα, ης, ἡ sea, inland sea, lake
13:2
συνάγω, συνάξω, συνήγαγον (2 aorist), συνῆγμαι, συνήχθην gather in, gather up, bring together; convene, come together, meet (passive)
ὥστε so that (conjunction)
πλοῖον, ου, τό ship, boat
ἐμβαίνω, ἐμβήσομαι, ἐνέβην, ἐμβέβηκα step in, embark
κάθημαι, καθήσομαι sit, stay, reside
αἰγιαλός, οῦ, ὁ shore, beach
ἵστημι, στήσω, ἔστησα, ἔστην (2 aorist), ἕστηκα, ἐστάθην put, place, set, cause to stand (transitive); stand, be (intransitive)

13:1 **ἐκάθητο** is a third person singular imperfect middle indicative of a deponent verb. The seaside provides an appropriate setting to teach large crowds.

13:2 **συνήχθησαν** is the third person plural first aorist passive indicative of συνάγω. **ὥστε αὐτὸν . . . καθῆσθαι**: *so that he sat down*; ὥστε, followed by the accusative with infinitive, introduces a result clause. **εἰς πλοῖον ἐμβάντα**: *after he had embarked the boat*; ἐμβάντα is a masculine singular aorist active participle that agrees in gender, number, and case with αὐτὸν. Since the action of the participle precedes that of the main verb, it is translated as a pluperfect. **εἱστήκει**: *stood*; the form is pluperfect and intransitive (cf. App. 53, F).

13:3 καὶ ἐλάλησεν αὐτοῖς πολλὰ ἐν παραβολαῖς λέγων, Ἰδοὺ ἐξῆλθεν ὁ σπείρων τοῦ σπείρειν. 13:4 καὶ ἐν τῷ σπείρειν αὐτὸν ἃ μὲν ἔπεσεν παρὰ τὴν ὁδόν, καὶ ἐλθόντα τὰ πετεινὰ κατέφαγεν αὐτά.

13:3

λαλέω, λαλήσω, ἐλάλησα, λελάληκα, λελάλημαι, ἐλαλήθην speak, address, preach

παραβολή, ῆς, ἡ comparison, parable, illustration

σπείρω, σπερῶ, ἔσπειρα, ἔσπαρμαι, ἐσπάρην sow

13:4

πίπτω, πεσοῦμαι, ἔπεσα, ἔπεσον (2 aorist), πέπτωκα fall, fall prostrate, fall down

παρά from (the side of), from, issuing from, by (preposition + genitive); with, by (+ dative); by, near to, along; to, at; by, near, at the side of (+ accusative)

πετεινόν, οῦ, τό bird, fowl

κατεσθίω, καταφάγομαι/κατέδομαι, κατέφαγον eat up, devour, consume

---

13:3 **ἐλάλησεν αὐτοῖς πολλὰ ἐν παραβολαῖς**: *He told them many examples in parables;* πολλὰ stands in close relationship to the verb and is a cognate accusative. For the sake of brevity (brachylogy) the verb omits the cognate noun and admits only a demonstrative pronoun or adjective as an object. In translating this construction more idiomatically an accusative noun may be supplied from the verbal form and added to the demonstrative pronoun. **τοῦ σπείρειν**: *to sow;* the construction is an articular infinitive. A purpose clause may be expressed by the neuter article in the genitive case, followed by an infinitive.

13:4 **ἐν τῷ σπείρειν αὐτὸν**: *while he was sowing* (literally: *in the time that he was sowing*); the construction is an articular infinitive. As a noun the infinitive takes an article which is the object of the preposition ἐν, which denotes the point of time while or when something occurs. As a verbal form the Greek infinitive may additionally take an accusative subject and object. In the event of two accusatives the context will be decisive. **ἃ μὲν ἔπεσεν**: *some seeds fell;* the neuter plural nominative relative pronoun and the particle are used correlatively in contrast with ἄλλα δὲ *others* in the verses below. Supply σπέρματα. Neuter plural subjects are considered as collective nouns and regularly take a singular verb.

13:5 ἄλλα δὲ ἔπεσεν ἐπὶ τὰ πετρώδη ὅπου οὐκ εἶχεν γῆν πολλήν,
καὶ εὐθέως ἐξανέτειλεν διὰ τὸ μὴ ἔχειν βάθος γῆς· 13:6 ἡλίου δὲ
ἀνατείλαντος ἐκαυματίσθη καὶ διὰ τὸ μὴ ἔχειν ῥίζαν ἐξηράνθη.
13:7 ἄλλα δὲ ἔπεσεν ἐπὶ τὰς ἀκάνθας, καὶ ἀνέβησαν αἱ ἄκανθαι καὶ
ἔπνιξαν αὐτά.

13:5

ἄλλος, η, ο other, another

πίπτω, πεσοῦμαι, ἔπεσα, ἔπεσον (2 aorist), πέπτωκα fall, fall prostrate, fall down

πετρώδης, ες rocky, stony; rocky ground (substantive)

ὅπου where (adverb)

εὐθέως at once, immediately (adverb)

ἐξανατέλλω, ἐξανατελῶ, ἐξανέτειλα spring up, rise up, sprout

βάθος, ους, τό depth

13:6

ἥλιος, ου, ὁ sun

ἀνατέλλω, ἀνατελῶ, ἀνέτειλα (1 aorist) cause to rise; rise, spring up (intransitive)

καυματίζω, καυματίσω, ἐκαυμάτισα, ἐκαυματίσθην burn up; be burned, be scorched (passive)

ῥίζα, ης, ἡ root

ξηραίνω, ξηρανῶ, ἐξήρανα, ἐξήραμμαι, ἐξηράνθην dry out, parch; become dry, dry up, wither (passive)

13:7

ἄλλος, η, ο other, another

πίπτω, πεσοῦμαι, ἔπεσα, ἔπεσον (2 aorist), πέπτωκα fall, fall prostrate, fall down

ἄκανθα, ης, ἡ thorn

ἀναβαίνω, ἀναβήσομαι, ἀνέβην, ἀναβέβηκα go up, ascend, rise; grow, spring up

πνίγω, πνίξω, ἔπνιξα choke, suffocate, strangle

13:5 **ἄλλα δὲ**: the neuter substantive distinguishes itself from the conjunction ἀλλά by the accent. **οὐκ εἶχεν**: the understood subject is τὰ σπέρματα. **διὰ τὸ μὴ ἔχειν βάθος γῆς**: *because they did not have depth of soil* (literally: *for this reason that they did not have depth of soil*); the understood accusative subject of the infinitive is τὰ σπέρματα. The infinitive additionally governs the accusative βάθος.

13:6 **ἡλίου δὲ ἀνατείλαντος**: *but when the sun rose*; the verb is intransitive.

13:8 ἄλλα δὲ ἔπεσεν ἐπὶ τὴν γῆν τὴν καλὴν καὶ ἐδίδου καρπόν, ὃ μὲν ἑκατόν, ὃ δὲ ἑξήκοντα, ὃ δὲ τριάκοντα. 13:9 ὁ ἔχων ὦτα ἀκουέτω.

13:10 Καὶ προσελθόντες οἱ μαθηταὶ εἶπαν αὐτῷ, Διὰ τί ἐν παραβολαῖς λαλεῖς αὐτοῖς;

13:8

ἄλλος, η, ο other, another

πίπτω, πεσοῦμαι, ἔπεσα, ἔπεσον (2 aorist), πέπτωκα fall, fall prostrate, fall down

καλός, ή, όν good, useful, choice

καρπός, οῦ, ὁ fruit, crop; result, gain

μέν on the one hand (the particle is used to contrast one term or clause with another, usually δέ *on the other*). If cumbersome it may be omitted in translation and δέ may be translated by *but*; ὅς μέν ... ὅς δέ = ὁ μέν ... ὁ δέ the one ... the other; οἱ μέν ... ἄλλοι δέ some ... others

ἑκατόν one hundred (a hundredfold yield of grain; indeclinable)

ἑξήκοντα sixty (a sixtyfold yield of grain; indeclinable)

τριάκοντα thirty (a thirtyfold yield of grain; indeclinable)

13:9

οὖς, ὠτός, τό ear

13:10

διὰ τί why?

παραβολή, ῆς, ἡ comparison, parable, illustration

13:8 **ἐδίδου**: *yielded*; the verbal form is a third person singular imperfect active indicative of δίδωμι (App. 58). **ὃ μὲν ἑκατόν**: *one seed a hundredfold*; the relative pronoun is neuter singular nominative and refers back to the plural ἄλλα. In this slight ellipsis supply ἐδίδου from the previous clause.

13:9 **ἀκουέτω**: the imperative verb refers especially to spiritual perception.

13:10 **Διὰ τί;** means *why?* in direct questions.

13:11 ὁ δὲ ἀποκριθεὶς εἶπεν αὐτοῖς, Ὅτι ὑμῖν δέδοται γνῶναι τὰ μυστήρια τῆς βασιλείας τῶν οὐρανῶν, ἐκείνοις δὲ οὐ δέδοται. 13:12 ὅστις γὰρ ἔχει, δοθήσεται αὐτῷ καὶ περισσευθήσεται· ὅστις δὲ οὐκ ἔχει, καὶ ὃ ἔχει ἀρθήσεται ἀπ' αὐτοῦ. 13:13 διὰ τοῦτο ἐν παραβολαῖς αὐτοῖς λαλῶ, ὅτι βλέποντες οὐ βλέπουσιν καὶ ἀκούοντες οὐκ ἀκούουσιν οὐδὲ συνίουσιν,

---

13:11

ἀποκρίνομαι, ἀπεκρινάμην, ἀπεκρίθην answer, reply

γινώσκω, γνώσομαι, ἔγνων, ἔγνωκα, ἔγνωσμαι, ἐγνώσθην know, learn, understand

μυστήριον, ου, τό secret, secret rite, secret teaching, mystery

13:12

περισσεύω, περισσεύσω, ἐπερίσσευσα be left over, abound; abundance is given, have great abundance, be gifted with abundance (passive)

αἴρω, ἀρῶ, ἦρα, ἦρκα, ἦρμαι, ἤρθην take up, bear, take away, lift, carry, remove; keep in suspense; destroy, kill

13:13

παραβολή, ῆς, ἡ comparison, parable, illustration

συνίημι/συνίω, συνήσω/συνήσομαι, συνῆκα (1 aorist) send together; understand, comprehend, perceive clearly

---

13:11 **ὑμῖν δέδοται γνῶναι**: *it has been granted to you to know*; the impersonal verb takes a dative and infinitive construction. The infinitive is the subject of the quasi-impersonal verb.

13:12 **ὅστις γὰρ ἔχει**: supply τὰ πνευματικά *the gifts of the Holy Spirit*, which include, among others, spiritual wisdom, knowledge, and faith (1 Cor 12:1–11). Since the understood third person singular pronoun which functions as antecedent of the indefinite relative pronoun has no main verb, the construction becomes an anacoluthon or a syntactic non sequitur in which the subject ends up as the object of the impersonal verbs δοθήσεται and περισσευθήσεται. The construction (*casus pendens*) imitates the compression of natural speech. **δοθήσεται**: the thought runs parallel to that in the previous verse: γνῶναι τὰ μυστήρια. **περισσευθήσεται**: *he will have a great abundance* (literally: *a great abundance will be given to him*); the transitive verb, used in the passive and impersonally with αὐτῷ, may be translated actively and personally. **ὅστις δὲ οὐκ ἔχει** introduces a negative anacoluthon. Supply again τὰ πνευματικά *the gifts of the Holy Spirit.*

13:13 **διὰ τοῦτο**: *for this reason*; the prepositional phrase anticipates the ὅτι clause. **ὅτι βλέποντες**: *because although they see*; the circumstantial participle expresses concession: the paronomasia or word play contrasts physical and spiritual sight.

13:14 καὶ ἀναπληροῦται αὐτοῖς ἡ προφητεία Ἠσαΐου ἡ λέγουσα,
Ἀκοῇ ἀκούσετε καὶ οὐ μὴ συνῆτε,
καὶ βλέποντες βλέψετε καὶ οὐ μὴ ἴδητε.
13:15 ἐπαχύνθη γὰρ ἡ καρδία τοῦ λαοῦ τούτου,
καὶ τοῖς ὠσὶν βαρέως ἤκουσαν
καὶ τοὺς ὀφθαλμοὺς αὐτῶν ἐκάμμυσαν,
μήποτε ἴδωσιν τοῖς ὀφθαλμοῖς
καὶ τοῖς ὠσὶν ἀκούσωσιν

13:14
ἀναπληρόω, ἀναπληρώσω, ἀνεπλήρωσα make complete, fulfill
προφητεία, ας, ἡ prophecy
ἀκοή, ῆς, ἡ hearing, fame, report, account
συνίημι/συνίω, συνήσω/συνήσομαι, συνῆκα (1 aorist) send together; understand, comprehend, perceive clearly
13:15
παχύνω, παχυνῶ, ἐπαχύνθην make fat, fatten; make impervious; render gross, dull, unfeeling
καρδία, ας, ἡ heart
λαός, οῦ, ὁ people
οὖς, ὠτός, τό ear
βαρέως heavily; with difficulty (adverb)
ὀφθαλμός, οῦ, ὁ eye
καμμύω, καμμύσω, ἐκαμμυσα shut, close
μήποτε not; that . . . not, lest, (in order) that . . . not

13:14 **αὐτοῖς**: *in them*; the case usage is a dative of reference. **Ἀκοῇ**: *by listening*; however, the noun may also refer to the ear: *with your ears*. **οὐ μὴ συνῆτε**: *you will never understand*; the double negative indicates a strong negation and usually takes an aorist subjunctive that is translated as a future. The hyperbole stresses the need to heed the Holy Spirit.

13:15 **ἐπαχύνθη**: *is rendered unfeeling*; the verb is used figuratively to describe the insensitivity of the people. By analogy to the following verbs, the people themselves are the responsible agent. This and the next two verbs **ἤκουσαν** and **ἐκάμμυσαν** are gnomic aorists. The aorist may be used to express a general truth where the experience of an action in the past suggests an action that is likely to be repeated. **μήποτε**: the conjunction introduces five negative clauses of purpose.

καὶ τῇ καρδίᾳ συνῶσιν καὶ ἐπιστρέψωσιν
καὶ ἰάσομαι αὐτούς.
13:16 ὑμῶν δὲ μακάριοι οἱ ὀφθαλμοὶ ὅτι βλέπουσιν καὶ τὰ ὦτα ὑμῶν
ὅτι ἀκούουσιν. 13:17 ἀμὴν γὰρ λέγω ὑμῖν ὅτι πολλοὶ προφῆται καὶ
δίκαιοι ἐπεθύμησαν ἰδεῖν ἃ βλέπετε καὶ οὐκ εἶδαν, καὶ ἀκοῦσαι ἃ
ἀκούετε καὶ οὐκ ἤκουσαν.
13:18 Ὑμεῖς οὖν ἀκούσατε τὴν παραβολὴν τοῦ σπείραντος.
13:19 παντὸς ἀκούοντος τὸν λόγον τῆς βασιλείας καὶ μὴ συνιέντος
ἔρχεται ὁ πονηρὸς

13:15
συνίημι/συνίω, συνήσω/συνήσομαι, συνῆκα (1 aorist) send together; understand, comprehend, perceive clearly
ἐπιστρέφω, ἐπιστρέψω, ἐπέστρεψα, ἐπέστραμμαι, ἐπεστρέφθην, ἐπεστράφην (2 aorist passive) turn, turn around, convert (transitive); turn oneself back, turn around, be converted (intransitive and middle)
ἰάομαι, ἰάσομαι, ἰασάμην, ἴαμαι, ἰάθην heal, cure, restore
13:16
μακάριος, ία, ιον blessed, happy, fortunate
οὖς, ὠτός, τό ear
13:17
δίκαιος, αία, αιον right, just, honest, good, righteous
ἐπιθυμέω, ἐπιθυμήσω, ἐπεθύμησα desire, long for
13:18
παραβολή, ῆς, ἡ comparison, parable, illustration
σπείρω, σπερῶ, ἔσπειρα, ἔσπαρμαι, ἐσπάρην sow
13:19
συνίημι/συνίω, συνήσω/συνήσομαι, συνῆκα (1 aorist) send together; understand, comprehend, perceive clearly

---

13:15 **ἰάσομαι**: after four subjunctive clauses a future indicative follows μήποτε instead of the subjunctive without change of meaning. In a classical tricolon the third member is regularly expanded, here forming another tricolon. The chiastic verse includes three tricola in all.

13:16 **μακάριοι**: supply εἰσίν. The adjective initiates a commonplace formula in Greek, Latin, and Hebrew literature.

13:17 **δίκαιοι**: *righteous men*; the masculine singular nominative adjective has been turned into a substantive. **εἶδαν**: occasionally second aorist stems take first aorist endings without the **σ**.

13:18 **ἀκούσατε**: the imperative has the sense of *understand*. **τοῦ σπείραντος**: *the sower*; the article and the participle combine to form a substantive.

13:19 **παντὸς ἀκούοντος ... καὶ μὴ συνιέντος**: *when anyone hears ... and does not understand*; only rarely does πᾶς combined with a participle have this meaning. However, it does so more frequently when combined with a participle in the negative. **τὸν λόγον τῆς βασιλείας** is being compared to the seed.

καὶ ἁρπάζει τὸ ἐσπαρμένον ἐν τῇ καρδίᾳ αὐτοῦ, οὗτός ἐστιν ὁ παρὰ τὴν ὁδὸν σπαρείς. 13:20 ὁ δὲ ἐπὶ τὰ πετρώδη σπαρείς, οὗτός ἐστιν ὁ τὸν λόγον ἀκούων καὶ εὐθὺς μετὰ χαρᾶς λαμβάνων αὐτόν, 13:21 οὐκ ἔχει δὲ ῥίζαν ἐν ἑαυτῷ ἀλλὰ πρόσκαιρός ἐστιν, γενομένης δὲ θλίψεως ἢ διωγμοῦ διὰ τὸν λόγον εὐθὺς σκανδαλίζεται.

13:19

ἁρπάζω, ἁρπάσω, ἥρπασα, ἡρπάσθην, ἡρπάγην (2 aorist passive) steal, carry off, drag away, take away

σπείρω, σπερῶ, ἔσπειρα, ἔσπαρμαι, ἐσπάρην sow

καρδία, ας, ἡ heart

παρά from (the side of), from, issuing from, by (preposition + genitive); with, by (+ dative); by, near to, along; to, at; by, near, at the side of (+ accusative)

13:20

πετρώδης, ες rocky, stony; rocky ground (substantive)

εὐθύς immediately, at once (adverb)

χαρά, ᾶς, ἡ joy

13:21

ῥίζα, ης, ἡ root

ἑαυτοῦ, ῆς, οῦ himself, herself, itself; themselves, ourselves, yourselves (in plural)

ἀλλά but, yet (conjunction)

πρόσκαιρος, ον lasting for a limited time, temporary, transitory, transient

θλῖψις, εως, ἡ oppression, affliction, trial, tribulation

διωγμός, ου, ὁ persecution

εὐθύς immediately, at once (adverb)

σκανδαλίζω, σκανδαλίσω, ἐσκανδάλισα, ἐσκανδαλίσθην offend, anger, shock

---

13:19 **τὸ ἐσπαρμένον**: *what was sown*; the verbal form is a neuter singular accusative perfect passive participle. The neuter gender is derived from σπέρμα *seed*. **οὗτός ἐστιν ὁ . . . σπαρείς**: *this is the seed sown*; σπαρείς is a masculine singular nominative second aorist passive participle (cf. App. 34). The masculine gender is derived from σπόρος *seed*. **παρὰ τὴν ὁδὸν**: the place where the seed is sown represents the receptivity of the human heart: ἐν τῇ καρδίᾳ.

13:20 **αὐτόν** refers to τὸν λόγον τῆς βασιλείας (18).

13:21 **οὐκ ἔχει δὲ ῥίζαν**: *he is not firmly rooted*; the noun is used figuratively. Supply ἐν τῷ λόγῳ τῆς βασιλείας. **γενομένης δὲ θλίψεως ἢ διωγμοῦ**: the construction is a genitive absolute.

13:22 ὁ δὲ εἰς τὰς ἀκάνθας σπαρείς, οὗτός ἐστιν ὁ τὸν λόγον ἀκούων,
καὶ ἡ μέριμνα τοῦ αἰῶνος καὶ ἡ ἀπάτη τοῦ πλούτου συμπνίγει τὸν
λόγον καὶ ἄκαρπος γίνεται. 13:23 ὁ δὲ ἐπὶ τὴν καλὴν γῆν σπαρείς,
οὗτός ἐστιν ὁ τὸν λόγον ἀκούων καὶ συνιείς, ὃς δὴ καρποφορεῖ καὶ
ποιεῖ ὃ μὲν ἑκατόν, ὃ δὲ ἑξήκοντα, ὃ δὲ τριάκοντα.

13:24 Ἄλλην παραβολὴν παρέθηκεν αὐτοῖς λέγων, Ὡμοιώθη
ἡ βασιλεία τῶν οὐρανῶν ἀνθρώπῳ σπείραντι καλὸν σπέρμα ἐν τῷ
ἀγρῷ αὐτοῦ.

13:22
ἄκανθα, ης, ἡ thorn
σπείρω, σπερῶ, ἔσπειρα, ἔσπαρμαι, ἐσπάρην sow
μέριμνα, ης, ἡ care
αἰών, αἰῶνος, ὁ eternity, perpetuity; period of time, life, age; world
ἀπάτη, ης, ἡ deceit, deception, seduction, delusion
πλοῦτος, ου, ὁ riches, wealth, opulence
συμπνίγω, συμπνιξοῦμαι, συνέπνιξα choke
ἄκαρπος, ον unfruitful, fruitless, barren; useless, unproductive
13:23
καλός, ή, όν good, useful, choice
σπείρω, σπερῶ, ἔσπειρα, ἔσπαρμαι, ἐσπάρην sow
συνίημι/συνίω, συνήσω/συνήσομαι, συνῆκα (1 aorist) send together; understand, comprehend, perceive clearly
καρποφορέω, καρποφορήσω, ἐκαρποφόρησα bear fruit; bear the fruit of good deeds
ἑκατόν one hundred (a hundredfold yield; indeclinable)
ἑξήκοντα sixty (a sixtyfold yield; indeclinable)
τριάκοντα thirty (a thirtyfold yield; indeclinable)
13:24
ἄλλος, η, ο other, another
παραβολή, ῆς, ἡ comparison, parable, illustration
παρατίθημι, παραθήσω, παρέθηκα set before, put before, propound
ὁμοιόω, ὁμοιώσω, ὁμοίωσα, ὡμοιώθην make like, liken, compare; be like, be made like, become like, resemble (passive)
σπείρω, σπερῶ, ἔσπειρα, ἔσπαρμαι, ἐσπάρην sow
καλός, ή, όν good, useful, choice
σπέρμα, ατος, τό seed; descendant, child, posterity
ἀγρός, οῦ, ὁ field

13:22 **ἡ ἀπάτη τοῦ πλούτου**: τοῦ πλούτου is a subjective genitive, i.e., the riches of the world deceive him.

13:23 **ποιεῖ ὃ μὲν ἑκατόν**: *produces that which is hundredfold.*

13:24 **Ὡμοιώθη ... ἀνθρώπῳ**: the verb governs the dative case.

13:25 ἐν δὲ τῷ καθεύδειν τοὺς ἀνθρώπους ἦλθεν αὐτοῦ ὁ ἐχθρὸς καὶ ἐπέσπειρεν ζιζάνια ἀνὰ μέσον τοῦ σίτου καὶ ἀπῆλθεν. 13:26 ὅτε δὲ ἐβλάστησεν ὁ χόρτος καὶ καρπὸν ἐποίησεν, τότε ἐφάνη καὶ τὰ ζιζάνια. 13:27 προσελθόντες δὲ οἱ δοῦλοι τοῦ οἰκοδεσπότου εἶπον αὐτῷ,

---

13:25
καθεύδω, καθευδήσω sleep, be fast asleep
ἐχθρός, ά, όν hostile, inimical; enemy, adversary (substantive)
ἐπισπείρω, ἐπισπερῶ, ἐπέσπειρα sow afterward
ζιζάνιον, ου, τό zizanium, darnel, false wheat, weed, tare
ἀνὰ μέσον among, between, in the midst, through the midst
σῖτος, ου, ὁ wheat, grain
13:26
ὅτε when, whenever (adverb)
βλαστάνω, βλαστήσω, ἐβλάστησα, ἔβλαστον (2 aorist) produce (transitive); bud, sprout, germinate, spring up
χόρτος, ου, ὁ grass, hay; stalks of grain, plant of corn
καρπός, οῦ, ὁ fruit, crop; result, gain
φαίνω, φανῶ, ἔφηνα, πέφαγκα, πέφηνα, πέφασμαι, ἐφάνθην, ἐφάνην shine, give light, be bright; be seen, be visible, appear, seem (middle and passive)
ζιζάνιον, ου, τό zizanium, darnel, false wheat, weed, tare
13:27
δοῦλος, ου, ὁ slave, servant
οἰκοδεσπότης, ου, ὁ master of the house

13:25 **ἐν δὲ τῷ καθεύδειν τοὺς ἀνθρώπους**: *while the people slept*; τοὺς ἀνθρώπους refers to the person just mentioned, the sower with his household. The construction is an articular infinitive. **ὁ ἐχθρὸς** is a personal enemy as opposed to ὁ πολέμιος, an enemy of the state. **ζιζάνια** are weeds resembling wheat.

13:26 **ἐφάνη καὶ τὰ ζιζάνια**: *the weeds also appeared*; καὶ functions as an adverb here. Neuter plural subjects are considered as collective nouns and regularly take a singular verb.

Κύριε, οὐχὶ καλὸν σπέρμα ἔσπειρας ἐν τῷ σῷ ἀγρῷ; πόθεν οὖν ἔχει
ζιζάνια; 13:28 ὁ δὲ ἔφη αὐτοῖς, Ἐχθρὸς ἄνθρωπος τοῦτο ἐποίησεν. οἱ
δὲ δοῦλοι λέγουσιν αὐτῷ, Θέλεις οὖν ἀπελθόντες συλλέξωμεν αὐτά;
13:29 ὁ δέ φησιν, Οὔ, μήποτε συλλέγοντες τὰ ζιζάνια ἐκριζώσητε
ἅμα αὐτοῖς τὸν σῖτον.

13:27
καλός, ή, όν good, useful, choice
σπέρμα, ατος, τό seed; descendant, child, posterity
σπείρω, σπερῶ, ἔσπειρα, ἔσπαρμαι, ἐσπάρην sow
ἀγρός, οῦ, ὁ field
πόθεν from where? how? in what way? (interrogative adverb)
ζιζάνιον, ου, τό zizanium, darnel, false wheat, weed, tare
13:28
φημί, φήσω, ἔφησα say, speak
ἐχθρός, ά, όν hostile, inimical; enemy, adversary (substantive)
δοῦλος, ου, ὁ slave, servant
συλλέγω, συλλέξω, συνέλεξα collect, gather
13:29
φημί, φήσω, ἔφησα say, speak
μήποτε not; that . . . not, lest, (in order) that . . . not
συλλέγω, συλλέξω, συνέλεξα collect, gather
ζιζάνιον, ου, τό zizanium, darnel, false wheat, weed, tare
ἐκριζόω, ἐκριζώσω, ἐξερίζωσα, ἐξεριζώθην pull out by the roots, uproot, eradicate; utterly destroy
ἅμα with, together with, at the same time (adverb; preposition + dative)
σῖτος, ου, ὁ wheat, grain

13:27 **οὐχὶ**: the negative is a strengthened form of οὐ; as an interrogative word in a question, it expects an affirmative answer. **ἔχει**: the subject is ὁ ἀγρός.

13:28 **Ἐχθρὸς ἄνθρωπος**: ἄνθρωπος is pleonastic but adds greater definiteness and emphasis. **Θέλεις . . . ἀπελθόντες συλλέξωμεν αὐτά**: *do you want us to go and gather them up*; the verb Θέλεις with a subjunctive (without a conjunction) introduces a deliberative question. The aorist participle may be changed into a finite verb and coordinated with the main verb in translation.

13:29 **μήποτε συλλέγοντες . . . ἐκριζώσητε**: *lest by gathering up . . . you uproot*; the conjunction introduces a negative clause of purpose. The present participle here expresses *means*, which regularly does not require an adverbial clause to bring out the idea latent in the participle, but it does indicate progressive, continued, and repeated action (aspect) in present time, which should not be slighted in translation.

13:30 ἄφετε συναυξάνεσθαι ἀμφότερα ἕως τοῦ θερισμοῦ, καὶ ἐν καιρῷ τοῦ θερισμοῦ ἐρῶ τοῖς θερισταῖς, Συλλέξατε πρῶτον τὰ ζιζάνια καὶ δήσατε αὐτὰ εἰς δέσμας πρὸς τὸ κατακαῦσαι αὐτά, τὸν δὲ σῖτον συναγάγετε εἰς τὴν ἀποθήκην μου.

13:31 Ἄλλην παραβολὴν παρέθηκεν αὐτοῖς λέγων, Ὁμοία ἐστὶν ἡ βασιλεία τῶν οὐρανῶν κόκκῳ σινάπεως, ὃν λαβὼν ἄνθρωπος ἔσπειρεν ἐν τῷ ἀγρῷ αὐτοῦ·

13:30

συναυξάνομαι, συναυξήσομαι grow together, grow side by side

ἀμφότεροι, αι, α both

θερισμός, οῦ, ὁ harvest

καιρός, οῦ, ὁ time, appointed time; season; time of crisis, end-time

θεριστής, οῦ, ὁ reaper, harvester

συλλέγω, συλλέξω, συνέλεξα collect, gather

πρῶτον first (in time; adverb)

ζιζάνιον, ου, τό zizanium, darnel, false wheat, weed, tare

δέω, δήσω, ἔδησα, δέδεκα, δέδεμαι, ἐδέθην bind, tie, impede

δέσμη, ης, ἡ bundle

κατακαίω, κατακαύσω, κατέκαυσα, κατεκαύθην light, cause to burn, kindle, burn up, burn down, consume by fire (active); burn, be burned, be consumed with fire (passive)

σῖτος, ου, ὁ wheat, grain

συνάγω, συνάξω, συνήγαγον (2 aorist), συνῆγμαι, συνήχθην gather in, gather up, bring together; convene, come together, meet (passive)

ἀποθήκη, ης, ἡ granary, storehouse, barn

13:31

ἄλλος, η, ο other, another

παραβολή, ῆς, ἡ comparison, parable, illustration

παρατίθημι, παραθήσω, παρέθηκα set before, put before, propound

ὅμοιος, οία, οιον like, similar to (+ dative)

κόκκος, ου, ὁ kernel, seed

σίναπι, εως, τό mustard

σπείρω, σπερῶ, ἔσπειρα, ἔσπαρμαι, ἐσπάρην sow

ἀγρός, οῦ, ὁ field

13:30 **ἄφετε** is a second person plural second aorist imperative of ἀφίημι (cf. App. 59). The verb takes an accusative infinitive construction. **ἐν καιρῷ**: *in the time*; the Greek article is frequently omitted in prepositional phrases. **ἐρῶ** is the first person singular future active indicative of λέγω. **πρὸς τὸ κατακαῦσαι αὐτά**: *to burn them*; the preposition πρὸς indicates purpose.

13:31 **λαβὼν** is a second aorist circumstantial participle of λαμβάνω.

13:32 ὃ μικρότερον μέν ἐστιν πάντων τῶν σπερμάτων, ὅταν δὲ
αὐξηθῇ μεῖζον τῶν λαχάνων ἐστὶν καὶ γίνεται δένδρον, ὥστε ἐλθεῖν
τὰ πετεινὰ τοῦ οὐρανοῦ καὶ κατασκηνοῦν ἐν τοῖς κλάδοις αὐτοῦ.
13:33 Ἄλλην παραβολὴν ἐλάλησεν αὐτοῖς· Ὁμοία ἐστὶν ἡ
βασιλεία τῶν οὐρανῶν ζύμῃ, ἣν λαβοῦσα γυνὴ ἐνέκρυψεν εἰς
ἀλεύρου σάτα τρία ἕως οὗ ἐζυμώθη ὅλον.

13:32

μικρότερος, έρα, ερον smaller, littler; smallest, least (the comparative of μικρός; also used as the superlative)

σπέρμα, ατος, τό seed; descendant, child, posterity

ὅταν when, whenever (conjunction)

αὐξάνω/αὔξω, αὐξήσω, ηὔξησα, ηὐξήθην grow, increase

μείζων, μεῖζον greater, larger; greatest, largest (the comparative of μέγας; also used as the superlative)

λάχανον, ου, τό garden herb, vegetable

δένδρον, ου, τό tree

ὥστε so that (conjunction)

πετεινόν, οῦ, τό bird, fowl

κατασκηνόω, κατασκηνώσω, κατεσκήνωσα pitch a tent; live, dwell; rest, abide; settle, nest

κλάδος, ου, ὁ branch, bough

13:33

ἄλλος, η, ο other, another

παραβολή, ῆς, ἡ comparison, parable, illustration

ὅμοιος, οία, οιον like, similar to (+ dative)

ζύμη, ης, ἡ leaven

γυνή, γυναικός, ἡ woman, wife

ἐγκρύπτω, ἐγκρύψω, ἐνέκρυψα hide, put, mix

ἄλευρον, ου, τό wheat flour

σάτον, ου, τό measure (of grain; about a peck and a half)

τρεῖς, τρία three

ζυμόω, ζυμώσω ferment, leaven

ὅλος, η, ον all, whole, entire, complete

13:32 **μικρότερον**: the context indicates that the comparative degree of the adjective stands for the superlative μικρότατον. **ὥστε**, followed by the accusative with infinitive, introduces a result clause.

13:33 **εἰς ἀλεύρου σάτα τρία**: *into three measures of flour*; the separation of the preposition and its object by a genitive is commonplace in Greek prose style. **ἕως οὗ . . . ὅλος**: *until the whole*; supply an article from the context to form the adjective into a noun: *until the whole batch of flour.*

13:34 Ταῦτα πάντα ἐλάλησεν ὁ Ἰησοῦς ἐν παραβολαῖς τοῖς ὄχλοις καὶ χωρὶς παραβολῆς οὐδὲν ἐλάλει αὐτοῖς, 13:35 ὅπως πληρωθῇ τὸ ῥηθὲν διὰ τοῦ προφήτου λέγοντος,

Ἀνοίξω ἐν παραβολαῖς τὸ στόμα μου,
ἐρεύξομαι κεκρυμμένα ἀπὸ καταβολῆς [κόσμου].

13:36 Τότε ἀφεὶς τοὺς ὄχλους ἦλθεν εἰς τὴν οἰκίαν.καὶ προσῆλθον αὐτῷ οἱ μαθηταὶ αὐτοῦ λέγοντες, Διασάφησον ἡμῖν τὴν παραβολὴν τῶν ζιζανίων τοῦ ἀγροῦ. 13:37 ὁ δὲ ἀποκριθεὶς εἶπεν, Ὁ σπείρων τὸ καλὸν σπέρμα ἐστὶν ὁ υἱὸς τοῦ ἀνθρώπου,

---

13:34
παραβολή, ῆς, ἡ comparison, parable, illustration
χωρίς without, apart from (preposition + genitive)
οὐδείς, οὐδεμία, οὐδέν no (adjective); no one, nobody, nothing (substantive)
13:35
πληρόω, πληρώσω, ἐπλήρωσα, πεπλήρωκα, πεπλήρωμαι, ἐπληρώθην fill, complete, fulfill
ἀνοίγω, ἀνοίξω, ἀνέῳξα/ἤνοιξα, ἀνέῳγα, ἀνέῳγμαι, ἠνεῴχθην open
παραβολή, ῆς, ἡ comparison, parable, illustration
στόμα, ατος, τό mouth
ἐρεύγομαι, ἐρεύξομαι vomit; utter, proclaim, declare openly
κρύπτω, κρύψω, ἔκρυψα, κέκρυμμαι, ἐκρύβην hide, conceal, cover
καταβολή, ῆς, ἡ beginning, foundation
κόσμος, ου, ὁ order, world, universe
13:36
διασαφέω, διασαφήσω, διεσάφησα make clear, explain; tell plainly, declare in detail, make known
παραβολή, ῆς, ἡ comparison, parable, illustration
ζιζάνιον, ου, τό zizanium, darnel, false wheat, weed, tare
ἀγρός, οῦ, ὁ field
13:37
σπείρω, σπερῶ, ἔσπειρα, ἔσπαρμαι, ἐσπάρην sow
σπέρμα, ατος, τό seed; descendant, child, posterity

13:34 **Ταῦτα πάντα ἐλάλησεν . . . ἐν παραβολαῖς τοῖς ὄχλοις**: *all these examples He told the crowds in parables*; Ταῦτα πάντα stands in close relationship to the verb and is a cognate accusative.

13:35 **τὸ ῥηθὲν**: *that which was spoken* (literally); the verbal form is a neuter singular nominative first aorist passive participle (cf. App. 53, G, 5; 34) of the verb λέγω.

13:36 **ἀφεὶς**: *after He had sent away*; the form is a masculine singular nominative second aorist active participle of ἀφίημι (cf. App. 34). Since the action of the aorist participle precedes that of the main verb and represents a single action in the past, it has the force of an English pluperfect.

13:37 **Ὁ σπείρων**: *he who sows.*

13:38 ὁ δὲ ἀγρός ἐστιν ὁ κόσμος, τὸ δὲ καλὸν σπέρμα οὗτοί εἰσιν
οἱ υἱοὶ τῆς βασιλείας· τὰ δὲ ζιζάνιά εἰσιν οἱ υἱοὶ τοῦ πονηροῦ,
13:39 ὁ δὲ ἐχθρὸς ὁ σπείρας αὐτά ἐστιν ὁ διάβολος, ὁ δὲ θερισμὸς
συντέλεια αἰῶνός ἐστιν, οἱ δὲ θερισταὶ ἄγγελοί εἰσιν. 13:40 ὥσπερ
οὖν συλλέγεται τὰ ζιζάνια καὶ πυρὶ [κατα]καίεται, οὕτως ἔσται ἐν τῇ
συντελείᾳ τοῦ αἰῶνος· 13:41 ἀποστελεῖ ὁ υἱὸς τοῦ ἀνθρώπου τοὺς
ἀγγέλους αὐτοῦ, καὶ συλλέξουσιν ἐκ τῆς βασιλείας αὐτοῦ

13:38
ἀγρός, οῦ, ὁ field
κόσμος, ου, ὁ order, world, universe
σπέρμα, ατος, τό seed; descendant, child, posterity
ζιζάνιον, ου, τό zizanium, darnel, false wheat, weed, tare
13:39
ἐχθρός, ά, όν hostile, inimical; enemy, adversary (substantive)
διάβολος, ου, ὁ slanderer, devil
θερισμός, οῦ, ὁ harvest
συντέλεια, ας, ἡ completion, close, end
αἰών, αἰῶνος, ὁ eternity, perpetuity; period of time, life, age; world
θεριστής, οῦ, ὁ reaper, harvester
ἄγγελος, ου, ὁ messenger, angel
13:40
ὥσπερ as, just as (adverb)
συλλέγω, συλλέξω, συνέλεξα collect, gather
ζιζάνιον, ου, τό zizanium, darnel, false wheat, weed, tare
κατακαίω, κατακαύσω, κατέκαυσα, κατεκαύθην light, cause to burn, kindle, burn up, burn down, consume by fire (active); burn, be burned, be consumed with fire (passive)
συντέλεια, ας, ἡ completion, close, end
αἰών, αἰῶνος, ὁ eternity, perpetuity; period of time, life, age; world
13:41
ἀποστέλλω, ἀποστελῶ, ἀπέστειλα, ἀπέσταλκα, ἀπέσταλμαι, ἀπεστάλην send, send away, send out
ἄγγελος, ου, ὁ messenger, angel
συλλέγω, συλλέξω, συνέλεξα collect, gather

13:38 **τὸ δὲ καλὸν σπέρμα οὗτοί εἰσιν οἱ υἱοὶ**: the demonstrative resumes τὸ καλὸν σπέρμα but agrees in gender and number with οἱ υἱοὶ.

13:39 **συντέλεια . . . ἄγγελοί**: a predicate nominative does not usually have an article. However, many predicates in these verses do.

13:40 **συλλέγεται τὰ ζιζάνια καὶ πυρί [κατα]καίεται**: neuter plural subjects are considered as collective nouns and regularly take a singular verb. πυρί is a dative of means.

13:41 **ἀποστελεῖ** is a third person singular liquid future. It shows a change in stem, is formed like verbs contracted with stem in **ε** (App. 56), and takes a circumflex over the contraction.

πάντα τὰ σκάνδαλα καὶ τοὺς ποιοῦντας τὴν ἀνομίαν 13:42 καὶ βαλοῦσιν αὐτοὺς εἰς τὴν κάμινον τοῦ πυρός· ἐκεῖ ἔσται ὁ κλαυθμὸς καὶ ὁ βρυγμὸς τῶν ὀδόντων. 13:43 Τότε οἱ δίκαιοι ἐκλάμψουσιν ὡς ὁ ἥλιος ἐν τῇ βασιλείᾳ τοῦ πατρὸς αὐτῶν. ὁ ἔχων ὦτα ἀκουέτω.

13:41
σκάνδαλον, ου, τό stumbling block, impediment; temptation to sin; that which gives offense, that which is offensive; scandal, offense
ἀνομία, ας, ἡ lawlessness, lawless deed, transgression, iniquity, sin
13:42
κάμινος, ου, ἡ oven, furnace
πῦρ, πυρός, τό fire
ἐκεῖ there, in that place (adverb)
κλαυθμός, ου, ὁ weeping, crying
βρυγμός, οῦ, ὁ chattering (of teeth), gnashing (of teeth)
ὀδούς, ὀδόντος, ὁ tooth
13:43
δίκαιος, αία, αιον right, just, honest, good, righteous
ἐκλάμπω, ἐκλάμψω, ἐξέλαμψα shine forth, be radiant, be resplendent
ἥλιος, ου, ὁ sun
οὖς, ὠτός, τό ear

13:41 **πάντα τὰ σκάνδαλα**: *all things that are offensive*; the neuter may include persons by analogy to the next coordinated clause **καὶ τοὺς ποιοῦντας τὴν ἀνομίαν**: *and those who commit iniquity* and the masculine object αὐτοὺς in the next verse.

13:42 **βαλοῦσιν** is a third person plural liquid future. It shows a change in stem, is formed like verbs contracted with stem in **ε** (App. 56), and takes a circumflex over the contraction. **κάμινον τοῦ πυρός**: τοῦ πυρός is an appositional genitive more specifically identifying κάμινον. **ἐκεῖ ἔσται**: *in that place there will be*. **ὁ βρυγμὸς τῶν ὀδόντων**: τῶν ὀδόντων is a subjective genitive, i.e., teeth will chatter.

13:43 **ὡς**: the conjunction introduces a comparison.

13:44 Ὁμοία ἐστὶν ἡ βασιλεία τῶν οὐρανῶν θησαυρῷ κεκρυμμένῳ ἐν τῷ ἀγρῷ, ὃν εὑρὼν ἄνθρωπος ἔκρυψεν, καὶ ἀπὸ τῆς χαρᾶς αὐτοῦ ὑπάγει καὶ πωλεῖ πάντα ὅσα ἔχει καὶ ἀγοράζει τὸν ἀγρὸν ἐκεῖνον.

13:45 Πάλιν ὁμοία ἐστὶν ἡ βασιλεία τῶν οὐρανῶν ἀνθρώπῳ ἐμπόρῳ ζητοῦντι καλοὺς μαργαρίτας·

13:44
ὅμοιος, οία, οιον like, similar to (+ dative)
θησαυρός, οῦ, ὁ treasure box, treasury, treasure
κρύπτω, κρύψω, ἔκρυψα, κέκρυμμαι, ἐκρύβην hide, conceal, cover
ἀγρός, οῦ, ὁ field
κρύπτω, κρύψω, ἔκρυψα, κέκρυμμαι, ἐκρύβην hide, conceal, cover
χαρά, ᾶς, ἡ joy
ὑπάγω, ὑπάξω, ὑπήγαγον, ὑπήχθην go, go away, go home
πωλέω, πωλήσω, ἐπώλησα sell
ὅσος, η, ον how large, how much, how great; as much as; as many as (plural)
ἀγοράζω, ἀγοράσω, ἠγόρασα, ἠγόρασμαι, ἠγοράσθην buy, purchase, acquire
ἀγρός, οῦ, ὁ field
13:45
πάλιν again (adverb)
ὅμοιος, οία, οιον like, similar to (+ dative)
ἔμπορος, ου, ὁ merchant
ζητέω, ζητήσω, ἐζήτησα, ἐζητήθην seek, desire, ask for
μαργαρίτης, ου, ὁ pearl

13:44 **ὃν**: the masculine singular accusative relative pronoun serves as an object for both the participle and the finite verb. **ἀπὸ τῆς χαρᾶς**: *in his joy*; the noun carries onomatopoeic qualities. **πάντα ὅσα**: *all that*; in conjuction with πάντα, ὅσα is translated as a relative pronoun.

13:45 **ἀνθρώπῳ ἐμπόρῳ**: *a merchant*; ἀνθρώπῳ is pleonastic but adds greater definiteness and emphasis.

13:46 εὑρὼν δὲ ἕνα πολύτιμον μαργαρίτην ἀπελθὼν πέπρακεν πάντα ὅσα εἶχεν καὶ ἠγόρασεν αὐτόν.

13:47 Πάλιν ὁμοία ἐστὶν ἡ βασιλεία τῶν οὐρανῶν σαγήνῃ βληθείσῃ εἰς τὴν θάλασσαν καὶ ἐκ παντὸς γένους συναγαγούσῃ· 13:48 ἣν ὅτε ἐπληρώθη ἀναβιβάσαντες ἐπὶ τὸν αἰγιαλὸν καὶ καθίσαντες συνέλεξαν τὰ καλὰ εἰς ἄγγη, τὰ δὲ σαπρὰ ἔξω ἔβαλον.

13:46
πολύτιμος, ον costly, precious, valuable
πιπράσκω, πέπρακα, πέπραμαι, ἐπράθην sell
ὅσος, η, ον how large, how much, how great; as much as; as many as (plural)
ἀγοράζω, ἀγοράσω, ἠγόρασα, ἠγόρασμαι, ἠγοράσθην buy, purchase, acquire
13:47
πάλιν again (adverb)
ὅμοιος, οία, οιον like, similar to (+ dative)
σαγήνη, ης, ἡ a large net, a large dragnet
θάλασσα, ης, ἡ sea, inland sea, lake
γένος, ους, τό offspring, progeny; nation, people; kind, sort, species
συνάγω, συνάξω, συνήγαγον (2 aorist), συνῆγμαι, συνήχθην gather in, gather up, bring together; convene, come together, meet (passive)
13:48
ὅτε when, whenever (adverb)
πληρόω, πληρώσω, ἐπλήρωσα, πεπλήρωκα, πεπλήρωμαι, ἐπληρώθην fill, complete, fulfill
ἀναβιβάζω, ἀναβιβάσω, ἀνεβίβασα draw up, pull up
αἰγιαλός, οῦ, ὁ shore, beach
καθίζω, καθίσω, ἐκάθισα, κεκάθικα cause to sit down, seat, set (transitive); sit, sit down; remain, stay, continue, rest (intransitive)
συλλέγω, συλλέξω, συνέλεξα collect, gather
ἄγγος, ους, τό vessel, container
σαπρός, ά, όν spoiled, rotten; bad, evil
ἔξω outside, out (adverb)

13:46 **ἀπελθὼν πέπρακεν**: *he went and sold*; a participle may receive as much emphasis as the finite verb and be coordinated with it. The perfect tense of πιπράσκω has aorist meaning. **πάντα ὅσα**: *all that*; in conjunction with πάντα, ὅσα is translated as a relative pronoun.

13:47 **βλησθείσῃ**: the feminine singular dative first aorist passive participle (cf. App. 53, G, 5; 34) of βάλλω stands in agreement with its subject σαγήνῃ. **γένους** is a third declension noun with stem in **σ** elided (App. 15). **συναγαγούσῃ**: the feminine singular dative second aorist active participle (cf. App. 54; 29) stands in agreement with its subject σαγήνῃ. Supply ἰχθύας *fish*.

13:48 **ἣν . . . ἀναβιβάσαντες**: *after they had pulled up the net*; the cumbersome nature of this sentence may be resolved by turning the relative into a noun and starting a new sentence. Since the action of the aorist participle precedes that of the main verb and represents a single action in the past, it has the force of an English pluperfect. **καθίσαντες** is an intransitive verb here. **ἄγγη** is a third declension noun with stem in **σ** elided (App. 15).

13:49 οὕτως ἔσται ἐν τῇ συντελείᾳ τοῦ αἰῶνος· ἐξελεύσονται οἱ
ἄγγελοι καὶ ἀφοριοῦσιν τοὺς πονηροὺς ἐκ μέσου τῶν δικαίων
13:50 καὶ βαλοῦσιν αὐτοὺς εἰς τὴν κάμινον τοῦ πυρός· ἐκεῖ ἔσται ὁ
κλαυθμὸς καὶ ὁ βρυγμὸς τῶν ὀδόντων.
13:51 Συνήκατε ταῦτα πάντα; λέγουσιν αὐτῷ, Ναί. 13:52 ὁ δὲ
εἶπεν αὐτοῖς, Διὰ τοῦτο πᾶς γραμματεὺς μαθητευθεὶς τῇ βασιλείᾳ
τῶν οὐρανῶν

13:49

συντέλεια, ας, ἡ completion, close, end

αἰών, αἰῶνος, ὁ eternity, perpetuity; period of time, life, age; world

ἄγγελος, ου, ὁ messenger, angel

ἀφορίζω, ἀφορίσω/ἀφοριῶ, ἀφώρισα, ἀφώρισμαι, ἀφορίσθην limit off; separate, take out, take away, exclude, excommunicate

μέσος, η, ον middle, in, among (as adjective + genitive); the middle (as noun τὸ μέσον)

δίκαιος, αία, αιον right, just, honest, good, righteous

13:50

κάμινος, ου, ἡ oven, furnace

πῦρ, πυρός, τό fire

ἐκεῖ there, in that place (adverb)

κλαυθμός, ου, ὁ weeping, crying

βρυγμός, οῦ, ὁ chattering (of teeth), gnashing (of teeth)

ὀδούς, ὀδόντος, ὁ tooth

13:51

συνίημι/συνίω, συνήσω/συνήσομαι, συνῆκα (1 aorist) send together; understand, comprehend, perceive clearly

ναί yes, indeed, certainly (particle of affirmation)

13:52

γραμματεύς, έως, ὁ secretary, clerk, scholar versed in law, scribe

μαθητεύω, μαθητεύσω, ἐμαθήτευσα become a disciple of, follow as a disciple (intransitive); make a disciple of, teach; be trained, be instructed (passive)

13:49 **ἐξελεύσονται** is the future of ἐξέρχομαι. **ἐκ μέσου**: *from among.*

13:50 **βαλοῦσιν** is a third person plural liquid future. It shows a change in stem, is formed like verbs contracted with stem in **ε** (App. 56), and takes a circumflex over the contraction.

13:51 **Συνήκατε**: *do you understand*; the perfect tense denotes action (aspect) that is completed near present time and continues with present result: have you understood (and do you understand now). The perfect is frequently translated as a present.

13:52 **μαθητευθεὶς τῇ βασιλείᾳ τῶν οὐρανῶν**: *instructed by the kingdom of heaven*; since the participle is passive, agency may be expressed by the dative of agency (27:57) rather than by the more usual preposition ὑπό and the genitive case.

ὅμοιός ἐστιν ἀνθρώπῳ οἰκοδεσπότῃ, ὅστις ἐκβάλλει ἐκ τοῦ θησαυροῦ αὐτοῦ καινὰ καὶ παλαιά.

13:53 Καὶ ἐγένετο ὅτε ἐτέλεσεν ὁ Ἰησοῦς τὰς παραβολὰς ταύτας, μετῆρεν ἐκεῖθεν. 13:54 καὶ ἐλθὼν εἰς τὴν πατρίδα αὐτοῦ ἐδίδασκεν αὐτοὺς ἐν τῇ συναγωγῇ αὐτῶν, ὥστε ἐκπλήσσεσθαι αὐτοὺς καὶ λέγειν, Πόθεν τούτῳ ἡ σοφία αὕτη καὶ αἱ δυνάμεις;

13:52

ὅμοιος, οία, οιον like, similar to (+ dative)

οἰκοδεσπότης, ου, ὁ master of the house

θησαυρός, οῦ, ὁ treasure box, treasury, treasure

καινός, ή, όν new

παλαιός, ά, όν old

13:53

ὅτε when, whenever (adverb)

τελέω, τελέσω, ἐτέλεσα, τετέλεκα, τετέλεσμαι, ἐτελέσθην finish, fulfill, accomplish, make an end

μεταίρω, μεταρῶ, μετῆρα go away, depart

ἐκεῖθεν from there, from that place (adverb)

13:54

πατρίς, πατρίδος, ἡ fatherland, homeland, hometown

διδάσκω, διδάξω, ἐδίδαξα, ἐδιδάχθην teach, instruct

ὥστε so that (conjunction)

ἐκπλήσσω, ἐκπλήξω, ἐξέπληξα, ἐξεπλάγην amaze, astound, overwhelm

πόθεν from where? how? in what way? (interrogative adverb)

σοφία, ας, ἡ wisdom, prudence

δύναμις, εως, ἡ power; ability; authority, deed of power, miracle, wonder

---

13:52 **ἐκ τοῦ θησαυροῦ αὐτοῦ καινὰ καὶ παλαιά** may refer to treasures of truth as revealed throughout the history of the world.

13:53 **Καὶ ἐγένετο**: the finite verb, usually omitted in translation, is translated in older versions: *and it came to pass.*

13:54 **ἐδιδάσκεν**: the imperfect tense denotes progressive, continued, and repeated action (aspect) in past time. It adds an augment and its endings to the present stem (cf. App. 53, C). **ὥστε ἐκπλήσσεσθαι αὐτοὺς**: *so that they were amazed*; ὥστε, followed by the accusative subject with infinitive, introduces a result clause. **Πόθεν τούτῳ ἡ σοφία αὕτη**: *from where does this man have this wisdom* (literally: *from where is this wisdom to this man*); the construction is a dative of possession. The verb ἐστιν is omitted and must be supplied. **καὶ αἱ δυνάμεις**: *and these miraculous powers;* Greek connects the demonstrative pronoun of the previous clause also with this noun.

13:55 οὐχ οὗτός ἐστιν ὁ τοῦ τέκτονος υἱός; οὐχ ἡ μήτηρ αὐτοῦ λέγεται Μαριὰμ καὶ οἱ ἀδελφοὶ αὐτοῦ Ἰάκωβος καὶ Ἰωσὴφ καὶ Σίμων καὶ Ἰούδας; 13:56 καὶ αἱ ἀδελφαὶ αὐτοῦ οὐχὶ πᾶσαι πρὸς ἡμᾶς εἰσιν; πόθεν οὖν τούτῳ ταῦτα πάντα; 13:57 καὶ ἐσκανδαλίζοντο ἐν αὐτῷ. ὁ δὲ Ἰησοῦς εἶπεν αὐτοῖς, Οὐκ ἔστιν προφήτης ἄτιμος εἰ μὴ ἐν τῇ πατρίδι καὶ ἐν τῇ οἰκίᾳ αὐτοῦ. 13:58 καὶ οὐκ ἐποίησεν ἐκεῖ δυνάμεις πολλὰς διὰ τὴν ἀπιστίαν αὐτῶν.

13:55
τέκτων, ονος, ὁ artisan; carpenter, wood-worker, builder
Μαρία, ας, ἡ Mary (Μαρίαμ indeclinable)
13:56
ἀδελφή, ῆς, ἡ sister
πόθεν from where? how? in what way? (interrogative adverb)
13:57
σκανδαλίζω, σκανδαλίσω, ἐσκανδάλισα, ἐσκανδαλίσθην offend, anger, shock
ἄτιμος, ον unhonored, dishonored, without honor
πατρίς, πατρίδος, ἡ fatherland, homeland, hometown
13:58
ἐκεῖ there, in that place (adverb)
δύναμις, εως, ἡ power; ability; authority, deed of power, miracle, wonder
ἀπιστία, ας, ἡ unfaithfulness, faithlessness, unbelief, lack of belief

---

13:55 **ὁ τοῦ τέκτονος** is an abbreviated form for ὁ υἱὸς τοῦ τέκτονος and stands in predicate position. **λέγεται**: *is called*; the verb applies also to the next slightly elliptical clause. The following names are in predicate position. **Ἰωσὴφ**: the name is also given as Ἰωσῆς (Mk 6:3).

13:56 **οὐχὶ πᾶσαι**: the negative is a strengthened form of οὐ; as an interrogative word in a question, it expects an affirmative answer. πᾶσαι resumes the original subject. **πρὸς ἡμᾶς**: *with us*. **τούτῳ ταῦτα πάντα**: *does this man have all these powers*; the construction is a dative of possession. The verb ἐστιν is omitted and must be supplied. The neuter plurals refer to His wisdom and miraculous powers as in the previous question (54).

13:57 **ἐσκανδαλίζοντο ἐν αὐτῷ**: *they were continually offended at Him*; the verb form is third person plural imperfect passive indicative (cf. App. 53, C). The imperfect tense denotes progressive, continued, and repeated action (aspect) in past time and should not be slighted in translation. **Οὐκ . . . ἄτιμος**: the assertion by means of negation or understatement, called *litotes*, intensifies meaning in the affirmative. **εἰ μὴ**: *except*.

14 Ἐν ἐκείνῳ τῷ καιρῷ ἤκουσεν Ἡρῴδης ὁ τετραάρχης τὴν ἀκοὴν Ἰησοῦ, 14:2 καὶ εἶπεν τοῖς παισὶν αὐτοῦ, Οὗτός ἐστιν Ἰωάννης ὁ βαπτιστής· αὐτὸς ἠγέρθη ἀπὸ τῶν νεκρῶν καὶ διὰ τοῦτο αἱ δυνάμεις ἐνεργοῦσιν ἐν αὐτῷ. 14:3 Ὁ γὰρ Ἡρῴδης κρατήσας τὸν Ἰωάννην ἔδησεν [αὐτὸν] καὶ ἐν φυλακῇ ἀπέθετο διὰ Ἡρῳδιάδα τὴν γυναῖκα Φιλίππου τοῦ ἀδελφοῦ αὐτοῦ·

14:1
καιρός, οῦ, ὁ time, appointed time; season; time of crisis, end-time
τετραάρχης/τετράρχης, ου, ὁ tetrarch
ἀκοή, ῆς, ἡ hearing, fame, report, account
14:2
παῖς, παιδός, ὁ child, boy, youth; servant
νεκρός, ά, όν dead
δύναμις, εως, ἡ power; ability; deed of power, miracle, wonder
ἐνεργέω, ἐνεργήσω, ἐνέργησα, ἐνέργηκα work, be at work, be active (intransitive); work, produce, effect (transitive)
14:3
κρατέω, κρατήσω, ἐκράτησα, κεκράτηκα, κεκράτημαι lay hold of, grasp; retain, not remit
δέω, δήσω, ἔδησα, δέδεκα, δέδεμαι, ἐδέθην bind, tie, impede
φυλακή, ῆς, ἡ watch, guard, prison
ἀποτίθημι, ἀποθήσω, ἀπεθέμην (2 aorist middle), ἀπετέθην put off, lay aside; lay down, put away
Ἡρῳδιάς, άδος, ἡ Herodias
γυνή, γυναικός, ἡ woman, wife

14:1 **ἤκουσεν . . . τὴν ἀκοὴν**: *heard of the fame.* **ὁ τετραάρχης**: the title distinguishes Herod Antipas from his father Herod the Great.

14:2 **τοῖς παισὶν αὐτοῦ**: *to his servants.* **αὐτὸς ἠγέρθη**: *he has risen*; αὐτὸς serves as the pronoun. The intransitive passive has the meaning *be raised* or *rise.* **διὰ τοῦτο**: *therefore.* **αἱ δυνάμεις ἐνεργοῦσιν**: *his powers are at work*; the article is used as an unemphatic possessive adjective where ownership or relationship is logically implied. The verb is intransitive. While John did not perform miraculous powers, he spoke and acted with power.

14:3 **διὰ Ἡρῳδιάδα**: *for the sake of Herodias*; with whom he had an illicit relationship.

14:4 ἔλεγεν γὰρ ὁ Ἰωάννης αὐτῷ, Οὐκ ἔξεστίν σοι ἔχειν αὐτήν. 14:5
καὶ θέλων αὐτὸν ἀποκτεῖναι ἐφοβήθη τὸν ὄχλον, ὅτι ὡς προφήτην
αὐτὸν εἶχον. 14:6 γενεσίοις δὲ γενομένοις τοῦ Ἡρῴδου ὠρχήσατο
ἡ θυγάτηρ τῆς Ἡρῳδιάδος ἐν τῷ μέσῳ καὶ ἤρεσεν τῷ Ἡρῴδῃ, 14:7
ὅθεν μεθ' ὅρκου ὡμολόγησεν αὐτῇ δοῦναι ὃ ἐὰν αἰτήσηται.

14:4

ἔξεστι(ν) it is permitted, it is possible (impersonal verb)

14:5

ἀποκτείνω, ἀποκτενῶ, ἀπέκτεινα, ἀπεκτάνθην kill

φοβέομαι, φοβηθήσομαι, ἐφοβήθην be afraid, become frightened

14:6

γενέσια, ίων, τά birthday celebration

ὀρχέομαι, ὀρχήσομαι, ὠρχησάμην dance

θυγάτηρ, τρός, ἡ daughter

Ἡρῳδιάς, άδος, ἡ Herodias

μέσος, η, ον middle, in, among (as adjective + genitive); the middle (as noun τὸ μέσον)

ἀρέσκω, ἀρέσω, ἤρεσα please, be pleasing

14:7

ὅθεν from where, whence, from which; from which fact, therefore, hence; wherefore, whereupon (adverb)

ὅρκος, ου, ὁ oath

ὁμολογέω, ὁμολογήσω, ὡμολόγησα assure, admit, confess, declare (publicly)

ὅς, ἥ, ὅ + ἄν (ἐάν) whoever, whatever

αἰτέω, αἰτήσω, ᾔτησα, ᾔτηκα ask, ask for, make a request whoever

---

14:4 **ἔξεστίν**: the verb calls for a dative and infinitive construction.

14:5 **θέλων . . . ἀποκτεῖναι**: *although he desired to kill*; the circumstantial participle expresses concession and takes a complementary infinitive. **ἐφοβήθη** is an first aorist passive deponent (App. 53, G, 1). Deponents have middle or passive voice forms but active meanings. **εἶχον**: *they considered*.

14:6 **γενέσιοις . . . γενομένοις τοῦ Ἡρῴδου**: *at the birthday festival celebrated for Herod*; γενέσιοις is a dative of time when. **ἤρεσεν**: the verb governs the dative case.

14:7 **δοῦναι**: the infinitive represents a future indicative in the direct statement: *I will give you*. **ὃ ἐὰν αἰτήσηται**: *whatever she asked*; is the protasis of a future more vivid condition (App. 70) in indirect statement. The middle voice denotes that the subject performs an action for itself or its own interest or its own benefit. The promise is a commonplace motif in literature that shows ἁμαρτία on the part of the person granting such a wish.

14:8 ἡ δὲ προβιβασθεῖσα ὑπὸ τῆς μητρὸς αὐτῆς, Δός μοι, φησίν, ὧδε ἐπὶ πίνακι τὴν κεφαλὴν Ἰωάννου τοῦ βαπτιστοῦ. 14:9 καὶ λυπηθεὶς ὁ βασιλεὺς διὰ τοὺς ὅρκους καὶ τοὺς συνανακειμένους ἐκέλευσεν δοθῆναι, 14:10 καὶ πέμψας ἀπεκεφάλισεν [τὸν] Ἰωάννην ἐν τῇ φυλακῇ.

14:8
προβιβάζω, προβιβάσω, προεβίβασα, προεβιβάσθην lead forward, put forward, push forward; incite, instigate, prompt
φημί, φήσω, ἔφησα say, speak
ὧδε here (adverb)
πίναξ, ακος, ἡ platter, dish
κεφαλή, ῆς, ἡ head
14:9
λυπέω, λυπήσω, ἐλύπησα, λελύπηκα, ἐλυπήθην vex, irritate, offend (active); be grieved, pained, distressed (passive)
βασιλεύς, έως, ὁ king
ὅρκος, ου, ὁ oath
συνανάκειμαι, συνανακείσομαι recline at table with, eat with
κελεύω, κελεύσω, ἐκέλευσα give order, command, urge, direct, bid
14:10
πέμπω, πέμψω, ἔπεμψα, πέπομφα, ἐπέμφθην send
ἀποκεφαλίζω, ἀποκεφαλίσω, ἀπεκεφάλισα behead
φυλακή, ῆς, ἡ watch, guard, prison

14:8 **προβιβασθεῖσα**: *since she had been prompted.* **φησίν**: *she said;* the verb is inserted after the first word or two of a quote to introduce direct discourse.

14:9 **λυπηθεὶς**: Herod at once recognizes his mistake. **ἐκέλευσεν δοθῆναι** may mean either *he ordered that her request be granted* in an impersonal construction or *that his head be given her,* where τὴν κεφαλὴν must be supplied in response to Δός μοι in the previous verse.

14:10 **πέμψας**: supply τοὺς ὑπηρέτας *his servants, assistants,* or *officers.*

14:11 καὶ ἠνέχθη ἡ κεφαλὴ αὐτοῦ ἐπὶ πίνακι καὶ ἐδόθη τῷ κορασίῳ,
καὶ ἤνεγκεν τῇ μητρὶ αὐτῆς. 14:12 καὶ προσελθόντες οἱ μαθηταὶ
αὐτοῦ ἦραν τὸ πτῶμα καὶ ἔθαψαν αὐτὸ[ν] καὶ ἐλθόντες ἀπήγγειλαν
τῷ Ἰησοῦ.
14:13 Ἀκούσας δὲ ὁ Ἰησοῦς ἀνεχώρησεν ἐκεῖθεν ἐν πλοίῳ εἰς
ἔρημον τόπον κατ᾽ ἰδίαν· καὶ ἀκούσαντες οἱ ὄχλοι ἠκολούθησαν
αὐτῷ πεζῇ ἀπὸ τῶν πόλεων. 14:14 καὶ ἐξελθὼν εἶδεν πολὺν ὄχλον καὶ
ἐσπλαγχνίσθη ἐπ᾽ αὐτοῖς καὶ ἐθεράπευσεν τοὺς ἀρρώστους αὐτῶν.

14:11
φέρω, οἴσω, ἤνεγκα (1 aorist), ἤνεγκον (2 aorist), ἠνέχθην bear, carry, bring
κεφαλή, ῆς, ἡ head
πίναξ, ακος, ἡ platter, dish
κοράσιον, ου, τό girl
14:12
αἴρω, ἀρῶ, ἦρα, ἦρκα, ἦρμαι, ἤρθην take up, bear, take away, lift, carry, remove; keep in suspense; destroy, kill
πτῶμα, ατος, τό that which has fallen; body, corpse
θάπτω, θάψω, ἔθαψα, τέταφα, ἐτάφην (2 aorist passive) bury
ἀπαγγέλλω, ἀπαγγελῶ, ἀπήγγειλα (1 aorist), ἀπηγγέλην (2 aorist passive) bring back word, report, declare, announce, tell
14:13
ἀναχωρέω, ἀναχωρήσω, ἀνεχώρησα go away, depart, withdraw, retire
ἐκεῖθεν from there, from that place (adverb)
πλοῖον, ου, τό ship, boat
ἔρημος, ον abandoned, empty, desolate, lonely; wilderness, desert, grassland (substantive)
τόπος, ου, ὁ place, position, region
ἴδιος, ία, ιον one's own; κατ᾽ ἰδίαν privately, by oneself, alone (adverb)
πεζῇ on foot; by land (adverb)
14:14
σπλαγχνίζομαι, σπλαγχνίσομαι, ἐσπλαγχνίσθην have compassion, feel sympathy, be moved with pity
ἄρρωστος, ον sick, ill, weak, infirm

14:11 **καὶ ἠνέχθη . . . καὶ ἐδόθη . . . καὶ ἤνεγκεν**: the formal chiastic tricolon of verbs and the polysyndeton produce a grotesque formality.

14:12 **ἦραν**: *they took*; the verbal form is the first aorist of the liquid verb αἴρω.

14:13 **ἠκολούθησαν** governs the dative case.

14:14 **εἶδεν** is the second aorist of ὁράω *see*. **ἐσπλανγχνίσθη** is a deponent verb.

14:15 ὀψίας δὲ γενομένης προσῆλθον αὐτῷ οἱ μαθηταὶ λέγοντες, Ἔρημός ἐστιν ὁ τόπος καὶ ἡ ὥρα ἤδη παρῆλθεν· ἀπόλυσον τοὺς ὄχλους, ἵνα ἀπελθόντες εἰς τὰς κώμας ἀγοράσωσιν ἑαυτοῖς βρώματα.
14:16 ὁ δὲ [Ἰησοῦς] εἶπεν αὐτοῖς, Οὐ χρείαν ἔχουσιν ἀπελθεῖν, δότε αὐτοῖς ὑμεῖς φαγεῖν. 14:17 οἱ δὲ λέγουσιν αὐτῷ, Οὐκ ἔχομεν ὧδε εἰ μὴ πέντε ἄρτους καὶ δύο ἰχθύας. 14:18 ὁ δὲ εἶπεν, Φέρετέ μοι ὧδε αὐτούς.

14:15
ὀψία, ας, ἡ evening
ἔρημος, ον abandoned, empty, desolate, lonely; wilderness, desert, grassland (substantive)
τόπος, ου, ὁ place, position, region
ὥρα, ας, ἡ hour
ἤδη now, already (adverb)
ἀπολύω, ἀπολύσω, ἀπέλυσα, ἀπολέλυκα, ἀπολέλυμαι, ἀπελύθην release, set free, allow to depart; pardon
κώμη, ης, ἡ village, small town
ἀγοράζω, ἀγοράσω, ἠγόρασα, ἠγόρασμαι, ἠγοράσθην buy, purchase, acquire
ἑαυτοῦ, ῆς, οῦ himself, herself, itself; themselves, ourselves, yourselves (in plural)
βρῶμα, ατος, τό food
14:16
χρεία, ας, ἡ need, necessity
ἐσθίω, φάγομαι, ἔφαγον (2 aorist) eat
14:17
ὧδε here (adverb)
πέντε five (indeclinable)
ἄρτος, ου, ὁ bread, loaf of bread
ἰχθύς, ύος, ὁ fish
14:18
φέρω, οἴσω, ἤνεγκα (1 aorist), ἤνεγκον (2 aorist), ἠνέχθην bear, carry, bring
ὧδε here (adverb)

14:15 **ὀψίας . . . γενομένης**: *when evening fell*; the construction is a genitive absolute. **Ἔρημός** is a predicate adjective. **ἡ ὥρα ἤδη παρῆλθεν**: *the time is already past.* **ἀπόλυσον** is a second person singular aorist active imperative (cf. App. 53, D, 3).

14:16 **Οὐ χρείαν ἔχουσιν**: *they do not need.* **δότε αὐτοῖς ὑμεῖς**: the collocation suggests their responsibility of surrounding care.

14:17 **εἰ μὴ**: *but*; the particles are equivalent to ἀλλά when preceded by **οὐκ**.

14:19 καὶ κελεύσας τοὺς ὄχλους ἀνακλιθῆναι ἐπὶ τοῦ χόρτου, λαβὼν τοὺς πέντε ἄρτους καὶ τοὺς δύο ἰχθύας, ἀναβλέψας εἰς τὸν οὐρανὸν εὐλόγησεν καὶ κλάσας ἔδωκεν τοῖς μαθηταῖς τοὺς ἄρτους, οἱ δὲ μαθηταὶ τοῖς ὄχλοις. 14:20 καὶ ἔφαγον πάντες καὶ ἐχορτάσθησαν, καὶ ἦραν τὸ περισσεῦον τῶν κλασμάτων δώδεκα κοφίνους πλήρεις. 14:21 οἱ δὲ ἐσθίοντες ἦσαν ἄνδρες ὡσεὶ πεντακισχίλιοι χωρὶς γυναικῶν καὶ παιδίων.

14:19
κελεύω, κελεύσω, ἐκέλευσα give order, command, urge, direct, bid
ἀνακλίνω, ἀνακλινῶ, ἀνέκλινα, ἀνεκλίθην cause to lie down; lie down, recline at meal (passive)
χόρτος, ου, ὁ grass
λαμβάνω, λήμψομαι, ἔλαβον, εἴληφα, εἴλημμαι, ἐλήφθην take, receive, accept
πέντε five (indeclinable)
ἄρτος, ου, ὁ bread, loaf of bread
ἰχθύς, ύος, ὁ fish
ἀναβλέπω, ἀναβλέψω, ἀνέβλεψα look up; regain sight, receive sight
εὐλογέω, εὐλογήσω, εὐλόγησα, εὐλόγηκα praise, bless
κλάω, κλάσω, ἔκλασα break
14:20
ἐσθίω, φάγομαι, ἔφαγον (2 aorist) eat
χορτάζω, χορτάω, εχόρτασα, ἐχορτάσθην feed, fill, satisfy
αἴρω, ἀρῶ, ἦρα, ἦρκα, ἦρμαι, ἤρθην take up, bear, take away, lift, carry, remove; keep in suspense; destroy, kill
περισσεύω, περισσεύσω, ἐπερίσσευσα be left over, abound
κλάσμα, ατος, τό fragment, morsel, piece
δώδεκα twelve (indeclinable)
κόφινος, ου, ὁ basket
πλήρης, ες full
14:21
ἐσθίω, φάγομαι, ἔφαγον (2 aorist) eat
ἀνήρ, ἀνδρός, ὁ man, male, husband
ὡσεί as if, as, like; about (adverb; with numerals)
πεντακισχίλιοι, αι, α five thousand
χωρίς without, apart from (preposition + genitive)

14:19 **κελεύσας . . . λαβών . . . ἀναβλέψας . . . κλάσας**: although translating these participles into finite verbs or breaking them up into several sentences would change the cumbersome nature of the sentence, it would also disturb its intended purpose: to slow down the rhythm of the language and inspire awe for the miracle being presently performed.

14:20 **τὸ περισσεῦον τῶν κλασμάτων**: *what was left over of the broken pieces.* **δώδεκα κοφίνους πλήρεις**: *namely twelve baskets full*; the phrase stands in apposition to τὸ περισσεύον.

14:22 Καὶ εὐθέως ἠνάγκασεν τοὺς μαθητὰς ἐμβῆναι εἰς τὸ πλοῖον καὶ προάγειν αὐτὸν εἰς τὸ πέραν, ἕως οὗ ἀπολύσῃ τοὺς ὄχλους. 14:23 καὶ ἀπολύσας τοὺς ὄχλους ἀνέβη εἰς τὸ ὄρος κατ' ἰδίαν προσεύξασθαι. ὀψίας δὲ γενομένης μόνος ἦν ἐκεῖ. 14:24 τὸ δὲ πλοῖον ἤδη σταδίους πολλοὺς ἀπὸ τῆς γῆς ἀπεῖχεν βασανιζόμενον ὑπὸ τῶν κυμάτων, ἦν γὰρ ἐναντίος ὁ ἄνεμος.

14:22

εὐθέως at once, immediately (adverb)

ἀναγκάζω, ἀναγκάσω, ἠνάγκασα, ἠναγκάσθην compel, force; constrain, urge

ἐμβαίνω, ἐμβήσομαι, ἐνέβην, ἐμβέβηκα step in, embark

πλοῖον, ου, τό ship, boat

προάγω, προάξω, προήγαγον (2 aorist) lead forward, bring out (transitive); go before, precede, go before (intransitive); go or come before *someone* (+ accusative of person)

πέραν across, beyond, on the other side of (preposition + genitive); τὸ πέραν farther side, the other side

ἀπολύω, ἀπολύσω, ἀπέλυσα, ἀπολέλυκα, ἀπολέλυμαι, ἀπελύθην release, set free, allow to depart; pardon

14:23

ἀναβαίνω, ἀναβήσομαι, ἀνέβην, ἀναβέβηκα go up, ascend, rise

ὄρος, ους, τό mountain, hill

ἴδιος, ία, ιον one's own; κατ' ἰδίαν privately, by oneself, alone (adverb)

προσεύχομαι, προσεύξομαι, προσηυξάμην pray

ὀψία, ας, ἡ evening

μόνος, η, ον only, alone

ἐκεῖ there, in that place (adverb)

14:24

πλοῖον, ου, τό ship, boat

ἤδη now, already (adverb)

στάδιον, ου, τό stade (measure of distance), arena, stadium, furlong (plural also οἱ στάδιοι)

ἀπέχω, ἀφέξω have in full, receive in full; be distant, be away

βασανίζω, βασανίσω, ἐβασάνισα, ἐβασανίσθην afflict, torment, torture; toss, harass

κῦμα, ατος, τό wave, surge, billow

ἐναντίος, α, ον opposite to, over against; contrary, adverse, hostile

---

14:22 **ἕως οὗ**: *while*; the temporal conjunction with the relative in the genitive may take an aorist indicative or aorist subjunctive.

14:23 **προσεύξασθαι** is an infinitive of purpose. This purpose construction is particularly prevalent after main verbs of motion like ἀναβαίνω. **ὀψίας . . . γενομένης**: *when evening fell*; the construction is a genitive absolute.

14:24 **σταδίους πολλοὺς** is an accusative of extent of space. **τὸ δὲ πλοῖον . . . βασανιζόμενον**: the hyperbaton emphasizes the separation of the ship from the land and its troubles. **ἐναντίος** is a predicate adjective.

14:25 τετάρτῃ δὲ φυλακῇ τῆς νυκτὸς ἦλθεν πρὸς αὐτοὺς περιπατῶν ἐπὶ τὴν θάλασσαν. 14:26 οἱ δὲ μαθηταὶ ἰδόντες αὐτὸν ἐπὶ τῆς θαλάσσης περιπατοῦντα ἐταράχθησαν λέγοντες ὅτι Φάντασμά ἐστιν, καὶ ἀπὸ τοῦ φόβου ἔκραξαν. 14:27 εὐθὺς δὲ ἐλάλησεν [ὁ Ἰησοῦς] αὐτοῖς λέγων, Θαρσεῖτε, ἐγώ εἰμι· μὴ φοβεῖσθε. 14:28 ἀποκριθεὶς δὲ αὐτῷ ὁ Πέτρος εἶπεν, Κύριε, εἰ σὺ εἶ, κέλευσόν με ἐλθεῖν πρός σε ἐπὶ τὰ ὕδατα. 14:29 ὁ δὲ εἶπεν, Ἐλθέ. καὶ καταβὰς ἀπὸ τοῦ πλοίου [ὁ] Πέτρος περιεπάτησεν ἐπὶ τὰ ὕδατα καὶ ἦλθεν πρὸς τὸν Ἰησοῦν.

14:25
τέταρτος, η, ον fourth
φυλακή, ῆς, ἡ watch, guard, prison
νύξ, νυκτός, ἡ night
περιπατέω, περιπατήσω, περιεπάτησα walk, walk about
θάλασσα, ης, ἡ sea, inland sea, lake
14:26
ταράσσω, ταράξω, ἐτάραξα, τετάραγμαι, ἐταράχθην stir up, disturb, trouble
φάντασμα, ατος, τό apparition, phantom, ghost
φόβος, ου, ὁ terror; fear, alarm, fright; reverence, respect
κράζω, κράξω, ἔκραξα, κέκραγα cry out, cry aloud
14:27
εὐθύς immediately, at once (adverb)
θαρσέω, θαρσήσω, ἐθάρσησα be of good courage, be cheerful
φοβέομαι, φοβηθήσομαι, ἐφοβήθην be afraid, become frightened
14:28
ἀποκρίνομαι, ἀπεκρινάμην, ἀπεκρίθην answer, reply
κελεύω, κελεύσω, ἐκέλευσα give order, command, urge, direct, bid
ὕδωρ, ὕδατος, τό water
14:29
καταβαίνω, καταβήσομαι, κατέβην, καταβέβηκα come down, go down, descend, fall
πλοῖον, ου, τό ship, boat
περιπατέω, περιπατήσω, περιεπάτησα walk, walk about
ὕδωρ, ὕδατος, τό water

14:25 **τέταρτῃ φυλακῇ**: watches of the night were divided into four equal periods according to Roman custom from 6 p.m. to 6 a.m.

14:26 **ὅτι** is used as our quotation marks to introduce direct discourse.

14:27 **ἐγώ εἰμι**: the context indicates the deeper meaning and more sacred use of the divine title **I Am**.

14:28 **κέλευσόν**: the first aorist imperative is followed by an accusative of person commanded and an aorist infinitive.

14:29 **Ἐλθέ** is a second person singular second aorist active imperative (cf. App. 54).

14:30 βλέπων δὲ τὸν ἄνεμον [ἰσχυρὸν] ἐφοβήθη, καὶ ἀρξάμενος
καταποντίζεσθαι ἔκραξεν λέγων, Κύριε, σῶσόν με. 14:31 εὐθέως
δὲ ὁ Ἰησοῦς ἐκτείνας τὴν χεῖρα ἐπελάβετο αὐτοῦ καὶ λέγει αὐτῷ,
Ὀλιγόπιστε, εἰς τί ἐδίστασας; 14:32 καὶ ἀναβάντων αὐτῶν εἰς τὸ
πλοῖον ἐκόπασεν ὁ ἄνεμος. 14:33 οἱ δὲ ἐν τῷ πλοίῳ προσεκύνησαν
αὐτῷ λέγοντες, Ἀληθῶς θεοῦ υἱὸς εἶ.
14:34 Καὶ διαπεράσαντες ἦλθον ἐπὶ τὴν γῆν εἰς Γεννησαρέτ.

14:30
ἄνεμος, ου, ὁ wind
ἰσχυρός, ά, όν strong, mighty, powerful
φοβέομαι, φοβηθήσομαι, ἐφοβήθην be afraid, become frightened
ἄρχω, ἄρξω, ἦρξα, ἦρχα, ἦργμαι, ἤρχθην rule (active); begin (middle)
καταποντίζω, καταποντίσω, κατεποντίσθην throw into the sea, drown; be sunk, be drowned; sink (passive)
κράζω, κράξω, ἔκραξα, κέκραγα cry out, cry aloud
σῴζω, σώσω, ἔσωσα, σέσωκα, σέσωσμαι, ἐσώθην save, rescue, preserve safe and unharmed
14:31
εὐθέως at once, immediately (adverb)
ἐκτείνω, ἐκτενῶ, ἐξέτεινα stretch out, hold out
ἐπιλαμβάνομαι, ἐπιέλαβόμην take hold of, grasp, catch, seize
ὀλιγόπιστος, ον of little faith
εἰς τί why?
διστάζω, διστάσω, ἐδίστασα doubt, hesitate, waver
14:32
ἀναβαίνω, ἀναβήσομαι, ἀνέβην, ἀναβέβηκα go up, ascend, rise; climb; embark
κοπάζω, κοπάσω, ἐκόπασα cease, abate, stop, rest
ἄνεμος, ου, ὁ wind
14:33
προσκυνέω, προσκυνήσω, προσεκύνησα worship, prostrate oneself before, reverence before, reverence
ἀληθῶς truly, certainly, of a truth
14:34
διαπεράω, διαπεράσω, διεπέρησα cross, cross over, pass through
Γεννησαρέτ, ἡ Gennesaret (indeclinable)

14:30 **ἀρξάμενος καταποντίζεσθαι**: *as he began to sink.*

14:31 **ἐπελάβετο** governs the genitive case. **Ὀλιγόπιστε** stands in the vocative case.

14:32 **ἀναβάντων αὐτῶν** is a genitive absolute construction.

14:33 **οἱ δὲ**: *but those who were*; the article followed by a prepositional phrase stands in attributive position as part of the substantive. **προσεκύνησαν αὐτῷ**: the verb governs the dative case.

14:34 **ἐπὶ τὴν γῆν εἰς Γεννησαρέτ**: *to the land of Gennesaret*; εἰς Γεννησαρέτ stands in apposition to ἐπὶ τὴν γῆν.

14:35 καὶ ἐπιγνόντες αὐτὸν οἱ ἄνδρες τοῦ τόπου ἐκείνου ἀπέστειλαν εἰς ὅλην τὴν περίχωρον ἐκείνην καὶ προσήνεγκαν αὐτῷ πάντας τοὺς κακῶς ἔχοντας 14:36 καὶ παρεκάλουν αὐτὸν ἵνα μόνον ἅψωνται τοῦ κρασπέδου τοῦ ἱματίου αὐτοῦ· καὶ ὅσοι ἥψαντο διεσώθησαν.

14:35

ἐπιγινώσκω, ἐπιγνώσομαι, ἐπέγνων (2 aorist), ἐπέγνωκα, ἐπεγνώσθην know, understand, recognize; discern, detect

τόπος, ου, ὁ place, position, region

ἀποστέλλω, ἀποστελῶ, ἀπέστειλα, ἀπέσταλκα, ἀπέσταλμαι, ἀπεστάλην send, send away, send out

ὅλος, η, ον all, whole, entire, complete

περίχωρος, ὁ, ἡ adjacent region, country around; inhabitants of the region around

προσφέρω, προσοίσω, προσήνεγκα, προσήνεγκον (2 aorist), προσηνέχθην bring to, bring before, offer, present

κακῶς ill, badly, wickedly, wrongly (adverb)

14:36

παρακαλέω, παρακαλέσω, παρεκάλεσα, παρακέκληκα, παρακέκλημαι, παρεκλήθην call upon, exhort, persuade; beg, entreat; comfort, encourage, cheer up

μόνον only (adverb); μὴ μόνον . . . ἀλλὰ καί not only . . . but also

ἅπτω, ἅψω, ἧψα fasten; light, kindle; touch (middle)

κράσπεδον, ου, τό edge, border, hem; tassel

ἱμάτιον, ου, τό garment, clothing; cloak, robe

ὅσος, η, ον how large, how great; as many as (plural)

διασῴζω, διασώσω, διεσώθην save, rescue; be cured, healed, restored to health (passive)

14:35 **ἀπέστειλαν**: supply *word* or *messengers.* **εἰς ὅλην τὴν περίχωρον ἐκείνην**: *that whole surrounding region.* **πάντας τοὺς κακῶς ἔχοντας**: *all who were sick*; ἔχω becomes intransitive with adverbs.

14:36 **ἵνα μόνον ἅψωνται τοῦ κρασπέδου**: *that they might only touch his hem*; the verb governs the genitive case.

15 Τότε προσέρχονται τῷ Ἰησοῦ ἀπὸ Ἱεροσολύμων Φαρισαῖοι καὶ γραμματεῖς λέγοντες, 15:2 Διὰ τί οἱ μαθηταί σου παραβαίνουσιν τὴν παράδοσιν τῶν πρεσβυτέρων; οὐ γὰρ νίπτονται τὰς χεῖρας [αὐτῶν] ὅταν ἄρτον ἐσθίωσιν. 15:3 ὁ δὲ ἀποκριθεὶς εἶπεν αὐτοῖς, Διὰ τί καὶ ὑμεῖς παραβαίνετε τὴν ἐντολὴν τοῦ θεοῦ διὰ τὴν παράδοσιν ὑμῶν; 15:4 ὁ γὰρ θεὸς εἶπεν, Τίμα τὸν πατέρα καὶ τὴν μητέρα, καί, Ὁ κακολογῶν πατέρα ἢ μητέρα θανάτῳ τελευτάτω.

15:1
Ἱεροσόλυμα, τά Jerusalem (indeclinable)
15:2
διὰ τί why?
παραβαίνω, παραβήσομαι, παρέβην (2 aorist) go aside, deviate, turn aside (intransitive); transgress, violate, break (transitive)
παράδοσις, εως, ἡ handing over; betrayal, arrest; teaching, doctrine; tradition
πρεσβύτερος, α, ον older, ancestor, elder (designation of an official); ancients, fathers (plural)
νίπτω, νίψω, ἔνιψα wash (active); wash oneself (middle)
ἄρτος, ου, ὁ bread, loaf of bread
ἐσθίω, φάγομαι, ἔφαγον (2 aorist) eat
15:3
διὰ τί why?
παραβαίνω, παραβήσομαι, παρέβην (2 aorist) go aside, deviate, turn aside (intransitive); transgress, violate, break (transitive)
ἐντολή, ῆς, ἡ command, commandment
παράδοσις, εως, ἡ handing over; betrayal, arrest; teaching, doctrine; tradition
15:4
τιμάω, τιμήσω, ἐτίμησα value, honor, revere
κακολογέω, κακολογήσω speak ill of, revile, insult, abuse
θάνατος, ου, ὁ death
τελευτάω, τελευτήσω, ἐτελεύτησα, τετελεύτηκα end one's life, finish, die

---

15:2 **τὴν παράδοσιν**: the tradition consisted of oral regulations of the Pharisees handed down for generations. Since they were not written down as part of the law of Moses, they were rejected by the Sadducees.

15:3 **τὴν ἐντολὴν τοῦ θεοῦ**: the new argument juxtaposes oral tradition to the law of Moses.

15:4 **θανάτῳ τελευτάτω**: *let him surely die*; the verb by itself is a euphemistic expression that generally means *to die*. However, the addition of θανάτῳ makes the phrase emphatic.

15:5 ὑμεῖς δὲ λέγετε, Ὃς ἂν εἴπῃ τῷ πατρὶ ἢ τῇ μητρί, Δῶρον ὃ
ἐὰν ἐξ ἐμοῦ ὠφεληθῇς, 15:6 οὐ μὴ τιμήσει τὸν πατέρα αὐτοῦ· καὶ
ἠκυρώσατε τὸν λόγον τοῦ θεοῦ διὰ τὴν παράδοσιν ὑμῶν.
15:7 ὑποκριταί, καλῶς ἐπροφήτευσεν περὶ ὑμῶν Ἠσαΐας λέγων,
15:8 Ὁ λαὸς οὗτος τοῖς χείλεσίν με τιμᾷ,
ἡ δὲ καρδία αὐτῶν πόρρω ἀπέχει ἀπ᾽ ἐμοῦ·

15:5
ὅς, ἥ, ὅ + ἄν (ἐάν) whoever, whatever
ὠφελέω, ὠφελήσω, ὠφέλησα, ὠφελήθην help, aid, benefit, be of use to, be of value; receive help, be benefitted (passive)
δῶρον, ου, τό gift, present; offering, sacrifice; consecration to God; contribution
15:6
οὐ μή never, certainly not
τιμάω, τιμήσω, ἐτίμησα value, honor, revere
ἀκυρόω, ἀκυρώσω, ἠκύρωσα make void, annul
παράδοσις, εως, ἡ handing over; betrayal, arrest; teaching, doctrine; tradition
15:7
καλῶς well (adverb)
προφητεύω, προφητεύσω, ἐπροφήτευσα proclaim a divine revelation, prophetically reveal, prophesy
περί about, concerning (preposition + genitive); about, around (+ accusative)
15:8
λαός, οῦ, ὁ people
χεῖλος, ους, τό lip
πόρρω forward; far, far off, far away, at a distance (adverb)
ἀπέχω, ἀφέξω have in full, receive in full; be distant, be away
μάτην in vain, without profit, fruitlessly (adverb)
σέβομαι worship, reverence
διδάσκω, διδάξω, ἐδίδαξα, ἐδιδάχθην teach, instruct
διδασκαλία, ας, ἡ precept, doctrine
ἔνταλμα, ατος, τό commandment

15:5 **Δῶρον ὃ ἐὰν ἐξ ἐμοῦ ὠφεληθῇς**: *whatever help you receive from me is a gift to God*; supply ἐστίν with Δῶρον. Mark more specifically defines the gift as Corban (7:11). According to the traditions of the Elders any financial obligation could be forgiven provided a vow was made, a Corban or sacrificial offering to God. In this case, the vow freed the adult children from the responsibility of supporting their aged parent no matter how much they were in need.

15:6 **οὐ μὴ τιμήσει**: *he shall not honor his father*; the double negative indicates a strong negation and takes a future indicative instead of the aorist subjunctive. The statement indicates the sentiment of the Pharisees that the son is not obliged to support his parent, a tradition that controverts the law of Moses.

15:8 **πόρρω ἀπέχει**: *is far from me*; ἔχω becomes intransitive with adverbs.

15:9 μάτην δὲ σέβονταί με
διδάσκοντες διδασκαλίας ἐντάλματα ἀνθρώπων.
15:10 Καὶ προσκαλεσάμενος τὸν ὄχλον εἶπεν αὐτοῖς, Ἀκούετε καὶ
συνίετε· 15:11 οὐ τὸ εἰσερχόμενον εἰς τὸ στόμα κοινοῖ τὸν ἄνθρωπον,
ἀλλὰ τὸ ἐκπορευόμενον ἐκ τοῦ στόματος τοῦτο κοινοῖ τὸν ἄνθρωπον.
15:12 Τότε προσελθόντες οἱ μαθηταὶ λέγουσιν αὐτῷ, Οἶδας ὅτι οἱ
Φαρισαῖοι ἀκούσαντες τὸν λόγον ἐσκανδαλίσθησαν; 15:13 ὁ δὲ
ἀποκριθεὶς εἶπεν, Πᾶσα φυτεία ἣν οὐκ ἐφύτευσεν ὁ πατήρ μου ὁ
οὐράνιος ἐκριζωθήσεται.

15:10
προσκαλέω, προσκαλέσω, προσεκάλεσα, προσκέκληκα, προσκέκλημαι, προσεκλήθην call on, summon, invite, call to oneself
συνίημι/συνίω, συνήσω/συνήσομαι, συνῆκα (1 aorist) send together; understand, comprehend, perceive clearly
15:11
στόμα, ατος, τό mouth
κοινόω, κοινώσω, ἐκοίνωσα, κεκοίνωκα make common, defile; profane, desecrate; render unclean, defile, pollute
ἀλλά but, yet (conjunction)
ἐκπορεύομαι, ἐκπορεύσομαι, ἐκπεπόρευμαι, ἐξεπορεύθην come out, go out, proceed
στόμα, ατος, τό mouth
15:12
οἶδα know
σκανδαλίζω, σκανδαλίσω, ἐσκανδάλισα, ἐσκανδαλίσθην offend, anger, shock
15:13
φυτεία, ας, ἡ plant
φυτεύω, φυτεύσω, ἐφύτευσα plant, set
οὐράνιος, ια, ιον heavenly, celestial
ἐκριζόω, ἐκριζώσω, ἐξερίζωσα, ἐξεριζώθην pull out by the roots, uproot, eradicate; utterly destroy

---

15:9 **διδασκαλίας** stands in predicate position to ἐντάλματα.

15:11 **κοινοῖ** is third person singular present active indicative of a contracted verb with stem in **ο** (cf. App. 57). **τοῦτο** resumes the subject τὸ ἐκπορευόμενον.

15:12 **Οἶδας ὅτι**: the verb introduces indirect discourse with the subordinating conjunction ὅτι. The construction takes a finite verb and the same mood and tense as would have been used in the direct statement.

15:13 **Πᾶσα φυτεία** is a reference to the Pharisees. They are not part of his vineyard.

15:14 ἄφετε αὐτούς· τυφλοί εἰσιν ὁδηγοί [τυφλῶν]· τυφλὸς δὲ
τυφλὸν ἐὰν ὁδηγῇ, ἀμφότεροι εἰς βόθυνον πεσοῦνται. 15:15
Ἀποκριθεὶς δὲ ὁ Πέτρος εἶπεν αὐτῷ, Φράσον ἡμῖν τὴν παραβολὴν
[ταύτην]. 15:16 ὁ δὲ εἶπεν, Ἀκμὴν καὶ ὑμεῖς ἀσύνετοί ἐστε; 15:17 οὐ
νοεῖτε ὅτι πᾶν τὸ εἰσπορευόμενον εἰς τὸ στόμα εἰς τὴν κοιλίαν χωρεῖ
καὶ εἰς ἀφεδρῶνα ἐκβάλλεται; 15:18 τὰ δὲ ἐκπορευόμενα ἐκ τοῦ
στόματος ἐκ τῆς καρδίας ἐξέρχεται, κἀκεῖνα κοινοῖ τὸν ἄνθρωπον.

15:14
τυφλός, ή, όν blind
ὁδηγός, ου, ὁ guide, leader; instructor, teacher
ἀμφότεροι, αι, α both
βόθυνος, ου, ὁ pit, well, cistern
πίπτω, πεσοῦμαι, ἔπεσα, ἔπεσον (2 aorist), πέπτωκα fall, fall prostrate, fall down
15:15
φράζω, φράσω, ἔφρασα explain, expound, interpret
15:16
ἀκμήν still, even now (adverb)
ἀσύνετος, ον without understanding, senseless, foolish
15:17
νοέω, νοήσω, ἐνόησα perceive, observe; understand, comprehend
εἰσπορεύομαι, εἰσπορεύσομαι go in, come in, enter, be put in
στόμα, ατος, τό mouth
κοιλία, ας, ἡ stomach, belly, womb
χωρέω, χωρήσω, ἐχώρησα move, pass; proceed; go forward, make progress; have room for, hold, contain; grasp, accept, comprehend, understand
ἀφεδρών, ῶνος, ὁ latrine, privy
15:18
ἐκπορεύομαι, ἐκπορεύσομαι, ἐκπεπόρευμαι, ἐξεπορεύθην come out, go out, proceed
στόμα, ατος, τό mouth
κοινόω, κοινώσω, ἐκοίνωσα, κεκοίνωκα make common, defile; profane, desecrate; render unclean, defile, pollute

---

15:14 **ἐὰν** introduces a future more vivid condition (App. 70).

15:15 **Φράσον** is second person singular aorist active imperative.

15:17 **οὐ νοεῖτε ὅτι**: the verb introduces indirect discourse with a subordinating conjunction ὅτι.

15:18 **κἀκεῖνα**: the combining of two words καὶ ἐκεῖνα to avoid vowel succession in adjoining words is called *crasis*.

15:19 ἐκ γὰρ τῆς καρδίας ἐξέρχονται διαλογισμοὶ πονηροί, φόνοι, μοιχεῖαι, πορνεῖαι, κλοπαί, ψευδομαρτυρίαι, βλασφημίαι. 15:20 ταῦτά ἐστιν τὰ κοινοῦντα τὸν ἄνθρωπον, τὸ δὲ ἀνίπτοις χερσὶν φαγεῖν οὐ κοινοῖ τὸν ἄνθρωπον.

15:21 Καὶ ἐξελθὼν ἐκεῖθεν ὁ Ἰησοῦς ἀνεχώρησεν εἰς τὰ μέρη Τύρου καὶ Σιδῶνος. 15:22 καὶ ἰδοὺ γυνὴ Χαναναία ἀπὸ τῶν ὁρίων ἐκείνων ἐξελθοῦσα ἔκραζεν λέγουσα, Ἐλέησόν με, κύριε υἱὸς Δαυίδ· ἡ θυγάτηρ μου κακῶς δαιμονίζεται.

15:19
διαλογισμός, ου, ὁ reasoning, thought, purpose; discourse, disputation, contention; doubt, hesitation
φόνος, ου, ὁ killing, murder
μοιχεία, ας, ἡ adultery
πορνεία, ας, ἡ immorality, prostitution, fornication
κλοπή, ῆς, ἡ theft
ψευδομαρτυρία, ας, ἡ false witness, false testimony
βλασφημία, ίας, ἡ slander, abusive speech, blasphemy
15:20
κοινόω, κοινώσω, ἐκοίνωσα, κεκοίνωκα make common, defile; profane, desecrate; render unclean, defile, pollute
ἄνιπτος, ον unwashed
15:21
ἐκεῖθεν from there, from that place (adverb)
ἀναχωρέω, ἀναχωρήσω, ἀνεχώρησα go away, depart, withdraw, retire
μέρος, ους, τό part, portion, share
15:22
Χαναναῖος, α, ον of Canaan, Canaanite, Canaanitish
ὅριον, ου, τό boundary; region, territory, district (plural)
κράζω, κράξω, ἔκραξα, κέκραγα cry out, cry aloud
ἐλεέω, ἐλεήσω, ἠλέησα, ἠλέημαι, ἠλεήθην pity, show mercy
θυγάτηρ, τρός, ἡ daughter
κακῶς ill, badly, wickedly, wrongly (adverb)
δαιμονίζομαι, δαιμονίσομαι, ἐδαιμονίσθην be possessed by a demon

---

15:20 **τὸ δὲ ἀνίπτοις χερσὶν φαγεῖν**: *eating with unwashed hands*; the articular infinitive is the subject of the sentence. χερσὶν is a dative of means.

15:21 **εἰς τὰ μέρη Τύρου καὶ Σιδῶνος**: the object of the preposition is a neuter plural accusative third declension noun with stem in **σ** elided (cf. App. 15). Τύρου and Σιδῶνος are partitive genitives or genitives of the whole since they follow a word denoting part of a whole (App. 65).

15:22 **Χαναναία**: the nation is traditionally associated as an enemy of Israel. **κύριε υἱὸς Δαυιδ**: *Lord, Son of David*; the nominative υἱὸς is used as a vocative.

15:23 ὁ δὲ οὐκ ἀπεκρίθη αὐτῇ λόγον. καὶ προσελθόντες οἱ μαθηταὶ
αὐτοῦ ἠρώτουν αὐτὸν λέγοντες, Ἀπόλυσον αὐτήν, ὅτι κράζει
ὄπισθεν ἡμῶν. 15:24 ὁ δὲ ἀποκριθεὶς εἶπεν, Οὐκ ἀπεστάλην εἰ μὴ
εἰς τὰ πρόβατα τὰ ἀπολωλότα οἴκου Ἰσραήλ. 15:25 ἡ δὲ ἐλθοῦσα
προσεκύνει αὐτῷ λέγουσα, Κύριε, βοήθει μοι.

15:23

ἐρωτάω, ἐρωτήσω, ἠρώτησα ask, inquire of, question, ask a question, request, beseech

ἀπολύω, ἀπολύσω, ἀπέλυσα, ἀπολέλυκα, ἀπολέλυμαι, ἀπελύθην release, set free, allow to depart, send away, let go, dismiss; pardon

κράζω, κράξω, ἔκραξα, κέκραγα cry out, cry aloud

ὄπισθεν from behind, behind, after (adverb; preposition + genitive)

15:24

ἀποστέλλω, ἀποστελῶ, ἀπέστειλα, ἀπέσταλκα, ἀπέσταλμαι, ἀπεστάλην send, send away, send out

εἰ μή unless, except

πρόβατον, ου, τό sheep

οἶκος, ου, ὁ house, dwelling

15:25

προσκυνέω, προσκυνήσω, προσεκύνησα worship, prostrate oneself before, reverence before, reverence

βοηθέω, βοηθήσω, ἐβοήθησα help, bring aid

15:23 **ἀπεκρίθη . . . λόγον**: *reply a word*; ἀπεκρίθη is a deponent verb. **ἠρώτουν**: *kept beseeching*; the imperfect tense denotes progressive, continued, and repeated action (aspect) in past time. In a Koine confusion of paradigms in contracted verbs with stem in **α** and **ε**, the third person plural imperfect active indicative ending ουν appears for ων (cf. App. 55; 56).

15:24 **ἀπεστάλην**: *I was sent*; some verbs show a second aorist passive. This passive omits θ, and the endings -ην, -ης, -η, -ημεν, -ητε, -ησαν (cf. App. 53, G, 1) are added directly to the stem.

15:25 **βοήθει** is a second person singular present active imperative of a contracted verb with stem in **ε** (cf. App. 56).

15:26 ὁ δὲ ἀποκριθεὶς εἶπεν, Οὐκ ἔστιν καλὸν λαβεῖν τὸν ἄρτον
τῶν τέκνων καὶ βαλεῖν τοῖς κυναρίοις. 15:27 ἡ δὲ εἶπεν, Ναὶ κύριε,
καὶ γὰρ τὰ κυνάρια ἐσθίει ἀπὸ τῶν ψιχίων τῶν πιπτόντων ἀπὸ τῆς
τραπέζης τῶν κυρίων αὐτῶν. 15:28 τότε ἀποκριθεὶς ὁ Ἰησοῦς εἶπεν
αὐτῇ, Ὦ γύναι, μεγάλη σου ἡ πίστις· γενηθήτω σοι ὡς θέλεις. καὶ
ἰάθη ἡ θυγάτηρ αὐτῆς ἀπὸ τῆς ὥρας ἐκείνης.
15:29 Καὶ μεταβὰς ἐκεῖθεν ὁ Ἰησοῦς ἦλθεν παρὰ τὴν θάλασσαν
τῆς Γαλιλαίας, καὶ ἀναβὰς εἰς τὸ ὄρος ἐκάθητο ἐκεῖ.

15:26
λαμβάνω, λήμψομαι, ἔλαβον, εἴληφα, εἴλημμαι, ἐλήφθην take, receive, accept
ἄρτος, ου, ὁ bread, loaf of bread
τέκνον, ου, τό child, descendant, posterity
κυνάριον, ίου, τό house-dog, little dog, dog (diminutive of κύων)
15:27
ναί yes, indeed, certainly (particle of affirmation)
ψιχίον, ου, τό crumb, bit
πίπτω, πεσοῦμαι, ἔπεσα, ἔπεσον (2 aorist), πέπτωκα fall, fall prostrate, fall down
τράπεζα, ης, ἡ table, counter
15:28
Ὦ O! (interjection)
μέγας, μεγάλη, μέγα large, great
πίστις, εως, ἡ faith, trust
15:28
ἰάομαι, ἰάσομαι, ἰασάμην, ἴαμαι, ἰάθην heal, cure, restore
θυγάτηρ, τρός, ἡ daughter
ὥρα, ας, ἡ hour
15:29
μεταβαίνω, μεταβήσομαι, μετέβην, μεταβέβηκα go, pass over, move
θάλασσα, ης, ἡ sea
Γαλιλαία, ας, ἡ Galilee
ἀναβαίνω, ἀναβήσομαι, ἀνέβην, ἀναβέβηκα go up, ascend, rise
ὄρος, ους, τό mountain, hill
κάθημαι, καθήσομαι sit, stay, reside
ἐκεῖ there, in that place (adverb)

15:26 **Οὐκ ἔστιν καλὸν λαβεῖν**: the infinitive is the subject of the quasi-impersonal verb.

15:27 **καὶ γὰρ**: *but even.*

15:28 **Ὦ γύναι** is in the vocative case and expresses a measure of surprise.

15:30 καὶ προσῆλθον αὐτῷ ὄχλοι πολλοὶ ἔχοντες μεθ' ἑαυτῶν
χωλούς, τυφλούς, κυλλούς, κωφούς, καὶ ἑτέρους πολλοὺς καὶ
ἔρριψαν αὐτοὺς παρὰ τοὺς πόδας αὐτοῦ, καὶ ἐθεράπευσεν αὐτούς·
15:31 ὥστε τὸν ὄχλον θαυμάσαι βλέποντας κωφοὺς λαλοῦντας,
κυλλοὺς ὑγιεῖς καὶ χωλοὺς περιπατοῦντας καὶ τυφλοὺς βλέποντας·
καὶ ἐδόξασαν τὸν θεὸν Ἰσραήλ.
15:32 Ὁ δὲ Ἰησοῦς προσκαλεσάμενος τοὺς μαθητὰς αὐτοῦ εἶπεν,
Σπλαγχνίζομαι ἐπὶ τὸν ὄχλον,

15:30
χωλός, ή, όν lame, crippled
τυφλός, ή, όν blind
κυλλός, ή, όν maimed, crippled, deformed; cripple, injured person (substantive)
κωφός, ή, όν blunt, dull; dull of hearing, deprived of hearing; deaf; dumb, mute
ἕτερος, α, ον other, another
ῥίπτω/ῥιπτέω, ῥίψω, ἔρριψα, ἔρριμαι hurl, throw; lay down, set on the ground; be dispersed, be scattered (passive)
πούς, ποδός, ὁ foot
15:31
ὥστε so that (conjunction)
θαυμάζω, θαυμάσομαι, ἐθαύμασα, ἐθαυμάσθην wonder, marvel, be astonished
κωφός, ή, όν blunt, dull; dull of hearing, deprived of hearing; deaf; dumb, mute
κυλλός, ή, όν maimed, crippled, deformed; cripple, injured person (substantive)
ὑγιής, ές healthy, sound
χωλός, ή, όν lame, crippled
περιπατέω, περιπατήσω, περιεπάτησα walk, walk about
τυφλός, ή, όν blind
δοξάζω, δοξάσω, ἐδόξασα, δεδόξασμαι, ἐδοξάσθην praise, honor, magnify, glorify
15:32
προσκαλέομαι, προσκαλέσομαι, προσεκαλεσάμην, προσκέκλημαι summon, call on, invite, call to oneself
σπλαγχνίζομαι, σπλαγχνίσομαι, ἐσπλαγχνίσθην have compassion, feel sympathy, be moved with pity

---

15:30 **προσῆλθον αὐτῷ**: the compound verb governs the dative case. **χωλούς**: *the lame*; this and the following three adjectives have been turned into substantives.

15:31 **ὥστε**, followed by the accusative with infinitive, introduces a result clause. **τὸν ὄχλον . . . βλέποντας**: *the multitude . . . as they saw*; the number shifts from singular to plural. **κωφοὺς λαλοῦντας, κυλλοὺς ὑγιεῖς καὶ χωλοὺς περιπατοῦντας καὶ τυφλοὺς βλέποντας**: *that the mute were speaking, the crippled were made well, and the lame were walking about, and the blind were seeing*; verbs of perceiving regularly introduce indirect discourse that takes a participle. The repetition of καὶ at the end slows down the rhythm of the language and inspires awe for the miracle being performed.

ὅτι ἤδη ἡμέραι τρεῖς προσμένουσίν μοι καὶ οὐκ ἔχουσιν τί φάγωσιν·
καὶ ἀπολῦσαι αὐτοὺς νήστεις οὐ θέλω, μήποτε ἐκλυθῶσιν ἐν τῇ ὁδῷ.
15:33 καὶ λέγουσιν αὐτῷ οἱ μαθηταί, Πόθεν ἡμῖν ἐν ἐρημίᾳ ἄρτοι
τοσοῦτοι ὥστε χορτάσαι ὄχλον τοσοῦτον; 15:34 καὶ λέγει αὐτοῖς ὁ
Ἰησοῦς, Πόσους ἄρτους ἔχετε; οἱ δὲ εἶπαν, Ἑπτὰ καὶ ὀλίγα ἰχθύδια.
15:35 καὶ παραγγείλας τῷ ὄχλῳ ἀναπεσεῖν ἐπὶ τὴν γῆν

15:32
ἤδη now, already (adverb)
τρεῖς, τρία three
προσμένω, προσμενῶ, προσέμεινα continue, remain; remain or stay with
ἀπολύω, ἀπολύσω, ἀπέλυσα, ἀπολέλυκα, ἀπολέλυμαι, ἀπελύθην release, set free, allow to depart, send away, let go, dismiss; pardon
νῆστις, ιος/ιδος, ὁ, ἡ hungry, not eating
μήποτε not; that . . . not, lest, (in order) that . . . not
ἐκλύομαι, ἐξελύθην become weary, exhausted, faint
15:33
πόθεν from where? how? in what way? (interrogative adverb)
ἐρημία, ας, ἡ uninhabited region, desert
τοσοῦτος, τοσαύτη, τοσοῦτο so great, so much, so large
ὥστε so that, so as to (conjunction)
χορτάζω, χορτάω, εχόρτασα, ἐχορτάσθην feed, fill, satisfy
15:34
πόσος, η, ον how great? how much?
ἑπτά seven (indeclinable)
ὀλίγος, η, ον little, small; few (plural)
ἰχθύδιον, ου, τό small fish
15:35
παραγγέλλω, παραγγελλῶ, παρήγγειλα announce, notify; command, direct
ἀναπίπτω, ἀναπεσοῦμαι, ἀνέπεσον lie down, recline, take one's place

---

15:32 **ὅτι ἤδη ἡμέραι τρεῖς προσμένουσίν μοι**: *because they have already spent three days with me*; ἡμέραι τρεῖς: the case may be construed as a parenthetical nominative. Supply εἰσιν καὶ: *three days have already passed and*; it is more usually an accusative of duration of time. The present tense plus the temporal adverb is equivalent to a perfect. **τί φάγωσιν**: *anything to eat* (literally: *what they will eat*); indirect questions retain the mood and the tense of the direct question. Since this is originally a deliberative question, it retains the subjunctive mood. The deliberative subjunctive (present or aorist) is used when the speaker is perplexed about *what he is to do* or *say* or *think*, etc.

15:33 **Πόθεν ἡμῖν . . . ἄρτοι τοσοῦτοι**: *from where do we have so many loaves of bread*; supply εἰσιν in this dative of possession construction. **ὥστε**, followed by the accusative with infinitive, introduces a result clause.

15:35 **παραγγείλας**: verbs of saying frequently introduce indirect discourse that takes an infinitive.

15:36 ἔλαβεν τοὺς ἑπτὰ ἄρτους καὶ τοὺς ἰχθύας καὶ εὐχαριστήσας
ἔκλασεν καὶ ἐδίδου τοῖς μαθηταῖς, οἱ δὲ μαθηταὶ τοῖς ὄχλοις.
15:37 καὶ ἔφαγον πάντες καὶ ἐχορτάσθησαν. καὶ τὸ περισσεῦον τῶν
κλασμάτων ἦραν ἑπτὰ σπυρίδας πλήρεις. 15:38 οἱ δὲ ἐσθίοντες
ἦσαν τετρακισχίλιοι ἄνδρες χωρὶς γυναικῶν καὶ παιδίων. 15:39 Καὶ
ἀπολύσας τοὺς ὄχλους ἐνέβη εἰς τὸ πλοῖον καὶ ἦλθεν εἰς τὰ ὅρια
Μαγαδάν.

15:36
λαμβάνω, λήμψομαι, ἔλαβον, εἴληφα, εἴλημμαι, ἐλήφθην take, receive, accept
ἑπτά seven (indeclinable)
ἰχθύς, ύος, ὁ fish
εὐχαριστέω, εὐχαριστήω, εὐχαρίστησα give thanks
κλάω, κλάσω, ἔκλασα break
15:37
χορτάζω, χορτάω, εχόρτασα, ἐχορτάσθην feed, fill, satisfy
περισσεύω, περισσεύσω, ἐπερίσσευσα be left over, abound
κλάσμα, ατος, τό fragment, morsel, piece
ἑπτά seven (indeclinable)
σπυρίς, ίδος, ἡ basket
πλήρης, ες full
15:38
τετρακισχίλιοι, αι, α four thousand
ἀνήρ, ἀνδρός, ὁ man, male, husband
χωρίς without, apart from (preposition + genitive)
15:39
ἀπολύω, ἀπολύσω, ἀπέλυσα, ἀπολέλυκα, ἀπολέλυμαι, ἀπελύθην release, set free, allow to depart, send away, let go, dismiss; pardon
ἐμβαίνω, ἐμβήσομαι, ἐνέβην, ἐμβέβηκα step in, embark
ὅριον, ου, τό boundary; region, territory, district (plural)
Μαγαδάν, ἡ Magadan (indeclinable)

15:36 **ἐδίδου**: *He continued to give*; the third person singular imperfect active indicative (App. 58). The imperfect tense denotes progressive, continued, and repeated action (aspect) in past time. The aspect may be of particular significance in the midst of this miracle.

15:37 **ἔφαγον** is the second aorist of ἐσθίω: *eat*. **τὸ περισσεῦον τῶν κλασμάτων**: *what was left over of the broken pieces*. **ἑπτὰ σπυρίδας πλήρεις**: *namely seven baskets full*; the phrase stands in apposition to τὸ περισσεῦον.

15:39 **Μαγαδάν**, otherwise unknown, may refer to Magdala.

16 Καὶ προσελθόντες οἱ Φαρισαῖοι καὶ Σαδδουκαῖοι πειράζοντες
ἐπηρώτησαν αὐτὸν σημεῖον ἐκ τοῦ οὐρανοῦ ἐπιδεῖξαι αὐτοῖς. 16:2
ὁ δὲ ἀποκριθεὶς εἶπεν αὐτοῖς, [Ὀψίας γενομένης λέγετε, Εὐδία,
πυρράζει γὰρ ὁ οὐρανός· 16:3 καὶ πρωΐ, Σήμερον χειμών, πυρράζει
γὰρ στυγνάζων ὁ οὐρανός.

16:1
πειράζω, πειράσω, ἐπείρασα, πεπείρασμαι, ἐπειράσθην try, test, tempt, prove
ἐπερωτάω, ἐπερωτήσω, ἐπηρώτησα ask, ask a question, interrogate, question; inquire after
σημεῖον, ου, τό sign, token, miracle
ἐπιδείκνυμι, ἐπιδείξω, ἐπέδειξα, ἐπιδέδειχα, ἐπιδέδειγμαι, ἐπεδείχθην show, point out, declare
16:2
ὀψία, ας, ἡ evening
εὐδία, ας, ἡ cloudless sky, fair weather; peace, tranquility
πυρράζω, πυρράσω be fiery red
16:3
πρωΐ early, early in the morning (adverb)
σήμερον today, this day (adverb)
χειμών, ῶνος, ἡ stormy weather, storm, tempest, winter
πυρράζω, πυρράσω be fiery red
στυγνάζω, στυγνάσω, ἐστύγνασα signal a gloomy look, be dark or gloomy

---

16:1 **ἐπηρώτησαν**: *requested*; verbs of saying frequently introduce indirect discourse that takes an infinitive. **αὐτὸν . . . επιδεῖξαι αὐτοῖς**: *that He show them*; the verb governs the dative case.

16:2 **Ὀψίας γενομένης**: *when it is evening*; the construction is a genitive absolute. **Εὐδία**: supply αὔριον: *tomorrow*.

16:3 **πυρράζει . . . στυγνάζων**: *is red and overcast*; a participle may receive as much emphasis as the finite verb and be coordinated with it.

τὸ μὲν πρόσωπον τοῦ οὐρανοῦ γινώσκετε διακρίνειν, τὰ δὲ σημεῖα τῶν καιρῶν οὐ δύνασθε;] 16:4 Γενεὰ πονηρὰ καὶ μοιχαλὶς σημεῖον ἐπιζητεῖ, καὶ σημεῖον οὐ δοθήσεται αὐτῇ εἰ μὴ τὸ σημεῖον Ἰωνᾶ. καὶ καταλιπὼν αὐτοὺς ἀπῆλθεν.

16:5 Καὶ ἐλθόντες οἱ μαθηταὶ εἰς τὸ πέραν

16:3

πρόσωπον, ου, τό face, countenance; appearance

γινώσκω, γνώσομαι, ἔγνων, ἔγνωκα, ἔγνωσμαι, ἐγνώσθην know, learn, understand

διακρίνω, διακρινῶ, διεκρίθην distinguish, discern, discriminate, judge; be at odds with oneself, hesitate, doubt, waver (middle or passive)

δέ and, but (conjunction, postpositive)

σημεῖον, ου, τό sign, token, miracle

καιρός, οῦ, ὁ time, appointed time; season; time of crisis, end-time

16:4

γενεά, ᾶς, ἡ progeny, generation, age

μοιχαλίς, ίδος, ἡ adulteress; adulterous, faithless, ungodly (adjective)

σημεῖον, ου, τό sign, token, miracle

ἐπιζητέω, ἐπιζητήσω, ἐπεζήτησα, ἐπεζητήθην search for, seek after; strive for, wish for; demand, desire

καταλείπω, καταλείψω, κατέλειψα, κατέλιπον (2 aorist), κατελείφθην leave behind (active); remain behind (passive)

16:5

πέραν across, beyond, on the other side of (preposition + genitive); τὸ πέραν farther side, the other side

---

16:3 **γινώσκετε . . . διακρίνειν**: supply *how* after γινώσκετε. **τὸ . . . πρόσωπον**: the sky is poetically personified. **οὐ δύνασθε**: supply διακρίνειν from the previous clause.

16:4 **μοιχαλὶς**: a generation becomes adulterous by abandoning its spiritual relationship with God and worshiping idols (Hos 1–3). **αὐτῇ**: the personal pronoun refers to Γενεὰ. **τὸ σημεῖον Ἰωνᾶ** is the burial of three days and three nights (12:40).

ἐπελάθοντο ἄρτους λαβεῖν. 16:6 ὁ δὲ Ἰησοῦς εἶπεν αὐτοῖς, Ὁρᾶτε καὶ προσέχετε ἀπὸ τῆς ζύμης τῶν Φαρισαίων καὶ Σαδδουκαίων. 16:7 οἱ δὲ διελογίζοντο ἐν ἑαυτοῖς λέγοντες ὅτι Ἄρτους οὐκ ἐλάβομεν. 16:8 γνοὺς δὲ ὁ Ἰησοῦς εἶπεν, Τί διαλογίζεσθε ἐν ἑαυτοῖς, ὀλιγόπιστοι, ὅτι ἄρτους οὐκ ἔχετε;

16:5
ἐπιλανθάνομαι, ἐπιλήσομαι, ἐπελαθόμην, ἐπιλέλησμαι forget
λαμβάνω, λήμψομαι, ἔλαβον, εἴληφα, εἴλημμαι, ἐλήφθην take, receive, accept
16:6
προσέχω, προσέξω, προσέσχον (2 aorist) pay attention to, give heed to, consider; beware of, take heed of, guard against (followed by ἀπό, μή)
ζύμη, ης, ἡ leaven
16:7
δέ and, but (conjunction, postpositive)
διαλογίζομαι, διαλογίσομαι reason, deliberate, ponder, consider
ἑαυτοῦ, ῆς, οῦ himself, herself, itself; themselves, ourselves, yourselves (in plural)
16:8
γινώσκω, γνώσομαι, ἔγνων, ἔγνωκα, ἔγνωσμαι, ἐγνώσθην know, learn, understand
διαλογίζομαι, διαλογίσομαι reason, deliberate, ponder, consider
ὀλιγόπιστος, ον of little faith

16:5 **ἐπελάθοντο ἄρτους λαβεῖν**: Mark mentions that they had only brought one loaf.

16:6 **τῆς ζύμης** is a fermenting ingredient, usually consisting of old highly fermented dough, which is added in small amounts when baking bread to raise the bread.

16:7 **ὅτι** here introduces a direct statement and is equivalent to our quotation marks. **Ἄρτους οὐκ ἐλάβομεν**: the disciples understand the warning literally as being about bread and reason that since the leaven of the Pharisees and Sadducees has grown old and sour, they are without resources.

16:8 **ὀλιγόπιστοι**: they are so called because they fail to recognize Him as the source of bread and life and to understand his warning about the Pharisees and Sadducees.

16:9 οὔπω νοεῖτε, οὐδὲ μνημονεύετε τοὺς πέντε ἄρτους τῶν
πεντακισχιλίων καὶ πόσους κοφίνους ἐλάβετε; 16:10 οὐδὲ τοὺς ἑπτὰ
ἄρτους τῶν τετρακισχιλίων καὶ πόσας σπυρίδας ἐλάβετε; 16:11
πῶς οὐ νοεῖτε ὅτι οὐ περὶ ἄρτων εἶπον ὑμῖν; προσέχετε δὲ ἀπὸ τῆς
ζύμης τῶν Φαρισαίων καὶ Σαδδουκαίων. 16:12 τότε συνῆκαν ὅτι οὐκ
εἶπεν προσέχειν ἀπὸ τῆς ζύμης τῶν ἄρτων ἀλλὰ ἀπὸ τῆς διδαχῆς τῶν
Φαρισαίων καὶ Σαδδουκαίων.

16:9
οὔπω not yet (adverb)
νοέω, νοήσω, ἐνόησα perceive, observe; understand, comprehend
μνημονεύω, μνημονεύσω, ἐμνημόνευσα remember, call to mind
πέντε five (indeclinable)
πεντακισχίλιοι, αι, α five thousand
πόσος, η, ον how great? how much?
κόφινος, ου, ὁ basket
λαμβάνω, λήμψομαι, ἔλαβον, εἴληφα, εἴλημμαι, ἐλήφθην take, get, get together, receive, accept
16:10
ἑπτά seven (indeclinable)
τετρακισχίλιοι, αι, α four thousand
σπυρίς, ίδος, ἡ basket
16:11
πῶς how? in what way? in what sense? (interrogative adverb)
νοέω, νοήσω, ἐνόησα perceive, observe; understand, comprehend
προσέχω, προσέξω, προσέσχον (2 aorist) pay attention to, give heed to, consider; beware of, take heed of, guard against (followed by ἀπό, μή)
ζύμη, ης, ἡ leaven
16:12
συνίημι/συνίω, συνήσω/συνήσομαι, συνῆκα (1 aorist) send together; understand, comprehend, perceive clearly
προσέχω, προσέξω, προσέσχον (2 aorist) pay attention to, give heed to, consider; beware of, take heed of, guard against (followed by ἀπό, μή)
ζύμη, ης, ἡ leaven
διδαχή, ῆς, ἡ teaching, instruction

16:9–10 **οὔπω νοεῖτε, οὐδὲ μνημονεύετε . . . οὐδὲ**: *do you not yet understand, do you remember neither . . . nor*; the lack of conjunction, or asyndeton, intensifies the relationship between the finite verbs. The arrangement of reversing the natural order of cognition, hysteron proteron, and placing the notion of understanding before that of remembering gives emphasis to the importance of understanding: by now the disciples should understand and should not need to be reminded. The two examples of the miracles of bread are joined by οὐδὲ . . . οὐδὲ.

16:11 **πῶς οὐ νοεῖτε** repeats the first verb and as the third member completes the tricolon of questions.

16:12 **τότε συνῆκαν·** the reminder of the miracles of the bread and the repetition of the original warning about the leaven of the Pharisees and Sadducees raise their level of spirituality and understanding. The verb of perceiving introduces a ὅτι clause in indirect discourse. **τῆς ζύμης . . . τῆς διδαχῆς**: their teachings have grown sour and old because of human traditions and regulations.

16:13 Ἐλθὼν δὲ ὁ Ἰησοῦς εἰς τὰ μέρη Καισαρείας τῆς Φιλίππου ἠρώτα τοὺς μαθητὰς αὐτοῦ λέγων, Τίνα λέγουσιν οἱ ἄνθρωποι εἶναι τὸν υἱὸν τοῦ ἀνθρώπου; 16:14 οἱ δὲ εἶπαν, Οἱ μὲν Ἰωάννην τὸν βαπτιστήν, ἄλλοι δὲ Ἠλίαν, ἕτεροι δὲ Ἰερεμίαν ἢ ἕνα τῶν προφητῶν. 16:15 λέγει αὐτοῖς, Ὑμεῖς δὲ τίνα με λέγετε εἶναι; 16:16 ἀποκριθεὶς δὲ Σίμων Πέτρος εἶπεν, Σὺ εἶ ὁ Χριστὸς ὁ υἱὸς τοῦ θεοῦ τοῦ ζῶντος. 16:17 ἀποκριθεὶς δὲ ὁ Ἰησοῦς εἶπεν αὐτῷ, Μακάριος εἶ, Σίμων Βαριωνᾶ, ὅτι σὰρξ καὶ αἷμα οὐκ ἀπεκάλυψέν σοι ἀλλ' ὁ πατήρ μου ὁ ἐν τοῖς οὐρανοῖς.

16:13
μέρος, ους, τό part, portion, share
Καισάρεια, ας, ἡ Caesarea
ἐρωτάω, ἐρωτήσω, ἠρώτησα ask, inquire of, question, ask a question, request, beseech
16:14
Ἰερεμίας, ου, ὁ Jeremiah
16:16
ζάω, ζήσω/ζήσομαι, ἔζησα, ἔζηκα live
16:17
μακάριος, ία, ιον blessed, happy, fortunate
σάρξ, σαρκός, ἡ flesh
αἷμα, ατος, τό blood
ἀποκαλύπτω, ἀποκαλύψω, ἀπεκάλυψα, ἀπεκαλύφθην uncover, reveal, disclose

---

16:13 **Καισαρείας τῆς Φιλίππου**: *Caesarea Philippi*; τῆς Φιλίππου is an abbreviated form for τῆς πόλεως Φιλίππου. The pagan city, originally named Paneas for the Greek rustic deity Pan and located at the southern foot of Mt Hermon about twenty miles north of the Sea of Galilee, was enlarged and renamed by the tetrarch in honor of Augustus, who had given it to Herod the Great in 20 BC. Perhaps the name of the city sparked an interest in the theme of name identification. **λέγουσιν** introduces an accusative and infinitive construction in indirect discourse.

16:14 **Οἱ μὲν**: *some*; supply λέγουσι σὲ εἶναι in this and the following four clauses. The consensus indicates that He is a prophet.

16:15 **Ὑμεῖς** stands in an emphatic position.

16:16 **Σὺ εἶ ὁ Χριστὸς**: the combination of the second person singular pronoun and the second person singular verb occurring at the beginning of the sentence makes an emphatic and revelatory statement. **ὁ υἱὸς** stands in apposition. **τοῦ θεοῦ** is a genitive of source.

16:17 **Μακάριος εἶ**: the formula, μακάριοι οἱ πτωχοὶ τῷ πνεύματι, heretofore used in a general way, applies to Peter specifically. His attitude suggests a reverence toward God and man and a recognition of his relationship to both: he recognizes where he stands in his relationship to Jesus.

16:18 κἀγὼ δέ σοι λέγω ὅτι σὺ εἶ Πέτρος, καὶ ἐπὶ ταύτῃ τῇ πέτρᾳ
οἰκοδομήσω μου τὴν ἐκκλησίαν καὶ πύλαι ᾅδου οὐ κατισχύσουσιν
αὐτῆς. 16:19 δώσω σοι τὰς κλεῖδας τῆς βασιλείας τῶν οὐρανῶν,
καὶ ὃ ἐὰν δήσῃς ἐπὶ τῆς γῆς ἔσται δεδεμένον ἐν τοῖς οὐρανοῖς, καὶ
ὃ ἐὰν λύσῃς ἐπὶ τῆς γῆς ἔσται λελυμένον ἐν τοῖς οὐρανοῖς. 16:20
τότε διεστείλατο τοῖς μαθηταῖς ἵνα μηδενὶ εἴπωσιν ὅτι αὐτός ἐστιν ὁ
Χριστός.

16:18
πέτρα, ας, ἡ rock
οἰκοδομέω, οἰκοδομήσω, ᾠκοδόμησα, ᾠκοδομήθην build, construct, establish
ἐκκλησία, ας, ἡ congregation, church
πύλη, ης, ἡ gate
ᾅδης, ου, ὁ Hades, underworld, abode of the dead; place of punishment, hell; the lowest place
κατισχύω, κατισχύσω, κατίσχυσα overpower, win victory over
16:19
κλεῖς, κλειδός, ἡ key
ὅς, ἥ, ὅ + ἄν (ἐάν) whoever, whatever
δέω, δήσω, ἔδησα, δέδεκα, δέδεμαι, ἐδέθην bind, tie, impede
λύω, λύσω, ἔλυσα, λέλυκα, λέλυμαι, ἐλύθην loose, unbind, unfasten, break, destroy
16:20
διαστέλλομαι, διαστελοῦμαι, διεστειλάμην order, give orders, admonish
μηδείς, μηδεμία, μηδέν not one, none, no one, nothing

16:18 **κἀγὼ δέ σοι λέγω**: the juxtaposition of the two pronouns emphasizes the solemnity and intimacy of the occasion. The verb of perceiving introduces a ὅτι clause in indirect discourse. **σὺ εἶ Πέτρος, καὶ ἐπὶ ταύτῃ τῇ πέτρᾳ**: the theme of name identification continues in a paronomasia. τῇ πέτρᾳ has been variously interpreted to mean Peter, Peter's revelation and confession, Christ, and the apostles as a whole. **οἰκοδομήσω μου τὴν ἐκκλησίαν**: the first person verb and the possessive pronoun are of fundamental importance indicating that this is not a human organization but Christ's church, that He is the corner stone and that it is additionally "built on the foundation of apostles and prophets" (Eph 2:20). Of the Gospel writers only Matthew uses this noun (also 18:17). **πύλαι ᾅδου οὐ κατισχύσουσιν αὐτῆς**: *gates of Hades*; by this metaphor an antithesis is created between the Church of Christ situated in the bright light of a rocky peak and the abode of Satan in the darkness of the shadows below. In the battle of the two kingdoms, the kingdom of light will prevail.

16:19 **τὰς κλεῖδας** symbolize powers, rights, and authority to preside and govern. **ὃ ἐὰν δήσῃς**: the actions include performing ordinances and covenants such as those made at baptism, at weddings, and in temples.

16:20 **ἵνα μηδενὶ εἴπωσιν**: He does not seek public attention or notoriety lest his mission be compromised.

16:21 Ἀπὸ τότε ἤρξατο ὁ Ἰησοῦς δεικνύειν τοῖς μαθηταῖς αὐτοῦ ὅτι δεῖ αὐτὸν εἰς Ἱεροσόλυμα ἀπελθεῖν καὶ πολλὰ παθεῖν ἀπὸ τῶν πρεσβυτέρων καὶ ἀρχιερέων καὶ γραμματέων καὶ ἀποκτανθῆναι καὶ τῇ τρίτῃ ἡμέρᾳ ἐγερθῆναι. 16:22 καὶ προσλαβόμενος αὐτὸν ὁ Πέτρος ἤρξατο ἐπιτιμᾶν αὐτῷ λέγων, Ἵλεώς σοι, κύριε· οὐ μὴ ἔσται σοι τοῦτο. 16:23 ὁ δὲ στραφεὶς εἶπεν τῷ Πέτρῳ, Ὕπαγε ὀπίσω μου, Σατανᾶ·

16:21

ἀπὸ τότε from then on, from that time on

ἄρχω, ἄρξω, ἦρξα, ἦρχα, ἦργμαι, ἤρχθην rule (active); begin (middle)

δείκνυμι/δεικνύω, δείξω, ἔδειξα, δέδειχα, ἐδείχθην show, point out, make known, demonstrate, announce

δεῖ it is necessary, it is proper (an impersonal verb from δέω)

πάσχω, πείσομαι, ἔπαθον, πέπονθα suffer, endure, undergo

πρεσβύτερος, α, ον older, ancestor, elder (designation of an official)

ἀρχιερεύς, έως, ὁ high priest

ἀποκτείνω, ἀποκτενῶ, ἀπέκτεινα, ἀπεκτάνθην kill

τρίτος, η, ον third

16:22

προσλαμβάνομαι, προσλήψομαι, προσελαβόμην take aside, draw to one's side

ἐπιτιμάω, ἐπιτιμήσω, ἐπετίμησα set a value on; assess a penalty; rebuke, reprove, censure, reprimand; admonish, enjoin

ἵλεως, ων gracious, merciful

16:23

στρέφω, στρέψω, ἔστρεψα, ἔστραμμαι, ἐστρέφθην, ἐστράφην (2 aorist passive) turn, make a change, change

ὑπάγω, ὑπάξω, ὑπήγαγον, ὑπήχθην go, go away, go home

ὀπίσω behind, after (adverb; preposition + genitive); εἰς τὰ ὀπίσω back, backward

---

16:21 **Ἀπὸ τότε**: *from then on*. **πολλὰ παθεῖν**: *to endure much suffering*; the construction is a cognate accusative. **τῇ τρίτῃ ἡμέρᾳ** is a dative of time when.

16:22 **Ἵλεώς σοι**: *may God forbid* (literally: *may God be merciful to you*; supply ὁ θεὸς εἴη. **Ἵλεώς**, a masculine singular nominative adjective, frequently used of God in the LXX, is the Attic form of ἵλαος. **οὐ μὴ ἔσται σοι τοῦτο**: *this will never happen to you*; the double negative indicates a strong negation and takes a future instead of the usual aorist subjunctive. σοι is an ethical dative or dative of reference.

16:23 **Ὕπαγε ὀπίσω μου**: not to be taken literally, the phrase means *get out of my sight* or *get away from me*.

σκάνδαλον εἶ ἐμοῦ, ὅτι οὐ φρονεῖς τὰ τοῦ θεοῦ ἀλλὰ τὰ τῶν ἀνθρώπων. 16:24 Τότε ὁ Ἰησοῦς εἶπεν τοῖς μαθηταῖς αὐτοῦ, Εἴ τις θέλει ὀπίσω μου ἐλθεῖν, ἀπαρνησάσθω ἑαυτὸν καὶ ἀράτω τὸν σταυρὸν αὐτοῦ καὶ ἀκολουθείτω μοι. 16:25 ὃς γὰρ ἐὰν θέλῃ τὴν ψυχὴν αὐτοῦ σῶσαι ἀπολέσει αὐτήν· ὃς δ' ἂν ἀπολέσῃ τὴν ψυχὴν αὐτοῦ ἕνεκεν ἐμοῦ εὑρήσει αὐτήν. 16:26 τί γὰρ ὠφεληθήσεται ἄνθρωπος ἐὰν τὸν κόσμον ὅλον κερδήσῃ τὴν δὲ ψυχὴν αὐτοῦ ζημιωθῇ; ἢ τί δώσει ἄνθρωπος ἀντάλλαγμα τῆς ψυχῆς αὐτοῦ;

16:23

σκάνδαλον, ου, τό stumbling block, impediment; temptation to sin; that which gives offense, that which is offensive; scandal, offense

φρονέω, φρονήσω, ἐφρόνησα think, take thought; take someone's side, espouse someone's cause

16:24

ὀπίσω behind, after (adverb; preposition + genitive); εἰς τὰ ὀπίσω back, backward

ἀπαρνέομαι, ἀπαρνήσομαι, ἀπηρνησάμην, ἀπήρνημαι deny; renounce, disregard

αἴρω, ἀρῶ, ἦρα, ἦρκα, ἦρμαι, ἤρθην take up, bear, take away, lift, carry, remove; keep in suspense; destroy, kill

σταυρός, οῦ, ὁ cross

16:25

ὅς, ἥ, ὅ + ἄν (ἐάν) whoever, whatever

ψυχή, ῆς, ἡ breath, life, soul, heart

σῴζω, σώσω, ἔσωσα, σέσωκα, σέσωσμαι, ἐσώθην save, rescue, preserve safe and unharmed

ἕνεκεν/ἕνεκα because of, on account of, for the sake of (preposition + genitive)

16:26

ὠφελέω, ὠφελήσω, ὠφέλησα, ὠφελήθην help, profit, aid, benefit, be of use to, be of value

κόσμος, ου, ὁ order, world, universe

ὅλος, η, ον all, whole, entire, complete

κερδαίνω, κερδήσω, ἐκέρδησα gain, acquire

ψυχή, ῆς, ἡ breath, life, soul, heart

ζημιόω, ζημιώσω, ἐζημιώθην suffer loss; lose, forfeit (passive)

ἀντάλλαγμα, ατος, τό price in exchange for, compensation

16:23 **σκάνδαλον**: Peter, who has just been praised for being like a rock, is called Satan and a stumbling block because his plans would subvert the plans of God.

16:24 **ὀπίσω μου ἐλθεῖν**: *to come after me*; here the phrase has the more usual sense.

16:25 **τὴν ψυχὴν αὐτοῦ σῶσαι**: to clarify the paradoxical statement supply ἄνευ μου: *without me* in this chiastic construction.

16:26 **τί γὰρ ὠφεληθήσεται ἄνθρωπος**: *how will a man profit* (literally: *how will a man be profited*). **τί δώσει**: the rhetorical question suggests that no riches can purchase eternal life.

16:27 μέλλει γὰρ ὁ υἱὸς τοῦ ἀνθρώπου ἔρχεσθαι ἐν τῇ δόξῃ τοῦ πατρὸς αὐτοῦ μετὰ τῶν ἀγγέλων αὐτοῦ, καὶ τότε ἀποδώσει ἑκάστῳ κατὰ τὴν πρᾶξιν αὐτοῦ. 16:28 ἀμὴν λέγω ὑμῖν ὅτι εἰσίν τινες τῶν ὧδε ἑστώτων οἵτινες οὐ μὴ γεύσωνται θανάτου ἕως ἂν ἴδωσιν τὸν υἱὸν τοῦ ἀνθρώπου ἐρχόμενον ἐν τῇ βασιλείᾳ αὐτοῦ.

16:27

μέλλω, μελλήσω be about to, be on the point of

δόξα, ης, ἡ glory, honor, majesty

ἀποδίδωμι, ἀποδώσω, ἀπέδωκα, ἀποδέδωκα, ἀποδέδομαι, ἀπεδόθην give away, pay; give back; render, reward, recompense

ἕκαστος, η, ον each, every; each one, every one (substantive)

πρᾶξις, εως, ἡ activity, way of acting; act, action, deed

16:28

ἀμήν in truth, verily (Hebrew)

ὧδε here (adverb)

ἵστημι, στήσω, ἔστησα, ἔστην (2 aorist), ἕστηκα, ἐστάθην put, place, set, cause to stand (transitive); stand, be (intransitive)

οὐ μή never, certainly not

γεύομαι, γεύσομαι, ἐγευσάμην taste; experience

θάνατος, ου, ὁ death

16:27 **μέλλει . . . ἔρχεσθαι**: unlike in Attic Greek, μέλλω is regularly followed by a present infinitive in Koine. The periphrastic future construction denotes the certainty of a future event. **κατὰ τὴν πρᾶξιν αὐτοῦ**: *according to his deeds.*

16:28 **εἰσίν τινες τῶν ὧδε ἑστώτων**: *there are some of those standing here;* ἑστώτων is a masculine plural genitive perfect active participle. It is intransitive and a partitive genitive (cf. App. 65). **οὐ μὴ γεύσωνται θανάτου**: the double negative indicates a strong negation and usually takes an aorist subjunctive that is translated as a future. The verb governs the genitive case. **ἕως ἂν ἴδωσιν**: *until they see;* the temporal conjunction with the aorist subjunctive and the particle ἄν refers indefinitely to the future and denotes that the commencement of one event is dependent on another.

17 Καὶ μεθ' ἡμέρας ἓξ παραλαμβάνει ὁ Ἰησοῦς τὸν Πέτρον καὶ
Ἰάκωβον καὶ Ἰωάννην τὸν ἀδελφὸν αὐτοῦ καὶ ἀναφέρει αὐτοὺς εἰς
ὄρος ὑψηλὸν κατ' ἰδίαν. 17:2 καὶ μετεμορφώθη ἔμπροσθεν αὐτῶν,
καὶ ἔλαμψεν τὸ πρόσωπον αὐτοῦ ὡς ὁ ἥλιος, τὰ δὲ ἱμάτια αὐτοῦ
ἐγένετο λευκὰ ὡς τὸ φῶς. 17:3 καὶ ἰδοὺ ὤφθη αὐτοῖς Μωϋσῆς καὶ
Ἠλίας συλλαλοῦντες μετ' αὐτοῦ. 17:4 ἀποκριθεὶς δὲ ὁ Πέτρος εἶπεν
τῷ Ἰησοῦ, Κύριε, καλόν ἐστιν ἡμᾶς ὧδε εἶναι· εἰ θέλεις, ποιήσω ὧδε
τρεῖς σκηνάς, σοὶ μίαν καὶ Μωϋσεῖ μίαν καὶ Ἠλίᾳ μίαν.

17:1
ἕξ six (indeclinable, numeral)
παραλαμβάνω, παραλήμψομαι, παρέλαβον, παρείληφα, παρείλημμαι, παρελήφθην take, receive, accept
ἀναφέρω, ἀνοίσω, ἀνήνεγκα, ἀνήνεγκον (2 aorist) bring, take up, lead
ὄρος, ους, τό mountain, hill
ὑψηλός, ή, όν high; exalted, proud, haughty
ἴδιος, ία, ιον one's own; κατ' ἰδίαν privately, by oneself, alone (adverb)
17:2
μεταμορφόω, μεταμορφώσω, μετεμορφώθην transform, change in form, transfigure
ἔμπροσθεν in front of, before, in the presence of (adverb; preposition + genitive)
λάμπω, λάμψω, ἔλαμψα shine, shine forth, give light
πρόσωπον, ου, τό face, countenance
ἥλιος, ου, ὁ sun
ἱμάτιον, ου, τό garment, clothing; cloak, robe
λευκός, ή, όν bright, shining, gleaming, white
φῶς, φωτός, τό light
17:3
συλλαλέω, συλλαλήσω, συνελάλησα talk, converse, confer
17:4
καλός, ή, όν good, useful, choice
ὧδε here (adverb)
τρεῖς, τρία three
σκηνή, ῆς, ἡ tent, tabernacle, dwelling, booth
σύ, σοῦ (σου) you (personal pronoun)
Ἠλίας, ου, ὁ Elijah

17:1 **κατ' ἰδίαν**: *by themselves.*

17:2 **ὡς ὁ ἥλιος**: *like the sun*; the conjunction introduces a comparison. **ὡς τὸ φῶς**: understand **τοῦ ἡλίου**.

17:3 **ὤφθη αὐτοῖς**: *appeared to them*; the verb is singular because it agrees only with the nearest subject and takes a dative of the person to whom they appear. **συλλαλοῦντες**: the participle in the plural agrees with both nominatives.

17:4 **καλόν ἐστιν** takes an accusative and infinitive construction. **μίαν** is the feminine singular nominative of the cardinal number εἷς (App. 50).

17:5 ἔτι αὐτοῦ λαλοῦντος ἰδοὺ νεφέλη φωτεινὴ ἐπεσκίασεν αὐτούς,
καὶ ἰδοὺ φωνὴ ἐκ τῆς νεφέλης λέγουσα, Οὗτός ἐστιν ὁ υἱός μου ὁ
ἀγαπητός, ἐν ᾧ εὐδόκησα· ἀκούετε αὐτοῦ. 17:6 καὶ ἀκούσαντες οἱ
μαθηταὶ ἔπεσαν ἐπὶ πρόσωπον αὐτῶν καὶ ἐφοβήθησαν σφόδρα.
17:7 καὶ προσῆλθεν ὁ Ἰησοῦς καὶ ἁψάμενος αὐτῶν εἶπεν, Ἐγέρθητε
καὶ μὴ φοβεῖσθε. 17:8 ἐπάραντες δὲ τοὺς ὀφθαλμοὺς αὐτῶν οὐδένα
εἶδον εἰ μὴ αὐτὸν Ἰησοῦν μόνον.

17:5
ἔτι yet, still (adverb)
νεφέλη, ης, ἡ cloud
φωτεινός, ή, όν radiant, bright, shining; full of light, enlightened, illuminated
ἐπισκιάζω, ἐπισκιάσω, ἐπεσκίασα overshadow, cast a shadow; cover
φωνή, ῆς, ἡ voice, sound
οὗτος, αὕτη, τοῦτο this, this one (demonstrative pronoun)
ἀγαπητός, ή, όν beloved, dear
εὐδοκέω, εὐδοκήσω, εὐδόκησα/ηὐδόκησα be well pleased, take delight
17:6
ἐπί on, to, upon, towards, against (+ accusative)
πρόσωπον, ου, τό face, countenance
φοβέομαι, φοβηθήσομαι, ἐφοβήθην be afraid, become frightened
σφόδρα greatly, exceedingly (adverb)
17:7
ἅπτω, ἅψω, ἧψα fasten; light, kindle; touch (middle)
17:8
ἐπαίρω, ἐπαρῶ, ἐπῆρα, ἐπήρθην lift up, hold up
οὐδείς, οὐδεμία, οὐδέν no (adjective); no one, nobody, nothing (substantive)
μόνος, η, ον only, alone

17:5 **ἔτι αὐτοῦ λαλοῦντος**: *while he was still speaking*; the construction is a genitive absolute. **εὐδόκησα**: *I am well pleased*; the verbal form is a gnomic aorist. The aorist may be used to express a general truth where the experience of an action in the past suggests an action that is likely to be repeated. **ἀκούετε αὐτοῦ**: the verb takes the genitive of the person.

17:6 **ἀκούσαντες**: *when they had heard this*; supply ταῦτα as the object of the circumstantial participle.

17:7 **ἁψάμενος αὐτῶν**: the participle governs the genitive case.

17:9 Καὶ καταβαινόντων αὐτῶν ἐκ τοῦ ὄρους ἐνετείλατο αὐτοῖς ὁ
Ἰησοῦς λέγων, Μηδενὶ εἴπητε τὸ ὅραμα ἕως οὗ ὁ υἱὸς τοῦ ἀνθρώπου
ἐκ νεκρῶν ἐγερθῇ. 17:10 καὶ ἐπηρώτησαν αὐτὸν οἱ μαθηταὶ λέγοντες,
Τί οὖν οἱ γραμματεῖς λέγουσιν ὅτι Ἠλίαν δεῖ ἐλθεῖν πρῶτον; 17:11
ὁ δὲ ἀποκριθεὶς εἶπεν, Ἠλίας μὲν ἔρχεται καὶ ἀποκαταστήσει πάντα·
17:12 λέγω δὲ ὑμῖν ὅτι Ἠλίας ἤδη ἦλθεν, καὶ οὐκ ἐπέγνωσαν αὐτὸν
ἀλλὰ ἐποίησαν ἐν αὐτῷ ὅσα ἠθέλησαν· οὕτως καὶ ὁ υἱὸς τοῦ ἀνθρώπου
μέλλει πάσχειν ὑπ' αὐτῶν.

17:9
καταβαίνω, καταβήσομαι, κατέβην, καταβέβηκα come down, go down, descend, fall
ὄρος, ους, τό mountain, hill
ἐντέλλομαι, ἐντελοῦμαι, ἐνετειλάμην, ἐντέταλμαι command, order, enjoin
μηδείς, μηδεμία, μηδέν not one, none, no one, nothing
ὅραμα, ατος, τό a thing seen, sight, appearance; vision
ἕως while, as long as, until; ἕως οὗ until
νεκρός, ά, όν dead
17:10
ἐπερωτάω, ἐπερωτήσω, ἐπηρώτησα ask, inquire of, question, ask a question, request, beseech
γραμματεύς, έως, ὁ secretary, clerk, scholar versed in law, scribe
δεῖ it is necessary, it is proper (an impersonal verb from δέω)
πρῶτον first (in time; adverb)
17:11
ἀποκαθίστημι/ἀποκαθιστάνω, ἀποκαταστήσω, ἀπεκατέστην (2 aorist), ἀπεκατεστάθην restore, bring back, give back
17:12
ἤδη now, already (adverb)
ἐπιγινώσκω, ἐπιγνώσομαι, ἐπέγνων (2 aorist), ἐπέγνωκα, ἐπεγνώσθην know, understand, recognize; discern, detect
ὅσος, η, ον how large, how great; as many as (plural); whosoever, whatsoever
μέλλω, μελλήσω be about to, be on the point of
πάσχω, πείσομαι, ἔπαθον, πέπονθα suffer, endure, undergo

17:9 **ἐκ τοῦ ὄρους**: the noun is a third declension with stem in **σ** elided (cf. App. 15). **εἴπητε** is a prohibitive subjunctive. **ἕως οὗ . . . ἐγερθῇ**: *until . . . has been raised*; the temporal conjunction with the relative in the genitive takes the aorist subjunctive.

17:10 **δεῖ ἐλθεῖν πρῶτον**: *must come first*; the impersonal verb introduces an accusative and infinitive construction.

17:11 **ἔρχεται**: the present tense connotes a future. Jesus turns their question into an affirmative response.

17:12 **ἤδε ἦλθεν**: *already came*. **ἐν αὐτῷ**: *to him*; John the Baptist was an Elijah in preparing the way of the Lord's first coming (11:11–14); Elijah the Tishbite will prepare the Lord's second coming.

17:13 τότε συνῆκαν οἱ μαθηταὶ ὅτι περὶ Ἰωάννου τοῦ βαπτιστοῦ εἶπεν αὐτοῖς.

17:14 Καὶ ἐλθόντων πρὸς τὸν ὄχλον προσῆλθεν αὐτῷ ἄνθρωπος γονυπετῶν αὐτὸν 17:15 καὶ λέγων, Κύριε, ἐλέησόν μου τὸν υἱόν, ὅτι σεληνιάζεται καὶ κακῶς πάσχει· πολλάκις γὰρ πίπτει εἰς τὸ πῦρ καὶ πολλάκις εἰς τὸ ὕδωρ. 17:16 καὶ προσήνεγκα αὐτὸν τοῖς μαθηταῖς σου, καὶ οὐκ ἠδυνήθησαν αὐτὸν θεραπεῦσαι. 17:17 ἀποκριθεὶς δὲ ὁ Ἰησοῦς εἶπεν, Ὦ γενεὰ ἄπιστος καὶ διεστραμμένη, ἕως πότε μεθ' ὑμῶν ἔσομαι; ἕως πότε ἀνέξομαι ὑμῶν; φέρετέ μοι αὐτὸν ὧδε.

17:13
συνίημι/συνίω, συνήσω/συνήσομαι, συνῆκα (1 aorist) send together; understand, comprehend, perceive clearly
περί about, concerning (preposition + genitive); about, around (+ accusative)
17:14
γονυπετέω, γονυπετήσω, ἐγονυπέτησα fall on one's knees before, kneel before
17:15
ἐλεέω, ἐλεήσω, ἠλέησα, ἠλέημαι, ἠλεήθην pity, show mercy
σεληνιάζομαι, σεληνιάσομαι be lunatic, be moon-struck
κακῶς ill, badly, wickedly, wrongly (adverb)
πάσχω, πείσομαι, ἔπαθον, πέπονθα suffer, endure, undergo
πολλάκις many times, often, frequently (adverb)
πῦρ, πυρός, τό fire
ὕδωρ, ὕδατος, τό water
17:16
δύναμαι, δυνήσομαι, ἠδυνήθην be able
17:17
γενεά, ᾶς, ἡ progeny, generation
ἄπιστος, ον unbelieving, incredulous
διαστρέφω, διαστρέψω, διέστραμμαι distort, pervert, corrupt
ἕως πότε; how long?
ἀνέχομαι, ἀνέξομαι endure, bear with; suffer
ὧδε here (adverb)

17:13 **συνῆκαν**: The verb of perceiving introduces a ὅτι clause in indirect discourse.

17:14 **ἐλθόντων**: supply *αὐτῶν* as the subject to complete the genitive absolute construction (9, 22).

17:15 **σεληνιάζεται**: the ancients probably associated epileptic seizures with the moon σελήνη, the Latin *luna*. The context suggests that the verb is equal to δαιμονίζεται.

17:16 **προσήνεγκα** is the first aorist of προσφέρω.

17:17 **ἄπιστος**: adjectives of two terminations have the same form for the masculine and feminine (cf. App. 18). **διέστραμμένη**: *perverse*.

17:18 καὶ ἐπετίμησεν αὐτῷ ὁ Ἰησοῦς καὶ ἐξῆλθεν ἀπ' αὐτοῦ τὸ
δαιμόνιον καὶ ἐθεραπεύθη ὁ παῖς ἀπὸ τῆς ὥρας ἐκείνης.
17:19 Τότε προσελθόντες οἱ μαθηταὶ τῷ Ἰησοῦ κατ' ἰδίαν εἶπον,
Διὰ τί ἡμεῖς οὐκ ἠδυνήθημεν ἐκβαλεῖν αὐτό; 17:20 ὁ δὲ λέγει
αὐτοῖς, Διὰ τὴν ὀλιγοπιστίαν ὑμῶν· ἀμὴν γὰρ λέγω ὑμῖν, ἐὰν ἔχητε
πίστιν ὡς κόκκον σινάπεως, ἐρεῖτε τῷ ὄρει τούτῳ, Μετάβα ἔνθεν
ἐκεῖ, καὶ μεταβήσεται· καὶ οὐδὲν ἀδυνατήσει ὑμῖν.

17:18

ἐπιτιμάω, ἐπιτιμήσω, ἐπετίμησα set a value on; assess a penalty; rebuke, reprove, censure, reprimand; admonish, enjoin

δαιμόνιον, ου, τό deity, divinity; demon, evil spirit

παῖς, παιδός, ὁ child, boy, youth; servant

ὥρα, ας, ἡ hour

17:19

ἴδιος, ία, ιον one's own; κατ' ἰδίαν privately, by oneself, alone (adverb)

διὰ τί why?

17:20

ὀλιγοπιστία, ας, ἡ weakness of faith, scantiness of faith, poverty of faith

πίστις, εως, ἡ faith, trust

κόκκος, ου, ὁ kernel, seed

σίναπι, εως, τό mustard

μεταβαίνω, μεταβήσομαι, μετέβην, μεταβέβηκα go, pass over, move

ἔνθεν hence, from here, from this place (adverb)

ἐκεῖ there, in that place; thither, to that place (adverb)

ἀδυνατέω, ἀδυνατήσω not to be able; be impossible

17:18 **αὐτῷ**: understand τῷ δαιμονίῳ.

17:20 **ἐρεῖτε** is the second person plural future active indicative of λέγω. The future is conjugated like the present active indicative of a contracted verb with stem in **ε** (cf. App. 56). **Μετάβα**: "to move a mountain" is a common idiom that means to overcome what is thought to be an ἀδύνατον, an impossible task. **μεταβήσεται**: the verb form is a third person singular future deponent indicative. Only the future tense of this verb is deponent. **οὐδὲν** is used as a substantive and is the subject of the sentence.

17:21 The best manuscripts omit this verse: **τοῦτο δὲ τὸ γένος οὐκ ἐκπορεύεται εἰ μὴ ἐν προσευχῇ καὶ νηστείᾳ**: *but this sort does not come out except by prayer and fasting.*

17:22 Συστρεφομένων δὲ αὐτῶν ἐν τῇ Γαλιλαίᾳ εἶπεν αὐτοῖς ὁ Ἰησοῦς, Μέλλει ὁ υἱὸς τοῦ ἀνθρώπου παραδίδοσθαι εἰς χεῖρας ἀνθρώπων, 17:23 καὶ ἀποκτενοῦσιν αὐτόν, καὶ τῇ τρίτῃ ἡμέρᾳ ἐγερθήσεται. καὶ ἐλυπήθησαν σφόδρα.

17:24 Ἐλθόντων δὲ αὐτῶν εἰς Καφαρναοὺμ προσῆλθον οἱ τὰ δίδραχμα λαμβάνοντες τῷ Πέτρῳ καὶ εἶπαν, Ὁ διδάσκαλος ὑμῶν οὐ τελεῖ [τὰ] δίδραχμα; 17:25 λέγει, Ναί.

17:22
συστρέφω, συστρέψω turn together; collect, gather
μέλλω, μελλήσω be about to, be on the point of
παραδίδωμι, παραδώσω, παρέδωκα, παρέδων (2 aorist), παραδέδωκα, παραδέδομαι, παρεδόθην give, hand over, give over, deliver, give up, betray
17:23
ἀποκτείνω, ἀποκτενῶ, ἀπέκτεινα, ἀπεκτάνθην kill
τρίτος, η, ον third
λυπέω, λυπήσω, ἐλύπησα, λελύπηκα, ἐλυπήθην vex, irritate, offend (active); be grieved, pained, distressed (passive)
σφόδρα greatly, exceedingly (adverb)
17:24
δίδραχμον, ου, τό a double drachma (paid to the temple treasury at Jerusalem)
διδάσκαλος, ου, ὁ master, teacher
τελέω, τελέσω, ἐτέλεσα, τετέλεκα, τετέλεσμαι, ἐτελέσθην finish, fulfill, accomplish, make an end; pay dues, pay tax
17:25
ναί yes, indeed, certainly (particle of affirmation)

17:22 **Μέλλει . . . παραδίδοσθαι**: unlike in Attic Greek, μέλλω is regularly followed by a present infinitive in Koine. The periphrastic future construction denotes the certainty of a future event. παραδίδοσθαι is the present passive infinitive (cf. App. 58).

17:23 **ἀποκτενοῦσιν**: the future is conjugated like the present active indicative of a contracted verb with stem in **ε** (cf. App. 56).

17:24 **οἱ τὰ δίδραχμα λαμβάνοντες**: *those who collect the double drachma tax*; the coin worth about 36 cents was the sum required of each person per year as a temple tax. **οὐ τελεῖ**: *does not pay, does he*; the negative used in direct questions expects an affirmative answer.

καὶ ἐλθόντα εἰς τὴν οἰκίαν προέφθασεν αὐτὸν ὁ Ἰησοῦς λέγων, Τί σοι δοκεῖ, Σίμων; οἱ βασιλεῖς τῆς γῆς ἀπὸ τίνων λαμβάνουσιν τέλη ἢ κῆνσον; ἀπὸ τῶν υἱῶν αὐτῶν ἢ ἀπὸ τῶν ἀλλοτρίων; 17:26 εἰπόντος δέ, Ἀπὸ τῶν ἀλλοτρίων, ἔφη αὐτῷ ὁ Ἰησοῦς, Ἄρα γε ἐλεύθεροί εἰσιν οἱ υἱοί. 17:27 ἵνα δὲ μὴ σκανδαλίσωμεν αὐτούς, πορευθεὶς εἰς θάλασσαν βάλε ἄγκιστρον καὶ τὸν ἀναβάντα πρῶτον ἰχθὺν ἆρον, καὶ ἀνοίξας τὸ στόμα αὐτοῦ εὑρήσεις στατῆρα· ἐκεῖνον λαβὼν δὸς αὐτοῖς ἀντὶ ἐμοῦ καὶ σοῦ.

17:25

προφθάνω, προφθάσω, προέφθασα outstrip, anticipate, be beforehand

δοκεῖ it seems; it seems good, best, or right (impersonal verb)

βασιλεύς, έως, ὁ king

τέλος, ους, τό end, fulfillment, completion; custom, tax, duty

ἤ either, or, than (conjunction)

κῆνσος, ου, ὁ tribute, tax, poll-tax

ἀλλότριος, ία, ιον strange, foreign; stranger, foreigner

17:26

ἄρα therefore, then, consequently (particle)

γε at least, indeed (an enclitic particle emphasizing the preceding word; often untranslatable)

ἐλεύθερος, α, ον free, independent

17:27

σκανδαλίζω, σκανδαλίσω, ἐσκανδάλισα, ἐσκανδαλίσθην offend, anger, shock

ἄγκιστρον, ου, τό hook, fish-hook

ἀναβαίνω, ἀναβήσομαι, ἀνέβην, ἀναβέβηκα go up, ascend, rise

πρῶτος, η, ον first, before, earlier, foremost

ἰχθύς, ύος, ὁ fish

αἴρω, ἀρῶ, ἦρα, ἦρκα, ἦρμαι, ἤρθην take up, bear, take away, lift, carry, remove; keep in suspense; destroy, kill

ἀνοίγω, ἀνοίξω, ἀνέῳξα/ἤνοιξα, ἀνέῳγα, ἀνέῳγμαι, ἠνεῴχθην open

στόμα, ατος, τό mouth

στατήρ, ῆρος, ὁ stater (an attic silver coin equivalent to a double drachma)

ἀντί in place of, for, upon (preposition + genitive)

17:25 **προέφθασεν . . . λέγων**: *was the first to address him*; λέγων is a supplementary participle. The meaning is that Jesus anticipated Peter's question about taxes. A supplementary participle completes the idea of the main verb. **Τί σοι δοκεῖ**: the idiom means *what do you think*. **ἀπὸ τίνων**: *from whom*; τίνων is an interrogative pronoun. Jesus employs a dialectical method of teaching Peter. **τέλη ἢ κῆνσον**: τέλη is a neuter plural accusative third declension noun with stem in **σ** elided (cf. App. 15). From κῆνσον derives our English *census*.

17:26 **εἰπόντος δέ**: *but when he said*; supply αὐτοῦ. The construction is a genitive absolute. **ἐλεύθεροί εἰσιν οἱ υἱοί**: the argument runs: just as the sons of mortal kings do not pay tribute, Jesus and the disciples as sons of the divine king are exempt from temple tax.

17:27 **πορευθεὶς . . . βάλε**: *go and cast*; proof follows instruction and argument.

18 Ἐν ἐκείνῃ τῇ ὥρᾳ προσῆλθον οἱ μαθηταὶ τῷ Ἰησοῦ λέγοντες,
Τίς ἄρα μείζων ἐστὶν ἐν τῇ βασιλείᾳ τῶν οὐρανῶν; 18:2 καὶ
προσκαλεσάμενος παιδίον ἔστησεν αὐτὸ ἐν μέσῳ αὐτῶν 18:3 καὶ
εἶπεν, Ἀμὴν λέγω ὑμῖν, ἐὰν μὴ στραφῆτε καὶ γένησθε ὡς τὰ παιδία,
οὐ μὴ εἰσέλθητε εἰς τὴν βασιλείαν τῶν οὐρανῶν. 18:4 ὅστις οὖν
ταπεινώσει ἑαυτὸν ὡς τὸ παιδίον τοῦτο, οὗτός ἐστιν ὁ μείζων ἐν τῇ
βασιλείᾳ τῶν οὐρανῶν.

18:1

ἄρα therefore, then, consequently (particle)

μείζων, μείζον greater, larger

18:2

προσκαλέω, προσκαλέσω, προσεκάλεσα, προσκέκληκα, προσκέκλημαι, προσεκλήθην call on, summon, invite, call to oneself

ἵστημι, στήσω, ἔστησα, ἔστην (2 aorist), ἕστηκα, ἐστάθην put, place, set, cause to stand (transitive); stand, be (intransitive)

μέσος, η, ον middle, in, among (as adjective + genitive); the middle (as noun τὸ μέσον)

18:3

στρέφω, στρέψω, ἔστρεψα, ἔστραμμαι, ἐστρέφθην, ἐστράφην (2 aorist passive) turn, make a change, change

18:4

ταπεινόω, ταπεινώσω, ἐταπείνωσα bring low; humble

μείζων, μείζον greater, larger

18:1 **μείζων**: the comparative stands for a superlative. The wrangling for rank takes place in the intimate circle of the twelve.

18:2 **ἔστησεν αὐτὸ**: *He placed*; the first aorist is transitive. The pronoun is pleonastic but adds greater definiteness and emphasis.

18:3 **ἐὰν μὴ στραφῆτε**: *unless you are converted*; the verb is a second aorist subjunctive. **οὐ μὴ εἰσέλθητε**: the double negative indicates a strong negation and usually takes an aorist subjunctive that is equivalent to a future indicative. It is the apodosis of a future more vivid condition (App. 70).

18:4 **ὅστις . . . ταπεινώσει** is the protasis of a simple or particular condition.

18:5 καὶ ὃς ἐὰν δέξηται ἓν παιδίον τοιοῦτο ἐπὶ τῷ ὀνόματί μου, ἐμὲ
δέχεται.
18:6 Ὃς δ' ἂν σκανδαλίσῃ ἕνα τῶν μικρῶν τούτων τῶν
πιστευόντων εἰς ἐμέ, συμφέρει αὐτῷ ἵνα κρεμασθῇ μύλος ὀνικὸς περὶ
τὸν τράχηλον αὐτοῦ καὶ καταποντισθῇ ἐν τῷ πελάγει τῆς θαλάσσης.

18:5

δέχομαι, δέξομαι, ἐδεξάμην, δέδεγμαι take, receive, welcome, accept

18:6

σκανδαλίζω, σκανδαλίσω, ἐσκανδάλισα, ἐσκανδαλίσθην offend, anger, shock

μικρός, ά, όν small, short, little; little one (substantive)

πιστεύω, πιστεύσω, ἐπίστευσα, πεπίστευκα, πεπίστευμαι, ἐπιστεύθην believe; entrust

συμφέρει it is profitable, expedient, advantageous, good or better (impersonal verb)

κρεμάννυμι, κρεμάσω, ἐκρέμασα, ἐκρεμάσθην hang, suspend

μύλος, ου, ὁ millstone

ὀνικός, ή, όν of an ass, for an ass, turned by an ass

τράχηλος, ου, ὁ neck

καταποντίζω, καταποντίσω, κατεπόντισα, κατεποντίσθην throw into the sea, sink, submerge

πέλαγος, εος, τό the high sea, the deep, open sea

18:5 **ὃς ἐὰν δέξηται** is the protasis of a present general condition.

18:6 **Ὃς δ' ἂν σκανδαλίσῃ ... συμφέρει αὐτῷ** is an anacoluthon or a syntactic non sequitur in which Ὃς starts as the subject, but ends up as the object of the verb. **ἕνα τῶν μικρῶν τούτων τῶν πιστευόντων εἰς ἐμέ**: μικρῶν is a partitive genitive (cf. App. 65). The article turns the adjective into a substantive. Jesus is now expanding the discussion to include warnings against members who would offend other members: *these little ones* are children of God, those who have humbled themselves like a child, and those who believe in Him. The **ἵνα** clause is the subject of the quasi-impersonal verb. **καταποντισθῇ ἐν τῷ πελάγει τῆς θαλάσσης**: the three references to the sea are pleonastic but add greater definiteness and emphasis.

18:7 οὐαὶ τῷ κόσμῳ ἀπὸ τῶν σκανδάλων· ἀνάγκη γὰρ ἐλθεῖν τὰ
σκάνδαλα, πλὴν οὐαὶ τῷ ἀνθρώπῳ δι' οὗ τὸ σκάνδαλον ἔρχεται.
18:8 Εἰ δὲ ἡ χείρ σου ἢ ὁ πούς σου σκανδαλίζει σε, ἔκκοψον αὐτὸν
καὶ βάλε ἀπὸ σοῦ· καλόν σοί ἐστιν εἰσελθεῖν εἰς τὴν ζωὴν κυλλὸν
ἢ χωλὸν ἢ δύο χεῖρας ἢ δύο πόδας ἔχοντα βληθῆναι εἰς τὸ πῦρ τὸ
αἰώνιον. 18:9 καὶ εἰ ὁ ὀφθαλμός σου σκανδαλίζει σε, ἔξελε αὐτὸν καὶ
βάλε ἀπὸ σοῦ·

18:7

οὐαί woe! alas! (interjection)

κόσμος, ου, ὁ order, world, universe

σκάνδαλον, ου, τό stumbling block, impediment; temptation to sin; that which gives offense, that which is offensive; scandal, offense

ἀνάγκη, ης, ἡ necessity, compulsion, obligation; ἀνάγκη (sc. ἐστὶν) it is necessary, inevitable, one must (with infinitive, or accusative and infinitive)

πλήν besides, except (adverb); but, however, nevertheless (conjunction)

18:8

πούς, ποδός, ὁ foot

σκανδαλίζω, σκανδαλίσω, ἐσκανδάλισα, ἐσκανδαλίσθην offend, anger, shock

ἐκκόπτω, ἐκκόψω, ἐξέκοψα, ἐξεκόπην cut out, cut off

ζωή, ῆς, ἡ life, life eternal

κυλλός, ή, όν crooked; lame, crippled

χωλός, ή, όν lame, crippled

δύο two

πῦρ, πυρός, τό fire

αἰώνιος, ον (αἰώνιος, ία, ιον) eternal, everlasting

18:9

σκανδαλίζω, σκανδαλίσω, ἐσκανδάλισα, ἐσκανδαλίσθην offend, anger, shock

ἐξαιρέω, ἐξελῶ, ἐξεῖλον take out, tear out

18:7 **οὐαὶ τῷ κόσμῳ**: *woe to the world*; the exclamatory interjection governs the dative of person or thing. **ἀνάγκη . . . ἐλθεῖν τὰ σκάνδαλα**: *offenses must come* (literally: *it is necessary that offenses come*); the infinitive clause is the subject of the quasi-impersonal verb. It is expected that offenses will come from the world.

18:8 **Εἰ δὲ . . . ἔκκοψον αὐτὸν**: the language in this and the following verse is similar to that of the warning about adultery (5:29–30). The metaphorical language stresses the seriousness of obligation of members to each other and the importance of rooting out and casting away, like a cancerous growth, from the body of the church those who commit offense or sin against those who are humble and believe. **καλόν σοί ἐστιν** is used like συμφέρει σοι: *it is better for you* in a comparison of two ideas. **τὴν ζωὴν** is *life eternal* in constrast to **τὸ πῦρ τὸ αἰώνιον**. **ἢ . . . ἢ . . . ἢ**: the first conjunction is *or,* joining two adjectives; the second *rather than,* joining two infinitives; the third *or,* joining two nouns.

καλόν σοί ἐστιν μονόφθαλμον εἰς τὴν ζωὴν εἰσελθεῖν ἢ δύο ὀφθαλμοὺς ἔχοντα βληθῆναι εἰς τὴν γέενναν τοῦ πυρός.

18:10 Ὁρᾶτε μὴ καταφρονήσητε ἑνὸς τῶν μικρῶν τούτων· λέγω γὰρ ὑμῖν ὅτι οἱ ἄγγελοι αὐτῶν ἐν οὐρανοῖς διὰ παντὸς βλέπουσι τὸ πρόσωπον τοῦ πατρός μου τοῦ ἐν οὐρανοῖς.

18:9

μονόφθαλμος, ον one-eyed; deprived of an eye

γέεννα, ης, ἡ Gehenna, Valley of Hinnom, hell, the fires of Tartarus (a place known for sacrifices to Moloch, pollution, pestilence, punishment of malefactors, and continually burning fires)

18:10

καταφρονέω, καταφρονήσω, κατεφρόνησα look down on, scorn, despise

μικρός, ά, όν small, short, little; little one (substantive)

διὰ παντός (sc. χρονοῦ) always, continuously, constantly

βλέπω, βλέψω, ἔβλεψα see, behold, perceive

πρόσωπον, ου, τό face, countenance

18:10 **Ὁρᾶτε μὴ καταφρονήσητε**: *see to it that you do not despise*; the verb is a second person plural present active imperative of a contracted verb with stem in **α** (cf. App. 55). μὴ introduces a negative clause of purpose. καταφρονήσητε governs the genitive case. **ἑνὸς τῶν μικρῶν τούτων**: μικρῶν is a partitive genitive (cf. App. 65). The article turns the adjective into a substantive. **οἱ ἄγγελοι αὐτῶν**: these children of God have divine representatives and messengers. **βλέπουσι τὸ πρόσωπον τοῦ πατρός**: they have direct access to the Father.

18:11 The best manuscripts omit this verse: **ἦλθεν γὰρ ὁ υἱὸς τοῦ ἀνθρώπου ζητῆσαι καὶ σῶσαι τὸ ἀπολωλός**: *for the Son of Man came to seek and save that which is lost*; the conjunction γὰρ is used to explain that the previous action of offending and leading astray is antithetical to the purposes of God and the mission of Jesus. ζητῆσαι και σῶσαι are infinitives of purpose. This purpose construction is particularly prevalent after main verbs of motion like ἔρχομαι.

18:12 Τί ὑμῖν δοκεῖ; ἐὰν γένηταί τινι ἀνθρώπῳ ἑκατὸν πρόβατα καὶ πλανηθῇ ἓν ἐξ αὐτῶν, οὐχὶ ἀφήσει τὰ ἐνενήκοντα ἐννέα ἐπὶ τὰ ὄρη καὶ πορευθεὶς ζητεῖ τὸ πλανώμενον; 18:13 καὶ ἐὰν γένηται εὑρεῖν αὐτό, ἀμὴν λέγω ὑμῖν ὅτι χαίρει ἐπ' αὐτῷ μᾶλλον ἢ ἐπὶ τοῖς ἐνενήκοντα ἐννέα τοῖς μὴ πεπλανημένοις.

18:12
δοκεῖ it seems; it seems good, best, or right (impersonal verb)
ἑκατόν, οἱ, αἱ, τά one hundred (indeclinable)
πρόβατον, ου, τό sheep
πλανάω, πλανήσω, ἐπλάνησα, πεπλάνημαι, ἐπλανήθην lead astray, cause to wander, mislead, deceive; go astray, wander about, stray (passive)
οὐχί not; no, by no means (adverb; more intensive form of οὐ)
ἐνενήκοντα ninety (indeclinable)
ἐννέα nine (indeclinable)
ὄρος, ους, τό mountain, hill
ζητέω, ζητήσω, ἐζήτησα, ἐζητήθην seek, desire, ask for
18:13
χαίρω, χαρήσομαι, ἐχάρην (2 aorist passive) rejoice, be glad; χαῖρε, χαίρετε hail, greetings, welcome (as a form of greeting)
μᾶλλον more, to a greater degree, rather (adverb)
ἐνενήκοντα ninety (indeclinable)
ἐννέα nine (indeclinable)
πλανάω, πλανήσω, ἐπλάνησα, πεπλάνημαι, ἐπλανήθην lead astray, cause to wander, mislead, deceive; go astray, wander about, stray (passive)

18:12 **Τί ὑμῖν δοκεῖ**: the idiom means *what do you think*. **ἐὰν γένηταί τινι ἀνθρώπῳ ἑκατὸν πρόβατα**: *if a certain man has a hundred sheep*; τινι ἀνθρώπῳ is a dative of possession. **ἀφήσει** is the third person singular future active indicative of ἀφίημι. **πλανώμενον**: *that is straying*; the verbal form is a neuter singular accusative present passive participle of a contracted verb with stem in **α** (cf. App. 55).

18:13 **ἐὰν γένηται εὑρεῖν αὐτό**: *if he actually finds it* (literally: *if it comes about that he finds it*). the construction emphasizes the actual occurrence of the action denoted by the infinitive. **ἐπ' αὐτῷ μᾶλλον ἤ**: *more over it than*; in this construction, both members being compared must be in the same case.

18:14 οὕτως οὐκ ἔστιν θέλημα ἔμπροσθεν τοῦ πατρὸς ὑμῶν τοῦ ἐν οὐρανοῖς ἵνα ἀπόληται ἓν τῶν μικρῶν τούτων.

18:15 Ἐὰν δὲ ἁμαρτήσῃ [εἰς σὲ] ὁ ἀδελφός σου, ὕπαγε ἔλεγξον αὐτὸν μεταξὺ σοῦ καὶ αὐτοῦ μόνου. ἐάν σου ἀκούσῃ, ἐκέρδησας τὸν ἀδελφόν σου· 18:16 ἐὰν δὲ μὴ ἀκούσῃ, παράλαβε μετὰ σοῦ ἔτι ἕνα ἢ δύο, ἵνα ἐπὶ στόματος δύο μαρτύρων ἢ τριῶν σταθῇ πᾶν ῥῆμα· 18:17 ἐὰν δὲ παρακούσῃ αὐτῶν, εἰπὲ τῇ ἐκκλησίᾳ· ἐὰν δὲ καὶ τῆς ἐκκλησίας παρακούσῃ, ἔστω σοι ὥσπερ ὁ ἐθνικὸς καὶ ὁ τελώνης.

18:14
θέλημα, ατος, τό will, desire
ἔμπροσθεν in front of, before, in the presence of (adverb; preposition + genitive)
μικρός, ά, όν small, short, little; little one (substantive)

18:15
ἁμαρτάνω, ἁμαρτήσω, ἡμάρτησα or ἥμαρτον, ἡμάρτηκα, ἡμάρτημαι, ἡμαρτήθην do wrong, sin
ὑπάγω, ὑπάξω, ὑπήγαγον, ὑπήχθην go, go away, go home
μεταξύ between (adverb, preposition + genitive)
μόνος, η, ον only, alone
κερδαίνω, κερδήσω, ἐκέρδησα gain, acquire

18:16
ἔτι yet, still (adverb)
στόμα, ατος, τό mouth
δύο two
μάρτυς, μάρτυρος, ὁ and ἡ witness
τρεῖς, τρία three
ῥῆμα, ατος, τό word, saying, expression, speech

18:17
παρακούω, παρακούσομαι fail to listen, disregard
ἐκκλησία, ας, ἡ congregation, church
ἐθνικός, ή, όν gentile, heathen
τελώνης, ου, ὁ tax-collector, publican

18:14 **οὕτως οὐκ ἔστιν θέλημα ἔμπροσθεν τοῦ πατρὸς ὑμῶν . . . ἵνα**: *so it is not your Father's will that*; the formal but untranslatable ἔμπροσθεν is used instead of the direct genitive out of reverence for deity. **ἀπόληται**: *perish*; the verb is third person singular second aorist middle subjunctive of ἀπόλλυμι (cf. App. 54).

18:15 **Ἐὰν δὲ ἁμαρτήσῃ [εἰς σε] ὁ ἀδελφός σου**: the theme of obligations of church members to each other continues. **ὕπαγε ἔλεγξον**: *go and tell*; ὕπαγε is a second person singular present active imperative (cf. App. 53, A, 3). Supply καὶ: the imperative is usually found without a conjunction when followed by another imperative. **σου ἀκούσῃ**: the verb governs the genitive of the person.

18:16 **σταθῇ**: *may be established*; the verb is third person singular aorist passive subjunctive.

18:17 **παρακούσῃ αὐτῶν**: the verb governs the genitive of the person. **ἔστω σοι ὥσπερ ὁ ἐθνικὸς καὶ ὁ τελώνης**: the injunction indicates that the unrepentant offender be disciplined and no longer be treated as a member of the community.

18:18 Ἀμὴν λέγω ὑμῖν· ὅσα ἐὰν δήσητε ἐπὶ τῆς γῆς ἔσται δεδεμένα ἐν οὐρανῷ, καὶ ὅσα ἐὰν λύσητε ἐπὶ τῆς γῆς ἔσται λελυμένα ἐν οὐρανῷ. 18:19 Πάλιν [ἀμὴν] λέγω ὑμῖν ὅτι ἐὰν δύο συμφωνήσωσιν ἐξ ὑμῶν ἐπὶ τῆς γῆς περὶ παντὸς πράγματος οὗ ἐὰν αἰτήσωνται, γενήσεται αὐτοῖς παρὰ τοῦ πατρός μου τοῦ ἐν οὐρανοῖς. 18:20 οὗ γάρ εἰσιν δύο ἢ τρεῖς συνηγμένοι εἰς τὸ ἐμὸν ὄνομα, ἐκεῖ εἰμι ἐν μέσῳ αὐτῶν.

18:18
δέω, δήσω, ἔδησα, δέδεκα, δέδεμαι, ἐδέθην bind, tie, impede
λύω, λύσω, ἔλυσα, λέλυκα, λέλυμαι, ἐλύθην loose, unbind, unfasten, break, destroy
18:19
πάλιν again (adverb)
συμφονέω, συμφονήσω sound together, be in unison, be in accord; agree, be in agreement; make an agreement
πᾶς, πᾶσα, πᾶν every, all, each, any
πρᾶγμα, ατος, τό that which is done, fact, deed, transaction, thing, matter, affair
αἰτέω, αἰτήσω, ᾔτησα, ᾔτηκα ask, ask for, make a request
18:20
οὗ where, in what place (adverb)
δύο two
τρεῖς, τρία three
συνάγω, συνάξω, συνήγαγον (2 aorist), συνῆγμαι, συνήχθην gather in, gather up, bring together; convene, come together, meet (passive)
μέσος, η, ον middle, in, among (as adjective + genitive); the middle (as noun τὸ μέσον)

18:18 **ὅσα ἐὰν δήσητε**: binding actions include performing ordinances and covenants such as those made at baptism, at weddings, and on other occasions. Proper actions taken by proper authority on the earth will be in effect in the eternities. **ὅσα ἐὰν λύσητε**: actions such as excommunication, disfellowshipping, or other measures of forgiving trespasses may be included in this category. They provide a thematic connection with the previous verse.

18:19 **δύο ἐξ ὑμῶν . . . αἰτήσωνται . . . αὐτοῖς**: the person shifts (enallage) from second to third person plural. **περὶ παντὸς πράγματος οὗ ἐὰν αἰτήσωνται**: *concerning anything at all for which they ask*; the case of the relative pronoun οὗ is a genitive of attraction. The case is not determined by its use in the clause but is simply attracted to the case of its antecedent πράγματος. It is translated as a neuter singular accusative ὃ according to its natural grammatical construction. **γενήσεται αὐτοῖς**: *it will be done for them*; the pronoun is a dative of advantage.

18:21 Τότε προσελθὼν ὁ Πέτρος εἶπεν αὐτῷ, Κύριε, ποσάκις ἁμαρτήσει εἰς ἐμὲ ὁ ἀδελφός μου καὶ ἀφήσω αὐτῷ; ἕως ἑπτάκις; 18:22 λέγει αὐτῷ ὁ Ἰησοῦς, Οὐ λέγω σοι ἕως ἑπτάκις ἀλλὰ ἕως ἑβδομηκοντάκις ἑπτά. 18:23 Διὰ τοῦτο ὡμοιώθη ἡ βασιλεία τῶν οὐρανῶν ἀνθρώπῳ βασιλεῖ, ὃς ἠθέλησεν συνᾶραι λόγον μετὰ τῶν δούλων αὐτοῦ. 18:24 ἀρξαμένου δὲ αὐτοῦ συναίρειν προσηνέχθη αὐτῷ εἷς ὀφειλέτης μυρίων ταλάντων.

18:21
ποσάκις how many times? how often? (interrogative adverb)
ἁμαρτάνω, ἁμαρτήσω, ἡμάρτησα or ἥμαρτον, ἡμάρτηκα, ἡμάρτημαι, ἡμαρτήθην do wrong, sin
ἕως while, as long as, as many as, until
ἑπτάκις seven times (adverb)
18:22
ἑβδομηκοντάκις seventy times (adverb)
ἑπτά seven (indeclinable)
18:23
ὁμοιόω, ὁμοιώσω, ὁμοίωσα, ὡμοιώθην make like, liken, compare; be like, be made like, become like, resemble (passive)
συναίρω, συναρῶ, συνῆρα settle
δοῦλος, ου, ὁ slave, servant
18:24
ἄρχω, ἄρξω, ἦρξα, ἦρχα, ἦργμαι, ἤρχθην rule (active); begin (middle)
συναίρω, συναρῶ, συνῆρα settle
προσφέρω, προσοίσω, προσήνεγκα, προσήνεγκον (2 aorist), προσηνέχθην bring, offer, present
ὀφειλέτης, ου, ὁ debtor; offender; sinner
μύριοι, αι, α ten thousand
τάλαντον, ου, τό talent

18:21 **ἀφήσω αὐτῷ**: the verb is a first person future active indicative of ἀφίημι. The verb takes the dative of the person and the accusative of the thing.

18:22 **Οὐ λέγω σοι ἕως ἑπτάκις**: *I do not say to you as many as seven times*; ἕως denotes the upper limit of the number expected. **ἕως ἑβδομηκοντάκις ἑπτά**: the number may mean either seventy times seven or seventy-seven. In either case the total suggests an immeasurable number: forgiveness has no limit.

18:23 **ὡμοιώθη . . . ἀνθρώπῳ βασιλεῖ**: ἀνθρώπῳ is pleonastically used with another noun but adds greater definiteness and emphasis: *a certain king*. **συνᾶραι λόγον**: *to settle account*.

18:24 **ἀρξαμένου . . . αὐτοῦ** is a genitive absolute. **ὀφειλέτης μυρίων ταλάντων**: *who owed ten thousand talents*; the hyperbolic number of money owed suggests an immeasurable sum only to show the matchless mercy of the king to forgive the debtor. A debt is commonly equated with sin, and the king or master with Jesus.

18:25 μὴ ἔχοντος δὲ αὐτοῦ ἀποδοῦναι ἐκέλευσεν αὐτὸν ὁ κύριος πραθῆναι καὶ τὴν γυναῖκα καὶ τὰ τέκνα καὶ πάντα ὅσα ἔχει, καὶ ἀποδοθῆναι. 18:26 πεσὼν οὖν ὁ δοῦλος προσεκύνει αὐτῷ λέγων, Μακροθύμησον ἐπ' ἐμοί, καὶ πάντα ἀποδώσω σοι. 18:27 σπλαγχνισθεὶς δὲ ὁ κύριος τοῦ δούλου ἐκείνου ἀπέλυσεν αὐτὸν καὶ τὸ δάνειον ἀφῆκεν αὐτῷ. 18:28 ἐξελθὼν δὲ ὁ δοῦλος ἐκεῖνος εὗρεν ἕνα τῶν συνδούλων αὐτοῦ,

---

18:25
ἔχω, ἕξω, ἔσχον (2 aorist), ἔσχηκα have, keep, cause, consider; be (with adverbs and indications of time and age); be able (with infinitive)
ἀποδίδωμι, ἀποδώσω, ἀπέδωκα, ἀποδέδωκα, ἀποδέδομαι, ἀπεδόθην give away, pay
κελεύω, κελεύσω, ἐκέλευσα give order, command, urge, direct, bid
πιπράσκω, πέπρακα, πέπραμαι, ἐπράθην sell
τέκνον, ου, τό child, descendant, posterity
18:26
δοῦλος, ου, ὁ slave, servant
προσκυνέω, προσκυνήσω, προσεκύνησα worship, prostrate oneself before, reverence before, reverence
μακροθυμέω, μακροθυμήσω, ἐμακροθύμησα have patience, wait; be patient, forbearing
ἀποδίδωμι, ἀποδώσω, ἀπέδωκα, ἀποδέδωκα, ἀποδέδομαι, ἀπεδόθην give away, pay
18:27
σπλαγχνίζομαι, σπλαγχνίσομαι, ἐσπλαγχνίσθην have compassion, feel sympathy, be moved with pity
δοῦλος, ου, ὁ slave, servant
ἀπολύω, ἀπολύσω, ἀπέλυσα, ἀπολέλυκα, ἀπολέλυμαι, ἀπελύθην release, set free, pardon
δάνειον, ου, τό loan, debt
18:28
σύνδουλος, ου, ὁ fellow slave, fellow servant

18:25 **μὴ ἔχοντος δὲ αὐτοῦ ἀποδοῦναι**: *but since he was not able to pay*; the negative μὴ regularly modifies a participle.

18:26 **ἐπ' ἐμοί**: *with me.* **πάντα ἀποδώσω σοι**: *I will pay you all debts*; πάντα is a cognate accusative.

18:27 **δάνειον ἀφῆκεν αὐτῷ**: *forgave him the debt*; ἀφῆκεν is the first aorist of ἀφίημι. The verb governs a dative of the person and an accusative of the thing.

ὃς ὤφειλεν αὐτῷ ἑκατὸν δηνάρια, καὶ κρατήσας αὐτὸν ἔπνιγεν λέγων, Ἀπόδος εἴ τι ὀφείλεις. 18:29 πεσὼν οὖν ὁ σύνδουλος αὐτοῦ παρεκάλει αὐτὸν λέγων, Μακροθύμησον ἐπ᾽ ἐμοί, καὶ ἀποδώσω σοι. 18:30 ὁ δὲ οὐκ ἤθελεν ἀλλὰ ἀπελθὼν ἔβαλεν αὐτὸν εἰς φυλακὴν ἕως ἀποδῷ τὸ ὀφειλόμενον. 18:31 ἰδόντες οὖν οἱ σύνδουλοι αὐτοῦ τὰ γενόμενα ἐλυπήθησαν σφόδρα καὶ ἐλθόντες διεσάφησαν τῷ κυρίῳ ἑαυτῶν πάντα τὰ γενόμενα.

18:28

ὀφείλω (only in present and imperfect) owe, ought, must, deserve

ἑκατόν, οἱ, αἱ, τά one hundred (indeclinable)

δηνάριον, ου, τό denarius (a Roman silver coin)

κρατέω, κρατήσω, ἐκράτησα, κεκράτηκα, κεκράτημαι lay hold of, grasp; retain, not remit

πνίγω, πνίξω, ἔπνιξα choke, suffocate, strangle

ἀποδίδωμι, ἀποδώσω, ἀπέδωκα, ἀποδέδωκα, ἀποδέδομαι, ἀπεδόθην give away, pay

18:29

σύνδουλος, ου, ὁ fellow slave, fellow servant

παρακαλέω, παρακαλέσω, παρεκάλεσα, παρακέκληκα, παρακέκλημαι, παρεκλήθην call upon, exhort, persuade; beg, entreat; comfort, encourage, cheer up

μακροθυμέω, μακροθυμήσω, ἐμακροθύμησα have patience, wait; be patient, forbearing

18:30

φυλακή, ῆς, ἡ watch, guard, prison

ὀφείλω (only in present and imperfect) owe, ought, must, deserve

18:31

σύνδουλος, ου, ὁ fellow slave, fellow servant

λυπέω, λυπήσω, ἐλύπησα, λελύπηκα, ἐλυπήθην vex, irritate, offend (active); be grieved, pained, distressed (passive)

σφόδρα greatly, exceedingly (adverb)

διασαφέω, διασαφήσω, διεσάφησα make clear, explain; tell plainly, declare in detail, make known

---

18:28 **ἔπνιγεν**: *began to choke*; the imperfect tense denotes inchoative action (aspect) in past time.

18:29 **Μακροθύμησον**: the plea of the fellow servant is the same that he had made earlier to the master.

18:30 **ὁ δὲ οὐκ ἤθελεν**: by not forgiving the debt, he proves himself false: he expects to be forgiven but will not forgive another.

18:31 **ἰδόντες . . . τὰ γενόμενα**: they see the injustice of what had happened.

18:32 τότε προσκαλεσάμενος αὐτὸν ὁ κύριος αὐτοῦ λέγει αὐτῷ,
Δοῦλε πονηρέ, πᾶσαν τὴν ὀφειλὴν ἐκείνην ἀφῆκά σοι, ἐπεὶ
παρεκάλεσάς με· 18:33 οὐκ ἔδει καὶ σὲ ἐλεῆσαι τὸν σύνδουλόν σου,
ὡς κἀγὼ σὲ ἠλέησα; 18:34 καὶ ὀργισθεὶς ὁ κύριος αὐτοῦ παρέδωκεν
αὐτὸν τοῖς βασανισταῖς ἕως οὗ ἀποδῷ πᾶν τὸ ὀφειλόμενον.
18:35 Οὕτως καὶ ὁ πατήρ μου ὁ οὐράνιος ποιήσει ὑμῖν, ἐὰν μὴ
ἀφῆτε ἕκαστος τῷ ἀδελφῷ αὐτοῦ ἀπὸ τῶν καρδιῶν ὑμῶν.

18:32

προσκαλέομαι, προσκαλέσομαι, προσεκαλεσάμην, προσκέκλημαι summon, call on, invite, call to oneself

δοῦλος, ου, ὁ slave, servant

ὀφειλή, ῆς, ἡ debt

ἐπεί when, after; since, because, for (conjunction)

παρακαλέω, παρακαλέσω, παρεκάλεσα, παρακέκληκα, παρακέκλημαι, παρεκλήθην call upon, exhort, persuade; beg, entreat; comfort, encourage, cheer up

18:33

δεῖ, δεήσει, ἐδέησε it is necessary, it is proper (impersonal verb from δέω)

ἐλεέω, ἐλεήσω, ἠλέησα, ἠλέημαι, ἠλεήθην pity, show mercy

σύνδουλος, ου, ὁ fellow slave, fellow servant

18:34

ὀργίζω, ὀργίσω, ὠργίσθην provoke to anger; be angry at, be enraged at (passive + dative)

παραδίδωμι, παραδώσω, παρέδωκα, παρέδων (2 aorist), παραδέδωκα, παραδέδομαι, παρεδόθην give, hand over, give over, deliver, give up, betray

βασανιστής, οῦ, ὁ torturer, tormentor, jailer

ὀφείλω (only in present and imperfect) owe, ought, must, deserve

18:35

καρδία, ας, ἡ heart

18:32 **Δοῦλε πονηρέ** are in the vocative case.

18:33 **οὐκ ἔδει καὶ σὲ ἐλεῆσαι**: *should you not also have had pity*; the impersonal construction may be changed to a personal one. The past tense of the impersonal verb is transferred to the infinitive in English.

18:34 **ἕως οὗ ἀποδῷ πᾶν τὸ ὀφειλόμενον**: having lost the mercy of the lord, he is now left to his own resources to pay his debts.

18:35 **ἐὰν μὴ ἀφῆτε ἕκαστος τῷ ἀδελφῷ αὐτοῦ**: *if you do not forgive, every one his brother*; ἕκαστος stands in apposition to the pronoun of the verb. The verb governs the dative case.

19 Καὶ ἐγένετο ὅτε ἐτέλεσεν ὁ Ἰησοῦς τοὺς λόγους τούτους,
μετῆρεν ἀπὸ τῆς Γαλιλαίας καὶ ἦλθεν εἰς τὰ ὅρια τῆς Ἰουδαίας
πέραν τοῦ Ἰορδάνου. 19:2 καὶ ἠκολούθησαν αὐτῷ ὄχλοι πολλοί, καὶ
ἐθεράπευσεν αὐτοὺς ἐκεῖ.
19:3 Καὶ προσῆλθον αὐτῷ Φαρισαῖοι πειράζοντες αὐτὸν καὶ
λέγοντες, Εἰ ἔξεστιν ἀνθρώπῳ ἀπολῦσαι τὴν γυναῖκα αὐτοῦ κατὰ
πᾶσαν αἰτίαν;

19:1
ὅτε when, whenever (adverb)
τελέω, τελέσω, ἐτέλεσα, τετέλεκα, τετέλεσμαι, ἐτελέσθην finish, fulfill, accomplish, make an end
μεταίρω, μεταρῶ, μετῆρα go away, depart
ὅριον, ου, τό boundary; region, territory, district (plural)
πέραν across, beyond, on the other side of (preposition + genitive)
19:3
πειράζω, πειράσω, ἐπείρασα, πεπείρασμαι, ἐπειράσθην try, test, tempt, prove
ἔξεστι(ν) it is permitted, it is possible (impersonal verb)
εἰ if, whether; εἰ μή unless, except; an interrogatory particle introducing a direct question
κατά near, towards, by, in accordance with, for the purpose of, for, after the manner of (preposition + accusative); down from, against (+ genitive)
αἰτία, ας, ἡ ground for complaint, fault

19:1 **Καὶ ἐγένετο**: the finite verb, usually omitted in translation, is translated in older versions: *and it came to pass.*

19:3 **πειράζοντες**: they wanted to see whether he would uphold the law of Moses. **Εἰ** is an interrogatory particle introducing a direct question. **ἔξεστιν ἀνθρωπῷ ἀπολῦσαι**: the impersonal verb is followed by the dative of the person and an aorist infinitive. **κατὰ πᾶσαν αἰτίαν**: *for any and every cause.*

19:4 ὁ δὲ ἀποκριθεὶς εἶπεν, Οὐκ ἀνέγνωτε ὅτι ὁ κτίσας ἀπ' ἀρχῆς ἄρσεν καὶ θῆλυ ἐποίησεν αὐτούς; 19:5 καὶ εἶπεν, Ἕνεκα τούτου καταλείψει ἄνθρωπος τὸν πατέρα καὶ τὴν μητέρα καὶ κολληθήσεται τῇ γυναικὶ αὐτοῦ, καὶ ἔσονται οἱ δύο εἰς σάρκα μίαν. 19:6 ὥστε οὐκέτι εἰσὶν δύο ἀλλὰ σὰρξ μία. ὃ οὖν ὁ θεὸς συνέζευξεν ἄνθρωπος μὴ χωριζέτω.

19:4

ἀναγινώσκω, ἀναγνώσομαι, ἀνέγνων (2 aorist), ἀνέγνωκα, ἀνέγνωσμαι, ἀνεγνώσθην read, read aloud, read in public

κτίζω, κτίσω, ἔκτισα, ἔκτισμαι, ἐκτίσθην create, frame

ἀρχή, ῆς, ἡ beginning; τὴν ἀρχὴν wholly, altogether, from the beginning (used adverbially)

ἄρσην, ἄρσεν, ενος, ὁ, τό male; τὸ ἄρσεν, sc. γένος offspring

θῆλυς, θήλεια, θῆλυ female; τὸ θῆλυ, sc. γένος offspring

19:5

ἕνεκεν/ἕνεκα because of, on account of, for the sake of (preposition + genitive)

καταλείπω, καταλείψω, κατέλειψα, κατέλιπον (2 aorist), κατελείφθην leave behind (active); remain behind (passive)

κολλάω, κολλήσω, ἐκολλήθην bind closely, unite; cling to, join oneself to, be joined to (passive)

δύο two

σάρξ, σαρκός, ἡ flesh

19:6

ὥστε so that (conjunction)

οὐκέτι no more, no longer, no further (adverb)

σάρξ, σαρκός, ἡ flesh

συζεύγνυμι, συζεύξω, συνέζευξα yoke together; join together, unite

χωρίζω, χωρίζω, ἐχώρισα, κεχώρισμαι, ἐχωρίσθην divide, separate, sever, sunder

---

19:4 **ὁ κτίσας**: *the Creator*; the article and the participle are used in an absolute sense. Jesus begins his response by giving a historical perspective on the subject.

19:5 **Ἕνεκα τούτου**: the union of male and female was divinely sanctioned. **καὶ ἔσονται οἱ δύο εἰς σάρκα μίαν**: *and the two will be one flesh*; under Semitic influence the predicate nominative after εἰμί may be replaced by εἰς with the accusative.

19:6 **ὃ οὖν ὁ θεὸς συνέζευξεν**: *therefore that which God has joined together*; marriage is a divine institution.

19:7 λέγουσιν αὐτῷ, Τί οὖν Μωϋσῆς ἐνετείλατο δοῦναι βιβλίον
ἀποστασίου καὶ ἀπολῦσαι [αὐτήν]; 19:8 λέγει αὐτοῖς ὅτι Μωϋσῆς
πρὸς τὴν σκληροκαρδίαν ὑμῶν ἐπέτρεψεν ὑμῖν ἀπολῦσαι τὰς
γυναῖκας ὑμῶν, ἀπ' ἀρχῆς δὲ οὐ γέγονεν οὕτως. 19:9 λέγω δὲ ὑμῖν
ὅτι ὃς ἂν ἀπολύσῃ τὴν γυναῖκα αὐτοῦ μὴ ἐπὶ πορνείᾳ καὶ γαμήσῃ
ἄλλην μοιχᾶται.

19:7

ἐντέλλομαι, ἐντελοῦμαι, ἐνετειλάμην, ἐντέταλμαι command, order, enjoin

βιβλίον, ου, τό roll, book, scroll, document, certificate, deed

ἀποστάσιον, ου, τό rebellion, abandonment; repudiation, divorce

19:8

σκληροκαρδίαν, ας, ἡ hardness of heart, obduracy, coldness, obstinacy, stubbornness

ἐπιτρέπω, ἐπιτρέψω, ἐπέτρεψα, ἐπιτέτραμμαι, ἐπετράπην (2 aorist passive) give over; permit, allow

ἀρχή, ῆς, ἡ beginning; τὴν ἀρχὴν wholly, altogether, from the beginning (used adverbially)

19:9

πορνεία, ας, ἡ immorality, prostitution, fornication, adultery

γαμέω, γαμήσω, ἔγημα/ἐγάμησα, γεγάμηκα, ἐγαμήθην marry, take a wife

μοιχάομαι, μοιχήσομαι defile a married woman, commit adultery, be guilty of adultery

---

19:7 **Μωϋσῆς ἐνετείλατο**: *did Moses give a command*; the verb has an absolute sense and takes an infinitive construction in indirect discourse.

19:8 **ὅτι** is used as our quotation marks to introduce direct discourse.

19:9 **μὴ ἐπὶ πορνείᾳ**: *except for adultery.* the man who divorces his wife is responsible of great crime when he divorces his wife for any reason other than adultery. **μοιχᾶται**: the man who marries her commits adultery because morally, not legally, he is still married to his first wife.

19:10 λέγουσιν αὐτῷ οἱ μαθηταὶ [αὐτοῦ], Εἰ οὕτως ἐστὶν ἡ αἰτία τοῦ
ἀνθρώπου μετὰ τῆς γυναικός, οὐ συμφέρει γαμῆσαι. 19:11 ὁ δὲ εἶπεν
αὐτοῖς, Οὐ πάντες χωροῦσιν τὸν λόγον [τοῦτον] ἀλλ' οἷς δέδοται.
19:12 εἰσὶν γὰρ εὐνοῦχοι οἵτινες ἐκ κοιλίας μητρὸς ἐγεννήθησαν
οὕτως, καὶ εἰσὶν εὐνοῦχοι οἵτινες εὐνουχίσθησαν ὑπὸ τῶν ἀνθρώπων,
καὶ εἰσὶν εὐνοῦχοι οἵτινες εὐνούχισαν ἑαυτοὺς διὰ τὴν βασιλείαν τῶν
οὐρανῶν. ὁ δυνάμενος χωρεῖν χωρείτω.

19:10
αἰτία, ας, ἡ cause, motive; ground for complaint, fault; case, relationship
συμφέρει it is profitable, expedient, advantageous, good or better (impersonal verb)
γαμέω, γαμήσω, ἔγημα/ἐγάμησα, γεγάμηκα, ἐγαμήθην marry, take a wife
19:11
χωρέω, χωρήσω, ἐχώρησα move, pass; proceed; go forward, make progress; have room for, hold, contain; grasp, accept, comprehend, understand
19:12
ευνοῦχος, ου, ὁ eunuch
κοιλία, ας, ἡ stomach, belly, womb
εὐνουχίζω, εὐνουχίσω, εὐνούχισα, εὐνουχίσθην castrate, emasculate; to impose chaste abstinence on
χωρέω, χωρήσω, ἐχώρησα move, pass; proceed; go forward, make progress; have room for, hold, contain; grasp, accept, comprehend, understand

---

19:10 **Εἰ οὕτως ἐστὶν ἡ αἰτία**: *if the relationship . . . is like this.* **οὐ συμφέρει γαμῆσαι**: *it is better not to marry*; the infinitive is the subject of the quasi-impersonal verb.

19:11 **οἷς δέδοται**: supply ἐκεῖνοι as the antecedent of the relative pronoun. δέδοται is an impersonal verb.

19:12 **εἰσὶν . . . εὐνοῦχοι οἵτινες**: *there are eunuchs who*; the first two classifications are those who are eunuchs for physical reasons. The third type is celibate for spiritual reasons in order to build up the kingdom of heaven.

19:13 Τότε προσηνέχθησαν αὐτῷ παιδία ἵνα τὰς χεῖρας ἐπιθῇ
αὐτοῖς καὶ προσεύξηται· οἱ δὲ μαθηταὶ ἐπετίμησαν αὐτοῖς. 19:14 ὁ δὲ
Ἰησοῦς εἶπεν, Ἄφετε τὰ παιδία καὶ μὴ κωλύετε αὐτὰ ἐλθεῖν πρός με,
τῶν γὰρ τοιούτων ἐστὶν ἡ βασιλεία τῶν οὐρανῶν. 19:15 καὶ ἐπιθεὶς
τὰς χεῖρας αὐτοῖς ἐπορεύθη ἐκεῖθεν.
19:16 Καὶ ἰδοὺ εἷς προσελθὼν αὐτῷ εἶπεν, Διδάσκαλε, τί ἀγαθὸν
ποιήσω ἵνα σχῶ ζωὴν αἰώνιον;

19:13
ἐπιτίθημι, ἐπιθήσω, ἐπέθηκα, ἐπιτέθεικα, ἐπιτέθειμαι, ἐπετέθην lay upon, put on
προσεύχομαι, προσεύξομαι, προσηυξάμην pray, offer prayer
ἐπιτιμάω, ἐπιτιμήσω, ἐπετίμησα set a value on; assess a penalty; rebuke, reprove, censure, reprimand; admonish, enjoin
19:14
κωλύω, κωλύσω, ἐκώλυσα, ἐκωλύθην hinder, restrain, prevent, prohibit
τοιοῦτος, τοιαύτη, τοιοῦτο such, of such kind, such as this, so great
ἐπιτίθημι, ἐπιθήσω, ἐπέθηκα, ἐπιτέθεικα, ἐπιτέθειμαι, ἐπετέθην lay upon, put on
19:16
διδάσκαλος, ου, ὁ master, teacher
ἀγαθός, ή, όν good, profitable, upright
ζωή, ῆς, ἡ life, life eternal
αἰώνιος, ον (αἰώνιος, ία, ιον) eternal, everlasting

19:13 **προσηνέχθησαν αὐτῷ παιδία**: the finite verb is third person plural first aorist passive indicative of προσφέρω. Neuter plural subjects are considered as collective nouns and regularly take a singular verb. However, a plural verb may be used when stress is laid on the plurality of persons or parts.

19:14 **ἀφέτε** is the second aorist imperative of ἀφίημι. **μὴ κωλύετε αὐτὰ ἐλθεῖν πρός με**: *and do not forbid them from coming to me*; the verb takes an accusative and infinitive construction.

19:15 **ἐπιθεὶς τὰς χεῖρας**: *after He had placed his hands*; the article is used as an unemphatic possessive adjective where ownership or relationship is logically implied.

19:16 **εἷς**: *someone*. **τί ἀγαθὸν ποιήσω**: *what good deed shall I perform*; the construction is a congnate accusative. **σχῶ** is a third person singular second aorist subjunctive of ἔχω. **ζωὴν αἰώνιον**: adjectives of two terminations have the same form for the masculine and feminine (cf. App. 18).

19:17 ὁ δὲ εἶπεν αὐτῷ, Τί με ἐρωτᾷς περὶ τοῦ ἀγαθοῦ; εἷς ἐστιν ὁ
ἀγαθός· εἰ δὲ θέλεις εἰς τὴν ζωὴν εἰσελθεῖν, τήρησον τὰς ἐντολάς.
19:18 λέγει αὐτῷ, Ποίας; ὁ δὲ Ἰησοῦς εἶπεν, Τὸ Οὐ φονεύσεις, Οὐ
μοιχεύσεις, Οὐ κλέψεις, Οὐ ψευδομαρτυρήσεις, 19:19 Τίμα τὸν
πατέρα καὶ τὴν μητέρα, καί, Ἀγαπήσεις τὸν πλησίον σου ὡς σεαυτόν.
19:20 λέγει αὐτῷ ὁ νεανίσκος, Πάντα ταῦτα ἐφύλαξα· τί ἔτι ὑστερῶ;
19:21 ἔφη αὐτῷ ὁ Ἰησοῦς, Εἰ θέλεις τέλειος εἶναι, ὕπαγε πώλησόν
σου τὰ ὑπάρχοντα καὶ δὸς [τοῖς] πτωχοῖς, καὶ ἕξεις θησαυρὸν ἐν
οὐρανοῖς, καὶ δεῦρο ἀκολούθει μοι.

19:17

ἀγαθός, ή, όν good, profitable, upright

ζωή, ῆς, ἡ life, life eternal

τηρέω, τηρήσω, ἐτήρησα, τετήρηκα, τετήρημαι, ἐτηρήθην guard, heed, preserve, reserve

ἐντολή, ῆς, ἡ command, commandment

19:18

ποῖος, ποία, ποῖον of what kind? of what sort? of what species? what? which?

φονεύω, φονεύσω, ἐφόνευσα murder, kill, commit murder

μοιχεύω, μοιχεύσω, ἐμοίχευσα commit adultery

κλέπτω, κλέψω, ἔκλεψα, κέκλοφα, ἐκλάπην (2 aorist passive) steal

ψευδομαρτυρέω, ψευδομαρτυρήσω bear false witness, bear false testimony

19:19

τιμάω, τιμήσω, ἐτίμησα value, honor, revere

ἀγαπάω, ἀγαπήσω, ἠγάπησα, ἠγάπηκα, ἠγάπημαι, ἠγαπήθην love, cherish, value

πλησίον near, close to (adverb, preposition + genitive); ὁ πλησίον neighbor; a friendly neighbor

σεαυτοῦ, ῆς, οῦ yourself (reflexive pronoun)

19:20

νεανίσκος, ου, ὁ young man, youth

φυλάσσω, φυλάξω, ἐφύλαξα watch, guard, defend, keep

ἔτι yet, still (adverb)

ὑστερέω, ὑστερήσω, ὑστέρησα, ὑστέρηκα, ὑστερήθην fail, lack, run short

19:21

φημί, φήσω, ἔφησα say, speak

τέλειος, εία, ειον complete, perfect, fully developed, consecrated

πωλέω, πωλήσω, ἐπώλησα sell

ὑπάρχω, ὑπάρξω begin; exist; be; τὰ ὑπάρχοντα possessions, goods, property

πτωχός, ή, όν poor, indigent, needy

θησαυρός, οῦ, ὁ treasure box, treasury, treasure

δεῦρο come! come here! (adverb)

19:17 **περὶ τοῦ ἀγαθοῦ**: *about what is good*; the neuter adjective preceded by the article is used as a substantive.

19:22 ἀκούσας δὲ ὁ νεανίσκος τὸν λόγον ἀπῆλθεν λυπούμενος· ἦν
γὰρ ἔχων κτήματα πολλά.
19:23 Ὁ δὲ Ἰησοῦς εἶπεν τοῖς μαθηταῖς αὐτοῦ, Ἀμὴν λέγω
ὑμῖν ὅτι πλούσιος δυσκόλως εἰσελεύσεται εἰς τὴν βασιλείαν τῶν
οὐρανῶν. 19:24 πάλιν δὲ λέγω ὑμῖν, εὐκοπώτερόν ἐστιν κάμηλον
διὰ τρυπήματος ῥαφίδος διελθεῖν ἢ πλούσιον εἰσελθεῖν εἰς τὴν
βασιλείαν τοῦ θεοῦ. 19:25 ἀκούσαντες δὲ οἱ μαθηταὶ ἐξεπλήσσοντο
σφόδρα λέγοντες, Τίς ἄρα δύναται σωθῆναι;

19:22
νεανίσκος, ου, ὁ young man, youth
λυπέω, λυπήσω, ἐλύπησα, λελύπηκα, ἐλυπήθην vex, irritate, offend (active); be grieved, pained, distressed (passive)
κτῆμα, ατος, τό possession, property
19:23
πλούσιος, α, ον rich, wealthy
δυσκόλως with difficulty, hardly
19:24
πάλιν again (adverb)
εὐκοπώτερος, α, ον easier
κάμηλος, ου, ὁ and ἡ camel
τρύπημα, ατος, τό hole, eye of a needle
ῥαφίς, ίδος, ἡ needle
διέρχομαι, διελεύσομαι, διῆλθον pass through, pass over, cross, pass along; proceed; travel through, wander about; transfix, pierce; spread abroad
πλούσιος, α, ον rich, wealthy
19:25
ἐκπλήσσω, ἐκπλήξω, ἐξέπληξα, ἐξεπλάγην amaze, astound, overwhelm
σφόδρα greatly, exceedingly (adverb)
ἄρα therefore, then, consequently (particle)
σῴζω, σώσω, ἔσωσα, σέσωκα, σέσωσμαι, ἐσώθην save, rescue, preserve safe and unharmed

---

19:22 **ἦν γὰρ ἔχων**: *for he owned*; the periphrasis of ἦν with the present participle is employed for the imperfect tense.

19:24 **εὐκοπώτερόν ἐστιν**: the impersonal verb takes an accusative and infinitive construction. **κάμηλον διὰ τρυπήματος ῥαφίδος**: the hyperbole stresses the simple truth that it is an ἀδύνατον, an impossibility, for a rich man to enter the kingdom of God without seeking the kingdom of God first (6:33).

19:25 **Τίς ἄρα δύναται σωθῆναι**: the disciples think that those who live in harmony with the laws of God will be materially blessed.

19:26 ἐμβλέψας δὲ ὁ Ἰησοῦς εἶπεν αὐτοῖς, Παρὰ ἀνθρώποις τοῦτο ἀδύνατόν ἐστιν, παρὰ δὲ θεῷ πάντα δυνατά. 19:27 Τότε ἀποκριθεὶς ὁ Πέτρος εἶπεν αὐτῷ, Ἰδοὺ ἡμεῖς ἀφήκαμεν πάντα καὶ ἠκολουθήσαμέν σοι· τί ἄρα ἔσται ἡμῖν; 19:28 ὁ δὲ Ἰησοῦς εἶπεν αὐτοῖς, Ἀμὴν λέγω ὑμῖν ὅτι ὑμεῖς οἱ ἀκολουθήσαντές μοι ἐν τῇ παλιγγενεσίᾳ, ὅταν καθίσῃ ὁ υἱὸς τοῦ ἀνθρώπου ἐπὶ θρόνου δόξης αὐτοῦ, καθήσεσθε καὶ ὑμεῖς ἐπὶ δώδεκα θρόνους κρίνοντες τὰς δώδεκα φυλὰς τοῦ Ἰσραήλ.

19:26

ἐμβλέπω, ἐμβλέψω, ἐνέβλεψα see, behold, perceive, look attentively at

παρά from (the side of), from, issuing from, by (preposition + genitive); with, by (+ dative); by, near to, along; to, at; by, near, at the side of (+ accusative)

ἀδύνατος, ον powerless, impotent; impossible

δυνατός, ή, όν able, powerful, strong, mighty; δυνατόν possible

19:28

παλιγγενεσία, ας, ἡ rebirth, resurrection, regeneration

καθίζω, καθίσω, ἐκάθισα, κεκάθικα cause to sit down, seat, set (transitive); sit, sit down; remain, stay, continue, rest (intransitive)

θρόνος, ου, ὁ seat, throne; power, dominion

δόξα, ης, ἡ glory, honor, majesty

κάθημαι, καθήσομαι sit, stay, reside

δώδεκα twelve (indeclinable)

κρίνω, κρινῶ, ἔκρινα, κέκρικα, κέκριμαι, ἐκρίθην separate, select, judge, condemn

φυλή, ῆς, ἡ tribe; people, nation

19:26 **τοῦτο**: the demonstrative pronoun refers back to εἰσελθεῖν εἰς τὴν βασιλείαν τοῦ θεοῦ of the previous verse. Entry into the kingdom of God is not made possible by man's accumulation of wealth but by God.

19:27 **ἀφήκαμεν** is first person plural first aorist active indicative of ἀφίημι. **τί ἄρα ἔσται ἡμῖν**: *what then will happen to us*; the verb governs the dative of the person.

19:28 **παλιγγενεσίᾳ** may refer to the general resurrection of the dead, to the regeneration of the earth, or to the new messianic age.

19:29 καὶ πᾶς ὅστις ἀφῆκεν οἰκίας ἢ ἀδελφοὺς ἢ ἀδελφὰς ἢ πατέρα ἢ μητέρα ἢ τέκνα ἢ ἀγροὺς ἕνεκεν τοῦ ὀνόματός μου, ἑκατονταπλασίονα λήμψεται καὶ ζωὴν αἰώνιον κληρονομήσει. 19:30 Πολλοὶ δὲ ἔσονται πρῶτοι ἔσχατοι καὶ ἔσχατοι πρῶτοι.

19:29
ἀδελφή, ῆς, ἡ sister
τέκνον, ου, τό child, descendant, posterity
ἀγρός, οῦ, ὁ field, cultivated field; lands, farms, villages (plural)
ἕνεκεν/ἕνεκα because of, on account of, for the sake of (preposition + genitive)
ἑκατονταπλασίων, ον a hundredfold
ζωή, ῆς, ἡ life, life eternal
αἰώνιος, ον (αἰώνιος, ία, ιον) eternal, everlasting
κληρονομέω, κληρονομήσω, ἐκληρονόμησα, κεκληρονόμηκα inherit; obtain, acquire, receive
19:30
πρῶτος, η, ον first, before, earlier, foremost
ἔσχατος, η, ον last

19:30 **Πολλοὶ . . . πρῶτοι**: *many who are first*; supply a relative clause. **πρῶτοι ἔσχατοι καὶ ἔσχατοι πρῶτοι**: the chiastic structure emphasizes the eschatological reversal.

20 Ὁμοία γάρ ἐστιν ἡ βασιλεία τῶν οὐρανῶν ἀνθρώπῳ
οἰκοδεσπότῃ, ὅστις ἐξῆλθεν ἅμα πρωῒ μισθώσασθαι ἐργάτας εἰς
τὸν ἀμπελῶνα αὐτοῦ. 20:2 συμφωνήσας δὲ μετὰ τῶν ἐργατῶν ἐκ
δηναρίου τὴν ἡμέραν ἀπέστειλεν αὐτοὺς εἰς τὸν ἀμπελῶνα αὐτοῦ.
20:3 καὶ ἐξελθὼν περὶ τρίτην ὥραν εἶδεν ἄλλους ἑστῶτας ἐν τῇ
ἀγορᾷ ἀργοὺς 20:4 καὶ ἐκείνοις εἶπεν,

20:1
ὅμοιος, οία, οιον like, similar (+ dative)
οἰκοδεσπότης, ου, ὁ master of the house
ἅμα with, together with, at the same time (adverb; preposition + dative); ἅμα πρωῒ early in the morning
πρωῒ early, early in the morning (adverb)
μισθόω, μισθώσω hire
ἐργάτης, ου, ὁ workman, laborer
ἀμπελών, ῶνος, ὁ vineyard
20:2
συμφονέω, συμφονήσω sound together, be in unison, be in accord; agree, be in agreement; make an agreement
ἐργάτης, ου, ὁ workman, laborer
ἐκ (ἐξ before a vowel) from, out of, of, by; to the sum of, for the price of, with (preposition + genitive)
δηνάριον, ου, τό denarius (a Roman silver coin)
ἀποστέλλω, ἀποστελῶ, ἀπέστειλα, ἀπέσταλκα, ἀπέσταλμαι, ἀπεστάλην send, send away, send out
ἀμπελών, ῶνος, ὁ vineyard
20:3
περί about, concerning (preposition + genitive); about, around (+ accusative)
τρίτος, η, ον third
ἵστημι, στήσω, ἔστησα, ἔστην (2 aorist), ἕστηκα, ἐστάθην put, place, set, cause to stand (transitive); stand, be (intransitive)
ἀγορά, ᾶς, ἡ marketplace
ἀργός, ή, όν inactive, unemployed; idle, lazy; useless, unproductive, careless, unprofitable, hollow

---

20:1 **ὅστις**: the indefinite relative pronoun has the force of a relative pronoun. **ἐξῆλθεν . . . μισθώσασθαι**: the infinitive of purpose is equivalent to the more commonly used ἵνα clause. It is particularly prevalent after main verbs of motion like ἔρχομαι.

20:2 **τὴν ἡμέραν**: *for the day*; the noun is an accusative of duration of time.

20:3 **περὶ τρίτην ὥραν**: the time would be approximately 9 a.m. Daytime hours begin at 6 a.m. and end at 6 p.m. **ἑστῶτας . . . ἀργοὺς**: *as they stood idly*; ἑστῶτας is masculine plural accusative perfect active participle (cf. App. 60; 33) modifying ἄλλους, the object of the main verb. The Greek frequently employs a predicate adjective where English uses an adverb.

Ὑπάγετε καὶ ὑμεῖς εἰς τὸν ἀμπελῶνα, καὶ ὃ ἐὰν ᾖ δίκαιον δώσω ὑμῖν. 20:5 οἱ δὲ ἀπῆλθον. πάλιν [δὲ] ἐξελθὼν περὶ ἕκτην καὶ ἐνάτην ὥραν ἐποίησεν ὡσαύτως. 20:6 περὶ δὲ τὴν ἑνδεκάτην ἐξελθὼν εὗρεν ἄλλους ἑστῶτας καὶ λέγει αὐτοῖς, Τί ὧδε ἑστήκατε ὅλην τὴν ἡμέραν ἀργοί; 20:7 λέγουσιν αὐτῷ, Ὅτι οὐδεὶς ἡμᾶς ἐμισθώσατο. λέγει αὐτοῖς, Ὑπάγετε καὶ ὑμεῖς εἰς τὸν ἀμπελῶνα. 20:8 ὀψίας δὲ γενομένης λέγει ὁ κύριος τοῦ ἀμπελῶνος τῷ ἐπιτρόπῳ αὐτοῦ, Κάλεσον τοὺς ἐργάτας καὶ ἀπόδος αὐτοῖς τὸν μισθὸν ἀρξάμενος ἀπὸ τῶν ἐσχάτων ἕως τῶν πρώτων.

20:4
ἀμπελών, ῶνος, ὁ vineyard
δίκαιος, αία, ιον right, just, honest, good, righteous
20:5
πάλιν again (adverb)
περί about, concerning (preposition + genitive); about, around (+ accusative)
ἕκτος, η, ον sixth
ἔνατος, άτη, ον ninth
ὡσαύτως in just the same way, likewise (adverb)
20:6
ἑνδέκατος, άτη, ατον eleventh
ἀργός, ή, όν inactive, unemployed; idle, lazy; useless, unproductive, careless, unprofitable, hollow
20:7
οὐδείς, οὐδεμία, οὐδέν no (adjective); no one, nobody, nothing (substantive)
μισθόω, μισθώσω hire
ἀμπελών, ῶνος, ὁ vineyard
20:8
ὀψία, ας, ἡ evening
ἐπίτροπος, ου, ὁ foreman, managers, steward; overseer, treasurer
ἐργάτης, ου, ὁ workman, laborer
μισθός, οῦ, ὁ pay, wages, reward
ἄρχω, ἄρξω, ἦρξα, ἦρχα, ἦργμαι, ἤρχθην rule (active); begin (middle)
ἔσχατος, η, ον last
πρῶτος, η, ον first, before, earlier, foremost

20:4 **ὃ ἐὰν ᾖ δίκαιον**: *whatever is right*; the clause is a future more vivid protasis.

20:6 **ἑστήκατε . . . ἀργοί**: the hyperbaton emphasizes the delay. **ὅλην τὴν ἡμέραν**: *the whole day long*; the adjective stands in predicate position. The noun is an accusative of duration of time.

20:7 **Ὅτι** is a causal conjunction.

20:8 **ὀψίας . . . γενομένης**: *when evening fell*; the construction is a genitive absolute. **ἀπὸ τῶν ἐσχάτων ἕως τῶν πρώτων**: *from the last to the first*; the adjectives are used as substantives.

20:9 καὶ ἐλθόντες οἱ περὶ τὴν ἑνδεκάτην ὥραν ἔλαβον ἀνὰ δηνάριον. 20:10 καὶ ἐλθόντες οἱ πρῶτοι ἐνόμισαν ὅτι πλεῖον λήμψονται· καὶ ἔλαβον [τὸ] ἀνὰ δηνάριον καὶ αὐτοί. 20:11 λαβόντες δὲ ἐγόγγυζον κατὰ τοῦ οἰκοδεσπότου 20:12 λέγοντες, Οὗτοι οἱ ἔσχατοι μίαν ὥραν ἐποίησαν, καὶ ἴσους ἡμῖν αὐτοὺς ἐποίησας τοῖς βαστάσασι τὸ βάρος τῆς ἡμέρας καὶ τὸν καύσωνα. 20:13 ὁ δὲ ἀποκριθεὶς ἑνὶ αὐτῶν εἶπεν, Ἑταῖρε, οὐκ ἀδικῶ σε·

20:9
ἑνδέκατος, άτη, ατον eleventh
ἀνά each, apiece (preposition + accusative; with numbers)
20:10
πρῶτος, η, ον first, before, earlier, foremost
νομίζω, νομίσω, ἐνόμισα, νενόμικα think, believe, consider
πλείων, πλεῖον or πλέον more, greater, larger; πλέον more (comparative adverb)
ἀνά each, apiece (preposition + accusative; with numbers)
20:11
γογγύζω, γογγύσω, ἐγόγγυσα murmur, grumble, mutter, complain, whisper
οἰκοδεσπότης, ου, ὁ master of the house
20:12
ἔσχατος, η, ον last
ἴσος, η, ον equal
βαστάζω, βαστάσω, ἐβάστασα lift, bear, take up; endure, suffer; carry away, remove, steal
βάρος, εος, τό weight, burden
καύσων, ωνος, ὁ scorching heat, scorching; hot weather, hot time
20:13
ἑταῖρος, ου, ὁ comrade, companion, fellow, friend
ἀδικέω, ἀδικήσω, ἠδίκησα, ἠδίκηκα, ἠδικήθην wrong, treat unjustly, cheat

---

20:9 **ἐλθόντες οἱ περὶ τὴν ἑνδεκάτην ὥραν**: *those who came at about the eleventh hour*; the article stands in attributive position and turns the prepositional phrase into a substantive.

20:10 **ἐνόμισαν ὅτι πλεῖον λήμψονται**: *thought that they would receive more*; the verb of thinking takes a ὅτι clause in indirect discourse. **καὶ αὐτοί**: *they likewise*; καὶ functions as an adverb here.

20:11 **ἐγόγγυζον**: *they kept murmuring*; the finite verb is an imperfect. The Greek, like the English verb, has onomatopoeic qualities.

20:12 **μίαν ὥραν** is an accusative of duration of time. **ἴσους ἡμῖν αὐτοὺς ἐποίησας**: *you have made them equal to us*; ἴσους stands in predicate position. **τοῖς βαστάσασι τὸ βάρος τῆς ἡμέρας καὶ τὸν καύσωνα**: *who have borne the burden and the heat of the day*; βαστάσασι is a masculine plural dative first aorist active participle in agreement with ἡμῖν.

20:13 **Ἑταῖρε** stands in the vocative case. **οὐχὶ**: the negative is a strengthened form of οὐ; as an interrogative word in a question, it expects an affirmative answer. **δηναρίου**: *on the price of a denarius*; the case is a genitive of price.

οὐχὶ δηναρίου συνεφώνησάς μοι; 20:14 ἆρον τὸ σὸν καὶ ὕπαγε. θέλω δὲ τούτῳ τῷ ἐσχάτῳ δοῦναι ὡς καὶ σοί· 20:15 [ἢ] οὐκ ἔξεστίν μοι ὃ θέλω ποιῆσαι ἐν τοῖς ἐμοῖς; ἢ ὁ ὀφθαλμός σου πονηρός ἐστιν ὅτι ἐγὼ ἀγαθός εἰμι; 20:16 Οὕτως ἔσονται οἱ ἔσχατοι πρῶτοι καὶ οἱ πρῶτοι ἔσχατοι.

20:17 Καὶ ἀναβαίνων ὁ Ἰησοῦς εἰς Ἱεροσόλυμα παρέλαβεν τοὺς δώδεκα [μαθητὰς] κατ' ἰδίαν καὶ ἐν τῇ ὁδῷ εἶπεν αὐτοῖς, 20:18 Ἰδοὺ ἀναβαίνομεν εἰς Ἱεροσόλυμα, καὶ ὁ υἱὸς τοῦ ἀνθρώπου παραδοθήσεται τοῖς ἀρχιερεῦσιν καὶ γραμματεῦσιν,

---

20:13
οὐχί not; no, by no means (adverb; more intensive form of οὐ)
δηνάριον, ου, τό denarius (a Roman silver coin)
συμφονέω, συμφονήσω sound together, be in unison, be in accord; agree, be in agreement
20:14
αἴρω, ἀρῶ, ἦρα, ἦρκα, ἦρμαι, ἤρθην take up, take, bear, take away, lift, carry, remove; keep in suspense; destroy, kill
ἔσχατος, η, ον last
20:15
ἔξεστι(ν) it is permitted, it is possible (impersonal verb)
ἀγαθός, ή, όν good, profitable, upright
20:16
ἔσχατος, η, ον last
πρῶτος, η, ον first, before, earlier, foremost
20:17
ἀναβαίνω, ἀναβήσομαι, ἀνέβην, ἀναβέβηκα go up, ascend, rise
δώδεκα twelve (indeclinable)
ἴδιος, ία, ιον one's own; κατ' ἰδίαν privately, by oneself, alone (adverb)
20:18
ἀναβαίνω, ἀναβήσομαι, ἀνέβην, ἀναβέβηκα go up, ascend, rise
παραδίδωμι, παραδώσω, παρέδωκα, παρέδων (2 aorist), παραδέδωκα, παραδέδομαι, παρεδόθην give, hand over, give over, deliver, give up, betray
ἀρχιερεύς, έως, ὁ high priest
γραμματεύς, έως, ὁ secretary, clerk, scholar versed in law, scribe

---

20:14 **τὸ σὸν**: *what is yours*; the adjective is used as a substantive. **ὡς καὶ σοί**: *even as to you.*

20:15 **ἐν τοῖς ἐμοῖς**: *with my own*; the adjective is used as a substantive. **ἢ ὁ ὀφθαλμός σου πονηρός ἐστιν**: *or are you envious*; the eye is evil because it looks with envy upon others. By metonymy or part for the whole the eye represents the whole person. The comparison is between the envy of the worker and the generosity of the master.

20:16 **Οὕτως**: the reversal comes about for the workers hired last because of the mercies of the master, for the workers hired first because of their envious disposition. Many manuscripts add at this point **πολλοὶ γάρ εἰσιν κλητοί, ὀλίγοι δὲ ἐκλεκτοί**: *many are called, but few are chosen.*

20:18 **παραδοθήσεται τοῖς ἀρχιερεῦσιν**: *will be betrayed to the high priests.*

καὶ κατακρινοῦσιν αὐτὸν θανάτῳ 20:19 καὶ παραδώσουσιν αὐτὸν τοῖς ἔθνεσιν εἰς τὸ ἐμπαῖξαι καὶ μαστιγῶσαι καὶ σταυρῶσαι, καὶ τῇ τρίτῃ ἡμέρᾳ ἐγερθήσεται.

20:20 Τότε προσῆλθεν αὐτῷ ἡ μήτηρ τῶν υἱῶν Ζεβεδαίου μετὰ τῶν υἱῶν αὐτῆς προσκυνοῦσα καὶ αἰτοῦσά τι ἀπ' αὐτοῦ. 20:21 ὁ δὲ εἶπεν αὐτῇ, Τί θέλεις; λέγει αὐτῷ, Εἰπὲ ἵνα καθίσωσιν οὗτοι οἱ δύο υἱοί μου εἷς ἐκ δεξιῶν σου καὶ εἷς ἐξ εὐωνύμων σου ἐν τῇ βασιλείᾳ σου.

20:18

κατακρίνω, κατακρινῶ, κατέκρινα, κατακέκρικα, κατακέκριμαι, κατεκρίθην condemn, pronounce sentence

θάνατος, ου, ὁ death

20:19

ἔθνος, ους, τό nation, people

ἐμπαίζω, ἐμπαίξω, ἐνέπαιξα, ἐνεπαίχθην ridicule, make fun of, mock, treat with scorn; deceive, trick

μαστιγόω, μαστιγώσω, ἐμαστίγωσα, ἐμαστιγώθην scourge, whip, flog, beat

σταυρόω, σταυρώσω, ἐσταύρωσα, ἐσταύρωμαι, ἐσταυρώθην crucify

τρίτος, η, ον third

20:20

αἰτέω, αἰτήσω, ᾔτησα, ᾔτηκα ask, ask for, make a request; desire

20:21

καθίζω, καθίσω, ἐκάθισα, κεκάθικα cause to sit down, seat, set (transitive); sit, sit down; remain, stay, continue, rest (intransitive)

δεξιός, ά, όν right (as opposed to *left*); ἐκ δεξιῶν τινός at someone's right

εὐώνυμος, ον left (as opposed to *right*); ἐκ εὐωνύμων τινός at someone's left

---

20:18 **θανάτῳ** is equivalent to εἰς θάνατον.

20:19 **εἰς τὸ ἐμπαῖξαι καὶ μαστιγῶσαι καὶ σταυρῶσαι**: *to mock and to flog and to crucify*; the preposition εἰς before the articular infinitives denotes purpose. The polysyndeton slows the narrative and emphasizes the tricolon of verbs. **τῇ τρίτῃ ἡμέρᾳ**: the threefold suffering will be resolved on the third day.

20:20 **αἰτοῦσά τι**: *making a request*; the neuter singular accusative indefinite pronoun is equal to an indefinite pronoun and is used as a cognate accusative.

20:21 **Τί** is the neuter interrogative pronoun. **Εἰπὲ ἵνα**: *grant that*; supply a demonstrative τοῦτο before ἵνα: *grant (this namely) that*; the purpose clause stands in apposition to the understood τοῦτο and explains it. **εἷς . . . εἷς**: *(the) one . . . the other.*

20:22 ἀποκριθεὶς δὲ ὁ Ἰησοῦς εἶπεν, Οὐκ οἴδατε τί αἰτεῖσθε. δύνασθε
πιεῖν τὸ ποτήριον ὃ ἐγὼ μέλλω πίνειν; λέγουσιν αὐτῷ, Δυνάμεθα.
20:23 λέγει αὐτοῖς, Τὸ μὲν ποτήριόν μου πίεσθε, τὸ δὲ καθίσαι ἐκ
δεξιῶν μου καὶ ἐξ εὐωνύμων οὐκ ἔστιν ἐμὸν [τοῦτο] δοῦναι, ἀλλ'
οἷς ἡτοίμασται ὑπὸ τοῦ πατρός μου. 20:24 Καὶ ἀκούσαντες οἱ δέκα
ἠγανάκτησαν περὶ τῶν δύο ἀδελφῶν.

20:22
οἶδα know
πίνω, πίομαι, ἔπιον, πέπωκα drink
ποτήριον, ου, τό cup
μέλλω, μελλήσω be about to, be on the point of
20:23
ποτήριον, ου, τό cup
πίνω, πίομαι, ἔπιον, πέπωκα drink
καθίζω, καθίσω, ἐκάθισα, κεκάθικα cause to sit down, seat, set (transitive); sit, sit down; remain, stay, continue, rest (intransitive)
δεξιός, ά, όν right (as opposed to *left*); ἐκ δεξιῶν τινός at someone's right
εὐώνυμος, ον left (as opposed to *right*); ἐκ εὐωνύμων τινός at someone's left
ἑτοιμάζω, ἑτοιμάσω, ἡτοίμασα, ἡτοίμακα, ἡτοίμασμαι, ἡτοιμάσθην make ready, prepare
20:24
δέκα ten (indeclinable)
ἀγανακτέω, ἀγανακτήσω, ἠγανάκτησα be indignant, angry (+ περί at)

20:22 **οἴδατε . . . αἰτεῖσθε**: the second person plural indicates a response to all three and reveals the mother as the mouthpiece for James and John. **τὸ ποτήριον**: by metonymy the cup represents its content. In this case it symbolizes sorrow and suffering. **μέλλω πίνειν**: unlike in Attic Greek, μέλλω is regularly followed by a present infinitive in Koine. The periphrastic future construction denotes the certainty of a future event.

20:23 **πίεσθε** is a second person plural deponent future indicative. **τὸ δὲ καθίσαι . . . οὐκ ἔστιν ἐμὸν δοῦναι**: *but sitting . . . is not my gift to bestow*; the infinitive is the subject of the verb. ἐμὸν is a predicate adjective that shows a cognate relationship with the infinitive. [**τοῦτο**] emphatically resumes the subject **τὸ . . . καθίσαι** at the beginning of the sentence.

20:25 ὁ δὲ Ἰησοῦς προσκαλεσάμενος αὐτοὺς εἶπεν, Οἴδατε ὅτι οἱ ἄρχοντες τῶν ἐθνῶν κατακυριεύουσιν αὐτῶν καὶ οἱ μεγάλοι κατεξουσιάζουσιν αὐτῶν. 20:26 οὐχ οὕτως ἔσται ἐν ὑμῖν, ἀλλ' ὃς ἐὰν θέλῃ ἐν ὑμῖν μέγας γενέσθαι ἔσται ὑμῶν διάκονος, 20:27 καὶ ὃς ἂν θέλῃ ἐν ὑμῖν εἶναι πρῶτος ἔσται ὑμῶν δοῦλος· 20:28 ὥσπερ ὁ υἱὸς τοῦ ἀνθρώπου οὐκ ἦλθεν διακονηθῆναι ἀλλὰ διακονῆσαι καὶ δοῦναι τὴν ψυχὴν αὐτοῦ λύτρον ἀντὶ πολλῶν.

20:29 Καὶ ἐκπορευομένων αὐτῶν ἀπὸ Ἰεριχὼ ἠκολούθησεν αὐτῷ ὄχλος πολύς.

20:25
προσκαλέομαι, προσκαλέσομαι, προσεκαλεσάμην, προσκέκλημαι summon, call on, invite, call to oneself
οἶδα know
ἄρχων, οντος, ὁ chief, ruler, magistrate, prince
ἔθνος, ους, τό nation, people
κατακυριεύω, κατακυριεύσω, κατεκυρίευσα, κατεκυριεύθην domineer over, gain dominion over, gain power over, lord it over
μέγας, μεγάλη, μέγα large, great
κατεξουσιάζω, κατεξουσιάσω exercise dominion over

20:26
μέγας, μεγάλη, μέγα large, great
διάκονος, ου, ὁ attendant, servant

20:27
πρῶτος, η, ον first, before, earlier, foremost
δοῦλος, ου, ὁ slave, servant

20:28
ὥσπερ as, just as (adverb)
διακονέω, διακονήσω, διηκόνησα, δεδιηκόνηκα, διηκονήθην wait on, attend upon, serve
ψυχή, ῆς, ἡ breath, life, soul, heart
λύτρον, ου, τό price paid, price of release, ransom
ἀντί in place of, for, upon (preposition + genitive)

20:29
ἐκπορεύομαι, ἐκπορεύσομαι, ἐκπεπόρευμαι, ἐξεπορεύθην come out, go out, proceed
Ἰεριχώ, ἡ Jericho (indeclinable)

20:25 **κατακυριεύουσιν . . . κατεξουσιάζουσιν** govern the genitive case. **οἱ μεγάλοι**: the adjective turned substantive is masculine plural nominative (App. 37).

20:26 **μέγας** is a predicate adjective. **ἔσται ὑμῶν διάκονος**: the verb is a deponent future indicative of εἰμί in this future more vivid apodosis. διάκονος is a predicate nominative.

20:28 **ὥσπερ** introduces an example. **λύτρον**: *as a ransom*; the noun is predicate accusative.

20:29 **ἐκπορευομένων αὐτῶν**: *as they were departing*; the construction is genitive absolute.

20:30 καὶ ἰδοὺ δύο τυφλοὶ καθήμενοι παρὰ τὴν ὁδὸν ἀκούσαντες ὅτι Ἰησοῦς παράγει, ἔκραξαν λέγοντες, Ἐλέησον ἡμᾶς, [κύριε,] υἱὸς Δαυίδ. 20:31 ὁ δὲ ὄχλος ἐπετίμησεν αὐτοῖς ἵνα σιωπήσωσιν· οἱ δὲ μεῖζον ἔκραξαν λέγοντες, Ἐλέησον ἡμᾶς, κύριε, υἱὸς Δαυίδ. 20:32 καὶ στὰς ὁ Ἰησοῦς ἐφώνησεν αὐτοὺς καὶ εἶπεν, Τί θέλετε ποιήσω ὑμῖν; 20:33 λέγουσιν αὐτῷ, Κύριε, ἵνα ἀνοιγῶσιν οἱ ὀφθαλμοὶ ἡμῶν. 20:34 σπλαγχνισθεὶς δὲ ὁ Ἰησοῦς ἥψατο τῶν ὀμμάτων αὐτῶν, καὶ εὐθέως ἀνέβλεψαν καὶ ἠκολούθησαν αὐτῷ.

20:30
τυφλός, ή, όν blind
κάθημαι, καθήσομαι sit, stay, reside
κράζω, κράξω, ἔκραξα, κέκραγα cry out, cry aloud
ἐλεέω, ἐλεήσω, ἠλέησα, ἠλέημαι, ἠλεήθην pity, show mercy
20:31
ἐπιτιμάω, ἐπιτιμήσω, ἐπετίμησα set a value on; assess a penalty; rebuke, reprove, censure, reprimand; admonish, enjoin
σιωπάω, σιωπήσω, ἐσιώπησα be silent, keep silent, hold one's peace
μείζων, μεῖζον greater, larger
ἐλεέω, ἐλεήσω, ἠλέησα, ἠλέημαι, ἠλεήθην pity, show mercy
20:32
φωνέω, φωνήσω, ἐφώνησα, ἐφωνήθην sound, call, summon
20:33
ἀνοίγω, ἀνοίξω, ἀνέῳξα/ἤνοιξα, ἀνέῳγα, ἀνέῳγμαι, ἠνεῴχθην open
20:34
σπλαγχνίζομαι, σπλαγχνίσομαι, ἐσπλαγχνίσθην have compassion, feel sympathy, be moved with pity
ἅπτω, ἅψω, ἧψα fasten; light, kindle; touch (middle)
ὄμμα, ατος, τό eye
εὐθέως at once, immediately (adverb)
ἀναβλέπω, ἀναβλέψω, ἀνέβλεψα look up; regain sight, receive sight

---

20:30 **δύο τυφλοὶ**: *two blind men*; the nominative adjective is used as a substantive and the subject of the verb. **υἱὸς**: the nominative is used as a vocative.

20:31 **μεῖζον ἔκραξαν**: *they cried out all the more*; μεῖζον is the comparative adverb of μέγας (App. 22, 37).

20:32 **Τί θέλετε ποιήσω ὑμῖν**: *what do you want me to do for you*; the verb θέλετε with a subjunctive (without a conjunction) introduces a deliberative question.

20:33 **ἵνα ἀνοιγῶσιν οἱ ὀφθαλμοὶ ἡμῶν**: *that our eyes may be opened*; the finite verb is a third person plural second aorist passive subjunctive.

20:34 **ἥψατο**: the verb governs the genitive case.

21 Καὶ ὅτε ἤγγισαν εἰς Ἱεροσόλυμα καὶ ἦλθον εἰς Βηθφαγὴ εἰς
τὸ Ὄρος τῶν Ἐλαιῶν, τότε Ἰησοῦς ἀπέστειλεν δύο μαθητὰς 21:2
λέγων αὐτοῖς, Πορεύεσθε εἰς τὴν κώμην τὴν κατέναντι ὑμῶν, καὶ
εὐθέως εὑρήσετε ὄνον δεδεμένην καὶ πῶλον μετ᾽ αὐτῆς· λύσαντες
ἀγάγετέ μοι. 21:3 καὶ ἐάν τις ὑμῖν εἴπῃ τι, ἐρεῖτε ὅτι Ὁ κύριος αὐτῶν
χρείαν ἔχει· εὐθὺς δὲ ἀποστελεῖ αὐτούς. 21:4 Τοῦτο δὲ γέγονεν ἵνα
πληρωθῇ τὸ ῥηθὲν διὰ τοῦ προφήτου λέγοντος,

21:1
ὅτε when, whenever (adverb)
ἐγγίζω, ἐγγίσω, ἤγγισα, ἤγγικα approach, draw near
βηθφαγή, ἡ Bethphage (indeclinable)
ὄρος, ους, τό mountain, hill
ἐλαία, ας, ἡ olive tree, olive
21:2
κώμη, ης, ἡ village, small town
κατέναντι opposite to, before (adverb; preposition + genitive)
εὐθέως at once, immediately (adverb)
ὄνος, ου, ὁ, ἡ donkey (male or female)
δέω, δήσω, ἔδησα, δέδεκα, δέδεμαι, ἐδέθην bind, tie, impede
πῶλος, ου, ὁ colt
λύω, λύσω, ἔλυσα, λέλυκα, λέλυμαι, ἐλύθην loose, unbind, unfasten, break, destroy
ἄγω, ἄξω, ἤγαγον (2 aorist), ἦχα, ἦγμαι, ἤχθην lead, bring, arrest
21:3
τις, τι anyone, anything, someone, something, a certain one, a certain thing (indefinite pronoun)
χρεία, ας, ἡ need, necessity
εὐθύς immediately, at once (adverb)

21:1 **βηθφαγὴ** is a place on the Mount of Olives.

21:2 **κατέναντι**: the preposition takes the genitive case.

21:3 **ἐρεῖτε** is the second person plural future active indicative of λέγω in the apodosis of a future more vivid condition introducing direct discourse. The future is conjugated like the present active indicative of a contracted verb with stem in **ε** (cf. App. 56). **αὐτῶν** is an objective genitive (cf. App. 65).

21:4 **τὸ ῥηθὲν**: *that which was spoken* (literally); the verbal form is a neuter singular nominative first aorist passive participle (cf. App. 53, G, 5; 34) of the verb λέγω that translates as a relative clause in conjunction with an article.

21:5 Εἴπατε τῇ θυγατρὶ Σιών,
Ἰδοὺ ὁ βασιλεύς σου ἔρχεταί σοι
πραῢς καὶ ἐπιβεβηκὼς ἐπὶ ὄνον
καὶ ἐπὶ πῶλον υἱὸν ὑποζυγίου.
21:6 πορευθέντες δὲ οἱ μαθηταὶ καὶ ποιήσαντες καθὼς συνέταξεν
αὐτοῖς ὁ Ἰησοῦς 21:7 ἤγαγον τὴν ὄνον καὶ τὸν πῶλον καὶ ἐπέθηκαν
ἐπ' αὐτῶν τὰ ἱμάτια, καὶ ἐπεκάθισεν ἐπάνω αὐτῶν.

21:5

θυγάτηρ, τρός, ἡ daughter

Σιών, ἡ Zion (indeclinable)

πραΰς, πραεῖα, πραΰ meek, gentle, humble, considerate, kind, forgiving; mild, benevolent, humane

ἐπιβαίνω, ἐπιβήσομαι, ἐπέβην (2 aorist), ἐπιβέβηκα go upon, mount, board

ὄνος, ου, ὁ, ἡ donkey (male or female)

πῶλος, ου, ὁ colt

υἱός, οῦ, ὁ son; young, offspring, foal

ὑποζύγιον, ου, τό beast for the yoke, beast of burden; oxen, horse, mule, donkey, ass

21:6

καθώς as, just as, how, inasmuch as (adverb)

συντάσσω, συντάξω, συνέταξα order, direct

21:7

ὄνος, ου, ὁ, ἡ donkey (male or female)

πῶλος, ου, ὁ colt

ἐπιτίθημι, ἐπιθήσω, ἐπέθηκα, ἐπιτέθεικα, ἐπιτέθειμαι, ἐπετέθην lay upon, put on

ἱμάτιον, ου, τό garment, clothing; cloak, robe; clothes, garments (plural)

ἐπικαθίζω, ἐπικαθίσω, ἐπεκάθισα sit, sit down (on)

ἐπάνω over, above, on (adverb; preposition + genitive)

21:5 **τῇ θυγατρὶ Σιών**: *to the daughter of Zion*; Σιών is an appositional genitive (cf. App. 65). **ἐπιβεβηκὼς** is a masculine singular nominative perfect active participle (cf. App. 33) modifying the subject of the main verb. The perfect is frequently translated as a present.

21:6 **συνέταξεν**: *had instructed*; since the action of the verb precedes that of the main verb ἤγαγον, it may be translated as a pluperfect.

21:7 **ἐπεκάθισεν**: the subject of the intransive verb is Jesus. The ride on a donkey and its foal fulfills messianic prophecy (Zech 9:9).

21:8 ὁ δὲ πλεῖστος ὄχλος ἔστρωσαν ἑαυτῶν τὰ ἱμάτια ἐν τῇ ὁδῷ,
ἄλλοι δὲ ἔκοπτον κλάδους ἀπὸ τῶν δένδρων καὶ ἐστρώννυον ἐν τῇ
ὁδῷ. 21:9 οἱ δὲ ὄχλοι οἱ προάγοντες αὐτὸν καὶ οἱ ἀκολουθοῦντες
ἔκραζον λέγοντες,

Ὡσαννὰ τῷ υἱῷ Δαυίδ·
Εὐλογημένος ὁ ἐρχόμενος ἐν ὀνόματι κυρίου·
Ὡσαννὰ ἐν τοῖς ὑψίστοις.

21:10 καὶ εἰσελθόντος αὐτοῦ εἰς Ἱεροσόλυμα ἐσείσθη πᾶσα ἡ πόλις
λέγουσα, Τίς ἐστιν οὗτος; 21:11 οἱ δὲ ὄχλοι ἔλεγον, Οὗτός ἐστιν ὁ
προφήτης Ἰησοῦς ὁ ἀπὸ Ναζαρὲθ τῆς Γαλιλαίας.

21:8

πλεῖστος, η, ον most, very great (superlative of πολύς)

στρωννύω, στρώσω, ἔστρωσα spread out

κόπτω, κόψω, ἔκοψα, ἐκόπην (2 aorist passive) smite, cut, cut off; beat one's breast (in mourning), mourn, lament (middle)

κλάδος, ου, ὁ branch, bough

δένδρον, ου, τό tree

21:9

προάγω, προάξω, προήγαγον (2 aorist) lead forward, bring out (transitive); go before, precede, go before (intransitive); go or come before someone (+ accusative of person)

κράζω, κράξω, ἔκραξα, κέκραγα cry out, cry aloud

ὡσαννά hosanna! save now, help now (Hebrew)

εὐλογέω, εὐλογήσω, εὐλόγησα, εὐλόγηκα praise, bless

ὕψιστος, η, ον highest, most exalted; ἐν τοῖς ὑψίστοις in the highest (heaven)

21:10

σείω, σείσω, ἔσεισα, ἐσείσθην shake, agitate, cause to quake; move, stir up, set in motion

---

21:8 **ὁ δὲ πλεῖστος ὄχλος ἔστρωσαν**: the singular subject takes a plural verb according to sense. **ἑαυτῶν τὰ ἱμάτια**: *their cloaks*; the reflexive pronoun is used instead of the personal possessive αὐτῶν (App. 40). The spreading of cloaks and branches indicates recognition of messianic prophecy that He is the Son of David.

21:9 **οἱ δὲ ὄχλοι οἱ προάγοντες αὐτὸν καὶ οἱ ἀκολουθοῦντες ἔκραζον**: the chiastic structure centers on Jesus in the middle, being surrounded by the large crowds in front of Him and behind Him. **Ὡσαννὰ τῷ υἱῷ Δαυίδ**: *Hosanna to the Son of David*; the original phrase meaning *save now* (Ps 118:25) may have become a traditional formulaic shout of praise at the time of Jesus. **Εὐλογημένος**: supply ἐστιν.

21:12 Καὶ εἰσῆλθεν Ἰησοῦς εἰς τὸ ἱερὸν καὶ ἐξέβαλεν πάντας
τοὺς πωλοῦντας καὶ ἀγοράζοντας ἐν τῷ ἱερῷ, καὶ τὰς τραπέζας τῶν
κολλυβιστῶν κατέστρεψεν καὶ τὰς καθέδρας τῶν πωλούντων τὰς
περιστεράς, 21:13 καὶ λέγει αὐτοῖς, Γέγραπται,

Ὁ οἶκός μου οἶκος προσευχῆς κληθήσεται,
ὑμεῖς δὲ αὐτὸν ποιεῖτε σπήλαιον λῃστῶν.

21:14 Καὶ προσῆλθον αὐτῷ τυφλοὶ καὶ χωλοὶ ἐν τῷ ἱερῷ, καὶ
ἐθεράπευσεν αὐτούς. 21:15 ἰδόντες δὲ οἱ ἀρχιερεῖς καὶ οἱ γραμματεῖς
τὰ θαυμάσια ἃ ἐποίησεν καὶ τοὺς παῖδας τοὺς κράζοντας ἐν τῷ ἱερῷ
καὶ λέγοντας, Ὡσαννὰ τῷ υἱῷ Δαυίδ, ἠγανάκτησαν 21:16 καὶ εἶπαν
αὐτῷ, Ἀκούεις τί οὗτοι λέγουσιν;

21:12
ἱερόν, οῦ, τό temple
πωλέω, πωλήσω, ἐπώλησα sell
ἀγοράζω, ἀγοράσω, ἠγόρασα, ἠγόρασμαι, ἠγοράσθην buy, purchase, acquire
τράπεζα, ης, ἡ table, counter
κολλυβιστής, οῦ, ὁ money changer
καταστρέφω, καταστρέψω, κατέστρεψα overturn, overthrow, throw down, upset
καθέδρα, ας, ἡ seat
περιστερά, ᾶς, ἡ dove, pigeon
21:13
γράφω, γράψω, ἔγραψα, γέγραφα, γέγραμμαι, ἐγράφθην engrave, write
οἶκος, ου, ὁ house, dwelling
προσευχή, ῆς, ἡ prayer
σπήλαιον, ου, τό cave, den
λῃστής, οῦ, ὁ robber, bandit
21:14
τυφλός, ή, όν blind
χωλός, ή, όν lame, crippled
ἱερόν, οῦ, τό temple
21:15
ἀρχιερεύς, έως, ὁ high priest
γραμματεύς, έως, ὁ secretary, clerk, scholar versed in law, scribe
θαυμάσιος, α, ον wonderful, marvelous; τὸ θαυμάσιον wonder, marvelous work
παῖς, παιδός, ὁ child, boy, youth; servant
κράζω, κράξω, ἔκραξα, κέκραγα cry out, cry aloud
ἱερόν, οῦ, τό temple
ὡσαννά hosanna! save now, help now (Hebrew)
ἀγανακτέω, ἀγανακτήσω, ἠγανάκτησα be indignant, angry (+ περί at)

21:13 **οἶκος** in second position is predicate nominative. **κληθήσεται** is a third person singular first future passive indicative of καλέω. In the active the verb takes a double accusative. **σπήλαιον** is a predicate accusative.

21:15 **ἰδόντες . . . ἠγανάκτησαν**: the hyperbaton emphasizes the protracted anger of the high priests and scribes. **τοὺς παῖδας**: members of the kingdom are by metonymy called children.

ὁ δὲ Ἰησοῦς λέγει αὐτοῖς, Ναί. οὐδέποτε ἀνέγνωτε ὅτι Ἐκ στόματος νηπίων καὶ θηλαζόντων κατηρτίσω αἶνον; 21:17 Καὶ καταλιπὼν αὐτοὺς ἐξῆλθεν ἔξω τῆς πόλεως εἰς Βηθανίαν καὶ ηὐλίσθη ἐκεῖ.

21:18 Πρωῒ δὲ ἐπανάγων εἰς τὴν πόλιν ἐπείνασεν. 21:19 καὶ ἰδὼν συκῆν μίαν ἐπὶ τῆς ὁδοῦ ἦλθεν ἐπ' αὐτὴν καὶ οὐδὲν εὗρεν ἐν αὐτῇ εἰ μὴ φύλλα μόνον, καὶ λέγει αὐτῇ, Μηκέτι ἐκ σοῦ καρπὸς γένηται εἰς τὸν αἰῶνα. καὶ ἐξηράνθη παραχρῆμα ἡ συκῆ.

21:16
ναί yes, indeed, certainly (particle of affirmation)
οὐδέποτε never (adverb)
ἀναγινώσκω, ἀναγνώσομαι, ἀνέγνων (2 aorist), ἀνέγνωκα, ἀνέγνωσμαι, ἀνεγνώσθην read, read aloud
νήπιος, ία, ιον unlearned, simple, young; infant, babe, child (substantive)
θηλάζω, θηλάσω, ἐθήλασα suckle; οἱ θηλάζοντες sucklings
καταρτίζω, καταρτίσω, κατήρτισα, κατήρτισμαι put in order; prepare, make, create; prepare for oneself (middle)
αἶνος, ου, ὁ praise
21:17
καταλείπω, καταλείψω, κατέλειψα, κατέλιπον (2 aorist), κατελείφθην leave behind (active)
ἔξω outside, out (adverb); out of (preposition)
Βηθανία, ας, ἡ Bethany
αὐλίζομαι, αὐλίσομαι, ηὐλίσθην spend the night, find lodging; stay
21:18
πρωΐ early, early in the morning (adverb)
ἐπανάγω, ἐπανάξω, ἐπανήγαγον (2 aorist) bring up; return (intransitive)
πεινάω, πεινάσω/πεινήσω, ἐπείνασα be hungry; hunger after, long for
21:19
συκῆ, ῆς, ἡ fig tree
φύλλον, ου, τό leaf
μόνον only (adverb)
μηκέτι no longer (adverb)
αἰών, αἰῶνος, ὁ eternity, perpetuity, life
ξηραίνω, ξηρανῶ, ἐξήρανα, ἐξήραμμαι, ἐξηράνθην dry up, parch; be withered (passive)
παραχρῆμα immediately, at once (adverb)

21:16 **Ἐκ στόματος νηπίων**: their expressions of praise in the sacred precinct of the temple are oracular (Ps 8:2).

21:17 **εἰς Βηθανίαν**, a village about two miles east of Jerusalem on the eastern slope of the Mount of Olives, the home of Mary, Martha, and Lazareth.

21:18 **ἐπανάγων** is intransitive. **ἐπείνασεν**: *He was hungry*; the verb has an absolute sense.

21:19 **μίαν** carries the force of an indefinite article. **εἰ μὴ**: *but*; the two particles are equivalent to ἀλλά when preceded by οὐδὲν. The tree, like the hypocrites, gave a false appearance and failed to fulfill the measure of its creation. **Μηκέτι . . . καρπὸς γένηται εἰς τὸν αἰῶνα**: *let fruit never again grow*; Μηκέτι introduces a prohibitive subjunctive. The aorist subjunctive may be in the second or third person. εἰς τὸν αἰῶνα intensifies the negative.

21:20 καὶ ἰδόντες οἱ μαθηταὶ ἐθαύμασαν λέγοντες, Πῶς παραχρῆμα ἐξηράνθη ἡ συκῆ; 21:21 ἀποκριθεὶς δὲ ὁ Ἰησοῦς εἶπεν αὐτοῖς, Ἀμὴν λέγω ὑμῖν, ἐὰν ἔχητε πίστιν καὶ μὴ διακριθῆτε, οὐ μόνον τὸ τῆς συκῆς ποιήσετε, ἀλλὰ κἂν τῷ ὄρει τούτῳ εἴπητε, Ἄρθητι καὶ βλήθητι εἰς τὴν θάλασσαν, γενήσεται· 21:22 καὶ πάντα ὅσα ἂν αἰτήσητε ἐν τῇ προσευχῇ πιστεύοντες λήμψεσθε.

21:23 Καὶ ἐλθόντος αὐτοῦ εἰς τὸ ἱερὸν προσῆλθον αὐτῷ διδάσκοντι οἱ ἀρχιερεῖς καὶ οἱ πρεσβύτεροι τοῦ λαοῦ λέγοντες, Ἐν ποίᾳ ἐξουσίᾳ ταῦτα ποιεῖς; καὶ τίς σοι ἔδωκεν τὴν ἐξουσίαν ταύτην;

21:20
θαυμάζω, θαυμάσομαι, ἐθαύμασα, ἐθαυμάσθην wonder, marvel, be astonished
πῶς how? in what way? in what sense? (interrogative adverb)
παραχρῆμα immediately, at once (adverb)
ξηραίνω, ξηρανῶ, ἐξήρανα, ἐξήραμμαι, ἐξηράνθην dry up, parch; be withered (passive)
συκῆ, ῆς, ἡ fig tree
21:21
πίστις, εως, ἡ faith, trust
διακρίνω, διακρινῶ, διεκρίθην distinguish, discern, judge; be at odds with oneself, hesitate, doubt, waver (middle or passive)
μόνον only (adverb); οὐ μόνον . . . ἀλλὰ καί not only . . . but also
συκῆ, ῆς, ἡ fig tree
θάλασσα, ης, ἡ sea
21:22
προσευχή, ῆς, ἡ prayer
πιστεύω, πιστεύσω, ἐπίστευσα, πεπίστευκα, πεπίστευμαι, ἐπιστεύθην believe; entrust
21:23
ἱερόν, οῦ, τό temple
διδάσκω, διδάξω, ἐδίδαξα, ἐδιδάχθην teach, instruct
ἀρχιερεύς, έως, ὁ high priest
πρεσβύτερος, α, ον older, ancestor, elder (designation of an official); ancients, fathers (plural)
λαός, οῦ, ὁ people
ποῖος, ποία, ποῖον of what kind? of what sort? what? which?
ἐξουσία, ας, ἡ authority, right, ability, might, power

21:21 **οὐ μόνον τὸ τῆς συκῆς ποιήσετε**: *you will perform not only the miracle of the fig*; supply σημεῖον in this cognate accusative construction. **κἂν** is crasis for καὶ ἄν: *even if*; the conditional particle introduces the protasis of a future more vivid condition. **Ἄρθητι**: *remove yourself*; the form is a second person singular first aorist passive imperative of αἴρω. Certain verbs in the aorist passive may have a reflexive or middle sense. The hyperbolic expression of moving mountains is commonplace for removing thorny difficulties by unwavering faith.

21:22 **πάντα ὅσα**: *all that*; in conjunction with πάντα, ὅσα is translated as a relative pronoun. **πιστεύοντες**: *if you believe*; the circumstantial participle may be interpreted conditionally.

21:23 **ταῦτα ποιεῖς**: *do you perform these miracles*; supply σημεῖα in this cognate accusative construction.

21:24 ἀποκριθεὶς δὲ ὁ Ἰησοῦς εἶπεν αὐτοῖς, Ἐρωτήσω ὑμᾶς κἀγὼ λόγον ἕνα, ὃν ἐὰν εἴπητέ μοι κἀγὼ ὑμῖν ἐρῶ ἐν ποίᾳ ἐξουσίᾳ ταῦτα ποιῶ· 21:25 τὸ βάπτισμα τὸ Ἰωάννου πόθεν ἦν; ἐξ οὐρανοῦ ἢ ἐξ ἀνθρώπων; οἱ δὲ διελογίζοντο ἐν ἑαυτοῖς λέγοντες, Ἐὰν εἴπωμεν, Ἐξ οὐρανοῦ, ἐρεῖ ἡμῖν, Διὰ τί οὖν οὐκ ἐπιστεύσατε αὐτῷ; 21:26 ἐὰν δὲ εἴπωμεν, Ἐξ ἀνθρώπων, φοβούμεθα τὸν ὄχλον, πάντες γὰρ ὡς προφήτην ἔχουσιν τὸν Ἰωάννην.

21:24
ἐρωτάω, ἐρωτήσω, ἠρώτησα ask, inquire of, question, ask a question, request, beseech
ποῖος, ποία, ποῖον of what kind? of what sort? of what species? what? which?
ἐξουσία, ας, ἡ authority, right, ability, might, power
21:25
βάπτισμα, ατος, τό immersion, baptism
πόθεν from where? how? in what way? (interrogative adverb)
διαλογίζομαι, διαλογίσομαι reason, deliberate, ponder, consider
πιστεύω, πιστεύσω, ἐπίστευσα, πεπίστευκα, πεπίστευμαι, ἐπιστεύθην believe; entrust

---

21:24 **Ἐρωτήσω ὑμᾶς κἀγὼ λόγον ἕνα**: *I will also ask you one question*; Ἐρωτήσω takes a double accusative: one of the person and one of the thing. The context suggests the translation of λόγον: they have asked him a question; he will ask one in turn. **ὃν** carries the force of a demonstrative pronoun. **ἐρῶ** is the first person singular future active indicative of λέγω. **ταῦτα**: supply σημεῖα in this cognate accusative construction.

21:25 **τὸ βάπτισμα τὸ Ἰωάννου . . . ἐξ οὐρανοῦ ἢ ἐξ ἀνθρώπων**: the source and authority of divine commission is also an important theme in the Gospel of John: the son μονογενής was sent παρὰ πατρός (1:14), John the Baptist was sent ἀπεσταλμένος παρὰ θεοῦ (1:6), the priests and Levites (1:19) were sent ἀπεσταλμένοι ἐκ τῶν Φαρισαίων. **διελογίζοντο**: *they kept deliberating*; the deponent verb is imperfect. The imperfect tense denotes progressive, continued, and repeated action (aspect) in past time. **Διὰ τί**: *why*.

21:26 **ἔχουσιν**: *regard*.

21:27 καὶ ἀποκριθέντες τῷ Ἰησοῦ εἶπαν, Οὐκ οἴδαμεν. ἔφη αὐτοῖς καὶ
αὐτός, Οὐδὲ ἐγὼ λέγω ὑμῖν ἐν ποίᾳ ἐξουσίᾳ ταῦτα ποιῶ.
21:28 Τί δὲ ὑμῖν δοκεῖ; ἄνθρωπος εἶχεν τέκνα δύο. καὶ προσελθὼν
τῷ πρώτῳ εἶπεν, Τέκνον, ὕπαγε σήμερον ἐργάζου ἐν τῷ ἀμπελῶνι.
21:29 ὁ δὲ ἀποκριθεὶς εἶπεν, Οὐ θέλω, ὕστερον δὲ μεταμεληθεὶς
ἀπῆλθεν. 21:30 προσελθὼν δὲ τῷ ἑτέρῳ εἶπεν ὡσαύτως.

21:27

οἶδα know

ποῖος, ποία, ποῖον of what kind? of what sort? of what species? what? which?

ἐξουσία, ας, ἡ authority, right, ability, might, power

21:28

δοκεῖ it seems; it seems good, best, or right (impersonal verb)

τέκνον, ου, τό child, descendant, posterity

πρῶτος, η, ον first, before, earlier, foremost

σήμερον today, this day (adverb)

ἐργάζομαι, ἐργάσομαι, ἠργασάμην/εἰργασάμην, εἴργασμαι work, do, accomplish, perform

ἀμπελών, ῶνος, ὁ vineyard

21:29

ὕστερος, α, ον later; ὕστερον later, afterwards (adverb)

μεταμέλομαι, μεταμελήσομαι, μετεμελήθην change one's mind, feel regret, repent

21:30

ἕτερος, α, ον other (of two), another

ὡσαύτως in just the same way, likewise (adverb)

21:27 **Οὐκ οἴδαμεν**: ironically they are compelled to speak the truth. **αὐτός**: contrary to classical usage, αὐτός stands here by itself in the nominative case as a personal pronoun (cf. App. 40, notes). **ταῦτα**: supply σημεῖα in this cognate accusative construction.

21:28 **Τί δὲ ὑμῖν δοκεῖ**: the idiom means *now what do you think*. **Τέκνον** is in the vocative case. **ὕπαγε . . . ἐργάζου**: *go and work*; ὕπαγε is a second person singular present active imperative (cf. App. 53, A, 3). Supply καὶ: the imperative is usually found without a conjunction when followed by another imperative.

21:29 **Οὐ θέλω**: *I will not*; the verb is used in an absolute sense.

ὁ δὲ ἀποκριθεὶς εἶπεν, Ἐγώ, κύριε, καὶ οὐκ ἀπῆλθεν. 21:31 τίς ἐκ τῶν δύο ἐποίησεν τὸ θέλημα τοῦ πατρός; λέγουσιν, Ὁ πρῶτος. λέγει αὐτοῖς ὁ Ἰησοῦς, Ἀμὴν λέγω ὑμῖν ὅτι οἱ τελῶναι καὶ αἱ πόρναι προάγουσιν ὑμᾶς εἰς τὴν βασιλείαν τοῦ θεοῦ. 21:32 ἦλθεν γὰρ Ἰωάννης πρὸς ὑμᾶς ἐν ὁδῷ δικαιοσύνης, καὶ οὐκ ἐπιστεύσατε αὐτῷ, οἱ δὲ τελῶναι καὶ αἱ πόρναι ἐπίστευσαν αὐτῷ· ὑμεῖς δὲ ἰδόντες οὐδὲ μετεμελήθητε ὕστερον τοῦ πιστεῦσαι αὐτῷ.

21:31

θέλημα, ατος, τό will, desire

πρῶτος, η, ον first, before, earlier, foremost

τελώνης, ου, ὁ tax-collector, publican

πόρνη, ης, ἡ harlot, prostitute

προάγω, προάξω, προήγαγον (2 aorist) lead forward, bring out (transitive); go before, precede, go before (intransitive); go or come before someone (+ accusative of person)

21:32

δικαιοσύνη, ης, ἡ justice, righteousness, godliness

πιστεύω, πιστεύσω, ἐπίστευσα, πεπίστευκα, πεπίστευμαι, ἐπιστεύθην believe; entrust

τελώνης, ου, ὁ tax-collector, publican

πόρνη, ης, ἡ harlot, prostitute

μεταμέλομαι, μεταμελήσομαι, μετεμελήθην change one's mind, feel regret, repent

ὕστερος, α, ον later; ὕστερον later, afterwards (adverb)

21:30 **Ἐγώ**: supply θέλω.

21:31 **προάγουσιν ὑμᾶς**: the verb governs the accusative case.

21:32 **ἐν ὁδῷ δικαιοσύνης**: δικαιοσύνης is an appositional genitive (cf. App. 65) more specifically identifying the metaphor ὁδῷ. **ἐπίστευσαν αὐτῷ**: the verb governs the dative case. **τοῦ πιστεῦσαι αὐτῷ**: *in order to believe Him*; the construction is an articular infinitive. A purpose clause may be expressed by the neuter article in the genitive case followed by an infinitive.

21:33 Ἄλλην παραβολὴν ἀκούσατε. Ἄνθρωπος ἦν οἰκοδεσπότης ὅστις ἐφύτευσεν ἀμπελῶνα καὶ φραγμὸν αὐτῷ περιέθηκεν καὶ ὤρυξεν ἐν αὐτῷ ληνὸν καὶ ᾠκοδόμησεν πύργον καὶ ἐξέδετο αὐτὸν γεωργοῖς καὶ ἀπεδήμησεν. 21:34 ὅτε δὲ ἤγγισεν ὁ καιρὸς τῶν καρπῶν, ἀπέστειλεν τοὺς δούλους αὐτοῦ πρὸς τοὺς γεωργοὺς λαβεῖν τοὺς καρποὺς αὐτοῦ.

21:33
οἰκοδεσπότης, ου, ὁ master of the house
φυτεύω, φυτεύσω, ἐφύτευσα, πεφύτευμαι, ἐφυτεύθην plant
ἀμπελών, ῶνος, ὁ vineyard
φραγμός, οῦ, ὁ fence, hedge
περιτίθημι, περιθήσω, περιέθηκα, περιέθην (2 aorist) place around, put about, attach
ὀρύσσω, ὀρύξω, ὤρυξα, ὠρύγην dig up, dig out, dig
ληνός, οῦ, ἡ tub; winepress; wine vat
οἰκοδομέω, οἰκοδομήσω, ᾠκοδόμησα, ᾠκοδομήθην build, construct, establish
πύργος, ου, ὁ tower; castle, palace
ἐκδίδωμι, ἐκδώσομαι, ἐξεδόμην (2 aorist) let out for hire, rent, lease (only in middle in N.T.)
γεωργός, οῦ, ὁ husbandman, farmer, tenant farmer, vinedresser
ἀποδημέω, ἀποδημήσω, ἀπεδήμησα be away from home, be abroad; go on a journey, go abroad
21:34
ἐγγίζω, ἐγγίσω, ἤγγισα, ἤγγικα approach, draw near
καιρός, οῦ, ὁ time, appointed time; season; time of crisis, end-time
γεωργός, οῦ, ὁ husbandman, tenant farmer, farmer, vinedresser

---

21:33 **Ἄνθρωπος . . . οἰκοδεσπότης**: Ἄνθρωπος is pleonastic but adds greater definiteness and emphasis. In this parable He is the Man of Holiness, God. **περιέθηκεν** is a third person singular aorist active indicative (cf. App. 59). The verb takes an accusative and a dative object of the preposition. **γεωργοῖς**: *tenant farmers*; they are given credit by the householder for the necessities of life, work the land, and receive a certain share of the value of the crop. They are identified as the Pharisees and the scribes (45). **ἀπεδήμησεν**: the householder lives abroad, a common practice of the time.

21:34 **ὁ καιρὸς τῶν καρπῶν**: *the time of picking fruit* or *time of harvest.* **τοὺς δούλους** are the prophets. **λαβεῖν**: *to collect*; the verbal form is the second aorist infinitive of λαμβάνω. The infinitive of purpose is particularly prevalent after main verbs of motion.

21:35 καὶ λαβόντες οἱ γεωργοὶ τοὺς δούλους αὐτοῦ ὃν μὲν ἔδειραν, ὃν δὲ ἀπέκτειναν, ὃν δὲ ἐλιθοβόλησαν. 21:36 πάλιν ἀπέστειλεν ἄλλους δούλους πλείονας τῶν πρώτων, καὶ ἐποίησαν αὐτοῖς ὡσαύτως. 21:37 ὕστερον δὲ ἀπέστειλεν πρὸς αὐτοὺς τὸν υἱὸν αὐτοῦ λέγων, Ἐντραπήσονται τὸν υἱόν μου. 21:38 οἱ δὲ γεωργοὶ ἰδόντες τὸν υἱὸν εἶπον ἐν ἑαυτοῖς, Οὗτός ἐστιν ὁ κληρονόμος· δεῦτε ἀποκτείνωμεν αὐτὸν καὶ σχῶμεν τὴν κληρονομίαν αὐτοῦ,

---

21:35
γεωργός, οῦ, ὁ husbandman, farmer, tenant farmer, vinedresser
ὅς, ἥ, ὅ who, which, what; he who, that (relative pronoun); ὃς μὲν . . . ὃς δέ the one . . . the other, one . . . another
δέρω, δερῶ, ἔδειρα skin, flay; beat, scourge, strike
ἀποκτείνω, ἀποκτενῶ, ἀπέκτεινα, ἀπεκτάνθην kill
λιθοβολέω, λιθοβολήσω, ἐλιθοβόλησα throw stones at; stone to death
21:36
πάλιν again (adverb)
πλείων, πλεῖον or πλέον more, greater, larger; πλέον more (comparative adverb)
ὡσαύτως in just the same way, likewise (adverb)
21:37
ὕστερος, α, ον later; ὕστερον later, afterwards (adverb)
ἐντρέπω, ἐντρέψω, ἐντρέπομαι, ἐνετράπην put to shame, make ashamed; be put to shame, be ashamed (passive); have regard for, respect, revere, reverence (with middle sense)
21:38
γεωργός, οῦ, ὁ husbandman, farmer, tenant farmer, vinedresser
κληρονόμος, ου, ὁ heir
δεῦτε come! come here! (adverb)
ἀποκτείνω, ἀποκτενῶ, ἀπέκτεινα, ἀπεκτάνθην kill
κληρονομία, ας, ἡ inheritance; possession, property

21:35 **λαβόντες οἱ γεωργοὶ . . . ὃν μὲν ἔδειραν**: *after they had seized . . . the tenants beat one*; the action of the participle precedes that of the main verb and may be translated as a pluperfect. **ἔδειραν . . . ἀπέκτειναν . . . ἐλιθοβόλησαν**: the tricolon of verbs emphasizes the brutality of their actions.

21:36 **πλείονας τῶν πρώτων**: *more than the first*; the comparative adjective takes a genitive of comparison (App. 65).

21:37 **τὸν υἱὸν αὐτοῦ** is the "Son of Man of Holiness," (33) Jesus; elsewhere abbreviated as the "Son of Man."

21:38 **ἀποκτείνωμεν . . . καὶ σχῶμεν**: *let us kill . . . and take*; the verbal forms are first person plural aorist active subjunctives (cf. App. 54). The hortatory subjunctive, like the prohibitive and deliberative, is an independent subjunctive. It is used to express an exhortation, a request, or a proposal in the first person. The difference between the present and aorist tense is one of aspect only: the present shows continuous, the aorist single action. σχῶμεν is the second aorist of ἔχω.

21:39 καὶ λαβόντες αὐτὸν ἐξέβαλον ἔξω τοῦ ἀμπελῶνος καὶ
ἀπέκτειναν. 21:40 ὅταν οὖν ἔλθῃ ὁ κύριος τοῦ ἀμπελῶνος, τί ποιήσει
τοῖς γεωργοῖς ἐκείνοις; 21:41 λέγουσιν αὐτῷ, Κακοὺς κακῶς
ἀπολέσει αὐτοὺς καὶ τὸν ἀμπελῶνα ἐκδώσεται ἄλλοις γεωργοῖς,
οἵτινες ἀποδώσουσιν αὐτῷ τοὺς καρποὺς ἐν τοῖς καιροῖς αὐτῶν.
21:42 λέγει αὐτοῖς ὁ Ἰησοῦς, Οὐδέποτε ἀνέγνωτε ἐν ταῖς γραφαῖς,

---

21:39

ἔξω outside, out (adverb); out of (preposition)

ἀμπελών, ῶνος, ὁ vineyard

ἀποκτείνω, ἀποκτενῶ, ἀπέκτεινα, ἀπεκτάνθην kill

21:40

ἀμπελών, ῶνος, ὁ vineyard

γεωργός, οῦ, ὁ husbandman, farmer, tenant farmer, vinedresser

21:41

κακός, ή, όν bad, evil, wrong; τὸ κακόν evil, wickedness, crime

κακῶς ill, badly; grievously, vehemently; wretchedly, miserably; wickedly, wrongly (adverb)

ἐκδίδωμι, ἐκδώσομαι, ἐξεδόμην (2 aorist) let out for hire, lease (only middle in N.T.)

γεωργός, οῦ, ὁ husbandman, farmer, tenant farmer, vinedresser

καιρός, οῦ, ὁ time, appointed time; season; time of crisis, end-time

21:42

οὐδέποτε never (adverb)

ἀναγινώσκω, ἀναγνώσομαι, ἀνέγνων (2 aorist), ἀνέγνωκα, ἀνέγνωσμαι, ἀνεγνώσθην read, read aloud, read in public

γραφή, ῆς, ἡ writing, Holy Scripture, passage of scripture

21:39 **αὐτὸν**, the object of the participle, also serves as the object of the two finite verbs.

21:40 **τοῖς γεωργοῖς ἐκείνοις**: *to those tenants*; the use of the case is a dative of disadvantage.

21:41 **Κακοὺς κακῶς ἀπολέσει αὐτοὺς**: *terribly he will destroy them as evildoers*; Κακοὺς, used as a substantive, is predicate accusative. **ἐν τοῖς καιροῖς αὐτῶν**: *in their seasons.*

Λίθον ὃν ἀπεδοκίμασαν οἱ οἰκοδομοῦντες,
οὗτος ἐγενήθη εἰς κεφαλὴν γωνίας·
παρὰ κυρίου ἐγένετο αὕτη
καὶ ἔστιν θαυμαστὴ ἐν ὀφθαλμοῖς ἡμῶν;

21:43 διὰ τοῦτο λέγω ὑμῖν ὅτι ἀρθήσεται ἀφ' ὑμῶν ἡ βασιλεία τοῦ
θεοῦ καὶ δοθήσεται ἔθνει ποιοῦντι τοὺς καρποὺς αὐτῆς. [21:44 Καὶ
ὁ πεσὼν ἐπὶ τὸν λίθον τοῦτον συνθλασθήσεται· ἐφ' ὃν δ' ἂν πέσῃ
λικμήσει αὐτόν.]

21:45 Καὶ ἀκούσαντες οἱ ἀρχιερεῖς καὶ οἱ Φαρισαῖοι τὰς
παραβολὰς αὐτοῦ ἔγνωσαν ὅτι περὶ αὐτῶν λέγει· 21:46 καὶ
ζητοῦντες αὐτὸν κρατῆσαι ἐφοβήθησαν τοὺς ὄχλους, ἐπεὶ εἰς
προφήτην αὐτὸν εἶχον.

21:42
λίθος, ου, ὁ stone
ἀποδοκιμάζω, ἀποδοκιμάσω, ἀπεδοκίμασα, ἀπεδοκιμάσθην reject
οἰκοδομέω, οἰκοδομήσω, ᾠκοδόμησα, ᾠκοδομήθην build, establish
κεφαλή, ῆς, ἡ head
γωνία, ας, ἡ corner
θαυμαστός, ή, όν wonderful, marvelous, remarkable
21:43
ἔθνος, ους, τό nation; pagans, Gentiles
21:44
πίπτω, πεσοῦμαι, ἔπεσα, ἔπεσον (2 aorist), πέπτωκα fall, fall prostrate, fall down
συνθλάω, συνθλάσω, συνεθλάσθην break in pieces, crush, dash to pieces, shatter
λικμάω, λικμήσω winnow grain; scatter like chaff; crush
21:45
ἀρχιερεύς, έως, ὁ high priest
21:46
κρατέω, κρατήσω, ἐκράτησα, κεκράτηκα, κεκράτημαι lay hold of, grasp; retain, not remit
φοβέομαι, φοβηθήσομαι, ἐφοβήθην fear, dread; be afraid, become frightened (only passive in N.T.)

21:42 **Λίθον ὃν**: *the stone which*; by inverse attraction the nominative noun assumes the accusative case of the relative pronoun. **ἐγενήθη εἰς κεφαλὴν γωνίας**: *has become the corner stone* (literally: *was made into the corner stone*); as the corner stone Jesus is the foundation of the kingdom of God. **αὕτη . . . θαυμαστὴ**: the gender refers to κεφαλὴν.

21:43 **δοθήσεται ἔθνει ποιοῦντι τοὺς κάρπους αὐτῆς**: *will be given to a nation that will produce its fruit*; a present participle agrees in time with the main verb.

21:44 **πέσῃ λικμήσει**: in this chiastic structure the subject of both verbs is ὁ λίθος.

21:45 **ἔγνωσαν ὅτι**: the verb of knowing takes a ὅτι clause in indirect discourse.

21:46 **ζητοῦντες . . . ἐφοβήθησαν**: *although they sought . . . they were afraid*; the adversative context invites a concessive interpretation of the participle.

22 Καὶ ἀποκριθεὶς ὁ Ἰησοῦς πάλιν εἶπεν ἐν παραβολαῖς αὐτοῖς
λέγων, 22:2 Ὡμοιώθη ἡ βασιλεία τῶν οὐρανῶν ἀνθρώπῳ βασιλεῖ,
ὅστις ἐποίησεν γάμους τῷ υἱῷ αὐτοῦ. 22:3 καὶ ἀπέστειλεν τοὺς
δούλους αὐτοῦ καλέσαι τοὺς κεκλημένους εἰς τοὺς γάμους, καὶ οὐκ
ἤθελον ἐλθεῖν. 22:4 πάλιν ἀπέστειλεν ἄλλους δούλους λέγων, Εἴπατε
τοῖς κεκλημένοις, Ἰδοὺ τὸ ἄριστόν μου ἡτοίμακα, οἱ ταῦροί μου καὶ
τὰ σιτιστὰ τεθυμένα καὶ πάντα ἕτοιμα· δεῦτε εἰς τοὺς γάμους.

22:1
πάλιν again (adverb)
22:2
ὁμοιόω, ὁμοιώσω, ὁμοίωσα, ὡμοιώθην make like, liken, compare; be like, be made like, become like, resemble (passive)
γάμος, ου, ὁ wedding, marriage
22:3
γάμος, ου, ὁ wedding, marriage
22:4
ἄριστον, ου, τό first meal; breakfast; luncheon, noon meal; meal
ἑτοιμάζω, ἑτοιμάσω, ἡτοίμασα, ἡτοίμακα, ἡτοίμασμαι, ἡτοιμάσθην make ready, prepare
ταῦρος, ου, ὁ bull
σιτιστός, ή, όν fattened; τὰ σιτιστά animals that have been fattened
θύω, θύσω, ἔθυσα, τέθυμαι, ἐτύθην sacrifice, slaughter, kill
ἕτοιμος, η, ον ready, prepared
δεῦτε come! come here! (adverb)

22:2 **ἀνθρώπῳ βασιλεῖ**: ἀνθρώπῳ is pleonastic but adds greater definiteness and emphasis: given the nature of a parable, the comparison is readily suggested between a mortal and the divine king. **ὅστις ἐποίησεν γάμους**: *who gave a wedding celebration*; the indefinite relative pronoun has the force of a relative pronoun. γάμους: the plural usually refers to a wedding celebration, the singular to a wedding.

22:3 **ἀπέστειλεν . . . καλέσαι**: *he sent . . . to call upon*; the infinitive of purpose is particularly prevalent after main verbs of motion. **τοὺς κεκλημένους**: *those who had been invited*; the perfect participle indicates action completed before the main verb. **οὐκ ἤθελον ἐλθεῖν**: *they would not come*; the imperfect tense denotes progressive, continued, and repeated action (aspect) in past time.

22:4 **οἱ ταῦροί μου καὶ τὰ σιτιστὰ τεθυμένα**: *my bulls and my fattened animals have been slaughtered*; the participle τεθυμένα agrees with the nearest subject in gender and number and requires ἐστιν to complete the periphrastic construction. Neuter plural subjects are considered as collective nouns and regularly take a singular verb. **πάντα ἕτοιμα**: supply ἐστίν.

22:5 οἱ δὲ ἀμελήσαντες ἀπῆλθον, ὃς μὲν εἰς τὸν ἴδιον ἀγρόν, ὃς δὲ ἐπὶ τὴν ἐμπορίαν αὐτοῦ· 22:6 οἱ δὲ λοιποὶ κρατήσαντες τοὺς δούλους αὐτοῦ ὕβρισαν καὶ ἀπέκτειναν. 22:7 ὁ δὲ βασιλεὺς ὠργίσθη καὶ πέμψας τὰ στρατεύματα αὐτοῦ ἀπώλεσεν τοὺς φονεῖς ἐκείνους καὶ τὴν πόλιν αὐτῶν ἐνέπρησεν. 22:8 τότε λέγει τοῖς δούλοις αὐτοῦ, Ὁ μὲν γάμος ἕτοιμός ἐστιν, οἱ δὲ κεκλημένοι οὐκ ἦσαν ἄξιοι· 22:9 πορεύεσθε οὖν ἐπὶ τὰς διεξόδους τῶν ὁδῶν καὶ ὅσους ἐὰν εὕρητε καλέσατε εἰς τοὺς γάμους. 22:10 καὶ ἐξελθόντες οἱ δοῦλοι ἐκεῖνοι εἰς τὰς ὁδοὺς συνήγαγον πάντας οὓς εὗρον, πονηρούς τε καὶ ἀγαθούς·

22:5
ἀμελέω, ἀμελήσω, ἠμέλησα, ἠμέληκα neglect, disregard; be careless
ὃς μὲν . . . ὃς δέ the one . . . the other
ἴδιος, ία, ιον one's own
ἐμπορία, ας, ἡ business, trade
22:6
λοιπός, ή, όν remaining; the rest
κρατέω, κρατήσω, ἐκράτησα, κεκράτηκα, κεκράτημαι lay hold of, grasp; retain, not remit
ὑβρίζω, ὑβρίσω, ὕβρισα mistreat, insult, scoff at
ἀποκτείνω, ἀποκτενῶ, ἀπέκτεινα, ἀπεκτάνθην kill
22:7
ὀργίζω, ὀργίσω, ὠργίσθην provoke to anger; be angry at (passive + dative)
πέμπω, πέμψω, ἔπεμψα, πέπομφα, ἐπέμφθην send
στράτευμα, ατος, τό army; armed force; troops, guards
φονεύς, έως, ὁ murderer
ἐμπί(μ)πρημι, ἐμπρήσω, ἐνέπρησα burn, set on fire
22:8
γάμος, ου, ὁ wedding, marriage
ἕτοιμος, η, ον ready, prepared
ἄξιος, ία, ιον worthy
22:9
διέξοδος, ου, ἡ highway, main road
ὅσος, η, ον how large, how great; as many as (plural); whosoever, whatsoever
γάμος, ου, ὁ wedding, marriage
22:10
συνάγω, συνάξω, συνήγαγον (2 aorist), συνῆγμαι, συνήχθην gather in, bring together; convene, come together, meet (passive)

22:5 **οἱ δὲ ἀμελήσαντες ἀπῆλθον**: *but they paid no attention and went away*; a participle may receive as much emphasis as the finite verb and be coordinated with it.

22:7 **φονεῖς**: the accusative plural looks like the nominative plural (cf. App. 13 note, 14).

22:9 **ἐπὶ τὰς διεξόδους τῶν ὁδῶν**: τῶν ὁδῶν is a partitive genitive. They are to go to major routes of the city where they are likely to find many people.

22:10 **πονηρούς τε καὶ ἀγαθούς**: *both bad and good*; the enclitic conjunction follows the word it modifies. The adjectives are used as substantives. All are invited into the kingdom.

καὶ ἐπλήσθη ὁ γάμος ἀνακειμένων. 22:11 εἰσελθὼν δὲ ὁ βασιλεὺς θεάσασθαι τοὺς ἀνακειμένους εἶδεν ἐκεῖ ἄνθρωπον οὐκ ἐνδεδυμένον ἔνδυμα γάμου, 22:12 καὶ λέγει αὐτῷ, Ἑταῖρε, πῶς εἰσῆλθες ὧδε μὴ ἔχων ἔνδυμα γάμου; ὁ δὲ ἐφιμώθη. 22:13 τότε ὁ βασιλεὺς εἶπεν τοῖς διακόνοις, Δήσαντες αὐτοῦ πόδας καὶ χεῖρας ἐκβάλετε αὐτὸν εἰς τὸ σκότος τὸ ἐξώτερον· ἐκεῖ ἔσται ὁ κλαυθμὸς καὶ ὁ βρυγμὸς τῶν ὀδόντων. 22:14 πολλοὶ γάρ εἰσιν κλητοί, ὀλίγοι δὲ ἐκλεκτοί.

22:10
πίμπλημι, πλήσω, ἐπλήστην fill, fulfill
ἀνάκειμαι, ἀνακείσομαι lie down, recline at table as a dinner guest
22:11
θεάομαι, θεάσομαι, ἐθεασάμην, τεθέαμαι see, look at, gaze upon, discern with the eyes
ἀνάκειμαι, ἀνακείσομαι lie down, recline at table as a dinner guest
ἐνδύω, ἐνδύσω, ἐνέδυσα dress, clothe; clothe oneself in, put on (middle)
ἔνδυμα, ατος, τό garment, clothing; cloak, mantle
γάμος, ου, ὁ wedding, marriage
22:12
ἑταῖρος, ου, ὁ comrade, companion, fellow, friend
πῶς how? in what way? in what sense? (interrogative adverb)
ἔνδυμα, ατος, τό garment, clothing; cloak, mantle
γάμος, ου, ὁ wedding, marriage
φιμόω, φιμώσω, ἐφίμωσα, πεφίμωμαι, ἐφιμώθην muzzle, silence; be silent, be speechless, be hushed (passive)
22:13
διάκονος, ου, ὁ attendant, servant
δέω, δήσω, ἔδησα, δέδεκα, δέδεμαι, ἐδέθην bind, tie, impede
πούς, ποδός, ὁ foot
σκότος, ους, τό darkness, gloom
ἐξώτερος, α, ον outer, external
κλαυθμός, ου, ὁ weeping, crying
βρυγμός, οῦ, ὁ chattering (of teeth), gnashing (of teeth)
ὀδούς, ὀδόντος, ὁ tooth
22:14
κλητός, ή, όν called, invited
ἐκλεκτός, ή, όν chosen, selected; elect; exalted; precious, choice

---

22:10 **ἐπλήσθη ὁ γάμος ἀνακειμένων**: *the hall was filled with guests*; the genitive is used with verbs meaning *to fill* and *full of*.

22:11 **οὐκ ἐνδεδυμένον ἔνδυμα γάμου**: *who was not wearing a wedding garment*; the participle is in the middle voice: he had not put on a wedding garment. The garment may represent righteousness or virtuous living. While all are invited (10), not all live the commandments and maintain their worthiness.

22:12 **πῶς εἰσῆλθες ὧδε**: *how did you get in here*. **μὴ ἔχων**: *if you did not have*; the circumstantial participle may be interpreted conditionally.

22:13 **Δήσαντες . . . ἐκβάλετε αὐτὸν**: *bind . . . and cast him out*; when a participle modifies an imperative, it is commonly changed into an imperative and the two verbs are coordinated in translation.

22:15 Τότε πορευθέντες οἱ Φαρισαῖοι συμβούλιον ἔλαβον ὅπως
αὐτὸν παγιδεύσωσιν ἐν λόγῳ. 22:16 καὶ ἀποστέλλουσιν αὐτῷ τοὺς
μαθητὰς αὐτῶν μετὰ τῶν Ἡρῳδιανῶν λέγοντες, Διδάσκαλε, οἴδαμεν
ὅτι ἀληθὴς εἶ καὶ τὴν ὁδὸν τοῦ θεοῦ ἐν ἀληθείᾳ διδάσκεις καὶ οὐ
μέλει σοι περὶ οὐδενός· οὐ γὰρ βλέπεις εἰς πρόσωπον ἀνθρώπων.
22:17 εἰπὲ οὖν ἡμῖν τί σοι δοκεῖ· ἔξεστιν δοῦναι κῆνσον Καίσαρι ἢ οὔ;

22:15
συμβούλιον, ίου, τό counsel, plan, consultation; συμβούλιον λαμβάνειν form a plan, consult, plot
παγιδεύω, παγιδεύσω set a snare, trap; entrap
22:16
Ἡρῳδιανοί, ῶν, οἱ the Herodians
διδάσκαλος, ου, ὁ master, teacher
οἶδα know
ἀληθής, ές true, real
ἀλήθεια, ας, ἡ truth
μέλει, μελήσει, ἐμέλησεν there is a care, it is a concern
βλέπω, βλέψω, ἔβλεψα see, behold, perceive
πρόσωπον, ου, τό face, countenance
22:17
ἔξεστι(ν) it is permitted, it is possible (impersonal verb)
κῆνσος, ου, ὁ tribute, tax, poll-tax
Καῖσαρ, ος, ὁ Caesar

22:15 **ὅπως . . . παγιδεύσωσιν**: the conjunction with the subjunctive is used to indicate purpose.

22:16 **οὐ μέλει σοι περὶ οὐδενός**: *you worry about no man,* i.e., *you court no man's favor*; the impersonal construction may be changed to a personal one. **οὐ γὰρ βλέπεις εἰς πρόσωπον ἀνθρώπων**: *for you do not regard the countenance of men*; the two statements of the same tenor are intended to encourage Jesus to speak freely without fear of repercussions from Herod or Caesar.

22:17 **τί σοι δοκεῖ**: the idiom means *what do you think.* **ἔξεστιν δοῦναι κῆνσον Καίσαρι ἢ οὔ**: the trap is: if He answers in the affirmative He runs the risk of alienating a large part of the population that despises the occupation of the Romans; if He answers in the negative He makes himself culpable of treason.

22:18 γνοὺς δὲ ὁ Ἰησοῦς τὴν πονηρίαν αὐτῶν εἶπεν, Τί με πειράζετε,
ὑποκριταί; 22:19 ἐπιδείξατέ μοι τὸ νόμισμα τοῦ κήνσου. οἱ δὲ
προσήνεγκαν αὐτῷ δηνάριον. 22:20 καὶ λέγει αὐτοῖς, Τίνος ἡ εἰκὼν
αὕτη καὶ ἡ ἐπιγραφή; 22:21 λέγουσιν αὐτῷ, Καίσαρος. τότε λέγει
αὐτοῖς, Ἀπόδοτε οὖν τὰ Καίσαρος Καίσαρι καὶ τὰ τοῦ θεοῦ τῷ θεῷ.
22:22 καὶ ἀκούσαντες ἐθαύμασαν, καὶ ἀφέντες αὐτὸν ἀπῆλθαν.

22:18

πονηρία, ας, ἡ evil disposition, wickedness, mischief

πειράζω, πειράσω, ἐπείρασα, πεπείρασμαι, ἐπειράσθην try, test, tempt, prove

ὑποκριτής, οῦ, ὁ hypocrite, pretender, dissembler

22:19

ἐπιδείκνυμι, ἐπιδείξω, ἐπέδειξα, ἐπιδέδειχα, ἐπιδέδειγμαι, ἐπεδείχθην show, point out, declare

νόμισμα, ατος, τό coin

κῆνσος, ου, ὁ tribute, tax, poll-tax

δηνάριον, ου, τό denarius (a Roman silver coin)

22:20

εἰκων, ονος, ἡ image, likeness, representation

ἐπιγραφή, ῆς, ἡ inscription

22:21

Καῖσαρ, ος, ὁ Caesar

22:22

θαυμάζω, θαυμάσομαι, ἐθαύμασα, ἐθαυμάσθην wonder, marvel, be astonished

---

22:19 **τό νόμισμα τοῦ κήνσου**: *the tribute coin.* **προσήνεγκαν**, the first aorist of προσφέρω, also shows a second aorist in προσήνεγκον. The distinction between the first and second aorist is only one of form, not of tense or meaning.

22:20 **Τίνος**: supply ἐστίν both in this clause and in the next.

22:21 **τὰ Καίσαρος**: *what is Caesar's.*

22:22 **ἀφέντες**: the second aorist participle of ἀφίημι is declined like the aorist passive participle of the **ω** verb (cf. App. 34).

22:23 Ἐν ἐκείνῃ τῇ ἡμέρᾳ προσῆλθον αὐτῷ Σαδδουκαῖοι, λέγοντες μὴ εἶναι ἀνάστασιν, καὶ ἐπηρώτησαν αὐτὸν 22:24 λέγοντες, Διδάσκαλε, Μωϋσῆς εἶπεν, Ἐάν τις ἀποθάνῃ μὴ ἔχων τέκνα, ἐπιγαμβρεύσει ὁ ἀδελφὸς αὐτοῦ τὴν γυναῖκα αὐτοῦ καὶ ἀναστήσει σπέρμα τῷ ἀδελφῷ αὐτοῦ. 22:25 ἦσαν δὲ παρ' ἡμῖν ἑπτὰ ἀδελφοί· καὶ ὁ πρῶτος γήμας ἐτελεύτησεν, καὶ μὴ ἔχων σπέρμα ἀφῆκεν τὴν γυναῖκα αὐτοῦ τῷ ἀδελφῷ αὐτοῦ· 22:26 ὁμοίως καὶ ὁ δεύτερος καὶ ὁ τρίτος ἕως τῶν ἑπτά.

22:23
ἀνάστασις, εως, ἡ rise, rising, resurrection
ἐπερωτάω, ἐπερωτήσω, ἐπηρώτησα ask, ask a question, interrogate, question; inquire after
22:24
διδάσκαλος, ου, ὁ master, teacher
Μωϋσῆς, έως, ὁ Moses
ἀποθνήσκω, ἀποθανοῦμαι, ἀπέθανον (2 aorist) die, face death, decay
τέκνον, ου, τό child, descendant, posterity
ἐπιγαμβρεύω, ἐπιγαμβρεύσω marry as next of kin
ἀνίστημι, ἀναστήσω, ἀνέστησα, ἀνέστην (2 aorist) cause to rise, raise, raise up; cause to be born (transitive); rise, stand up, get up (2 aorist and all middle forms are intransitive)
σπέρμα, ατος, τό seed; descendant, child, posterity
22:25
ἑπτά seven (indeclinable)
γαμέω, γαμήσω, ἔγημα/ἐγάμησα, γεγάμηκα, ἐγαμήθην marry, take a wife
τελευτάω, τελευτήσω, ἐτελεύτησα, τετελεύτηκα end one's life, finish, die
σπέρμα, ατος, τό seed; descendant, child, posterity
22:26
ὁμοίως likewise, also, similarly (adverb)
δεύτερος, α, ον second
τρίτος, η, ον third
ἕως even, as many as (of number)
ἑπτά seven (indeclinable)

22:23 **λέγοντες μὴ εἶναι ἀνάστασιν**: *who maintain that there is no resurrection;* the Sadducees rejected any teachings beyond those made explicit in the Pentateuch, the five books of Moses, or the Law.

22:24 **Ἐάν** introduces a future more vivid condition (App. 70). The levirate law protects the widow and assures family succession.

22:25 **παρ' ἡμῖν**: *among us;* the prepositional phrase adds a touch of reality in an otherwise feigned story. **γήμας**: *after he had married.* **ἐτελεύτησεν** is a euphemism that almost aways connotes death.

22:27 ὕστερον δὲ πάντων ἀπέθανεν ἡ γυνή. 22:28 ἐν τῇ
ἀναστάσει οὖν τίνος τῶν ἑπτὰ ἔσται γυνή; πάντες γὰρ ἔσχον
αὐτήν· 22:29 ἀποκριθεὶς δὲ ὁ Ἰησοῦς εἶπεν αὐτοῖς, Πλανᾶσθε μὴ
εἰδότες τὰς γραφὰς μηδὲ τὴν δύναμιν τοῦ θεοῦ· 22:30 ἐν γὰρ τῇ
ἀναστάσει οὔτε γαμοῦσιν οὔτε γαμίζονται, ἀλλ' ὡς ἄγγελοι ἐν τῷ
οὐρανῷ εἰσιν.

22:27

ὕστερος, α, ον later; ὕστερον later, afterwards; finally; last (adverb)

ἀποθνήσκω, ἀποθανοῦμαι, ἀπέθανον (2 aorist) die, face death, decay

22:28

ἀνάστασις, εως, ἡ rise, rising, resurrection

ἑπτά seven (indeclinable)

22:29

πλανάω, πλανήσω, ἐπλάνησα, πεπλάνημαι, ἐπλανήθην lead astray, cause to wander, mislead, deceive; go astray, wander about, stray, be deceived, err (passive)

γραφή, ῆς, ἡ writing, Holy Scripture, passage of scripture

μηδέ and not, but not; nor (following a negation)

δύναμις, εως, ἡ power; strength, ability; authority; might, majesty; omnipotence; miraculous power, miracle

22:30

ἀνάστασις, εως, ἡ rise, rising, resurrection

οὔτε and not, not even (conjunction); οὔτε . . . οὔτε neither . . . nor

γαμέω, γαμήσω, ἔγημα/ἐγάμησα, γεγάμηκα, ἐγαμήθην marry, take a wife

γαμίζω, γαμίσω give in marriage

22:27 **ὕστερον . . . πάντων**: *last of all*; ὕστερον is used adverbially.

22:28 **τίνος τῶν ἑπτὰ ἔσται γυνή**: whose wife will she be of the seven. **πάντες γὰρ ἔσχον αὐτήν**: *for all married her*; the idiom understands the addition of γυναῖκα: *as wife*.

22:29 **Πλανᾶσθε**: in addition to not believing in the resurrection, the Sadducees fail to understand that according to the Law and by the power of God, binding actions such as those performed at weddings by proper authority on the earth will be in effect in the eternities (16:19, 18:18).

22:30 **ἐν γὰρ τῇ ἀναστάσει**: marriages are ordinances and covenants performed on the earth in mortality. **οὔτε γαμοῦσιν οὔτε γαμίζονται**: the Greek language traditionally distinguishes between the action of marriage partners: the groom marries; the bride is given in marriage. **ὡς ἄγγελοι**: since she is not married by the power that binds on earth and in heaven, the wife will be married to none of the Sadducee brothers in heaven.

22:31 περὶ δὲ τῆς ἀναστάσεως τῶν νεκρῶν οὐκ ἀνέγνωτε τὸ ῥηθὲν ὑμῖν ὑπὸ τοῦ θεοῦ λέγοντος, 22:32 Ἐγώ εἰμι ὁ θεὸς Ἀβραὰμ καὶ ὁ θεὸς Ἰσαὰκ καὶ ὁ θεὸς Ἰακώβ; οὐκ ἔστιν [ὁ] θεὸς νεκρῶν ἀλλὰ ζώντων. 22:33 καὶ ἀκούσαντες οἱ ὄχλοι ἐξεπλήσσοντο ἐπὶ τῇ διδαχῇ αὐτοῦ.

22:34 Οἱ δὲ Φαρισαῖοι ἀκούσαντες ὅτι ἐφίμωσεν τοὺς Σαδδουκαίους συνήχθησαν ἐπὶ τὸ αὐτό, 22:35 καὶ ἐπηρώτησεν εἷς ἐξ αὐτῶν [νομικὸς] πειράζων αὐτόν,

---

22:31

ἀνάστασις, εως, ἡ rise, rising, resurrection

νεκρός, ά, όν dead

ἀναγινώσκω, ἀναγνώσομαι, ἀνέγνων (2 aorist), ἀνέγνωκα, ἀνέγνωσμαι, ἀνεγνώσθην read, read aloud, read in public

22:32

νεκρός, ά, όν dead

ζάω, ζήσω/ζήσομαι, ἔζησα, ἔζηκα live

22:33

ἐκπλήσσω, ἐκπλήξω, ἐξέπληξα, ἐξεπλάγην amaze, astound, overwhelm

διδαχή, ῆς, ἡ teaching, instruction

22:34

φιμόω, φιμώσω, ἐφίμωσα, πεφίμωμαι, ἐφιμώθην muzzle, silence; be silent, be speechless, be hushed (passive)

συνάγω, συνάξω, συνήγαγον (2 aorist), συνῆγμαι, συνήχθην gather in, gather up, bring together; convene, come together, meet (passive)

22:35

ἐπερωτάω, ἐπερωτήσω, ἐπηρώτησα ask, ask a question, interrogate, question; inquire after

νομικός, ή, όν pertaining to law; a jurist, lawyer, an interpreter and teacher of the Mosaic law (substantive)

πειράζω, πειράσω, ἐπείρασα, πεπείρασμαι, ἐπειράσθην try, test, tempt, prove

---

22:31 **τὸ ῥηθὲν**: *that which was spoken*; the verbal form is a neuter singular nominative first aorist passive participle (cf. App. 53, G, 5; 34) of the verb λέγω.

22:32 **Ἐγώ εἰμι ὁ θεὸς Ἀβραὰμ**: *I am the God of Abraham*; the present tense suggests that Abraham and the Abrahamic covenants are alive and well in the resurrection. **οὐκ ἔστιν [ὁ] θεὸς**: *He is not the God*; the predicate nominative takes an article.

22:34 **ἐπὶ τὸ αὐτό**: *at the same place.*

22:35 **[νομικὸς]** stands in apposition.

22:36 Διδάσκαλε, ποία ἐντολὴ μεγάλη ἐν τῷ νόμῳ; 22:37 ὁ δὲ ἔφη
αὐτῷ, Ἀγαπήσεις κύριον τὸν θεόν σου ἐν ὅλῃ τῇ καρδίᾳ σου καὶ
ἐν ὅλῃ τῇ ψυχῇ σου καὶ ἐν ὅλῃ τῇ διανοίᾳ σου· 22:38 αὕτη ἐστὶν ἡ
μεγάλη καὶ πρώτη ἐντολή. 22:39 δευτέρα δὲ ὁμοία αὐτῇ, Ἀγαπήσεις
τὸν πλησίον σου ὡς σεαυτόν. 22:40 ἐν ταύταις ταῖς δυσὶν ἐντολαῖς
ὅλος ὁ νόμος κρέμαται καὶ οἱ προφῆται.

22:41 Συνηγμένων δὲ τῶν Φαρισαίων ἐπηρώτησεν αὐτοὺς ὁ
Ἰησοῦς 22:42 λέγων, Τί ὑμῖν δοκεῖ περὶ τοῦ Χριστοῦ; τίνος υἱός
ἐστιν; λέγουσιν αὐτῷ, Τοῦ Δαυίδ.

22:36
διδάσκαλος, ου, ὁ master, teacher
ποῖος, ποία, ποῖον of what kind? of what sort? of what species? what? which?
ἐντολή, ῆς, ἡ command, commandment
νόμος, ου, ὁ law, custom, ordinance
22:37
ἀγαπάω, ἀγαπήσω, ἠγάπησα, ἠγάπηκα, ἠγάπημαι, ἠγαπήθην love, cherish, value
διάνοια, ας, ἡ mind, intellect, understanding
22:38
ἐντολή, ῆς, ἡ command, commandment
22:39
δεύτερος, α, ον second
ὅμοιος, οία, οιον like, similar (+ dative)
ἀγαπάω, ἀγαπήσω, ἠγάπησα, ἠγάπηκα, ἠγάπημαι, ἠγαπήθην love, cherish, value
πλησίον near, close to (adverb, preposition + genitive); ὁ πλησίον neighbor; a friendly neighbor
σεαυτοῦ, ῆς, οῦ yourself (reflexive pronoun)
22:40
ἐντολή, ῆς, ἡ command, commandment
νόμος, ου, ὁ law, custom, ordinance
κρεμάννυμι, κρεμάσω, ἐκρέμασα, ἐκρεμάσθην hang, suspend; depend
22:41
ἐπερωτάω, ἐπερωτήσω, ἐπηρώτησα ask, ask a question, interrogate, question; inquire after

---

22:36 **ποία ἐντολὴ μεγάλη**: supply ἐστιν.

22:37 **κύριον**: supply τὸν.

22:38 **ἡ μεγάλη . . . πρώτη ἐντολή**: μεγάλη may have a superlative sense with πρώτη. The noun and the adjectives stand in predicate position.

22:39 **δευτέρα**: supply ἡ and ἐστιν.

22:40 **κρέμαται**: the verb depends on the closest noun to it for its number.

22:41 **Συνηγμένων δὲ τῶν Φαρισαίων**: *while the Pharisees were gathered together*; the construction is a genitive absolute.

22:42 **Τί ὑμῖν δοκεῖ**: the idiom means *what do you think*.

22:43 λέγει αὐτοῖς, Πῶς οὖν Δαυὶδ ἐν πνεύματι καλεῖ αὐτὸν κύριον λέγων,

22:44 Εἶπεν κύριος τῷ κυρίῳ μου,
Κάθου ἐκ δεξιῶν μου,
ἕως ἂν θῶ τοὺς ἐχθρούς σου ὑποκάτω τῶν ποδῶν σου;

22:45 εἰ οὖν Δαυὶδ καλεῖ αὐτὸν κύριον, πῶς υἱὸς αὐτοῦ ἐστιν; 22:46
καὶ οὐδεὶς ἐδύνατο ἀποκριθῆναι αὐτῷ λόγον οὐδὲ ἐτόλμησέν τις ἀπ'
ἐκείνης τῆς ἡμέρας ἐπερωτῆσαι αὐτὸν οὐκέτι.

22:43
πνεῦμα, ατος, τό wind, spirit, mind, Holy Spirit
22:44
κάθημαι, καθήσομαι sit, stay, reside
δεξιός, ά, όν right (as opposed to *left*); ἐκ δεξιῶν τινός at someone's right
τίθημι, θήσω, ἔθηκα, τέθεικα, τέθειμαι, ἐτέθην place, set, lay, render, serve, give
ἐχθρός, ά, όν hostile, inimical; enemy, adversary (substantive)
ὑποκάτω under (adverb + genitive)
πούς, ποδός, ὁ foot
22:46
τολμάω, τολμήσω, ἐτόλμησα, dare, have the courage (+ infinitive)
οὐκέτι no more, no longer, no further (adverb)

22:43 **ἐν πνεύματι**: *by the gift of the Spirit.* **καλεῖ αὐτὸν κύριον**: *does call Him Lord*; the verb takes a double accusative; in addition to the direct object it takes a predicate accusative. Their answer causes Jesus to try to raise their understanding to a greater level of awareness of his divinity as the Son of God.

22:44 **κύριος τῷ κυρίῳ μου**: David gives an account of the Father speaking to the Son messianically (Ps 110). David's refererence to both the Father and the Son by the title κύριος may confuse the Pharisees. **ἕως ἂν θῶ**: *until I place*; the temporal conjunction with the aorist subjunctive and the particle ἂν refers indefinitely to the future and denotes that the commencement of one event is dependent on another.

22:45 **πῶς υἱὸς αὐτοῦ ἐστιν**: *how is He his Son*; Jesus continues to press the Pharisees about his divine sonship.

22:46 **οὐδεὶς ἐδύνατο ἀποκριθῆναι αὐτῷ λόγον**: they fail to understand that He is the Son of God who will come through the lineage of David and will ultimately sit at the right hand of God as the Messiah.

23 Τότε ὁ Ἰησοῦς ἐλάλησεν τοῖς ὄχλοις καὶ τοῖς μαθηταῖς αὐτοῦ
23:2 λέγων, Ἐπὶ τῆς Μωϋσέως καθέδρας ἐκάθισαν οἱ γραμματεῖς
καὶ οἱ Φαρισαῖοι. 23:3 πάντα οὖν ὅσα ἐὰν εἴπωσιν ὑμῖν ποιήσατε
καὶ τηρεῖτε, κατὰ δὲ τὰ ἔργα αὐτῶν μὴ ποιεῖτε· λέγουσιν γὰρ καὶ οὐ
ποιοῦσιν. 23:4 δεσμεύουσιν δὲ φορτία βαρέα [καὶ δυσβάστακτα]
καὶ ἐπιτιθέασιν ἐπὶ τοὺς ὤμους τῶν ἀνθρώπων, αὐτοὶ δὲ τῷ δακτύλῳ
αὐτῶν οὐ θέλουσιν κινῆσαι αὐτά.

23:2
καθέδρα, ας, ἡ seat
καθίζω, καθίσω, ἐκάθισα, κεκάθικα cause to sit down, seat, set (transitive); sit, sit down; remain, stay, continue, rest (intransitive)
23:3
τηρέω, τηρήσω, ἐτήρησα, τετήρηκα, τετήρημαι, ἐτηρήθην guard, heed, preserve, reserve
ἔργον, ου, τό work, deed, action
23:4
δεσμεύω, δεσμεύσω bind, bind up
φορτίον, ου, τό load, burden
βαρύς, εῖα, ύ heavy; burdensome, oppressive; weighty, important, momentous
δυσβάστακτος, ον hard to bear, oppressive
ἐπιτίθημι, ἐπιθήσω, ἐπέθηκα, ἐπιτέθεικα, ἐπιτέθειμαι, ἐπετέθην lay upon, put on
ὦμος, ου, ὁ shoulder
δάκτυλος, ου, ὁ finger
κινέω, κινήσω, ἐκίνησα to move; to excite; to shake

23:2 **Ἐπὶ τῆς Μωϋσέως καθέδρας ἐκάθισαν**: καθέδρας is probably used metaphorically as the seat of authority. ἐκάθισαν: *they sit*; the verbal form is a gnomic aorist. The aorist may be used to express a general truth where the experience of an action in the past suggests an action that is likely to be repeated.

23:3 **πάντα . . . ὅσα**: *all that*; in conjunction with πάντα, ὅσα is translated as a relative pronoun. **κατὰ . . . τὰ ἔργα αὐτῶν**: *after the manner of their works*.

23:4 **ἐπιτιθέασιν**: supply αὐτὰ, the personal pronoun. **αὐτοὶ δὲ**: *but they themselves*; αὐτοὶ in the nominative is used as an intensive pronoun (App. 40, note 2).

23:5 πάντα δὲ τὰ ἔργα αὐτῶν ποιοῦσιν πρὸς τὸ θεαθῆναι
τοῖς ἀνθρώποις· πλατύνουσιν γὰρ τὰ φυλακτήρια αὐτῶν καὶ
μεγαλύνουσιν τὰ κράσπεδα, 23:6 φιλοῦσιν δὲ τὴν πρωτοκλισίαν ἐν
τοῖς δείπνοις καὶ τὰς πρωτοκαθεδρίας ἐν ταῖς συναγωγαῖς 23:7 καὶ
τοὺς ἀσπασμοὺς ἐν ταῖς ἀγοραῖς καὶ καλεῖσθαι ὑπὸ τῶν ἀνθρώπων,
Ῥαββί. 23:8 ὑμεῖς δὲ μὴ κληθῆτε, Ῥαββί· εἷς γάρ ἐστιν ὑμῶν ὁ
διδάσκαλος, πάντες δὲ ὑμεῖς ἀδελφοί ἐστε. 23:9 καὶ πατέρα μὴ
καλέσητε ὑμῶν ἐπὶ τῆς γῆς, εἷς γάρ ἐστιν ὑμῶν ὁ πατὴρ ὁ οὐράνιος.

23:5
ἔργον, ου, τό work, deed, action
θεάομαι, θεάσομαι, ἐθεασάμην, τεθέαμαι, ἐθεάθην see, look at, gaze upon, discern with the eyes
πλατύνω, πλατυνῶ, πεπλάτυμαι, ἐπλατύνθην to widen, enlarge
φυλακτήριον, ου, τό station of a guard; safeguard; phylactery (a small box containing scriptural verses, bound on forehead and arm during prayer)
μεγαλύνω, μεγαλυνῶ, ἐμεγάλυνα enlarge, amplify, magnify; exalt, glorify, praise
κράσπεδον, ου, τό edge, border, hem; tassel

23:6
πρωτοκλισία, ας, ἡ first place of reclining at the table, the most honorable place at the table
δεῖπνον, ου, τό dinner, supper
πρωτοκαθεδρία, ας, ἡ the first seat, the most honorable seat
συναγωγή, ῆς, ἡ synagogue

23:7
ἀσπασμός, οῦ, ὁ greeting
ἀγορά, ᾶς, ἡ marketplace

23:9
γῆ, γῆς, ἡ earth, soil, land, region, country
οὐράνιος, ία, ιον heavenly, celestial

23:5 **πρὸς τὸ θεαθῆναι τοῖς ἀνθρώποις**: *to be seen by men*; πρὸς τὸ θεαθῆναι is an articular infinitive. As a noun the infinitive takes an article which is the object of the preposition πρὸς: *for the purpose of*. Since the verbal noun is passive, agency is expressed by the dative case.

23:8 **εἷς**: the primary authority as teacher is Christ (10).

23:9 **εἷς**: the primary father figure is God.

23:10 μηδὲ κληθῆτε καθηγηταί, ὅτι καθηγητὴς ὑμῶν ἐστιν εἷς ὁ Χριστός. 23:11 ὁ δὲ μείζων ὑμῶν ἔσται ὑμῶν διάκονος. 23:12 ὅστις δὲ ὑψώσει ἑαυτὸν ταπεινωθήσεται καὶ ὅστις ταπεινώσει ἑαυτὸν ὑψωθήσεται.

23:13 Οὐαὶ δὲ ὑμῖν, γραμματεῖς καὶ Φαρισαῖοι ὑποκριταί, ὅτι κλείετε τὴν βασιλείαν τῶν οὐρανῶν ἔμπροσθεν τῶν ἀνθρώπων· ὑμεῖς γὰρ οὐκ εἰσέρχεσθε οὐδὲ τοὺς εἰσερχομένους ἀφίετε εἰσελθεῖν.

23:10
καθηγητής, οῦ, ὁ leader; teacher, instructor
23:11
μείζων, μεῖζον greater, larger
διάκονος, ου, ὁ attendant, servant
23:12
ὑψόω, ὑψώσω, ὕψωσα, ὑψώθην lift up, raise high, exalt
ταπεινόω, ταπεινώσω, ἐταπείνωσα bring low; humble
23:13
οὐαί woe! alas! (interjection)
ὑποκριτής, οῦ, ὁ hypocrite, pretender, dissembler
κλείω, κλείσω, ἔκλεισα, κέκλεισμαι, ἐκλείσθην close, shut, lock

---

23:10 **ὁ Χριστός** stands in apposition to **εἷς**.

23:11 **ὁ δὲ μείζων ὑμῶν**: *but he who is the greatest among you*; the comparative stands for a superlative.

23:12 **ὅστις δὲ ὑψώσει ἑαυτὸν ταπεινωθήσεται**: the indefinite relative pronoun introduces a future most vivid condition instead of εἰ and takes a future in both the protasis and apodosis. The chiastic structure in the sentence emphasizes the eschatological reversal.

23:13 **Οὐαὶ δὲ ὑμῖν**: *but woe to you*; the exclamatory interjection governs the dative of person or thing. The formulaic pattern occurs throughout the chapter. **κλείετε τὴν βασιλείαν** means *you shut the doors of the kingdom.* **ἔμπροσθεν τῶν ἀνθρώπων**: *in the face of men.*

23:14 The verse is not shown in the Fourth Revised Edition and not included in the better manuscripts. The apparatus criticus reads: **Οὐαὶ δὲ ὑμῖν, γραμματεῖς καὶ Φαρισαῖοι ὑποκριταί, ὅτι κατεσθίετε τὰς οἰκίας τῶν χηρῶν καὶ προφάσει μακρὰ προσευχόμενοι· διὰ τοῦτο λήμψεσθε περισσότερον κρίμα**: *but woe to you scribes and Pharisees, hypocrites! because you consume the homes of widows and as a pretext you offer long prayers. For this reason you will receive greater condemnation.* (cf. Mk 12:40; Lk 20:47).

23:15 Οὐαὶ ὑμῖν, γραμματεῖς καὶ Φαρισαῖοι ὑποκριταί, ὅτι περιάγετε τὴν θάλασσαν καὶ τὴν ξηρὰν ποιῆσαι ἕνα προσήλυτον, καὶ ὅταν γένηται ποιεῖτε αὐτὸν υἱὸν γεέννης διπλότερον ὑμῶν.
23:16 Οὐαὶ ὑμῖν, ὁδηγοὶ τυφλοὶ οἱ λέγοντες, Ὃς ἂν ὀμόσῃ ἐν τῷ ναῷ, οὐδέν ἐστιν· ὃς δ' ἂν ὀμόσῃ ἐν τῷ χρυσῷ τοῦ ναοῦ, ὀφείλει.
23:17 μωροὶ καὶ τυφλοί, τίς γὰρ μείζων ἐστίν, ὁ χρυσὸς ἢ ὁ ναὸς ὁ ἁγιάσας τὸν χρυσόν;

23:15
οὐαί woe! alas! (interjection)
περιάγω, περιάξω lead around; traverse
θάλασσα, ης, ἡ sea
ξηρός, ά, όν dried up, withered, paralyzed; ἡ ξηρά (γῆ) dry land, land
προσήλυτος, ου, ὁ, ἡ proselyte, convert
γέεννα, ης, ἡ Gehenna, Valley of Hinnom, hell, the fires of Tartarus (a place known for sacrifices to Moloch, pollution, pestilence, punishment of malefactors, and continually burning fires)
διπλότερον twofold more, twice more (comparative adverb of διπλοῦς, ῆ, οῦν double, twofold)
23:16
οὐαί woe! alas! (interjection)
ὁδηγός, ου, ὁ guide, leader; instructor, teacher
τυφλός, ή, όν blind
ὀμνύω/ὄμνυμι, ὀμοῦμαι, ὤμοσα, ὀμώμοκα swear, promise with an oath
ναός, οῦ, ὁ dwelling, temple
χρυσός, οῦ, ὁ gold
ὀφείλω (only in present and imperfect) owe, ought, must, deserve
23:17
μωρός, ά, όν foolish, wicked, impious
μείζων, μεῖζον greater, larger
χρυσός, οῦ, ὁ gold
ναός, οῦ, ὁ dwelling, temple
ἁγιάζω, ἁγιάσω, ἡγίασα, ἡγίακα, ἡγίασμαι, ἡγιάσθην separate, consecrate; cleanse, purify, sanctify; regard as holy

---

23:15 **περιάγετε . . . ποιῆσαι**: *you traverse . . . to win*; the verb of motion introduces an infinitive of purpose. **ὅταν γένηται**: *whenever he becomes*; supply προσήλυτος. **ποιεῖτε αὐτὸν υἱὸν γεέννης διπλότερον ὑμῶν**: *you make him twofold more a son of Gehenna than yourselves*; ποιεῖτε takes a double accusative. ὑμῶν is a genitive of comparison.

23:16 **ὁδηγοὶ τυφλοί**: the oxymoron emphasizes the untenable nature of their position. **Ὃς ἂν ὀμόσῃ . . . οὐδέν ἐστιν**: *if any one swears . . .* (his oath) *is worthless* (literally: *it is nothing*); the relative clause forms virtually the protasis of a condition. **ὀφείλει**: *he is obligated* (by his oath); the verb is used in an absolute sense.

23:17 **μωροὶ καὶ τυφλοὶ**: *you blind fools*; the figure of speech, hendiadys, expands a single idea into a compound one for purposes of emphasis: you are blind and foolish men. The adjectives are used as substantives. **τίς**: *which of two*; the masculine interrogative pronoun agrees with both **ὁ χρυσὸς** and **ὁ ναὸς**.

23:18 καί, Ὃς ἂν ὀμόσῃ ἐν τῷ θυσιαστηρίῳ, οὐδέν ἐστιν· ὃς δ᾽ ἂν
ὀμόσῃ ἐν τῷ δώρῳ τῷ ἐπάνω αὐτοῦ, ὀφείλει. 23:19 τυφλοί, τί γὰρ
μεῖζον, τὸ δῶρον ἢ τὸ θυσιαστήριον τὸ ἁγιάζον τὸ δῶρον; 23:20
ὁ οὖν ὀμόσας ἐν τῷ θυσιαστηρίῳ ὀμνύει ἐν αὐτῷ καὶ ἐν πᾶσι τοῖς
ἐπάνω αὐτοῦ· 23:21 καὶ ὁ ὀμόσας ἐν τῷ ναῷ ὀμνύει ἐν αὐτῷ καὶ ἐν τῷ
κατοικοῦντι αὐτόν,

23:18
ὀμνύω/ὄμνυμι, ὀμοῦμαι, ὤμοσα, ὀμώμοκα swear, promise with an oath
θυσιαστήριον, ίου, τό altar
δῶρον, ου, τό gift, present
ἐπάνω over, above, on (adverb; preposition + genitive)
ὀφείλω (only in present and imperfect) owe, ought, must, deserve
23:19
μείζων, μεῖζον greater, larger
δῶρον, ου, τό gift, present
θυσιαστήριον, ίου, τό altar
ἁγιάζω, ἁγιάσω, ἡγίασα, ἡγίακα, ἡγίασμαι, ἡγιάσθην separate, consecrate; cleanse, purify, sanctify; regard as holy
23:20
ὀμνύω/ὄμνυμι, ὀμοῦμαι, ὤμοσα, ὀμώμοκα swear, promise with an oath
θυσιαστήριον, ίου, τό altar
ἐπάνω over, above, on (adverb; preposition + genitive)
23:21
ναός, οῦ, ὁ dwelling, temple
κατοικέω, κατοικήσω, κατῴκησα inhabit (transitive); live, dwell, reside, settle down (intransitive)

23:18 **οὐδέν ἐστιν**: (his oath) *is worthless*. **ὀφείλει**: *he is obligated* (by his oath); the verb is used in an absolute sense.

23:19 **τί γὰρ μεῖζον**: *which of the two is greater*; the neuter interrogative pronoun agrees with both **τὸ δῶρον** and **τὸ θυσιαστήριον**. **τὸ ἁγιάζον τὸ δῶρον**: *that sanctifies the gift*; the present active participle in attributive position agrees with its antecedent and takes an accusative object.

23:20 **ἐν πᾶσι τοῖς**: supply δώροις.

23:21 **καὶ ἐν τῷ κατοικοῦντι αὐτόν**: *and by Him who inhabits it*; the temple, as the Mercy Seat of the Ark of the Covenant before it (Ex 25:22, Lev 16:2, Num 7:89), was considered the earthly dwelling place of God (1 Kgs 8:11).

23:22 καὶ ὁ ὀμόσας ἐν τῷ οὐρανῷ ὀμνύει ἐν τῷ θρόνῳ τοῦ θεοῦ καὶ ἐν τῷ καθημένῳ ἐπάνω αὐτοῦ.

23:23 Οὐαὶ ὑμῖν, γραμματεῖς καὶ Φαρισαῖοι ὑποκριταί, ὅτι ἀποδεκατοῦτε τὸ ἡδύοσμον καὶ τὸ ἄνηθον καὶ τὸ κύμινον καὶ ἀφήκατε τὰ βαρύτερα τοῦ νόμου, τὴν κρίσιν καὶ τὸ ἔλεος καὶ τὴν πίστιν· ταῦτα [δὲ] ἔδει ποιῆσαι κἀκεῖνα μὴ ἀφιέναι. 23:24 ὁδηγοὶ τυφλοί, οἱ διϋλίζοντες τὸν κώνωπα, τὴν δὲ κάμηλον καταπίνοντες.

23:22

ὀμνύω/ὄμνυμι, ὀμοῦμαι, ὤμοσα, ὀμώμοκα swear, promise with an oath

θρόνος, ου, ὁ seat, throne; power, dominion

ἐπάνω over, above, on (adverb; preposition + genitive)

23:23

οὐαί woe! alas! (interjection)

ὑποκριτής, οῦ, ὁ hypocrite, pretender, dissembler

ἀποδεκατόω, ἀποδεκατώσω pay tithes of, give one-tenth of, tithe

ἡδύοσμον, ου, τό garden mint, mint

ἄνηθον, ου, τό anethum, dill

κύμινον, ου, τό cum(m)in, the fruit or seed of the cumin

βαρύς, εῖα, ύ heavy; burdensome, oppressive; weighty, important, momentous

νόμος, ου, ὁ law, custom, ordinance

ἔλεος, εως, τό/ὁ pity, mercy, compassion, clemency

πίστις, εως, ἡ faith, trust

δεῖ, δεήσει, ἐδέησε it is necessary, it is proper (impersonal verb from δέω)

23:24

ὁδηγός, ου, ὁ guide, leader; instructor, teacher

διϋλίζω, διϋλίσω filter out, strain out

κώνωψ, ωπος, ὁ gnat, mosquito

κάμηλος, ου, ὁ and ἡ camel

καταπίνω, καταπίομαι, κατέπιον (2 aorist), κατεπόθην drink, swallow, gulp down

---

23:22 **καὶ ἐν τῷ καθημένῳ ἐπάνω αὐτοῦ**: *and by Him who sits on it.*

23:23 **τὰ βαρύτερα**: *the more important matters*; the form is the comparative degree of the adjective that is used as a substantive. **τὴν κρίσιν . . . τὸ ἔλεος . . . τὴν πίστιν**: the nouns stand in apposition to τὰ βαρύτερα. Abstract nouns are generally modified by an article, which is omitted in translation. **ταῦτα [δὲ] ἔδει ποιῆσαι κἀκεῖνα μὴ ἀφιέναι**: *you should have performed the latter and not omitted the former*; the impersonal construction may be changed to a personal one.

23:24 **οἱ διϋλίζοντες τὸν κώνωπα, τὴν δὲ κάμηλον καταπίνοντες**: the chiastic construction expresses a hyperbole and juxtaposes the smallest to the largest unclean animal. Some Pharisees used to strain their water through a cloth to avoid drinking anything unclean.

23:25 Οὐαὶ ὑμῖν, γραμματεῖς καὶ Φαρισαῖοι ὑποκριταί, ὅτι
καθαρίζετε τὸ ἔξωθεν τοῦ ποτηρίου καὶ τῆς παροψίδος, ἔσωθεν
δὲ γέμουσιν ἐξ ἁρπαγῆς καὶ ἀκρασίας. 23:26 Φαρισαῖε τυφλέ,
καθάρισον πρῶτον τὸ ἐντὸς τοῦ ποτηρίου, ἵνα γένηται καὶ τὸ ἐκτὸς
αὐτοῦ καθαρόν.
23:27 Οὐαὶ ὑμῖν, γραμματεῖς καὶ Φαρισαῖοι ὑποκριταί, ὅτι
παρομοιάζετε τάφοις κεκονιαμένοις, οἵτινες ἔξωθεν μὲν φαίνονται
ὡραῖοι,

23:25
οὐαί woe! alas! (interjection)
ὑποκριτής, οῦ, ὁ hypocrite, pretender, dissembler
καθαρίζω, καθαρίσω, ἐκαθάρισα cleanse, render pure
ἔξωθεν outwardly, externally (adverb); τὸ ἔξωθεν the exterior, outside
ποτήριον, ου, τό cup
παροποψίς, ίδος, ἡ dish
ἔσωθεν from inside; inside, within (adverb)
γέμω be full
ἁρπαγή, ῆς, ἡ robbery, plunder, prey, spoil; greediness
ἀκρασίας, ας, ἡ intemperance, incontinence, self-indulgence
23:26
καθαρίζω, καθαρίσω, ἐκαθάρισα cleanse, render pure
πρῶτον first (in time; adverb)
ἐντός inside, within (adverb); τὸ ἐντός the interior, inside
ποτήριον, ου, τό cup
ἐκτός outside (adverb); τὸ ἐκτός the outside
καθαρός, ά, όν clean, pure
23:27
οὐαί woe! alas! (interjection)
ὑποκριτής, οῦ, ὁ hypocrite, pretender, dissembler
παρομοιάζω, παρομοιάσω be like, resemble
τάφος, ου, ὁ grave, tomb, sepulchre
κονιάω, κονιάσω, κεκονίαμαι whitewash, plaster
ἔξωθεν outwardly, externally (adverb); τὸ ἔξωθεν the exterior, outside
φαίνω, φανῶ, ἔφηνα, πέφαγκα, πέφηνα, πέφασμαι, ἐφάνθην, ἐφάνην shine, give light, be bright; be seen, appear, seem (middle or passive)
ὡραῖος, α, ον timely, seasonable, in bloom; beautiful, fair, lovely

---

23:25 **τὸ ἔξωθεν τοῦ ποτηρίου καὶ τῆς παροψίδος**: the vessels metaphorically represent the bodies of the scribes and Pharisees: they appear clean on the outside but are unclean on the inside. **γέμουσιν ἐκ ἁρπαγῆς**: *they are full of greed*; the preposition is used in conjunction with verbs of filling.

23:26 **Φαρισαῖε** stands in the vocative case. **καθαρόν** is a predicate adjective.

23:27 **παρομοιάζετε τάφοις κεκονιαμένοις**: the verb governs the dative case.

ἔσωθεν δὲ γέμουσιν ὀστέων νεκρῶν καὶ πάσης ἀκαθαρσίας. 23:28 οὕτως καὶ ὑμεῖς ἔξωθεν μὲν φαίνεσθε τοῖς ἀνθρώποις δίκαιοι, ἔσωθεν δέ ἐστε μεστοὶ ὑποκρίσεως καὶ ἀνομίας.

23:29 Οὐαὶ ὑμῖν, γραμματεῖς καὶ Φαρισαῖοι ὑποκριταί, ὅτι οἰκοδομεῖτε τοὺς τάφους τῶν προφητῶν καὶ κοσμεῖτε τὰ μνημεῖα τῶν δικαίων, 23:30 καὶ λέγετε, Εἰ ἤμεθα ἐν ταῖς ἡμέραις τῶν πατέρων ἡμῶν, οὐκ ἂν ἤμεθα αὐτῶν κοινωνοὶ ἐν τῷ αἵματι τῶν προφητῶν.

23:27
ἔσωθεν from inside; inside, within (adverb)
γέμω be full
ὀστέον, ου, (contracted to ὀστοῦν, ὀστοῦ) τό bone
νεκρός, ά, όν dead
ἀκαθαρσία, ας, ἡ impurity, refuse; immorality, lewdness
23:28
ἔξωθεν outwardly, externally (adverb); τὸ ἔξωθεν the exterior, outside
φαίνω, φανῶ, ἔφηνα, πέφαγκα, πέφηνα, πέφασμαι, ἐφάνθην, ἐφάνην shine, give light, be bright; be seen, appear, seem (middle or passive)
δίκαιος, αία, αιον right, just, honest, good, righteous
ἔσωθεν from inside; inside, within (adverb)
μεστός, ή, όν full
ὑπόκρισις, ως, ἡ acting; hypocrisy, simulation
ἀνομία, ας, ἡ lawlessness, iniquity, sin
23:29
οἰκοδομέω, οἰκοδομήσω, ᾠκοδόμησα, ᾠκοδομήθην build, construct, establish
τάφος, ου, ὁ grave, tomb, sepulchre
κοσμέω, κοσμήσω, ἐκόσμησα, κεκόσμηκα, κεκόσμημαι set in order, arrange; prepare, trim; decorate, adorn
μνημεῖον, ου, τό monument, grave, tomb
δίκαιος, αία, αιον right, just, honest, good, righteous
23:30
κοινωνός, οῦ, ὁ companion, partner, sharer
αἷμα, ατος, τό blood

23:27 **γέμουσιν ὀστέων νεκρῶν**: *full of dead men's bones*; the genitive is used with verbs signifying *to fill*. **πάσης ἀκαθαρσίας**: all content in the grave causes ritual impurity.

23:28 **φαίνεσθε τοῖς ἀνθρώποις δίκαιοι**: the verb governs the dative case. δίκαιοι is a predicate adjective.

23:30 **Εἰ ἤμεθα . . . ἤμεθα αὐτῶν κοινωνοὶ**: *if we had lived . . . we would not have been their partners*; the verbal form is an optional first person plural imperfect active indicative of εἰμί. The imperfect functions as an aorist to form a past contrary to fact condition.

23:31 ὥστε μαρτυρεῖτε ἑαυτοῖς ὅτι υἱοί ἐστε τῶν φονευσάντων τοὺς προφήτας. 23:32 καὶ ὑμεῖς πληρώσατε τὸ μέτρον τῶν πατέρων ὑμῶν. 23:33 ὄφεις, γεννήματα ἐχιδνῶν, πῶς φύγητε ἀπὸ τῆς κρίσεως τῆς γεέννης; 23:34 διὰ τοῦτο ἰδοὺ ἐγὼ ἀποστέλλω πρὸς ὑμᾶς προφήτας καὶ σοφοὺς καὶ γραμματεῖς· ἐξ αὐτῶν ἀποκτενεῖτε καὶ σταυρώσετε καὶ ἐξ αὐτῶν μαστιγώσετε ἐν ταῖς συναγωγαῖς ὑμῶν καὶ διώξετε ἀπὸ πόλεως εἰς πόλιν·

23:31

μαρτυρέω, μαρτυρήσω, ἐμαρτύρησα, μεμαρτύρηκα, μεμαρτύρημαι, ἐμαρτυρήθην bear witness, witness

φονεύω, φονεύσω, ἐφόνευσα murder, kill, commit murder

23:32

μέτρον, ου, τό measure

23:33

ὄφις, εως, ὁ snake, serpent

γέννημα, ατος, τό offspring, progeny, brood

ἔχιδνα, ης, ἡ viper, poisonous serpent

φεύγω, φεύξομαι, ἔφυγον (2 aorist) flee, flee from, avoid, shun

γέεννα, ης, ἡ Gehenna, Valley of Hinnom, hell, the fires of Tartarus (a place known for sacrifices to Moloch, pollution, pestilence, punishment of malefactors, and continually burning fires)

23:34

σοφός, ή, όν wise; clever, skillful; learned, intelligent

ἀποκτείνω, ἀποκτενῶ, ἀπέκτεινα, ἀπεκτάνθην kill, put to death, murder

σταυρόω, σταυρώσω, ἐσταύρωσα, ἐσταύρωμαι, ἐσταυρώθην crucify

μαστιγόω, μαστιγώσω, ἐμαστίγωσα, ἐμαστιγώθην scourge, whip, flog, beat

συναγωγή, ῆς, ἡ synagogue

διώκω, διώξω, ἐδίωξα, δεδίωγμαι, ἐδιώχθην persecute, pursue, seek after

---

23:31 **ὥστε μαρτυρεῖτε ἑαυτοῖς ὅτι**: *therefore you bear witness against yourselves that;* the illative particle introduces an independent clause.

23:32 **πληρώσατε τὸ μέτρον**: *fill the measure*; the phrase means to fill to capacity the measure that someone else has partly filled.

23:33 **πῶς φύγητε**: *how will you flee*; the deliberative subjunctive (present or aorist) is used when the speaker is perplexed about an action. Since the future is also used in deliberative questions, the subjunctive is appropriately translated by the future.

23:34 **διὰ τοῦτο**: *for this reason*; the prepositional phrase resumes the preceding theme of wickedness. **ἐξ αὐτῶν**: *some of them*; supply τινας as the object of the verb. ἐξ is used with the partitive genitive after the indefinite pronoun.

23:35 ὅπως ἔλθῃ ἐφ᾽ ὑμᾶς πᾶν αἷμα δίκαιον ἐκχυννόμενον ἐπὶ τῆς γῆς ἀπὸ τοῦ αἵματος Ἅβελ τοῦ δικαίου ἕως τοῦ αἵματος Ζαχαρίου υἱοῦ Βαραχίου, ὃν ἐφονεύσατε μεταξὺ τοῦ ναοῦ καὶ τοῦ θυσιαστηρίου. 23:36 ἀμὴν λέγω ὑμῖν, ἥξει ταῦτα πάντα ἐπὶ τὴν γενεὰν ταύτην.

23:37 Ἰερουσαλὴμ Ἰερουσαλήμ, ἡ ἀποκτείνουσα τοὺς προφήτας καὶ λιθοβολοῦσα τοὺς ἀπεσταλμένους πρὸς αὐτήν,

---

23:35
αἷμα, ατος, τό blood
δίκαιος, αία, αιον right, just, honest, good, righteous
ἐκχύνω, ἐκχυνῶ pour out, shed
Ἅβελ, ὁ Abel (indeclinable)
Ζαχαρίας, ου, ὁ Zacharias, Zechariah
Βαραχίας, ου, ὁ Barachias, Barachiah
φονεύω, φονεύσω, ἐφόνευσα murder, kill, commit murder
μεταξύ between (adverb)
ναός, οῦ, ὁ dwelling, temple
θυσιαστήριον, ίου, τό altar
23:36
γενεά, ᾶς, ἡ progeny, generation
23:37
Ἱεροσόλυμα, τά and ἡ, and Ἰερουσαλήμ, ἡ Jerusalem (indeclinable)
λιθοβολέω, λιθοβολήσω, ἐλιθοβόλησα throw stones at; stone to death

---

23:35 **ὅπως ἔλθῃ ἐφ᾽ ὑμας πᾶν αἷμα**: the scribes and Pharisees will be held accountable for the bloodshed of the righteous. **ἕως τοῦ αἵματος**: *even to the blood.*

23:36 **ἐπὶ τὴν γενεὰν ταύτην**: the phrase suggests immediacy of time rather than an eschatological event.

23:37 **Ἰερουσαλὴμ Ἰερουσαλήμ**: the change from normal discourse to the direct address of an audience that is inanimate in the second person, called *apostrophe,* is a poetic figure that enhances the foreboding lament over the destruction of Jerusalem. **ἡ ἀποκτείνουσα τοὺς προφήτας**: *you who kill the prophets.*

ποσάκις ἠθέλησα ἐπισυναγαγεῖν τὰ τέκνα σου, ὃν τρόπον ὄρνις ἐπισυνάγει τὰ νοσσία αὐτῆς ὑπὸ τὰς πτέρυγας, καὶ οὐκ ἠθελήσατε.
23:38 ἰδοὺ ἀφίεται ὑμῖν ὁ οἶκος ὑμῶν ἔρημος. 23:39 λέγω γὰρ ὑμῖν,
οὐ μή με ἴδητε ἀπ' ἄρτι ἕως ἂν εἴπητε, Εὐλογημένος ὁ ἐρχόμενος ἐν ὀνόματι κυρίου.

23:37

ποσάκις how many times? how often? (interrogative adverb)

ἐπισυνάγω, ἐπισυνάξω gather (together)

τέκνον, ου, τό child, descendant, posterity

τρόπος, ου, ὁ mode, manner, way; ὃν τρόπον in which manner, as, even as

ὄρνις, ιθος, ὁ, ἡ bird; hen

νοσσίον, ου, τό the young of birds, a chick; a brood of young birds (plural)

πτέρυξ, υγος, ἡ wing

23:38

οἶκος, ου, ὁ house, dwelling

ἔρημος, η, ον abandoned, empty, desolate, lonely

23:39

ἄρτι now, at the present time, at once, immediately; just (adverb); ἀπ' ἄρτι from now, from this time, henceforth

εὐλογέω, εὐλογήσω, εὐλόγησα, εὐλόγηκα praise, bless

23:37 **ὃν τρόπον**: *just as* (literally: *in the manner in which*); the case usage is an accusative of respect. It introduces a simile. **καὶ οὐκ ἠθελήσατε**: *and you were not willing*; the verb is used in an absolute sense. The pronoun changes from a second singular σου, addressing the city, to a second person plural, addressing the people.

23:38 **ἀφίεται . . . ἔρημος**: *is left desolate*; the adjective stands in predicate position.

23:39 **οὐ μή**: the double negative indicates a strong negation and usually takes an aorist subjunctive that is translated as a future. The negation stresses the certainty of the statement. **ἀπ' ἄρτι**: *from now on*. **ἕως ἂν εἴπητε**: *until you will say*; the temporal conjunction with the aorist subjunctive and the particle ἂν refers indefinitely to the future and denotes that the commencement of one event is dependent on another. **Εὐλογημένος**: supply ἐστιν.

24 Καὶ ἐξελθὼν ὁ Ἰησοῦς ἀπὸ τοῦ ἱεροῦ ἐπορεύετο, καὶ προσῆλθον οἱ μαθηταὶ αὐτοῦ ἐπιδεῖξαι αὐτῷ τὰς οἰκοδομὰς τοῦ ἱεροῦ. 24:2 ὁ δὲ ἀποκριθεὶς εἶπεν αὐτοῖς, Οὐ βλέπετε ταῦτα πάντα; ἀμὴν λέγω ὑμῖν, οὐ μὴ ἀφεθῇ ὧδε λίθος ἐπὶ λίθον ὃς οὐ καταλυθήσεται.

24:3 Καθημένου δὲ αὐτοῦ ἐπὶ τοῦ Ὄρους τῶν Ἐλαιῶν προσῆλθον αὐτῷ οἱ μαθηταὶ κατ' ἰδίαν λέγοντες, Εἰπὲ ἡμῖν πότε ταῦτα ἔσται καὶ τί τὸ σημεῖον τῆς σῆς παρουσίας καὶ συντελείας τοῦ αἰῶνος;

24:1
ἱερόν, οῦ, τό temple
ἐπιδείκνυμι, ἐπιδείξω, ἐπέδειξα, ἐπιδέδειχα, ἐπιδέδειγμαι, ἐπεδείχθην show, point out, declare
οἰκοδομή, ῆς, ἡ building, structure
24:2
βλέπω, βλέψω, ἔβλεψα see, behold, perceive
λίθος, ου, ὁ stone
καταλύω, καταλύσω, κατελύθην destroy, demolish, overthrow, throw down

24:3
ὄρος, ους, τό mountain, hill
ἐλαία, ας, ἡ olive tree, olive
ἴδιος, ία, ιον one's own; κατ' ἰδίαν privately, by oneself, alone (adverb)
πότε when? (interrogative adverb)
σημεῖον, ου, τό sign, token, miracle
παρουσία, ας, ἡ presence; coming, arrival
συντέλεια, ας, ἡ completion, close, end
αἰών, αἰῶνος, ὁ eternity, perpetuity; life, age, era; world

24:1 **προσῆλθον . . . ἐπιδεῖξαι**: the infinitive of purpose construction is particularly prevalent after main verbs of motion.

24:2 **Οὐ βλέπετε**: Jesus is speaking of the activity of their spiritual eyes. **οὐ μὴ ἀφεθῇ**: *there will not be left*; the double negative indicates a strong negation and usually takes an aorist subjunctive that is translated as a future. The negation stresses the certainty of the statement. ἀφεθῇ is a third person singular first aorist passive subjunctive (cf. App. 53, G, 2).

24:3 **ἔσται**: supply the verb also in the following clause.

24:4 καὶ ἀποκριθεὶς ὁ Ἰησοῦς εἶπεν αὐτοῖς, Βλέπετε μή τις ὑμᾶς
πλανήσῃ· 24:5 πολλοὶ γὰρ ἐλεύσονται ἐπὶ τῷ ὀνόματί μου λέγοντες,
Ἐγώ εἰμι ὁ Χριστός, καὶ πολλοὺς πλανήσουσιν. 24:6 μελλήσετε δὲ
ἀκούειν πολέμους καὶ ἀκοὰς πολέμων· ὁρᾶτε μὴ θροεῖσθε· δεῖ γὰρ
γενέσθαι, ἀλλ' οὔπω ἐστὶν τὸ τέλος. 24:7 ἐγερθήσεται γὰρ ἔθνος ἐπὶ
ἔθνος καὶ βασιλεία ἐπὶ βασιλείαν καὶ ἔσονται λιμοὶ καὶ σεισμοὶ κατὰ
τόπους·

24:4

πλανάω, πλανήσω, ἐπλάνησα, πεπλάνημαι, ἐπλανήθην lead astray, cause to wander, mislead, deceive; go astray, wander about, stray, be deceived, err (passive)

24:6

μέλλω, μελλήσω be about to, be on the point of

πόλεμος, ου, ὁ war

ἀκοή, ῆς, ἡ hearing; fame, report, rumor; account

θροέω, θροήσω cry aloud; be disturbed, alarmed, terrified (passive)

δεῖ, δεήσει, ἐδέησε it is necessary, it is proper (impersonal verb from δέω)

οὔπω not yet (adverb)

τέλος, ους, τό end, fulfillment, completion; custom, tax, duty

24:7

ἐγείρω, ἐγερῶ, ἤγειρα, ἠγήγερμαι, ἠγέρθην awaken, raise up from the dead, restore; be raised, rise (passive)

ἔθνος, ους, τό nation, people

λιμός, οῦ, ὁ hunger, famine

σεισμός, ου, ὁ shaking; earthquake; tempest

τόπος, ου, ὁ place, position, region

24:4 **Βλέπετε μή τις**: *see to it that no one*; the verb is followed by μὴ and the aorist subjunctive.

24:5 **ἐλεύσονται** is the third person plural future deponent indicative of ἔρχομαι.

24:6 **μελλήσετε . . . ἀκούειν**: unlike in Attic Greek, μέλλω is regularly followed by a present infinitive in Koine. The periphrastic future construction denotes the certainty of a future event. **ὁρᾶτε μὴ θροεῖσθε**: *take care and do not be troubled*; supply καὶ: asyndeton is frequently found when an imperative follows another imperative. **δεῖ**: supply ταῦτα as the object of the impersonal verb and the subject of the infinitive.

24:8 πάντα δὲ ταῦτα ἀρχὴ ὠδίνων. 24:9 τότε παραδώσουσιν ὑμᾶς εἰς θλῖψιν καὶ ἀποκτενοῦσιν ὑμᾶς, καὶ ἔσεσθε μισούμενοι ὑπὸ πάντων τῶν ἐθνῶν διὰ τὸ ὄνομά μου. 24:10 καὶ τότε σκανδαλισθήσονται πολλοὶ καὶ ἀλλήλους παραδώσουσιν καὶ μισήσουσιν ἀλλήλους· 24:11 καὶ πολλοὶ ψευδοπροφῆται ἐγερθήσονται καὶ πλανήσουσιν πολλούς·

24:8

ἀρχή, ῆς, ἡ beginning; τὴν ἀρχὴν wholly, altogether, from the beginning (used adverbially)

ὠδίν, ὠδῖνος, ἡ birth pain, pain

24:9

θλῖψις, εως, ἡ affliction, tribulation, trouble

μισέω, μισήσω, ἐμίσησα, μεμίσηκα hate, detest, abhor

24:10

σκανδαλίζω, σκανδαλίσω, ἐσκανδάλισα, ἐσκανδαλίσθην offend, anger, shock

ἀλλήλων, οις, ους each other, one another (reciprocal pronoun)

24:11

ψευδοπροφήτης, ου, ὁ false prophet

πλανάω, πλανήσω, ἐπλάνησα, πεπλάνημαι, ἐπλανήθην lead astray, cause to wander, mislead, deceive; go astray, wander about, stray, be deceived, err (passive)

24:8 **πάντα δὲ ταῦτα**: supply ἐστιν. **ἀρχὴ ὠδίνων**: *the beginning of the end-time birth pangs*; ἀρχὴ stands in predicate position. The symbolic language aptly describes the prelude of terror, turmoil, and torments as labor pains before the appearance of Christ at the end of history.

24:9 **ἔσεσθε μισούμενοι** is a periphrastic construction. The periphrase of εἰμί in the future (App. 63) and a present participle (cf. App. 56) to form a future tense is not an unusual construction.

24:10 **σκανδαλισθήσονται πολλοὶ**: *many will fall away*; πολλοὶ is a substantive. σκανδαλισθήσονται because of loss of faith.

24:11 **πολλοὶ . . . πολλούς**: the chiastic construction emphasizes the great number that will deceive and be deceived.

24:12 καὶ διὰ τὸ πληθυνθῆναι τὴν ἀνομίαν ψυγήσεται ἡ ἀγάπη τῶν πολλῶν. 24:13 ὁ δὲ ὑπομείνας εἰς τέλος οὗτος σωθήσεται. 24:14 καὶ κηρυχθήσεται τοῦτο τὸ εὐαγγέλιον τῆς βασιλείας ἐν ὅλῃ τῇ οἰκουμένῃ εἰς μαρτύριον πᾶσιν τοῖς ἔθνεσιν, καὶ τότε ἥξει τὸ τέλος.

24:12

πληθύνω, πληθυνῶ, ἐπλήθυνα, ἐπληθύνθην increase, multiply (active and passive)

ἀνομία, ας, ἡ lawlessness, iniquity, sin

ψύχω, ψύξω, ἐψύγην breathe, cool; grow cold, be extinguished (passive)

ἀγάπη, ης, ἡ love

24:13

ὑπομένω, ὑπομενῶ remain; remain constant, persevere, endure

τέλος, ους, τό end, fulfillment, completion; custom, tax, duty

σῴζω, σώσω, ἔσωσα, σέσωκα, σέσωσμαι, ἐσώθην save, rescue, preserve safe and unharmed

24:14

κηρύσσω, κηρύξω, ἐκήρυξα, ἐκηρύχθην announce openly, proclaim aloud

εὐαγγέλιον, ου, τό good news, gospel, glad tidings

οἰκουμένη, ης, ἡ inhabited earth, world (literally *inhabited:* supply γῆ)

μαρτύριον, ιου, τό testimony, witness

τέλος, ους, τό end, fulfillment, completion; custom, tax, duty

---

24:12 **διὰ τὸ πληθυνθῆναι τὴν ἀνομίαν**: *because wickedness increases;* the construction is an articular infinitive. As a verbal form the Greek infinitive may additionally have an accusative subject. **ἡ ἀγάπη τῶν πολλῶν**: the use of the genitive may be a subjective or objective genitive or both.

24:13 **ὁ . . . ὑπομείνας**: *he who endures;* the verbal form is the first aorist active participle of the liquid verb μένω. The basic stem ends in a liquid (**λ**, **μ**, **ν**, or **ρ**). The aorist stem passes through two changes: intervocalic **σ** drops out and the **ε** is lengthened in compensation (compensatory lengthening).

24:14 **εἰς μαρτύριον**: *as a witness;* the preposition denotes purpose.

24:15 Ὅταν οὖν ἴδητε τὸ βδέλυγμα τῆς ἐρημώσεως τὸ ῥηθὲν διὰ Δανιὴλ τοῦ προφήτου ἑστὸς ἐν τόπῳ ἁγίῳ, ὁ ἀναγινώσκων νοείτω, 24:16 τότε οἱ ἐν τῇ Ἰουδαίᾳ φευγέτωσαν εἰς τὰ ὄρη, 24:17 ὁ ἐπὶ τοῦ δώματος μὴ καταβάτω ἆραι τὰ ἐκ τῆς οἰκίας αὐτοῦ,

---

24:15
βδέλυγμα, ατος, τό abomination, abominable thing
ἐρήμωσις, εως, ἡ desolation, destruction, devastation
Δανιήλ, ὁ Daniel (indeclinable)
τόπος, ου, ὁ place, position, region
ἅγιος, ια, ιον hallowed, pure, holy
ἀναγινώσκω, ἀναγνώσομαι, ἀνέγνων (2 aorist), ἀνέγνωκα, ἀνέγνωσμαι, ἀνεγνώσθην read, read aloud, read in public
νοέω, νοήσω, ἐνόησα perceive, observe; understand, comprehend

24:16
Ἰουδαία, ας, ἡ Judaea
φεύγω, φεύξομαι, ἔφυγον (2 aorist) flee, flee from; avoid, shun

24:17
δῶμα, ατος, τό house; housetop, roof
καταβαίνω, καταβήσομαι, κατέβην, καταβέβηκα come down, go down, descend, fall
αἴρω, ἀρῶ, ἦρα, ἦρκα, ἦρμαι, ἤρθην take up, take, bear, take away, lift, carry, remove; keep in suspense; destroy, kill

---

24:15 **τὸ βδέλυγμα . . . ἑστὸς**: *the abomination . . . standing*; ἑστὸς is neuter singular accusative perfect active participle of ἵστημι agreeing in gender, number, and case with its subject τὸ βδέλυγμα. **ὁ ἀναγινώσκων νοείτω**: *let the reader understand*; supply ταῦτα τὰ ῥήματα: *these words*. νοείτω is third person singular present active imperative (cf. App. 56).

24:16 **οἱ . . . φευγέτωσαν**: *let those . . . flee*; the form is a third person plural present active imperative (cf. App. 53, A, 3).

24:17 **ὁ ἐπὶ τοῦ δώματος**: people enjoyed some of their leisure activities on top of their flat roof. **μὴ καταβάτω ἆραι τὰ**: καταβάτω is the third person singular second aorist active imperative. ἆραι is the aorist infinitive of αἴρω: *take*. The infinitive of purpose construction is particularly prevalent after main verbs of motion. Supply ὑπάρχοντα with τὰ: *his possessions*; the article is used as an unemphatic possessive adjective where ownership or relationship is logically implied.

24:18 καὶ ὁ ἐν τῷ ἀγρῷ μὴ ἐπιστρεψάτω ὀπίσω ἆραι τὸ ἱμάτιον
αὐτοῦ. 24:19 οὐαὶ δὲ ταῖς ἐν γαστρὶ ἐχούσαις καὶ ταῖς θηλαζούσαις ἐν
ἐκείναις ταῖς ἡμέραις. 24:20 προσεύχεσθε δὲ ἵνα μὴ γένηται ἡ φυγὴ
ὑμῶν χειμῶνος μηδὲ σαββάτῳ. 24:21 ἔσται γὰρ τότε θλῖψις μεγάλη
οἵα οὐ γέγονεν ἀπ' ἀρχῆς κόσμου ἕως τοῦ νῦν οὐδ' οὐ μὴ γένηται.

24:18

ἐπιστρέφω, ἐπιστρέψω, ἐπέστρεψα, ἐπέστραμμαι, ἐπεστρέφθην, ἐπεστράφην (2 aorist passive) turn, turn around

ὀπίσω back, backwards, behind, after (adverb; preposition + genitive); εἰς τὰ ὀπίσω back, backwards

ἱμάτιον, ου, τό garment, clothing; cloak, robe; clothes, garments (plural)

24:19

οὐαί woe! alas! (interjection)

γαστήρ, τρός, ἡ belly, womb; ἐν γαστρὶ ἔχειν be with child, be pregnant

θηλάζω, θηλάσω, ἐθήλασα nurse, suckle; suck; οἱ θηλάζοντες sucklings

24:20

προσεύχομαι, προσεύξομαι, προσηυξάμην pray, offer prayer

φυγή, ῆς, ἡ flight

χειμών, ῶνος, ἡ stormy weather, storm, tempest, winter

σάββατον, ου, τό Sabbath; week (both in singular and plural)

24:21

θλῖψις, εως, ἡ affliction, tribulation, trouble

οἷος, οἵα, οἷον of what sort, (such) as

ἀρχή, ῆς, ἡ beginning; τὴν ἀρχὴν wholly, altogether, from the beginning (used adverbially)

κόσμος, ου, ὁ order, world, universe

νῦν now, at the present time, just now, of late (adverb); τὸ νῦν the present time, now (noun)

24:19 **ταῖς ἐν γαστρὶ ἐχούσαις**: γαστρὶ is a third declension noun that declines like μήτηρ (App. 12). The idiom is easily understood if παιδίον: *child* is supplied as the accusative object of the participle.

24:20 **ἵνα μὴ** introduces a negative clause of purpose. **χειμῶνος**: the genitive of time expresses time at or within which an action takes place. **σαββάτῳ** is a dative of time when.

24:21 **ἔσται**: *there will be*. **ἕως τοῦ νῦν**: *until now*. **οὐδ' οὐ μὴ γένηται**: *nor will it ever happen again*; the double negative indicates a strong negation and usually takes an aorist subjunctive that is translated as a future.

24:22 καὶ εἰ μὴ ἐκολοβώθησαν αἱ ἡμέραι ἐκεῖναι, οὐκ ἂν ἐσώθη πᾶσα σάρξ· διὰ δὲ τοὺς ἐκλεκτοὺς κολοβωθήσονται αἱ ἡμέραι ἐκεῖναι. 24:23 τότε ἐάν τις ὑμῖν εἴπῃ, Ἰδοὺ ὧδε ὁ Χριστός, ἤ, Ὧδε, μὴ πιστεύσητε· 24:24 ἐγερθήσονται γὰρ ψευδόχριστοι καὶ ψευδοπροφῆται καὶ δώσουσιν σημεῖα μεγάλα καὶ τέρατα ὥστε πλανῆσαι, εἰ δυνατόν, καὶ τοὺς ἐκλεκτούς.

24:22
κολοβόω, κολοβώσω, ἐκολόβωσα, ἐκολοβώθην shorten, cut short, curtail
σῴζω, σώσω, ἔσωσα, σέσωκα, σέσωσμαι, ἐσώθην save, rescue, preserve safe and unharmed
σάρξ, σαρκός, ἡ flesh
ἐκλεκτός, ή, όν chosen, selected; elect; exalted; precious, choice
24:23
ὧδε here, hither, to this place; ὧδε ἤ ὧδε here or there
24:24
ψευδόχριστος, ου, ὁ false Christ
ψευδοπροφήτης, ου, ὁ false prophet
σημεῖον, ου, τό sign, token, miracle
τέρας, ατος, τό portent, omen, wonder
πλανάω, πλανήσω, ἐπλάνησα, πεπλάνημαι, ἐπλανήθην lead astray, cause to wander, mislead, deceive; go astray, wander about, stray, be deceived, err (passive)
δυνατός, ή, όν able, powerful, strong, mighty; δυνατόν possible
ἐκλεκτός, ή, όν chosen, selected; elect; exalted; precious, choice

---

24:22 **εἰ μὴ ἐκολοβώθησαν αἱ ἡμέραι ἐκεῖναι, οὐκ ἂν ἐσώθη πᾶσα σάρξ**: *if those days had not been shortened, no flesh would have been saved*; the past contrary to fact condition indicates that the action is not fulfilled in the past time. Here the decision to shorten the days had been made by God in the past about the future. If the the abomination of desolation had been prolonged, even the righteous would have perished. **διὰ δὲ τοὺς ἐκλεκτοὺς**: the reference may simply be to the righteous.

24:23 **ὧδε**: supply ἐστιν. **μὴ πιστεύσητε** is a prohibitive subjunctive. It has the force of (take care that you) *do not believe*.

24:24 **ὥστε πλανῆσαι**: ὥστε followed by the infinitive without the accusative introduces a result clause. However, the intended result here scarcely differs in meaning from a ἵνα purpose clause.

24:25 ἰδοὺ προείρηκα ὑμῖν. 24:26 ἐὰν οὖν εἴπωσιν ὑμῖν, Ἰδοὺ ἐν
τῇ ἐρήμῳ ἐστίν, μὴ ἐξέλθητε· Ἰδοὺ ἐν τοῖς ταμείοις, μὴ πιστεύσητε·
24:27 ὥσπερ γὰρ ἡ ἀστραπὴ ἐξέρχεται ἀπὸ ἀνατολῶν καὶ φαίνεται
ἕως δυσμῶν, οὕτως ἔσται ἡ παρουσία τοῦ υἱοῦ τοῦ ἀνθρώπου·
24:28 ὅπου ἐὰν ᾖ τὸ πτῶμα, ἐκεῖ συναχθήσονται οἱ ἀετοί.

24:29 Εὐθέως δὲ μετὰ τὴν θλῖψιν τῶν ἡμερῶν ἐκείνων
ὁ ἥλιος σκοτισθήσεται,
καὶ ἡ σελήνη οὐ δώσει τὸ φέγγος αὐτῆς,
καὶ οἱ ἀστέρες πεσοῦνται ἀπὸ τοῦ οὐρανοῦ,
καὶ αἱ δυνάμεις τῶν οὐρανῶν σαλευθήσονται.

24:25
προλέγω, προλέξω, προεῖπα, προεῖπον (2 aorist), προείρηκα tell beforehand, foretell
24:26
ἔρημος, ου, ἡ and ἔρημος, η, ον abandoned, empty, desolate; wilderness, desert, grassland (noun)
ταμεῖον, ου, τό storehouse, barn; inner chamber, secret room
24:27
ἀστραπή, ῆς, ἡ lightning; light, ray
ἀνατολή, ῆς, ἡ rising, rising of the sun, east, orient
φαίνω, φανῶ, ἔφηνα, πέφαγκα, πέφηνα, πέφασμαι, ἐφάνθην, ἐφάνην shine, give light, be bright
δυσμή, ῆς, ἡ sinking, setting; setting of the sun, west (plural)
παρουσία, ας, ἡ presence; coming, arrival
24:28
ὅπου where (adverb)
πτῶμα, ατος, τό dead body, corpse
ἀετός, οῦ, ὁ eagle
24:29
εὐθέως at once, immediately (adverb)
θλῖψις, εως, ἡ affliction, tribulation, trouble
ἥλιος, ου, ὁ sun
σκοτίζω, σκοτίσω, ἐσκοτίσθην darken; be darkened, obscured (passive)
σελήνη, ης, ἡ moon
φέγγος, εος, τό light, radiance
ἀστήρ, ἀστέρος, ὁ star
δύναμις, εως, ἡ power; ability; authority; might, majesty; omnipotence; miraculous power, miracle
σαλεύω, σαλεύσω, ἐσάλευσα, ἐσαλεύθην shake; shake down or together; agitate, disturb

---

24:26 **μὴ ἐξέλθητε** is a prohibitive subjunctive.

24:27 **ὥσπερ** introduces a simile. **ἕως δυσμῶν**: *even to the west.*

24:28 **τὸ πτῶμα . . . οἱ ἀετοί**: the language may metaphorically refer to the body of the Church, which becomes a gathering place for the Son of Man as the head of the body (Col 1:18) and the elect who are gathered from the four corners of the earth (31; Mk 13:26–27). The simile expresses a single complete thought: the gathering.

24:29 **πεσοῦνται** is the third person plural deponent future indicative of πίπτω: *fall.*

24:30 καὶ τότε φανήσεται τὸ σημεῖον τοῦ υἱοῦ τοῦ ἀνθρώπου ἐν οὐρανῷ, καὶ τότε κόψονται πᾶσαι αἱ φυλαὶ τῆς γῆς καὶ ὄψονται τὸν υἱὸν τοῦ ἀνθρώπου ἐρχόμενον ἐπὶ τῶν νεφελῶν τοῦ οὐρανοῦ μετὰ δυνάμεως καὶ δόξης πολλῆς· 24:31 καὶ ἀποστελεῖ τοὺς ἀγγέλους αὐτοῦ μετὰ σάλπιγγος μεγάλης, καὶ ἐπισυνάξουσιν τοὺς ἐκλεκτοὺς αὐτοῦ ἐκ τῶν τεσσάρων ἀνέμων ἀπ' ἄκρων οὐρανῶν ἕως [τῶν] ἄκρων αὐτῶν.

24:32 Ἀπὸ δὲ τῆς συκῆς μάθετε τὴν παραβολήν· ὅταν ἤδη ὁ κλάδος αὐτῆς γένηται ἁπαλὸς καὶ τὰ φύλλα ἐκφύῃ, γινώσκετε ὅτι ἐγγὺς τὸ θέρος· 24:33 οὕτως καὶ ὑμεῖς, ὅταν ἴδητε πάντα ταῦτα, γινώσκετε ὅτι ἐγγύς ἐστιν ἐπὶ θύραις.

24:30
σημεῖον, ου, τό sign, token, miracle
κόπτω, κόψω, ἔκοψα, ἐκόπην (2 aorist passive) smite, cut, cut off; beat one's breast (in mourning), mourn, lament (middle)
φυλή, ῆς, ἡ tribe; people, nation
γῆ, γῆς, ἡ earth, soil, land, region, country
νεφέλη, ης, ἡ cloud
δύναμις, εως, ἡ power; strength, ability; authority; might, majesty; omnipotence; miraculous power, miracle
δόξα, ης, ἡ glory, honor, majesty
24:31
σάλπιγξ, ιγγος, ἡ trumpet
ἐπισυνάγω, ἐπισυνάξω gather (together)
ἐκλεκτός, ή, όν chosen, selected; elect; exalted; precious, choice
τέσσαρες, τέσσαρα (neuter), ων four
ἄνεμος, ου, ὁ wind
ἄκρον, ου, τό top, tip, end
24:32
συκῆ, ῆς, ἡ fig-tree
κλάδος, ου, ὁ branch
ἁπαλός, ή, όν soft, tender
φύλλον, ου, τό leaf
ἐκφύω, ἐκφύσω generate; put forth, shoot, produce
ἐγγύς near (adverb)
θέρος, εος, τό summer
24:33
θύρα, ας, ἡ door, entrance

24:30 **φανήσεται** is a third person singular first future passive of φαίνω. **τὸ σημεῖον τοῦ υἱοῦ τοῦ ἀνθρώπου**: τοῦ υἱοῦ is an appositional genitive—the sign is the Son of Man. **ὄψονται** is the deponent future of ὁράω.

24:31 **ἀπ' ἄκρων οὐρανῶν ἕως [τῶν] ἄκρων αὐτῶν**: *from one end of heaven to the other.*

24:32 **Ἀπὸ δὲ τῆς συκῆς μάθετε τὴν παραβολήν**: *learn this lesson from the fig tree*; the article may be used as a demonstrative. **ἐκφύῃ**: the subject is ὁ κλάδος.

24:33 **ὅταν ἴδητε . . . γινώσκετε** is a present general condition (cf. App. 70). **πάντα ταῦτα**: supply σημεῖα. **ἐγγύς . . . ἐπὶ θύραις**: *at your very door.*

24:34 ἀμὴν λέγω ὑμῖν ὅτι οὐ μὴ παρέλθῃ ἡ γενεὰ αὕτη ἕως ἂν πάντα
ταῦτα γένηται. 24:35 ὁ οὐρανὸς καὶ ἡ γῆ παρελεύσεται, οἱ δὲ λόγοι
μου οὐ μὴ παρέλθωσιν.
24:36 Περὶ δὲ τῆς ἡμέρας ἐκείνης καὶ ὥρας οὐδεὶς οἶδεν, οὐδὲ
οἱ ἄγγελοι τῶν οὐρανῶν οὐδὲ ὁ υἱός, εἰ μὴ ὁ πατὴρ μόνος. 24:37
ὥσπερ γὰρ αἱ ἡμέραι τοῦ Νῶε, οὕτως ἔσται ἡ παρουσία τοῦ υἱοῦ τοῦ
ἀνθρώπου.

24:34
γενεά, ᾶς, ἡ progeny, generation
24:35
γῆ, γῆς, ἡ earth, soil, land, region, country
παρέρχομαι, παρελεύσομαι, παρῆλθον (2 aorist), ἐλήλυθα pass along, pass by; pass away
24:36
ὥρα, ας, ἡ hour
οἶδα know
μόνος, η, ον only, alone
24:37
ὥσπερ as, just as (adverb)
Νῶε, ὁ Noah (indeclinable)
παρουσία, ας, ἡ presence; coming, arrival

24:34 **οὐ μὴ παρέλθῃ ἡ γενεὰ ἄυτη**: although τὸ βδέλυγματῆς ἐρημώσεως was fulfilled in part in His generation by the destruction of Jerusalem and its temple in AD 70, it is clear that many of the signs spoken of in verses 4–31 are yet to come. However, in the asseveration Jesus bears in mind that His generation includes some disciples to whom He uttered the promise that they would not see death until his return (Mk 9:1, Lk 9:27), and the disciple *whom Jesus loved* may have been among them (Jn 21:20–23).

24:35 **παρελεύσεται** agrees with the nearest subject in number.

24:36 **οὐδὲ . . . οὐδὲ**: *neither . . . nor.*

24:37 **τοῦ Νῶε**: supply ἦσαν.

24:38 ὡς γὰρ ἦσαν ἐν ταῖς ἡμέραις [ἐκείναις] ταῖς πρὸ τοῦ κατακλυσμοῦ τρώγοντες καὶ πίνοντες, γαμοῦντες καὶ γαμίζοντες, ἄχρι ἧς ἡμέρας εἰσῆλθεν Νῶε εἰς τὴν κιβωτόν, 24:39 καὶ οὐκ ἔγνωσαν ἕως ἦλθεν ὁ κατακλυσμὸς καὶ ἦρεν ἅπαντας, οὕτως ἔσται [καὶ] ἡ παρουσία τοῦ υἱοῦ τοῦ ἀνθρώπου. 24:40 τότε δύο ἔσονται ἐν τῷ ἀγρῷ, εἷς παραλαμβάνεται καὶ εἷς ἀφίεται· 24:41 δύο ἀλήθουσαι ἐν τῷ μύλῳ, μία παραλαμβάνεται καὶ μία ἀφίεται.

24:38
κατακλυσμός, οῦ, ὁ flood, deluge, inundation
τρώγω, τρώξομαι, ἔτραγον eat
πίνω, πίομαι, ἔπιον, πέπωκα drink
γαμέω, γαμήσω, ἔγημα/ἐγάμησα, γεγάμηκα, ἐγαμήθην marry, take a wife
γαμίζω, γαμίσω give in marriage
ἄχρι until (preposition + genitive)
Νῶε, ὁ Noah (indeclinable)
κιβωτός, οῦ, ἡ box, chest; ark (of Noah); ark (of the covenant)
24:39
κατακλυσμός, οῦ, ὁ flood, deluge, inundation
ἅπας, ἅπασα, ἅπασαν all, whole, every
παρουσία, ας, ἡ presence; coming, arrival
24:41
ἀλήθω, ἀλήσω grind
μύλος, ου, ὁ mill; millstone

24:38 **ἦσαν . . . τρώγοντες καὶ πίνοντες, γαμοῦντες καὶ γαμίζοντες**: the periphrasis of ἦσαν with the present participle is employed for the imperfect tense. **ἄχρι ἧς ἡμέρας**: *until the day when*; the case of the relative pronoun ἧς is a genitive of attraction. The case is not determined by its use in the clause but is simply attracted to the case of its antecedent ἡμέρας. It is translated as a feminine singular dative according to its natural grammatical construction: ἄχρι ἡμέρας ᾗ. ᾗ is a dative of time when.

24:39 **ἕως**: *until*; the temporal conjunction may simply take the indicative.

24:40 **εἷς . . . εἷς**: they enjoy the same occupation but their spiritual standing brings about differing results: the one is lifted up by the angels; the other is left to perish as stubble (Mal 4:1).

24:41 **δύο ἀλήθουσαι**: *two women will be grinding*; supply ἔσονται from the previous verse to complete the future periphrastic. ἀλήθουσαι is a feminine plural nominative present active participle.

24:42 γρηγορεῖτε οὖν, ὅτι οὐκ οἴδατε ποίᾳ ἡμέρᾳ ὁ κύριος ὑμῶν ἔρχεται. 24:43 ἐκεῖνο δὲ γινώσκετε ὅτι εἰ ᾔδει ὁ οἰκοδεσπότης ποίᾳ φυλακῇ ὁ κλέπτης ἔρχεται, ἐγρηγόρησεν ἂν καὶ οὐκ ἂν εἴασεν διορυχθῆναι τὴν οἰκίαν αὐτοῦ. 24:44 διὰ τοῦτο καὶ ὑμεῖς γίνεσθε ἕτοιμοι, ὅτι ᾗ οὐ δοκεῖτε ὥρᾳ ὁ υἱὸς τοῦ ἀνθρώπου ἔρχεται.

24:42
γρηγορέω, γρηγορήσω, ἐγρηγόρησα be awake, watch; be alive; be watchful, attentive, vigilant
οἶδα know
ποῖος, ποία, ποῖον of what kind? of what sort? of what species? what? which?
24:43
οἰκοδεσπότης, ου, ὁ master of the house
ποῖος, ποία, ποῖον of what kind? of what sort? of what species? what? which?
φυλακή, ῆς, ἡ watch, guard, prison
κλέπτης, ου, ὁ thief
γρηγορέω, γρηγορήσω, ἐγρηγόρησα be awake, watch; be alive; be watchful, attentive, vigilant
ἐάω, ἐάσω, εἴασα allow, permit
διορύσσω, διορύξω break through, break in
24:44
ἕτοιμος, η, ον ready, prepared
δοκέω, δόξω, ἔδοξα think (mistakenly), believe, suppose, consider

---

24:42 **ποίᾳ ἡμέρᾳ** is a dative of time when.

24:43 **ἐκεῖνο δὲ γινώσκετε**: *but know this*; ἐκεῖνο is used as ὅδε: *this, the following.* **εἰ ᾔδει ὁ οἰκοδεσπότης . . . ἐγρηγόρησεν ἂν καὶ οὐκ ἂν εἴασεν**: *if the master had known . . . he would have watched and would not have let*; the contrary to fact condition is formed with εἰ plus the pluperfect indicative in the protasis and the aorist indicative plus ἄν in the two apodoses. The pluperfect ᾔδει (App. 62) is used as an aorist. **ποίᾳ φυλακῇ ὁ κλέπτης ἔρχεται**: *in what watch the thief was coming*; φυλακῇ is a dative of time when. ποίᾳ introduces an indirect question. In indirect questions Greek retains the original mood and tense. In the original question the mood is indicative and the tense present. In English the verb of the indirect question matches the tense of the verb introducing the indirect question. Since ᾔδει is a past tense, ἔρχεται is translated as a past.

24:44 **ᾗ . . . ὥρᾳ**: *at an hour when*; both case uses are datives of time when.

24:45 Τίς ἄρα ἐστὶν ὁ πιστὸς δοῦλος καὶ φρόνιμος ὃν κατέστησεν ὁ κύριος ἐπὶ τῆς οἰκετείας αὐτοῦ τοῦ δοῦναι αὐτοῖς τὴν τροφὴν ἐν καιρῷ; 24:46 μακάριος ὁ δοῦλος ἐκεῖνος ὃν ἐλθὼν ὁ κύριος αὐτοῦ εὑρήσει οὕτως ποιοῦντα· 24:47 ἀμὴν λέγω ὑμῖν ὅτι ἐπὶ πᾶσιν τοῖς ὑπάρχουσιν αὐτοῦ καταστήσει αὐτόν. 24:48 ἐὰν δὲ εἴπῃ ὁ κακὸς δοῦλος ἐκεῖνος ἐν τῇ καρδίᾳ αὐτοῦ, Χρονίζει μου ὁ κύριος,

---

24:45
ἄρα therefore, then, consequently (particle)
πιστός, ή, όν faithful, true; believing, trusting
φρόνιμος, η, ον thoughtful, prudent, wise
καθίστημι and καθιστάνω, καταστήσω, κατέστησα, κατεστάθην place, set, constitute, appoint, put in charge
οἰκετεία, ας, ἡ household
τροφή, ῆς, ἡ nourishment, food
καιρός, οῦ, ὁ time, appointed time

24:46
μακάριος, ία, ιον blessed, happy, fortunate

24:47
ὑπάρχω, ὑπάρξω begin; exist; be; τὰ ὑπάρχοντα possessions, goods, property
καθίστημι and καθιστάνω, καταστήσω, κατέστησα, κατεστάθην place, set, constitute, appoint, put in charge

24:48
κακός, ή, όν bad, evil, wrong
χρονίζω, χρονίσω, ἐχρόνισα take time, linger, delay, fail to come for a long time

---

24:45 **ὁ πιστὸς δοῦλος καὶ φρόνιμος** is a general reference to anyone who is in charge of the care and welfare of others. **τοῦ δοῦναι**: the construction is an articular infinitive. A purpose clause may be expressed by the neuter article in the genitive case followed by an infinitive. **αὐτοῖς** refers to the servants of the household.

24:46 **μακάριος**: supply ἐστιν. **ἐλθὼν ὁ κύριος αὐτοῦ**: *his lord upon his coming.*

24:49 καὶ ἄρξηται τύπτειν τοὺς συνδούλους αὐτοῦ, ἐσθίῃ δὲ καὶ πίνῃ μετὰ τῶν μεθυόντων, 24:50 ἥξει ὁ κύριος τοῦ δούλου ἐκείνου ἐν ἡμέρᾳ ᾗ οὐ προσδοκᾷ καὶ ἐν ὥρᾳ ᾗ οὐ γινώσκει, 24:51 καὶ διχοτομήσει αὐτὸν καὶ τὸ μέρος αὐτοῦ μετὰ τῶν ὑποκριτῶν θήσει· ἐκεῖ ἔσται ὁ κλαυθμὸς καὶ ὁ βρυγμὸς τῶν ὀδόντων.

24:49

ἄρχω, ἄρξω, ἦρξα, ἦρχα, ἦργμαι, ἤρχθην rule (active); begin (middle)

τύπτω, τύψω, ἔτυψα beat, strike, smite

σύνδουλος, ου, ὁ fellow slave, fellow servant

πίνω, πίομαι, ἔπιον, πέπωκα drink

μεθύω be intoxicated, be drunk

24:50

ἥκω, ἥξω have come, be present (the present is supplied by ἔρχομαι)

προσδοκάω, προσδοκήσω, προσεδόκησα wait for, look for, expect; think, anticipate

24:51

διχοτομέω, διχοτομήσω cut in two; punish severely

μέρος, ους, τό part, portion, share

τίθημι, θήσω, ἔθηκα, τέθεικα, τέθειμαι, ἐτέθην place, set, lay, render, serve, give, allocate, assign

ὑποκριτής, οῦ, ὁ hypocrite, pretender, dissembler

κλαυθμός, ου, ὁ weeping, crying

βρυγμός, οῦ, ὁ chattering (of teeth), gnashing (of teeth)

ὀδούς, ὀδόντος, ὁ tooth

24:49 **μετὰ τῶν μεθυόντων**: *with those who are drunk.*

24:50 **ᾗ**: *when*; the relative pronoun is a dative of time when.

25 Τότε ὁμοιωθήσεται ἡ βασιλεία τῶν οὐρανῶν δέκα παρθένοις,
αἵτινες λαβοῦσαι τὰς λαμπάδας ἑαυτῶν ἐξῆλθον εἰς ὑπάντησιν τοῦ
νυμφίου. 25:2 πέντε δὲ ἐξ αὐτῶν ἦσαν μωραὶ καὶ πέντε φρόνιμοι.
25:3 αἱ γὰρ μωραὶ λαβοῦσαι τὰς λαμπάδας αὐτῶν οὐκ ἔλαβον μεθ'
ἑαυτῶν ἔλαιον. 25:4 αἱ δὲ φρόνιμοι ἔλαβον ἔλαιον ἐν τοῖς ἀγγείοις
μετὰ τῶν λαμπάδων ἑαυτῶν. 25:5 χρονίζοντος δὲ τοῦ νυμφίου
ἐνύσταξαν πᾶσαι καὶ ἐκάθευδον.

25:1
ὁμοιόω, ὁμοιώσω, ὁμοίωσα, ὡμοιώθην make like, liken, compare; be like, be made like, become like, resemble (passive)
δέκα ten (indeclinable)
παρθένος, ου, ἡ virgin
λαμπάς, άδος, ἡ light, lamp, torch
ὑπάντησις, εως, ἡ coming to meet; εἰς ὑπάντησιν to meet (+ dative or genitive)
νυμφίος, ου, ὁ bridegroom
25:2
πέντε five (indeclinable)
μωρός, ά, όν foolish, wicked, impious
φρόνιμος, η, ον thoughtful, prudent, wise
25:3
λαμπάς, άδος, ἡ light, lamp, torch
ἔλαιον, ου, τό olive oil, oil
25:4
ἀγγεῖον, ου, τό vessel, flask, container
25:5
χρονίζω, χρονίσω, ἐχρόνισα take time, linger, delay, fail to come for a long time
νυμφίος, ου, ὁ bridegroom
νυστάζω, νυστάσω nod, become drowsy
καθεύδω, καθευδήσω sleep, be fast asleep

25:1 **Τότε** refers to the Coming of the Son of Man in the previous verse. **τὰς λαμπάδας ἑαυτων**: *their lamps*; the reflexive pronoun is used as a possessive. **εἰς ὑπάντησιν τοῦ νυμφίου**: *to meet the bridegroom*; the prepositional phrase takes an objective genitive.

25:2 **φρόνιμοι**: adjectives of two terminations have the same form for the masculine and feminine (cf. App. 18).

25:3 **αἱ . . . μωραὶ**: the article has substantivizing force.

25:6 μέσης δὲ νυκτὸς κραυγὴ γέγονεν, Ἰδοὺ ὁ νυμφίος, ἐξέρχεσθε
εἰς ἀπάντησιν [αὐτοῦ]. 25:7 τότε ἠγέρθησαν πᾶσαι αἱ παρθένοι
ἐκεῖναι καὶ ἐκόσμησαν τὰς λαμπάδας ἑαυτῶν. 25:8 αἱ δὲ μωραὶ ταῖς
φρονίμοις εἶπαν, Δότε ἡμῖν ἐκ τοῦ ἐλαίου ὑμῶν, ὅτι αἱ λαμπάδες
ἡμῶν σβέννυνται. 25:9 ἀπεκρίθησαν δὲ αἱ φρόνιμοι λέγουσαι,
Μήποτε οὐ μὴ ἀρκέσῃ ἡμῖν καὶ ὑμῖν· πορεύεσθε μᾶλλον πρὸς τοὺς
πωλοῦντας καὶ ἀγοράσατε ἑαυταῖς.

25:6
μέσος, η, ον middle, in the middle; in, among (as adjective + genitive); the middle (as noun τὸ μέσον)
κραυγή, ῆς, ἡ cry, shouting, clamor
νυμφίος, ου, ὁ bridegroom
ἀπάντησις, εως, ἡ coming to meet; εἰς ἀπάντησιν to meet (+ dative or genitive)
25:7
παρθένος, ου, ἡ virgin
κοσμέω, κοσμήσω, ἐκόσμησα, κεκόσμηκα, κεκόσμημαι set in order, arrange; prepare, trim; decorate, adorn
λαμπάς, άδος, ἡ light, lamp, torch
25:8
μωρός, ά, όν foolish, wicked, impious
φρόνιμος, η, ον thoughtful, prudent, wise
ἔλαιον, ου, τό olive oil, oil
σβέννυμι, σβέσω, ἔσβεσα extinguish, put out
25:9
μήποτε not, never; that . . . not, lest, (in order) that . . . not (conjunction)
ἀρκέω, ἀρκήσω, ἤρκεσα be enough, be sufficient
μᾶλλον more, to a greater degree, rather (adverb)
πωλέω, πωλήσω, ἐπώλησα sell
ἀγοράζω, ἀγοράσω, ἠγόρασα, ἠγόρασμαι, ἠγοράσθην buy, purchase, acquire

---

25:6 **μέσης . . . νυκτὸς**: *at midnight*; supply οὔσης to complete the genitive absolute. **εἰς ἀπάντησιν [αὐτοῦ]**: *to meet him*; the prepositional phrase takes an objective genitive.

25:8 **Δότε ἡμῖν**: supply τι: *some.*

25:9 **Μήποτε οὐ μὴ ἀρκέσῃ**: *no, certainly there will never be enough*; the double negative indicates a strong negation and usually takes an aorist subjunctive that is translated as a future. Μήποτε may introduce either a weakened negation: *perhaps, probably,* or one more intense in tone. The context suggests the latter. The simile expresses a single complete thought: preparation.

25:10 ἀπερχομένων δὲ αὐτῶν ἀγοράσαι ἦλθεν ὁ νυμφίος, καὶ αἱ ἕτοιμοι εἰσῆλθον μετ᾽ αὐτοῦ εἰς τοὺς γάμους καὶ ἐκλείσθη ἡ θύρα. 25:11 ὕστερον δὲ ἔρχονται καὶ αἱ λοιπαὶ παρθένοι λέγουσαι, Κύριε κύριε, ἄνοιξον ἡμῖν. 25:12 ὁ δὲ ἀποκριθεὶς εἶπεν, Ἀμὴν λέγω ὑμῖν, οὐκ οἶδα ὑμᾶς. 25:13 Γρηγορεῖτε οὖν, ὅτι οὐκ οἴδατε τὴν ἡμέραν οὐδὲ τὴν ὥραν.

25:14 Ὥσπερ γὰρ ἄνθρωπος ἀποδημῶν ἐκάλεσεν τοὺς ἰδίους δούλους καὶ παρέδωκεν αὐτοῖς τὰ ὑπάρχοντα αὐτοῦ,

---

25:10
νυμφίος, ου, ὁ bridegroom
ἕτοιμος, η, ον ready, prepared
γάμος, ου, ὁ wedding, marriage
κλείω, κλείσω, ἔκλεισα, κέκλεισμαι, ἐκλείσθην close, shut, lock
θύρα, ας, ἡ door, entrance
25:11
ὕστερος, α, ον later; ὕστερον later, afterwards; finally; last (adverb)
λοιπός, ή, όν remaining; the rest, remainder
παρθένος, ου, ἡ virgin
ἀνοίγω, ἀνοίξω, ἀνέῳξα/ἤνοιξα, ἀνέῳγα, ἀνέῳγμαι, ἠνεῴχθην open
25:12
οἶδα know
25:13
γρηγορέω, γρηγορήσω, ἐγρηγόρησα be awake, watch; be alive; be watchful, attentive, vigilant
ὥρα, ας, ἡ hour
25:14
ὥσπερ as, just as (adverb)
ἀποδημέω, ἀποδημήσω, ἀπεδήμησα be away from home, be abroad; go on a journey, go abroad
ἴδιος, ία, ιον one's own
ὑπάρχω, ὑπάρξω begin; exist; be; τὰ ὑπάρχοντα possessions, goods, property

---

25:11 **ἄνοιξον ἡμῖν**: supply τὴν θύραν.

25:13 **Γρηγορεῖτε**: the imperative summarizes the theme of the parable.

25:14 **Ὥσπερ γὰρ**: *for it is just like;* supply ἡ βασιλεῖα τῶν οὐρανῶν as the subject of the adverbial clause. The ὥσπερ clause is at times shortened and needs to be supplemented and connected with what goes on before. **ἄνθρωπος ἀποδημῶν ἐκάλεσεν**: *a man who, before he went on a journey, called.* ἀποδημῶν is a circumstantial participle.

25:15 καὶ ᾧ μὲν ἔδωκεν πέντε τάλαντα, ᾧ δὲ δύο, ᾧ δὲ ἕν, ἑκάστῳ
κατὰ τὴν ἰδίαν δύναμιν, καὶ ἀπεδήμησεν. εὐθέως 25:16 πορευθεὶς ὁ
τὰ πέντε τάλαντα λαβὼν ἠργάσατο ἐν αὐτοῖς καὶ ἐκέρδησεν ἄλλα
πέντε· 25:17 ὡσαύτως ὁ τὰ δύο ἐκέρδησεν ἄλλα δύο. 25:18 ὁ δὲ τὸ ἓν
λαβὼν ἀπελθὼν ὤρυξεν γῆν καὶ ἔκρυψεν τὸ ἀργύριον τοῦ κυρίου
αὐτοῦ.

25:15
ὃς μὲν . . . ὃς δέ one . . . another
πέντε five (indeclinable)
τάλαντον, ου, τό talent
ἕκαστος, η, ον each, every; each one, every one (substantive)
ἀποδημέω, ἀποδημήσω, ἀπεδήμησα be away from home, be abroad; go on a journey, go abroad
εὐθέως at once, immediately (adverb)
25:16
ἐργάζομαι, ἐργάσομαι, ἠργασάμην/εἰργασάμην, εἴργασμαι work, do, accomplish, perform; trade, do business
κερδαίνω, κερδήσω, ἐκέρδησα gain, acquire
πέντε five (indeclinable)
25:17
ὡσαύτως in just the same way, likewise (adverb)
κερδαίνω, κερδήσω, ἐκέρδησα gain, acquire
25:18
ὀρύσσω, ὀρύξω, ὤρυξα, ὠρύγην dig up, dig out, dig
κρύπτω, κρύψω, ἔκρυψα, κέκρυμμαι, ἐκρύβην hide, conceal, cover
ἀργύριον, ίου, τό silver, silver shekel, silver drachma, silver money

---

25:15 **εὐθέως**: the adverb regularly precedes the participle or verb in Matthew.

25:16 **πορευθεὶς . . . ἠργάσατο**: *he went on his way and traded*; a participle may receive as much emphasis as the finite verb and be coordinated with it. **ἄλλα πέντε**: *five more*; supply τάλαντα.

25:17 **ὁ τὰ δύο**: supply λαβών.

25:18 **ἀπελθὼν ὤρυξεν . . . καὶ ἔκρυψεν**: *went off, dug up . . . and hid.*

25:19 μετὰ δὲ πολὺν χρόνον ἔρχεται ὁ κύριος τῶν δούλων ἐκείνων καὶ συναίρει λόγον μετ᾽ αὐτῶν. 25:20 καὶ προσελθὼν ὁ τὰ πέντε τάλαντα λαβὼν προσήνεγκεν ἄλλα πέντε τάλαντα λέγων, Κύριε, πέντε τάλαντά μοι παρέδωκας· ἴδε ἄλλα πέντε τάλαντα ἐκέρδησα. 25:21 ἔφη αὐτῷ ὁ κύριος αὐτοῦ, Εὖ, δοῦλε ἀγαθὲ καὶ πιστέ, ἐπὶ ὀλίγα ἦς πιστός, ἐπὶ πολλῶν σε καταστήσω· εἴσελθε εἰς τὴν χαρὰν τοῦ κυρίου σου. 25:22 προσελθὼν [δὲ] καὶ ὁ τὰ δύο τάλαντα εἶπεν, Κύριε, δύο τάλαντά μοι παρέδωκας· ἴδε ἄλλα δύο τάλαντα ἐκέρδησα. 25:23 ἔφη αὐτῷ ὁ κύριος αὐτοῦ, Εὖ, δοῦλε ἀγαθὲ καὶ πιστέ, ἐπὶ ὀλίγα ἦς πιστός, ἐπὶ πολλῶν σε καταστήσω· εἴσελθε εἰς τὴν χαρὰν τοῦ κυρίου σου.

25:19

μετά with (preposition + genitive); after (+ accusative)

πολύς, πολλή, πολύ much, large, many (in plural)

συναίρω, συναρῶ, συνῆρα settle

25:20

πέντε five (indeclinable)

τάλαντον, ου, τό talent

ἴδε lo! behold! (interjection; imperative of εἴδω see)

κερδαίνω, κερδήσω, ἐκέρδησα gain, acquire

25:21

εὖ well, happily, rightly; well done, it is well (adverb)

πιστός, ή, όν faithful, true; believing, trusting

ἐπί on, to, against, towards, over (+ accusative)

ὀλίγος, η, ον little, small; few (plural)

καθίστημι and καθιστάνω, καταστήσω, κατέστησα, κατεστάθην place, set, constitute, appoint, put in charge

χαρά, ᾶς, ἡ joy

25:22

κερδαίνω, κερδήσω, ἐκέρδησα gain, acquire

25:23

εὖ well, happily, rightly; well done, it is well (adverb)

πιστός, ή, όν faithful, true; believing, trusting

ἐπί on, to, against, towards, over (+ accusative)

ὀλίγος, η, ον little, small; few (plural)

καθίστημι and καθιστάνω, καταστήσω, κατέστησα, κατεστάθην place, set, constitute, appoint, put in charge

χαρά, ᾶς, ἡ joy

25:19 **συναίρει λόγον**: *settled his accounts.*

25:20 **προσήνεγκεν** is the third person singular second aorist active indicative of προσφέρω. **παρέδωκας** is the second person singular first aorist indicative of παραδίδωμι.

25:21 **δοῦλε** stands in the vocative case.

25:22 **ὁ τὰ δύο**: supply λαβὼν.

25:24 προσελθὼν δὲ καὶ ὁ τὸ ἓν τάλαντον εἰληφὼς εἶπεν, Κύριε,
ἔγνων σε ὅτι σκληρὸς εἶ ἄνθρωπος, θερίζων ὅπου οὐκ ἔσπειρας
καὶ συνάγων ὅθεν οὐ διεσκόρπισας, 25:25 καὶ φοβηθεὶς ἀπελθὼν
ἔκρυψα τὸ τάλαντόν σου ἐν τῇ γῇ· ἴδε ἔχεις τὸ σόν. 25:26 ἀποκριθεὶς
δὲ ὁ κύριος αὐτοῦ εἶπεν αὐτῷ, Πονηρὲ δοῦλε καὶ ὀκνηρέ, ᾔδεις ὅτι
θερίζω ὅπου οὐκ ἔσπειρα καὶ συνάγω ὅθεν οὐ διεσκόρπισα; 25:27
ἔδει σε οὖν βαλεῖν τὰ ἀργύριά μου τοῖς τραπεζίταις,

25:24
σκληρός, ά, όν hard, harsh
θερίζω, θερίσω, ἐθέρισα reap, harvest
ὅπου where (adverb)
ὅθεν from where, from the place where, whence, from which; from which fact, therefore, hence; wherefore, whereupon (adverb)
διασκορπίζω, διασκορπίσω, διεσκόρπισα, διεσκορπίσθην scatter, disperse, strew

25:25
κρύπτω, κρύψω, ἔκρυψα, κέκρυμμαι, ἐκρύβην hide, conceal, cover
ἴδε lo! behold! (interjection; imperative of εἴδω see)
σός, σή, σόν your, yours

25:26
ὀκνηρός, ά, όν lazy, indolent, idle
θερίζω, θερίσω, ἐθέρισα reap, harvest
ὅπου where (adverb)
ὅθεν from where, from the place where, whence, from which; from which fact, therefore, hence; wherefore, whereupon (adverb)
διασκορπίζω, διασκορπίσω, διεσκόρπισα, διεσκορπίσθην scatter, disperse, strew

25:27
ἀργύριον, ίου, τό silver, silver shekel, silver drachma, silver money
τραπεζίτης, ου, ὁ money changer, broker, banker

25:24 **ὁ . . . εἰληφὼς**: *the man who had received*; εἰληφὼς is a masculine singular nominative perfect active participle (cf. App. 33) of λαμβάνω. Since the action of the participle precedes that of the main verb, the participle is treated as a pluperfect.

25:25 **καὶ φοβηθεὶς ἀπελθὼν ἔκρυψα**: *and since I was afraid I went and hid.*

25:26 **ᾔδεις**: *you knew*; the verb form is a second person singular pluperfect active indicative. Since the perfect οἶδα: *know* is used as a present, the pluperfect is taken as an imperfect (App. 62).

25:27 **ἔδει σε . . . βαλεῖν**: *you ought to have brought*; the impersonal construction may be changed to a personal one.

καὶ ἐλθὼν ἐγὼ ἐκομισάμην ἂν τὸ ἐμὸν σὺν τόκῳ. 25:28 ἄρατε οὖν ἀπ' αὐτοῦ τὸ τάλαντον καὶ δότε τῷ ἔχοντι τὰ δέκα τάλαντα· 25:29 τῷ γὰρ ἔχοντι παντὶ δοθήσεται καὶ περισσευθήσεται, τοῦ δὲ μὴ ἔχοντος καὶ ὃ ἔχει ἀρθήσεται ἀπ' αὐτοῦ. 25:30 καὶ τὸν ἀχρεῖον δοῦλον ἐκβάλετε εἰς τὸ σκότος τὸ ἐξώτερον· ἐκεῖ ἔσται ὁ κλαυθμὸς καὶ ὁ βρυγμὸς τῶν ὀδόντων.

25:27

κομίζω, κομίσω, ἐκόμισα bring; carry off, get, receive, obtain, get back, recover (middle)

σύν with, together with (+ dative)

τόκος, ου, ὁ offspring; interest (on money loaned)

25:28

τάλαντον, ου, τό talent

25:29

περισσεύω, περισσεύσω, ἐπερίσσευσα be left over, abound; abundance is given, have great abundance, be gifted with abundance (passive)

25:30

ἀχρεῖος, α, ον useless, unprofitable, worthless, miserable

σκότος, ους, τό darkness, gloom

ἐξώτερος, α, ον outer, external

κλαυθμός, ου, ὁ weeping, crying

βρυγμός, οῦ, ὁ chattering (of teeth), gnashing (of teeth)

ὀδούς, ὀδόντος, ὁ tooth

25:27 **ἐλθὼν . . . ἐκομισάμην**: *if I had gone, I would have received*; supply the participle with πρὸς αὐτοὺς. The circumstantial participle replaces the protasis of this past contrary to fact condition.

25:28 **ἄρατε . . . δότε**: the master is speaking to a group of attendants.

25:29 **τῷ γὰρ ἔχοντι παντὶ δοθήσεται**: *for to everyone who has, more will be given*; the context suggests the subject πλεῖον. **περισσευθήσεται**: *he will have a great abundance*; the passive has a middle sense. **τοῦ δὲ μὴ ἔχοντος καὶ ὃ ἔχει ἀρθήσεται ἀπ' αὐτοῦ**: *from him who gained nothing even that which he had will be taken*; ἔχοντος carries the meaning *to bring about* or *to be able (to do)*. The principle has universal applications.

25:30 **ἐκβάλετε**: the Master is speaking to a group of attendants.

25:31 Ὅταν δὲ ἔλθῃ ὁ υἱὸς τοῦ ἀνθρώπου ἐν τῇ δόξῃ αὐτοῦ καὶ
πάντες οἱ ἄγγελοι μετ' αὐτοῦ, τότε καθίσει ἐπὶ θρόνου δόξης αὐτοῦ·
25:32 καὶ συναχθήσονται ἔμπροσθεν αὐτοῦ πάντα τὰ ἔθνη, καὶ
ἀφορίσει αὐτοὺς ἀπ' ἀλλήλων, ὥσπερ ὁ ποιμὴν ἀφορίζει τὰ πρόβατα
ἀπὸ τῶν ἐρίφων, 25:33 καὶ στήσει τὰ μὲν πρόβατα ἐκ δεξιῶν αὐτοῦ,
τὰ δὲ ἐρίφια ἐξ εὐωνύμων. 25:34 τότε ἐρεῖ ὁ βασιλεὺς τοῖς ἐκ δεξιῶν
αὐτοῦ,

25:31
δόξα, ης, ἡ glory, honor, majesty
καθίζω, καθίσω, ἐκάθισα, κεκάθικα cause to sit down, seat, set (transitive); sit, sit down; remain, stay, continue, rest (intransitive)
θρόνος, ου, ὁ seat, throne; power, dominion
25:32
ἀφορίζω, ἀφορίσω/ἀφοριῶ, ἀφώρισα, ἀφώρισμαι, ἀφορίσθην limit off; separate, take out, take away, exclude, excommunicate
ἀλλήλων, οις, ους each other, one another (reciprocal pronoun)
ὥσπερ as, just as (adverb)
ποιμήν, ένος, ὁ shepherd, herdsman, guardian
πρόβατον, ου, τό sheep
ἔριφος, ου, ὁ kid, goat
25:33
δεξιός, ά, όν right (as opposed to *left*); ἐκ δεξιῶν τινός at someone's right
ἐρίφιον, ιου, τό kid, goat (diminutive)
εὐώνυμος, ον left (as opposed to *right*); ἐκ εὐωνύμων τινός at someone's left

---

25:31 **Ὅταν**: the indefinite relative adverb replaces ἐάν or ἄν in this future more vivid condition (App. 70).

25:33 **στήσει** is the third person singular future active indicative of ἵστημι.

25:34 **ἐρεῖ** is the second person singular future active indicative of λέγω. The future is conjugated like the present active indicative of a contracted verb with stem in **ε** (cf. App. 56).

Δεῦτε οἱ εὐλογημένοι τοῦ πατρός μου, κληρονομήσατε τὴν ἡτοιμασμένην ὑμῖν βασιλείαν ἀπὸ καταβολῆς κόσμου. 25:35 ἐπείνασα γὰρ καὶ ἐδώκατέ μοι φαγεῖν, ἐδίψησα καὶ ἐποτίσατέ με, ξένος ἤμην καὶ συνηγάγετέ με, 25:36 γυμνὸς καὶ περιεβάλετέ με, ἠσθένησα καὶ ἐπεσκέψασθέ με, ἐν φυλακῇ ἤμην καὶ ἤλθατε πρός με. 25:37 τότε ἀποκριθήσονται αὐτῷ οἱ δίκαιοι λέγοντες, Κύριε, πότε σε εἴδομεν πεινῶντα καὶ ἐθρέψαμεν, ἢ διψῶντα καὶ ἐποτίσαμεν;

25:34
δεῦτε come! come here! (adverb)
εὐλογέω, εὐλογήσω, εὐλόγησα, εὐλόγηκα praise, bless
κληρονομέω, κληρονομήσω, ἐκληρονόμησα, κεκληρονόμηκα inherit; obtain, acquire, receive
ἑτοιμάζω, ἑτοιμάσω, ἡτοίμασα, ἡτοίμακα, ἡτοίμασμαι, ἡτοιμάσθην make ready, prepare
καταβολή, ῆς, ἡ beginning, foundation
κόσμος, ου, ὁ order, world, universe
25:35
πεινάω, πεινάσω/πεινήσω, ἐπείνασα hunger, be hungry; hunger after, long for
ἐσθίω, φάγομαι, ἔφαγον eat
διψάω, διψήσω, ἐδίψησα thirst, be thirsty
ποτίζω, ποτίσω, ἐπότισα, πεπότικα cause someone to drink, give someone something to drink
ξένος, ου, ὁ strange, foreign; stranger, foreigner (substantive)
25:36
γυμνός, ή, όν naked, without an outer garment, uncovered
περιβάλλω, περιβαλῶ, περέβαλον, περιβέβληκα, περεβλήθην cast around, throw around; clothe; clothe oneself, be clothed (middle)
ἀσθενέω, ἀσθενήσω, ἠσθένησα be weak, be sick
ἐπισκέπτομαι, ἐπισκέψομαι, ἐπεσκεψάμην look for; go to see, visit
φυλακή, ῆς, ἡ watch, guard, prison
25:37
πεινάω, πεινάσω/πεινήσω, ἐπείνασα hunger, be hungry; hunger after, long for
τρέφω, θρέψω, ἔθρεψα feed, nourish, support
διψάω, διψήσω, ἐδίψησα thirst, be thirsty
ποτίζω, ποτίσω, ἐπότισα, πεπότικα cause someone to drink, give someone something to drink

---

25:34 **οἱ εὐλογημένοι τοῦ πατρός μου**: *you who are blessed by my Father*; the genitive is used with the substantivized perfect passive participle to indicate the agent.

25:35 **ἐδώκατέ μοι φαγεῖν**: *you gave me something to eat*; supply τι. **φαγεῖν** is an infinitive of purpose. **ἤμην** is the first person singular imperfect active indicative of εἰμί (App. 63).

25:36 **γυμνὸς**: supply ἤμην.

25:37 **εἴδομεν** is the second aorist of ὁράω. **ἐθρέψαμεν . . . ἐποτίσαμεν**: supply **σε** from earlier in the sentence.

25:38 πότε δέ σε εἴδομεν ξένον καὶ συνηγάγομεν, ἢ γυμνὸν καὶ
περιεβάλομεν; 25:39 πότε δέ σε εἴδομεν ἀσθενοῦντα ἢ ἐν φυλακῇ
καὶ ἤλθομεν πρός σε; 25:40 καὶ ἀποκριθεὶς ὁ βασιλεὺς ἐρεῖ αὐτοῖς,
Ἀμὴν λέγω ὑμῖν, ἐφ᾽ ὅσον ἐποιήσατε ἑνὶ τούτων τῶν ἀδελφῶν μου
τῶν ἐλαχίστων, ἐμοὶ ἐποιήσατε.

25:41 Τότε ἐρεῖ καὶ τοῖς ἐξ εὐωνύμων, Πορεύεσθε ἀπ᾽ ἐμοῦ [οἱ]
κατηραμένοι εἰς τὸ πῦρ τὸ αἰώνιον τὸ ἡτοιμασμένον τῷ διαβόλῳ καὶ
τοῖς ἀγγέλοις αὐτοῦ.

25:38

ξένος, ου, ὁ strange, foreign; stranger, foreigner (substantive)

γυμνός, ή, όν naked, without an outer garment, uncovered

περιβάλλω, περιβαλῶ, περέβαλον, περιβέβληκα, περεβλήθην cast around, throw around; clothe; clothe oneself, be clothed (middle)

25:39

πότε when? (interrogative adverb)

ἀσθενέω, ἀσθενήσω, ἠσθένησα be weak, be sick

φυλακή, ῆς, ἡ watch, guard, prison

25:40

ὅσος, η, ον how large, how great; as many as (plural); whosoever, whatsoever; ἐφ᾽ ὅσον while, as long as, inasmuch as

ἐλάχιστος, η, ον smallest, least

25:41

εὐώνυμος, ον left (as opposed to *right*); ἐκ εὐωνύμων τινός at someone's left

καταράομαι, καταράσομαι, κατηρασάμην curse

πῦρ, πυρός, τό fire

αἰώνιος, ον (αἰώνιος, ία, ιον) eternal, everlasting

ἑτοιμάζω, ἑτοιμάσω, ἡτοίμασα, ἡτοίμακα, ἡτοίμασμαι, ἡτοιμάσθην make ready, prepare

διάβολος, ου, ὁ slanderer, devil

25:40 **ἐρεῖ** is the second person singular future active indicative of λέγω. The future is conjugated like the present active indicative of a contracted verb with stem in **ε** (cf. App. 56). **ἐποιήσατε**: supply τοῦτο.

25:41 **ἐξ εὐωνύμων**: the adjective literally means *of good name, of good omen, fortunate, prosperous*. The euphemism substitutes a disagreeable word ἀριστερός: *left, on the left hand* with an agreeable one to avoid a word of ill omen. 25:41 [**οἱ**] **κατηραμένοι**: *you who are accursed;* κατηραμένοι: the perfect passive participle stands in agreement with **Πορεύεσθε**. Verbs beginning with a short vowel lengthen the vowel to show reduplication. The perfect is frequently translated as a present. **τὸ ἡτοιμασμένον τῷ διαβόλῳ**: *which has been prepared for the devil;* the perfect passive participle agreees with its subject τὸ πῦρ and takes a dative object. τῷ διαβόλῳ: inherent in his name διάβολος, commonly translated as *slanderer,* is also the notion of *missing the mark,* a primary meaning of the verb διαβάλλω and a metaphor from the field of archery. As one who profoundly missed the mark in choosing to oppose the will of God, he causes others to do the same—to miss the mark.

25:42 ἐπείνασα γὰρ καὶ οὐκ ἐδώκατέ μοι φαγεῖν, ἐδίψησα καὶ οὐκ ἐποτίσατέ με, 25:43 ξένος ἤμην καὶ οὐ συνηγάγετέ με, γυμνὸς καὶ οὐ περιεβάλετέ με, ἀσθενὴς καὶ ἐν φυλακῇ καὶ οὐκ ἐπεσκέψασθέ με. 25:44 τότε ἀποκριθήσονται καὶ αὐτοὶ λέγοντες, Κύριε, πότε σε εἴδομεν πεινῶντα ἢ διψῶντα ἢ ξένον ἢ γυμνὸν ἢ ἀσθενῆ ἢ ἐν φυλακῇ καὶ οὐ διηκονήσαμέν σοι; 25:45 τότε ἀποκριθήσεται αὐτοῖς λέγων, Ἀμὴν λέγω ὑμῖν, ἐφ᾽ ὅσον οὐκ ἐποιήσατε ἑνὶ τούτων τῶν ἐλαχίστων, οὐδὲ ἐμοὶ ἐποιήσατε. 25:46 καὶ ἀπελεύσονται οὗτοι εἰς κόλασιν αἰώνιον, οἱ δὲ δίκαιοι εἰς ζωὴν αἰώνιον.

25:42

πεινάω, πεινάσω/πεινήσω, ἐπείνασα hunger, be hungry; hunger after, long for

ἐσθίω, φάγομαι, ἔφαγον eat

διψάω, διψήσω, ἐδίψησα thirst, be thirsty

ποτίζω, ποτίσω, ἐπότισα, πεπότικα cause someone to drink, give someone something to drink

25:43

ξένος, ου, ὁ strange, foreign; stranger, foreigner (substantive)

γυμνός, ή, όν naked, without an outer garment, uncovered

περιβάλλω, περιβαλῶ, περέβαλον, περιβέβληκα, περεβλήθην cast around, throw around; clothe; clothe oneself, be clothed (middle)

ἀσθενέω, ἀσθενήσω, ἠσθένησα be weak, be sick

φυλακή, ῆς, ἡ watch, guard, prison

ἐπισκέπτομαι, ἐπισκέψομαι, ἐπεσκεψάμην look for; go to see, visit

25:44

πότε when? (interrogative adverb)

πεινάω, πεινάσω/πεινήσω, ἐπείνασα hunger, be hungry; hunger after, long for

διψάω, διψήσω, ἐδίψησα thirst, be thirsty

ξένος, ου, ὁ strange, foreign; stranger, foreigner (substantive)

γυμνός, ή, όν naked, without an outer garment, uncovered

ἀσθενής, ές weak; sick, ill

φυλακή, ῆς, ἡ watch, guard, prison

διακονέω, διακονήσω, διηκόνησα, δεδιηκόνηκα, διηκονήθην wait on, attend upon, serve

25:45

ὅσος, η, ον how large, how great; as many as (plural); whosoever, whatsoever; ἐφ᾽ ὅσον while, as long as, inasmuch as

ἐλάχιστος, η, ον smallest, least

25:46

κόλασις, εως, ἡ punishment

αἰώνιος, ον (αἰώνιος, ία, ιον) eternal, everlasting

ζωή, ῆς, ἡ life, life eternal

25:46 **ἀπελεύσονται** is the future middle indicative of ἀπέρχομαι. **αἰώνιον**: adjectives of two terminations have the same form for the masculine and feminine (cf. App. 18).

26 Καὶ ἐγένετο ὅτε ἐτέλεσεν ὁ Ἰησοῦς πάντας τοὺς λόγους
τούτους, εἶπεν τοῖς μαθηταῖς αὐτοῦ, 26:2 Οἴδατε ὅτι μετὰ δύο
ἡμέρας τὸ πάσχα γίνεται, καὶ ὁ υἱὸς τοῦ ἀνθρώπου παραδίδοται
εἰς τὸ σταυρωθῆναι. 26:3 Τότε συνήχθησαν οἱ ἀρχιερεῖς καὶ οἱ
πρεσβύτεροι τοῦ λαοῦ εἰς τὴν αὐλὴν τοῦ ἀρχιερέως τοῦ λεγομένου
Καϊάφα 26:4 καὶ συνεβουλεύσαντο ἵνα τὸν Ἰησοῦν δόλῳ
κρατήσωσιν καὶ ἀποκτείνωσιν· 26:5 ἔλεγον δέ, Μὴ ἐν τῇ ἑορτῇ, ἵνα
μὴ θόρυβος γένηται ἐν τῷ λαῷ.

26:1

ὅτε when, whenever (adverb)

τελέω, τελέσω, ἐτέλεσα, τετέλεκα, τετέλεσμαι, ἐτελέσθην finish, fulfill, accomplish, make an end

26:2

ὅτι that, because, since (conjunction)

πάσχα, τό feast of the passover (indeclinable)

σταυρόω, σταυρώσω, ἐσταύρωσα, ἐσταύρωμαι, ἐσταυρώθην crucify

26:3

ἀρχιερεύς, έως, ὁ high priest

πρεσβύτερος, α, ον older, ancestor, elder (designation of an official); ancients, fathers (plural)

λαός, οῦ, ὁ people

αὐλή, ῆς, ἡ fold; courtyard; palace

Καϊάφας, α, ὁ Caiaphas

26:4

συμβουλεύω, συμβουλεύσω counsel, advise; consult together, plot (middle)

δόλος, ου, ὁ fraud, deceit, guile

κρατέω, κρατήσω, ἐκράτησα, κεκράτηκα, κεκράτημαι lay hold of, grasp; retain, not remit

26:5

ἑορτή, ῆς, ἡ feast, festival

θόρυβος, ου, ὁ noise; turmoil, uproar

λαός, οῦ, ὁ people

26:1 **Καὶ ἐγένετο**: the finite verb, usually omitted in translation, is translated in older versions: *and it came to pass.*

26:2 **τὸ πάσχα**: the Greek verb πάσχω means *to suffer, suffer death*; the Hebrew means *to pass over.* **γίνεται . . . παραδίδοται**: the present tense connotes a future. **εἰς τὸ σταυρωθῆναι**: *to be crucified*; the articular infinitive expresses purpose.

26:3 **τοῦ λεγομένου**: *who was called.*

26:4 **δόλῳ**: *by cunning*; the dative of manner indicates the way in which something is done.

26:6 Τοῦ δὲ Ἰησοῦ γενομένου ἐν Βηθανίᾳ ἐν οἰκίᾳ Σίμωνος τοῦ λεπροῦ, 26:7 προσῆλθεν αὐτῷ γυνὴ ἔχουσα ἀλάβαστρον μύρου βαρυτίμου καὶ κατέχεεν ἐπὶ τῆς κεφαλῆς αὐτοῦ ἀνακειμένου. 26:8 ἰδόντες δὲ οἱ μαθηταὶ ἠγανάκτησαν λέγοντες, Εἰς τί ἡ ἀπώλεια αὕτη; 26:9 ἐδύνατο γὰρ τοῦτο πραθῆναι πολλοῦ καὶ δοθῆναι πτωχοῖς. 26:10 γνοὺς δὲ ὁ Ἰησοῦς εἶπεν αὐτοῖς, Τί κόπους παρέχετε τῇ γυναικί; ἔργον γὰρ καλὸν ἠργάσατο εἰς ἐμέ·

26:6
λεπρός, οῦ, ὁ leper
26:7
ἀλάβαστρον, ου, τό alabaster flask, alabaster box
μύρον, ου, τό ointment, unguent, perfume
βαρύτιμος, ον very expensive, very precious
καταχέω, καταχεύσω pour out, pour down
κεφαλή, ῆς, ἡ head
ἀνάκειμαι, ἀνακείσομαι lie down, recline
26:8
ἀγανακτέω, ἀγανακτήσω, ἠγανάκτησα be indignant, angry (+ περί at)
ἀπώλεια, ας, ἡ destruction; waste; misery, eternal ruin
26:9
πιπράσκω, πέπρακα, πέπραμαι, ἐπράθην sell
πτωχός, ή, όν poor, indigent, needy
26:10
κόπος, ου, ὁ work, labor, toil; trouble, difficulty
παρέχω, παρέξω, παρέσχον (2 aorist) give up, offer, present; grant, show; cause, bring about
ἔργον, ου, τό work, deed, action
ἐργάζομαι, ἐργάσομαι, ἠργασάμην/εἰργασάμην, εἴργασμαι work, do, accomplish, perform

---

26:7 **ἀλάβαστρον μύρου**: the genitive expresses material or contents. **ἀνακειμένου**: *as he was reclining at the table.*

26:8 **ἰδόντες**: *when they saw this*; supply τοῦτο. **Εἰς τί;** means *why?* in direct questions.

26:9 **πολλοῦ**: *at a high price*; the use of the case is a genitive of price or value. In the context of buying or selling the genitive is used to indicate what something is worth.

26:10 **εἰς ἐμέ**: *on my behalf*; the preposition is used as a dative of advantage.

26:11 πάντοτε γὰρ τοὺς πτωχοὺς ἔχετε μεθ' ἑαυτῶν, ἐμὲ δὲ οὐ
πάντοτε ἔχετε· 26:12 βαλοῦσα γὰρ αὕτη τὸ μύρον τοῦτο ἐπὶ τοῦ
σώματός μου πρὸς τὸ ἐνταφιάσαι με ἐποίησεν. 26:13 ἀμὴν λέγω
ὑμῖν, ὅπου ἐὰν κηρυχθῇ τὸ εὐαγγέλιον τοῦτο ἐν ὅλῳ τῷ κόσμῳ,
λαληθήσεται καὶ ὃ ἐποίησεν αὕτη εἰς μνημόσυνον αὐτῆς.
26:14 Τότε πορευθεὶς εἷς τῶν δώδεκα, ὁ λεγόμενος Ἰούδας
Ἰσκαριώτης, πρὸς τοὺς ἀρχιερεῖς 26:15 εἶπεν, Τί θέλετέ μοι δοῦναι,
κἀγὼ ὑμῖν παραδώσω αὐτόν; οἱ δὲ ἔστησαν αὐτῷ τριάκοντα
ἀργύρια. 26:16 καὶ ἀπὸ τότε ἐζήτει εὐκαιρίαν ἵνα αὐτὸν παραδῷ.

26:11
πάντοτε always, at all times, ever (adverb)
πτωχός, ή, όν poor, indigent, needy
26:12
μύρον, ου, τό ointment, unguent, perfume
σῶμα, ατος, τό body
ἐνταφιάζω, ἐνταφιάσω, ἐνεταφίασα prepare for burial, bury
26:13
κηρύσσω, κηρύξω, ἐκήρυξα, ἐκηρύχθην announce openly, proclaim aloud
εὐαγγέλιον, ου, τό good news, gospel, glad tidings
κόσμος, ου, ὁ order, world, universe
μνημόσυνον, ου, τό memorial; remembrance
26:14
δώδεκα twelve (indeclinable)
ἀρχιερεύς, έως, ὁ high priest
26:15
τριάκοντα thirty (indeclinable)
ἀργύριον, ίου, τό silver, silver shekel, silver drachma, silver money
26:16
εὐκαιρία, ας, ἡ convenient opportunity, favorable occasion, suitable moment

---

26:11 **μεθ' ἑαυτῶν**: the third person plurals of the third person reflexive pronouns frequently substitute for the first and second person plurals of the reflexive pronouns (App. 45, 46).

26:12 **βαλοῦσα**: *when she poured.* **πρὸς τὸ ἐνταφιάσαι με**: *to prepare me for burial*; the preposition introduces an articular infinitive of purpose. **ἐποίησεν**: supply τοῦτο.

26:13 **λαληθήσεται καὶ ὃ**: *also that will be told which*; supply ἐκεῖνο as the subject of the verb and the antecedent of the relative pronoun. **εἰς μνημόσυνον αὐτῆς**: *in memory of her*; αὐτῆς is an objective genitive: future generations will remember her.

26:14–15 **πορευθεὶς . . . εἶπεν**: *went and said.*

26:15 **Τί θέλετέ μοι δοῦναι**: *what are you willing to pay me.* **οἱ δὲ ἔστησαν**: *and they weighed out* (on the scales); the first aorist is transitive.

26:17 Τῇ δὲ πρώτῃ τῶν ἀζύμων προσῆλθον οἱ μαθηταὶ τῷ Ἰησοῦ λέγοντες, Ποῦ θέλεις ἑτοιμάσωμέν σοι φαγεῖν τὸ πάσχα; 26:18 ὁ δὲ εἶπεν, Ὑπάγετε εἰς τὴν πόλιν πρὸς τὸν δεῖνα καὶ εἴπατε αὐτῷ, Ὁ διδάσκαλος λέγει, Ὁ καιρός μου ἐγγύς ἐστιν, πρὸς σὲ ποιῶ τὸ πάσχα μετὰ τῶν μαθητῶν μου. 26:19 καὶ ἐποίησαν οἱ μαθηταὶ ὡς συνέταξεν αὐτοῖς ὁ Ἰησοῦς καὶ ἡτοίμασαν τὸ πάσχα. 26:20 Ὀψίας δὲ γενομένης ἀνέκειτο μετὰ τῶν δώδεκα. 26:21 καὶ ἐσθιόντων αὐτῶν εἶπεν, Ἀμὴν λέγω ὑμῖν ὅτι εἷς ἐξ ὑμῶν παραδώσει με. 26:22 καὶ λυπούμενοι σφόδρα ἤρξαντο λέγειν αὐτῷ εἷς ἕκαστος, Μήτι ἐγώ εἰμι, κύριε;

26:17
ἄζυμος, ον unleavened; τὰ ἄζυμα the festival of unleavened bread
ποῦ where? in what place? (interrogative adverb)
ἑτοιμάζω, ἑτοιμάσω, ἡτοίμασα, ἡτοίμακα, ἡτοίμασμαι, ἡτοιμάσθην make ready, prepare
ἐσθίω, φάγομαι, ἔφαγον eat
πάσχα, τό feast of the passover (indeclinable)
26:18
δεῖνα, δεῖνος, ὁ, ἡ, τό certain man, somebody
καιρός, οῦ, ὁ time, appointed time
ἐγγύς near, close at hand (adverb)
πάσχα, τό feast of the passover (indeclinable)
26:19
συντάσσω, συντάξω, συνέταξα arrange; order, charge, direct
ἑτοιμάζω, ἑτοιμάσω, ἡτοίμασα, ἡτοίμακα, ἡτοίμασμαι, ἡτοιμάσθην make ready, prepare
26:20
ὀψία, ας, ἡ evening
ἀνάκειμαι, ἀνακείσομαι, lie down, recline
δώδεκα twelve (indeclinable)
26:21
ἐσθίω, φάγομαι, ἔφαγον eat
26:22
λυπέω, λυπήσω, ἐλύπησα, λελύπηκα, ἐλυπήθην vex, irritate, offend (active); be grieved, pained, distressed (passive)
σφόδρα greatly, exceedingly (adverb)
ἄρχω, ἄρξω, ἦρξα, ἦρχα, ἦργμαι, ἤρχθην rule (active); begin (middle)
ἕκαστος, η, ον each, every; each one, every one (substantive)

26:17 **Τῇ δὲ πρώτῃ**: supply ἡμέρᾳ. The case usage is a dative of time when. **προσῆλθον . . . τῷ Ἰησοῦ**: the compound verb takes the dative of the person. **Ποῦ θέλεις ἑτοιμάσωμέν σοι**: *where do you want us to make preparations for you*; the verb θέλεις with a subjunctive (without a conjunction) introduces a doubtful or deliberative question.

26:18 **πρὸς σὲ**: *at your house.*

26:22 **Μήτι ἐγώ εἰμι**: *surely I am not the one*; the interrogative particle in questions expects a negative answer.

26:23 ὁ δὲ ἀποκριθεὶς εἶπεν, Ὁ ἐμβάψας μετ᾽ ἐμοῦ τὴν χεῖρα ἐν τῷ
τρυβλίῳ οὗτός με παραδώσει. 26:24 ὁ μὲν υἱὸς τοῦ ἀνθρώπου ὑπάγει
καθὼς γέγραπται περὶ αὐτοῦ, οὐαὶ δὲ τῷ ἀνθρώπῳ ἐκείνῳ δι᾽ οὗ ὁ
υἱὸς τοῦ ἀνθρώπου παραδίδοται· καλὸν ἦν αὐτῷ εἰ οὐκ ἐγεννήθη ὁ
ἄνθρωπος ἐκεῖνος. 26:25 ἀποκριθεὶς δὲ Ἰούδας ὁ παραδιδοὺς αὐτὸν
εἶπεν, Μήτι ἐγώ εἰμι, ῥαββί; λέγει αὐτῷ, Σὺ εἶπας.
26:26 Ἐσθιόντων δὲ αὐτῶν λαβὼν ὁ Ἰησοῦς ἄρτον καὶ εὐλογήσας
ἔκλασεν καὶ δοὺς τοῖς μαθηταῖς εἶπεν, Λάβετε φάγετε, τοῦτό ἐστιν
τὸ σῶμά μου. 26:27 καὶ λαβὼν ποτήριον καὶ εὐχαριστήσας ἔδωκεν
αὐτοῖς λέγων, Πίετε ἐξ αὐτοῦ πάντες,

26:23
ἐμβάπτω, ἐμβάψω, ἐνέβαψα dip (in, into)
τρύβλιον, ου, τό bowl, dish
26:24
καθώς as, just as, how, inasmuch as (adverb)
γράφω, γράψω, ἔγραψα, γέγραφα, γέγραμμαι, ἐγράφθην engrave, write
οὐαί woe! alas! (interjection)
26:26
ἐσθίω, φάγομαι, ἔφαγον eat
εὐλογέω, εὐλογήσω, εὐλόγησα, εὐλόγηκα praise, bless
κλάω, κλάσω, ἔκλασα break
σῶμα, ατος, τό body
26:27
ποτήριον, ου, τό cup
εὐχαριστέω, εὐχαριστήω, εὐχαρίστησα give thanks
πίνω, πίομαι, ἔπιον, πέπωκα drink

26:23 **Ὁ ἐμβάψας**: since all do so, He is simply restating: εἷς ἐξ ὑμῶν.

26:24 **γέγραπται**: *it is written*; the verb form is impersonal use of the third person singular perfect passive indicative of γράφω (cf. App. 53, E, 1). **καλὸν ἦν αὐτῷ**: *it would be* or *it would have been better for him*; the neuter predicate adjective indicates the impersonal nature of the verb. The positive degree of the adjective is used instead of the comparative by analogy to the Semitic pattern which lacks the comparative degree. ἦν provides a degree of uncertainty as to tense in the contrary to fact apodosis because εἰμί lacks a pluperfect tense. **εἰ οὐκ ἐγεννήθη**: *if . . . had not been born*; is a past contrary to fact protasis (cf. App. 70).

26:25 **Σὺ εἶπας** is a positive affirmation.

26:26 **λαβὼν . . . εὐλογήσας ἔκλασεν**: the participles may be translated as the finite verbs and be coordinated with ἔκλασεν.

26:27 **ποτήριον**: by metonymy the cup represents its content. In this case the γένημα τῆς ἀμπέλου symbolizes τὸ αἷμά μου. **πάντες**: *all of you*.

26:28 τοῦτο γάρ ἐστιν τὸ αἷμά μου τῆς διαθήκης τὸ περὶ πολλῶν
ἐκχυννόμενον εἰς ἄφεσιν ἁμαρτιῶν. 26:29 λέγω δὲ ὑμῖν, οὐ μὴ πίω
ἀπ' ἄρτι ἐκ τούτου τοῦ γενήματος τῆς ἀμπέλου ἕως τῆς ἡμέρας
ἐκείνης ὅταν αὐτὸ πίνω μεθ' ὑμῶν καινὸν ἐν τῇ βασιλείᾳ τοῦ πατρός
μου. 26:30 Καὶ ὑμνήσαντες ἐξῆλθον εἰς τὸ Ὄρος τῶν Ἐλαιῶν.
26:31 Τότε λέγει αὐτοῖς ὁ Ἰησοῦς, Πάντες ὑμεῖς
σκανδαλισθήσεσθε ἐν ἐμοὶ ἐν τῇ νυκτὶ ταύτῃ, γέγραπται γάρ,

Πατάξω τὸν ποιμένα,
καὶ διασκορπισθήσονται τὰ πρόβατα τῆς ποίμνης.

26:28
αἷμα, ατος, τό blood
διαθήκη, ης, ἡ covenant
ἐκχύνω, ἐκχυνῶ pour out, shed
ἄφεσις, εως, ἡ release; remission, forgiveness
ἁμαρτία, ας, ἡ error, sin
26:29
πίνω, πίομαι, ἔπιον, πέπωκα drink
γένημα, ατος, τό product, fruit
ἄμπελος, ου, ἡ vine, grapevine
καινός, ή, όν new
26:30
ὑμνέω, ὑμνήσω, ὕμνησα praise, celebrate with hymns; sing a hymn
ἐλαία, ας, ἡ olive tree, olive
26:31
νύξ, νυκτός, ἡ night
πατάσσω, πατάξω, ἐπάταξα strike, smite; kill
ποιμήν, ένος, ὁ shepherd, herdsman, guardian
διασκορπίζω, διασκορπίσω, διεσκόρπισα, διεσκορπίσθην scatter, disperse, strew
πρόβατον, ου, τό sheep
ποίμνη, ης, ἡ flock

26:28 **τὸ αἷμά μου τῆς διαθήκης**: μου is emphatic. The covenant that formerly required the blood of sacrificial animals is now fulfilled and surpassed by the ultimate sacrifice of Jesus. **εἰς ἄφεσιν ἁμαρτιῶν**: *for forgiveness of sins*; the preposition indicates purpose. ἁμαρτιῶν is an objective genitive: by His blood He redeems our sins.

26:29 **οὐ μὴ πίω**: *I will never drink*; the double negative indicates a strong negation and usually takes an aorist subjunctive that is translated as a future. **ἀπ' ἄρτι**: *from now on*. **ἕως**: *until*; the preposition takes the genitive case. **αὐτὸ . . . καινὸν**: *it anew*; the predicate adjective is used as an adverb.

26:30 **ὑμνήσαντες**: *after they had sung a hymn.*

26:31 **ὑμεῖς σκανδαλισθήσεσθε**: *you will fall away*; σκανδαλισθήσεσθε because of temporary loss of faith they will all flee (26:56). **ἐν ἐμοὶ ἐν τῇ νυκτὶ ταύτῃ**: *because of me this night*; νυκτὶ is a dative of time when.

26:32 μετὰ δὲ τὸ ἐγερθῆναί με προάξω ὑμᾶς εἰς τὴν Γαλιλαίαν.
26:33 ἀποκριθεὶς δὲ ὁ Πέτρος εἶπεν αὐτῷ, Εἰ πάντες
σκανδαλισθήσονται ἐν σοί, ἐγὼ οὐδέποτε σκανδαλισθήσομαι.
26:34 ἔφη αὐτῷ ὁ Ἰησοῦς, Ἀμὴν λέγω σοι ὅτι ἐν ταύτῃ τῇ νυκτὶ πρὶν
ἀλέκτορα φωνῆσαι τρὶς ἀπαρνήσῃ με. 26:35 λέγει αὐτῷ ὁ Πέτρος,
Κἂν δέῃ με σὺν σοὶ ἀποθανεῖν, οὐ μή σε ἀπαρνήσομαι. ὁμοίως καὶ
πάντες οἱ μαθηταὶ εἶπαν.

26:32
προάγω, προάξω, προήγαγον (2 aorist) lead forward, bring out (transitive); go before, precede, go before (intransitive); go or come before *someone* (+ accusative of person)
26:33
οὐδέποτε never (adverb)
26:34
νύξ, νυκτός, ἡ night
πρίν before (adverb)
ἀλέκτωρ, ορος, ὁ cock, rooster
φωνέω, φωνήσω, ἐφώνησα, ἐφωνήθην sound, crow, call, summon
τρίς three times (adverb)
ἀπαρνέομαι, ἀπαρνήσομαι, ἀπηρνησάμην, ἀπήρνημαι deny, disown, repudiate
26:35
δεῖ, δεήσει, ἐδέησε it is necessary, it is proper (impersonal verb from δέω)
σύν with, together with (+ dative)
ἀποθνήσκω, ἀποθανοῦμαι, ἀπέθανον (2 aorist) die, face death, decay
ὁμοίως likewise, also, similarly (adverb)

26:32 **μετὰ δὲ τὸ ἐγερθῆναί με**: *but after I have risen.*

26:33 **Εἰ πάντες . . . ἐγὼ οὐδέποτε**: the future most vivid expresses an enlarged sense of confidence most intently.

26:34 **πρὶν ἀλέκτορα φωῆσαι**: *before the cock crows*; πρὶν is followed by an infinitive with a subject accusative. **ἀπαρνήσῃ** is second person singular future middle indicative of a deponent verb (cf. App. 53, B, 1).

26:35 **Κἂν δέῃ με σὺν σοὶ ἀποθανεῖν**: *even if I have to die with you*; Κἂν introduces the protasis of a future more vivid condition. The impersonal verb, followed by an infinitive with a subject accusative, may be translated personally. **ὁμοίως . . . εἶπαν**: *spoke in the same manner*; εἶπαν: occasionally this second aorist stem takes first aorist endings without the σ. The present tense of this second aorist form (cf. App. 54) has gone out of use and is supplied by λέγω, φημί, or ἀγορεύω.

26:36 Τότε ἔρχεται μετ' αὐτῶν ὁ Ἰησοῦς εἰς χωρίον λεγόμενον Γεθσημανὶ καὶ λέγει τοῖς μαθηταῖς, Καθίσατε αὐτοῦ ἕως [οὗ] ἀπελθὼν ἐκεῖ προσεύξωμαι. 26:37 καὶ παραλαβὼν τὸν Πέτρον καὶ τοὺς δύο υἱοὺς Ζεβεδαίου ἤρξατο λυπεῖσθαι καὶ ἀδημονεῖν. 26:38 τότε λέγει αὐτοῖς, Περίλυπός ἐστιν ἡ ψυχή μου ἕως θανάτου· μείνατε ὧδε καὶ γρηγορεῖτε μετ' ἐμοῦ. 26:39 καὶ προελθὼν μικρὸν ἔπεσεν ἐπὶ πρόσωπον αὐτοῦ προσευχόμενος καὶ λέγων,

---

26:36
Γεθσημανί Gethsemane (indeclinable; an olive orchard on the Mount of Olives)
καθίζω, καθίσω, ἐκάθισα, κεκάθικα cause to sit down, seat, set (transitive); sit, sit down; remain, stay, continue, rest (intransitive)
αὐτοῦ here, in this place (adverb)
26:37
λυπέω, λυπήσω, ἐλύπησα, λελύπηκα, ἐλυπήθην vex, irritate, offend (active); be grieved, pained, distressed, sorrowful (passive)
ἀδημονέω, ἀδημονήσω be anxious, be distressed, be full of anguish
26:38
περίλυπος, ον greatly grieved, exceedingly sorrowful
θάνατος, ου, ὁ death
μένω, μενῶ, ἔμεινα, μεμένηκα stay, rest, dwell
γρηγορέω, γρηγορήσω, ἐγρηγόρησα be awake, watch; be alive; be watchful, attentive, vigilant
26:39
προέρχομαι, προελεύσομαι, προῆλθον, προελήλυθα go forward, advance, proceed; go before
μικρός, ά, όν small, short, little; little one (substantive); μικρόν short time; short distance
πρόσωπον, ου, τό face, countenance; person, personage

26:36 **ἕως [οὗ] ἀπελθὼν ἐκεῖ προσεύξωμαι**: *while I go and pray there*; ἕως [οὗ] is followed by the aorist subjunctive.

26:37 **τοὺς δύο υἱοὺς Ζεβεδαίου**: *James and John*. **ἤρξατο** means *to begin* in the middle and takes a complementary infinitive.

26:38 **ἕως θανάτου**: *unto death*.

26:39 **προελθὼν μικρὸν**: *walking a little way*; μικρὸν is a cognate accusative.

Πάτερ μου, εἰ δυνατόν ἐστιν, παρελθάτω ἀπ' ἐμοῦ τὸ ποτήριον
τοῦτο· πλὴν οὐχ ὡς ἐγὼ θέλω ἀλλ' ὡς σύ. 26:40 καὶ ἔρχεται πρὸς
τοὺς μαθητὰς καὶ εὑρίσκει αὐτοὺς καθεύδοντας, καὶ λέγει τῷ Πέτρῳ,
Οὕτως οὐκ ἰσχύσατε μίαν ὥραν γρηγορῆσαι μετ' ἐμοῦ; 26:41
γρηγορεῖτε καὶ προσεύχεσθε, ἵνα μὴ εἰσέλθητε εἰς πειρασμόν· τὸ
μὲν πνεῦμα πρόθυμον ἡ δὲ σὰρξ ἀσθενής. 26:42 πάλιν ἐκ δευτέρου
ἀπελθὼν προσηύξατο λέγων, Πάτερ μου, εἰ οὐ δύναται τοῦτο
παρελθεῖν ἐὰν μὴ αὐτὸ πίω, γενηθήτω τὸ θέλημά σου.

26:39

δυνατός, ή, όν able, powerful, strong, mighty; δυνατόν possible

παρέρχομαι, παρελεύσομαι, παρῆλθον (2 aorist), ἐλήλυθα pass, pass along, pass by; pass away, come to an end

ποτήριον, ου, τό cup

πλήν besides, except (adverb); but, however, nevertheless (conjunction)

26:40

καθεύδω, καθευδήσω sleep, be fast asleep

ἰσχύω, ἰσχύσω, ἴσχυσα be good, be strong, be powerful, have power, be able, be well

γρηγορέω, γρηγορήσω, ἐγρηγόρησα be awake, watch; be alive; be watchful, attentive, vigilant

26:41

πειρασμός, οῦ, ὁ test, trial; temptation

πνεῦμα, ατος, τό wind, spirit, mind, Holy Spirit

πρόθυμος, ον ready, willing, eager

σάρξ, σαρκός, ἡ flesh

ἀσθενής, ές weak; sick, ill

26:42

δεύτερος, α, ον second; ἐκ δευτέρου again, the second time, another time

παρέρχομαι, παρελεύσομαι, παρῆλθον (2 aorist), ἐλήλυθα pass, pass along, pass by; pass away, come to an end

πίνω, πίομαι, ἔπιον, πέπωκα drink

θέλημα, ατος, τό will, desire

26:39 **τὸ ποτήριον**: by metonymy the cup represents its content. In this case it symbolizes sorrow and suffering. **πλὴν** is used as a conjunction: *but.*

26:40 **Οὕτως** introduces a question: *so.* **μίαν ὥραν** is an accusative of duration of time.

26:41 **τὸ μὲν πνεῦμα . . . ἡ δὲ σὰρξ**: supply ἐστιν. The juxtaposition of the nouns points out a basic antithesis between the two.

26:42 **τοῦτο**: supply τὸ ποτήριον.

26:43 καὶ ἐλθὼν πάλιν εὗρεν αὐτοὺς καθεύδοντας, ἦσαν γὰρ αὐτῶν οἱ ὀφθαλμοὶ βεβαρημένοι. 26:44 καὶ ἀφεὶς αὐτοὺς πάλιν ἀπελθὼν προσηύξατο ἐκ τρίτου τὸν αὐτὸν λόγον εἰπὼν πάλιν. 26:45 τότε ἔρχεται πρὸς τοὺς μαθητὰς καὶ λέγει αὐτοῖς, Καθεύδετε [τὸ] λοιπὸν καὶ ἀναπαύεσθε· ἰδοὺ ἤγγικεν ἡ ὥρα καὶ ὁ υἱὸς τοῦ ἀνθρώπου παραδίδοται εἰς χεῖρας ἁμαρτωλῶν. 26:46 ἐγείρεσθε ἄγωμεν· ἰδοὺ ἤγγικεν ὁ παραδιδούς με.

26:43
καθεύδω, καθευδήσω sleep, be fast asleep
βαρέω, βαρήσω, βεβάρημαι weigh down; become heavy, be burdened, be overcome (passive)
26:44
τρίτος, η, ον third; ἐκ τρίτου the third time, for the third time
26:45
καθεύδω, καθευδήσω sleep, be fast asleep
λοιπός, ή, όν remaining; the rest, remainder; (τὸ) λοιπόν from now on, in the future, henceforth
ἀναπαύω, ἀναπαύσω, ἀνέπαυσα, ἀναπέπαυμαι, ἀνεπαύθην give rest, refresh, revive; rest, take rest
ἐγγίζω, ἐγγίσω, ἤγγισα, ἤγγικα approach, draw near
ἁμαρτωλός, όν sinful; sinner (substantive)
26:46
ἄγω, ἄξω, ἤγαγον, ἦχα, ἦγμαι, ἤχθην lead, bring, arrest; go

26:44 **ἀφεὶς αὐτοὺς πάλιν ἀπελθὼν**: *after he had left them and departed again*; supply καὶ to coordinate the two participles. πάλιν, collocated between the participles, may modify both and govern a double syntactic function called *apo koinou* (ἀπὸ κοινοῦ). **τὸν αὐτὸν λόγον εἰπὼν**: *saying the same words*; αὐτὸν carries this meaning in attributive position (App. 40, note 3). λόγον is a cognate accusative.

26:45 **Καθεύδετε . . . ἀναπαύεσθε** may be a statement, an imperative, or a question.

26:46 **ἄγωμεν**: *let us go*; like the prohibitive and deliberative, the hortatory is an independent subjunctive. It is used to express a request or a proposal in the first person. The verb is intransitive. **ἤγγικεν** is third person singular perfect active indicative. The perfect tense denotes action (aspect) that is completed near present time and continues with present result. Verbs beginning with a short vowel lengthen the vowel to show reduplication. The reduplication or doubling of the sound at the beginning of a word occurs especially in the perfect, pluperfect, and future perfect tenses to indicate completed action. **ὁ παραδιούς με**: *has approached* (and is now here). The verb expresses urgency.

26:47 Καὶ ἔτι αὐτοῦ λαλοῦντος ἰδοὺ Ἰούδας εἷς τῶν δώδεκα ἦλθεν καὶ μετ' αὐτοῦ ὄχλος πολὺς μετὰ μαχαιρῶν καὶ ξύλων ἀπὸ τῶν ἀρχιερέων καὶ πρεσβυτέρων τοῦ λαοῦ. 26:48 ὁ δὲ παραδιδοὺς αὐτὸν ἔδωκεν αὐτοῖς σημεῖον λέγων, Ὃν ἂν φιλήσω αὐτός ἐστιν, κρατήσατε αὐτόν. 26:49 καὶ εὐθέως προσελθὼν τῷ Ἰησοῦ εἶπεν, Χαῖρε, ῥαββί, καὶ κατεφίλησεν αὐτόν. 26:50 ὁ δὲ Ἰησοῦς εἶπεν αὐτῷ, Ἑταῖρε, ἐφ' ὃ πάρει. τότε προσελθόντες ἐπέβαλον τὰς χεῖρας ἐπὶ τὸν Ἰησοῦν καὶ ἐκράτησαν αὐτόν.

26:47
μάχαιρα, ας, ἡ sword
ξύλον, ου, τό wood; club, cudgel; cross; tree
ἀρχιερεύς, έως, ὁ high priest
πρεσβύτερος, α, ον older, ancestor, elder (designation of an official); ancients, fathers (plural)

26:48
σημεῖον, ου, τό sign, token, miracle
φιλέω, φιλήσω, ἐφίλησα, πεφίληκα love, regard with affection, have affection for, like; kiss
κρατέω, κρατήσω, ἐκράτησα, κεκράτηκα, κεκράτημαι lay hold of, grasp, seize, apprehend; retain, not remit

26:49
χαίρω, χαρήσομαι, ἐχάρην (2 aorist passive) rejoice, be glad; χαῖρε, χαίρετε hail, greetings, welcome (as a form of greeting)
καταφιλέω, καταφιλήσω kiss

26:50
ἑταῖρος, ου, ὁ comrade, companion, fellow, friend
ἐφ' ὅ why?
πάρειμι be present, be here, have come
ἐπιβάλλω, ἐπιβαλῶ, ἐπέβαλον, ἐπιβέβληκα, ἐπεβλήθην lay, put on
κρατέω, κρατήσω, ἐκράτησα, κεκράτηκα, κεκράτημαι lay hold of, grasp, seize, apprehend; retain, not remit

---

26:47 **ἔτι αὐτοῦ λαλοῦντος**: *while He was still speaking*; **ἀπὸ τῶν ἀρχιερέων**: *sent by the high priests*; supply ἀπεσταλμένοι. ἀπὸ sometimes replaces ὑπό with verbs in the passive voice.

26:48 **ἔδωκεν αὐτοῖς σημεῖον**: *had given them a sign*; the aorist is equivalent to a pluperfect: the time of the arrangement of the sign precedes that of his coming.

26:49 **ῥαββί**: the honorary title mocks. Of the disciples, only Judas calls Him by this form of address in this Gospel (25).

26:51 καὶ ἰδοὺ εἷς τῶν μετὰ Ἰησοῦ ἐκτείνας τὴν χεῖρα ἀπέσπασεν
τὴν μάχαιραν αὐτοῦ καὶ πατάξας τὸν δοῦλον τοῦ ἀρχιερέως ἀφεῖλεν
αὐτοῦ τὸ ὠτίον. 26:52 τότε λέγει αὐτῷ ὁ Ἰησοῦς, Ἀπόστρεψον τὴν
μάχαιράν σου εἰς τὸν τόπον αὐτῆς· πάντες γὰρ οἱ λαβόντες μάχαιραν
ἐν μαχαίρῃ ἀπολοῦνται. 26:53 ἢ δοκεῖς ὅτι οὐ δύναμαι παρακαλέσαι
τὸν πατέρα μου, καὶ παραστήσει μοι ἄρτι πλείω δώδεκα λεγιῶνας
ἀγγέλων; 26:54 πῶς οὖν πληρωθῶσιν αἱ γραφαὶ ὅτι οὕτως δεῖ
γενέσθαι;

26:51

ἐκτείνω, ἐκτενῶ, ἐξέτεινα stretch out, hold out

ἀποσπάω, ἀποσπάσω draw, draw out; draw away, attract

μάχαιρα, ας, ἡ sword

πατάσσω, πατάξω, ἐπάταξα strike, smite; kill

ἀρχιερεύς, έως, ὁ high priest

ἀφαιρέω, ἀφαιρήσω, ἀφεῖλον (2 aorist) take away, remove; take off, remove by cutting off, cut off

ὠτίον, ου, τό ear

26:52

ἀποστρέφω, ἀποστρέψω, ἀπέστρεψα, ἀπέστραμμαι, ἀπεστράφην (2 aorist passive) turn away, remove; turn away (intransitive in middle and 2 aorist passive)

μάχαιρα, ας, ἡ sword

τόπος, ου, ὁ place, position, region

26:53

παρακαλέω, παρακαλέσω, παρεκάλεσα, παρακέκληκα, παρακέκλημαι, παρεκλήθην call upon, exhort, persuade; beg, entreat; comfort, encourage, cheer up

παρίστημι, παραστήσω place beside, put at one's disposal, present, offer, show; stand by, be present (intransitive)

ἄρτι now, at the present time, at once, immediately (adverb)

πλείων, πλεῖον or πλέον more, greater, larger; πλέον more (comparative adverb)

λεγιών, ῶνος, ὁ legion

26:54

γραφή, ῆς, ἡ writing, Holy Scripture, passage of scripture

δεῖ, δεήσει, ἐδέησε it is necessary, it is proper (impersonal verb from δέω)

26:51 **εἷς τῶν**: *one of those*; τῶν is a partitive genitive.

26:52 **ἀπολοῦνται** is a third person plural future middle indicative of ἀπόλλυμι.

26:53 **πλείω δώδεκα λεγιῶνας**: *more than twelve legions*; πλείω is the neuter plural accusative optional form of the comparative adjective of πολύς (cf. App. 22). After the comparative adjective the conjunction ἤ: *than* is omitted before numerals.

26:54 **πῶς οὖν πληρωθῶσιν αἱ γραφαὶ**: *how then are the scriptures fulfilled*; πληρωθῶσιν is a third person plural first aorist passive subjunctive. The mood indicates a rhetorical question. **ὅτι οὕτως δεῖ γενέσθαι**: *that it must be so*; supply αἱ λέγοντες: *that say* before the ὅτι clause.

26:55 Ἐν ἐκείνῃ τῇ ὥρᾳ εἶπεν ὁ Ἰησοῦς τοῖς ὄχλοις, Ὡς ἐπὶ λῃστὴν
ἐξήλθατε μετὰ μαχαιρῶν καὶ ξύλων συλλαβεῖν με; καθ᾽ ἡμέραν ἐν
τῷ ἱερῷ ἐκαθεζόμην διδάσκων καὶ οὐκ ἐκρατήσατέ με. 26:56 τοῦτο
δὲ ὅλον γέγονεν ἵνα πληρωθῶσιν αἱ γραφαὶ τῶν προφητῶν. Τότε οἱ
μαθηταὶ πάντες ἀφέντες αὐτὸν ἔφυγον.
26:57 Οἱ δὲ κρατήσαντες τὸν Ἰησοῦν ἀπήγαγον πρὸς Καϊάφαν
τὸν ἀρχιερέα, ὅπου οἱ γραμματεῖς καὶ οἱ πρεσβύτεροι συνήχθησαν.
26:58 ὁ δὲ Πέτρος ἠκολούθει αὐτῷ ἀπὸ μακρόθεν ἕως τῆς αὐλῆς τοῦ
ἀρχιερέως καὶ εἰσελθὼν ἔσω ἐκάθητο μετὰ τῶν ὑπηρετῶν ἰδεῖν τὸ
τέλος.

26:55

λῃστής, οῦ, ὁ robber, bandit

μάχαιρα, ας, ἡ sword

ξύλον, ου, τό wood; club, cudgel; cross; tree

συλλαμβάνω, συλλήψομαι, συνέλαβον, συνείληφα, συνελήφθην seize, apprehend, arrest

καθ᾽ ἡμέραν daily, every day

ἱερόν, οῦ, τό temple

καθέζομαι, καθεδοῦμαι sit, sit down

κρατέω, κρατήσω, ἐκράτησα, κεκράτηκα, κεκράτημαι lay hold of, grasp, seize, apprehend; retain, not remit

26:56

γραφή, ῆς, ἡ writing, Holy Scripture, passage of scripture

φεύγω, φεύξομαι, ἔφυγον (2 aorist) flee, flee from; avoid, shun

26:57

ἀπάγω, ἀπάξω, ἀπήγαγον, ἀπήχθην lead away; lead away (of a road; intransitive)

Καϊάφας, α, ὁ Caiaphas

ὅπου where (adverb)

26:58

μακρόθεν far off, at a distance, from afar (adverb)

αὐλή, ῆς, ἡ fold; courtyard; palace

ἔσω in, inside (adverb)

ὑπηρέτης, ου, ὁ servant, helper, assistant, attendant, officer

τέλος, ους, τό end, fulfillment, completion; custom, tax, duty

---

26:55 **Ὡς** introduces a simile and a question. **συλλαβεῖν** introduces a purpose clause after a main verb of motion.

26:57 **τὸν ἀρχιερέα**: Caiaphas was appointed the high priest and president of the Sanhedrin by the procurator Valerius Gratus.

26:58 **εἰσελθὼν ἔσω**: the prefixed preposition is commonly repeated either by the same or by a similar preposition or adverb.

26:59 οἱ δὲ ἀρχιερεῖς καὶ τὸ συνέδριον ὅλον ἐζήτουν ψευδομαρτυρίαν κατὰ τοῦ Ἰησοῦ ὅπως αὐτὸν θανατώσωσιν, 26:60 καὶ οὐχ εὗρον πολλῶν προσελθόντων ψευδομαρτύρων. ὕστερον δὲ προσελθόντες δύο 26:61 εἶπαν, Οὗτος ἔφη, Δύναμαι καταλῦσαι τὸν ναὸν τοῦ θεοῦ καὶ διὰ τριῶν ἡμερῶν οἰκοδομῆσαι. 26:62 καὶ ἀναστὰς ὁ ἀρχιερεὺς εἶπεν αὐτῷ, Οὐδὲν ἀποκρίνῃ τί οὗτοί σου καταμαρτυροῦσιν;

26:59

συνέδριον, ίου, τό assembly, high council, Sanhedrin

ψευδομαρτυρία, ας, ἡ false witness, false testimony

θανατόω, θανατώσω, ἐθανάτωσα kill, put to death, deliver to death

26:60

ψευδομάρτυς, υρος, ὁ one who gives false testimony, false witness

ὕστερος, α, ον later; ὕστερον later, afterwards; finally; last (adverb)

26:61

φημί, φήσω, ἔφησα say, speak

καταλύω, καταλύσω, κατέλυσα, κατελύθην throw down, destroy, abolish

ναός, οῦ, ὁ dwelling, temple

τρεῖς, τρία three

οἰκοδομέω, οἰκοδομήσω, ᾠκοδόμησα, ᾠκοδομήθην build, construct, establish

26:62

ἀνίστημι, ἀναστήσω, ἀνέστησα, ἀνέστην (2 aorist) cause to rise, raise, raise up; cause to be born (transitive); rise, stand up, get up (2 aorist and all middle forms are intransitive)

καταμαρτυρέω, καταμαρτυρήσω bear witness against, witness against

---

26:59 **τὸ συνέδριον ὅλον**: *the whole Sanhedrin*; ὅλον never stands in attributive position. **ἐζήτουν ψευδομαρτυρίαν**: *kept looking for false testimony*; the imperfect tense denotes progressive, continued, and repeated action (aspect) in past time. **θανατώσωσιν** is an aorist subjunctive.

26:60 **καὶ οὐχ εὗρον**: *yet they did not find anyone*; supply the indefinite pronoun τινα. **πολλῶν προσελθόντων ψευμαρτύρων**: *although many false witnesses came forward*; the adversative context invites a concessive interpretation of the genitive absolute.

26:61 **καταλῦσαι . . . οἰκοδομῆσαι** are complementary infinitives. **διὰ τριῶν ἡμερῶν**: *within three days*; the preposition with the genitive expresses time within which something occurs.

26:62 **Οὐδὲν ἀποκρίνῃ τί**: *do you give no response to what*; Οὐδὲν is a cognate accusative.

26:63 ὁ δὲ Ἰησοῦς ἐσιώπα. καὶ ὁ ἀρχιερεὺς εἶπεν αὐτῷ, Ἐξορκίζω σε
κατὰ τοῦ θεοῦ τοῦ ζῶντος ἵνα ἡμῖν εἴπῃς εἰ σὺ εἶ ὁ Χριστὸς ὁ υἱὸς τοῦ
θεοῦ. 26:64 λέγει αὐτῷ ὁ Ἰησοῦς, Σὺ εἶπας· πλὴν λέγω ὑμῖν,
ἀπ' ἄρτι ὄψεσθε τὸν υἱὸν τοῦ ἀνθρώπου
καθήμενον ἐκ δεξιῶν τῆς δυνάμεως
καὶ ἐρχόμενον ἐπὶ τῶν νεφελῶν τοῦ οὐρανοῦ.
26:65 τότε ὁ ἀρχιερεὺς διέρρηξεν τὰ ἱμάτια αὐτοῦ λέγων,
Ἐβλασφήμησεν· τί ἔτι χρείαν ἔχομεν μαρτύρων; ἴδε νῦν ἠκούσατε
τὴν βλασφημίαν· 26:66 τί ὑμῖν δοκεῖ; οἱ δὲ ἀποκριθέντες εἶπαν,
Ἔνοχος θανάτου ἐστίν.

26:63

σιωπάω, σιωπήσω, ἐσιώπησα be silent, keep silent, hold one's peace

ἐξορκίζω, ἐξορκίσω adjure, charge under oath

ζάω, ζήσω/ζήσομαι, ἔζησα, ἔζηκα live

26:64

πλήν besides, except (adverb); but, however, nevertheless (conjunction)

ἄρτι now, at the present time, at once, immediately; just (adverb); ἀπ' ἄρτι from now, from this time, henceforth

δεξιός, ά, όν right (as opposed to *left*); ἐκ δεξιῶν τινός at someone's right

νεφέλη, ης, ἡ cloud

26:65

διαρρήγνυμι and διαρρήσσω, διαρρήξω, διέρρηξα rend, tear, burst

ἱμάτιον, ου, τό garment, clothing; cloak, robe; clothes, garments (plural)

βλασφημέω, βλασφημήσω, ἐβλασφήμησα, βεβλασφήμηκα, ἐβλασφημήθην blaspheme, speak irreverently of

ἔτι yet, still (adverb)

χρεία, ας, ἡ need, necessity

μάρτυς, μάρτυρος, ὁ and ἡ witness

νῦν now, at the present time, just now, of late (adverb); τὸ νῦν the present time, now (noun)

βλασφημία, ίας, ἡ slander, abusive speech, blasphemy

26:66

δοκεῖ it seems; it seems good, best or right (impersonal verb)

ἔνοχος, ον subjected to, liable to; guilty

26:63 **ἐσιώπα**: *remained silent*; the imperfect tense denotes progressive, continued, and repeated action (aspect) in past time.

26:64 **Σὺ εἶπας** is a positive affirmation.

26:65 **διέρρηξεν τὰ ἱμάτια αὐτοῦ**: *he tore his (own) clothing*; the personal pronoun αὐτοῦ stands for the reflexive αὑτοῦ (App. 46, note). The action indicates a show of anger. **χρείαν . . . μαρτύρων**: μαρτύρων is an objective genitive.

26:66 **Ἔνοχος θανάτου**: the adjective denotes the punishment θανάτου and takes a judicial genitive.

26:67 Τότε ἐνέπτυσαν εἰς τὸ πρόσωπον αὐτοῦ καὶ ἐκολάφισαν αὐτόν, οἱ δὲ ἐράπισαν 26:68 λέγοντες, Προφήτευσον ἡμῖν, Χριστέ, τίς ἐστιν ὁ παίσας σε;

26:69 Ὁ δὲ Πέτρος ἐκάθητο ἔξω ἐν τῇ αὐλῇ· καὶ προσῆλθεν αὐτῷ μία παιδίσκη λέγουσα, Καὶ σὺ ἦσθα μετὰ Ἰησοῦ τοῦ Γαλιλαίου. 26:70 ὁ δὲ ἠρνήσατο ἔμπροσθεν πάντων λέγων, Οὐκ οἶδα τί λέγεις. 26:71 ἐξελθόντα δὲ εἰς τὸν πυλῶνα εἶδεν αὐτὸν ἄλλη καὶ λέγει τοῖς ἐκεῖ, Οὗτος ἦν μετὰ Ἰησοῦ τοῦ Ναζωραίου. 26:72 καὶ πάλιν ἠρνήσατο μετὰ ὅρκου ὅτι Οὐκ οἶδα τὸν ἄνθρωπον.

26:67
ἐμπτύω, ἐμπτύσω, ἐνέπτυσα spit upon
πρόσωπον, ου, τό face, countenance; person, personage
κολαφίζω, κολαφίσω strike with the fist, beat with the fist
ῥαπίζω, ῥαπίσω, ἐρράπισα beat with rods; strike with the palm of the hands; strike, slap
26:68
προφητεύω, προφητεύσω, ἐπροφήτευσα proclaim a divine revelation, prophetically reveal, prophesy
παίω, παίσω, ἔπαισα, πέπαικα strike, smite
26:69
ἔξω outside, out (adverb); out of (preposition)
αὐλή, ῆς, ἡ fold; courtyard; palace
παιδίσκη, ης, ἡ girl, maiden, servant girl
26:70
ἀρνέομαι, ἀρνήσομαι, ἠρνησάμην, ἤρνημαι deny, disown
26:71
πυλών, ῶνος, ὁ gate, gateway, entrance, vestibule
26:72
ἀρνέομαι, ἀρνήσομαι, ἠρνησάμην, ἤρνημαι deny, disown
ὅρκος, ου, ὁ oath

26:67 **ἐνέπτυσαν . . . ἐκολάφισαν . . . ἐράπισαν**: the tricolon of verbs emphasizes the abusive nature of their actions.

26:70 **ἠρνήσατο**: supply αὐτὸν.

26:71 **ἄλλη**: supply παιδίσκη from verse 69.

26:72 **ἠρνήσατο μετὰ ὅρκου**: supply αὐτὸν.

26:73 μετὰ μικρὸν δὲ προσελθόντες οἱ ἑστῶτες εἶπον τῷ Πέτρῳ, Ἀληθῶς καὶ σὺ ἐξ αὐτῶν εἶ, καὶ γὰρ ἡ λαλιά σου δῆλόν σε ποιεῖ. 26:74 τότε ἤρξατο καταθεματίζειν καὶ ὀμνύειν ὅτι Οὐκ οἶδα τὸν ἄνθρωπον. καὶ εὐθέως ἀλέκτωρ ἐφώνησεν. 26:75 καὶ ἐμνήσθη ὁ Πέτρος τοῦ ῥήματος Ἰησοῦ εἰρηκότος ὅτι Πρὶν ἀλέκτορα φωνῆσαι τρὶς ἀπαρνήσῃ με· καὶ ἐξελθὼν ἔξω ἔκλαυσεν πικρῶς.

26:73
μικρός, ά, όν small, short, little; little one (substantive); μικρόν short time; short distance
ἀληθῶς truly, certainly, of a truth
λαλιά, ᾶς, ἡ speech
δῆλος, η, ον clear, plain, evident
26:74
καταθεματίζω καταθεματίσω curse
ὀμνύω/ὄμνυμι, ὀμοῦμαι, ὤμοσα, ὀμώμοκα swear, promise with an oath
ἀλέκτωρ, ορος, ὁ cock, rooster
φωνέω, φωνήσω, ἐφώνησα, ἐφωνήθην sound, crow, call, summon
26:75
μιμνήσκομαι, μνησθήσομαι, μέμνημαι, ἐμνήσθην remember, recollect, call to mind
ῥῆμα, ατος, τό word, saying, expression, speech
πρίν before (adverb)
ἀπαρνέομαι, ἀπαρνήσομαι, ἀπηρνησάμην, ἀπήρνημαι deny; renounce, disregard
ἔξω outside, out (adverb); out of (preposition)
κλαίω, κλαύσω/κλαύσομαι, ἔκλαυσα weep, shed tears
πικρῶς bitterly (adverb)

26:73 **προσελθόντες . . . εἶπον τῷ Πέτρῳ**: *came to Peter and said*; both verbs govern the dative case. **σὺ ἐξ αὐτῶν**: supply εἶς. **δῆλόν σε ποιεῖ**: *reveals you.*

26:74 **ἤρξατο** means *to begin* in the middle and takes a complementary infinitive. **ὅτι** is used as our quotation marks to introduce direct disourse.

26:75 **ἐμνήσθη . . . τοῦ ῥήματος**: verbs of remembering govern the genitive case. **Ἰησοῦ εἰρηκότος**: *of Jesus when He said.* **Πρὶν ἀλέκτορα φωῆσαι**: *before the cock crows*; πρὶν is followed by an infinitive with a subject accusative. **καὶ ἐξελθὼν ἔξω**: *and as he went out*; the prefixed preposition is commonly repeated either by the same or by a similar preposition or adverb.

27 Πρωΐας δὲ γενομένης συμβούλιον ἔλαβον πάντες οἱ ἀρχιερεῖς
καὶ οἱ πρεσβύτεροι τοῦ λαοῦ κατὰ τοῦ Ἰησοῦ ὥστε θανατῶσαι αὐτόν·
27:2 καὶ δήσαντες αὐτὸν ἀπήγαγον καὶ παρέδωκαν Πιλάτῳ τῷ
ἡγεμόνι.

27:3 Τότε ἰδὼν Ἰούδας ὁ παραδιδοὺς αὐτὸν ὅτι κατεκρίθη,
μεταμεληθεὶς ἔστρεψεν τὰ τριάκοντα ἀργύρια τοῖς ἀρχιερεῦσιν καὶ
πρεσβυτέροις 27:4 λέγων,

27:1

πρωΐα, ας, ἡ morning, morning hour

συμβούλιον, ίου, τό counsel, plan, consultation; συμβούλιον λαμβάνειν form a plan, consult, plot

πρεσβύτερος, α, ον older, ancestor, elder (designation of an official); ancients, fathers (plural)

θανατόω, θανατώσω, ἐθανάτωσα kill, put to death, deliver to death

27:2

δέω, δήσω, ἔδησα, δέδεκα, δέδεμαι, ἐδέθην bind, tie, impede

ἀπάγω, ἀπάξω, ἀπήγαγον, ἀπήχθην lead away; lead away (of a road; intransitive)

Πιλᾶτος, ου, ὁ Pilate

ἡγεμών, όνος, ὁ guide, leader, prince, governor; prefect, procurator

27:3

κατακρίνω, κατακρινῶ, κατέκρινα, κατακέκρικα, κατακέκριμαι, κατεκρίθην condemn, pronounce sentence

μεταμέλομαι, μεταμελήσομαι, μετεμελήθην change one's mind, feel regret, repent

στρέφω, στρέψω, ἔστρεψα, ἔστραμμαι, ἐστρέφθην, ἐστράφην (2 aorist passive) turn, make a turn, change; bring back, return; turn around, change inwardly, be converted (passive)

τριάκοντα thirty (indeclinable)

ἀργύριον, ίου, τό silver, silver shekel, silver drachma, silver money

πρεσβύτερος, α, ον older, ancestor, elder (designation of an official); ancients, fathers (plural)

27:1 **ὥστε**, followed by the accusative with infinitive, introduces also intended result which is scarcely distinguishable from a purpose clause. The missing accusative subject is readily supplied from the context.

27:2 **τῷ ἡγεμόνι**: Pilate was procurator of Judea from 26 to 36 AD and as such had authority to execute criminals.

27:3 **μεταμεληθεὶς ἔστρεψεν**: *repented and returned.*

Ἥμαρτον παραδοὺς αἷμα ἀθῷον. οἱ δὲ εἶπαν, Τί πρὸς ἡμᾶς; σὺ ὄψῃ.
27:5 καὶ ῥίψας τὰ ἀργύρια εἰς τὸν ναὸν ἀνεχώρησεν, καὶ ἀπελθὼν
ἀπήγξατο. 27:6 οἱ δὲ ἀρχιερεῖς λαβόντες τὰ ἀργύρια εἶπαν, Οὐκ
ἔξεστιν βαλεῖν αὐτὰ εἰς τὸν κορβανᾶν, ἐπεὶ τιμὴ αἵματός ἐστιν.
27:7 συμβούλιον δὲ λαβόντες ἠγόρασαν ἐξ αὐτῶν τὸν ἀγρὸν τοῦ
κεραμέως εἰς ταφὴν τοῖς ξένοις.

27:4
ἁμαρτάνω, ἁμαρτήσω, ἡμάρτησα or ἥμαρτον, ἡμάρτηκα, ἡμάρτημαι, ἡμαρτήθην do wrong, sin
αἷμα, ατος, τό blood
ἀθῷος, ον innocent
27:5
ῥίπτω/ῥιπτέω, ῥίψω, ἔρριψα, ἔρριμαι hurl, throw; lay down, set on the ground; be dispersed, be scattered (passive)
ἀργύριον, ίου, τό silver, silver shekel, silver drachma, silver money
ναός, οῦ, ὁ dwelling, temple
ἀναχωρέω, ἀναχωρήσω, ἀνεχώρησα go away, depart, withdraw, retire
ἀπάγχομαι, ἀπάγξομαι, ἀπηγξάμην hang oneself
27:6
ἀργύριον, ίου, τό silver, silver shekel, silver drachma, silver money
ἔξεστι(ν) it is permitted, it is possible (impersonal verb)
κορβανᾶς, ᾶ, ὁ temple treasury
ἐπεί when, after; since, because, for (conjunction)
τιμή, ῆς, ἡ price, value
αἷμα, ατος, τό blood
27:7
συμβούλιον, ίου, τό counsel, plan, consultation; συμβούλιον λαμβάνειν form a plan, consult, plot
ἀγοράζω, ἀγοράσω, ἠγόρασα, ἠγόρασμαι, ἠγοράσθην buy, purchase, acquire
ἀγρός, οῦ, ὁ field, cultivated field; lands, farms, villages (plural)
κεραμεύς, έως, ὁ potter
ταφή, ῆς, ἡ burial place
ξένος, ου, ὁ strange, foreign; stranger, foreigner (substantive)

27:4 **Ἥμαρτον παραδοὺς**: *I sinned by betraying*; the context of the circumstantial participle suggests the interpretation of means. **Τί πρὸς ἡμᾶς**: *what is that to us*; supply ἐστιν ἐκεῖνο in this expression of indifference. **σὺ ὄψῃ**: *see to that yourself*; the verb is second person singular deponent future indicative of the verb ὁράω. The future indicative may be used to express a command, like the imperative. The pronoun σὺ with the second person verb is used emphatically. They are saying that the matter is his responsibility.

27:6 **Οὐκ ἔξεστιν βαλεῖν**: the impersonal construction is followed by an accusative infinitive construction. The missing accusative subject ἡμᾶς is readily supplied from the context. **τιμὴ ἅιματός**: *blood money*; τιμὴ is predicate nominative referring to αὐτὰ. The genitive of value indicates what something is worth. The genitive also stands in apposition to its noun: the price is blood.

27:7 **εἰς ταφὴν**: *as a burial place*; the preposition introduces the notion of purpose.

27:8 διὸ ἐκλήθη ὁ ἀγρὸς ἐκεῖνος Ἀγρὸς Αἵματος ἕως τῆς σήμερον.
27:9 τότε ἐπληρώθη τὸ ῥηθὲν διὰ Ἰερεμίου τοῦ προφήτου λέγοντος, Καὶ ἔλαβον τὰ τριάκοντα ἀργύρια, τὴν τιμὴν τοῦ τετιμημένου ὃν ἐτιμήσαντο ἀπὸ υἱῶν Ἰσραήλ,
27:10 καὶ ἔδωκαν αὐτὰ εἰς τὸν ἀγρὸν τοῦ κεραμέως, καθὰ συνέταξέν μοι κύριος.

27:8
διό therefore, for this reason (conjunction)
ἀγρός, οῦ, ὁ field, cultivated field; lands, farms, villages (plural)
αἷμα, ατος, τό blood
σήμερον today, this day (adverb)
27:9
ἀργύριον, ίου, τό silver, silver shekel, silver drachma, silver money
τιμή, ῆς, ἡ price, value
τιμάω, τιμήσω, ἐτίμησα value, honor, revere
Ἰσραήλ, ὁ Israel (indeclinable)
27:10
ἀγρός, οῦ, ὁ field, cultivated field; lands, farms, villages (plural)
κεραμεύς, έως, ὁ potter
καθά as, just as (adverb)
συντάσσω, συντάξω, συνέταξα arrange; order, charge, direct

27:9 **τὸ ῥηθὲν**: *that which was spoken* (literally); the verbal form is a neuter singular nominative first aorist passive participle (cf. App. 53, G, 5; 34) of the verb λέγω. Although Jeremiah speaks of the simile of the potter (18:6) and the purchase of a field (Jer 32:6–9), perhaps a more precise reference is found in Zechariah, where he speaks messianically about the thirty silver pieces and the potter (11:12–13). This passage may represent a conflation of stories and Jeremiah may be the first to come to mind. **τὴν τιμὴν τοῦ τετιμημένου**: *the price of Him who was valued*; τιμὴν stands in apposition to ἀργύρια. **ὃν ἐτιμήσαντο ἀπὸ υἱῶν Ἰσραήλ**: *upon whom they of the sons of Israel set a price*; ἐτιμήσαντο has a middle sense: they did this in their own interest. The subject of the verb is ἀρχιερεῖς καὶ οἱ πρεσβύτεροι τοῦ λαοῦ (1) who were plotting to kill Him and who set the price. ἀπὸ υἱῶν is used as a partitive genitive.

27:10 **εἰς τὸν ἀγρὸν**: *for the field*; the preposition introduces the notion of purpose: to purchase the field. **καθὰ συνέταξέν μοι κύριος**: the formulaic phrase emphasizes the prophet's source and authority.

27:11 Ὁ δὲ Ἰησοῦς ἐστάθη ἔμπροσθεν τοῦ ἡγεμόνος· καὶ ἐπηρώτησεν αὐτὸν ὁ ἡγεμὼν λέγων, Σὺ εἶ ὁ βασιλεὺς τῶν Ἰουδαίων; ὁ δὲ Ἰησοῦς ἔφη, Σὺ λέγεις. 27:12 καὶ ἐν τῷ κατηγορεῖσθαι αὐτὸν ὑπὸ τῶν ἀρχιερέων καὶ πρεσβυτέρων οὐδὲν ἀπεκρίνατο. 27:13 τότε λέγει αὐτῷ ὁ Πιλᾶτος, Οὐκ ἀκούεις πόσα σου καταμαρτυροῦσιν; 27:14 καὶ οὐκ ἀπεκρίθη αὐτῷ πρὸς οὐδὲ ἓν ῥῆμα, ὥστε θαυμάζειν τὸν ἡγεμόνα λίαν.

27:11
ἡγεμών, όνος, ὁ guide, leader, prince, governor; prefect, procurator
ἐπερωτάω, ἐπερωτήσω, ἐπηρώτησα ask, ask a question, interrogate, question; inquire after
27:12
κατηγορέω, κατηγορήσω, κατηγόρησα accuse, speak against
πρεσβύτερος, α, ον older, ancestor, elder (designation of an official); ancients, fathers (plural)
οὐδείς, οὐδεμία, οὐδέν no (adjective); no one, nobody, nothing (substantive)
27:13
πόσος, η, ον how great? how much? how many? (plural)
καταμαρτυρέω, καταμαρτυρήσω bear witness against, witness against
27:14
ῥῆμα, ατος, τό word, saying, expression, speech
θαυμάζω, θαυμάσομαι, ἐθαύμασα, ἐθαυμάσθην wonder, marvel, be astonished
ἡγεμών, όνος, ὁ guide, leader, prince, governor; prefect, procurator
λίαν greatly, exceedingly (adverb)

27:11 **ἐστάθη**: *stood*; the aorist passive of ἵστημι is intransitive. **Σὺ λέγεις**: the bold agreement does not seem to concern Pilate.

27:12 **καὶ ἐν τῷ κατηγορεῖσθαι αὐτὸν**: *and when He was accused*; ἐν introduces the point of time when something occurs and an articular infinitive with a subject accusative. **οὐδὲν ἀπεκρίνατο**: *He gave no response*; οὐδὲν is a cognate accusative.

27:13 **πόσα σου καταμαρτυροῦσιν**: *how many testimonies they are bringing against you*; πόσα is a cognate accusative.

27:14 **οὐκ ἀπεκρίθη αὐτῷ**: *He gave no response to him*; the verb is used in an absolute sense. **πρὸς οὐδὲ ἓν ῥῆμα**: *not even to a single charge*; ῥῆμα often takes its significance from the context. **ὥστε**, followed by the subject accusative with infinitive, introduces a result clause.

27:15 Κατὰ δὲ ἑορτὴν εἰώθει ὁ ἡγεμὼν ἀπολύειν ἕνα τῷ ὄχλῳ δέσμιον ὃν ἤθελον. 27:16 εἶχον δὲ τότε δέσμιον ἐπίσημον λεγόμενον [Ἰησοῦν] Βαραββᾶν. 27:17 συνηγμένων οὖν αὐτῶν εἶπεν αὐτοῖς ὁ Πιλᾶτος, Τίνα θέλετε ἀπολύσω ὑμῖν, [Ἰησοῦν τὸν] Βαραββᾶν ἢ Ἰησοῦν τὸν λεγόμενον Χριστόν; 27:18 ᾔδει γὰρ ὅτι διὰ φθόνον παρέδωκαν αὐτόν. 27:19 Καθημένου δὲ αὐτοῦ ἐπὶ τοῦ βήματος ἀπέστειλεν πρὸς αὐτὸν ἡ γυνὴ αὐτοῦ λέγουσα, Μηδὲν σοὶ καὶ τῷ δικαίῳ ἐκείνῳ·

27:15
ἑορτή, ῆς, ἡ feast, festival
εἴωθα be accustomed
ἡγεμών, όνος, ὁ guide, leader, prince, governor; prefect, procurator
δέσμιος, ου, ὁ prisoner
27:16
ἐπίσημος, ον noted, prominent; notorious
Βαραββᾶς, ᾶ, ὁ Barabbas
27:18
φθόνος, ου, ὁ envy, jealousy, spite
27:19
βῆμα, ατος, τό step; tribunal, judicial bench
μηδείς, μηδεμία, μηδέν not one, none, no one, nothing

27:15 **εἰώθει**: *was accustomed*; the form of the verb is a third person singular pluperfect active indicative of εἴωθα, the perfect of an obsolete present ἔθω. Since the perfect is used as a present, the pluperfect (cf. App. 53, F) is taken as an imperfect.

27:16 **εἶχον**: *they were holding*; the verb form is a third person plural imperfect active indicative of ἔχω.

27:17 **Τίνα θέλετε ἀπολύσω ὑμῖν**: *whom do you want me to release for you*; the verb θέλετε with a subjunctive (without a conjunction) introduces a deliberative question.

27:18 **ᾔδει**: *he knew*; the verb form is a third person singular pluperfect active indicative. Since the perfect οἶδα is used as a present, the pluperfect is taken as an imperfect (App. 62).

27:19 **Καθημένου δὲ αὐτοῦ**: *while he was sitting*; the subject of the genitive absolute is Pilate. **Μηδὲν σοὶ καὶ τῷ δικαίῳ ἐκείνῳ**: *there is naught between you and that innocent man*; the idiomatic expression is pregnant with meaning and suggests that there is no reason to fear, no hostility, and no cause to condemn.

πολλὰ γὰρ ἔπαθον σήμερον κατ' ὄναρ δι' αὐτόν. 27:20 Οἱ δὲ ἀρχιερεῖς καὶ οἱ πρεσβύτεροι ἔπεισαν τοὺς ὄχλους ἵνα αἰτήσωνται τὸν Βαραββᾶν, τὸν δὲ Ἰησοῦν ἀπολέσωσιν. 27:21 ἀποκριθεὶς δὲ ὁ ἡγεμὼν εἶπεν αὐτοῖς, Τίνα θέλετε ἀπὸ τῶν δύο ἀπολύσω ὑμῖν; οἱ δὲ εἶπαν, Τὸν Βαραββᾶν. 27:22 λέγει αὐτοῖς ὁ Πιλᾶτος, Τί οὖν ποιήσω Ἰησοῦν τὸν λεγόμενον Χριστόν; λέγουσιν πάντες, Σταυρωθήτω.

27:19

πάσχω, πείσομαι, ἔπαθον, πέπονθα suffer, endure, undergo

σήμερον today, this day (adverb)

ὄναρ, τό dream (indeclinable)

27:20

πρεσβύτερος, α, ον older, ancestor, elder (designation of an official); ancients, fathers (plural)

πείθω, πείσω, ἔπεισα, πέπεικα, πέπεισμαι, ἐπείσθην persuade, influence by persuasion; pacify, conciliate, win over

27:21

ἡγεμών, όνος, ὁ guide, leader, prince, governor; prefect, procurator

27:22

σταυρόω, σταυρώσω, ἐσταύρωσα, ἐσταύρωμαι, ἐσταυρώθην crucify

27:19 **πολλὰ γὰρ ἔπαθον σήμερον κατ' ὄναρ δι' αὐτόν**: *for I received many warnings in a dream last night because of Him.* πολλὰ is a cognate accusative. ἔπαθον: although the verb frequently expresses the passive idea of suffering, it does not always carry the passive meaning with a negative connotation. The context of a dream from God may suggest a more neutral or even positive sense: *to experience.* In her dream the wife of Pilate was deeply impressed with a warning about the innocence of Jesus. The theme of experiencing warnings, omens, and signs in a dream is commonplace in Greek and Latin literature and her warning would readily be acknowledged by the pagan Pilate. σήμερον: since the Jewish day began at sundown, the whole night is part of the one twenty-four-hour period.

27:20 **ἀπωλέσωσιν** is the third person plural aorist active subjunctive of ἀπόλλυμι.

27:22 **Τί οὖν ποιήσω Ἰησοῦν**: *then what shall I do with Jesus*; the verb takes a double accusative. **Σταυρωθήτω**: *let Him be crucified*; the verb form is a third person singular first aorist passive imperative (cf. App. 53, G, 3).

27:23 ὁ δὲ ἔφη, Τί γὰρ κακὸν ἐποίησεν; οἱ δὲ περισσῶς ἔκραζον λέγοντες, Σταυρωθήτω. 27:24 ἰδὼν δὲ ὁ Πιλᾶτος ὅτι οὐδὲν ὠφελεῖ ἀλλὰ μᾶλλον θόρυβος γίνεται, λαβὼν ὕδωρ ἀπενίψατο τὰς χεῖρας ἀπέναντι τοῦ ὄχλου λέγων, Ἀθῷός εἰμι ἀπὸ τοῦ αἵματος τούτου· ὑμεῖς ὄψεσθε. 27:25 καὶ ἀποκριθεὶς πᾶς ὁ λαὸς εἶπεν, Τὸ αἷμα αὐτοῦ ἐφ' ἡμᾶς καὶ ἐπὶ τὰ τέκνα ἡμῶν.

27:23

κακός, ή, όν bad, evil, wrong; τὸ κακόν evil, wickedness, crime

περισσός, ή, όν over and above, extraordinary, excessive; περισσῶς in full abundance, exceedingly, vehemently (adverb); περισσότερος, α, ον more, greater (comparative)

κράζω, κράξω, ἔκραξα, κέκραγα cry out, cry aloud

σταυρόω, σταυρώσω, ἐσταύρωσα, ἐσταύρωμαι, ἐσταυρώθην crucify

27:24

ὠφελέω, ὠφελήσω, ὠφέλησα, ὠφελήθην help, aid, benefit, be of use to, be of value

μᾶλλον more, to a greater degree, rather (adverb)

θόρυβος, ου, ὁ noise; turmoil, uproar

ὕδωρ, ὕδατος, τό water

ἀπονίπτω, ἀπονίψω, ἀπένιψα wash (active); wash off (for) oneself (middle)

ἀπέναντι before; opposite (adverb; preposition + genitive)

ἀθῷος, ον innocent

αἷμα, ατος, τό blood

27:23 **Τί . . . κακὸν**: Τί is an interrogative adjective. **περισσῶς**: the positive degree of the adverb is used instead of the comparative by analogy to the Semitic pattern which lacks the comparative degree.

27:24 **ὅτι οὐδὲν ὠφελεῖ**: *that he was accomplishing nothing.* **λαβὼν ὕδωρ ἀπενίψατο τὰς χεῖρας**: the act symbolizes ritual expiation of murder. **ὑμεῖς ὄψεσθε**: *see to that yourselves*; the verb is second person plural deponent future indicative of the verb ὁράω. The future indicative may be used to express a command, like the imperative. The pronoun ὑμεῖς with the second person verb is used emphatically. He is saying that the outcome is their responsibility.

27:25 **Τὸ αἷμα αὐτοῦ ἐφ' ἡμᾶς**: they willingly acknowledge their responsibility in committing ἁμαρτία.

27:26 τότε ἀπέλυσεν αὐτοῖς τὸν Βαραββᾶν, τὸν δὲ Ἰησοῦν
φραγελλώσας παρέδωκεν ἵνα σταυρωθῇ.
27:27 Τότε οἱ στρατιῶται τοῦ ἡγεμόνος παραλαβόντες τὸν
Ἰησοῦν εἰς τὸ πραιτώριον συνήγαγον ἐπ' αὐτὸν ὅλην τὴν σπεῖραν.
27:28 καὶ ἐκδύσαντες αὐτὸν χλαμύδα κοκκίνην περιέθηκαν αὐτῷ,
27:29 καὶ πλέξαντες στέφανον ἐξ ἀκανθῶν ἐπέθηκαν ἐπὶ τῆς
κεφαλῆς αὐτοῦ καὶ κάλαμον ἐν τῇ δεξιᾷ αὐτοῦ,

27:26
φραγελλόω, φραγελλώσω flog, scourge
σταυρόω, σταυρώσω, ἐσταύρωσα, ἐσταύρωμαι, ἐσταυρώθην crucify
27:27
στρατιώτης, ου, ὁ soldier
ἡγεμών, όνος, ὁ guide, leader, prince, governor; prefect, procurator
πραιτώριον, ου, τό general's tent, governor's official residence
σπεῖρα, ας, ἡ band, company, troop; maniple, cohort
27:28
ἐκδύω, ἐκδύσω strip, take off
χλαμύς, χλαμύδος, ἡ (a Roman military commander's) cloak
κόκκινος, η, ον red, crimson, scarlet
περιτίθημι, περιθήσω, περιέθην (2 aorist), περιέθηκα place around, put about, attach
27:29
πλέκω, πλέξω, ἔπλεξα weave, braid, plait
στέφανος, ου, ὁ garland, wreath, crown
ἄκανθα, ης, ἡ thorn
ἐπιτίθημι, ἐπιθήσω, ἐπέθηκα, ἐπιτέθεικα, ἐπιτέθειμαι, ἐπετέθην lay upon, put on
κεφαλή, ῆς, ἡ head
κάλαμος, ου, ὁ reed, cane; staff
δεξιός, ά, όν right (as opposed to left); ἡ δεξιά (χείρ) right hand

---

27:26 **φραγελλώσας**: verbs ending in -όω in particular and other active verbs in general are causative, denoting *to cause* or *to make,* and indicate an action performed at the bidding of the subject. So here: Pilate had Him flogged. The Romans often flogged slaves and non-Romans after a death penalty had been imposed and before crucifixion. The action and the benefit are prophesied by Isaiah (53:5).

27:27 **ὅλην**: the adjective never stands in attributive position. **σπεῖραν**: the reference is technically to a Roman *cohors,* a military unit of about 600 Roman soldiers, but the number varied. It was led by a military tribune.

27:28–29 **χλαμύδα κοκκίνην . . . στέφανον ἐξ ἀκανθῶν . . . κάλαμον . . . γονυπετήσαντες . . . ἐνέπαιξαν**: they decked Him out with symbols of mock royal trappings and mocked Him as king.

καὶ γονυπετήσαντες ἔμπροσθεν αὐτοῦ ἐνέπαιξαν αὐτῷ λέγοντες, Χαῖρε, βασιλεῦ τῶν Ἰουδαίων, 27:30 καὶ ἐμπτύσαντες εἰς αὐτὸν ἔλαβον τὸν κάλαμον καὶ ἔτυπτον εἰς τὴν κεφαλὴν αὐτοῦ. 27:31 καὶ ὅτε ἐνέπαιξαν αὐτῷ, ἐξέδυσαν αὐτὸν τὴν χλαμύδα καὶ ἐνέδυσαν αὐτὸν τὰ ἱμάτια αὐτοῦ καὶ ἀπήγαγον αὐτὸν εἰς τὸ σταυρῶσαι.

27:32 Ἐξερχόμενοι δὲ εὗρον ἄνθρωπον Κυρηναῖον ὀνόματι Σίμωνα, τοῦτον ἠγγάρευσαν ἵνα ἄρῃ τὸν σταυρὸν αὐτοῦ.

27:29
γονυπετέω, γονυπετήσω, ἐγονυπέτησα fall on one's knees before, kneel before
ἐμπαίζω, ἐμπαίξω, ἐνέπαιξα, ἐνεπαίχθην ridicule, make fun of, mock, treat with scorn; deceive, trick
χαίρω, χαρήσομαι, ἐχάρην (2 aorist passive) rejoice, be glad; χαῖρε, χαίρετε hail, greetings, welcome (as a form of greeting)
27:30
ἐμπτύω, ἐμπτύσω, ἐνέπτυσα spit upon
κάλαμος, ου, ὁ reed, cane; staff
τύπτω, τύψω, ἔτυψα beat, strike, smite
κεφαλή, ῆς, ἡ head
27:31
ἐμπαίζω, ἐμπαίξω, ἐνέπαιξα, ἐνεπαίχθην ridicule, make fun of, mock, treat with scorn; deceive, trick
ἐκδύω, ἐκδύσω strip, take off
χλαμύς, χλαμύδος, ἡ (a Roman military commander's) cloak
ἐνδύω, ἐνδύσω, ἐνέδυσα put on, dress, clothe; clothe oneself in, put on (middle)
ἱμάτιον, ου, τό garment, clothing; cloak, robe; clothes, garments (plural)
ἀπάγω, ἀπάξω, ἀπήγαγον, ἀπήχθην lead away; lead away (of a road; intransitive)
σταυρόω, σταυρώσω, ἐσταύρωσα, ἐσταύρωμαι, ἐσταυρώθην crucify
27:32
Κυρηναῖος, ου, ὁ Cyrenian
ἀγγαρεύω, ἀγγαρεύσω, ἠγγάρευσα force, compel
σταυρός, οῦ, ὁ cross

27:30 **ἔτυπτον**: *kept smiting Him*; supply αὐτὸν. The imperfect tense denotes progressive, continued, and repeated action (aspect) in past time.

27:31 **ἐξέδυσαν . . . ἐνέδυσαν**: the verbs take a double accusative. **εἰς τὸ σταυρῶσαι**: *to crucify Him*; supply αὐτόν from the context. The preposition introduces an articular infinitive of purpose.

27:32 **ὀνόματι Σίμωνα**: *Simon by name* (literally: *in respect to his name*); ὀνόματι is a dative of respect.

27:33 Καὶ ἐλθόντες εἰς τόπον λεγόμενον Γολγοθᾶ, ὅ ἐστιν Κρανίου Τόπος λεγόμενος, 27:34 ἔδωκαν αὐτῷ πιεῖν οἶνον μετὰ χολῆς μεμιγμένον· καὶ γευσάμενος οὐκ ἠθέλησεν πιεῖν. 27:35 σταυρώσαντες δὲ αὐτὸν διεμερίσαντο τὰ ἱμάτια αὐτοῦ βάλλοντες κλῆρον, 27:36 καὶ καθήμενοι ἐτήρουν αὐτὸν ἐκεῖ. 27:37 καὶ ἐπέθηκαν ἐπάνω τῆς κεφαλῆς αὐτοῦ τὴν αἰτίαν αὐτοῦ γεγραμμένην· Οὗτός ἐστιν Ἰησοῦς ὁ βασιλεὺς τῶν Ἰουδαίων.

27:33

τόπος, ου, ὁ place, position, region

Γολγοθᾶ, ἡ Golgotha (= place of a skull) (indeclinable)

κρανίον, ου, τό skull

27:34

πίνω, πίομαι, ἔπιον, πέπωκα drink

οἶνος, ου, ὁ wine

χολή, ῆς, ἡ bile, gall

μίγνυμι/μίγνυω, μίξω, ἔμιξα, μέμιγμαι mix, mingle

γεύομαι, γεύσομαι, ἐγευσάμην taste, partake of, enjoy; eat; come to know, experience

27:35

σταυρόω, σταυρώσω, ἐσταύρωσα, ἐσταύρωμαι, ἐσταυρώθην crucify

διαμερίζω, διαμερίσω, διεμέρισα divide and distribute, divide

κλῆρος, ου, ὁ lot (= pebble, potsherd, etc.)

27:36

τηρέω, τηρήσω, ἐτήρησα, τητήρηκα, τητήρημαι, ἐτηρήθην guard, heed, preserve, reserve

27:37

ἐπιτίθημι, ἐπιθήσω, ἐπέθηκα, ἐπιτέθεικα, ἐπιτέθειμαι, ἐπετέθην lay upon, put on

ἐπάνω over, above, on (adverb; preposition + genitive)

αἰτία, ας, ἡ cause, motive; ground for complaint, fault; case, relationship; accusation, crime

---

27:33 **ὅ ἐστιν Κρανίου Τόπος λεγόμενος**: *which means Place of a Skull*; the phrase is frequently used to explain foreign terms and names and may be translated more idiomatically. Supply ὄνομα as the antecedent of the neuter relative pronoun. λεγόμενος agrees in gender with the nearest noun instead of the relative and may be omitted as a pleonastic addition.

27:34 **χολῆς** is a bitter ingredient, perhaps even a poison, intended either to mock or to end His life before the cross. **οὐκ ἠθέλησεν πιεῖν**: *he refused to drink*.

27:37 **τὴν αἰτίαν αὐτοῦ γεγραμμένην**: *the charge against Him in writing*.

27:38 Τότε σταυροῦνται σὺν αὐτῷ δύο λῃσταί, εἷς ἐκ δεξιῶν καὶ εἷς ἐξ εὐωνύμων. 27:39 Οἱ δὲ παραπορευόμενοι ἐβλασφήμουν αὐτὸν κινοῦντες τὰς κεφαλὰς αὐτῶν 27:40 καὶ λέγοντες, Ὁ καταλύων τὸν ναὸν καὶ ἐν τρισὶν ἡμέραις οἰκοδομῶν, σῶσον σεαυτόν, εἰ υἱὸς εἶ τοῦ θεοῦ, [καὶ] κατάβηθι ἀπὸ τοῦ σταυροῦ. 27:41 ὁμοίως καὶ οἱ ἀρχιερεῖς ἐμπαίζοντες μετὰ τῶν γραμματέων καὶ πρεσβυτέρων ἔλεγον,

---

27:38
σταυρόω, σταυρώσω, ἐσταύρωσα, ἐσταύρωμαι, ἐσταυρώθην crucify
σύν with, together with (+ dative)
λῃστής, οῦ, ὁ robber, bandit
εὐώνυμος, ον left (as opposed to *right*); ἐκ εὐωνύμων τινός at someone's left
27:39
παραπορεύομαι, παραπορεύσομαι pass by, pass along, go
βλασφημέω, βλασφημήσω, ἐβλασφήμησα, βεβλασφήμηκα, ἐβλασφημήθην blaspheme, speak irreverently of
κινέω, κινήσω, ἐκίνησα to move; to excite; to shake
27:40
καταλύω, καταλύσω, κατέλυσα, κατελύθην throw down, destroy, abolish
ναός, οῦ, ὁ dwelling, temple
τρεῖς, τρία three
οἰκοδομέω, οἰκοδομήσω, ᾠκοδόμησα, ᾠκοδομήθην build, construct, establish
σῴζω, σώσω, ἔσωσα, σέσωκα, σέσωσμαι, ἐσώθην save, rescue, preserve safe and unharmed
σεαυτοῦ, ῆς, οῦ yourself (reflexive pronoun)
καταβαίνω, καταβήσομαι, κατέβην, καταβέβηκα come down, go down, descend, fall
27:41
ὁμοίως likewise, also, similarly (adverb)
ἐμπαίζω, ἐμπαίξω, ἐνέπαιξα, ἐνεπαίχθην ridicule, make fun of, mock, treat with scorn; deceive, trick
γραμματεύς, έως, ὁ secretary, clerk, scholar versed in law, scribe
πρεσβύτερος, α, ον older, ancestor, elder (designation of an official); ancients, fathers (plural)

27:38 **σταυροῦνται . . . δύο λῃσταί**: *two robbers were crucified*; the verb form is a third person plural present passive indicative. The present used for a past tense is called *historical present* and is frequently seen in vivid narrative accounts.

27:39 **ἐβλασφήμουν αὐτὸν κινοῦντες**: *kept insulting Him as they shook*; the imperfect tense denotes progressive, continued, and repeated action (aspect) in past time.

27:40 **Ὁ καταλύων . . . σῶσον σεαυτόν**: *you who are going to destroy . . . save yourself*; the article stands for a relative pronoun. The participle connotes a future.

27:42 Ἄλλους ἔσωσεν, ἑαυτὸν οὐ δύναται σῶσαι· βασιλεὺς Ἰσραήλ ἐστιν, καταβάτω νῦν ἀπὸ τοῦ σταυροῦ καὶ πιστεύσομεν ἐπ᾽ αὐτόν. 27:43 πέποιθεν ἐπὶ τὸν θεόν, ῥυσάσθω νῦν εἰ θέλει αὐτόν· εἶπεν γὰρ ὅτι Θεοῦ εἰμι υἱός. 27:44 τὸ δ᾽ αὐτὸ καὶ οἱ λησταὶ οἱ συσταυρωθέντες σὺν αὐτῷ ὠνείδιζον αὐτόν.

27:45 Ἀπὸ δὲ ἕκτης ὥρας σκότος ἐγένετο ἐπὶ πᾶσαν τὴν γῆν ἕως ὥρας ἐνάτης.

27:42

καταβαίνω, καταβήσομαι, κατέβην, καταβέβηκα come down, go down, descend, fall

νῦν now, at the present time, just now, of late (adverb); τὸ νῦν the present time, now (noun)

σταυρός, οῦ, ὁ cross

πιστεύω, πιστεύσω, ἐπίστευσα, πεπίστευκα, πεπίστευμαι, ἐπιστεύθην believe; entrust

27:43

πείθω, πείσω, ἔπεισα, πέπεικα, πέποιθα (2 perfect), πέπεισμαι, ἐπείσθην persuade, influence by persuasion; pacify, conciliate, win over

ῥύομαι, ῥύσομαι, ἐρ(ρ)υσάμην, ἐρ(ρ)ύσθην save, deliver, rescue, preserve

νῦν now, at the present time, just now, of late (adverb); τὸ νῦν the present time, now (noun)

27:44

λῃστής, οῦ, ὁ robber, bandit

συσταυρόω, συσταυρώσω, συνεσταύρωσα, συνεσταύρωμαι, συνεσταυρώθην crucify with

ὀνειδίζω, ὀνειδίσω, ὠνείδισα reproach, revile, heap insults upon

27:45

ἕκτος, η, ον sixth

σκότος, ους, τό darkness, gloom

ἔνατος, άτη, ατον ninth

27:43 **πέποιθεν ἐπὶ**: *He trusts*; the second perfect has present meaning and a change in meaning: *depend on, trust in, put one's confidence in*. **ῥυσάσθω νῦν . . . αὐτόν**: *let God save Him now*; the verb is a third person singular aorist middle imperative (cf. App. 53, D, 3) of a deponent verb. It requires a change of subject.

27:44 **τὸ . . . αὐτὸ**: *in the same way*; the construction is adverbial.

27:45 **Ἀπὸ δὲ ἕκτης ὥρας**: the time would approximately be noon. Daytime hours begin at 6 a.m. and end at 6 p.m.

27:46 περὶ δὲ τὴν ἐνάτην ὥραν ἀνεβόησεν ὁ Ἰησοῦς φωνῇ μεγάλῃ λέγων, Ηλι ηλι λεμα σαβαχθανι; τοῦτ' ἔστιν, Θεέ μου θεέ μου, ἱνατί με ἐγκατέλιπες; 27:47 τινὲς δὲ τῶν ἐκεῖ ἑστηκότων ἀκούσαντες ἔλεγον ὅτι Ἠλίαν φωνεῖ οὗτος. 27:48 καὶ εὐθέως δραμὼν εἷς ἐξ αὐτῶν καὶ λαβὼν σπόγγον πλήσας τε ὄξους καὶ περιθεὶς καλάμῳ ἐπότιζεν αὐτόν.

27:46
ἀναβοάω, ἀναβήσομαι, ἀνέβησα cry out, exclaim
φωνή, ῆς, ἡ voice, sound
ἠλι my God! (Aramaic)
λεμα why? (Aramaic)
σαβαχθανι hast thou forsaken me? (Aramaic)
θεός, οῦ, ὁ God, god
ἱνατι why? why is it that? for what reason? (adverb)
ἐγκαταλείπω, ἐγκαταλείψω, ἐγκατέλιπον (2 aorist) leave, leave behind; forsake, abandon
27:47
φωνέω, φωνήσω, ἐφώνησα, ἐφωνήθην sound, crow, call, summon
27:48
τρέχω, θρέξομαι/δραμοῦμαι, ἔδραμον (2 aorist) run
σπόγγος, ου, ὁ sponge
πίμπλημι, πλήσω, ἔπλησα, ἐπλήσθην fill
ὄξος, ους, τό vinegar, sour wine, common wine
περιτίθημι, περιθήσω, περιέθην (2 aorist), περιέθηκα place around, put about, attach
κάλαμος, ου, ὁ reed, cane; staff
ποτίζω, ποτίσω, ἐπότισα, πεπότικα cause someone to drink, give someone something to drink

---

27:46 **φωνῇ μεγάλῃ** is an ablative of means. **Θεέ** is a vocative. **ἐγκατέλιπες**: the aorist aspect expresses a single act (aspect) in past time that quickly moves on.

27:47 **τινὲς δὲ τῶν**: *but some of those*; τῶν is a partitive genitive. **Ἠλίαν**: they misunderstand and hear Ἠλία, the vocative of Ἠλίας, instead of Ηλι.

27:48 **δραμὼν . . . καὶ λαβὼν . . . ἐπότιζεν**: a participle may receive as much emphasis as the finite verb and be coordinated with it. **πλήσας τε ὄξους καὶ περιθεὶς καλάμῳ**: *and after he had filled it with wine vinegar and attached it to a reed*; the genitive is used with verbs signifying *to fill*. The compound verb takes the dative case.

27:49 οἱ δὲ λοιποὶ ἔλεγον, Ἄφες ἴδωμεν εἰ ἔρχεται Ἠλίας σώσων
αὐτόν. 27:50 ὁ δὲ Ἰησοῦς πάλιν κράξας φωνῇ μεγάλῃ ἀφῆκεν τὸ
πνεῦμα. 27:51 Καὶ ἰδοὺ τὸ καταπέτασμα τοῦ ναοῦ ἐσχίσθη ἀπ'
ἄνωθεν ἕως κάτω εἰς δύο καὶ ἡ γῆ ἐσείσθη καὶ αἱ πέτραι ἐσχίσθησαν,
27:52 καὶ τὰ μνημεῖα ἀνεῴχθησαν καὶ πολλὰ σώματα τῶν
κεκοιμημένων ἁγίων ἠγέρθησαν,

27:49
λοιπός, ή, όν remaining; the rest, remainder
27:50
φωνή, ῆς, ἡ voice, sound
27:51
καταπέτασμα, ατος, τό veil, curtain
ναός, οῦ, ὁ dwelling, temple
σχίζω, σχίσω, ἔσχισα, ἐσχίσθην split, tear asunder, divide
ἄνωθεν from above, again, anew (adverb)
κάτω downward, down, below (adverb)
σείω, σείσω, ἔσεισα, ἐσείσθην shake, agitate, cause to quake; stir up, set in motion
πέτρα, ας, ἡ rock; crags, clefts, rock formation; stony ground
27:52
μνημεῖον, ου, τό monument, grave, tomb
σῶμα, ατος, τό body
κοιμάω, κοιμήσω, ἐκοίμησα, κεκοίμημαι lull to sleep; sleep, fall asleep, die, pass away (passive)
ἅγιος, ια, ιον hallowed, pure, holy; οἱ ἅγιοι God's people, saints

---

27:49 **Ἄφες ἴδωμεν**: *let us see*; the imperatives ἄφες and ἄφετε are commonly used with the first person subjunctive. **εἰ ἔρχεται Ἠλίας σώσον αὐτόν**: *whether Elijah will come to save him*; ἔρχεται connotes a future. σώσον: the future active participle expresses purpose, especially when combined with a verb of motion.

27:50 **φωνῇ μεγάλῃ** is an ablative of means.

27:51–52 **τὸ καταπέτασμα . . . ἐσχίσθη . . . ἡ γῆ ἐσείσθη . . . αἱ πέτραι ἐσχίσθησαν . . . τὰ μνημεῖα ἀνεῴχθησαν . . . πολλὰ σώματα . . . ἠγέρθησαν**: the cry summons a passive but dramatic cosmic response. The physical phenomena attest to the cosmic significance of the death and resurrection. ἀνεῴχθησαν is a third person plural first aorist passive indicative of ἀνοίγω. It takes a double augment of the stem but the preposition is not augmented.

27:53 καὶ ἐξελθόντες ἐκ τῶν μνημείων μετὰ τὴν ἔγερσιν αὐτοῦ
εἰσῆλθον εἰς τὴν ἁγίαν πόλιν καὶ ἐνεφανίσθησαν πολλοῖς. 27:54 Ὁ
δὲ ἑκατόνταρχος καὶ οἱ μετ' αὐτοῦ τηροῦντες τὸν Ἰησοῦν ἰδόντες
τὸν σεισμὸν καὶ τὰ γενόμενα ἐφοβήθησαν σφόδρα, λέγοντες,
Ἀληθῶς θεοῦ υἱὸς ἦν οὗτος. 27:55 Ἦσαν δὲ ἐκεῖ γυναῖκες πολλαὶ
ἀπὸ μακρόθεν θεωροῦσαι, αἵτινες ἠκολούθησαν τῷ Ἰησοῦ ἀπὸ τῆς
Γαλιλαίας διακονοῦσαι αὐτῷ· 27:56 ἐν αἷς ἦν Μαρία ἡ Μαγδαληνὴ
καὶ Μαρία ἡ τοῦ Ἰακώβου καὶ Ἰωσὴφ μήτηρ καὶ ἡ μήτηρ τῶν υἱῶν
Ζεβεδαίου.

27:53
μνημεῖον, ου, τό monument, grave, tomb
ἔγερσις, εως, ἡ resurrection
ἅγιος, ια, ιον hallowed, pure, holy
ἐμφανίζω, ἐμφανίσω, ἐνεφάνισα, ἐνεφανίσθην reveal, make known
27:54
ἑκατόνταρχος, ου, ὁ commander of 100 men, centurion
τηρέω, τηρήσω, ἐτήρησα, τετήρηκα, τετήρημαι, ἐτηρήθην guard, heed, preserve, reserve
σεισμός, ου, ὁ shaking; earthquake; tempest
σφόδρα greatly, exceedingly (adverb)
ἀληθῶς truly, certainly, of a truth
27:55
μακρόθεν far off, at a distance, from afar (adverb)
θεωρέω, θεωρήσω, ἐθεώρησα see, look at, observe, perceive, experience; view
διακονέω, διακονήσω, διηκόνησα, δεδιηκόνηκα, διηκονήθην wait on, attend upon, serve
27:56
Μαγδαληνή, ῆς, ἡ Magdalene, woman from Magdala

27:53 **εἰς τὴν ἁγίαν πόλιν**: Jerusalem with its temple is dedicated to God.

27:54 **θεοῦ υἱὸς ἦν οὗτος**: *this was the Son of God;* a predicate nominative does not usually carry an article. Their testimony is all the more powerful given that they are hostile witnesses and have nothing to gain by confession.

27:56 **Μαρία ἡ τοῦ Ἰακώβου καὶ Ἰωσὴφ**: Mary, the mother of James and Joses; the name is also given as Ἰωσῆς (Mk 6:3, 15:47), one of the brothers of Jesus. John also records that the mother of Jesus was present (19:25).

27:57 Ὀψίας δὲ γενομένης ἦλθεν ἄνθρωπος πλούσιος ἀπὸ
Ἁριμαθαίας, τοὔνομα Ἰωσήφ, ὃς καὶ αὐτὸς ἐμαθητεύθη τῷ Ἰησοῦ·
27:58 οὗτος προσελθὼν τῷ Πιλάτῳ ᾐτήσατο τὸ σῶμα τοῦ Ἰησοῦ.
τότε ὁ Πιλᾶτος ἐκέλευσεν ἀποδοθῆναι. 27:59 καὶ λαβὼν τὸ σῶμα ὁ
Ἰωσὴφ ἐνετύλιξεν αὐτὸ [ἐν] σινδόνι καθαρᾷ

27:57

ὄψιος, ία, ιον late; ὀψία, ας, ἡ evening

πλούσιος, ία, ιον rich, wealthy; rich man (substantive)

Ἁριμαθαία, ας, ἡ Arimathaea

μαθητεύω, μαθητεύσω, ἐμαθήτευσα become a disciple of, follow as a disciple (intransitive active and passive deponent); make a disciple of, teach; be trained, be instructed (passive)

27:58

κελεύω, κελεύσω, ἐκέλευσα give order, command, urge, direct, bid

27:59

ἐντυλίσσω, ἐντυλίξω, ἐνετύλιξα, ἐντετύλιγμαι wrap (up), envelope; fold together

σινδών, όνος, ἡ linen cloth, linen sheet; sheet, tunic

καθαρός, ά, όν clean, pure

27:57 **πλούσιος** is used as a substantive. **τοὔνομα** is crasis for τὸ ὄνομα: *by name*; the use of the case is an accusative of specification. **ἐμαθητεύθη τῷ Ἰησοῦ**: *who had become a disciple of Jesus*; the action of the verb precedes that of the aorist ἦλθεν and has the force of a pluperfect. τῷ Ἰησοῦ is a dative of reference.

27:58 **ᾐτήσατο τὸ σῶμα**: the verb is third person singular first aorist middle indicative of αἰτέω. The middle voice denotes that the subject performs an action for itself or its own interest or for its own benefit. The verb takes an accusative of the thing asked for and may also govern an accusative of the person asked. **ἐκέλευσεν ἀποδοθῆναι**: *ordered that it be given to him*; verbs indicating *will* or *desire* are often followed by an accusative infinitive construction. The accusative subject of the infinitive may not be included but σῶμα is readily supplied from the context. So also αὐτῷ, the person to whom the body is given.

27:60 καὶ ἔθηκεν αὐτὸ ἐν τῷ καινῷ αὐτοῦ μνημείῳ ὃ ἐλατόμησεν ἐν τῇ πέτρᾳ καὶ προσκυλίσας λίθον μέγαν τῇ θύρᾳ τοῦ μνημείου ἀπῆλθεν. 27:61 ἦν δὲ ἐκεῖ Μαριὰμ ἡ Μαγδαληνὴ καὶ ἡ ἄλλη Μαρία καθήμεναι ἀπέναντι τοῦ τάφου.

27:62 Τῇ δὲ ἐπαύριον, ἥτις ἐστὶν μετὰ τὴν παρασκευήν, συνήχθησαν οἱ ἀρχιερεῖς καὶ οἱ Φαρισαῖοι πρὸς Πιλᾶτον 27:63 λέγοντες, Κύριε, ἐμνήσθημεν ὅτι ἐκεῖνος ὁ πλάνος εἶπεν ἔτι ζῶν, Μετὰ τρεῖς ἡμέρας ἐγείρομαι.

27:60
καινός, ή, όν new
μνημεῖον, ου, τό monument, grave, tomb
λατομέω, λατομήσω, ἐλατόμησα, λελατόμηκα cut out of stone, hew out of rock
πέτρα, ας, ἡ rock; crags, clefts, rock formation; stony ground
προσκυλίω, προσκυλίσω to roll (up to, against)
λίθος, ου, ὁ stone
θύρα, ας, ἡ door, entrance
27:61
ἀπέναντι before; opposite (adverb; preposition + genitive)
τάφος, ου, ὁ grave, tomb, sepulchre
27:62
ἐπαύριον following (adverb); ἡ ἐπαύριον the next day, the following day (understand ἡμέρα)
παρασκευή, ῆς, ἡ preparation (= day of preparation for a festival)
27:63
μιμνήσκομαι, μνησθήσομαι, μέμνημαι, ἐμνήσθην remember, recollect, call to mind
πλάνος, η, ον wanderer, vagabond; deceiver, imposter
ἔτι yet, still (adverb)
ζάω, ζήσω/ζήσομαι, ἔζησα, ἔζηκα live
τρεῖς, τρία three

27:60 **ὃ ἐλατόμησεν . . . καὶ προσκυλίσας λίθον μέγαν τῇ θύρᾳ**: *which he had hewn . . . and after he had a great stone rolled up to the entrance*; the aorist verb and participle are causative, denoting *to cause* or *to make*, and indicate an action performed at the bidding of the subject.

27:61 **ἦν . . . Μαριὰμ . . . καθήμεναι**: the singular number of the verb agrees with the nearest Μαριὰμ. The participle agrees with both in number. **ἡ ἄλλη Μαρία** is the mother of James and Joses (cf. Mk 15:40, 47). ἄλλη differentiates and distinguishes her from Mary Magdalene.

27:62 **Τῇ δὲ ἐπαύριον** is a dative of time when with an adverb. Supply ἡμέρᾳ with the article.

27:63 **ἔτι ζῶν**: *while he was still living*; the temporal adverb at the beginning of the participial clause helps to clarify the interpretation of the participle. **ἐγείρομαι**: *I will rise again*; the present passive intransitive verb connotes a future tense.

27:64 κέλευσον οὖν ἀσφαλισθῆναι τὸν τάφον ἕως τῆς τρίτης ἡμέρας, μήποτε ἐλθόντες οἱ μαθηταὶ αὐτοῦ κλέψωσιν αὐτὸν καὶ εἴπωσιν τῷ λαῷ, Ἠγέρθη ἀπὸ τῶν νεκρῶν, καὶ ἔσται ἡ ἐσχάτη πλάνη χείρων τῆς πρώτης. 27:65 ἔφη αὐτοῖς ὁ Πιλᾶτος, Ἔχετε κουστωδίαν· ὑπάγετε ἀσφαλίσασθε ὡς οἴδατε.

27:64
κελεύω, κελεύσω, ἐκέλευσα give order, command, urge, direct, bid
ἀσφαλίζω, ἀσφαλίσω to make safe, to make secure
τάφος, ου, ὁ grave, tomb, sepulchre
τρίτος, η, ον third
μήποτε not, never; that . . . not, lest, (in order) that . . . not (conjunction)
κλέπτω, κλέψω, ἔκλεψα, κέκλοφα, ἐκλάπην (2 aorist passive) steal
νεκρός, ά, όν dead
ἔσχατος, η, ον last
πλάνη, ης, ἡ wandering; deceit, deception, delusion
χείρων, ον worse, more severe (comparative of κακός)
27:65
κουστωδία, ας, ἡ watch, guard (composed of soldiers)
ἀσφαλίζω, ἀσφαλίσω to make safe, to make secure

27:64 **κέλευσον**: the infinitive with the subject accusative is used as the object of the verb of commanding in indirect discourse. The aorist is the usual tense after verbs of *will* or *desire*. **μήποτε ἐλθόντες . . . κλέψωσιν . . . καὶ εἴπωσιν**: *lest by coming . . . they steal . . . and say*; the conjunction introduces a negative clause of purpose. **καὶ ἔσται ἡ ἐσχάτη πλάνη χείρων τῆς πρώτης**: *and the last deception will be worse than the first*; the comparative adjective takes a genitive of comparison. Ironically the only deception from beginning to end has been that of the Jewish leadership (28:12).

27:65 **Ἔχετε κουστωδίαν**: *take a guard*; the verb may be construed either as a present indicative or as an imperative. In the indicative, Pilate suggests that they enlist their own temple officers. In the imperative, he tells them to take his soldiers (cf. 28:12–14). Since Pilate seems to agree to the request of guarding the tomb in principle, he would trust his Roman soldiers to be able to do so. **ὑπάγετε ἀσφαλίσασθε ὡς οἴδατε**: *go and make the tomb as secure as you can*; supply καὶ: the imperative is usually found without a conjunction when followed by another imperative. Supply also τὸ τάφον as the object of ἀσφαλίσασθε. **ὡς οἴδατε** is used in an absolute sense. It literally means: *as you know how (to do)*.

27:66 οἱ δὲ πορευθέντες ἠσφαλίσαντο τὸν τάφον σφραγίσαντες τὸν λίθον μετὰ τῆς κουστωδίας.

27:66
τάφος, ου, ὁ grave, tomb, sepulchre
σφραγίζω, σφραγίσω, ἐσφράγισα, ἐσφράγισμαι, ἐσφραγίσθην seal (up), attest, certify
κουστωδία, ας, ἡ watch, guard (composed of soldiers)

27:66 **σφραγίσαντες τὸν λίθον μετὰ τῆς κουστωδίας**: *by sealing the stone with the guard*; σφραγίσαντες τὸν λίθον means that they are keeping anyone from moving the stone. Thus the tomb is sealed by a stone and the stone is sealed by guards.

28 Ὀψὲ δὲ σαββάτων, τῇ ἐπιφωσκούσῃ εἰς μίαν σαββάτων ἦλθεν Μαριὰμ ἡ Μαγδαληνὴ καὶ ἡ ἄλλη Μαρία θεωρῆσαι τὸν τάφον.
28:2 καὶ ἰδοὺ σεισμὸς ἐγένετο μέγας· ἄγγελος γὰρ κυρίου καταβὰς ἐξ οὐρανοῦ καὶ προσελθὼν ἀπεκύλισεν τὸν λίθον καὶ ἐκάθητο ἐπάνω αὐτοῦ. 28:3 ἦν δὲ ἡ εἰδέα αὐτοῦ ὡς ἀστραπὴ καὶ τὸ ἔνδυμα αὐτοῦ λευκὸν ὡς χιών. 28:4 ἀπὸ δὲ τοῦ φόβου αὐτοῦ ἐσείσθησαν οἱ τηροῦντες καὶ ἐγενήθησαν ὡς νεκροί.

28:1
ὀψέ late (in the day), in the evening (adverb); ὀψὲ σαββάτων after the close of the sabbath (preposition + genitive)
ἐπιφώσκω shine forth, dawn
εἷς, μία, ἕν one, single (numeral); equivalent to πρῶτος, η, ον first
θεωρέω, θεωρήσω, ἐθεώρησα see, look at, observe, perceive, experience; view
τάφος, ου, ὁ grave, tomb, sepulchre
28:2
σεισμός, ου, ὁ shaking; earthquake; tempest
ἀποκυλίω, ἀποκυλίσω to roll away
λίθος, ου, ὁ stone
ἐπάνω over, above, on (adverb; preposition + genitive)
28:3
εἰδέα, ας, ἡ form; appearance, look, aspect
ἀστραπή, ῆς, ἡ lightning; light, ray
ἔνδυμα, ατος, τό garment, clothing; cloak, mantle
λευκός, ή, όν bright, shining, gleaming, white
χιών, όνος, ἡ snow
28:4
φόβος, ου, ὁ terror; fear, alarm, fright; reverence, respect
σείω, σείσω, ἔσεισα, ἐσείσθην shake, agitate, cause to quake; stir up, set in motion
τηρέω, τηρήσω, ἐτήρησα, τετήρηκα, τετήρημαι, ἐτηρήθην guard, heed, preserve, reserve
νεκρός, ά, όν dead

28:1 **Ὀψὲ . . . σαββάτων**: *after the Sabbath*; the adverb is used as a preposition with the genitive case. **τῇ ἐπιφωσκούσῃ εἰς μίαν σαββάτων**: as dawn ushered in the first day *of the week*. τῇ ἐπιφωσκούσῃ is a dative of time when. εἰς μίαν: supply ἡμέραν. σαββάτων is a partitive genitive.

28:2 **ἐγένετο**: *there was.*

28:3 **ὡς** introduces a simile to describe brightness.

28:4 **ἀπὸ . . . τοῦ φόβου αὐτοῦ**: *for fear of him*; αὐτοῦ is an objective genitive. **καὶ ἐνεγνήθησαν ὡς νεκροί**: *and they became like dead men*; νεκροί is a substantive.

28:5 ἀποκριθεὶς δὲ ὁ ἄγγελος εἶπεν ταῖς γυναιξίν, Μὴ φοβεῖσθε ὑμεῖς, οἶδα γὰρ ὅτι Ἰησοῦν τὸν ἐσταυρωμένον ζητεῖτε· 28:6 οὐκ ἔστιν ὧδε, ἠγέρθη γὰρ καθὼς εἶπεν· δεῦτε ἴδετε τὸν τόπον ὅπου ἔκειτο. 28:7 καὶ ταχὺ πορευθεῖσαι εἴπατε τοῖς μαθηταῖς αὐτοῦ ὅτι Ἠγέρθη ἀπὸ τῶν νεκρῶν, καὶ ἰδοὺ προάγει ὑμᾶς εἰς τὴν Γαλιλαίαν, ἐκεῖ αὐτὸν ὄψεσθε· ἰδοὺ εἶπον ὑμῖν. 28:8 καὶ ἀπελθοῦσαι ταχὺ ἀπὸ τοῦ μνημείου μετὰ φόβου καὶ χαρᾶς μεγάλης ἔδραμον ἀπαγγεῖλαι τοῖς μαθηταῖς αὐτοῦ.

28:6

καθώς as, just as, how, inasmuch as (adverb)

δεῦτε come! come here! (adverb)

τόπος, ου, ὁ place, position, region

ὅπου where (adverb)

κεῖμαι, κείσομαι lie, be laid, be placed, be set

28:7

ταχύς, εῖα, ύ quick, swift, fleet; ταχύ quickly, speedily, hastily (adverb)

28:8

μνημεῖον, ου, τό monument, grave, tomb

φόβος, ου, ὁ terror; fear, alarm, fright; reverence, respect

χαρά, ᾶς, ἡ joy

τρέχω, θρέξομαι/δραμοῦμαι, ἔδραμον (2 aorist) run

ἀπαγγέλλω, ἀπαγγελῶ, ἀπήγγειλα (1 aorist), ἀπηγγέλην (2 aorist passive) bring back word, report, declare, announce, tell

---

28:5 **ὑμεῖς** with the second person plural imperative is emphatic and stands in contrast to the soldiers.

28:6 **ἠγέρθη**: *He has risen.*

28:7 **ὄψεσθε** is the future deponent verb of ὁράω.

28:8 **μετὰ φόβου καὶ χαρᾶς**: φόβου is different from the fear that seized the soldiers (4). The women are filled *with reverence.* χαρᾶς: the noun carries onomatopoeic qualities. **ἀπαγγεῖλαι**: *to bring back word*; the verb is used in an absolute sense.

28:9 καὶ ἰδοὺ Ἰησοῦς ὑπήντησεν αὐταῖς λέγων, Χαίρετε. αἱ δὲ
προσελθοῦσαι ἐκράτησαν αὐτοῦ τοὺς πόδας καὶ προσεκύνησαν
αὐτῷ. 28:10 τότε λέγει αὐταῖς ὁ Ἰησοῦς, Μὴ φοβεῖσθε· ὑπάγετε
ἀπαγγείλατε τοῖς ἀδελφοῖς μου ἵνα ἀπέλθωσιν εἰς τὴν Γαλιλαίαν,
κἀκεῖ με ὄψονται.

28:11 Πορευομένων δὲ αὐτῶν ἰδού τινες τῆς κουστωδίας
ἐλθόντες εἰς τὴν πόλιν ἀπήγγειλαν τοῖς ἀρχιερεῦσιν ἅπαντα
τὰ γενόμενα. 28:12 καὶ συναχθέντες μετὰ τῶν πρεσβυτέρων
συμβούλιόν τε λαβόντες ἀργύρια ἱκανὰ ἔδωκαν τοῖς στρατιώταις
28:13 λέγοντες,

28:9
ὑπαντάω, ὑπαντήσω, ὑπήντησα meet (+ dative)
χαίρω, χαρήσομαι, ἐχάρην (2 aorist passive) rejoice, be glad; χαῖρε, χαίρετε hail, greetings, welcome (as a form of greeting)
πούς, ποδός, ὁ foot
28:10
ἀπαγγέλλω, ἀπαγγελῶ, ἀπήγγειλα (1 aorist), ἀπηγγέλην (2 aorist passive) bring back word, report, declare, announce, tell
28:11
κουστωδία, ας, ἡ watch, guard (composed of soldiers)
ἅπας, ἅπασα, ἅπασαν all, whole, every
28:12
συμβούλιον, ίου, τό counsel, plan, consultation; συμβούλιον λαμβάνειν form a plan, consult, plot
ἀργύριον, ίου, τό silver, silver shekel, silver drachma, silver money
ἱκανός, ή, όν sufficient, enough; adequate, competent, qualified; fit, worthy
στρατιώτης, ου, ὁ soldier

28:9 **ἐκράτησαν**: *they took a hold of*; the verb takes an accusative of the person or thing.

28:10 **ἀπαγγείλατε τοῖς ἀδελφοῖς μου**: the message confirms that of the angel at the tomb (7).

28:11 **τινες τῆς κουστωδίας**: the case usage of the noun is a partitive genitive. **ἅπαντα**: ἅπας is a strengthened form of πᾶς (App. 27). The prefix ἁ- or ἀ- (alpha copulative) may indicate union, likeness, and intensity and is derived from ἅμα: *together.*

28:12 **συμβούλιόν τε λαβόντες**: their final plot and their ἡ ἐσχάτη πλάνη.

Εἴπατε ὅτι Οἱ μαθηταὶ αὐτοῦ νυκτὸς ἐλθόντες ἔκλεψαν αὐτὸν ἡμῶν κοιμωμένων. 28:14 καὶ ἐὰν ἀκουσθῇ τοῦτο ἐπὶ τοῦ ἡγεμόνος, ἡμεῖς πείσομεν [αὐτὸν] καὶ ὑμᾶς ἀμερίμνους ποιήσομεν. 28:15 οἱ δὲ λαβόντες τὰ ἀργύρια ἐποίησαν ὡς ἐδιδάχθησαν. Καὶ διεφημίσθη ὁ λόγος οὗτος παρὰ Ἰουδαίοις μέχρι τῆς σήμερον [ἡμέρας].

28:16 Οἱ δὲ ἕνδεκα μαθηταὶ ἐπορεύθησαν εἰς τὴν Γαλιλαίαν εἰς τὸ ὄρος οὗ ἐτάξατο αὐτοῖς ὁ Ἰησοῦς,

---

28:13
νύξ, νυκτός, ἡ night
κλέπτω, κλέψω, ἔκλεψα, κέκλοφα, ἐκλάπην (2 aorist passive) steal
κοιμάω, κοιμήσω, ἐκοίμησα, κεκοίμημαι lull to sleep; sleep, fall asleep, die, pass away (passive)
28:14
ἡγεμών, όνος, ὁ guide, leader, prince, governor; prefect, procurator
πείθω, πείσω, ἔπεισα, πέπεικα, πέποιθα (2 perfect), πέπεισμαι, ἐπείσθην persuade, influence by persuasion; pacify, conciliate, win over
ἀμέριμνος, ον free from care
28:15
ἀργύριον, ίου, τό silver, silver shekel, silver drachma, silver money
διαφημίζω, διαφημίσω, διεφήμισα report, proclaim, spread news about, spread widely, disseminate
μέχρι to, even to; until, till (preposition + genitive)
σήμερον today, this day (adverb)
28:16
ἕνδεκα eleven (indeclinable)
οὗ where, in what place (adverb)
τάσσω, τάξω, ἔταξα, τέταγμαι, ἐτάχθην, ἐτάγην (2 aorist passive) arrange, appoint, determine

---

28:13 **νυκτὸς**: *at night*; the genitive of time expresses time at which an action takes place.

28:14 **ἐὰν ἀκουσθῇ τοῦτο ἐπὶ τοῦ ἡγεμόνος**: *if this should come to the procurator's ears*; ἐὰν introduces the protasis of a future more vivid condition (App. 70). τοῦτο: supply τὸ συμβούλιον. **ὑμᾶς ἀμερίμνους ποιήσομεν**: *we will keep you out of trouble*; ἀμερίμνους is a predicate accusative adjective.

28:15 **ὡς ἐδιδάχθησαν**: *as they were instructed.*

28:16 **οὗ ἐτάξατο αὐτοῖς**: *where he had appointed them to go*; supply πορεύεσθαι. ἐτάξατο is an aorist middle.

28:17 καὶ ἰδόντες αὐτὸν προσεκύνησαν, οἱ δὲ ἐδίστασαν. 28:18
καὶ προσελθὼν ὁ Ἰησοῦς ἐλάλησεν αὐτοῖς λέγων, Ἐδόθη μοι
πᾶσα ἐξουσία ἐν οὐρανῷ καὶ ἐπὶ [τῆς] γῆς. 28:19 πορευθέντες οὖν
μαθητεύσατε πάντα τὰ ἔθνη, βαπτίζοντες αὐτοὺς εἰς τὸ ὄνομα τοῦ
πατρὸς καὶ τοῦ υἱοῦ καὶ τοῦ ἁγίου πνεύματος, 28:20 διδάσκοντες
αὐτοὺς τηρεῖν πάντα ὅσα ἐνετειλάμην ὑμῖν· καὶ ἰδοὺ ἐγὼ μεθ᾽ ὑμῶν
εἰμι πάσας τὰς ἡμέρας ἕως τῆς συντελείας τοῦ αἰῶνος.

28:17

διστάζω, διστάσω, ἐδίστασα doubt, hesitate, waver

28:18

ἐξουσία, ας, ἡ authority, right, ability, might, power

28:19

μαθητεύω, μαθητεύσω, ἐμαθήτευσα become a disciple of, follow as a disciple (intransitive active and passive deponent); make a disciple of, teach; be trained, be instructed (passive)

βαπτίζω, βαπτίσω, ἐβάπτισα, βεβάπτισμαι, ἐβαπτίσθην dip, immerse, baptize

ἅγιος, ια, ιον hallowed, pure, holy

28:20

τηρέω, τηρήσω, ἐτήρησα, τετήρηκα, τετήρημαι, ἐτηρήθην guard, heed, preserve, reserve, keep, observe

ἐντέλλομαι, ἐντελοῦμαι, ἐνετειλάμην, ἐντέταλμαι command, order, enjoin

συντέλεια, ας, ἡ completion, close, end

αἰών, αἰῶνος, ὁ eternity, perpetuity; life, age, era; world

28:17 **οἱ δὲ ἐδίστασαν**: *some doubted*; perhaps those who were not present wanted to be eyewitnesses also.

28:19 **πορευθέντες . . . μαθητεύσατε**: *go and teach.*

28:20 **πάντα ὅσα**: *whatsoever.* **πάσας τὰς ἡμέρας**: *all the days*; the case usage is an accusative of duration of time. **ἕως τῆς συντελείας τοῦ αἰῶνος**: *even to the end of the age*; the promise of divine presence and divine assistance extends to the end of the world.

GRAMMATICAL APPENDIX

Content of Grammatical Appendix

20. Contracted adjectives in **οος**: ἁπλοῦς (-οος), ἁπλῆ (-εα), ἁπλοῦν (-οον)
21. Adjectives of the third or consonant declension: ἀληθής, ἀληθές
22. Third declension comparative: μείζων, μεῖζον
23. Third declension comparative: βελτίων, βέλτιον
24. Third declension adjectives with stems in **υ** (**υς**, **εια**, **υ**): ἡδύς, ἡδεῖα, ἡδύ
25. Third declension adjectives with stems in **ν** (**ας**, **αινα**, **αν**): μέλας, μέλαινα, μέλαν
26. Third declension adjectives with stems in **ντ**: χαρίεις, χαρίεσσα, χαρίεν
27. Third declension adjectives with stems in **ντ**: πᾶς, πᾶσα, πᾶν
28. The present participle of εἰμί: ὤν, οὖσα, ὄν
29. The present active participle of λύω: λύων, λύουσα, λῦον
30. The present middle and passive participle: λυόμενος, λυομένη, λυόμενον
31. The aorist active participle of λύω: λύσας, λύσασα, λῦσαν
32. The aorist middle participle of λύω: λυσάμενος, λυσαμένη, λυσάμενον
33. The perfect active participle of λύω: λελυκώς, λελυκυῖα, λελυκός
34. The aorist passive participle of λύω: λυθείς, λυθεῖσα, λυθέν
35. The present active participle of contracted verbs in **αω**: τιμῶν (-αω), τιμῶσα (-αου), τιμῶν (-αο)
36. The present active participle of contracted verbs in **εω**: ποιῶν (-εω), ποιοῦσα (-εου), ποιοῦν (-εο)
37. Adjectives of irregular declension with the stems of **μεγα** and **μεγαλο**: μέγας, μεγάλη, μέγα
38. Adjectives of irregular declension with the stems of **πολυ** and **πολλο**: πολύς, πολλή, πολύ
39. First, second, and third person personal pronouns: ἐγώ, σύ, ἐκεῖνος/οὗτος
40. Personal and intensive pronouns: αὐτός, αὐτή, αὐτό

41. Demonstrative pronoun/adjective: οὗτος, αὕτη, τοῦτο
42. Demonstrative pronoun/adjective: ἐκεῖνος, ἐκείνη, ἐκεῖνο
43. Reciprocal pronoun: ἀλλήλων
44. First person reflexive pronouns: ἐμαυτοῦ, ἐμαυτῆς
45. Second person reflexive pronouns: σεαυτοῦ, σεαυτῆς
46. Third person reflexive pronouns: ἑαυτοῦ, ἑαυτῆς, ἑαυτοῦ
47. Interrogative pronouns/adjectives: τίς, τί
48. Indefinite pronouns: τις, τι
49. Relative pronouns: ὅς, ἥ, ὅ
50. The cardinal number εἷς
51. The cardinal numbers δύο and τρεῖς
52. The cardinal number τέσσαρες
53. The conjugation of the regular **ω** verbs: λύω
54. The second aorist: ἔλιπον
55. Contracted verb with stem in **α**: τιμῶ (αω)
56. Contracted verb with stem in **ε**: φιλῶ (εω)
57. Contracted verb with stem in **ο**: δηλῶ (οω)
58. The conjugation of the **μι** verbs with stem in **δο**: δίδωμι
59. The conjugation of the **μι** verbs with stem in **θε**: τίθημι
60. The conjugation of the **μι** verbs with stem in **στα**: ἵστημι
61. The second aorist of ἵστημι and γινώσκω: ἔστην, ἔγνων
62. The conjugation of οἶδα
63. The conjugation of εἰμί
64. Uses of the nominative case
65. Uses of the genitive case
66. Uses of the dative case
67. Uses of the accusative case
68. Use of the vocative case
69. Apposition
70. Conditions

GRAMMATICAL APPENDIX

The Article

1. The article includes three genders: masculine, feminine, and neuter.

		M.	F.	N.
Sing.	Nominative	ὁ	ἡ	τό
	Genitive	τοῦ	τῆς	τοῦ
	Dative	τῷ	τῇ	τῷ
	Accusative	τόν	τήν	τό
Plur.	Nominative	οἱ	αἱ	τά
	Genitive	τῶν	τῶν	τῶν
	Dative	τοῖς	ταῖς	τοῖς
	Accusative	τούς	τάς	τά

N.B.: The nominative masculine and feminine articles, in both the singular and plural, are proclitics and have no accent.

First Declension Nouns

2. The first declension includes feminine nouns ending in **α** or **η**:

Sing.	N., V.	ἀρχή	ἡμέρα	δόξα
	G.	ἀρχῆς	ἡμέρας	δόξης
	D.	ἀρχῇ	ἡμέρᾳ	δόξῃ
	A.	ἀρχήν	ἡμέραν	δόξαν
Plur.	N., V.	ἀρχαί	ἡμέραι	δόξαι
	G.	ἀρχῶν	ἡμερῶν	δοξῶν
	D.	ἀρχαῖς	ἡμέραις	δόξαις
	A.	ἀρχάς	ἡμέρας	δόξας

N.B.: Three patterns emerge in the singular: 1) a noun ending with **η** in the nominative keeps the **η** in the other cases; 2) a noun retains the final **α** after **ε**, **ι**, or **ρ**; 3) in all other nouns the **α**will change to an **η** in the genitive and dative cases. The plural endings are consistent.

3. The first declension also includes some masculine nouns ending in **ης** or **ας**:

Sing.	N.	μαθητής	προφήτης	νεανίας
	G.	μαθητοῦ	προφήτου	νεανίου
	D.	μαθητῇ	προφήτῃ	νεανίᾳ
	A.	μαθητήν	προφήτην	νεανίαν
	V.	μαθητά	προφῆτα	νεανία
Plur.	N., V.	μαθηταί	προφῆται	νεανίαι
	G.	μαθητῶν	προφητῶν	νεανιῶν
	D.	μαθηταῖς	προφήταις	νεανίαις
	A.	μαθητάς	προφήτας	νεανίας

N.B.: Except for the nominative and genitive singular the endings follow the feminine declensional pattern but they are masculine nouns and all modifiers must agree in gender. The genitive singular form is derived from the second declension.

Second Declension Nouns

4. The second declension includes masculine nouns ending in **ος**:

Sing.	N.	λόγος	ἄνθρωπος	υἱός
	G.	λόγου	ἀνθρώπου	υἱοῦ
	D.	λόγῳ	ἀνθρώπῳ	υἱῷ
	A.	λόγον	ἄνθρωπον	υἱόν
	V.	λόγε	ἄνθρωπε	υἱέ
Plur.	N., V.	λόγοι	ἄνθρωποι	υἱοί
	G.	λόγων	ἀνθρώπων	υἱῶν
	D.	λόγοις	ἀνθρώποις	υἱοῖς
	A.	λόγους	ἀνθρώπους	υἱούς

5. The second declension includes neuter nouns ending in **ον** and a few feminines ending in **ος**:

Sing.	N., V.	τέκνον	δῶρον	N.	ὁδός
	G.	τέκνου	δώρου	G.	ὁδοῦ
	D.	τέκνῳ	δώρῳ	D.	ὁδῷ
	A.	τέκνον	δῶρον	A.	ὁδόν
				V.	ὁδέ
Plur.	N., V.	τέκνα	δῶρα	ὁδοί	
	G.	τέκνων	δώρων	ὁδῶν	
	D.	τέκνοις	δώροις	ὁδοῖς	
	A.	τέκνα	δῶρα	ὁδούς	

N.B.: Neuter nouns look alike in the nominative and accusative cases, both in the singular and in the plural. Although feminine nouns ending in **ος** follow the masculine declensional pattern they are feminine and all modifiers must agree in gender.

Third Declension Nouns

6. The third declension includes all genders. The stem of this declension can usually be found by removing the **ος** from the genitive singular.

7. Stems in gutturals (**κ, γ, χ**):

Sing.	N., V.	σάρξ	αἴξ	θρίξ
	G.	σαρκός	αἰγός	τριχός
	D.	σαρκί	αἰγί	τριχί
	A.	σάρκα	αἶγα	τρίχα
Plur.	N., V.	σάρκες	αἶγες	τρίχες
	G.	σαρκῶν	αἰγῶν	τρίχῶν
	D.	σαρξί(ν)	αἰξί(ν)	θριξί(ν)
	A.	σάρκας	αἶγας	τρίχας

8. Stems in dentals (**τ, δ, θ**):

Sing.	N.	χάρις	ἐλπίς	ὄρνις
	G.	χάριτος	ἐλπίδος	ὄρνιθος
	D.	χάριτι	ἐλπίδι	ὄρνιθι
	A.	χάριν (χάριτα)	ἐλπίδα	ὄρνιν
	V.	χάρι	ἐλπί	ὄρνι
Plur.	N., V.	χάριτες	ἐλπίδες	ὄρνιθες
	G.	χαρίτων	ἐλπίδων	ὀρνίθων
	D.	χάρισι(ν)	ἐλπίσι(ν)	ὄρνισι(ν)
	A.	χάριτας	ἐλπίδας	ὄρνιθας

9. Stems in a labial (**π, β, φ**):

Sing.	N., V.	κλώψ	φλέψ
	G.	κλωπός	φλεβός
	D.	κλωπί	φλεβί
	A.	κλῶπα	φλέβα
Plur.	N., V.	κλῶπες	φλέβες
	G.	κλωπῶν	φλεβῶν
	D.	κλωψί(ν)	φλέψί(ν)
	A.	κλῶπας	φλέβας

10. Neuters with stems in **τ**:

Sing.	N., V.	ὄνομα	φῶς	τέρας
	G.	ὀνόματος	φωτός	τέρατος
	D.	ὀνόματι	φωτί	τέρατι
	A.	ὄνομα	φῶς	τέρας
Plur.	N., V.	ὀνόματα	φῶτα	τέρατα
	G.	ὀνομάτων	φώτων	τεράτων
	D.	ὀνόμασι(ν)	φωσί(ν)	τέρασι(ν)
	A.	ὀνόματα	φῶτα	τέρατα

11. Stems in a liquid (**λ, ρ**) or a nasal (**ν**):

Sing.	N., V.	ἅλς	σωτήρ	δαίμων
	G.	ἁλός	σωτῆρος	δαίμονος
	D.	ἁλί	σωτῆρι	δαίμονι
	A.	ἅλα	σωτῆρα	δαίμονα
Plur.	N., V.	ἅλες	σωτῆρες	δαίμονες
	G.	ἁλῶν	σωτήρων	δαιμόνων
	D.	ἁλσί(ν)	σωτῆρσι(ν)	δαίμοσι(ν)
	A.	ἅλας	σωτῆρας	δαίμονας

12. Stems in **ερ** alternating with **ρ**:

Sing.	N.	πατήρ	μήτηρ	ἀνήρ
	G.	πατρός	μητρός	ἀνδρός
	D.	πατρί	μητρί	ἀνδρί
	A.	πατέρα	μητέρα	ἄνδρα
	V.	πάτερ	μῆτερ	ἄνερ
Plur.	N., V.	πατέρες	μητέρες	ἄνδρες
	G.	πατέρων	μητέρων	ἀνδρῶν
	D.	πατράσι(ν)	μητράσι(ν)	ἀνδράσι(ν)
	A.	πατέρας	μητέρας	ἄνδρας

13. Stems in **ι** and **υ**:

Sing.	N.	πόλις	ἰχθύς	πῆχυς
	G.	πόλεως	ἰχθύος	πήχεως/πήχεος
	D.	πόλει (ει)	ἰχθύι	πήχει (ει)
	A.	πόλιν	ἰχθύν	πῆχυν
	V.	πόλι	ἰχθύ	πῆχυ
Plur.	N., V.	πόλεις (εε)	ἰχθύες	πήχεις (εε)
	G.	πόλεων	ἰχθύων	πηχῶν/πήχεων
	D.	πόλεσι(ν)	ἰχθύσι(ν)	πήχεσι(ν)
	A.	πόλεις	ἰχθύας	πήχεις

N.B.: The stem in **ι** usually changes to **ε** in all cases except in the nominative, accusative, and vocative singular. Occasionally the same phenomenon occurs in the **υ** stem. Both stems show **ω** after **ε** in the genitive singular. When the stem in **ε** precedes **ε, ι,** or **α** contraction takes place (**ε** + **ε** = **ει**, **ε** + **ι** = **ει**, **ε** + **α** = **η**).

14. Stems in **ευ**, **αυ**, and **ου**:

Sing.	N.	βασιλεύς	ναῦς	βοῦς
	G.	βασιλέως	νεώς	βοός
	D.	βασιλεῖ	νηΐ	βοΐ
	A.	βασιλέα	ναῦν	βοῦν
	V.	βασιλεῦ	ναῦ	βοῦ
Plur.	N., V.	βασιλεῖς	νῆες	βόες
	G.	βασιλέων	νεῶν	βοῶν
	D.	βασιλεῦσι(ν)	ναυσί(ν)	βουσί(ν)
	A.	βασιλέας	ναῦς	βοῦς

15. Stems in **σ** (elided):

Sing.	N.	γένος	τριήρης	γέρας
	G.	γένους	τριήρους	γέρως
	D.	γένει	τριήρει	γέραι
	A.	γένος	τριήρη	γέρας
	V.	γένος	τριῆρες	γέρας
Plur.	N., V.	γένη	τριήρεις	γέρα
	G.	γενῶν	τριήρων	γερῶν
	D.	γένεσι(ν)	τριήρεσι(ν)	γέρασι(ν)
	A.	γένη	τριήρεις	γέρα

N.B.: The intervocalic **ς** drops out of the stem ending (γένεσος, τριήρεσος, γέρασος); the vowels contract: **ε** + **ο** = **ου**, **ε** + **ι** = **ει**, **ε** + **α** = **η**, **ε** + **ω** = **ω**, **α** + **ο** = **ω**, **α** + **ι** = **αι**, **α** + **α** = **α**, **α** + **ω** = **ω**, and a double **σ** in the dative plural (γένεσσι) becomes a single consonant.

First and Second Declension Adjectives

16. The second and first declension adjectives include all genders and have three endings:

		M.	F.	N.
Sing.	N.	ἀγαθός	ἀγαθή	ἀγαθόν
	G.	ἀγαθοῦ	ἀγαθῆς	ἀγαθοῦ
	D.	ἀγαθῷ	ἀγαθῇ	ἀγαθῷ
	A.	ἀγαθόν	ἀγαθήν	ἀγαθόν
	V.	ἀγαθέ	ἀγαθή	ἀγαθόν
Plur.	N., V.	ἀγαθοί	ἀγαθαί	ἀγαθά
	G.	ἀγαθῶν	ἀγαθῶν	ἀγαθῶν
	D.	ἀγαθοῖς	ἀγαθαῖς	ἀγαθοῖς
	A.	ἀγαθούς	ἀγαθάς	ἀγαθά

17. After **ε**, **ι**, or **ρ** the **α** remains constant in the singular of the feminine adjective:

		M.	F.	N.
Sing.	N.	μικρός	μικρά	μικρόν
	G.	μικροῦ	μικρᾶς	μικροῦ
	D.	μικρῷ	μικρᾷ	μικρῷ
	A.	μικρόν	μικράν	μικρόν
	V.	μικρέ	μικρά	μικρόν
Plur.	N., V.	μικροί	μικραί	μικρά
	G.	μικρῶν	μικρῶν	μικρῶν
	D.	μικροῖς	μικραῖς	μικροῖς
	A.	μικρούς	μικράς	μικρά

18. Some adjectives have similar forms in the masculine and feminine—two endings:

		M. & F.	N.	M. & F.	N.
Sing.	N.	ἄδικος	ἄδικον	φρόνιμος	φρόνιμον
	G.	ἀδίκου	ἀδίκου	φρονίμου	φρονίμου
	D.	ἀδίκῳ	ἀδίκῳ	φρονίμῳ	φρονίμῳ
	A.	ἄδικον	ἄδικον	φρόνιμον	φρόνιμον
	V.	ἄδικε	ἄδικον	φρόνιμε	φρόνιμον
Plur.	N., V.	ἄδικοι	ἄδικα	φρόνιμοι	φρόνιμα
	G.	ἀδίκων	ἀδίκων	φρονίμων	φρονίμων
	D.	ἀδίκοις	ἀδίκοις	φρονίμοις	φρονίμοις
	A.	ἀδίκους	ἄδικα	φρονίμους	φρόνιμα

N.B.: While a few masculine and feminine uncompounded adjectives like φρόνιμος share the same form, most compounds like ἄδικος, ἀθάνατος, πρόθυμος do.

19. Contracted adjectives in **εος**:

		M.	F.	N.
Sing.	N., V.	χρυσοῦς (-εος)	χρυσῆ (-εα)	χρυσοῦν (-εον)
	G.	χρυσοῦ (-εου)	χρυσῆς (-εας)	χρυσοῦ (-εου)
	D.	χρυσῷ (-εῳ)	χρυσῇ (-εᾳ)	χρυσῷ (-εῳ)
	A.	χρυσοῦν (-εον)	χρυσῆν (-εα)	χρυσοῦν (-εον)
Plur.	N., V.	χρυσοῖ (-εοι)	χρυσαῖ (-εαι)	χρυσᾶ (-εα)
	G.	χρυσῶν (-εων)	χρυσῶν (-εων)	χρυσῶν (-εων)
	D.	χρυσοῖς (-εοις)	χρυσαῖς (-εαις)	χρυσοῖς (-εοις)
	A.	χρυσοῦς (-εους)	χρυσᾶς (-εας)	χρυσᾶ (-εα)

N.B.: A circumflex accent (perispomenon) falls on the contraction.

20. Contracted adjectives in **οος**:

		M.		F.		N.	
Sing.	N., V.	ἁπλοῦς	(-οος)	ἁπλῆ	(-εα)	ἁπλοῦν	(-οον)
	G.	ἁπλοῦ	(-οου)	ἁπλῆς	(-εας)	ἁπλοῦ	(-οου)
	D.	ἁπλῷ	(-οῳ)	ἁπλῇ	(-εᾳ)	ἁπλῷ	(-οῳ)
	A.	ἁπλοῦν	(-οον)	ἁπλῆν	(-εα)	ἁπλοῦν	(-οον)
Plur.	N., V.	ἁπλοῖ	(-οοι)	ἁπλαῖ	(-εαι)	ἁπλᾶ	(-οα)
	G.	ἁπλῶν	(-οων)	ἁπλῶν	(-εων)	ἁπλῶν	(-οων)
	D.	ἁπλοῖς	(-οοις)	ἁπλαῖς	(-εαις)	ἁπλοῖς	(-οοις)
	A.	ἁπλοῦς	(-οους)	ἁπλᾶς	(-εας)	ἁπλᾶ	(-οα)

N.B.: A circumflex accent falls on the contraction (perispomenon).

Third Declension Adjectives

21. Adjectives of the third or consonant declension have two endings:

		M. & F.		N.	
Sing.	N.	ἀληθής		ἀληθές	
	G.	ἀληθοῦς	(-εος)	ἀληθοῦς	(-εος)
	D.	ἀληθεῖ	(-ει)	ἀληθεῖ	(-ει)
	A.	ἀληθῆ	(-εα)	ἀληθές	(-εα)
	V.	ἀληθές		ἀληθές	
Plur.	N., V.	ἀληθεῖς	(-εες)	ἀληθῆ	(-εα)
	G.	ἀληθῶν	(-εων)	ἀληθῶν	(-εων)
	D.	ἀληθέσι(ν)	(-εσσι)	ἀληθέσι(ν)	(-εσσι)
	A.	ἀληθεῖς	(-οους)	ἀληθῆ	(-εα)

22. Third declension comparative with stems in **ον**: μείζων

		M. & F.	N.
Sing.	N.	μείζων	μεῖζον
	G.	μείζονος	μείζονος
	D.	μείζονι	μείζονι
	A.	μείζονα/μείζω	μεῖζον
	V.	μεῖζον	μεῖζον
Plur.	N., V.	μείζονες/μείζους	μείζονα/μείζω
	G.	μειζόνων	μειζόνων
	D.	μείζοσι(ν)	μείζοσι(ν)
	A.	μείζονας/μείζους	μείζονα/μείζω

23. Third declension comparative with stems in **ον**: βελτίων

		M. & F.	N.
Sing.	N.	βελτίων	βέλτιον
	G.	βελτίονος	βελτίονος
	D.	βελτίονι	βελτίονι
	A.	βελτίονα/βελτίω	βέλτιον
	V.	βέλτιον	βέλτιον
Plur.	N., V.	βελτίονες/βελτίους	βελτίονα/βελτίω
	G.	βελτιόνων	βελτιόνων
	D.	βελτίοσι(ν)	βελτιόνων
	A.	βελτίονας/βελτίους	βελτίονα/βελτίω

N.B.: The accusative plural in the masculine and feminine forms borrows the nominative abbreviated form. The shorter forms were more prominent in speech.

First and Third Declension Adjectives

24. The masculine and neuter adjectives are in the third declension pattern, the feminine in the first. Stems in **υ** (**υς, εια, υ**):

		M.	F.	N.
Sing.	N.	ἡδύς	ἡδεῖα	ἡδύ
	G.	ἡδέος	ἡδείας	ἡδέος
	D.	ἡδεῖ (ει)	ἡδείᾳ	ἡδεῖ (ει)
	A.	ἡδύν	ἡδεῖαν	ἡδύ
	V.	ἡδύ	ἡδεῖα	ἡδύ
Plur.	N., V.	ἡδεῖς	ἡδεῖαι	ἡδέα
	G.	ἡδέων	ἡδειῶν	ἡδέων
	D.	ἡδέσι(ν)	ἡδείαις	ἡδέσι(ν)
	A.	ἡδεῖς	ἡδείας	ἡδέα

25. The masculine and neuter adjectives are in the third declension pattern, the feminine in the first. Stems in **ν** (**ας, αινα, αν**):

		M.	F.	N.
Sing.	N.	μέλας	μέλαινα	μέλαν
	G.	μέλανος	μελαίνης	μέλανος
	D.	μέλανι	μελαίνῃ	μέλανι
	A.	μέλανα	μέλαιναν	μέλαν
	V.	μέλαν	μέλαινα	μέλαν
Plur.	N., V.	μέλανες	μέλαιναι	μέλανα
	G.	μελάνων	μελαινῶν	μελάνων
	D.	μέλασι(ν)	μελαίναις	μέλασι(ν)
	A.	μέλανας	μελαίνας	μέλανα

26. The masculine and neuter adjectives are in the third declension pattern, the feminine in the first. Stems in **ντ**:

		M.	F.	N.
Sing.	N.	χαρίεις	χαρίεσσα	χαρίεν
	G.	χαρίεντος	χαριέσσης	χαρίεντος
	D.	χαρίεντι	χαριέσσῃ	χαρίεντι
	A.	χαρίεντα	χαρίεσσαν	χαρίεν
	V.	χαρίεν	χαρίεσσα	χαρίεν
Plur.	N., V.	χαρίεντες	χαρίεσσαι	χαρίεντα
	G.	χαριέντων	χαριεσσῶν	χαριέντων
	D.	χαρίεσι(ν)	χαριέσσαις	χαρίεσι(ν)
	A.	χαρίεντας	χαριέσσας	χαρίεντα

27. The masculine and neuter adjectives are in the third declension pattern, the feminine in the first. Stems in **ντ**:

		M.	F.	N.
Sing.	N.	πᾶς	πᾶσα	πᾶν
	G.	παντός	πάσης	παντός
	D.	παντί	πάσῃ	παντί
	A.	πάντα	πᾶσαν	πᾶν
	V.	πᾶς	πᾶσα	πᾶν
Plur.	N., V.	πάντες	πᾶσαι	πάντα
	G.	πάντων	πασῶν	πάντων
	D.	πᾶσι(ν)	πάσαις	πᾶσι(ν)
	A.	πάντας	πάσας	πάντα

Declension of Participles

28. The present participle of εἰμί:

		M.	F.	N.
Sing.	N., V.	ὤν	οὖσα	ὄν
	G.	ὄντος	οὔσης	ὄντος
	D.	ὄντι	οὔσῃ	ὄντι
	A.	ὄντα	οὖσαν	ὄν
Plur.	N., V.	ὄντες	οὖσαι	ὄντα
	G.	ὄντων	οὐσῶν	ὄντων
	D.	οὖσι(ν)	οὔσαις	οὖσι(ν)
	A.	ὄντας	οὔσας	ὄντα

29. The present active participle of λύω:

		M.	F.	N.
Sing.	N., V.	λύων	λύουσα	λῦον
	G.	λύοντος	λυούσης	λύοντος
	D.	λύοντι	λυούσῃ	λύοντι
	A.	λύοντα	λύουσαν	λῦον
Plur.	N., V.	λύοντες	λύουσαι	λύοντα
	G.	λυόντων	λυουσῶν	λυόντων
	D.	λύουσι(ν)	λυούσαις	λύουσι(ν)
	A.	λύοντας	λυούσας	λύοντα

N.B.: Like λύων in endings is λιπών but with accent changes. γνούς, διδούς, and δούς take the same endings except in the masculine nominative singular.

30. The present middle and passive participle: λυόμενος, λυομένη, λυομένον

		M.	F.	N.
Sing.	N., V.	λυόμενος	λυομένη	λυόμενον
	G.	λυομένου	λυομένης	λυομένου
	D.	λυομένῳ	λυομένῃ	λυομένῳ
	A.	λυόμενον	λυομένην	λυόμενον
Plur.	N., V.	λυόμενοι	λυόμεναι	λυόμενα
	G.	λυομένων	λυομένων	λυομένων
	D.	λυομένοις	λυομέναις	λυομένοις
	A.	λυομένους	λυομένας	λυομένα

N.B.: The endings are those of the second and first declension adjectives. They are also the endings of the deponent participle.

31. The aorist active participle of λύω:

		M.	F.	N.
Sing.	N., V.	λύσας	λύσασα	λῦσαν
	G.	λύσαντος	λυσάσης	λύσαντος
	D.	λύσαντι	λυσάσῃ	λύσαντι
	A.	λύσαντα	λύσασαν	λῦσαν
Plur.	N., V.	λύσαντες	λύσασαι	λύσαντα
	G.	λυσάντων	λυσασῶν	λυσάντων
	D.	λύσασι(ν)	λυσάσαις	λύσασι(ν)
	A.	λύσαντας	λυσάσας	λύσαντα

N.B.: Like λύσας in endings, but with accent changes, are the present participle of ἵστημι (ἱστάς, ἱστᾶσα, ἱστάν) and the aorist participle (στάς, στᾶσα, στάν).

32. The aorist middle participle of λύω:

		M.	F.	N.
Sing.	N., V.	λυσάμενος	λυσαμένη	λυσάμενον
	G.	λυσαμένου	λυσαμένης	λυσαμένου
	D.	λυσαμένῳ	λυσαμένῃ	λυσαμένῳ
	A.	λυσάμενον	λυσαμένην	λυσάμενον
Plur.	N., V.	λυσάμενοι	λυσάμεναι	λυσάμενα
	G.	λυσαμένων	λυσαμένων	λυσαμένων
	D.	λυσαμένοις	λυσαμέναις	λυσαμένοις
	A.	λυσαμένους	λυσαμένας	λυσάμενα

N.B.: The endings are those of the second and first declension adjectives.

33. The perfect active participle of λύω:

		M.	F.	N.
Sing.	N., V.	λελυκώς	λελυκυῖα	λελυκός
	G.	λελυκότος	λελυκυίας	λελυκότος
	D.	λελυκότι	λελυκυίᾳ	λελυκότι
	A.	λελυκότα	λελυκυῖαν	λελυκός
Plur.	N., V.	λελυκότες	λελυκυῖαι	λελυκότα
	G.	λελυκότων	λελυκυιῶν	λελυκότων
	D.	λελυκόσι(ν)	λελυκυίαις	λελυκόσι(ν)
	A.	λελυκότας	λελυκυίας	λελυκότα

34. The aorist passive participle of λύω:

		M.	F.	N.
Sing.	N., V.	λυθείς	λυθεῖσα	λυθέν
	G.	λυθέντος	λυθείσης	λυθέντος
	D.	λυθέντι	λυθείσῃ	λυθέντι
	A.	λυθέντα	λυθεῖσαν	λυθέν
Plur.	N., V.	λυθέντες	λυθεῖσαι	λυθέντα
	G.	λυθέντων	λυθεισῶν	λυθέντων
	D.	λυθεῖσι(ν)	λυθείσαις	λυθεῖσι(ν)
	A.	λυθέντας	λυθείσας	λυθέντα

N.B.: Like λυθείς in endings are τιθείς and θείς.

35. The present active participle of contracted verbs in **αω**:

		M.		F.		N.	
Sing.	N., V.	τιμῶν	(-αω)	τιμῶσα	(-αου)	τιμῶν	(-αο)
	G.	τιμῶντος	(-αο)	τιμώσης	(-αου)	τιμῶντος	(-αο)
	D.	τιμῶντι	(-αο)	τιμώσῃ	(-αου)	τιμῶντι	(-αο)
	A.	τιμῶντα	(-αο)	τιμῶσαν	(-αου)	τιμῶν	(-αο)
Plur.	N., V.	τιμῶντες	(-αο)	τιμῶσαι	(-αου)	τιμῶντα	(-αο)
	G.	τιμώντων	(-αο)	τιμωσῶν	(-αου)	τιμώντων	(-αο)
	D.	τιμῶσι	(-αου)	τιμώσαις	(-αου)	τιμῶσι	(-αου)
	A.	τιμῶντας	(-αο)	τιμώσας	(-αου)	τιμῶντα	(-αο)

36. The present active participle of contracted verbs in **εω**:

		M.		F.		N.	
Sing.	N., V.	ποιῶν	(-εω)	ποιοῦσα	(-εου)	ποιοῦν	(-εο)
	G.	ποιοῦντος	(-εο)	ποιούσης	(-εου)	ποιοῦντος	(-εο)
	D.	ποιοῦντι	(-εο)	ποιούσῃ	(-εου)	ποιοῦντι	(-εο)
	A.	ποιοῦντα	(-εο)	ποιοῦσαν	(-εου)	ποιοῦν	(-εο)
Plur.	N., V.	ποιοῦντες	(-εο)	ποιοῦσαι	(-εου)	ποιοῦντα	(-εο)
	G.	ποιούντων	(-εο)	ποιουσῶν	(-εου)	ποιοῦντων	(-εο)
	D.	ποιοῦσι(ν)	(-εο)	ποιούσαις	(-εου)	ποιοῦσι(ν)	(-εου)
	A.	ποιοῦντας	(-εο)	ποιούσας	(-εου)	ποιοῦντα	(-εο)

Adjectives of Irregular Declension

37. Adjectives with the stems of **μεγα** and **μεγαλο**:

		M.	F.	N.
Sing.	N.	μέγας	μεγάλη	μέγα
	G.	μεγάλου	μεγάλης	μεγάλου
	D.	μεγάλῳ	μεγάλῃ	μεγάλῳ
	A.	μέγαν	μεγάλην	μέγα
	V.	μεγάλε	μεγάλη	μέγα
Plur.	N., V.	μεγάλοι	μεγάλαι	μεγάλα
	G.	μεγάλων	μεγάλων	μεγάλων
	D.	μεγάλοις	μεγάλαις	μεγάλοις
	A.	μεγάλους	μεγάλας	μεγάλα

38. Adjectives with the stems of **πολυ** and **πολλο**:

		M.	F.	N.
Sing.	N.	πολύς	πολλή	πολύ
	G.	πολλοῦ	πολλῆς	πολλοῦ
	D.	πολλῷ	πολλῇ	πολλῷ
	A.	πολύν	πολλήν	πολύ
Plur.	N., V.	πολλοί	πολλαί	πολλά
	G.	πολλῶν	πολλῶν	πολλῶν
	D.	πολλοῖς	πολλαῖς	πολλοῖς
	A.	πολλούς	πολλάς	πολλά

39. First, second, and third person personal pronouns:

Sing.	N.	ἐγώ	σύ	ἐκεῖνος/οὗτος
	G.	ἐμοῦ/μου	σοῦ/σου	αὐτοῦ
	D.	ἐμοί/μοι	σοῖ/σοι	αὐτῷ
	A.	ἐμέ/με	σέ/σε	αὐτόν
Plur.	N., V.	ἡμεῖς	ὑμεῖς	σφεῖς
	G.	ἡμῶν	ὑμῶν	σφῶν
	D.	ἡμῖν	ὑμῖν	σφίσι(ν)
	A.	ἡμᾶς	ὑμᾶς	σφᾶς

N.B.: The accented forms are more emphatic than the enclitic. Third person personal pronouns in the nominative singular are usually expressed by a demonstrative like ἐκεῖνος or οὗτος, in the oblique cases of the singular by the appropriate form of αὐτός.

40. Personal and intensive pronouns:

		M.	F.	N.
Sing.	N.	αὐτός	αὐτή	αὐτό
	G.	αὐτοῦ	αὐτῆς	αὐτοῦ
	D.	αὐτῷ	αὐτῇ	αὐτῷ
	A.	αὐτόν	αὐτήν	αὐτό
Plur.	N., V.	αὐτοί	αὐταί	αὐτά
	G.	αὐτῶν	αὐτῶν	αὐτῶν
	D.	αὐτοῖς	αὐταῖς	αὐτοῖς
	A.	αὐτούς	αὐτάς	αὐτά

N.B.: αὐτός has three uses:

1. Standing by itself in the oblique cases (i.e., all but the nominative and vocative) it is a personal pronoun.
2. It is an intensive pronoun standing in predicate position with the verb: αὐτός ἔφη means *he himself said*, or in agreement with a noun or pronoun in the oblique case τοῦ ἀνθρώπου αὐτοῦ means *of the man himself.*
3. When in the attributive position (i.e., between article and noun) it is an adjective meaning *same*: τὸν αὐτὸν ἄνδρα *the same man.*

41. Demonstrative pronoun/adjective οὗτος:

		M.	F.	N.
Sing.	N.	οὗτος	αὕτη	τοῦτο
	G.	τούτου	ταύτης	τούτου
	D.	τούτῳ	ταύτῃ	τούτῳ
	A.	τοῦτον	ταύτην	τοῦτο
Plur.	N., V.	οὗτοι	αὗται	ταῦτα
	G.	τούτων	τούτων	τούτων
	D.	τούτοις	ταύταις	τούτοις
	A.	τούτους	ταύτας	ταῦτα

42. Demonstrative pronoun/adjective ἐκεῖνος:

		M.	F.	N.
Sing.	N.	ἐκεῖνος	ἐκείνη	ἐκεῖνο
	G.	ἐκείνου	ἐκείνης	ἐκείνου
	D.	ἐκείνῳ	ἐκείνῃ	ἐκείνῳ
	A.	ἐκεῖνον	ἐκείνην	ἐκεῖνο
Plur.	N., V.	ἐκεῖνοι	ἐκεῖναι	ἐκεῖνα
	G.	ἐκείνων	ἐκείνων	ἐκείνων
	D.	ἐκείνοις	ἐκείναις	ἐκείνοις
	A.	ἐκείνους	ἐκείνας	ἐκεῖνα

43. Reciprocal pronoun:

		M.	F.	N.
Plur.	G.	ἀλλήλων	ἀλλήλων	ἀλλήλων
	D.	ἀλλήλοις	ἀλλήλαις	ἀλλήλοις
	A.	ἀλλήλους	ἀλλήλας	ἀλλήλα

44. First person reflexive pronouns:

		M.	F.
Sing.	G.	ἐμαυτοῦ	ἐμαυτῆς
	D.	ἐμαυτῷ	ἐμαυτῇ
	A.	ἐμαυτόν	ἐμαυτήν
Plur.	G.	ἡμῶν αὐτῶν	ἡμῶν αὐτῶν
	D.	ἡμῖν αὐτοῖς	ἡμῖν αὐταῖς
	A.	ἡμᾶς αὐτούς	ἡμᾶς αὐτάς

45. Second person reflexive pronouns:

		M.	F.
Sing.	G.	σεαυτοῦ	σεαυτῆς
	D.	σεαυτῷ	σεαυτῇ
	A.	σεαυτόν	σεαυτήν
Plur.	G.	ὑμῶν αὐτῶν	ὑμῶν αὐτῶν
	D.	ὑμῖν αὐτοῖς	ὑμῖν αὐταῖς
	A.	ὑμᾶς αὐτούς	ὑμᾶς αὐτάς

N.B.: A variant form exists without the **ε** in the singular.

46. Third person reflexive pronouns:

		M.	F.	N.
Sing.	G.	ἑαυτοῦ	ἑαυτῆς	ἑαυτοῦ
	D.	ἑαυτῷ	ἑαυτῇ	ἑαυτῷ
	A.	ἑαυτόν	ἑαυτήν	ἑαυτό
Plur.	G.	ἑαυτῶν	ἑαυτῶν	ἑαυτῶν
	D.	ἑαυτοῖς	ἑαυταῖς	ἑαυτοῖς
	A.	ἑαυτούς	ἑαυτάς	ἑαυτά

N.B.: A variant form exists in the singular without the initial **ε** and with the rough breathing on the **αυ**. The third person plurals frequently substitute for the first and second person plurals.

47. Interrogative pronouns or adjectives:

		M. & F.	N.
Sing.	N.	τίς	τί
	G.	τίνος/τοῦ	τίνος/τοῦ
	D.	τίνι/τῷ	τίνι/τῷ
	A.	τίνα	τί
Plur.	N., V.	τίνες	τίνα
	G.	τίνων	τίνων
	D.	τίσι	τίσι
	A.	τίνας	τίνα

48. Indefinite pronouns:

		M. & F.	N.
Sing.	N.	τις	τι
	G.	τινός/του	τινός/του
	D.	τινί/τῳ	τινί/τῳ
	A.	τινά	τι
Plur.	N., V.	τινές	τινά
	G.	τινῶν	τινῶν
	D.	τισί	τισί
	A.	τινάς	τινά

49. Relative pronouns:

		M.	F.	N.
Sing.	N.	ὅς	ἥ	ὅ
	G.	οὗ	ἧς	οὗ
	D.	ᾧ	ᾗ	ᾧ
	A.	ὅν	ἥν	ὅ
Plur.	N., V.	οἵ	ἅι	ἅ
	G.	ὧν	ὧν	ὧν
	D.	οἷς	αἷς	οἷς
	A.	οὕς	ἅς	ἅ

N.B.: Gender and number of the relative are determined by the antecedent, the case by the use in its own clause.

Numerals

50. The cardinal number εἷς:

		M.	F.	N.
Sing.	N.	εἷς	μία	ἕν
	G.	ἑνός	μιᾶς	ἑνός
	D.	ἑνί	μιᾷ	ἑνί
	A.	ἕνα	μίαν	ἕν

51. The cardinal numbers δύο and τρεῖς:

		M., F., N.	M. & F.	N.
Plur.	N.	δύο	τρεῖς	τρία
	G.	δύο	τριῶν	τριῶν
	D.	δυσίν	τρισί(ν)	τρισί(ν)
	A.	δύο	τρεῖς	τρία

N.B.: The cardinal number δύο may be treated as indeclinable.

52. The cardinal number τέσσαρες:

		M. & F.	N.
Plur.	N.	τέσσαρες	τέσσαρα
	G.	τεσσάρων	τεσσάρων
	D.	τέσσαρσι(ν)	τέσσαρσι(ν)
	A.	τέσσαρας	τέσσαρα

Verbs

53. The conjugation of the regular **ω** verbs:

A. Present

	Active	Middle or Passive	
1. Indicative	λύω	First Person Sing.	λύομαι
	λύεις	Second Person Sing.	λύῃ/λύει
	λύει	Third Person Sing.	λύεται
	λύομεν	First Person Plur.	λυόμεθα
	λύετε	Second Person Plur.	λύεσθε
	λύουσι(ν)	Third Person Plur.	λύονται
2. Subjunctive	λύω		λύωμαι
	λύῃς		λύῃ
	λύῃ		λύηται
	λύωμεν		λυώμεθα
	λύητε		λύησθε
	λύωσι(ν)		λύωνται

3.	Imperative	λῦε	λύου
		λυέτω	λυέσθω
		λύετε	λύεσθε
		λυέτωσαν	λυέσθωσαν
4.	Infinitive	λύειν	λύεσθαι
5.	Participle	λύων	λυόμενος
		λύουσα	λυομένη
		λῦον	λυόμενον

B. Future

		Active	Middle
1.	Indicative	λύσω	λύομαι
		λύσεις	λύσῃ/λύσει
		λύσει	λύσεται
		λύσομεν	λυσόμεθα
		λύσετε	λύσεσθε
		λύσουσι(ν)	λύσονται
2.	Infinitive	λύσειν	λύσεσθαι
3.	Participle	λύσων	λυσόμενος
		λύσουσα	λυσομένη
		λῦσον	λυσόμενον

N.B.: The future passive will be cited below with the aorist passive.

C. Imperfect

	Active	Middle or Passive
Indicative	ἔλυον	ἐλυόμην
	ἔλυες	ἐλύου
	ἔλυε(ν)	ἐλύετο
	ἐλύομεν	ἐλυόμεθα
	ἐλύετε	ἐλύεσθε
	ἔλυον	ἐλύοντο

D. First Aorist

		Active	Middle
1.	Indicative	ἔλυσα	ἐλυσάμην
		ἔλυσας	ἐλύσω
		ἔλυσε(ν)	ἐλύσατο
		ἐλύσαμεν	ἐλυσάμεθα
		ἐλύσατε	ἐλύσασθε
		ἔλυσαν	ἐλύσαντο
2.	Subjunctive	λύσω	λύσωμαι
		λύσῃς	λύσῃ
		λύσῃ	λύσηται
		λύσωμεν	λυσώμεθα
		λύσητε	λύσησθε
		λύσωσι(ν)	λύσωνται
3.	Imperative	λύσον	λῦσαι
		λυσάτω	λυσάσθω
		λύσατε	λύσασθε
		λυσάτωσαν	λυσάσθωσαν
4.	Infinitive	λῦσαι	λύσασθαι
5.	Participle	λύσας	λυσάμενος
		λύσασα	λυσαμένη
		λῦσαν	λυσάμενον

E. First Perfect

		Active	Middle or Passive
1.	Indicative	λέλυκα	λέλυμαι
		λέλυκας	λέλυσαι
		λέλυκε(ν)	λέλυται
		λελύκαμεν	λελύμεθα
		λελύκατε	λέλυσθε
		λελύκασι(ν)	λέλυνται

2.	Infinitive	λελυκέναι	λελύσθαι
3.	Participle	λελυκώς	λελυμένος
		λελυκυῖα	λελυμένη
		λελυκός	λελυμένον

F. Pluperfect

	Active	Middle or Passive
Indicative	(ἐ)λελύκειν	(ἐ)λελύμην
	(ἐ)λελύκεις	(ἐ)λέλυσο
	(ἐ)λελύκει(ν)	(ἐ)λέλυτο
	(ἐ)λελύκειμεν	(ἐ)λελύμεθα
	(ἐ)λελύκειτε	(ἐ)λέλυσθε
	(ἐ)λελύκεισαν	(ἐ)λέλυντο

G. First Aorist Passive / First Future Passive

1.	Indicative	ἐλύθην	λυθήσομαι
		ἐλύθης	λυθήσῃ/λυθήσει
		ἐλύθη	λυθήσεται
		ἐλύθημεν	λυθησόμεθα
		ἐλύθητε	λυθήσεσθε
		ἐλύθησαν	λυθήσονται
2.	Subjunctive	λυθῶ	
		λυθῇς	
		λυθῇ	
		λυθῶμεν	
		λυθῆτε	
		λυθῶσι	
3.	Imperative	λύθητι	
		λυθήτω	
		λύθητε	
		λυθήτωσαν	
4.	Infinitive	λυθῆναι	λυθήσεσθαι

5.	Participle	λυθείς	λυθησόμενος
		λυθεῖσα	λυθησομένη
		λυθέν	λυθησόμενον

54. Some verbs show a second aorist:

Second Aorist

	Active	Middle or Passive
Indicative	ἔλιπον	ἐλιπόμην
	ἔλιπες	ἐλίπου
	ἔλιπε(ν)	ἐλίπετο
	ἐλίπομεν	ἐλιπόμεθα
	ἐλίπετε	ἐλίπεσθε
	ἔλιπον	ἐλιπόντο
Subjunctive	λίπω	λίπωμαι
	λίπῃς	λίπῃ
	λίπῃ	λίπηται
	λίπωμεν	λιπώμεθα
	λίπητε	λίπησθε
	λίπωσι	λίπωνται
Imperative	λίπε	λίπου
	λιπέτω	λιπέσθω
	λίπετε	λίπεσθε
	λιπέτωσαν	λιπέσθωσαν
Infinitive	λιπεῖν	λιπέσθαι
Participle	λιπών	λιπόμενος
	λιποῦσα	λιπομένη
	λιπόν	λιπόμενον

55. Contracted verb with stem in **α**:

Present

	Active		Middle or Passive	
Indicative	τιμῶ	(αω)	τιμῶμαι	(αω)
	τιμᾷς	(αει)	τιμᾷ	(αη)
	τιμᾷ	(αει)	τιμᾶται	(αε)
	τιμῶμεν	(αο)	τιμώμεθα	(αο)
	τιμᾶτε	(αε)	τιμᾶσθε	(αε)
	τιμῶσι(ν)	(αου)	τιμῶνται	(αο)
Subjunctive	τιμῶ	(αω)	τιμῶμαι	(αω)
	τιμᾷς	(αῃ)	τιμᾷ	(αῃ)
	τιμᾷ	(αῃ)	τιμᾶται	(αη)
	τιμῶμεν	(αω)	τιμώμεθα	(αω)
	τιμᾶτε	(αη)	τιμᾶσθε	(αη)
	τιμῶσι(ν)	(αω)	τιμῶνται	(αω)
Imperative	τίμα	(αε)	τιμῶ	(αου)
	τιμάτω	(αε)	τιμάσθω	(αε)
	τιμᾶτε	(αε)	τιμᾶσθε	(αε)
	τιμάτωσαν	(αε)	τιμάσθωσαν	(αε)
Infinitive	τιμᾶν	(αει)	τιμᾶσθαι	(αε)
Participle	τιμῶν	(αω)	τιμώμενος	(αο)
	τιμῶσα	(αου)	τιμωμένη	(αο)
	τιμῶν	(αο)	τιμώμενον	(αο)

Imperfect

	Active		Middle or Passive	
Indicative	ἐτίμων	(αο)	ἐτιμώμην	(αο)
	ἐτίμας	(αε)	ἐτιμῶ	(αου)
	ἐτίμα	(αε)	ἐτιμᾶτο	(αε)
	ἐτιμῶμεν	(αο)	ἐτιμώμεθα	(αο)
	ἐτιμᾶτε	(αε)	ἐτιμᾶσθε	(αε)
	ἐτίμων	(αο)	ἐτιμῶντο	(αο)

56. Contracted verb with stem in **ε**:

Present

	Active		Middle or Passive	
Indicative	φιλῶ	(εω)	φιλοῦμαι	(εο)
	φιλεῖς	(εει)	φιλῇ	(εη)
	φιλεῖ	(εει)	φιλεῖται	(εε)
	φιλοῦμεν	(εο)	φιλούμεθα	(εο)
	φιλεῖτε	(εε)	φιλεῖσθε	(εε)
	φιλοῦσι(ν)	(εου)	φιλοῦνται	(εο)
Subjunctive	φιλῶ	(εω)	φιλῶμαι	(εω)
	φιλῇς	(εη)	φιλῇ	(εη)
	φιλῇ	(εη)	φιλῆται	(εη)
	φιλῶμεν	(εω)	φιλώμεθα	(εω)
	φιλῆτε	(εη)	φιλῆσθε	(εη)
	φιλῶσι(ν)	(εω)	φιλῶνται	(εω)
Imperative	φίλει	(εε)	φιλοῦ	(εο)
	φιλείτω	(εε)	φιλείσθω	(εε)
	φιλεῖτε	(εε)	φιλεῖσθε	(εε)
	φιλείτωσαν	(εε)	φιλείσθωσαν	(εε)
Infinitive	φιλεῖν	(εε)	φιλεῖσθαι	(εε)
Participle	φιλῶν	(εω)	φιλούμενος	(εο)
	φιλοῦσα	(εου)	φιλουμένη	(εο)
	φιλοῦν	(εο)	φιλούμενος	(εο)

Imperfect

	Active		Middle or Passive	
Indicative	ἐφίλουν	(εο)	ἐφιλούμην	(εο)
	ἐφίλεις	(εε)	ἐφιλοῦ	(εου)
	ἐφίλει	(εε)	ἐφιλεῖτο	(εε)
	ἐφιλοῦμεν	(εο)	ἐφιλούμεθα	(εο)
	ἐφιλεῖτε	(εε)	ἐφιλεῖσθε	(εε)
	ἐφίλουν	(εο)	ἐφιλοῦντο	(εο)

57. Contracted verb with stem in **o**:

Present

	Active		Middle or Passive	
Indicative	δηλῶ	(οω)	δηλοῦμαι	(οο)
	δηλοῖς	(οει)	δηλοῖ	(οῃ)
	δηλοῖ	(οει)	δηλοῦται	(οε)
	δηλοῦμεν	(οο)	δηλούμεθα	(οο)
	δηλοῦτε	(οε)	δηλοῦσθε	(οε)
	δηλοῦσι(ν)	(οου)	δηλοῦνται	(οο)
Subjunctive	δηλῶ	(οω)	δηλῶμαι	(οω)
	δηλοῖς	(οῃ)	δηλοῖ	(οῃ)
	δηλοῖ	(οῃ)	δηλῶται	(οη)
	δηλῶμεν	(οω)	δηλώμεθα	(οω)
	δηλῶτε	(οη)	δηλῶσθε	(οη)
	δηλῶσι(ν)	(οω)	δηλῶνται	(οω)
Imperative	δήλου	(οε)	δηλοῦ	(οου)
	δηλούτω	(οε)	δηλούσθω	(οε)
	δηλοῦτε	(οε)	δηλοῦσθε	(οε)
	δηλούτωσαν	(οε)	δηλούσθωσαν	(οε)
Infinitive	δηλοῦν	(οει)	δηλοῦσθαι	(οε)
Participle	δηλῶν	(οω)	δηλούμενος	(οο)
	δηλοῦσα	(οου)	δηλουμένη	(οο)
	δηλοῦν	(οο)	δηλούμενον	(οο)

Imperfect

	Active		Middle or Passive	
Indicative	ἐδήλουν	(οο)	ἐδηλούμην	(οο)
	ἐδήλους	(οε)	ἐδηλοῦ	(οου)
	ἐδήλου	(οε)	ἐδηλοῦτο	(οε)
	ἐδηλοῦμεν	(οο)	ἐδηλούμεθα	(οο)
	ἐδηλοῦτε	(οε)	ἐδηλούσθε	(οε)
	ἐδήλουν	(οο)	ἐδηλοῦντο	(οο)

58. The conjugation of the **μι** verbs with stem in **δο**:

Present

	Active	Middle or Passive
Indicative	δίδωμι	δίδομαι
	δίδως	δίδοσαι
	δίδωσι(ν)	δίδοται
	δίδομεν	διδόμεθα
	δίδοτε	δίδοσθε
	διδόασι(ν)	δίδονται
Subjunctive	διδῶ	διδῶμαι
	διδῷς	διδῷ
	διδῷ	διδῶται
	διδῶμεν	διδώμεθα
	διδῶτε	διδῶσθε
	διδῶσι	διδῶνται
Imperative	δίδου	δίδοσο
	διδότω	διδόσθω
	δίδοτε	δίδοσθε
	διδότωσαν	διδόσθωσαν
Infinitive	διδόναι	δίδοσθαι
Participle	διδούς	διδόμενος
	διδοῦσα	διδομένη
	διδόν	διδόμενον

Imperfect

	Active	Middle or Passive
Indicative	ἐδίδουν	ἐδιδόμην
	ἐδίδους	ἐδίδοσο
	ἐδίδου	ἐδίδοτο
	ἐδίδομεν	ἐδιδόμεθα
	ἐδίδοτε	ἐδίδοσθε
	ἐδίδοσαν/ἐδίδουν	ἐδίδοντο

Aorist

	Active	Middle
Indicative	ἔδωκα	ἐδόμην
	ἔδωκας	ἔδου
	ἔδωκε	ἔδοτο
	ἐδώκαμεν	ἐδόμεθα
	ἐδώκατε	ἔδοσθε
	ἔδωκαν	ἔδοντο

N.B. The second aorist active indicative shows forms only in the plural: ἔδομεν, ἔδοτε, ἔδοσαν.

Subjunctive	δῶ	δῶμαι
	δῷς	δῷ
	δῷ	δῶται
	δῶμεν	δώμεθα
	δῶτε	δῶσθε
	δῶσι(ν)	δῶνται
Imperative	δός	δοῦ
	δότω	δόσθω
	δότε	δόσθε
	δότωσαν	δόσθωσαν
Infinitive	δοῦναι	δόσθαι
Participle	δούς	δόμενος
	διδοῦσα	δομένη
	δόν	δόμενον

59. The conjugation of the **μι** verbs with stem in **θε**:

Present

	Active	Middle or Passive
Indicative	τίθημι	τίθεμαι
	τίθης	τίθεσαι
	τίθησι(ν)	τίθεται
	τίθεμεν	τιθέμεθα
	τίθετε	τίθεσθε
	τιθέασι(ν)	τίθενται
Subjunctive	τιθῶ	τιθῶμαι
	τιθῇς	τιθῇ
	τιθῇ	τιθῆται
	τιθῶμεν	τιθώμεθα
	τιθῆτε	τιθῆσθε
	τιθῶσι(ν)	τιθῶνται
Imperative	τίθει	τίθεσο
	τίθετω	τιθέσθω
	τιθέτε	τιθέσθε
	τιθέτωσαν	τιθέσθωσαν
Infinitive	τιθέναι	τιθέσθαι
Participle	τιθείς	τιθέμενος
	τιθεῖσα	τιθεμένη
	τιθέν	τιθέμενον

Imperfect

	Active	Middle or Passive
Indicative	ἐτίθην	ἐτιθέμην
	ἐτίθεις	ἐτίθεσο
	ἐτίθει	ἐτίθετο
	ἐτίθεμεν	ἐτιθέμεθα
	ἐτίθετε	ἐτίθεσθε
	ἐτίθεσαν	ἐτίθεντο

Aorist

	Active	Middle
Indicative	ἔθηκα	ἐθέμην
	ἔθηκας	ἔθου
	ἔθηκε	ἔθετο
	ἐθήκαμεν	ἐθέμεθα
	ἐθήκατε	ἔθεσθε
	ἔθηκαν	ἔθεντο
Subjunctive	θῶ	θῶμαι
	θῇς	θῇ
	θῇ	θῆται
	θῶμεν	θώμεθα
	θῆτε	θῆσθε
	θῶσι(ν)	θῶνται
Imperative	θές	θοῦ
	θέτω	θέσθω
	θέτε	θέσθε
	θέτωσαν	θέσθωσαν
Infinitive	θεῖναι	θέσθαι
Participle	θείς	θέμενος
	θεῖσα	θεμένη
	θέν	θέμενον

60. The conjugation of the **μι** verbs with stem in **στα**:

Present

	Active	Middle or Passive
Indicative	ἵστημι	ἵσταμαι
	ἵστης	ἵστασαι
	ἵστησι(ν)	ἵσταται
	ἵσταμεν	ἱστάμεθα
	ἵστατε	ἵστασθε
	ἱστᾶσι(ν)	ἵστανται
Subjunctive	ἱστῶ	ἱστῶμαι
	ἱστῇς	ἱστῇ
	ἱστῇ	ἱστῆται
	ἱστῶμεν	ἱστώμεθα
	ἱστῆτε	ἱστῆσθε
	ἱστῶσι(ν)	ἱστῶνται
Imperative	ἵστη	ἵστασο
	ἱστάτω	ἱστάσθω
	ἵστατε	ἵστασθε
	ἱστάτωσαν	ἱστάσθωσαν
Infinitive	ἱστάναι	ἵστασθαι
Participle	ἱστάς	ἱστάμενος
	ἱστᾶσα	ἱσταμένη
	ἱστάν	ἱστάμενον

Imperfect

	Active	Middle or Passive
Indicative	ἵστην	ἱστάμην
	ἵστης	ἵστασο
	ἵστη	ἵστατο
	ἵσταμεν	ἱστάμεθα
	ἵστατε	ἵστασθε
	ἵστασαν	ἵσταντο

61. The second aorist of ἵστημι and γινώσκω:

	Active	
Indicative	ἔστην	ἔγνων
	ἔστης	ἔγνως
	ἔστη	ἔγνω
	ἔστημεν	ἔγνωμεν
	ἔστητε	ἔγνωτε
	ἔστησαν	ἔγνωσαν
Subjunctive	στῶ	γνῶ
	στῇς	γνῷς
	στῇ	γνῷ
	στῶμεν	γνῶμεν
	στῆτε	γνῶτε
	στῶσι(ν)	γνῶσι
Imperative	στῆθι	γνῶθι
	στήτω	γνώτω
	στῆτε	γνώτε
	στήτωσαν	γνώτωσαν
Infinitive	στῆναι	γνῶναι
Participle	στάς	γνούς
	στᾶσα	γνοῦσα
	στάν	γνόν

N.B.: The second aorist of ἵστημι is intransitive.

62. The conjugation of οἶδα:

	Perfect	Pluperfect
Indicative	οἶδα	ᾔδειν
	οἶδας	ᾔδεις
	οἶδε(ν)	ᾔδει
	οἴδαμεν	ᾔδειμεν
	οἴδατε	ᾔδειτε
	οἴδασι(ν)	ᾔδεισαν
Subjunctive	εἰδῶ	
	εἰδῇς	
	εἰδῇ	
	εἰδῶμεν	
	εἰδῆτε	
	εἰδῶσι(ν)	
Imperative	ἴσθι	
	ἴστω	
	ἴστε	
	ἴστωσαν	
Infinitive	εἰδέναι	
Participle	εἰδώς, εἰδυῖα, εἰδός	

63. The conjugation of εἰμί:

	Present	Imperfect	Future
Indicative	εἰμί	ἤμην	ἔσομαι
	εἶ	ἦς	ἔσῃ
	ἐστί(ν)	ἦν	ἔσται
	ἐσμέν	ἦμεν	ἐσόμεθα
	ἐστέ	ἦτε	ἔσεσθε
	εἰσί(ν)	ἦσαν	ἔσονται
Subjunctive	ὦ		
	ᾖς		
	ᾖ		
	ὦμεν		
	ἦτε		
	ὦσι(ν)		
Imperative	ἴσθι		
	ἔστω		
	ἔστε		
	ἔστωσαν		
Infinitive	εἶναι		
Participle	ὤν, οὖσα, ὄν		

64. **Nominative Case**

The nominative case names the subject of the finite or conjugated verb, predicate nouns, and predicate adjectives.

1. ἐγένετο **Ἰωάννης**. ***John*** *came.*
2. **πᾶσα ἡ Ἰουδαία χώρα** ἐξεπορεύετο. ***The whole Judean countryside*** *continually went out.*
3. **ἐγὼ** ἐβάπτισα ὑμᾶς. ***I*** *baptized you.*
4. ἦσαν γὰρ **ἁλιεῖς**. *For they were* ***fishermen***. (predicate nominative)

5. **κύριός** ἐστιν . . . τοῦ σαββάτου. *He is **Lord** of the Sabbath.* (predicate nominative)
6. Ἰωσὴφ δὲ ὁ ἀνὴρ αὐτῆς ἦν **δίκαιος**. *But Joseph her husband was **just**.* (predicate adjective)

65. **Genitive Case**

The genitive case frequently indicates possession and depends on another noun.

The genitive of **possession** denotes ownership or belonging:

1. ἰδοὺ ἄγγελος **κυρίου** . . . ἐφάνη. *Behold an angel of the **Lord** appeared.*
2. τὰ **Καίσαρος**. *What is **Caesar's**.*
3. τὸν ἄγγελόν **μου**. ***My** messenger.*

The genitive **absolute** consists of a noun and a circumstantial participle in the genitive case. They are syntactically independent of the main clause. A circumstantial participle may express time, cause, concession, condition, and other circumstances. It needs to be sensitively interpreted and translated into English as a clause:

1. **Ὀψίας δὲ γενομένης**. ***but when evening came.***
2. **γενομένης θλίψεως** διὰ τὸν λόγον. ***when trouble comes** because of the word.*
3. ὁ γὰρ Ἰησοῦς ἐξένευσεν **ὄχλου ὄντος** ἐν τῷ τόπῳ. *For Jesus had withdrawn **because a crowd was** in the place.*
4. ἥ τε θάλασσα **ἀνέμου μεγάλου πνέοντος** διεγείρετο. *And the sea arose **because a great wind was blowing**.*

The **appositional** genitive gives a more explicit identification to a more general word:

1. Ἀρχὴ τοῦ εὐαγγελίου Ἰησοῦ Χριστοῦ [**υἱοῦ θεοῦ**]. *The beginning of the gospel of Jesus Christ, **the Son of God**.*
2. ἀπῆλθεν ὁ Ἰησοῦς πέραν τῆς θαλάσσης **τῆς Γαλιλαίας**. *Jesus went beyond the sea **of Galilee**.*

The genitive of **comparison** is used with comparative adjectives or adverbs to indicate a comparison:

1. τὸ ἀγαπᾶν αὐτὸν . . . περισσότερόν ἐστιν **πάντων τῶν ὁλοκαυτωμάτων καὶ θυσιῶν**. *To love Him . . . is more* ***than all whole burnt offerings and sacrifices.***
2. ἡ χήρα αὕτη πλεῖον ἡ πτωχὴ **πάντων** ἔβαλεν **τῶν βαλλόντων** εἰς τὸ γαζοφυλάκιον. *This poor widow cast in more* ***than all who cast into the treasury.***
3. μείζω **τούτων** ὄψῃ. *You will see greater things* ***than these.***
4. μὴ σὺ μείζων εἶ **τοῦ πατρὸς** ἡμῶν; *You are not greater* ***than our father,*** *are you?*
5. μείζονα **τούτων** δείξει αὐτῷ ἔργα. *He will show Him greater works* ***than these.***

The genitive of **measure** with the preposition expresses distance of space:

1. ἦν δὲ ἡ Βηθανία ὡς **ἀπὸ σταδίων δεκαπέντε**. *But Bethany was about* ***fifteen stades away.***
2. οὐ γὰρ ἦσαν μακρὰν ἀπὸ τῆς γῆς ἀλλὰ ὡς **ἀπὸ πηχῶν διακοσίων**. *They were not far from the land, but about* ***two hundred cubits away.***

The **objective** genitive is the object of a verbal noun:

1. ἐγένετο Ἰωάννης . . . κηρύσσων βάπτισμα μετανοίας εἰς ἄφεσιν **ἁμαρτιῶν**. *John came . . . preaching baptism of repentence for the remission* ***of sins.***
2. ποιήσω ὑμᾶς γενέσθαι ἁλιεῖς **ἀνθρώπων**. *I will make you fishers* ***of men.***
3. οὐδεὶς μέντοι παρρησίᾳ ἐλάλει περὶ αὐτοῦ διὰ τὸν φόβον **τῶν Ἰουδαίων**. *Yet no one spoke openly about Him for fear* ***of the Jews.***
4. ἤγειρεν αὐτὴν κρατήσας **τῆς χειρός**. *After He had taken a hold* ***of her hand,*** *He lifted her.*

The **partitive** genitive expresses part of the whole. The partitive idea is frequently expressed with ἐκ and the genitive:

1. ὅς . . . μικρότερον ὂν **πάντων τῶν σπερμάτων** τῶν ἐπὶ τῆς γῆς. *Which . . . is the smallest **of all the seeds** that are upon the earth.*
2. Οὗτος **ἐξ αὐτῶν** ἐστιν. *This is one **of them**.*
3. ἰδόντες τινὰς **τῶν μαθητῶν** αὐτοῦ ὅτι . . . ἐσθίουσιν. *When they saw that some of his disciples were eating.*
4. ἀλλ' εἰσὶν **ἐξ ὑμῶν** τινες οἳ οὐ πιστεύουσιν. *But there are some **of you** who do not believe.*

The genitive of **price** or **value** indicates the price at which something is sold or bought:

1. Ἀπελθόντες ἀγοράσωμεν **δηναρίων διακοσίων** ἄρτους; *Shall we go and buy bread **at the price of two hundred denarii**?*
2. **Διακοσίων δηναρίων** ἄρτοι οὐκ ἀρκοῦσιν αὐτοῖς. *Loaves of bread **at the price of two hundred denarii** are not sufficient for them.*
3. Διὰ τί τοῦτο τὸ μύρον οὐκ ἐπράθη **τριακοσίων δηναρίων**; *Why was this ointment not sold **for three hundred denarii**?*

The genitive of **time** expresses time within which an action takes place:

1. **νυκτὸς καὶ ἡμέρας**. ***By night and day.***
2. Οὐχὶ δώδεκα ὧραί εἰσιν **τῆς ἡμέρας**; *Are there not twelve hours **in the day**?*
3. οὗτος ἦλθεν πρὸς αὐτὸν **νυκτὸς**. *He came to Him **at night**.*
4. **Ὄρθρου** δὲ πάλιν παρεγένετο εἰς τὸ ἱερόν. *And **in the early morning** He again came into the temple.*
5. **ἀλεκτοροφωνίας**. ***At cockcrow.***

66. **Dative Case**

The dative case often expresses the person *to whom* the action of a verb pertains other than the subject or direct object. It is frequently rendered in English by the prepositions *to* or *for.*

The dative case is the **indirect object** of the verb:

1. ὕπαγε σεαυτὸν δεῖξον **τῷ ἱερεῖ**. *Go and show yourself* ***to the priest.***
2. ἔδωκεν ἐξουσίαν **τοῖς μαθηταῖς**. *He gave power* ***to the disciples.***
3. πάντα ἔδωκεν **τῷ υἱῷ** ὁ πατὴρ. *The Father gave all things* ***to the Son.***
4. ἐφανέρωσεν ἑαυτὸν πάλιν ὁ Ἰησοῦς **τοῖς μαθηταῖς**. *Jesus showed Himself again* ***to the disciples.***
5. μὴ δυνάμενοι προσενέγκαι **αὐτῷ**. *Since they were not able to bring him* ***to Him.***

The dative case expresses **means**:

1. ἐγὼ ἐβάπτισα ὑμᾶς **ὕδατι**. *I baptized you* ***with water.***
2. ἐὰν μὴ **πυγμῇ** νίψωνται τὰς χεῖρας. *unless they wash their hands* ***with a fist.***
3. καὶ ἐξέμαξεν **ταῖς θριξὶν** αὐτῆς τοὺς πόδας αὐτοῦ. *And she wiped His feet* ***with*** *her* ***hair.***
4. καὶ νῦν δόξασόν με σύ, πάτερ, **τῇ δόξῃ**. *And now, O Father, magnify me* ***with glory.***
5. ὁ δὲ Ἰησοῦς **τῷ δακτύλῳ** κατέγραφεν εἰς τὴν γῆν. *But Jesus wrote* ***with His finger*** *on the ground.*

The dative case expresses **manner**:

1. τὸ πνεῦμα τὸ ἀκάθαρτον . . . φωνῆσαν **φωνῇ μεγάλῃ** ἐξῆλθεν ἐξ αὐτοῦ. *The unclean spirit, after crying out* ***with a loud voice,*** *departed.*
2. ἐξέστησαν εὐθὺς **ἐκστάσει μεγάλῃ**. *They were at once amazed* ***with great amazement.***
3. **θανάτῳ** τελευτάτω. *Let him end his life* ***by death.***

The dative case shows **possession**:

1. Πόθεν **τούτῳ** ταῦτα; *From where does* ***He*** *have these precepts?*
2. γνώσονται πάντες ὅτι **ἐμοὶ** μαθηταί ἐστε. *All will know that you are* ***my*** *disciples.*
3. Πόσος χρόνος ἐστὶν ὡς τοῦτο γέγονεν **αὐτῷ**; *How long has* ***he*** *had this?*
4. πάντες γὰρ ἐκ τοῦ περισσεύοντος **αὐτοῖς** ἔβαλον. *They all cast in from* ***their*** *surplus.*
5. Τί ὄνομά **σοι**; *What is* ***your*** *name?*

The dative of **time** indicates a specified period of time when something takes place:

1. **τοῖς σάββασιν** . . . ἐδίδασκεν. *He taught* **on the Sabbath.**
2. **τῇ ἡμέρᾳ τῇ τρίτῃ** γάμος ἐγένετο. **On the third day** *there was a marriage.*
3. **Τεσσαράκοντα καὶ ἓξ ἔτεσιν** οἰκοδομήθη ὁ ναὸς οὗτος. *This temple was built in* ***forty-six years.***
4. καὶ ἀπέστειλεν . . . **τῷ καιρῷ** δοῦλον. *And he sent a servant* ***at the proper time.***

The dative of **degree of difference** is used with a comparative adjective to indicate by how much one item differs from another:

1. ὁ δὲ **πολλῷ μᾶλλον** ἔκραζεν. *But he cried out* ***all the more*** (literally: *more by much*).
2. **πολλῷ** πλείους ἐπίστευσαν διὰ τὸν λόγον αὐτοῦ. ***Many*** *more* (literally: *more by much*) *believed because of* His *word.*

The dative of **advantage** or **disadvantage** pertains to persons or things that are either helped or harmed by an action.

1. ἐν ᾧ μέτρῳ μετρεῖτε μετρηθήσεται **ὑμῖν**. *For with what measure you measure, it will be measured out* ***to you.***
2. τοὺς δύο ἰχθύας ἐμέρισεν **πᾶσιν**. *He divided the two fishes* ***among them all.***
3. Τίς ἀποκυλίσει **ἡμῖν** τὸν λίθον ἐκ τῆς θύρας τοῦ μνημείου; *Who will roll away the stone from the tomb* ***for us?***

The **ethical dative** makes reference to a first or second person to denote interest of the speaker or the person spoken to in something said or done:

1. Τί ἐποίησέν **σοι**; *What did He do* ***for you****?*
2. Γινώσκετε τί πεποίηκα **ὑμῖν**; *Do you know what I have done* ***for you****?*
3. Τί **σοι** θέλεις ποιήσω; *What do you want me to do* ***for you****?*

67. **Accusative Case**

The accusative case commonly designates the direct object of a verb.

The accusative is the **direct object** of the verb:

1. Ἰδοὺ ἀποστέλλω **τὸν ἄγγελόν** μου. *Behold, I will send my* ***messenger****.*
2. ὅς κατασκευάσει **τὴν ὁδόν** σου. *Who will prepare your* ***way****.*
3. εἶδεν σχιζομένους **τοὺς οὐρανοὺς**. *He saw* ***the heavens*** *as they were opening.*
4. ἦλθες ἀπολέσαι **ἡμᾶς**; *Have You come to destroy* ***us****?*
5. ὕπαγε **σεαυτὸν** δεῖξον τῷ ἱερεῖ. *Go and show* ***yourself*** *to the priest.*

A noun in the accusative showing the same root or meaning as the verb is a **cognate** accusative. Occasionally the cognate accusative construction admits only a demonstrative pronoun or adjective as an object:

1. Τί **ταῦτα** διαλογίζεσθε; *Why do you ponder* ***these thoughts****?*
2. τὴν δικαίαν **κρίσιν** κρίνετε. *Judge righteous* ***judgment****.*
3. **πολλὰ** ἐπετίμα αὐτοῖς. *He gave them* ***many strict orders.***
4. Οὐκ ἀποκρίνῃ **οὐδέν** τί οὗτοί σου καταμαρτυροῦσιν; *Do you give* ***no response*** *to what these men testify against you?*

The accusative denotes **duration of time**:

1. ἦν ἐν τῇ ἐρήμῳ **τεσσαράκοντα ἡμέρας**. *He had been in the desert* ***forty days****.*

2. οὖσα ἐν ῥύσει αἵματος **δώδεκα ἔτη**. *Who had suffered from hemorrhages **twelve years**.*
3. ἔμεινεν ἐκεῖ **δύο ἡμέρας**. *He stayed there **two days**.*
4. Ἔτι **χρόνον μικρὸν** μεθ' ὑμῶν εἰμι. *I am still with you **a little time**.*

The accusative of **respect** limits a verb or an adjective in respect to parts of the body, qualities, or attributes:

1. ἀνέπεσαν οὖν οἱ ἄνδρες **τὸν ἀριθμὸν** ὡς πεντακισχίλιοι. *Then the men sat down, about five thousand **in number**.*

The accusative expresses the **subject** of an infinitive:

1. οὐκ ἤφιεν λαλεῖν **τὰ δαιμόνια**. *He would not allow **the demons** to speak.*
2. ὥστε ἐξίστασθαι **πάντας** καὶ δοξάζειν. *So that **all** were amazed and contined to glorify.*
3. Καὶ ἐγένετο κατακεῖσθαι **αὐτὸν.** *And it came to pass that **He** was reclining at the table.*
4. ὑψωθῆναι δεῖ **τὸν υἱὸν** τοῦ ἀνθρώπου. ***The Son** of Man must be lifted up.*
5. διὰ τὸ **αὐτὸν** πολλάκις . . . δεδέσθαι. *Because **he** had often been bound.*
6. πρὶν ἢ δὶς **ἀλέκτορα** φωνῆσαι. *Before **the cock** crows twice.*
7. ἰδὼν **αὐτοὺς** βασανιζομένους ἐν τῷ ἐλαύνειν. *When He saw that **they** were straining at the oars.*

Some verbs take a **double accusative**:

1. **οὓς** καὶ **ἀποστόλους** ὠνόμασεν. ***Whom** He also called **apostles**.*
2. ἐποίησεν **τὸ ὕδωρ οἶνον**. *He made **the water wine**.*
3. **πατέρα ἴδιον** ἔλεγεν **τὸν θεόν**. *He called **God His own Father**.*
4. ἠρώτων **αὐτὸν τὰς παραβολάς**. *They kept asking **Him about the parables.***
5. ἤρξατο διδάσκειν **αὐτοὺς πολλά**. *He began to teach **them many doctrines.***

68. **Vocative Case**

The vocative case is the case of **direct address.**

1. **Διδάσκαλε,** οὐ μέλει σοι ὅτι ἀπολλύμεθα; ***Master,*** *do you not care that we perish?*
2. Ἰ**ησοῦ υἱὲ** τοῦ θεοῦ τοῦ ὑψίστου. ***Jesus, Son*** *of the Most High God.*
3. Ἔξελθε **τὸ πνεῦμα τὸ ἀκάθαρτον** ἐκ τοῦ ἀνθρώπου. *Come out of this man,* ***evil spirit.***
4. **Θυγάτηρ,** ἡ πίστις σου σέσωκέν σε. ***Daughter,*** *your faith has saved you.*

69. **Apposition**

An appositive is a noun added to another noun or pronoun, further identifying it and standing in the same case with it unless it is an appositional genitive. It may appear in all cases.

1. Καθὼς γέγραπται ἐν τῷ Ἠσαΐᾳ **τῷ προφήτῃ.** *As it is written in Isaiah,* ***the prophet.***
2. παράγων παρὰ τὴν θάλασσαν **τῆς Γαλιλαίας.** *As He walked along the* ***Sea of Galilee.***
3. εἶδεν Σίμωνα καὶ Ἀνδρέαν **τὸν ἀδελφὸν** Σίμωνος. *He saw Simon and Andrew,* ***the brother*** *of Simon.*
4. ἦραν κλάσματα δώδεκα κοφίνων **πληρώματα.** *They gathered the broken pieces,* ***the contents*** *of twelve baskets full.*

70. **Conditions**

Conditions consist of a protasis, i.e., that which is put forth or proposed, and an apodosis, the conclusion. The protasis may precede or follow the apodosis. The negative of the protasis is usually μή, of the apodosis mostly οὐ.

A **simple** or **particular** condition (present or past) refers to an act that occurs or has occurred. The protasis expresses a general or particular truth: *if ever* (*whenever*); the apodosis describes the logical consequence of that condition as a repeated action or general truth. The verbs in both clauses frequently stand in the indicative. The apodosis may be in the subjunctive or imperative.

1. ὅταν αὐτὸν ἐθεώρουν, προσέπιπτον αὐτῷ. *Whenever they saw Him, they fell down before Him.*
2. εἰ ὁ Σατανᾶς ἀνέστη ἐφ' ἑαυτὸν καὶ ἐμερίσθη, οὐ δύναται στῆναι. *If Satan rises against himself and is divided, he cannot stand.*
3. ὃς γὰρ οὐκ ἔστιν καθ' ἡμῶν, ὑπὲρ ἡμῶν ἐστιν. *For whoever is not against us is for us.*
4. εἰ σὺ εἶ ὁ Χριστός, εἰπὲ ἡμῖν παρρησίᾳ. *If you are Christ, tell us openly.*
5. εἰ οὐ ποιῶ τὰ ἔργα τοῦ πατρός μου, μὴ πιστεύετέ μοι. *If I do not perform the works of my Father, do not believe me.*

A **future more vivid** condition makes a more positive statement that an action is likely to take place in the future. It is formed by ἐάν or ἄν with a subjunctive in the protasis and a future indicative or an equivalent form in the apodosis. The apodosis of a negative future more vivid condition frequently takes a subjunctive which is equivalent to a future indicative. οὐ μή strengthens a negation. A protasis may also be introduced by a relative pronoun or adverb instead of ἐάν. Since the subjunctive commonly connotes a future, the tenses refer to aspect rather than time: the present indicates progressive/repeated action; the aorist expresses a single act.

1. ὅταν ἀπαρθῇ ἀπ' αὐτῶν ὁ νυμφίος, καὶ τότε νηστεύσουσιν. *When the bridegroom is taken from them, even then they will fast.*
2. Ἐὰν ἅψωμαι τῶν ἱματίων αὐτοῦ, σωθήσομαι. *If I touch His garments, I will get well.*
3. Ὅπου ἐὰν εἰσέλθητε εἰς οἰκίαν, ἐκεῖ μένετε. *Wherever you go into a house, remain there.*
4. ἐὰν ἀπολύσω αὐτοὺς νήστεις εἰς οἶκον, ἐν τῇ ὁδῷ ἐκλυθήσονται. *If I let them go hungry to their homes, they will grow faint on their journey.*
5. ὃς γὰρ ἐὰν θέλῃ τὴν ψυχὴν αὐτοῦ σῶσαι ἀπολέσει αὐτήν. *Whoever wishes to save his life will lose it.*
6. ὅταν ἔλθῃ ἐκεῖνος, ἀναγγελεῖ ἡμῖν ἅπαντα. *When that one comes, He will tell us all things.*

A **present general** condition makes a factual statement about an action that is always true in present time. It is introduced by ἐάν or ἄν with a subjunctive in the protasis and a present indicative in the apodosis. A protasis may also be introduced by a relative pronoun or adverb with ἐάν or ἄν.

1. Ἐὰν θέλῃς δύνασαί με καθαρίσαι. *If you are willing, you are able to cleanse me.*
2. ἐὰν βασιλεία ἐφ' ἑαυτὴν μερισθῇ, οὐ δύναται σταθῆναι ἡ βασιλεία ἐκείνη. *If a kingdon is divided against itself, that kingdom cannot stand.*
3. ὃς δ' ἂν βλασφημήσῃ εἰς τὸ πνεῦμα τὸ ἅγιον, οὐκ ἔχει ἄφεσιν εἰς τὸν αἰῶνα. *Whoever blasphemes against the Holy Spirit does not ever have forgiveness.*
4. ὃς ἂν ποιήσῃ τὸ θέλημα τοῦ θεοῦ, οὗτος ἀδελφός μου καὶ ἀδελφὴ καὶ μήτηρ ἐστίν. *Whoever does the will of God, this is my brother and my sister and my mother.*
5. ἃ γὰρ ἂν ἐκεῖνος ποιῇ, ταῦτα καὶ ὁ υἱὸς ὁμοίως ποιεῖ. *For whatever He does, these also the Son does likewise.*
6. ὃς ἂν ἐμὲ δέχηται, οὐκ ἐμὲ δέχεται ἀλλὰ τὸν ἀποστείλαντά με. *Whoever receives me does not receive me but Him who sent me.*

A **present contrary to fact** condition indicates that the action is not fulfilled in the present time. It is constructed with εἰ and an imperfect indicative in the protasis and an imperfect indicative plus ἄν in the apodosis. However, ἄν is not required in New Testament usage.

1. εἰ γὰρ ἐπιστεύετε Μωϋσεῖ, ἐπιστεύετε ἂν ἐμοί. *For if you believed Moses, you would believe me.*
2. Εἰ ὁ θεὸς πατὴρ ὑμῶν ἦν, ἠγαπᾶτε ἂν ἐμέ. *If God were your Father you would love me.*
3. εἰ μὴ ἦν οὗτος παρὰ θεοῦ, οὐκ ἠδύνατο ποιεῖν οὐδέν. *If this man were not of God, He could do nothing.*
4. Εἰ τυφλοὶ ἦτε, οὐκ ἂν εἴχετε ἁμαρτίαν. *If you were blind, you would have no sin.*

A **past contrary to fact** condition indicates that the action is not fulfilled in the past time. It is formed with εἰ plus the aorist indicative in the protasis and the aorist indicative plus ἄν in the apodosis. Past and present contrary to fact conditions are frequently mixed.

1. εἰ μὴ ἐκολόβωσεν κύριος τὰς ἡμέρας, οὐκ ἂν ἐσώθη πᾶσα σάρξ. *If the Lord had not shortened the days, no flesh would have been saved;*
2. καλὸν αὐτῷ εἰ οὐκ ἐγεννήθη ὁ ἄνθρωπος ἐκεῖνος. *It would have been/be better for him, if that man had not been born.* (The protasis could also be a present contrary to fact).
3. εἰ ἦς ὧδε οὐκ ἂν ἀπέθανεν ὁ ἀδελφός μου. *If you had been here, my brother would not have died.* (Since εἰμί lacks a pluperfect tense, the imperfect ἦς is equivalent to an aorist here.)
4. εἰ δὲ μή, εἶπον ἂν ὑμῖν. *If it were not so, I would have told you.* (The apodosis only is past contrary to fact.)
5. εἰ μὴ ἦλθον καὶ ἐλάλησα αὐτοῖς, ἁμαρτίαν οὐκ εἴχοσαν. *If I had not come and spoken to them, they would not (now) be guilty of sin.* (The protases only show past contrary to fact.)

VOCABULARY

α

Ἄβελ, ὁ Abel (indeclinable)
Ἀβιά, ὁ Abijah (indeclinable)
Ἀβιούδ, ὁ Abiud (indeclinable)
Ἀβραάμ, ὁ Abraham (indeclinable)
ἀγαθός, ή, όν good, profitable, upright
ἀγαλλιάω, ἀγαλλιάσω, ἠγαλλίασα celebrate, praise, rejoice (usually deponent)
ἀγανακτέω, ἀγανακτήσω, ἠγανάκτησα be indignant, angry (+ περί at)
ἀγαπάω, ἀγαπήσω, ἠγάπησα, ἠγάπηκα, ἠγάπημαι, ἠγαπήθην love, cherish, value
ἀγάπη, ης, ἡ love
ἀγαπητός, ή, όν beloved, dear
ἀγγαρεύω, ἀγγαρεύσω, ἠγγάρευσα force, press, compel (someone) to go
ἀγγεῖον, ου, τό vessel, flask, container
ἄγγελος, ου, ὁ messenger, angel
ἄγγος, ους, τό vessel, container
ἀγέλη, ής, ἡ herd
ἁγιάζω, ἁγιάσω, ἡγίασα, ἡγίακα, ἡγίασμαι, ἡγιάσθην separate, consecrate; cleanse, purify, sanctify; regard as holy, hold in reverence, hallow
ἅγιος, ια, ιον hallowed, pure, holy; οἱ ἅγιοι God's people, saints
ἄγκιστρον, ου, τό hook, fish-hook
ἄγναφος, ον unbleached, unshrunken, unsized, new
ἀγορά, ᾶς, ἡ marketplace
ἀγοράζω, ἀγοράσω, ἠγόρασα, ἠγόρασμαι, ἠγοράσθην buy, purchase, acquire
ἄγριος, ία, ιον wild
ἀγρός, οῦ, ὁ field, cultivated field; lands, farms, villages (plural)
ἄγω, ἄξω, ἤγαγον, ἦχα, ἦγμαι, ἤχθην lead, bring, arrest
ἀδελφή, ῆς, ἡ sister
ἀδελφός, οῦ, ὁ brother
ἀδημονέω, ἀδημονήσω be anxious, be distressed, be full of anguish
ᾅδης, ου, ὁ Hades, underworld, abode of the dead; place of punishment, hell; the lowest place
ἀδικέω, ἀδικήσω, ἠδίκησα, ἠδίκηκα, ἠδικήθην wrong, treat unjustly, cheat
ἄδικος, ον unjust, unrighteous, dishonest, untrustworthy
ἀδυνατέω, ἀδυνατήσω not be able; be impossible
ἀδύνατος, ον powerless, impotent; impossible

ἀετός, οῦ, ὁ eagle
ἄζυμος, ον unleavened; τὰ ἄζυμα the festival of unleavened bread
Ἀζώρ, ὁ Azor (indeclinable)
ἀθῷος, ον innocent
αἰγιαλός, οῦ, ὁ shore, beach
Αἴγυπτος, ου, ἡ Egypt
αἷμα, ατος, τό blood
αἱμορροέω, αἱμορροήσω suffer with hemorrhage, have a flux of blood
αἶνος, ου, ὁ praise
αἱρετίζω, αἱρετίσω, ᾑρέτισα choose
αἴρω, ἀρῶ, ἦρα, ἦρκα, ἦρμαι, ἤρθην take up, take, bear, take away, lift, carry, remove; keep in suspense; destroy, kill
αἰτέω, αἰτήσω, ᾔτησα, ᾔτηκα ask, ask for, make a request; desire
αἰτία, ας, ἡ cause, motive; ground for complaint, fault; case, relationship; accusation, crime
αἰών, αἰῶνος, ὁ eternity, perpetuity; period of time, life, age; world
αἰώνιος, ον (αἰώνιος, ία, ιον) eternal, everlasting
ἀκαθαρσία, ας, ἡ impurity, refuse; immorality, lewdness
ἀκάθαρτος, ον unclean, impure; lewd; foul
ἄκανθα, ης, ἡ thorn
ἄκαρπος, ον unfruitful, fruitless, barren; useless, unproductive
ἀκέραιος, ον unmixed; pure, innocent, sincere, without guile, blameless
ἀκμήν still, even now (adverb)
ἀκοή, ῆς, ἡ hearing; fame, report, rumor; account
ἀκολουθέω, ἀκολουθήσω, ἠκολούθησα, ἠκολούθηκα follow (+ dative)
ἀκούω, ἀκούσω, ἤκουσα, ἀκήκοα, ἤκουσμαι, ἠκούσθην hear, obey, understand
ἀκρασίας, ας, ἡ intemperance, incontinence, self-indulgence
ἀκριβόω, ἀκριβώσω, ἠκρίβωσα, ἠκρίβωκα ascertain exactly
ἀκριβῶς diligently, accurately (adverb)
ἀκρίς, ίδος, ἡ grasshopper, locust
ἄκρον, ου, τό top, tip, end
ἀκυρόω, ἀκυρώσω, ἠκύρωσα make void, annul
ἀλάβαστρον, ου, τό alabaster flask, alabaster box
ἅλας, ατος, τό salt
ἀλείφω, ἀλείψω, ἤλειψα anoint
ἀλέκτωρ, ορος, ὁ cock, rooster
ἄλευρον, ου, τό wheat flour
ἀλήθεια, ας, ἡ truth
ἀληθής, ές true, real
ἀλήθω, ἀλήσω grind
ἀληθῶς truly, certainly, of a truth
ἁλιεύς, έως, ὁ fisherman
ἁλίζω, ἁλίσω, ἡλίσθην salt
ἀλλ' = ἀλλά but, yet (conjunction)
ἀλλά but, yet (conjunction)
ἀλλήλων, οις, ους each other, one another (reciprocal pronoun)
ἄλλος, η, ο other, another; ἄλλος . . . ἄλλος one . . . another

ἀλλότριος, ία, ιον strange, foreign; stranger, foreigner (substantive)
Ἁλφαῖος, ου, ὁ Alphaeus
ἅλων, ωνος, ἡ threshing floor
ἀλώπηξ, ἀλώπεκος, ἡ fox; crafty man
ἅμα with, together with, at the same time (adverb; preposition + dative); ἅμα πρωῒ early in the morning
ἁμαρτάνω, ἁμαρτήσω, ἡμάρτησα or ἥμαρτον, ἡμάρτηκα, ἡμάρτημαι, ἡμαρτήθην do wrong, sin
ἁμαρτία, ας, ἡ error, sin
ἁμαρτωλός, όν sinful; sinner (substantive)
ἀμελέω, ἀμελήσω, ἠμέλησα, ἠμέληκα neglect, be unconcerned, disregard; be careless, heedless, negligent
ἀμέριμνος, ον free from care
ἀμήν in truth, verily (Hebrew)
Ἀμιναδάβ, ὁ Aminadab, Amminadab (indeclinable)
ἄμμος, ου, ἡ sand
ἄμπελος, ου, ἡ vine, grapevine
ἀμπελών, ῶνος, ὁ vineyard
ἀμφίβληστρον, ου, τό casting-net
ἀμφιέννυμι, ἀμφιέσω, ἠμφίεσμαι clothe, dress
ἀμφότεροι, αι, α both
Ἀμώς, ὁ Amos, Amon (indeclinable)
ἄν (a conditional particle indicating contingency in certain constructions)
ἀνά each, apiece (preposition + accusative; with numbers)
ἀναβαίνω, ἀναβήσομαι, ἀνέβην, ἀναβέβηκα go up, ascend, rise; climb; embark
ἀναβιβάζω, ἀναβιβάσω, ἀνεβίβασα draw up, pull up
ἀναβλέπω, ἀναβλέψω, ἀνέβλεψα look up; regain sight, receive sight
ἀναβοάω, ἀναβήσομαι, ἀνέβησα cry out, exclaim
ἀναγινώσκω, ἀναγνώσομαι, ἀνέγνων (2 aorist), ἀνέγνωκα, ἀνέγνωσμαι, ἀνεγνώσθην read, read aloud, read in public
ἀναγκάζω, ἀναγκάσω, ἠνάγκασα, ἠναγκάσθην compel, force; constrain, urge
ἀνάγκη, ης, ἡ necessity, compulsion, obligation; ἀνάγκη (sc. ἐστὶν) it is necessary, inevitable, one must (with infinitive, or accusative and infinitive)
ἀνάγω, ἀνάξω, ἀνήγαγον (2 aorist), ἀνήχθην lead up, bring up
ἀναιρέω, ἀναιρήσω, ἀνεῖλον (2 aorist), ἀνηρέθην take away, destroy, kill, put to death, murder
ἀναίτιος, ον blameless, guiltless, innocent
ἀνακάμπτω, ἀνακάμψω, ἀνέκαμψα return
ἀνάκειμαι, ἀνακείσομαι lie down, recline at table as a dinner guest
ἀνακλίνω, ἀνακλινῶ, ἀνέκλινα, ἀνεκλίθην cause to lie down; lie down, recline at meal (passive)

ἀνάπαυσις, εως, ἡ ceasing; rest; resting place
ἀναπαύω, ἀναπαύσω, ἀνέπαυσα, ἀναπέπαυμαι, ἀνεπαύθην give rest, refresh, revive; rest, take rest
ἀναπίπτω, ἀναπεσοῦμαι, ἀνέπεσον lie down, recline, take one's place
ἀναπληρόω, ἀναπληρώσω, ἀνεπλήρωσα make complete, fulfill
ἀνάστασις, εως, ἡ rise, rising, resurrection
ἀνατέλλω, ἀνατελῶ, ἀνέτειλα (1 aorist) cause to rise; rise, spring up (intransitive)
ἀνατολή, ῆς, ἡ rising, rising of the sun, east, orient
ἀναφέρω, ἀνοίσω, ἀνήνεγκα, ἀνήνεγκον (2 aorist) bring, take up, lead
ἀναχωρέω, ἀναχωρήσω, ἀνεχώρησα go away, depart, withdraw, retire
Ἀνδρέας, ου, ὁ Andrew
ἀνεκτότερος, α, ον more bearable, endurable, tolerable (comparative of ἀνεκτός, ή, όν)
ἄνεμος, ου, ὁ wind
ἄνευ without (preposition + genitive)
ἀνέχομαι, ἀνέξομαι endure, bear with; suffer
ἄνηθον, ου, τό anethum, dill
ἀνήρ, ἀνδρός, ὁ man, male, husband
ἀνθίστημι, ἀντέστην (2 aorist), ἀνθέστηκα, ἀντεστάθην oppose, resist, withstand (+ dative)
ἄνθρωπος, ου, ὁ human being, person, man
ἄνιπτος, ον unwashed
ἀνίστημι, ἀναστήσω, ἀνέστησα, ἀνέστην (2 aorist) cause to rise, raise, raise up; cause to be born (transitive); rise, stand up, get up (2 aorist and all middle forms are intransitive)
ἀνοίγω, ἀνοίξω, ἀνέῳξα/ἤνοιξα, ἀνέῳγα, ἀνέῳγμαι, ἠνεῴχθην open
ἀνομία, ας, ἡ lawlessness, lawless deed, transgression, iniquity, sin
ἀντάλλαγμα, ατος, τό price in exchange for, compensation
ἀντέχω, ἀνθέξομαι cling to, adhere to, be devoted to
ἀντί in place of, for, upon (preposition + genitive)
ἀντίδικος, ου, ὁ opponent, adversary, enemy
ἄνυδρος, ον waterless, dry, barren
ἄνωθεν from above, again, anew (adverb)
ἀξίνη, ης, ἡ ax
ἄξιος, ία, ιον worthy
ἀπαγγέλλω, ἀπαγγελῶ, ἀπήγγειλα (1 aorist), ἀπηγγέλην (2 aorist passive) bring back word, report, declare, announce, tell
ἀπάγχομαι, ἀπάγξομαι, ἀπηγξάμην hang oneself
ἀπάγω, ἀπάξω, ἀπήγαγον, ἀπήχθην lead away; lead away (of a road; intransitive)
ἀπαίρω, ἀπαρῶ, ἀπήρθην take away; be taken away (passive)

ἁπαλός, ή, όν soft, tender

ἀπαρνέομαι, ἀπαρνήσομαι, ἀπηρνησάμην, ἀπήρνημαι deny; renounce, disregard

ἅπας, ἅπασα, ἅπασαν all, whole, every

ἀπάτη, ης, ἡ deceit, deception, seduction, delusion

ἀπέναντι before; opposite (adverb; preposition + genitive)

ἀπέρχομαι, ἀπελεύσομαι, ἀπῆλθον, ἀπελήλυθα go, go away, depart; go forth, pervade

ἀπέχω, ἀφέξω have in full, receive in full; be distant, be away

ἀπιστία, ας, ἡ unfaithfulness, faithlessness, unbelief, lack of belief

ἄπιστος, ον unbelieving, incredulous

ἁπλοῦς, ῆ, οῦν simple, single, sincere; clear, sound, healthy

ἀπό from, because of, out of, by (preposition + genitive); ἀπὸ τότε from then on

ἀποδεκατόω, ἀποδεκατώσω pay tithes of, give one-tenth of, tithe

ἀποδημέω, ἀποδημήσω, ἀπεδήμησα be away from home, be abroad; go on a journey, go abroad

ἀποδίδωμι, ἀποδώσω, ἀπέδωκα, ἀπέδων (2 aorist), ἀποδέδωκα, ἀποδέδομαι, ἀπεδόθην give, give away, give out; give back, return; render in full, reward, recompense; pay, keep, perform

ἀποδημέω, ἀποδημήσω, ἀπεδήμησα be away from home, be abroad; go on a journey, go abroad

ἀποδοκιμάζω, ἀποδοκιμάσω, ἀπεδοκίμασα, ἀπεδοκιμάσθην reject

ἀποθήκη, ης, ἡ granary, storehouse, barn

ἀποθνήσκω, ἀποθανοῦμαι, ἀπέθανον (2 aorist) die, face death, decay

ἀποκαθίστημι/ἀποκαθιστάνω, ἀποκαταστήσω, ἀπεκατέστην (2 aorist), ἀπεκατεστάθην restore, bring back, give back

ἀποκαλύπτω, ἀποκαλύψω, ἀπεκάλυψα, ἀπεκαλύφθην uncover, reveal, disclose

ἀποκεφαλίζω, ἀποκεφαλίσω, ἀπεκεφάλισα behead

ἀποκρίνομαι, ἀπεκρινάμην, ἀπεκρίθην answer, reply

ἀποκτείνω/ἀποκτέννω, ἀποκτενῶ, ἀπέκτεινα, ἀπεκτάνθην kill, put to death, murder

ἀποκυλίω, ἀποκυλίσω to roll away

ἀπόλλυμι/ἀπολλύω, ἀπολέσω/ἀπολῶ, ἀπώλεσα, ἀπολώλεκα, ἀπόλωλα (2 perfect) lose, destroy, ruin, kill; perish, die, be lost (middle)

ἀπολύω, ἀπολύσω, ἀπέλυσα, ἀπολέλυκα, ἀπολέλυμαι, ἀπελύθην release, set free, allow to depart; send away, let go, dismiss; pardon, divorce

ἀπονίπτω, ἀπονίψω, ἀπένιψα wash (active); wash off (for) oneself (middle)
ἀποσπάω, ἀποσπάσω draw, draw out; draw away, attract
ἀποστάσιον, ου, τό rebellion, abandonment; repudiation, divorce
ἀποστέλλω, ἀποστελῶ, ἀπέστειλα, ἀπέσταλκα, ἀπέσταλμαι, ἀπεστάλην send, send away, send out
ἀπόστολος, ου, ὁ messenger, agent, delegate, apostle
ἀποστρέφω, ἀποστρέψω, ἀπέστρεψα, ἀπέστραμμαι, ἀπεστράφην (2 aorist passive) turn away, remove; turn away (intransitive in middle and 2 aorist passive)
ἀποτίθημι, ἀποθήσω, ἀπεθέμην (2 aorist middle), ἀπετέθην put off, lay aside; lay down, put away
ἀποχωρέω, ἀποχωρήσω go from, go away, depart
ἅπτω, ἅψω, ἧψα fasten; light, kindle; touch, take hold of, hold (middle)
ἀπώλεια, ας, ἡ destruction; waste; misery, eternal ruin
ἄρα therefore, then, consequently (particle)
Ἀράμ, ὁ Aram (indeclinable)
ἀργός, ή, όν inactive, unemployed; idle, lazy; useless, unproductive, careless, unprofitable, hollow
ἀργύριον, ίου, τό silver, silver shekel, silver drachma, silver money
ἄργυρος, ου, ὁ silver; money
ἀρέσκω, ἀρέσω, ἤρεσα please, be pleasing
ἀριθμέω, ἀριθμήσω, ἠρίθμησα, ἠρίθμημαι count, number
Ἀριμαθαία, ας, ἡ Arimathaea
ἀριστερός, ά, όν left
ἄριστον, ου, τό first meal; breakfast; luncheon, noon meal; meal
ἀρκετός, ή, όν sufficient, enough, adequate
ἀρκέω, ἀρκήσω, ἤρκεσα be enough, be sufficient
ἀρνέομαι, ἀρνήσομαι, ἠρνησάμην, ἤρνημαι deny, disown
ἁρπαγή, ῆς, ἡ robbery, plunder, prey, spoil; greediness
ἁρπάζω, ἁρπάσω, ἥρπασα, ἡρπάσθην, ἡρπάγην (2 aorist passive) steal, carry off, drag away, take away
ἅρπαξ, αγος ravenous; rapacious
ἄρρωστος, ον sick, ill, weak, infirm
ἄρσην, ἄρσεν, ενος, ὁ, τό male; τὸ ἄρσεν, sc. γένος offspring
ἄρτι now, at the present time, at once, immediately; just (adverb); ἀπ' ἄρτι from now, from this time, henceforth
ἄρτος, ου, ὁ bread, loaf of bread
ἀρχαῖος, αία, αῖον old, ancient
Ἀρχέλαος, ου, ὁ Archelaus
ἀρχή, ῆς, ἡ beginning; τὴν ἀρχὴν wholly, altogether, from the beginning (used adverbially)
ἀρχιερεύς, έως, ὁ high priest
ἄρχω, ἄρξω, ἦρξα, ἦρχα, ἦργμαι, ἤρχθην rule (active); begin (middle)

ἄρχων, οντος, ὁ chief, ruler, magistrate, prince
Ἀσάφ, ὁ Asa(ph) (indeclinable)
ἄσβεστος, ον inextinguishable, unquenchable
ἀσθένεια, ας, ἡ weakness, sickness, disease
ἀσθενέω, ἀσθενήσω, ἠσθένησα be weak, be sick
ἀσθενής, ές weak; sick, ill
ἀσκός, οῦ, ὁ leather bag, wine-skin
ἀσπάζομαι, ἀσπάσομαι, ἠσπασάμην, ἤσπασμαι salute, greet, welcome; treat with affection, be fond of, cherish; embrace
ἀσπασμός, οῦ, ὁ greeting
ἀσσάριον, ου, τό as, assarian, (Roman) copper coin
ἀστήρ, ἀστέρος, ὁ star
ἀστραπή, ῆς, ἡ lightning; light, ray
ἀσύνετος, ον without understanding, senseless, foolish
ἀσφαλίζω, ἀσφαλίσω make safe, make secure
ἄτιμος, ον unhonored, dishonored, without honor
αὐλέω, αὐλήσω, ηὔλησα play the flute
αὐλή, ῆς, ἡ fold; courtyard; palace
αὐλητής, οῦ, ὁ flute player
αὐλίζομαι, αὐλίσομαι, ηὐλίσθην spend the night, find lodging, lodge at night; stay
αὐξάνω/αὔξω, αὐξήσω, ηὔξησα, ηὐξήθην grow, increase
αὔριον tomorrow (adverb)
αὐτός, αὐτή, αὐτό self; same; he, she, it, they
αὐτοῦ here, in this place (adverb)
ἀφαιρέω, ἀφαιρήσω, ἀφεῖλον (2 aorist) take away, remove; take off, remove by cutting off, cut off
ἀφανίζω, ἀφανίσω, ἠφανίσθην render unrecognizable; destroy, consume; spoil, deform, disfigure
ἀφεδρών, ῶνος, ὁ latrine, privy
ἄφεσις, εως, ἡ release; remission, forgiveness
ἀφίημι, ἀφήσω, ἀφῆκα, ἀφῆν (2 aorist), ἀφεῖκα, ἀφεῖμαι, ἀφέθην let go, send away; forgive, pardon; leave, let, permit, suffer, allow
ἀφορίζω, ἀφορίσω/ἀφοριῶ, ἀφώρισα, ἀφώρισμαι, ἀφορίσθην limit off; separate, take out, take away, exclude, excommunicate
Ἀχάζ, ὁ Achaz, Ahaz (indeclinable)
Ἀχίμ, ὁ Achim (indeclinable)
ἀχρεῖος, α, ον useless, unprofitable, worthless, miserable
ἄχρι until (preposition + genitive)
ἄχυρον, ου, τό chaff, straw

β

Βαβυλών, ῶνος, ἡ Babylon
βάθος, ους, τό depth
βάλλω, βαλῶ, ἔβαλον, βέβληκα, βέβλημαι, ἐβλήθην throw, sow, cast, place, put, pour, bring
βαπτίζω, βαπτίσω, ἐβάπτισα, βεβάπτισμαι, ἐβαπτίσθην dip, immerse, baptize

βάπτισμα, ατος, τό immersion, baptism
βαπτιστής, οῦ, ὁ one who baptizes, Baptist, Baptizer
Βαραββᾶς, ᾶ, ὁ Barabbas
Βαραχίας, ου, ὁ Barachias, Barachiah
βαρέω, βαρήσω, βεβάρημαι weigh down; become heavy, be burdened, be overcome
βαρέως heavily; with difficulty (adverb)
Βαρθολομαίος, ου, ὁ Bartholomew
βάρος, εος, τό weight, burden
βαρύς, εῖα, ύ heavy; burdensome, oppressive; weighty, important, momentous
βαρύτιμος, ον very expensive, very precious
βασανίζω, βασανίσω, ἐβασάνισα, ἐβασανίσθην afflict, torment, torture; toss, harass
βασανιστής, οῦ, ὁ torturer, tormentor, jailer
βάσανος, ου, ἡ torture, torment
βασιλεία, ας, ἡ kingship, royal power, kingdom
βασιλεύς, έως, ὁ king
βασίλισσα, ης, ἡ queen
βαστάζω, βαστάσω, ἐβάστασα lift, bear, take up; endure, suffer; carry away, remove, steal
βατταλογέω, βατταλογήσω babble, prate, speak idly, use vain repetitions
βδέλυγμα, ατος, τό abomination, abominable thing
βεβηλόω, βεβηλώσω, ἐβεβήλωσα desecrate, profane, pollute, violate
βεελζεβούλ/βεελζεβούβ and βεεζεβούλ, ὁ Beelzebub (indeclinable)
Βηθανία, ας, ἡ Bethany
Βηθλέεμ, ἡ Bethlehem (indeclinable)
Βηθσαϊδά, ἡ Bethsaida (indeclinable)
βηθφαγή, ἡ Bethphage (indeclinable)
βῆμα, ατος, τό step; tribunal, judicial bench
βιάζω, βιάσω apply force, urge, overpower; press forward; be oppressed, suffer violence (passive)
βιαστής, ου, ὁ violent man, impetuous man
βιβλίον, ου, τό roll, book, scroll, document, certificate, deed
βίβλος, ου, ἡ scroll, roll, book
βλαστάνω, βλαστήσω, ἐβλάστησα, ἔβλαστον (2 aorist) produce (transitive); bud, sprout, germinate, spring up
βλασφημέω, βλασφημήσω, ἐβλασφήμησα, βεβλασφήμηκα, ἐβλασφημήθην blaspheme, speak irreverently of
βλασφημία, ίας, ἡ slander, abusive speech, blasphemy
βλέπω, βλέψω, ἔβλεψα see, behold, perceive
βοάω, βοήσω, ἐβόησα shout, cry out

Βόες, ὁ Booz, Boaz (indeclinable)
βοηθέω, βοηθήσω, ἐβοήθησα help, bring aid
βόθυνος, ου, ὁ pit, well, cistern
βόσκω, βοσκήσω, ἐβόσκησα feed, tend; graze, feed (passive)
βούλομαι, βουλήσομαι, βεβούλημαι, ἐβουλήθην wish, be willing, desire, want
βρέχω, βρέξω, ἔβρεξα wet, moisten; rain, cause to rain, send rain
βροχή, ῆς, ἡ rain
βρυγμός, οῦ, ὁ chattering (of teeth), gnashing (of teeth)
βρῶμα, ατος, τό food
βρῶσις, εως, ἡ eating; food, meat; canker, rust, corrosion

γ

Γαδαρηνός, ή, όν from Gadara
γαλήνη, ης, ἡ calm, tranquility
Γαλιλαία, ας, ἡ Galilee
γαμέω, γαμήσω, ἔγημα/ἐγάμησα, γεγάμηκα, ἐγαμήθην marry, take a wife
γαμίζω, γαμίσω give in marriage
γάμος, ου, ὁ wedding, marriage
γάρ for, indeed, but (conjunction)
γαστήρ, τρός, ἡ belly, womb; ἐν γαστρὶ ἔχειν be with child, be pregnant
γε at least, indeed (an enclitic particle emphasizing the preceding word; often untranslatable)
γέεννα, ης, ἡ Gehenna, Valley of Hinnom, hell, the fires of Tartarus (a place known for sacrifices to Moloch, pollution, pestilence, punishment of malefactors, and continually burning fires)
Γεθσημανί Gethsemane (indeclinable; an olive orchard on the Mount of Olives)
γέμω be full
γενεά, ᾶς, ἡ progeny, generation
γενέσια, ίων, τά birthday celebration
γένεσις, εως, ἡ birth; generation, descent, lineage
γένημα, ατος, τό product, fruit
γεννάω, γεννήσω, ἐγέννησα, γεγέννηκα, γεγέννημαι, ἐγεννήθην beget, give birth to, bear, bring forth; be born (in passive)
Γεννησαρέτ, ἡ Gennesaret (indeclinable)
γεννητός, ή, όν born
γένος, ους, τό offspring, progeny; nation, people; kind, sort, species
γεύομαι, γεύσομαι, ἐγευσάμην taste, partake of, enjoy; eat; come to know, experience
γεωργός, οῦ, ὁ husbandman, farmer, vinedresser
γῆ, γῆς, ἡ earth, soil, land, region, country
γίνομαι, γενήσομαι, ἐγενόμην, γέγονα/γεγένημαι, ἐγενήθην become, be made, be done, be created, be born, come, arrive, be present, take place

γινώσκω, γνώσομαι, ἔγνων, ἔγνωκα, ἔγνωσμαι, ἐγνώσθην know, learn, understand, know carnally

γογγύζω, γογγύσω, ἐγόγγυσα murmur, grumble, mutter, complain, whisper

Γολγοθᾶ, ἡ Golgotha (= place of a skull) (indeclinable)

Γόμορρα, ων, τά and ας, ἡ Gomorrah

γονεύς, έως, ὁ father; parents (plural)

γονυπετέω, γονυπετήσω, ἐγονυπέτησα fall on one's knees before, kneel before

γραμματεύς, έως, ὁ secretary, clerk, scholar versed in law, scribe

γραφή, ῆς, ἡ writing, Holy Scripture, passage of scripture

γράφω, γράψω, ἔγραψα, γέγραφα, γέγραμμαι, ἐγράφθην engrave, write

γρηγορέω, γρηγορήσω, ἐγρηγόρησα be awake, watch; be alive; be watchful, attentive, vigilant

γυμνός, ή, όν naked, without an outer garment, uncovered

γυνή, γυναικός, ἡ woman, wife

γωνία, ας, ἡ corner

δ

δαιμονίζομαι, δαιμονίσομαι, ἐδαιμονίσθην be possessed, tormented, afflicted (by a demon)

δαιμόνιον, ου, τό deity, divinity; demon, evil spirit

δαίμων, ονος, ὁ demon, evil spirit

δάκτυλος, ου, ὁ finger

δαν(ε)ίζω, δανίσω, ἐδάνισα lend money (active); borrow money (middle)

δάνειον, ου, τό loan, debt

Δανιήλ, ὁ Daniel (indeclinable)

Δαυίδ, ὁ David (indeclinable)

δέ and, but, now (conjunction, postpositive)

δεῖ, δεήσει, ἐδέησε it is necessary, it is proper (impersonal verb from δέω)

δειγματίζω, δειγματίσω, ἐδειγμάτισα disgrace, make a public spectacle of

δείκνυμι/δεικνύω, δείξω, ἔδειξα, δέδειχα, ἐδείχθην show, point out, make known, demonstrate, announce

δειλός, ή, όν timid, fearful

δεῖνα, δεῖνος, ὁ, ἡ, τό certain man, somebody

δεινῶς terribly, dreadfully, grievously, greatly, vehemently (adverb)

δεῖπνον, ου, τό dinner, supper

δέκα ten (indeclinable)

Δεκάπολις, εως, ἡ Decapolis

δεκατέσσαρες, ων, οἱ, αἱ fourteen

δένδρον, ου, τό tree

δεξιός, ά, όν right (as opposed to *left*); ἡ δεξιά (χείρ) right hand; ἐκ δεξιῶν τινός at someone's right

δέομαι, δεήσομαι, ἐδεήθην ask, request; pray, beseech, supplicate

δερμάτινος, η, ον made of skin, leather
δέρω, δερῶ, ἔδειρα skin, flay; beat, scourge, strike
δέσμη, ης, ἡ bundle
δέσμιος, ου, ὁ prisoner
δεσμεύω, δεσμεύσω bind, bind up
δέσμιος, ου, ὁ prisoner
δεσμωτήριον, ίου, τό prison
δεῦρο come! come here! (adverb)
δεῦτε come! come here! (adverb)
δεύτερος, α, ον second; ἐκ δευτέρου again, the second time, another time
δέχομαι, δέξομαι, ἐδεξάμην, δέδεγμαι take, receive, welcome, accept
δέω, δήσω, ἔδησα, δέδεκα, δέδεμαι, ἐδέθην bind, tie, impede
δῆλος, η, ον clear, plain, evident
δηνάριον, ου, τό denarius (a Roman silver coin)
διά through, by (preposition + genitive); διὰ παντός (sc. χρονοῦ) always, continuously, constantly; because of, for the sake of (+ accusative); διὰ τοῦτο therefore, for this reason
διαβλέπω, διαβλέψω, διέβλεψα look intently; see clearly (+ infinitive)
διάβολος, ου, ὁ slanderer, devil
διαθήκη, ης, ἡ covenant
διακαθαρίζω, διακαθαριῶ clean out
διακονέω, διακονήσω, διηκόνησα, δεδιηκόνηκα, διηκονήθην wait on, attend upon, serve
διάκονος, ου, ὁ attendant, servant
διακρίνω, διακρινῶ, διεκρίθην distinguish, discern, discriminate, judge; be at odds with oneself, hesitate, doubt, waver (middle or passive)
διακωλύω, διακωλύσω hinder, restrain, prevent, prohibit
διαλλάσσομαι, διηλλάγην (2 aorist passive) become reconciled to (+ dative)
διαλογίζομαι, διαλογίσομαι reason, deliberate, ponder, consider
διαλογισμός, ου, ὁ reasoning, thought, purpose; discourse, disputation, contention; doubt, hesitation
διαμερίζω, διαμερίσω, διεμέρισα divide and distribute, divide
διάνοια, ας, ἡ mind, intellect, understanding
διαπεράω, διαπεράσω, διεπέρησα cross, cross over, pass through
διαρπάζω, διαρπάσω plunder, rob, steal; snatch, abduct, take captive
διαρρήγνυμι and διαρρήσσω, διαρρήξω, διέρρηξα rend, tear, burst
διασαφέω, διασαφήσω, διεσάφησα make clear, explain; tell plainly, declare in detail, make known
διασκορπίζω, διασκορπίσω, διεσκόρπισα, διεσκορπίσθην scatter, disperse, strew
διαστέλλομαι, διαστελοῦμαι, διεστειλάμην order, give orders, admonish

διαστρέφω, διαστρέψω, διέστραμμαι distort, pervert, corrupt
διασῴζω, διασώσω, διεσώθην save, rescue; be cured, healed, restored to health (passive)
διατάσσω, διατάξω, διέταξα, διετάχθην order, direct, charge, command
διὰ τί why?
διαφέρω, διοίσω, διήνεγκα carry through; differ, be different; be better, be worth more than, be superior to
διαφημίζω, διαφημίσω, διεφήμισα report, proclaim, spread news about, spread widely, disseminate
διδασκαλία, ας, ἡ precept, doctrine
διδάσκαλος, ου, ὁ master, teacher
διδάσκω, διδάξω, ἐδίδαξα, ἐδιδάχθην teach, instruct; direct, admonish
διδαχή, ῆς, ἡ teaching, instruction
δίδραχμον, ου, τό a double drachma (paid to the temple treasury at Jerusalem)
δίδωμι, δώσω, ἔδωκα, ἔδων (2 aorist), δέδωκα, δέδομαι, ἐδόθην give
διέξοδος, ου, ἡ thoroughfare, highway, main road
διέρχομαι, διελεύσομαι, διῆλθον pass through, pass over, cross, pass along; proceed; travel through, wander about; transfix, pierce; spread abroad
διετής, ές two years old
δίκαιος, αία, αιον right, just, honest, good, righteous
δικαιοσύνη, ης, ἡ justice, righteousness, godliness, generosity, alms
δικαιόω, δικαιώσω, ἐδικαίωσα, ἐδικαιώθην justify, vindicate
δίκτυον, ου, τό net
διό therefore, for this reason (conjunction)
διορύσσω, διορύξω break through, break in
διπλότερον twofold more, twice more (comparative adverb of διπλοῦς, ῆ, οῦν double, twofold)
διστάζω, διστάσω, ἐδίστασα doubt, hesitate, waver
διϋλίζω, διϋλίσω filter out, strain out
διχάζω, διχάσω, ἐδίχασα divide, separate; turn someone against someone
διχοτομέω, διχοτομήσω cut in two; punish severely
διψάω, διψήσω, ἐδίψησα thirst, be thirsty
διωγμός, ου, ὁ persecution
διώκω, διώξω, ἐδίωξα, δεδίωγμαι, ἐδιώχθην persecute, pursue, seek after
δοκεῖ it seems; it seems good, best, or right (impersonal verb)
δοκέω, δόξω, ἔδοξα think (mistakenly), believe, suppose, consider
δοκός, οῦ, ἡ beam of wood
δόλος, ου, ὁ fraud, deceit, guile
δόμα, ατος, τό gift, present

δόξα, ης, ἡ glory, honor, majesty
δοξάζω, δοξάσω, ἐδόξασα, δεδόξασμαι, ἐδοξάσθην praise, honor, magnify, glorify
δουλεύω, δουλεύσω, ἐδούλευσα, δεδούλευκα be a slave, be subjected, serve as a slave, serve
δοῦλος, ου, ὁ slave, servant
δύναμαι, δυνήσομαι, ἠδυνήθην be able
δύναμις, εως, ἡ power; strength, ability; authority; might, majesty; omnipotence; miraculous power, miracle, wonder
δυνατός, ή, όν able, powerful, strong, mighty; δυνατόν possible
δύο two
δυσβάστακτος, ον hard to bear, oppressive
δυσκόλως with difficulty, hardly
δυσμή, ῆς, ἡ sinking, setting; setting of the sun, west (plural)
δώδεκα twelve (indeclinable)
δῶμα, ατος, τό house; housetop, roof
δωρεάν as a gift, without payment, freely (used as an adverb)
δῶρον, ου, τό gift, present; offering, sacrifice; consecration to God; contribution

ε

ἐάν if (conditional particle); ἐὰν μή if not, unless, except
ἑαυτοῦ, ῆς, οῦ himself, herself, itself; themselves, ourselves, yourselves (in plural)
ἐάω, ἐάσω, εἴασα allow, permit
ἑβδομηκοντάκις seventy times (adverb)
ἐγγίζω, ἐγγίσω, ἤγγισα, ἤγγικα approach, draw near
ἐγγύς near, close at hand (adverb)
ἐγείρω, ἐγερῶ, ἤγειρα, ἠγήγερμαι, ἠγέρθην awaken, raise up from the dead, restore, rebuild; be raised, rise (passive); arise! get up! come! (intransitive, only in imperative)
ἔγερσις, εως, ἡ resurrection
ἐγκαταλείπω, ἐγκαταλείψω, ἐγκατέλιπον (2 aorist) leave, leave behind; forsake, abandon
ἐγκρύπτω, ἐγκρύψω, ἐνέκρυψα hide, put, mix
ἐγώ, ἐμοῦ (μου) I (personal pronoun)
Ἑζεκίας, ου, ὁ Ezekias, Hezekiah
ἐθνικός, ή, όν gentile, heathen
ἔθνος, ους, τό nation, people
εἰ if, whether; εἰ μή unless, except (an interrogatory particle introducing a direct question)
εἰ δὲ μή if not, otherwise
εἰδέα, ας, ἡ form; appearance, look, aspect
εἰκων, ονος, ἡ image, likeness, representation
εἰμί, ἔσομαι be
εἰρήνη, ης, ἡ peace
εἰρηνοποιός, οῦ, ὁ/ἡ peace-maker
εἰς to, into, on, in; for, as; by (in oaths); with respect to (preposition + accusative)

εἷς, μία, ἕν one, single (numeral and indefinite article); εἷς καθ' εἷς one after the other; equivalent to πρῶτος

εἰσακούω, εἰσακούσομαι, εἰσήκουσα, εἰσηκούσθην listen to, hear, obey

εἰσέρχομαι, εἰσελεύσομαι, εἰσῆλθον (2 aorist), εἰσελήλυθα come (in, into), go (in, into), enter into, share in, come to enjoy

εἰσπορεύομαι, εἰσπορεύσομαι go in, come in, enter, be put in

εἰσφέρω, εἰσοίσω, εἰσήνεγκα (1 aorist), εἰσήνεγκον (2 aorist), εἰσηνέχθην bear in, carry to; bring or lead (someone) into

εἴωθα be accustomed

ἐκ (ἐξ before a vowel) from, out of, of, by; to the sum of, for the price of, with (preposition + genitive)

ἕκαστος, η, ον each, every; each one, every one (substantive)

ἑκατόν one hundred (a hundredfold yield of grain; indeclinable)

ἑκατονταπλασίων, ον a hundredfold

ἑκατόνταρχος, ου, ὁ commander of 100 men, centurion

ἐκβάλλω, ἐκβαλῶ, ἐξέβαλον, ἐκβέβληκα, ἐξεβλήθην drive out, expel, disdain, spurn, send out, lead out, take out, bring out

ἐκδίδωμι, ἐκδώσομαι, ἐξεδόμην (2 aorist) let out for hire, lease (only in middle in N.T.)

ἐκδύω, ἐκδύσω strip, take off

ἐκεῖ there, in that place; thither, to that place (adverb)

ἐκεῖθεν from there, from that place (adverb)

ἐκεῖνος, η, ον that, that one, the former

ἐκκλησία, ας, ἡ congregation, church

ἐκκόπτω, ἐκκόψω, ἐξέκοψα, ἐξεκόπην cut out, cut off

ἐκλάμπω, ἐκλάμψω, ἐξέλαμψα shine forth, be radiant, be resplendent

ἐκλεκτός, ή, όν chosen, selected; elect; exalted; precious, choice

ἐκλύομαι, ἐξελύθην become weary, exhausted, faint

ἐκπειράζω, ἐκπειράσω, ἐκεπείρασα, ἐκπεπείρασμαι, ἐκεπειράσθην try, put to the test, tempt

ἐκπλήσσω, ἐκπλήξω, ἐξέπληξα, ἐξεπλάγην amaze, astound, overwhelm

ἐκπορεύομαι, ἐκπορεύσομαι, ἐκπεπόρευμαι, ἐξεπορεύθην come out, go out, proceed

ἐκριζόω, ἐκριζώσω, ἐξερίζωσα, ἐξεριζώθην pull out by the roots, uproot, eradicate; utterly destroy

ἐκτείνω, ἐκτενῶ, ἐξέτεινα stretch out, hold out

ἐκτινάσσω, ἐκτινάξω, ἐξετίναξα shake off

ἐκτός outside (adverb); τὸ ἐκτός the outside

ἕκτος, η, ον sixth

ἐκφύω, ἐκφύσω generate; put forth, shoot, produce

ἐκχέω, ἐκχέω/ἐκχεῶ, ἐξέχεα (1 aorist), ἐκκέχυκα, ἐκκέχυμαι, ἐξεχύθην pour out, spill, scatter

ἐκχύνω, ἐκχυνῶ pour out, shed
ἐλαία, ας, ἡ olive tree, olive
ἔλαιον, ου, τό olive oil, oil
ἐλαφρός, ά, όν light, easy to bear
ἐλάχιστος, η, ον smallest, least
Ἐλεάζαρ, ὁ Eleazar (indeclinable)
ἐλεέω, ἐλεήσω, ἠλέησα, ἠλέημαι, ἠλεήθην pity, show mercy
ἐλεημοσύνη, ης, ἡ kind deed, alms, charitable giving
ἐλεήμων, ον merciful, compassionate
ἔλεος, εως, τό/ὁ pity, mercy, compassion, clemency
ἐλεύθερος, α, ον free, independent
Ἐλιακίμ, ὁ Eliakim (indeclinable)
Ἐλιούδ, ὁ Eliud
ἐλπίζω, ἐλπίσω/ἐλπιῶ, ἤλπισα, ἤλπικα hope, hope for, expect
ἐμαυτοῦ, ῆς myself
ἐμβαίνω, ἐμβήσομαι, ἐνέβην, ἐμβέβηκα step in, embark, go upon, mount, board
ἐμβάπτω, ἐμβάψω, ἐνέβαψα dip (in, into)
ἐμβλέπω, ἐμβλέψω, ἐνέβλεψα see, behold, perceive, look attentively at
ἐμβριμάομαι, ἐμβριμήσομαι, ἐνεβριμησάμην, ἐνεβριμήθην be deeply moved, groan deeply; charge, forbid, warn sternly
Ἐμμανουήλ, ὁ Emmanuel (indeclinable)
ἐμπαίζω, ἐμπαίξω, ἐνέπαιξα, ἐνεπαίχθην ridicule, make fun of, mock, treat with scorn; deceive, trick
ἐμπί(μ)πρημι, ἐμπρήσω, ἐνέπρησα burn, set on fire
ἐμπίπτω, ἐμπεσοῦμαι, ἐνέπεσον (2 aorist) fall (in, into, among)
ἐμπορία, ας, ἡ business, trade
ἔμπορος, ου, ὁ merchant
ἔμπροσθεν in front of, before, in the presence of (adverb; preposition + genitive)
ἐμπτύω, ἐμπτύσω, ἐνέπτυσα spit upon
ἐμφανίζω, ἐμφανίσω, ἐνεφάνισα, ἐνεφανίσθην reveal, make known
ἐν in, on, among; with, by (proclitic; preposition + dative)
ἐναντίος, α, ον opposite to, over against; contrary, adverse, hostile
ἔνατος, άτη, ατον ninth
ἕνδεκα eleven (indeclinable)
ἑνδέκατος, άτη, ατον eleventh
ἔνδυμα, ατος, τό garment, clothing; cloak, mantle
ἐνδύω, ἐνδύσω, ἐνέδυσα dress, clothe; clothe oneself in, put on, wear (middle)
ἕνεκεν/ἕνεκα because of, on account of, for the sake of (preposition + genitive)
ἐνενήκοντα ninety (indeclinable)
ἐνεργέω, ἐνεργήσω, ἐνέργησα, ἐνέργηκα work, be at work, be active (intransitive); work, produce, effect (transitive)
ἔνθεν hence, from here, from this place (adverb)

ἐνθυμέομαι, ἐνθυμήσομαι, ἐνεθυμήθην reflect on, ponder, consider, think

ἐνθύμησις, εως, ἡ thought, reflection, idea

ἐννέα nine (indeclinable)

ἔνοχος, ον subjected to, liable to; guilty

ἐντάλμα, ατος, τό commandment

ἐνταφιάζω, ἐνταφιάσω, ἐνεταφίασα prepare for burial, bury

ἐντέλλομαι, ἐντελοῦμαι, ἐνετειλάμην, ἐντέταλμαι command, order, enjoin

ἐντολή, ῆς, ἡ command, commandment

ἐντός inside, within (adverb); τὸ ἐντός the interior, inside

ἐντρέπω, ἐντρέψω, ἐντρέπομαι, ἐνετράπην put to shame, make ashamed; be put to shame, be ashamed (passive); have regard for, respect, revere, reverence (with middle sense)

ἐντυλίσσω, ἐντυλίξω, ἐνετύλιξα, ἐντετύλιγμαι wrap (up), envelop; fold together

ἕξ six (indeclinable, numeral)

ἐξαιρέω, ἐξελῶ, ἐξεῖλον take out, tear out

ἐξανατέλλω, ἐξανατελῶ, ἐξανέτειλα spring up, rise up, sprout

ἐξέρχομαι, ἐξελεύσομαι, ἐξῆλθον (2 aorist), ἐξελήλυθα go or come out of, go out

ἔξεστι(ν) it is permitted, it is possible (impersonal verb)

ἐξετάζω, ἐξετάσω, ἐξήτασα search out, inquire, interrogate

ἑξήκοντα sixty (a sixtyfold yield of grain; indeclinable)

ἐξίστημι/ἐξιστάω, ἐκστήσω, ἐξέστησα, ἐξέστην (2 aorist), ἐξέστακα put out of its place; astonish, amaze; be astonished (2 aorist and middle)

ἐξομολογέω, ἐξομολογήσω, ἐξωμολόγησα consent, agree; confess, admit, acknowledge; praise, give praise (middle)

ἐξόν it is possible, it is proper, it is permitted (participle of ἔξεστι(ν), an impersonal verb)

ἐξορκίζω, ἐξορκίσω adjure, charge under oath

ἐξουσία, ας, ἡ authority, command, right, ability, might, power

ἔξω outside, out (adverb); out of (preposition + genitive)

ἔξωθεν outwardly, externally (adverb); τὸ ἔξωθεν the exterior, outside

ἐξώτερος, α, ον outer, external

ἑορτή, ῆς, ἡ feast, festival

ἐπαίρω, ἐπαρῶ, ἐπῆρα, ἐπήρθην lift up, hold up

ἐπάν whenever, as soon as (conjunction)

ἐπανάγω, ἐπανάξω, ἐπανήγαγον (2 aorist) bring up; return (intransitive)

ἐπανίστημι raise up against; rise up against (middle)

ἐπάνω over, above, on (adverb; preposition + genitive)
ἐπαύριον following (adverb); ἡ ἐπαύριον the next day, the following day (understand ἡμέρα)
ἐπεί when, after; since, because, for (conjunction)
ἐπερωτάω, ἐπερωτήσω, ἐπηρώτησα ask, ask a question, interrogate, question; inquire after, request
ἐπί upon, on, at the time of, during, by, in the presence of (preposition + genitive); on, in, above, at, by, near, during, at the time of (+ dative); on, to, against, towards, over (+ accusative)
ἐπιβαίνω, ἐπιβήσομαι, ἐπέβην (2 aorist), ἐπιβέβηκα go upon, mount, board
ἐπιβάλλω, ἐπιβαλῶ, ἐπέβαλον, ἐπιβέβληκα, ἐπεβλήθην lay, put on
ἐπίβλημα, ατος, τό patch
ἐπιγαμβρεύω, ἐπιγαμβρεύσω marry as next of kin
ἐπιγινώσκω, ἐπιγνώσομαι, ἐπέγνων (2 aorist), ἐπέγνωκα, ἐπεγνώσθην know, understand, recognize; discern, detect
ἐπιγραφή, ῆς, ἡ inscription
ἐπιδείκνυμι, ἐπιδείξω, ἐπέδειξα, ἐπιδέδειχα, ἐπιδέδειγμαι, ἐπεδείχθην show, point out, declare
ἐπιδίδωμι, ἐπιδώσω give to
ἐπιζητέω, ἐπιζητήσω, ἐπεζήτησα, ἐπεζητήθην search for, seek after; strive for, wish for; demand, desire
ἐπιούσιος, ιον daily
ἐπιθυμέω, ἐπιθυμήσω, ἐπεθύμησα desire, long for
ἐπικαθίζω, ἐπικαθίσω, ἐπεκάθισα sit, sit down (on)
ἐπικαλέω, ἐπικαλέσω, ἐπεκάλεσα, ἐπικέκληκα, ἐπικέκλημαι, ἐπεκλήθην call, name
ἐπιλαμβάνομαι, ἐπιελαβόμην take hold of, grasp, catch, seize
ἐπιλανθάνομαι, ἐπιλήσομαι, ἐπελαθόμην, ἐπιλέλησμαι forget
ἐπιορκέω, ἐπιορκήσω swear falsely, perjure oneself; break one's oath
ἐπίσημος, ον noted, prominent; notorious
ἐπισκέπτομαι, ἐπισκέψομαι, ἐπεσκεψάμην look for; go to see, visit
ἐπισκιάζω, ἐπισκιάσω, ἐπεσκίασα cast a shadow, overshadow
ἐπισπείρω, ἐπισπερῶ, ἐπέσπειρα sow afterward
ἐπιστρέφω, ἐπιστρέψω, ἐπέστρεψα, ἐπέστραμμαι, ἐπεστρέφθην, ἐπεστράφην (2 aorist passive) turn, turn around, convert (transitive); turn oneself back, turn around, be converted (intransitive and middle)
ἐπισυνάγω, ἐπισυνάξω gather (together)

ἐπιτίθημι, ἐπιθήσω, ἐπέθηκα, ἐπιτέθεικα, ἐπιτέθειμαι, ἐπετέθην lay upon, put on
ἐπιτιμάω, ἐπιτιμήσω, ἐπετίμησα set a value on; assess a penalty; rebuke, reprove, censure, reprimand; admonish, enjoin
ἐπιτρέπω, ἐπιτρέψω, ἐπέτρεψα, ἐπιτέτραμμαι, ἐπετράπην (2 aorist passive) give over; permit, allow
ἐπίτροπος, ου, ὁ foreman, manager, steward; overseer, treasurer
ἐπιφώσκω shine forth, dawn
ἑπτά seven (indeclinable)
ἑπτάκις seven times (adverb)
ἐργάζομαι, ἐργάσομαι, ἠργασάμην/εἰργασάμην, εἴργασμαι work, do, accomplish, perform; trade, do business
ἐργάτης, ου, ὁ workman, laborer
ἔργον, ου, τό work, deed, action
ἐρεύγομαι, ἐρεύξομαι vomit; utter, proclaim, declare openly
ἐρημία, ας, ἡ uninhabited region, desert
ἔρημος, η, ον abandoned, empty, desolate, lonely; ἔρημος, ου, ἡ wilderness, desert, grassland (noun)
ἐρημόω, ἐρημώσω, ἠρήμωμαι, ἠρημώθην lay waste, bring to ruin, depopulate
ἐρήμωσις, εως, ἡ desolation, destruction, devastation
ἐρίζω, ἐρίσω quarrel, wrangle
ἐρίφιον, ιου, τό kid, goat (diminutive)
ἔριφος, ου, ὁ kid, goat
ἔρχομαι, ἐλεύσομαι, ἦλθον (2 aorist), ἐλήλυθα come, go
ἐρωτάω, ἐρωτήσω, ἠρώτησα ask, inquire of, question, ask a question, request, beseech
ἐσθίω, φάγομαι, ἔφαγον (2 aorist) eat
Ἑσρώμ, ὁ Esrom, Hezron (indeclinable)
ἔσχατος, η, ον last
ἔσω in, inside (adverb)
ἔσωθεν from inside; inside, within (adverb)
ἑταῖρος, ου, ὁ comrade, companion, fellow, friend
ἕτερος, α, ον other, another
ἔτι yet, still (adverb)
ἑτοιμάζω, ἑτοιμάσω, ἡτοίμασα, ἡτοίμακα, ἡτοίμασμαι, ἡτοιμάσθην make ready, prepare
ἕτοιμος, η, ον ready, prepared
ἔτος, ους, τό year
εὖ well, happily, rightly; well done, it is well (adverb)
εὐαγγελίζω, εὐαγγελίσω, εὐηγγέλισα, εὐηγγέλισμαι, εὐηγγελίσθην bring or announce good news, address with good tidings, announce good tidings
εὐαγγέλιον, ου, τό good news, gospel, glad tidings
εὐδία, ας, ἡ cloudless sky, fair weather; peace, tranquility
εὐδοκέω, εὐδοκήσω, εὐδόκησα/ ηὐδόκησα be well pleased, take delight

εὐδοκία, ας, ἡ good will; favor, good pleasure, purpose, intention; wish, desire

εὐθέως at once, immediately (adverb)

εὐθύς immediately, at once (adverb)

εὐθύς, εῖα, ύ straight; right, upright, true

εὐκαιρία, ας, ἡ convenient opportunity, favorable occasion, suitable moment

εὐκοπώτερος, α, ον easier

εὐλογέω, εὐλογήσω, εὐλόγησα, εὐλόγηκα praise, bless

εὐνοέω be well disposed to, make friends with (+ dative)

εὐνουχίζω, εὐνουχίσω, εὐνούχισα, εὐνουχίσθην castrate, emasculate; to impose chaste abstinence on

εὐνοῦχος, ου, ὁ eunuch

εὑρίσκω, εὑρήσω, εὗρον, ηὕρηκα/εὕρηκα, εὑρέθην find, meet, discover, recognize

εὐρύχωρος, ον broad, spacious, wide

εὐχαριστέω, εὐχαριστήω, εὐχαρίστησα give thanks

εὐώνυμος, ον left (as opposed to *right*); ἐκ εὐωνύμων τινός at someone's left

ἐχθρός, ά, όν hostile, hated, hating, inimical; enemy, adversary (substantive)

ἔχιδνα, ης, ἡ viper, poisonous serpent

ἔχω, ἕξω, ἔσχον, ἔσχηκα have, keep, cause, consider; be (with adverbs and indications of time and age); be able (with infinitive)

ἕως while, as long as, until; ἕως ἄνω to the brim; ἕως (+ genitive) until, unto, even to, as far as; ἕως οὗ until; ἕως πότε; how long? even, as many as (of number)

ζ

Ζάρα, ὁ Zara, Zerah (indeclinable)

Ζαχαρίας, ου, ὁ Zacharias, Zechariah

ζάω, ζήσω/ζήσομαι, ἔζησα, ἔζηκα live

Ζεβεδαῖος, ου, ὁ Zebedee

ζημιόω, ζημιώσω, ἐζημιώθην suffer loss; lose, forfeit (passive)

ζητέω, ζητήσω, ἐζήτησα, ἐζητήθην seek, desire, ask for

ζιζάνιον, ου, τό zizanium, darnel, false wheat, weed, tare

Ζοροβαβέλ, ὁ Zorobabel, Zerubbabel

ζυγός, οῦ, ὁ yoke

ζύμη, ης, ἡ leaven

ζυμόω, ζυμώσω ferment, leaven

ζωή, ῆς, ἡ life, life eternal

ζώνη, ης, ἡ belt, girdle

η

ἤ either, or, than (conjunction)

ἡγεμών, όνος, ὁ guide, leader, prince, governor; prefect, procurator

ἡγέομαι, ἡγήσομαι lead, preside, govern, rule

ἤδη now, already (adverb)

ἡδύοσμον, ου, τό garden mint, mint

ἥκω, ἥξω have come, be present (the present is supplied by ἔρχομαι)
ἠλί my God! (Aramaic)
Ἠλίας, ου, ὁ Elijah
ἡλικία, ας, ἡ age, time of life; stature
ἥλιος, ου, ὁ sun
ἡμέρα, ας, ἡ day; καθ' ἡμέραν daily, every day
Ἡρῴδης, ου, ὁ Herod
Ἡρῳδιανοί, ῶν, οἱ the Herodians
Ἡρῳδιάς, άδος, ἡ Herodias
Ἠσαΐας, ου, ὁ Isaiah

θ

Θαδδαῖος, ου, ὁ Thaddaeus
θάλασσα, ης, ἡ sea, inland sea, lake
Θαμάρ, ἡ Thamar, Tamar (indeclinable)
θάνατος, ου, ὁ death
θανατόω, θανατώσω, ἐθανάτωσα kill, put to death, deliver to death
θάπτω, θάψω, ἔθαψα, τέταφα, ἐτάφην (2 aorist passive) bury
θαρσέω, θαρσήσω, ἐθάρσησα be of good courage, be cheerful
θαυμάζω, θαυμάσομαι, ἐθαύμασα, ἐθαυμάσθην wonder, marvel, be astonished
θαυμάσιος, α, ον wonderful, marvelous; τὸ θαυμάσιον wonder, marvellous work
θαυμαστός, ή, όν wonderful, marvelous, remarkable; τὸ θαυμαστόν the remarkable thing
θεάομαι, θεάσομαι, ἐθεασάμην, τεθέαμαι, ἐθεάθην see, look at, gaze upon, discern with the eyes
θέλημα, ατος, τό will, desire
θέλω, θελήσω, ἠθέλησα wish to have, desire, purpose, want
θεμελιόω, θεμελιώσω, ἐθεμελίωσα, τεθεμελίωκα, τεθεμελίωμαι found, establish
θεός, θεοῦ, ὁ God, god
θεραπεύω, θεραπεύσω, ἐθεράπευσα, ἐθεραπεύθην care for, heal, restore
θερίζω, θερίσω, ἐθέρισα reap, harvest
θερισμός, οῦ, ὁ harvest
θεριστής, οῦ, ὁ reaper, harvester
θέρος, εος, τό summer
θεωρέω, θεωρήσω, ἐθεώρησα see, look at, observe, perceive, experience; view
θηλάζω, θηλάσω, ἐθήλασα suckle; suck; οἱ θηλάζοντες sucklings
θῆλυς, θήλεια, θῆλυ female; τὸ θῆλυ, sc. γένος offspring
θησαυρίζω, θησαυρίσω, ἐθησαύρισα store up, gather, save
θησαυρός, οῦ, ὁ treasure box, treasury, treasure
θλίβω, θλίψω, τέθλιμμαι press upon, make narrow; be restricted, narrow (passive)
θλῖψις, εως, ἡ affliction, tribulation, trouble
θνήσκω, θανοῦμαι, ἔθανον (2 aorist), τέθνηκα die, face death
θορυβέω, θορυβήσω disturb, throw into disorder; be troubled, be distressed (passive)

θόρυβος, ου, ὁ noise; turmoil, uproar
θρηνέω, θρηνήσω, ἐθρήνησα lament, mourn
θρίξ, τριχός, ἡ hair
θροέω, θροήσω cry aloud; be disturbed, alarmed, terrified (passive)
θρόνος, ου, ὁ seat, throne; power, dominion
θυγάτηρ, τρός, ἡ daughter
θυμόω, θυμώσω, ἐθυμώθην provoke to anger, make angry; become angry, enraged (passive)
θύρα, ας, ἡ door, entrance
θυσία, ας, ἡ sacrifice, offering; victim
θυσιαστήριον, ίου, τό altar
θύω, θύσω, ἔθυσα, τέθυμαι, ἐτύθην sacrifice, slaughter, kill
Θωμᾶς, ᾶ, ὁ Thomas (Aramaic = "twin")

ι

Ἰακώβ, ὁ Jacob (indeclinable)
Ἰάκωβος, ου, ὁ Jacob = James (Greek form of Ἰακώβ)
ἰάομαι, ἰάσομαι, ἰασάμην, ἴαμαι, ἰάθην heal, cure, restore
ἰατρός, οῦ, ὁ physician
ἴδε lo! behold! (interjection; imperative of εἴδω see)
ἴδιος, ία, ιον one's own; κατ' ἰδίαν privately, by oneself, alone (adverb)
ἰδού see, look, behold (demonstrative particle)
Ἰερεμίας, ου, ὁ Jeremiah
ἱερεύς, έως, ὁ priest
Ἱεριχώ, ἡ Jericho (indeclinable)
ἱερόν, οῦ, τό temple
Ἱεροσόλυμα, τά and ἡ, and Ἰερουσαλήμ, ἡ Jerusalem (indeclinable)
Ἰεσσαί, ὁ Jesse (indeclinable)
Ἰεχονίας, ου, ὁ Jechonias, Jechoniah
Ἰησοῦς, οῦ, ὁ Jesus
ἱκανός, ή, όν sufficient, enough; adequate, competent, qualified; fit, worthy
ἵλεως, ων gracious, merciful
ἱμάτιον, ου, τό garment, clothing; cloak, robe; clothes, garments (plural)
ἵνα to, in order to, in order that, that (conjunction)
ἱνατί why? why is it that? for what reason? (adverb)
Ἰόρδάνης, ου, ὁ Jordan
Ἰσαάκ, ὁ Isaac (indeclinable)
Ἰσκαριώτης, ου, ὁ Iscariot
ἴσος, η, ον equal
ἵστημι, στήσω, ἔστησα, ἔστην (2 aorist), ἕστηκα, ἐστάθην put, place, set, cause to stand; set out, weigh out, pay (transitive); stand, be (intransitive)
ἰσχυρός, ά, όν strong, mighty, powerful
ἰσχύω, ἰσχύσω, ἴσχυσα be good, be strong, be powerful, have power, be able, be well
Ἰουδαία, ας, ἡ Judaea
Ἰουδαῖος, αία, αῖον Jewish, Jew

Ἰούδας, α, ὁ Judas (Greek), Judah (Hebrew)
Ἰσραήλ, ὁ Israel (indeclinable)
ἰσχύω, ἰσχύσω, ἴσχυσα be strong, be well; have power, be able
ἰχθύδιον, ου, τό small fish
ἰχθύς, ύος, ὁ fish
Ἰωαθάμ, ὁ Joatham, Jotham (indeclinable)
Ἰωάννης, ου, ὁ John
Ἰωβήδ, ὁ Obed (indeclinable)
Ἰωνᾶς, ᾶ, ὁ Jonah
Ἰωράμ, ὁ Joram (indeclinable)
Ἰωσαφάτ, ὁ Josaphat, Jehoshaphat (indeclinable)
Ἰωσήφ, ὁ Joseph (indeclinable)
Ἰωσίας, ου, ὁ Josias, Josiah
ἰῶτα, τό iota, yod, jot, the least bit (indeclinable)

κ

κἀγώ = καὶ ἐγώ
καθά as, just as (adverb)
καθαρίζω, καθαρίσω, ἐκαθάρισα cleanse, render pure
καθαρός, ά, όν clean, pure
καθέδρα, ας, ἡ seat
καθέζομαι, καθεδοῦμαι sit, sit down
καθεύδω, καθευδήσω sleep, be fast asleep
καθηγητής, οῦ, ὁ leader; teacher, instructor
κάθημαι, καθήσομαι sit, stay, reside
καθίζω, καθίσω, ἐκάθισα, κεκάθικα cause to sit down, seat, set (transitive); sit, sit down; remain, stay, continue, rest (intransitive)
καθίστημι and καθιστάνω, καταστήσω, κατέστησα, κατεστάθην place, set, constitute, appoint, put in charge
καθώς as, just as, how, inasmuch as (adverb)
καί and (conjunction); even, also, likewise, and yet (adverb); καί . . . καί both . . . and, not only . . . but also
Καϊάφας, α, ὁ Caiaphas
καινός, ή, όν new
καιρός, οῦ, ὁ time, appointed time; season; time of crisis, end-time
Καῖσαρ, ος, ὁ Caesar
Καισάρεια, ας, ἡ Caesarea
κἀκεῖ = καί ἐκεῖ and there, and in that place (adverb)
κακία, ας, ἡ depravity, wickedness, vice; evil, trouble, misfortune
κακολογέω, κακολογήσω speak ill of, revile, insult, abuse
κακός, ή, όν bad, evil, wrong; τὸ κακόν evil, wickedness, crime
κακῶς ill, badly; grievously, vehemently; wretchedly, miserably; wickedly, wrongly (adverb)
κάλαμος, ου, ὁ reed, cane; staff
καλέω, καλέσω, ἐκάλεσα, κέκληκα, κέκλημαι, ἐκλήθην call, summon, invite
καλός, ή, όν good, useful, choice
καλύπτω, καλύψω, ἐκάλυψα, κεκάλυμμαι cover; hide, conceal

καλῶς well (adverb)
κάμηλος, ου, ὁ and ἡ camel
κάμινος, ου, ἡ oven, furnace
καμμύω, καμμύσω, ἐκαμμυσα shut, close
Κανανaῖος, ου, ὁ Cananaean
καρδία, ας, ἡ heart
καρπός, οῦ, ὁ fruit, crop; result, gain
καρποφορέω, καρποφορήσω, ἐκαρποφόρησα bear fruit; bear the fruit of good deeds
κάρφος, ους, τό speck, bit, small particle (of straw, chaff, wood)
κατά in, during, near, towards, by, in accordance with, for the purpose of, for, after the manner of (preposition + accusative); by (in oaths), down from, against (+ genitive)
καταβαίνω, καταβήσομαι, κατέβην, καταβέβηκα come down, go down, descend, fall
καταβολή, ῆς, ἡ beginning, foundation
καταγελάω, καταγελάσω/ καταγελάσομαι laugh at, deride, jeer, ridicule
κατάγνυμι, κατεάξω, κατέαξα, κατεάγην (2 aorist passive) break, break in pieces, break in two, crush
καταδικάζω, καταδικάσω, κατεδίσα, κατεδικάσθην condemn, find guilty
καταθεματίζω καταθεματίσω curse
κατακαίω, κατακαύσω, κατέκαυσα, κατεκαύθην light, cause to burn, kindle, burn up, burn down, consume by fire (active); burn, be burned, be consumed with fire (passive)
κατακλυσμός, οῦ, ὁ flood, deluge, inundation
κατακρίνω, κατακρινῶ, κατέκρινα, κατακέκρικα, κατακέκριμαι, κατεκρίθην condemn, pronounce sentence
κατακυριεύω, κατακυριεύσω, κατεκυρίευσα, κατεκυριεύθην domineer over, gain dominion over, gain power over, lord it over
καταλείπω, καταλείψω, κατέλειψα, κατέλιπον (2 aorist), κατελείφθην leave behind (active); remain behind (passive)
καταλύω, καταλύσω, κατελύθην destroy, demolish, overthrow, throw down
καταμανθάνω, καταμαθήσομαι, κατέμαθον (2 aorist), καταμεμάθηκα observe, consider, contemplate
καταμαρτυρέω, καταμαρτυρήσω bear witness against, witness against
κατανοέω, κατανοήσω notice, observe; look at, mark, discern; consider
καταπατέω, καταπατήσω, κατεπάτησα, κατεπατήθην trample underfoot; treat with disdain

καταπέτασμα, ατος, τό veil, curtain
καταπίνω, καταπίομαι, κατέπιον (2 aorist), κατεπόθην drink, swallow, gulp down
καταποντίζω, καταποντίσω, κατεποντίσθην throw into the sea, drown; be sunk, be drowned; sink (passive)
καταράομαι, καταράσομαι, κατηρασάμην curse
καταρτίζω, καταρτίσω, κατήρτισα, κατήρτισμαι put in order, restore to its former condition; prepare, make, create; prepare for oneself (middle)
κατασκευάζω, κατασκευάσω, κατεκεύασα, κατεκευάσθην prepare, make ready; build, construct
κατασκήνοσις, εως, ἡ tent; dwelling-place, place to live; nest (of birds)
κατασκηνόω, κατασκηνώσω, κατεσκήνωσα pitch a tent; live, dwell; rest, abide; settle, nest
καταστρέφω, καταστρέψω, κατέστρεψα overturn, overthrow, throw down, upset
καταφιλέω, καταφιλήσω kiss
καταφρονέω, καταφρονήσω, κατεφρόνησα look down on, scorn, despise
καταχέω, καταχεύσω pour out, pour down
κατέναντι opposite to, before (adverb; preposition + genitive)
κατεξουσιάζω, κατεξουσιάσω exercise dominion over
κατεσθίω, καταφάγομαι/κατέδομαι, κατέφαγον eat up, devour, consume
κατηγορέω, κατηγορήσω, κατηγόρησα accuse, bring charges against, speak against
κατισχύω, κατισχύσω, κατίσχυσα overpower, win victory over
κατοικέω, κατοικήσω, κατῴκησα live, dwell, reside (intransitive); inhabit (transitive)
κάτω downward, down, below (adverb)
κατωτέρω under; lower, further down (adverb)
καυματίζω, καυματίσω, ἐκαυμάτισα, ἐκαυματίσθην burn up; be burned, be scorched (passive)
καύσων, ωνος, ὁ scorching heat, scorching; hot weather, hot time
Καφαρναούμ, ἡ Capernaum (indeclinable)
κεῖμαι, κείσομαι lie, be laid, be placed, be set
κελεύω, κελεύσω, ἐκέλευσα give order, command, urge, direct, bid
κεραία, ας, ἡ point, tittle, minutest part
κεραμεύς, έως, ὁ potter
κερδαίνω, κερδήσω, ἐκέρδησα gain, acquire
κεφαλή, ῆς, ἡ head
κῆνσος, ου, ὁ tribute, tax, poll-tax
κήρυγμα, ατος, τό proclaiming, preaching

κηρύσσω, κηρύξω, ἐκήρυξα, ἐκηρύχθην announce openly, proclaim aloud
κῆτος, ους, τό large fish, sea monster, whale
κιβωτός, οῦ, ἡ box, chest; ark (of Noah); ark (of the covenant)
κινέω, κινήσω, ἐκίνησα move; excite; shake
κλάδος, ου, ὁ branch, bough
κλαίω, κλαύσω/κλαύσομαι, ἔκλαυσα weep, shed tears
κλάσμα, ατος, τό fragment, morsel, piece
κλαυθμός, ου, ὁ weeping, crying
κλάω, κλάσω, ἔκλασα break
κλεῖς, κλειδός, ἡ key
κλείω, κλείσω, ἔκλεισα, κέκλεισμαι, ἐκλείσθην close, shut, lock
κλέπτης, ου, ὁ thief
κλέπτω, κλέψω, ἔκλεψα, κέκλοφα, ἐκλάπην (2 aorist passive) steal
κληρονομέω, κληρονομήσω, ἐκληρονόμησα, κεκληρονόμηκα inherit; obtain, acquire, receive
κληρονομία, ας, ἡ inheritance; possession, property
κληρονόμος, ου, ὁ heir
κλῆρος, ου, ὁ lot (= pebble, potsherd, etc.)
κλητός, ή, όν called, invited
κλίβανος, ου, ὁ oven, furnace
κλίνη, ης, ἡ bed, couch; pallet, stretcher
κλίνω, κλινῶ, ἔκλινα (1 aorist), κέκλικα bend, bow; lay down (to rest)
κλοπή, ῆς, ἡ theft
κοδράντης, ου, ὁ Roman brass coin, penny, cent (the actual value is approximately one quarter of an as)
κοιλία, ας, ἡ stomach, belly, womb
κοιμάω, κοιμήσω, ἐκοίμησα, κεκοίμημαι lull to sleep; sleep, fall asleep, die, pass away (passive)
κοινόω, κοινώσω, ἐκοίνωσα, κεκοίνωκα make common, defile; profane, desecrate; render unclean, defile, pollute
κοινωνός, οῦ, ὁ companion, partner, sharer
κόκκινος, η, ον red, crimson, scarlet
κόκκος, ου, ὁ kernel, seed
κόλασις, εως, ἡ punishment
κολαφίζω, κολαφίσω strike with the fist, beat with the fist
κολλάω, κολλήσω, ἐκολλήθην bind closely, unite; cling to, join oneself to, be joined to (passive)
κολλυβιστής, οῦ, ὁ money changers
κολοβόω, κολοβώσω, ἐκολόβωσα, ἐκολοβώθην shorten, cut short, curtail
κομίζω, κομίσω, ἐκόμισα bring; carry off, get, receive, obtain, get back, recover (middle)
κονιάω, κονιάσω, κεκονίαμαι whitewash, plaster
κονιορτός, οῦ, ὁ dust
κοπάζω, κοπάσω, ἐκόπασα cease, abate, stop, rest

κοπιάω, κοπιάσω, ἐκοπίασα, κεκοπίακα be weary, be tired, work hard, toil
κόπος, ου, ὁ work, labor, toil; trouble, difficulty
κόπτω, κόψω, ἔκοψα, ἐκόπην (2 aorist passive) smite, cut, cut off; beat one's breast (in mourning), mourn, lament (middle)
κοράσιον, ου, τό girl
κορβανᾶς, ᾶ, ὁ temple treasury
κοσμέω, κοσμήσω, ἐκόσμησα, κεκόσμηκα, κεκόσμημαι set in order, arrange; prepare, trim; decorate, adorn
κόσμος, ου, ὁ order, world, universe
κουστωδία, ας, ἡ watch, guard (composed of soldiers)
κόφινος, ου, ὁ basket
κράζω, κεκράξομαι/κράξω, ἐκέκραξα/ἔκραξα, κέκραγα cry out, cry aloud, scream; call, call out, cry
κρανίον, ου, τό skull
κράσπεδον, ου, τό edge, border, hem; tassel
κρατέω, κρατήσω, ἐκράτησα, κεκράτηκα, κεκράτημαι lay hold of, grasp, seize, apprehend; retain, not remit
κραυγάζω, κραυγάσω, ἐκραύγασα cry out, exclaim
κραυγή, ῆς, ἡ shouting, clamor
κρεμάννυμι, κρεμάσω, ἐκρέμασα, ἐκρεμάσθην hang, suspend; depend
κρημνός, οῦ, ὁ precipice, steep slope or bank, cliff
κρίμα, ατος, τό judging, judgment, condemnation
κρίνον, ου, τό lily
κρίνω, κρινῶ, ἔκρινα, κέκρικα, κέκριμαι, ἐκρίθην separate, select, judge, condemn; dispute, quarrel, debate, sue (middle and passive)
κρίσις, εως, ἡ judgment, justice, righteousness, condemnation
κριτής, ου, ὁ judge
κρούω, κρούσω, ἔκρουσα knock (at a door)
κρυπτός, ή, όν hidden, concealed, secret (adjective); hidden thing, hidden place, secret (noun)
κρύπτω, κρύψω, ἔκρυψα, κέκρυμμαι, ἐκρύβην hide, conceal, cover
κρυφαῖος, αία, αῖον secret, hidden; ἐν τῷ κρυφαίῳ in secret
κτάομαι, κτήσομαι, ἐκτησάμην, κέκτημαι procure, acquire, get; make gain, gain; preserve, save
κτῆμα, ατος, τό possession, property
κτίζω, κτίσω, ἔκτισα, ἔκτισμαι, ἐκτίσθην create, frame
κυλλός, ή, όν maimed, crippled, deformed; cripple, injured person (substantive)
κῦμα, ατος, τό wave, surge, billow
κύμινον, ου, τό cum(m)in, the fruit or seed of the cumin
κυνάριον, ίου, τό house-dog, little dog, dog (diminutive of κύων)

Κυρηναῖος, ου, ὁ Cyrenian
κύριος, ου, ὁ lord, Lord, master
κύων, κυνός, ὁ dog
κωλύω, κωλύσω, ἐκώλυσα, ἐκωλύθην hinder, restrain, prevent, prohibit
κώμη, ης, ἡ village, small town
κώνωψ, ωπος, ὁ gnat, mosquito
κωφός, ή, όν blunt, dull; dull of hearing, deprived of hearing; deaf; dumb, mute

λ

λάθρᾳ in secret, secretly (adverb)
λαλέω, λαλήσω, ἐλάλησα, λελάληκα, λελάλημαι, ἐλαλήθην speak, address, preach
λαλιά, ᾶς, ἡ speech
λαμβάνω, λήμψομαι, ἔλαβον, εἴληφα, εἴλημμαι, ἐλήφθην take, get, get together, receive, accept
λαμπάς, άδος, ἡ light, lamp, torch
λάμπω, λάμψω, ἔλαμψα shine, shine forth, give light
λαός, οῦ, ὁ people
λατομέω, λατομήσω, ἐλατόμησα, λελατόμηκα cut out of stone, hew out of rock
λατρεύω, λατρεύσω, ἐλάτρευσα serve
λάχανον, ου, τό garden herb, vegetable
λεγιών, ῶνος, ὁ legion
λέγω, ἐρῶ, εἶπον (2 aorist), εἴρηκα, εἴρημαι, ἐρρέθην/ἐρρήθην say, assert, proclaim, tell, declare
λεμά why? (Aramaic)
λευκός, ή, όν bright, shining, gleaming, white
λέπρα, ας, ἡ leprosy
λεπρός, οῦ, ὁ leper
ληνός, οῦ, ἡ tub; winepress; wine vat
λῃστής, οῦ, ὁ robber, bandit
λίαν greatly, exceedingly (adverb)
λίβανος, ου, ὁ frankincense
λιθοβολέω, λιθοβολήσω, ἐλιθοβόλησα throw stones at, stone to death
λίθος, ου, ὁ stone
λικμάω, λικμήσω winnow grain; scatter like chaff
λιμός, οῦ, ὁ hunger, famine
λίνον, ου, τό flax, linen; flaxen wick, lamp-wick
λόγος, ου, ὁ word, doctrine, account, reason, statement, saying, talk, speech
λοιπός, ή, όν remaining; the rest, remainder; (τὸ) λοιπόν from now on, in the future, henceforth
λύκος, ου, ὁ wolf
λυπέω, λυπήσω, ἐλύπησα, λελύπηκα, ἐλυπήθην vex, irritate, offend (active); be grieved, pained, distressed, sorrowful (passive)
λύτρον, ου, τό price paid, price of release, ransom
λυχνία, ας, ἡ lampstand, stand
λύχνος, ου, ὁ lamp
λύω, λύσω, ἔλυσα, λέλυκα, λέλυμαι, ἐλύθην loose, unbind, unfasten, break, destroy

μ

Μαγαδάν, ἡ Magadan (indeclinable)
Μαγδαληνή, ῆς, ἡ Magdalene, woman from Magdala
μάγος, ου, ὁ magus, wise man, magian
μαθητεύω, μαθητεύσω, ἐμαθήτευσα become a disciple of, follow as a disciple (intransitive active and passive deponent); make a disciple of, teach; be trained, be instructed (passive)
μαθητής, οῦ, ὁ disciple
Μαθθαῖος/Ματθαῖος, ου, ὁ Matthew
μακάριος, ία, ιον blessed, happy, fortunate
μακράν far, far off, far away (adverb)
μακρόθεν far off, at a distance, from afar (adverb)
μακροθυμέω, μακροθυμήσω, ἐμακροθύμησα have patience, wait; be patient, forbearing
μαλακία, ας, ἡ softness, weakness, infirmity
μαλακός, ή, όν soft, delicate
μᾶλλον more, to a greater degree, rather (adverb)
μαμωνᾶς, ᾶ, ὁ wealth, property, Mammon
Μανασσῆς, ῆ, ὁ Manasses, Manasseh
μανθάνω, μαθήσομαι, ἔμαθον (2 aorist), μεμάθηκα learn
μαργαρίτης, ου, ὁ pearl
Μαρία, ας, ἡ Mary (Μαρίαμ indeclinable)
μαρτυρέω, μαρτυρήσω, ἐμαρτύρησα, μεμαρτύρηκα, μεμαρτύρημαι, ἐμαρτυρήθην bear witness, witness
μαρτύριον, ίου, τό proof, testimony, evidence
μάρτυς, μάρτυρος, ὁ and ἡ witness
μαστιγόω, μαστιγώσω, ἐμαστίγωσα, ἐμαστιγώθην scourge, whip, flog, beat
μάτην in vain, without profit, fruitlessly (adverb)
Ματθάν, ὁ Matthan (indeclinable)
μάχαιρα, ας, ἡ sword
μεγαλύνω, μεγαλυνῶ, ἐμεγάλυνα enlarge, amplify, magnify; exalt, glorify, praise
μέγας, μεγάλη, μέγα large, great
μεθερμηνεύω, μεθερμηνεύσω translate, interpret
μεθύω be intoxicated, be drunk
μείζων, μεῖζον greater, larger; greatest, largest (the comparative of μέγας; also used as the superlative)
μέλας, αινα, αν black
μέλει, μελήσει, ἐμέλησεν there is a care, it is a concern
μέλι, ιτος, τό honey
μέλλω, μελλήσω be about to, be on the point of
μέλος, ους, τό member, limb, part

μέν on the one hand (the particle is used to contrast one term or clause with another, usually δέ *on the other*. If cumbersome it may be omitted in translation and δέ may be translated by *but*). ὁ μέν . . . ὁ δέ the one . . . the other; οἱ μέν . . . ἄλλοι δέ some . . . others
μένω, μενῶ, ἔμεινα, μεμένηκα stay, rest, dwell
μερίζω, μερίσω, ἐμέρισα, μεμέρικα, μεμέρισμαι, ἐμερίσθην divide, separate; be at variance (passive)
μέριμνα, ης, ἡ care
μεριμνάω, μεριμνήσω, ἐμερίμνησα have anxiety, be anxious; expend careful thought, concern oneself
μέρος, ους, τό part, portion, share
μέσος, η, ον middle, in the middle; in, among (as adjective + genitive); the middle (as noun τὸ μέσον); ἀνὰ μέσον among, between, in the midst, through the midst
μεστός, ή, όν full
μετά (μεθ' before a rough breathing) with (preposition + genitive); after (+ accusative)
μεταβαίνω, μεταβήσομαι, μετέβην, μεταβέβηκα go, pass over, move; go away, depart
μεταίρω, μεταρῶ, μετῆρα go away, depart
μεταμέλομαι, μεταμελήσομαι, μετεμελήθην change one's mind, feel regret, repent
μεταμορφόω, μεταμορφώσω, μετεμορφώθην transform, change in form, transfigure
μετανοέω, μετανοήσω, μετανόησα change one's mind, repent
μετάνοια, ας, ἡ change of mind, remorse, repentance
μεταξύ between (adverb, preposition + genitive)
μετοικεσία, ας, ἡ migration, removal, deportation, captivity
μετρέω, μετρήσω, ἐμέτρησα measure; give out, apportion
μέτρον, ου, τό measure
μέχρι to, even to; until, till (preposition + genitive)
μή not, except that (particle of negation); that not, lest (conjunction); (interrogative particle expecting a negative answer)
μηδέ and not, but not; nor (following a negation)
μηδείς, μηδεμία, μηδέν not one, none, no one, nothing
μηκέτι no longer, not from now on (adverb)
μήποτε not, never; that . . . not, lest, (in order) that . . . not (conjunction)
μήτε . . . μήτε neither . . . nor
μήτι (interrogative particle in questions expecting a negative answer)
μήτηρ, τρος, ἡ mother
μίγνυμι/μίγνυω, μίξω, ἔμιξα, μέμιγμαι mix, mingle

μικρός, ά, όν small, short, little, humble; little one (substantive); μικρόν short time; short distance
μικρότερος, έρα, ερον smaller, littler; smallest, least (the comparative of μικρός; also used as the superlative)
μίλιον, ίου, τό (Roman) mile = 1000 paces
μιμνήσκομαι, μνησθήσομαι, μέμνημαι, ἐμνήσθην remember, recollect, call to mind
μισέω, μισήσω, ἐμίσησα, μεμίσηκα hate, detest, abhor; love less, esteem less
μισθός, οῦ, ὁ pay, wages, reward
μισθόω, μισθώσω hire
μνημεῖον, ου, τό monument, grave, tomb
μνημονεύω, μνημονεύσω, ἐμνημόνευσα remember, call to mind
μνημόσυνον, ου, τό memorial; remembrance
μνηστεύω, μνηστεύσω, ἐμνηστεύθην to betroth (active); be betrothed (passive)
μόδιος, ου, ὁ corn measure, vessel, bushel
μοιχαλίς, ίδος, ἡ adulteress; adulterous, faithless, ungodly (adjective)
μοιχάομαι, μοιχήσομαι defile a married woman, commit adultery, be guilty of adultery
μοιχεία, ας, ἡ adultery
μοιχεύω, μοιχεύσω, ἐμοίχευσα commit adultery with, debauch (+ accusative)
μόνον only (adverb); μὴ μόνον . . . ἀλλὰ καί not only . . . but also
μόνος, η, ον only, alone
μονόφθαλμος, ον one-eyed; deprived of an eye
μύλος, ου, ὁ mill; millstone
μύριοι, αι, α ten thousand
μύρον, ου, τό ointment, unguent, perfume
μυστήριον, ου, τό secret, secret rite, secret teaching, mystery
μωραίνω, μωρανῶ, ἐμώρανα, ἐμωράνθην make foolish, make tasteless; become foolish, become tasteless, become insipid (passive)
μωρός, ά, όν foolish, wicked, impious
Μωϋσῆς, έως, ὁ Moses

ν

Ναασσών, ὁ Naasson, Nahshon (indeclinable)
Ναζαρέτ, ἡ Nazareth (indeclinable)
Ναζωραῖος, ου, ὁ Nazorean, Nazarene, inhabitant of Nazareth
ναί yes, indeed, certainly (particle of affirmation)
ναός, οῦ, ὁ dwelling, temple
νεανίσκος, ου, ὁ young man, youth
νεκρός, ά, όν dead
νέος, α, ον new, fresh, young
νεφέλη, ης, ἡ cloud

νήθω, νήσω spin
νήπιος, ία, ιον unlearned, simple, young; infant, babe, child (substantive)
νηστεύω, νηστεύσω, ἐνήστευσα fast
νῆστις, ιος/ιδος, ὁ, ἡ hungry, not eating
νῖκος, ους, τό victory
Νινευίτης, ου, ὁ Ninevite
νίπτω, νίψω, ἔνιψα wash (active); wash oneself (middle)
νοέω, νοήσω, ἐνόησα perceive, observe; understand, comprehend
νομίζω, νομίσω, ἐνόμισα, νενόμικα think, believe, consider
νομικός, ή, όν pertaining to law; a jurist, lawyer, an interpreter and teacher of the Mosaic law (substantive)
νόμισμα, ατος, τό coin
νόμος, ου, ὁ law, custom, ordinance
νόσος, ου, ἡ disease, sickness, illness
νοσσίον, ου, τό the young of birds, a chick; a brood of young birds (plural)
νότος, ου, ὁ south wind; south
νύμφη, ης, ἡ bride; daughter-in-law
νυμφίος, ου, ὁ bridegroom
νυμφών, ῶνος, ὁ wedding hall, bridal chamber
νῦν now, at the present time, just now, of late (adverb); τὸ νῦν the present time, now (noun)
νύξ, νυκτός, ἡ night
νυστάζω, νυστάσω nod, become drowsy
Νῶε, ὁ Noah (indeclinable)

ξ

ξένος, ου, ὁ strange, foreign; stranger, foreigner (substantive)
ξηραίνω, ξηρανῶ, ἐξήρανα, ἐξήραμμαι, ἐξηράνθην dry out, parch; become dry, dry up, wither (passive)
ξηρός, ά, όν dried up, withered, paralyzed; ἡ ξηρά (γῆ) dry land, land
ξύλον, ου, τό wood; club, cudgel; cross; tree

ο

ὁ, ἡ, τό the (definite article)
ὁδηγός, ου, ὁ guide, leader; instructor, teacher
ὁδός, οῦ, ἡ road, way, path, journey
ὀδούς, ὀδόντος, ὁ tooth
ὀδυρμός, ου, ὁ lamentation, mourning
Ὀζίας, ου, ὁ Ozias, Uzziah
ὅθεν from where, from the place where, whence, from which; from which fact, therefore, hence; wherefore, whereupon (adverb)
οἶδα know; know how to (+ infinitive)
οἰκετεία, ας, ἡ household
οἰκία, ας, ἡ house, household, family

οἰκιακός, ου, ὁ member of a household
οἰκοδεσπότης, ου, ὁ master of the house
οἰκοδομέω, οἰκοδομήσω, ᾠκοδόμησα, ᾠκοδομήθην build, construct, establish
οἰκοδομή, ῆς, ἡ building, structure
οἶκος, ου, ὁ house, dwelling
οἰκουμένη, ης, ἡ inhabited earth, world (literally *inhabited;* supply γῆ)
οἰνοπότης, ου, ὁ wine-drinker, drunkard
οἶνος, ου, ὁ wine
οἷος, οἵα, οἷον of what sort, (such) as
ὀκνηρός, ά, όν lazy, indolent, idle
ὀλιγοπιστία, ας, ἡ weakness of faith, scantiness of faith, poverty of faith
ὀλιγόπιστος, ον of little faith
ὀλίγος, η, ον little, small; few (plural)
ὅλος, η, ον all, whole, entire, complete; δι᾽ ὅλου throughout
ὅλως wholly, altogether; at all (adverb; with a negative)
ὄμμα, ατος, τό eye
ὀμνύω/ὄμνυμι, ὀμοῦμαι, ὤμοσα, ὀμώμοκα swear, promise with an oath
ὅμοιος, οία, οιον like, similar to (+ dative)
ὁμοιόω, ὁμοιώσω, ὁμοίωσα, ὡμοιώθην make like, liken, compare; be like, be made like, become like, resemble (passive)
ὁμοίως likewise, also, similarly (adverb)
ὁμολογέω, ὁμολογήσω, ὡμολόγησα assure, admit, confess, declare (publicly)
ὄναρ, τό dream (indeclinable)
ὀνειδίζω, ὀνειδίσω, ὠνείδισα reproach, revile, heap insults upon
ὀνικός, ή, όν of an ass, for an ass, turned by an ass
ὄνομα, ατος, τό name
ὄνος, ου, ὁ, ἡ donkey (male or female)
ὄξος, ους, τό vinegar, sour wine, common wine
ὄπισθεν from behind, behind, after (adverb; preposition + genitive)
ὀπίσω back, backward, behind, after (adverb; preposition + genitive); εἰς τὰ ὀπίσω back, backward
ὅπου where (adverb); ὅπου ἐάν wherever (with present subjunctive)
ὅπως that, in order that (conjunction)
ὅραμα, ατος, τό a thing seen, sight, appearance; vision
ὁράω, ὄψομαι, εἶδον (2 aorist), ἑώρακα/ἑόρακα, ὤφθην see, catch sight of, notice, look, observe, perceive, experience, witness
ὀργή, ῆς, ἡ anger, wrath, indignation
ὀργίζω, ὀργίσω, ὠργίσθην provoke to anger; be angry at, be enraged at (passive + dative)

ὅριον, ου, τό boundary; region, territory, district (plural)
ὅρκος, ου, ὁ oath
ὁρμάω, ὁρμήσω, ὥρμησα put in motion, incite; rush (intransitive)
ὄρνις, ιθος, ὁ, ἡ bird; hen
ὄρος, ους, τό mountain, hill
ὀρύσσω, ὀρύξω, ὤρυξα, ὠρύγην dig up, dig out, dig
ὀρχέομαι, ὀρχήσομαι, ὠρχησάμην dance
ὅς, ἥ, ὅ who, which, what; he who, that (relative pronoun); ἐφ' ὅ why? ὃς μὲν . . . ὃς δέ the one . . . the other, one . . . another; ὅς, ἥ, ὅ + ἄν (ἐάν) whoever, whatever
ὅσος, η, ον how large, how much, how great; as much as; as many as (plural); whosoever, whatsoever; ἐφ' ὅσον while, as long as, inasmuch as
ὀστέον, ου, (contracted to ὀστοῦν, ὀστοῦ) τό bone
ὅστις, ἥτις, ὅ τι whoever, whatever (indefinite relative pronoun)
ὀσφύς, ύος, ἡ waist
ὅταν when, whenever (conjunction)
ὅτε when, whenever (adverb)
ὅτι that, because, since (conjunction); (used as our quotation marks to introduce direct discourse)
οὗ where, in what place (adverb)
οὐ not (οὐκ before vowels with a smooth breathing, οὐχ before a rough breathing, adverb)
οὐ μή never, certainly not; οὐ μόνον . . . ἀλλὰ καί . . . not only but also
οὐαί woe! alas! (interjection)
οὐδαμῶς by no means (adverb)
οὐδέ not even (when single); and not, neither, nor (conjunction and adverb)
οὐδείς, οὐδεμία, οὐδέν no (adjective); no one, nobody, nothing (substantive)
οὐδέποτε never (adverb)
οὐκ not (a form of οὐ used before vowels with a smooth breathing, adverb)
οὐκέτι no more, no longer, no further (adverb)
οὖν therefore, then, so (conjunction, postpositive)
οὔπω not yet (adverb)
οὐράνιος, ία, ιον heavenly, celestial
οὐρανός, οῦ, ὁ heaven
Οὐρίας, ου, ὁ Urias (Greek), Uriah (Hebrew)
οὖς, ὠτός, τό ear
οὔτε and not, not even (conjunction); οὔτε . . . οὔτε neither . . . nor
οὗτος, αὕτη, τοῦτο this, this one (demonstrative pronoun)
οὕτως so, thus, in this manner (adverb)
οὐχί not; no, by no means (adverb; more intensive form of οὐ)
ὀφειλέτης, ου, ὁ debtor; offender; sinner
ὀφειλή, ῆς, ἡ debt

ὀφείλημα, ατος, τό debts; offense, fault, sin
ὀφείλω (only in present and imperfect) owe, ought, must, deserve
ὀφθαλμός, οῦ, ὁ eye
ὄφις, εως, ὁ snake, serpent
ὄχλος, ου, ὁ crowd, throng, multitude
ὀψέ late (in the day), in the evening (adverb); ὀψὲ σαββάτων after the close of the sabbath (preposition + genitive)
ὀψία, ας, ἡ evening
ὄψιος, ία, ιον late

π

παγιδεύω, παγιδεύσω set a snare, trap; entrap
παιδίον, ου, τό infant, young child, little boy, little girl
παιδίσκη, ης, ἡ girl, maiden, servant girl
παῖς, παιδός, ὁ child, boy, youth; servant
παίω, παίσω, ἔπαισα, πέπαικα strike, smite
πάλαι long ago, formerly; for a long time; already (adverb)
παλαιός, ά, όν old
παλιγγενεσία, ας, ἡ rebirth, resurrection, regeneration
πάλιν again (adverb)
πάντοτε always, at all times, ever (adverb)
παρ' = παρά from (the side of), from, issuing from, by (preposition + genitive)
παρά from (the side of), from, issuing from, by (preposition + genitive); with, by, among, in the sight of, in the judgment of (+ dative); by, near to, along, to, at (+ accusative)
παραβαίνω, παραβήσομαι, παρέβην (2 aorist) go aside, deviate, turn aside (intransitive); transgress, violate, break (transitive)
παραβολή, ῆς, ἡ comparison, parable, illustration
παραγγέλλω, παραγγελλῶ announce, notify; command, direct
παραγίνομαι, παραγενήσομαι, παρεγενόμην come, arrive, be present
παράγω, παράξω lead beside, bring in (transitive); pass by, depart, go away (intransitive)
παραδίδωμι, παραδώσω, παρέδωκα, παρέδων (2 aorist), παραδέδωκα, παραδέδομαι, παρεδόθην give, hand over, give over, deliver up, give up, arrest, betray
παράδοσις, εως, ἡ handing over; betrayal, arrest; teaching, doctrine; tradition
παραθαλάσσιος, ία, ιον by the sea, maritime, by the lake
παρακαλέω, παρακαλέσω, παρεκάλεσα, παρακέκληκα, παρακέκλημαι, παρεκλήθην call upon, call for, summon, invite, appeal to, request, urge, exhort, persuade; beg, implore, entreat; comfort, encourage, cheer up

παρακούω, παρακούσομαι fail to listen, disregard

παραλαμβάνω, παραλήμψομαι, παρέλαβον (2 aorist), παρείληφα, παρείλημμαι, παρελήφθην take, receive, accept

παραλυτικός, ή, όν lame person, paralytic, palsied

παραπορεύομαι, παραπορεύσομαι pass by, pass along, go

παράπτωμα, ατος, τό transgression, sin

παρασκευή, ῆς, ἡ preparation (= day of preparation for a festival)

παρατίθημι, παραθήσω, παρέθηκα set before, put before, propound

παραχρῆμα immediately, at once (adverb)

πάρειμι be present, be here, have come

παρεκτός except for, apart from (preposition + genitive)

παρέρχομαι, παρελεύσομαι, παρῆλθον (2 aorist), παρελήλυθα pass, pass along, pass by; pass away, come to an end

παρέχω, παρέξω, παρέσχον (2 aorist) give up, offer, present; grant, show; cause, bring about

παρθένος, ου, ἡ virgin

παρίστημι, παραστήσω place beside, put at one's disposal, present, offer, show; stand by, be present (intransitive)

παρομοιάζω, παρομοιάσω be like, resemble

παροψίς, ίδος, ἡ dish

παρουσία, ας, ἡ presence; coming, arrival

πᾶς, πᾶσα, πᾶν every, all, each, any; διὰ παντός (sc. χρονοῦ) always, continuously, constantly

πάσχα, τό feast of the passover (indeclinable)

πάσχω, πείσομαι, ἔπαθον, πέπονθα suffer, endure, undergo

πατάσσω, πατάξω, ἐπάταξα strike, smite; kill

πατήρ, πατρός, ὁ father, parent, ancestor; God

πατρίς, πατρίδος, ἡ fatherland, homeland, hometown

παχύνω, παχυνῶ, ἐπαχύνθην make fat, fatten; make impervious, render gross, dull, unfeeling

πεζῇ on foot; by land (adverb)

πείθω, πείσω, ἔπεισα, πέπεικα, πέποιθα (2 perfect), πέπεισμαι, ἐπείσθην persuade, influence by persuasion; pacify, conciliate, win over

πεινάω, πεινάσω/πεινήσω, ἐπείνασα hunger, be hungry; hunger after, long for

πειρασμός, οῦ, ὁ test, trial; temptation

πειράζω, πειράσω, ἐπείρασα, πεπείρασμαι, ἐπειράσθην try, test, tempt, prove

πέλαγος, εος, τό the high sea, the deep, open sea

πέμπω, πέμψω, ἔπεμψα, πέπομφα, ἐπέμφθην send; send word

πενθερά, ᾶς, ἡ mother-in-law

πενθέω, πενθήσω, ἐπένθησα be sad, grieve, lament, mourn
πεντακισχίλιοι, αι, α five thousand
πέντε five (indeclinable)
πέραν across, beyond, on the other side of (preposition + genitive); τὸ πέραν farther side, the other side
πέρας, ατος, τό end, limit, boundary
περί about, concerning, at (preposition + genitive); about, around (+ accusative)
περιάγω, περιάξω lead around; traverse
περιβάλλω, περιβαλῶ, περέβαλον, περιβέβληκα, περεβλήθην cast around, throw around; clothe; put (something) on oneself, clothe oneself, be clothed (middle)
περίλυπος, ον greatly grieved, exceedingly sorrowful
περιπατέω, περιπατήσω, περιεπάτησα walk, walk about
περίσσευμα, ατος, τό abundance, fullness, exuberance
περισσεύω, περισσεύσω, ἐπερίσσευσα be left over, abound; abundance is given, have great abundance, be gifted with abundance (passive)
περισσός, ή, όν over and above, extraordinary, excessive; περισσῶς in full abundance (adverb); περισσότερος, α, ον more, greater (comparative)
περιστερά, ᾶς, ἡ dove, pigeon
περιτίθημι, περιθήσω, περιέθην (2 aorist), περιέθηκα place around, put about, attach
περίχωρος, ὁ, ἡ adjacent region, country around; inhabitants of the region around
πετεινόν, οῦ, τό bird, fowl
πέτρα, ας, ἡ rock; crags, clefts, rock formation; stony ground
Πέτρος, ου, ὁ Peter
πετρώδης, ες rocky, stony; rocky ground (substantive)
πήρα, ας, ἡ leather bag, traveler's bag, knapsack
πῆχυς, εως, ὁ cubit (17 to 18 inches)
πικρῶς bitterly (adverb)
Πιλᾶτος, ου, ὁ Pilate
πίμπλημι, πλήσω, ἐπλήστην fill, fulfill
πίναξ, ακος, ἡ platter, dish
πίνω, πίομαι, ἔπιον, πέπωκα drink
πιπράσκω, πέπρακα, πέπραμαι, ἐπράθην sell
πίπτω, πεσοῦμαι, ἔπεσα, ἔπεσον (2 aorist), πέπτωκα fall, fall prostrate, fall down
πιστεύω, πιστεύσω, ἐπίστευσα, πεπίστευκα, πεπίστευμαι, ἐπιστεύθην believe; entrust
πίστις, εως, ἡ faith, trust
πιστός, ή, όν faithful, true; believing, trusting
πλανάω, πλανήσω, ἐπλάνησα, πεπλάνημαι, ἐπλανήθην lead astray, cause to wander, mislead, deceive; go astray, wander about, stray, be deceived, err (passive)

πλάνη, ης, ἡ wandering; deceit, deception, delusion
πλάνος, η, ον wanderer, vagabond; deceiver, imposter
πλατεῖα, ας, ἡ wide road, street
πλατύνω, πλατυνῶ, πεπλάτυμαι, ἐπλατύνθην widen, enlarge
πλατύς, εῖα, ύ broad, wide
πλεῖστος, η, ον most, very great (superlative of πολύς)
πλείων, πλεῖον or πλέον more, greater, larger; πλέον more (comparative adverb)
πλέκω, πλέξω, ἔπλεξα weave, braid, plait
πληθύνω, πληθυνῶ, ἐπλήθυνα, ἐπληθύνθην increase, multiply (active and passive)
πλήν besides, except (adverb); but, however, nevertheless (conjunction)
πλήρης, ες full
πληρόω, πληρώσω, ἐπλήρωσα, πεπλήρωκα, πεπλήρωμαι, ἐπληρώθην fill, complete, fulfill
πλήρωμα, ατος, τό that which fills, that which replaces, patch
πλησίον near, close to (adverb, preposition + genitive); ὁ πλησίον neighbor; a friendly neighbor
πλοῖον, ου, τό ship, boat
πλούσιος, ία, ιον rich, wealthy; rich man (substantive)
πλοῦτος, ου, ὁ riches, wealth, opulence
πνεῦμα, ατος, τό wind, spirit, mind, Holy Spirit
πνέω, πνεύσω, ἔπνευσα blow
πνίγω, πνίξω, ἔπνιξα choke, suffocate, strangle
πόθεν from where? how? in what way? (interrogative adverb)
ποιέω, ποιήσω, ἐποίησα, πεποίηκα, πεποίημαι, ἐποιήθην make, do; keep, obey; bring about, produce; spend (time), continue for a (time); give, keep, celebrate (a festival)
ποικίλος, η, ον various, diverse
ποιμαίνω, ποιμανῶ, ἐποίμανα feed, herd, tend
ποίμνη, ης, ἡ flock
ποιμήν, ένος, ὁ shepherd, herdsman, guardian
ποῖος, ποία, ποῖον of what kind? of what sort? of what species? what? which?
πόλεμος, ου, ὁ war
πόλις, εως, ἡ city
πολλάκις many times, often, frequently (adverb)
πολυλογία, ας, ἡ wordiness
πολύς, πολλή, πολύ much, large, great, many (in plural); πολλῷ by far (adverb)
πολύτιμος, ον costly, precious, valuable
πονηρία, ας, ἡ evil disposition, wickedness, mischief
πονηρός, ά, όν bad, evil, wicked
πονηρότερος, α, ον more evil, more wicked (comparative of πονηρός)

πορεύομαι, πορεύσομαι, πεπόρευμαι, ἐπορεύθην go, proceed, travel; go away, depart
πορνεία, ας, ἡ immorality, prostitution, fornication, adultery
πόρνη, ης, ἡ harlot, prostitute
πόρρω forward; far, far off, far away, at a distance (adverb)
ποσάκις how many times? how often? (interrogative adverb)
πόσος, η, ον how great? how much?
ποταμός, οῦ, ὁ river, stream, torrent
ποταπός, ή, όν what? of what manner? of what sort?
πότε when? ἕως πότε; how long? (interrogative adverb)
ποτήριον, ου, τό cup
ποτίζω, ποτίσω, ἐπότισα, πεπότικα cause someone to drink, give someone something to drink
ποῦ where? in what place? (interrogative adverb)
πούς, ποδός, ὁ foot
πρᾶγμα, ατος, τό that which is done, fact, deed, transaction, thing, matter, affair
πραιτώριον, ου, τό general's tent, governor's official residence
πρᾶξις, εως, ἡ activity, way of acting; act, action, deed
πραῢς, πραεῖα, πραΰ meek, gentle, humble, considerate, kind, forgiving; mild, benevolent, humane
πρέπον fitting, proper, right (+ dative and infinitive)
πρεσβύτερος, α, ον older, ancestor, elder (designation of an official); ancients, fathers (plural)
πρίν before (adverb)
πρίν ἤ sooner than, before (adverb)
πρό before (preposition + genitive)
προάγω, προάξω, προήγαγον (2 aorist) lead forward, bring out (transitive); go before, precede, go before (intransitive); go or come before *someone* (+ accusative of person)
προβαίνω, προβήσομαι, προέβην (2 aorist) go forward, go ahead, advance
πρόβατον, ου, τό sheep
προβιβάζω, προβιβάσω, προεβίβασα, προεβιβάσθην lead forward, put forward, push forward; incite, instigate, prompt
προέρχομαι, προελεύσομαι, προῆλθον, προελήλυθα go forward, advance, proceed; go before
πρόθεσις, εως, ἡ putting out, setting forth, presentation
πρόθυμος, ον ready, willing, eager
προλέγω, προλέξω, προεῖπα, προεῖπον (2 aorist), προείρηκα tell beforehand, foretell
πρός for, for the purpose of (preposition + genitive); with, to, towards, unto, for, for the purpose of, by, at, with reference to, in relation to, of, concerning, against (+ accusative); near, at, by (preposition + dative)

προσδοκάω, προσδοκήσω, προσεδόκησα wait for, look for, expect; think, anticipate
προσέρχομαι, προσελεύσομαι, προσῆλθον, προσελήλυθα come to, go to, approach
προσευχή, ῆς, ἡ prayer
προσεύχομαι, προσεύξομαι, προσηυξάμην pray, offer prayer
προσέχω, προσέξω, προσέσχον (2 aorist) pay attention to, give heed to, consider; beware of, take heed of, guard against (followed by ἀπό, μή)
προσήλυτος, ου, ὁ, ἡ proselyte, convert
πρόσκαιρος, ον lasting for a limited time, temporary, transitory, transient
προσκαλέομαι, προσκαλέσομαι, προσεκαλεσάμην, προσκέκλημαι summon, call on, invite, call to oneself
προσκαλέω, προσκαλέσω, προσεκάλεσα, προσκέκληκα, προσκέκλημαι, προσεκλήθην call on, summon, invite, call to oneself
προσκόπτω, προσκόψω, προσέκοψα dash against, beat upon, strike (the foot) against; stumble
προσκυλίω, προσκυλίσω to roll (up to, against)
προσκυνέω, προσκυνήσω, προσεκύνησα worship, prostrate oneself before, reverence before, reverence
προσλαμβάνομαι, προσλήψομαι, προσελαβόμην take aside, draw to one's side
προσμένω, προσμενῶ, προσέμεινα continue, remain; remain or stay with
προσπίπτω, προσπεσοῦμαι, προέπεσον (2 aorist) fall upon; rush upon, beat against
προστάσσω, προστάξω, προσέταξα, προστέταγμαι, προσετάχθην command, order
προστίθημι, προσθήσω, προσέθηκα, προστέθεικα, προστέθειμαι, προσετέθην add, add to; provide, give, grant, do
προσφέρω, προσοίσω, προσήνεγκα, προσήνεγκον (2 aorist), προσηνέχθην bring to, bring before, offer, present
προσφωνέω, προσφωνήσω, προσεφώνησα call out, address
πρόσωπον, ου, τό face, countenance; appearance; person, personage
προφητεία, ας, ἡ prophecy
προφθάνω, προφθάσω, προέφθασα outstrip, anticipate, be beforehand
προφητεύω, προφητεύσω, ἐπροφήτευσα proclaim a divine revelation, prophetically reveal, prophesy
προφήτης, ου, ὁ prophet, seer, revelator
προφθάνω, προφθάσω, προέφθασα outstrip, anticipate, be beforehand

πρωΐ early, early in the morning (adverb)
πρωΐα, ας, ἡ morning, morning hour
πρωτοκαθεδρία, ας, ἡ the first seat, the most honorable seat
πρωτοκλισία, ας, ἡ first place of reclining at the table, the most honorable place at the table
πρῶτον first (in time; adverb)
πρῶτος, η, ον first, before, earlier, foremost
πτερύγιον, ου, τό little wing; pinnacle, summit
πτέρυξ, υγος, ἡ wing
πτύον, ου, τό winnowing shovel
πτῶμα, ατος, τό that which has fallen; body, dead body, corpse, carcass
πτῶσις, εως, ἡ fall, crash, ruin
πτωχός, ή, όν poor, indigent, needy, lowly, contrite
πύλη, ης, ἡ gate
πυλών, ῶνος, ὁ gate, gateway, entrance, vestibule
πυνθάνομαι, πεύσομαι, ἐπυθόμην (2 aorist) inquire, ask
πῦρ, πυρός, τό fire
πύργος, ου, ὁ tower; castle, palace
πυρέσσω, πυρέξω suffer with a fever
πυρετός, οῦ, ὁ fever
πυρράζω, πυρράσω be fiery red
πωλέω, πωλήσω, ἐπώλησα sell
πῶλος, ου, ὁ colt
πῶς how? in what way? in what sense? (interrogative adverb)

ρ

ῥαββί, ὁ my master, teacher (Hebrew)
ῥάβδος, ου, ἡ rod, staff, stick
ῥακά empty one, empty-head, numbskull, fool (Aramaic term of abuse and derision)
ῥάκος, ους, τό tattered garment; piece of cloth, patch
Ῥαμά, ἡ Rama (indeclinable)
ῥαπίζω, ῥαπίσω, ἐρράπισα beat with rods; strike with the palm of the hands; strike, slap
ῥαφίς, ίδος, ἡ needle
Ῥαχήλ, ἡ Rachel (indeclinable)
Ῥαχάβ, ἡ Rachab, Rahab (indeclinable)
ῥήγνυμι/ῥήσσω, ῥήξω, ἔρ(ρ)ηξα tear in pieces; break, burst
ῥῆμα, ατος, τό word, saying, speech, declaration, expression
ῥίζα, ης, ἡ root
ῥίπτω/ῥιπτέω, ῥίψω, ἔρριψα, ἔρριμαι hurl, throw; lay down, set on the ground; be dispersed, be scattered (passive)
Ῥοβοάμ, ὁ Roboam, Rehoboam (indeclinable)
Ῥούθ, ἡ Ruth (indeclinable)
ῥύμη, ης, ἡ narrow street, lane, alley
ῥύομαι, ῥύσομαι, ἐρ(ρ)υσάμην, ἐρ(ρ)ύσθην save, deliver, rescue, preserve

σ

σαβαχθανί hast thou forsaken me? (Aramaic)

σάββατον, ου, τό Sabbath; week (both in singular and in plural)
σαγήνη, ης, ἡ a large net, a large dragnet
Σαδδουκαῖος, ου, ὁ Sadducee
Σαδώκ, ὁ Sadoc, Zadok (indeclinable)
σάκκος, ου, ὁ sack, sackcloth
Σαλαθιήλ, ὁ Salathiel, Shealtiel (indeclinable)
σαλεύω, σαλεύσω, ἐσάλευσα, ἐσαλεύθην shake; shake down or together; agitate, disturb
Σαλμών, ὁ Salmon (indeclinable)
σάλπιγξ, ιγγος, ἡ trumpet
σαλπίζω, σαλπίσω, ἐσάλπισα sound a trumpet, trumpet forth
Σαμαρίτης, ου, ὁ Samaritan
σαπρός, ά, όν spoiled, rotten; bad, evil
σάρξ, σαρκός, ἡ flesh
σαρόω, σαρώσω, ἐσάρωσα, σεσάρωμαι, ἐσαρώθην sweep clean, cleanse with a broom, cleanse
Σατανᾶς, ᾶ, ὁ Satan
σάτον, ου, τό measure (of grain; about a peck and a half)
σβέννυμι, σβέσω, ἔσβεσα extinguish, put out
σεαυτοῦ, ῆς, οῦ yourself (reflexive pronoun)
σέβομαι worship, reverence
σεισμός, ου, ὁ shaking; earthquake; tempest
σείω, σείσω, ἔσεισα, ἐσείσθην shake, agitate, cause to quake; stir up, set in motion
σελήνη, ης, ἡ moon
σεληνιάζομαι, σεληνιάσομαι be lunatic, be moon-struck
σημεῖον, ου, τό sign, token, miracle
σήμερον today, this day, now, our time (adverb)
σής, σεός/σητός, ὁ moth
σιαγών, όνος, ἡ cheek
Σιδών, ῶνος, ἡ Sidon
Σίμων, Σίμωνος, ὁ Simon
σίναπι, εως, τό mustard
σινδών, όνος, ἡ linen cloth, linen sheet; sheet, tunic
σιτιστός, ή, όν fattened; τὰ σιτιστά animals that have been fattened
σῖτος, ου, ὁ wheat, grain
Σιών, ἡ Zion (indeclinable)
σιωπάω, σιωπήσω, ἐσιώπησα be silent, keep silent, hold one's peace
σκανδαλίζω, σκανδαλίσω, ἐσκανδάλισα, ἐσκανδαλίσθην offend, anger, shock
σκάνδαλον, ου, τό stumbling block, impediment; temptation to sin; that which gives offense, that which is offensive; scandal, offense
σκεῦος, ους, τό vessel, jar, container
σκηνή, ῆς, ἡ tent, tabernacle, dwelling, booth
σκιά, ᾶς, ἡ shade, shadow; gloom; darkness
σκληροκαρδίαν, ας, ἡ hardness of heart, obduracy, coldness, obstinacy, stubbornness

σκληρός, ά, όν hard, harsh
σκορπίζω, σκορπίσω, ἐσκόρπισα, ἐσκορπίσθην scatter, disperse
σκοτεινός, ή, όν dark
σκοτία, ας, ἡ darkness, gloom
σκοτίζω, σκοτίσω, ἐσκοτίσθην darken; be darkened, obscured (passive)
σκότος, ους, τό darkness, gloom
σκυθροπός, ή, όν with a sad face, of a gloomy countenance, with a sullen look
σκύλλω, σκυλλῶ, ἔσκυλμαι weary, harass; trouble, bother, annoy
σμύρνα, ης, ἡ myrrh
Σόδομα, ων, τά Sodom
Σολομών, ῶνος, ὁ Solomon
σός, σή, σόν your, yours
σοφία, ας, ἡ wisdom, prudence
σοφός, ή, όν wise; clever, skillful; learned, intelligent
σπεῖρα, ας, ἡ band, company, troop; maniple, cohort
σπείρω, σπερῶ, ἔσπειρα, ἔσπαρμαι, ἐσπάρην sow
σπέρμα, ατος, τό seed; descendant, child, posterity
σπήλαιον, ου, τό cave, den
σπλαγχνίζομαι, σπλαγχνίσομαι, ἐσπλαγχνίσθην have compassion, feel sympathy, be moved with pity
σπόγγος, ου, ὁ sponge
σποδός, οῦ, ἡ ashes
σπόριμος, ου, ὁ sown; standing grain, fields of grain, cornfields (plural)
σπυρίς, ίδος, ἡ basket
στάδιον, ου, τό stade (measure of distance), arena, stadium, furlong (plural also οἱ στάδιοι)
στατήρ, ῆρος, ὁ stater (an attic silver coin equivalent to a double drachma)
σταυρός, οῦ, ὁ cross
σταυρόω, σταυρώσω, ἐσταύρωσα, ἐσταύρωμαι, ἐσταυρώθην crucify
σταφυλή, ῆς, ἡ cluster or bunch of grapes, grapes
στάχυς, υος, ὁ ear of corn, head of wheat
στέγη, ης, ἡ roof
στενός, ή, όν narrow, straight
στέφανος, ου, ὁ garland, wreath, crown
στόμα, ατος, τό mouth
στράτευμα, ατος, τό army; armed force; troops, guards
στρατιώτης, ου, ὁ soldier
στρέφω, στρέψω, ἔστρεψα, ἔστραμμαι, ἐστρέφθην, ἐστράφην (2 aorist passive) turn, make a turn, change; bring back, return; turn around, change inwardly, be converted (passive)
στρουθίον, ίου, τό small bird; sparrow
στρωννύω, στρώσω, ἔστρωσα spread (out)
στυγνάζω, στυγνάσω, ἐστύγνασα signal a gloomy look, be dark or gloomy
σύ, σοῦ (σου) you (personal pronoun)

συζεύγνυμι, συζεύξω, συνέζευξα yoke together; join together, unite
συκῆ, ῆς, ἡ fig-tree
σῦκον, ου, τό fig
συλλαλέω, συλλαλήσω, συνελάλησα talk, converse, confer
συλλαμβάνω, συλλήψομαι, συνέλαβον, συνείληφα, συνελήφθην seize, apprehend, arrest
συλλέγω, συλλέξω, συνέλεξα collect, gather
συμβουλεύω, συμβουλεύσω counsel, advise; consult together, plot (middle)
συμβούλιον, ίου, τό counsel, plan, consultation; συμβούλιον λαμβάνειν form a plan, consult, plot
συμπνίγω, συμπνιξοῦμαι, συνέπνιξα choke
συμφέρει it is profitable, expedient, advantageous, good, or better (impersonal verb)
συμφονέω, συμφονήσω sound together, be in unison, be in accord; agree, be in agreement; make an agreement
συνάγω, συνάξω, συνήγαγον, συνῆγμαι, συνήχθην gather in, gather up, bring together, receive as guest; convene, come together, meet (passive)
συναγωγή, ῆς, ἡ synagogue
συναίρω, συναρῶ, συνῆρα settle
συνανάκειμαι, συνανακείσομαι recline at table with, eat with
συναυξάνομαι, συναυξήσομαι grow together, grow side by side
σύνδουλος, ου, ὁ fellow slave, fellow servant
συνέδριον, ίου, τό assembly, high council, Sanhedrin
συνέρχομαι, συνελεύσομαι, συνῆλθον (2 aorist), συνελήλυθα come together, go or come with (anyone), accompany
συνετός, ή, όν intelligent, wise, prudent
συνέχω, συνέξω hold together; be seized with, be affected with (passive)
συνθλάω, συνθλάσω, συνεθλάσθην crush, dash to pieces, shatter
συνίημι/συνίω, συνήσω/συνήσομαι, συνῆκα (1 aorist) send together; understand, comprehend, perceive clearly
συντάσσω, συντάξω, συνέταξα arrange; order, charge, direct
συντέλεια, ας, ἡ completion, close, end
συντηρέω, συντηρήσω protect, defend; be saved, be preserved (passive)
συντρίβω, συντρίψω, συνέτριψα, συντέτριμμαι, συνετρίβην rub together; shiver; break, bruise, crush; deprive of strength, debilitate; be broken in heart, be contrite (passive)
Συρία, ας, ἡ Syria

συσταυρόω, συσταυρώσω, συνεσταύρωσα, συνεσταύρωμαι, συνεσταυρώθην crucify with
συστρέφω, συστρέψω turn together; collect, gather
σφόδρα greatly, exceedingly (adverb)
σφραγίζω, σφραγίσω, ἐσφράγισα, ἐσφράγισμαι, ἐσφραγίσθην seal (up); attest, certify
σχίζω, σχίσω, ἔσχισα, ἐσχίσθην split, tear asunder, divide
σχίσμα, ατος, τό split, tear, division, dissension
σχολάζω, σχολάσω, ἐσχόλασα be at leisure; be unoccupied, be empty
σῴζω, σώσω, ἔσωσα, σέσωκα, σέσωσμαι, ἐσώθην save, rescue, preserve safe and unharmed
σῶμα, ατος, τό body

τ

τάλαντον, ου, τό talent
ταμεῖον, ου, τό storehouse, barn; inner chamber, private room, secret room
ταπεινός, ή, όν humble, poor, lowly
ταπεινόω, ταπεινώσω, ἐταπείνωσα bring low; humble
ταράσσω, ταράξω, ἐτάραξα, τετάραγμαι, ἐταράχθην stir up, disturb, trouble
τάσσω, τάξω, ἔταξα, τέταγμαι, ἐτάχθην, ἐτάγην (2 aorist passive) arrange, appoint, determine
ταῦρος, ου, ὁ bull
ταφή, ῆς, ἡ burial place
τάφος, ου, ὁ grave, tomb, sepulchre
ταχύς, εῖα, ύ quick, swift, fleet; ταχύ quickly, speedily, hastily (adverb)
τεκνίον, ου, τό little child
τέκνον, ου, τό child, descendant, posterity
τέκτων, ονος, ὁ artisan; carpenter, wood-worker, builder
τέλειος, εία, ειον complete, perfect, fully developed, consecrated
τελευτάω, τελευτήσω, ἐτελεύτησα, τετελεύτηκα end one's life, finish, die
τελευτή, ῆς, ἡ end; end of life, death
τελέω, τελέσω, ἐτέλεσα, τετέλεκα, τετέλεσμαι, ἐτελέσθην finish, end, fulfill, accomplish, make an end; pay dues, pay tax
τέλος, ους, τό end, fulfillment, completion; custom, tax, duty
τελώνης, ου, ὁ tax-collector, publican
τελώνιον, ου, τό tax office, custom house, toll office
τέρας, ατος, τό portent, omen, wonder
τέσσαρες, τέσσαρα (neuter), ων four
τεσσεράκοντα forty (indeclinable)
τέταρτος, η, ον fourth
τετραάρχης/τετράρχης, ου, ὁ tetrarch

τετρακισχίλιοι, αι, α four thousand
τηρέω, τηρήσω, ἐτήρησα, τετήρηκα, τετήρημαι, ἐτηρήθην guard, heed, preserve, reserve, keep, observe
τίθημι, θήσω, ἔθηκα, τέθεικα, τέθειμαι, ἐτέθην place, set, put, lay, serve, give, render, allocate, assign; add; provide, give, grant, do
τίκτω, τέξομαι, ἔτεκον (2 aorist), τέτοκα, ἐτέχθην give birth, bear, bring forth
τίλλω, τιλῶ pick, pluck
τιμάω, τιμήσω, ἐτίμησα value, honor, revere
τιμή, ῆς, ἡ price, value
τόκος, ου, ὁ offspring; interest (on money loaned)
τολμάω, τολμήσω, ἐτόλμησα, dare, have the courage (+ infinitive)
τόπος, ου, ὁ place, position, region
τότε then, at that time, thereupon, thereafter; ἀπὸ τότε from then on (adverb)
τις, τι anyone, anything, someone, something; a certain one, a certain thing; some, certain, several (plural; indefinite pronoun)
τίς, τί, (τίνος) who? what? τί why? how? (interrogative pronoun); διὰ τί why? εἰς τί why? how! (in exclamations)
τοιοῦτος, τοιαύτη, τοιοῦτο such, of such kind, such as this, so great
τοσοῦτος, τοσαύτη, τοσοῦτο so great, so much, so large
τράπεζα, ης, ἡ table, counter
τραπεζίτης, ου, ὁ money changer, broker, banker
τράχηλος, ου, ὁ neck
τρεῖς, τρία three
τρέφω, θρέψω, ἔθρεψα feed, nourish, support
τρέχω, θρέξομαι/δραμοῦμαι, ἔδραμον (2 aorist) run
τριάκοντα thirty (a thirtyfold yield of grain; indeclinable)
τρίβολος, ου, ὁ thistle
τρίβος, ου, ἡ a beaten track; path, road, highway
τρίς three times (adverb)
τρίτος, η, ον third; ἐκ τρίτου the third time, for the third time
τρόπος, ου, ὁ mode, manner, way; ὃν τρόπον in which manner, as, even as
τροφή, ῆς, ἡ nourishment, food
τρύβλιον, ου, τό bowl, dish
τρύπημα, ατος, τό hole, eye of a needle
τρώγω, τρώξομαι, ἔτραγον eat
τύπτω, τύψω, ἔτυψα beat, strike, smite
Τύρος, ου, ἡ Tyre
τυφλός, ή, όν blind
τύφω, θύψω give off smoke; smoke, smolder (passive)

υ

ὑβρίζω, ὑβρίσω, ὕβρισα treat in an arrogant manner, mistreat, insult, scoff at
ὑγιής, ές healthy, sound
ὕδωρ, ὕδατος, τό water

υἱός, οῦ, ὁ son; young, offspring, foal

ὑμνέω, ὑμνήσω, ὕμνησα praise, celebrate with hymns; sing a hymn

ὑπάγω, ὑπάξω, ὑπήγαγον, ὑπήχθην go, go away, go home

ὑπακούω, ὑπακούσομαι hear, listen, obey

ὑπαντάω, ὑπαντήσω, ὑπήντησα meet (+ dative)

ὑπάντησις, εως, ἡ coming to meet; εἰς ὑπάντησιν to meet (+ dative)

ὑπάρχω, ὑπάρξω begin; exist; be; τὰ ὑπάρχοντα possessions, goods, property

ὑπέρ above, in behalf of, about, for (preposition + genitive); over, beyond; more than (+ accusative)

ὑπηρέτης, ου, ὁ servant, helper, assistant, attendant, officer

ὕπνος, ου, ὁ sleep

ὑπό by (preposition + genitive of personal agent); under (+ accusative)

ὑποδείκνυμι/ὑποδεικνύω, ὑποδείξω, ὑπέδειξα, ὑποδέδειχα, ὑπεδείχθην show, point out, make known, demonstrate, announce

ὑπόδημα, ατος, τό sandal

ὑποζύγιον, ου, τό beast for the yoke, beast of burden; oxen, horse, mule, donkey, ass

ὑποκάτω under (adverb + genitive)

ὑπόκρισις, ως, ἡ acting; hypocrisy, simulation

ὑποκριτής, οῦ, ὁ hypocrite, pretender, dissembler

ὑπομένω, ὑπομενῶ remain; remain constant, persevere, endure

ὑποπόδιον, ιου, τό footstool

ὑστερέω, ὑστερήσω, ὑστέρησα, ὑστέρηκα, ὑστερήθην fail, lack, run short

ὕστερος, α, ον later; ὕστερον later, afterwards; finally; last (adverb)

ὑψηλός, ή, όν high; exalted, proud, haughty

ὕψιστος, η, ον highest, most exalted; ἐν τοῖς ὑψίστοις in the highest (heaven)

ὑψόω, ὑψώσω, ὕψωσα, ὑψώθην lift up, raise high, exalt

φ

φάγος, ου, ὁ glutton

φαίνω, φανῶ, ἔφηνα, πέφαγκα, πέφηνα, πέφασμαι, ἐφάνθην, ἐφάνην shine, give light, be bright; be seen, appear, be visible (middle and passive)

φανερός, ά, όν visible, clear, known

φάντασμα, ατος, τό apparition, phantom, ghost

Φάρες, ὁ Phares, Perez (indeclinable)

Φαρισαῖος, ου, ὁ a Pharisee

φέγγος, εος, τό light, radiance

φέρω, οἴσω, ἤνεγκα (1 aorist), ἤνεγκον (2 aorist), ἠνέχθην bear, carry, bring

φεύγω, φεύξομαι, ἔφυγον (2 aorist) flee, flee from; avoid, shun

φήμη, ης, ἡ fame, rumor, report
φημί, φήσω, ἔφησα say, speak
φθάνω, φθήσομαι, φθάσω, ἔφθασα, ἔφθην (2 aorist passive) outstrip; advance, come before, precede; come, arrive; come upon, overtake
φθόνος, ου, ὁ envy, jealousy, spite
φιλέω, φιλήσω, ἐφίλησα, πεφίληκα love, like, be fond of, regard with affection, have affection for; kiss
Φίλιππος, ου, ὁ Philip
φίλος, ου, ὁ friend
φιμόω, φιμώσω, ἐφίμωσα, πεφίμωμαι, ἐφιμώθην muzzle, silence; be silent, be speechless, be hushed (passive)
φοβέομαι, φοβηθήσομαι, ἐφοβήθην fear, dread; be afraid, become frightened (only passive in N.T.)
φόβος, ου, ὁ terror; fear, alarm, fright; reverence, respect
φονεύς, έως, ὁ murderer
φονεύω, φονεύσω, ἐφόνευσα murder, kill, commit murder
φόνος, ου, ὁ killing, murder
φορέω, φορήσω/φορέσω, ἐφόρεσα, πεφόρηκα bear, wear
φορτίζω, φορτίσω, πεφόρτισμαι load, burden
φορτίον, ου, τό load, burden
φραγελλόω, φραγελλώσω flog, scourge
φραγμός, οῦ, ὁ fence, hedge
φράζω, φράσω, ἔφρασα explain, expound, interpret
φρονέω, φρονήσω, ἐφρόνησα think, take thought; take someone's side, espouse someone's cause
φρόνιμος, η, ον thoughtful, prudent, wise
φυγή, ῆς, ἡ flight
φυλακή, ῆς, ἡ watch, guard, prison
φυλακτήριον, ου, τό station of a guard; safeguard; phylactery (a small box containing scriptural verses, bound on forehead and arm during prayer)
φυλάσσω, φυλάξω, ἐφύλαξα watch, guard, defend, keep
φυλή, ῆς, ἡ tribe; people, nation
φύλλον, ου, τό leaf
φυτεία, ας, ἡ plant
φυτεύω, φυτεύσω, ἐφύτευσα plant, set
φωλεός, οῦ, ὁ den, lair, hole
φωνέω, φωνήσω, ἐφώνησα, ἐφωνήθην sound, crow, call, summon
φωνή, ῆς, ἡ voice, sound
φῶς, φωτός, τό light
φωτεινός, ή, όν radiant, bright, shining; full of light, enlightened, illuminated

χ

χαίρω, χαρήσομαι, ἐχάρην (2 aorist passive) rejoice, be glad; χαῖρε, χαίρετε hail, greetings, welcome (as a form of greeting)
χαλεπός, ή, όν hard, difficult; hard to deal with, violent, dangerous; bad, evil

χαλκός, οῦ, ὁ copper, bronze; copper money; money
Χαναναῖος, α, ον of Canaan, Canaanite, Canaanitish
χαρά, ᾶς, ἡ joy
χεῖλος, ους, τό lip
χειμών, ῶνος, ἡ stormy weather, storm, tempest, winter
χείρ, χειρός, ἡ hand
χείρων, ον worse, more severe (comparative of κακός)
χιτών, ῶνος, ὁ tunic, inner garment, shirt
χιών, όνος, ἡ snow
χλαμύς, χλαμύδος, ἡ (a Roman military commander's) cloak
χοῖρος, ου, ὁ young pig, swine
χολή, ῆς, ἡ bile, gall
Χοραζίν, ἡ Chorazin (indeclinable)
χορτάζω, χορτάω, εχόρτασα, ἐχορτάσθην feed, fill, satisfy
χόρτος, ου, ὁ grass, hay; stalks of grain, plant of corn
χρεία, ας, ἡ need, necessity
χρῄζω need, have need of, want, desire
χρηματίζω, χρηματίσω, ἐχρημάτισα, κεχρημάτισμαι, ἐχρημάτισθην have dealings, negotiate; be divinely instructed, receive a revelation or warning from God
χρηστός, ἡ, όν useful, suitable, worthy; good, pleasant, agreeable; easy; gentle, kind, gracious
Χριστός, οῦ, ὁ Christ
χρονίζω, χρονίσω, ἐχρόνισα take time, linger, delay, fail to come for a long time
χρόνος, ου, ὁ time
χρυσός, οῦ, ὁ gold
χωλός, ή, όν lame, crippled
χώρα, ας, ἡ country, land, field
χωρέω, χωρήσω, ἐχώρησα move, pass; proceed; go forward, make progress; have room for, hold, contain; grasp, accept, comprehend, understand
χωρίζω, χωρίζω, ἐχώρισα, κεχώρισμαι, ἐχωρίσθην divide, separate, sever, sunder
χωρίον, ου, τό place, piece of land, field
χωρίς without, apart from (preposition + genitive)

ψ

ψεύδομαι, ψεύσομαι, ἐψευσάμην lie, tell a falsehood
ψευδομαρτυρέω, ψευδομαρτυρήσω bear false witness, bear false testimony
ψευδομαρτυρία, ας, ἡ false witness, false testimony
ψευδομάρτυς, υρος, ὁ one who gives false testimony, false witness
ψευδοπροφήτης, ου, ὁ false prophet
ψευδόχριστος, ου, ὁ false Christ
ψιχίον, ου, τό crumb, bit
ψυχή, ῆς, ἡ breath, life, soul, heart
ψυχρός, ά, όν cool, cold; cold water (substantive)

ψύχω, ψύξω, ἐψύγην breathe, cool; grow cold, be extinguished (passive)

ω

ὦ O! (interjection)
ὧδε here, hither, to this place; ὧδε ἢ ὧδε here or there
ὠδίν, ὠδῖνος, ἡ birth pain, pain
ὦμος, ου, ὁ shoulder
ὥρα, ας, ἡ hour
ὡραῖος, α, ον timely, seasonable, in bloom; beautiful, fair, lovely
ὡς as, like, just as, when, after, about (with numerals), how, provided that (adverb, conjunction)
ὡσαννά hosanna! save now, help now (Hebrew)
ὡσαύτως in just the same way, likewise (adverb)
ὡσεί as if, as, like; about (adverb; with numerals)
ὥσπερ as, just as (adverb)
ὥστε so that, so as to (conjunction)
ὠτίον, ου, τό ear
ὠφελέω, ὠφελήσω, ὠφέλησα, ὠφελήθην help, aid, benefit, be of use to, be of value

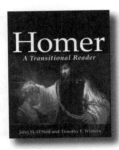

Further Readings

Origins of the Gospel According to St. Matthew

The Textual and Source Study

G.D. Kilpatrick

vi + 167 pp. (1950, reprint 2007) Paperback, ISBN 978-0-86516-667-7

This book is an exact reprint of the 1950 Oxford University Press edition, with a new foreword by J. K. Elliott and a biography by A. M. Devine.

A pioneering study on Matthew's Gospel, The Origins of the Gospel according to St. Matthew has stood the test of time and for the past sixty years has been regularly referred to and discussed in many a learned monograph or article on Matthew as well as in the standard commentaries on that Gospel.... Kilpatrick's investigation had revitalized and rejuvenated New Testament source criticism in general and Matthaean studies in particular.

–J. K. Elliott, Foreword

The Vulgate of Mark with the Synoptic Parallels

Dale A. Grote

xxii + 442 pp., 1 map (2016)
Paperback, ISBN 978-0-86515-835-0

The Vulgate of Mark with the Synoptic Parallels empowers intermediate Latin students to read an engaging narrative in accessible prose. Parallel passages from Matthew and Luke, along with historical and grammatical notes, introduce students to a historical-textual approach to reading and interpreting these texts.

www.BOLCHAZY.com

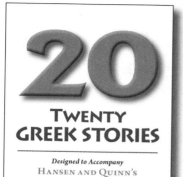

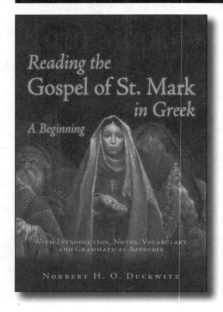